THE GERMAN ECONOMY

Eric Owen Smith

ROUTLEDGE

London and New York

First published 1994
by Routledge
11 New Fetter Lane, London EC4P 4EE

Simultaneously published in the USA and Canada
by Routledge
29 West 35th Street, New York, NY 10001

© 1994 Eric Owen Smith

Typeset in Garamond by
Florencetype Ltd, Kewstoke, Avon
Printed and bound in Great Britain by
TJ Press (Padstow) Ltd, Padstow, Cornwall

British Library Cataloguing in Publication Data
A catalogue record for this book is available from the British Library

Library of Congress Cataloging in Publication Data
Owen Smith, E.
The Germany economy / Eric Owen Smith.
p. cm.
Includes bibliographical references and index.
1. Germany–Economic conditions–1945–1990.
2. Germany–Economic policy–1945–1990.
3. Germany–Economic conditions–1990–
4. Germany–Economic policy–1900–
I. Title.
HC286.5.0925 1994
330.943′ 087–dc20
93-34911

ISBN 0-415-06288-8.
ISBN 0-415-06289-6 (pbk.)

CONTENTS

CONTENTS

CONTENTS

CONTENTS

FIGURES

FIGURES

FIGURES

TABLES

PREFACE

When I wrote *The West German Economy* (1983), I was concerned mainly with the period 1950–80. However, the book was completed during part of the recession which began in 1979. I therefore had to conclude by reporting that, by post-war German standards, interest rates, inflation, the general budget deficit, the current account deficit and unemployment were all high. Because of the more propitious trend in crude-oil prices, I was able to give a more encouraging view of these indicators in my chapter on economic policy in *West Germany Today* (1989), although unemployment still remained obstinately high during the period reviewed. The present book was written following unification when the former West German economy initially enjoyed a boom but there was an economic collapse in the East. However, the Bundesbank raised interest rates to record heights, thereby repeating its reaction to the first two crude-oil price shocks (see Chapter 4). This had a deflationary effect both within Germany and in other economies. As well as these two contrastin effects of unification on aggregate demand, there were also many supply-s policy issues with which West Germany was only just coming to grips enormous economic strains of transforming the derelict East German omy badly exacerbated West Germany's economic problems. German tion therefore became one of two dominant European economic iss 1990s, the other being European economic, monetary and social Many of the lessons learned from unification influenced Germa further European integration. On the other hand, prepar European Single Market (EC 1993) were already underway wall fell. Meanwhile, in the world economy at large, economics of protection had intensified. Evidence of afforded by the tortuous GATT negotiations. In Germa emerged from the protection of agriculture, steel and

The moral is that economic activity is cyclical concentrate as far as possible on long-term trends three German terms indicated crucial trends and all of which are analysed in this book. Fir

Germany's potential as a competitive industrial base, indicated the fear in some quarters that costs were no longer being related to expected revenue (Chapters 3, 5, 6 and 8). High labour costs, but not the associated high productivity in the west, were selected for particular attention (Chapter 6). It would be difficult to believe, however, that the elaborate social-policy system and industrial democracy are under fundamental threat (Chapters 5 and 6). After all, the Constitutional Court has enjoined the government to ensure decent living standards for families with children. The same court has also affirmed the Codetermination Act (1976). Second, *Allfinanz*, or the widest possible range of financial services being supplied over a bank's counter, reveals a linking of banking and insurance services which was part of the preparations for the EC 1993 – albeit a trend which somewhat backfired when French companies succeeded in gaining at least a transient foothold in the West German market (Chapter 7). The response from the German financial institutions was to erect fairly effective barriers to entry. Similarly, the third term – *Finanzplatz Deutschland* – represented attempts to improve the general provision of financial services in order to compete with London and other major financial centres (Chapters 7 and 8). It will be seen that the attempts to reform equity finance led to further demands for the recognition of share-holders' rights. The reader is asked to bear this search for longer terms trends in mind. It can then be shown that unification represents only one dimension of recent trends in the German economy, albeit a highly significant dimension.

Since *The West German Economy* appeared many of my interpretations of the post-war recovery have become conventional wisdom. The Bibliography has been accordingly extended. (Where a choice existed, preference has been given to works in English in both the Bibliography and the citations which appear in the text.) In particular, Abelshauser's outstanding research work is responsible for the new knowledge on the post-war recovery and reconstruction. Moreover, Berghahn has produced an authoritative assessment of anti-trust developments and Riha has provided invaluable insights into German political economy. These works must be added to the classic texts by Stolper and Wallich. All of these publications were extremely valuable for the purpose of drawing comparisons between the post-war recovery and the abject hopes raised in the east after the fall of the Berlin wall. Obviously, a large number of other research results have also appeared and many of them are included in the bibliography.

Many myths about the post-Second World War economy of West Germany have therefore been exposed. Chief among these is the misapprehension about the nature of the social market economy (SME). A close second is the belief that German industry lay in complete ruins after the Second World War. There is also the conviction that Germans work harder than other nationals, as opposed to working in better organised ways with technically superior equip-

ment. Even the sloppy translation of *das Wirtschaftswunder* as 'the economic miracle' connotes a need for theological discourse rather than economic analysis, although Giersch *et al.* (1992: xi) contend that miracles emerge when spontaneity prevails over regulation, and they fade when corporatist rigidities impair the flexibility (required) for smooth adjustments. Nonetheless, the near-mystical interpretation accorded to the post-war reconstruction and recovery of the West German economy engendered the expectation following unification that the same magic wand would resolve the economic ills of East Germany overnight. For example, Stille (1990: 8) suggested:

Recollections of the economic miracle years, combined with a positive assessment of the overall workings of the SME, clearly pointed towards doing the trick again.

Yet it will be seen as early as the first chapter in this book that the recovery phase in the West was not completed until 1949, while reconstruction took until 1958. As Schmieding pointed out in the *Financial Times* (25 February 1991), favourable economic conditions existed in 1948, whereas a complex cost explosion eradicated any chances of the SME being an overnight success in 1990.

Regrettably, the SME has become a political banner slogan for adherents of the free-market doctrine. For example, the Introductions detract from the two otherwise extremely useful volumes by Peacock and Willgerodt. As pointed out by the *Economic Journal* reviewer (June 1990: 630), there are a number of misconceptions in one introduction, not least about the nature and history of German economic thought. The other introduction is of a party-political nature, referring to their original editorial conference being held during the 'touch and go' tussle within the British Labour government of 1977 between supporters of collectivism and the mixed economy. Yet Tony Benn (whom they nominate as the leader of the former 'intellectual entourage') had effectively been demoted two years previously and the Letter of Intent to the IMF (1976) had tightly constrained policy options (Fishbein, 1984: 156 and 186–78; Healey 1989: 432 and 447).

There is an even more important distinction between the German and Anglo-Saxon models of market competition. It will be shown in this book that both an extremely wide-ranging social framework and an adequate social safety net were created as *part* of the SME. This derived logically from German economic history, although it will also be shown that the Allies influenced and encouraged the post-war incorporation of many traditional social and economic features of the modern German economy. Moreover, the SME model assumes dominant firms to be as harmful as government barriers to competition. But dominant firms are not illegal *per se*. They must be shown to be abusing their economic power. This philosophy is a critical feature of anti-trust policy – a general policy framework viewed within Germany as 'competition-policy *regulation*' (see Chapter 8). A strict regulatory framework was also developed with the aim of modifying the behaviour of the financial, labour and other markets. A high degree of post-war policy consensus thus emerged as a result of the SME. Each pillar of this policy edifice plays a critically important part in maintaining such a degree of consensus. It is fallacious to believe that any of the pillars can be simply moved. Seeking consensus in the drawing up of a solidarity pact to cover the costs of integrating east Germany in 1993 is an excellent example of German economic policy making. Another example is afforded by Federal government ministers appearing at mass meetings and running the gauntlet of hostility of disenchanted Ruhr coal miners and steel workers. Their efforts to reach agreement on rationalisation measures stands in stark contrast to the approach adopted in supply-side Britain and the USA. ⁓

If the Reagan and Thatcher eras represented the Anglo-Saxon approach to market competition, it follows that there are fundamental differences from the German approach. These differences include the apparent lack in the US and UK models of any priorities on social policy, the hostility shown to trade unions, deregulation and (in Britain) the intensive privatisation of intact monopolies. One refers, of course, to the supply-side revolution in economic thinking. This school was rather more crudely known as 'monetarist' in order to emphasise their view that the single task of macro-economic policy was the adoption of an anti-inflationary stance. Economic growth and welfare were best stimulated by private economic agents operating in a free market. The excesses of bus deregulation – with buses owned by different companies competing on the same route – followed by the consequential but predictable bankruptcy of several companies, were viewed with astonishment by German economists who visited the writer during the 1980s. (They at least politely referred to the contrasting liveries!) Airline deregulation as pursued in the USA also provoked criticism from many German economists with whom this writer is in communication. Similarly, on a longer-term note, German visitors to Loughborough regard the Victorian efforts to promote competition by building three railway lines and stations to serve London as a misallocation of resources. Perhaps above all, however, the disastrous effects of Reagonomics and Thatcherism on the financial systems of the USA and UK usually cause pause for thought in Germany. There are thus several inconsistencies between, on the one hand, supply-side economics and, on the other, the theory and, in most cases, the practice of the SME. This writer finds it difficult to believe that the Anglo-Saxons have much to teach the Germans about economic performance. The West German profile stood out in international comparisons even in the mid-1970s as an enclave of relative prosperity and stability (Riemer 1983: 41). 'Model Germany' was admired at home and abroad. It will also be demonstrated that during the 1980s, Germany's trade surpluses were quite substantial (Chapter 8). During the 1990s the Germans would be far better advised to observe the economy with many similarities to their own, namely Japan (also see Chapter 8). Economies geared to product innovation and technological change are far preferable to the Anglo-Saxon financial system which breeds hostile takeovers and short-term dividend maximisation.

In view of what has just been said, it is essential to note that there are German economists who believe that the West German approach to economic policy was not widely understood outside their country (Helmstädter 1988: 412). Other countries, including Britain, 'appear to have begun to adopt a quite similar approach in the 1980s' (*ibid.*). The Council of Economic Advisers (SVR – see Chapter 3) insisted in their annual report for 1976/77 that 'demand-oriented overall management' should be supplemented by a 'supply-oriented policy'. Yet this report only confirmed the second of two 'paradigm shifts' in West German economic policy (Riemer 1983: 86 and 154). The first shift, in the 1960s, was from the neo-liberal Freiburg school to an accommodation of Keynesianism. Professor Schiller (SPD) and the SVR cleared the way for the introduction of certain Keynesian principles and practices (*ibid.*: 115). 'Concerted Action' with the wage bargainers represented the anti-inflation approach – an approach considered to be 'less punitive' than the Bundesbank-induced stabilisation crises (*ibid.*: 88). It can, of course, be argued that an attempted synthesising of the pure theory of the Freiburg and Keynesian schools was a dubious undertaking where the history of economic doctrines was concerned (*ibid.*: 113). Moreover, the Bundesbank view resembled the (British) Treasury view. This approach caused confused thinking on fiscal policy, debt management and monetary policy: the question 'how much public spending can be financed?' (the Treasury view) held sway over the modern Keynesian view of 'how much public money is needed?' (*ibid.*: 135). In short, it was the Bundesbank which came to be identified by the SVR with a 'traditional stabilisation strategy' that dictated monetary and fiscal stringency but disregarded the costs (social, political and even economic) of interrupted growth (*ibid.*: 148). Hence, the second paradigm shift may have resulted in the SVR becoming a closer ally of the Bundesbank, but it still did not markedly influence the pragmatic approach to the SME. This foreign observer would have the temerity to suggest that the SME in practice delineates the fundamental differences between, on the one hand, Reaganomics and Thatcherism, and, on the other, the SME. The cleavage between the Bundesbank and Keynesian views also undermined the process of integrating east Germany into the SME. Initially, the ostrich-like attitude of Federal government politicians set the whole process off in a specious manner. It is at the very least arguable that the combination of fiscal, incomes and exchange-rate policies invoked by the SVR and Schiller as part of their Keynesian design was more relevant to the needs of

German unification than either the Bundesbank view, or the supply-side doctrines of the USA and UK. Above all else, however, developments in the West German economy during the 1980s differed fundamentally from developments in the USA and UK.

There was nonetheless some contemporaneous enthusiasm for increasing the role of market forces in West Germany – see for example Giersch (1983). In particular, however, one supply-side agenda for Germany was based on experience in the United States and Britain (Fels and von Furstenberg (eds) 1989). It represented a valuable analysis of this vitally important school of economic thought – particularly its appraisal of privatisation. But there was also some evidence of the almost blind prejudice towards trade unions characteristic of Reaganomics and Thatcherism. The editors (page 11) inaccurately imply that one contributor to their volume (Walters, page 187) had said that British trade unions dislike decentralisation. Perhaps the work of the Donovan Commission should be required reading, even though its work pre-dated the supply-side revolution. The Commission's central thesis was that British trade unions were *too* decentralised. The editors go on to apply their notion of centralisation to German trade unions, which is another matter. But did German unions become centralised as a result of their role in reconstructing the West German economy (see Chapter 6 below)? Similarly, another contributor (Rose, page 8) seems to be used by the editors as an authority for the statement that '100 per cent of the TUC's General Council supports the Labour Party'. This is not what Rose writes on page 256. He is in any case referring to a bygone era. Moreover, if this statement means *financial* support from all unions represented on the General Council, it is patently incorrect. I am also doubtful about the *Zussammenfassung* of Rose's contribution. Does it fully bring out the numerous qualifications the author correctly makes about Thatcherite privatisation? Finally, the German trade unions are held partly responsible for the fading economic miracle in Giersch *et al.* (1992). There had been 'a long series of management scandals in union-owned firms – notably *Neue Heimat*' (page 216). What were the other scandals in this *long* series? Are the authors referring to the Co-op? Moreover, why is there no entry under the name of Flick in their index? The Flick financial scandal affected the conservative and liberal political parties in the 1980s. The Federal Constitutional Court ruled their type of 'support' to be unconstitutional. The family was also involved in an Anglo-Saxon style hostile takeover, the first of its kind in Germany (see Chapter 8 below). Hostile takeovers in turn reveal a lot about how capital markets function. They therefore merit attention. In short, the supply-siders' lack of balance caused problems in the USA and the UK without resolving – indeed making a positive contribution to – the fundamental disequilibria in budgetary and trade policies. Why should Germany want to emulate those errors?

A central hypothesis of this book is that most of the economic problems encountered on unification were not unique to this phase in Germany's economic development. Nearly every chapter gives examples of similar problems experienced by West German policy makers well before unification. A few major examples are:

- regional disparities (Chapter 2)
- budget deficits (Chapter 3)
- high interest rates (Chapter 4)
- social-insurance problems (Chapter 5)
- high unemployment (Chapter 6)
- anti-trust problems (Chapters 7 and 8)

On the other hand – notwithstanding sustained economic recovery and record Bundesbank profits – the 1980s saw some progress towards budgetary consolidation and tax reform. Nonetheless, even with the deficient data base in the east – which in some respects may take at least a decade to remedy – it became quite obvious that all the above issues would be further exacerbated by the shock of unification.

The evolution of policies and institutions naturally receive a lot of attention throughout this book. Such institutions, and therefore policies, are not confined to governments and parliaments. As Perlman lucidly puts it (in his introduction to Giersch et al. 1992) 'economic ideas are most obviously revealed through economic policies, which in turn create and are implemented by economic institutions'. Hence, a cursory glance down the list of abbreviations used below reveals how a number of critically important statutes have produced a rich institutional framework. Two good longer-term examples of such institutional development are the banks (Chapter 7) and the trade unions (Chapter 6). The nature of the cooperative banks has resulted in an endeavour to combine small units which involve shareholders in decision making with a larger institution at the top of the pyramid (also see Kirchner's discussion in Bonus and Schmidt 1990: 211). In other words, how can owners influence management in times of increasing power and market shares on the part of large companies? This problem will emerge in a wider context when corporate finance, control and ownership are discussed in Chapters 7 and 8. In addition to the special features of the capital market, the special-purpose banks will provide yet further examples of German ingenuity when it comes to establishing *ad hoc* institutions. Trade unions, in some ways at the expense of losing direct influence, have been instrumental in the introduction of a system of industrial democracy; such a development has probably affected – in a positive manner – labour turnover rates, recruitment, absenteeism and productivity (also see Frick 1992b). This is not to say that politicians have had no economic impact. For instance, in spite of the economic problems alluded to in the previous paragraph, an undertaking was given that monetary union between the two Germanies would be achieved in accordance with the Paretian principle: 'no one will be worse off and many will be better off' (Schrettl 1992: 146). The abrupt rise in public debt was only one indication that such an undertaking was unsustainable. Moreover, the monetary policy pursued bears re-emphasis, not least because of the inherent contradiction between the narrow Bundesbank view and macroeconomic policies which had wider aims. As a result of a further increase in wage and price inflation, the independent Bundesbank raised interest rates to unprecedented post-war levels. Yet the trade unions were not prepared to accept cuts in living standards and potential wage competition between eastern and western members.

Any consideration of the international dimension of the German economy inevitably involves an appreciation of Germany's importance as a trading nation, along with the external influence of her monetary policies. For example, higher interest rates and the consequential appreciation of European currencies against the US$ completely offset or even reversed the direct expansionary effect of unification on Germany's European partners, just as these countries were faced with a major slowdown in growth (Chauffour *et al.* 1992: 251 and 254). It could, however, be argued that the broadly positive effect of unification was concealed by other factors affecting the global economy – the Gulf crisis, the recession in the Anglo-Saxon economies and the end of the investment boom (*ibid.*). Both the Gulf crisis and events in the former Soviet Union exerted upward pressure on the dollar, while the easing of US short-term interest rates fuelled the downward pressure (*ibid.*: 258). Some of these factors may also have played a role in the west German recession which commenced in 1992. The fact remains, however, that inflationary pressure and short-term interest rates were increasing in West Germany well before unification. In general recognition of the monetary and trade importance of Germany, therefore, Chapters 4 and 8 respectively offer more detail on these topics.

After the manuscript of this book was completed, the proposals in the Maastricht treaty were still going through the machinations of referenda and vituperative debates in the British Parliament with the treaty's principles being challenged before the German Federal Constitutional Court. I therefore concluded that it would be best to continue using the abbreviation EC when referring to the then still extant European Communities. The list of abbreviations and the index make it clear, however, that I was conscious of the policy implications of the European Union (EU). There are numerous references in the text to EMU, the less ambitious EMS (including its ill-fated ERM) and the arguably decisive step towards the EU taken by the introduction of EC 1993. These references are concerned with both the decisively reactive and, less significantly, the proactive aspects of German policy making in terms of

EMU, the ERM and EC 1993. Some attention is also paid to the widening of the EC (or EU) so as to include, with varying degrees of certainty as this Preface is being written, Austria, Finland, Norway and Sweden. In short, the fluid course of events indicated in this paragraph led me to prefer the abbreviation EC, thus avoiding unnecessarily anticipating political and constitutional decisions.

I gratefully acknowledge a number of sources of intellectual stimulation. Among my colleagues at Loughborough University, Professor Brian Tew made me clarify my thoughts on monetary policy; Tony Westaway did likewise in respect of fiscal policy and Dr Eric Pentecost contributed in both of these fields. My colleague Peter Maunder has for many years passed on invaluable information on developments in Germany, all of which were derived from his incredibly perceptive scanning of the quality newspapers in the UK. James Johnson – a postgraduate – kindly commented on some features of Chapter 7. My friend and colleague Professor Eckhard Knappe of Trier University helped me to understand social policy in Germany so much better. Drs T-W Eser, B Frick, M Walger and A Winkler of the same institution respectively commented on some of my interpretations of German regional policy, collective bargaining, social policy and fiscal and monetary policy. Subject to the conventional academic rider, Figure 4.1 represents, for example, the results of valuable conversations with Brian Tew, Eric Pentecost and Adalbert Winkler. In addition, Professor Horst Tomann (Freie Universität, Berlin) kindly commented on my draft account of housing policy, while David Lauder and Hsueh-Fang Lin provided research assistance for Chapters 2 and 5 respectively. Without Mr Lauder's and Ms Lin's expertise in German and computing, along with the many hours we spent discussing draft work, the numerous complexities of regional and social policies would remain untranslated into English. Professor Peffekoven of Mainz University made valuable comments on Mr Lauder's early drafts on fiscal equalisation. Similarly, Herr Seffen of the Institut der Deutschen Wirtschaft answered queries from Ms Lin, whose stay in Loughborough was generously financed by Colonia Versicherung AG. The writer is also grateful to Herr Lange, librarian at the Bundesministerium der Finanzen, who kindly located some historical data on fiscal-policy matters, as well as forwarding more recent material.

I particularly enjoyed working on parts of Chapter 8 with Stephan Burger and Lothar Funk, also of Trier University. My pleasure derived not least from the fact that – as undergraduates – they had both participated in my ERASMUS exchange programme. Herr Burger diligently concentrated on privatisation, while Herr Funk immersed himself in the international trade section. We were able to discuss this work in Trier during my sabbatical leave from Loughborough University. Both of these colleagues additionally looked through a draft of the Bibliography. Also during my sabbatical, I visited another former (English) ERASMUS student who now works in Frankfurt. Both he and one of his colleagues commented on parts of Chapter 7. By way of coincidence, a close relative of yet another former ERASMUS student worked at the same location and he commented on other parts of Chapter 7. In connection with my sabbatical, I would also wish to record my sincere thanks to the DAAD (the German Academic Exchange Service) for the generous financial assistance which enabled me to spend three valuable months at Trier University.

Gloria Brentnall typed the Bibliography and several of the figures and tables, as well as early drafts of Chapters 6, 7 and 8. Lorraine Whittington typed drafts of the tables for Chapters 4 and 6. Graham Gerrard again transformed computer data files into a form in which I could use them, while Mike Hopkins, Eric Davis and other members of the library staff at Loughborough University provided their usual helpful and expert assistance. I am also grateful to Sue Smith of Leicester University's library for some urgently required OECD data which she supplied. A vote of thanks is also due to my publisher, particularly their Economics Editor, Alan Jarvis. Alan never once put pressure on me to deliver a manuscript before we had finally agreed the extent to which I should deal with the transformation process in eastern Germany.

A more long-term note of deep appreciation is due to my final-year teachers at Abbey Street Secondary Modern School, Derby, and to the staff at Derby Technical College, Newbattle Abbey College, Dalkeith and Sheffield University. My wife and family were also the usual tower of strength – thank you for being there!

I alone, of course, remain responsible for the final product.

Eric Owen Smith
Loughborough, August 1993.

ABBREVIATIONS

(See Chapter 7 for the numerous Banking and Finance abbreviations.)

AdwF	Working Party of the six economics research institutes (Arbeitsgemeinschaft deutscher wirtschaftswissenschaflicher Forschungsinstitute – see DIW, HWWA, Ifo, IWA, IfW and RWI)
AEG	Allgemeine Elektrizitätsgesellschaft
AFG	Employment Promotion Act 1969 (Arbeitsförderungsgesetz)
AG	Public Limited Company (Aktiengesellschaft)
AOK	State health-insurance office(s) (Allgemeineortskrankenkasse(n))
AR	Non-executive or supervisory board (Aufsichtsrat)
ARSt	Non-executive overseas directors' fees tax (Aufsichtsratsteuer)
AWG	External Trade and Payments Act 1961 (Außenwirtschaftsgesetz)
BA	Federal Labour Office (Bundesanstalt für Arbeit)
BAFÖG	Act to Promote Education and Training 1971 (Bundesausbildungsförderungsgesetz)
BAG	Federal Labour Court (Bundesarbeitsgericht)
BAK	Federal Banking Supervisory Authority (Bundesaufsichtsamt für das Kreditwesen)
BASF	Badische Anilin- und Sodafabriken AG
BAV	Federal Insurance Supervisory Authority (Bundesaufsichtsamt für das Versicherungswesen)
BBankG	Federal Bank Act 1957 (Deutsche Bundesbankgesetz)
BBk	Deutsche Bundesbank (also see BdL)
BDA	National Confederation of German Employers' Associations (Bundesvereinigung der Deutschen Arbeitgeberverbände)
BdB	Federal Association of (private) German Banks (Bundesverband deutscher Banken)
BDI	Federal Association of German Industry (Bundesverband der Deutschen Industrie)

BdL	Bank deutscher Länder (predecessor of BBk)
BerlinFG	Berlin Development Act (Berlinförderungsgesezt)
BetrVG	Company Constitution Acts 1952 and 1972 (Betriebsverfassungsgesetze)
BFM	Federal Finance Ministry (Bundesfinanzminiserium)
BGH	Federal Supreme Court (Bundesgerichtshof)
BHG	Berlin Assistance Act (Berlinhilfegesetz)
BHO	Federal Budget Act 1969 (Bundeshaushaltsordnunggesetz)
BKA	Federal Cartel Office (Bundeskartellamt)
BMA	Federal Minister(try) of Employment and Social Planning (Bundesminister(ium) für Arbeit und Sozialordnung)
BMF	Federal Minister(try) (Bundesminister(ium) der Finanzen)
BMW	Bayerische Motorenwerke AG
BMWi	Federal Economics Minister(try) (Bundesminister(ium) für Wirtschaft)
BRD	The Federal Republic of Germany, both before (West Germany) and after unification (Bundesrepublik Deutschland)
BSHG	Federal Social Assistance Act (Bundessozialhilfegesetz)
BVerwG	Federal Administration Court (Bundesverwaltungsgericht)
BVG	Federal Constitutional Court (Bundesverfassungsgericht)
BVR	Federal Association of Co-operative Banks (Bundesverband der Deutschen Volksbanken und Raiffeisenbanken)
CDU	die Christlich-Demokratische Union Deutschlands (Christian Democrats)
CSU	die Christlich-Soziale Union in Bayern (Bavarian sister party of the CDU)
DAG	Union of German White-Collar Employees (Deutsche Angestellten-Gewerkschaft)
DBB	Federation of (Senior) Public-Sector Employees (Deutscher Beamtenbund)
DDR	German Democratic Republic, or East Germany prior to unification (Deutsche Demokratische Republik)
DGB	German Trade Union Federation (Deutscher Gewerkschaftsbund – also see Table 6.1)
DIHT	Deutsche Industrie- und Handelstag
DIW	Deutsches Institut für Wirtschaftsforschung, Berlin
DSGV	(Federal) Association of German Savings Banks and Giros (Landesbanken) (Deutscher Sparkassen- und Giroverband)
EC	European Communities (the post-Maastricht European Union)
EC 1993	The EC Single Market
ECBC	European Central Bank Council (see ECBS)
ECBS	European Central Bank System (part of EMU proposals)

ABBREVIATIONS

ECSC	European Coal and Steel Community
ECU	European Currency Unit (introduced as part of EMS; envisaged single currency in EMU)
EMS	European Monetary System
EMU	European Economic and Monetary Union (now usually applied specifically to EC's Maastricht Treaty)
EPU	European Payments Union
ERM	Exchange Rate Mechanism of EMS
ERP	European Recovery Programme (Marshall Plan or Aid)
ESt[G]	Income Tax [Act] (Einkommensteuer[gesetz])
EU	European Union
eV	Registered Charity (eingetragener Verein)
FAZ	Frankfurter Allgemeine Zeitung
FDI	Foreign Direct Investment
FDP	die Freie Demokratische Partei (liberal party)
FT	Financial Times
GARIOA	Government and Relief in Occupied Areas
GEMSU	German Economic, Monetary and Social Union (1 July 1990)
GewSt	Trade tax (Gewerbesteuer)
GG	'Basic Law' or Federal Constitution 1949 (Grundgesetz)
GHH	Gutehoffnungshütte Aktienverein – subsumed by MAN in 1980s
GKV	Statutory Health Insurance (Gesetzliche Krankenversicherung)
GmbH	Private Limited Company (Gesellschaft mit beschränkter Haftung)
GNP	Gross national product in nominal terms
GNRP	Gross national product in real terms
GüW	Investment Companies' Act (Gesetz über Kapitalanlagegesellschaften)
GWB	Act against Restraints on Competition 1957 (Gesetz gegen Wettbewerbsbeschränkungen)
HGrG	Act containing the basic principles for Federal and Länder budgets 1969 (Haushaltsgrundsätzegesetz)
HWWA	Institut für Wirtschaftsforschung, Hamburg
IAB	Institut für Arbeitsmarkt- und Berufsforschung, Nürnberg (Research institute of BA above)
IDS	Incomes Data Services Ltd
Ifo	Institut für Wirtschaftsforschung, München
IfW	Institut für Weltwirtschaft, Kiel
IG	Industriegewerkschaft
IMF	International Monetary Fund
IW	Institut der Deutschen Wirtschaft, Köln (Employers' Research Institute)

IWA	Institut für Wirtschaftsforschung, Halle
KESt	Capital yield or withholding tax (Kapitalertragsteuer)
KfW	Reconstruction and Development Loan Corporation (Kreditanstalt für Wiederaufbau)
KGAAG	Investment Regulation Act (Investmentgesetz)
KSt	Corporation tax (Körperschaftsteuer)
KWG	Banking Act 1961 (Gesetz über das Kreditwesen)
LFAG	Länder Revenue Sharing Act 1969 (Länderfinanzausgleichsgesetz)
LSt	Tax on income from employment (Lohnsteuer)
M&A	Mergers and Acquisitions
MAN	Maschinenfabrik Augsburg-Nürnberg AG
MBB	Messerschmitt-Bölkow-Blohm
MBR	Midland Bank Review
MitbestG	Codetermination Acts 1951 and 1976 (Mitbestimmungsgesetzt[e])
MK	Monopolies Commission (Monopolkommission)
MRDB	Monthly Report of the Deutsche Bundesbank
MRRs	Minimum Reserve Requirements
MTU	Motoren und Turbinen Union
MWSt	Value-added tax (Mehrwertsteuer)
Nazi	(*or* NSDAP) Nationalsozialistische Deutsche Arbeiterpartei (Hitlerite national socialists)
OECD	Organisation for Economic Co-operation and Development
OM	Ostmark (East Mark – currency unit in DDR before GEMSU)
PSBR	Public sector borrowing requirement (Netto Kreditaufnahme)
R&D	Research and Development (Forschung und Entwicklung – FuE)
RWE	Rheinisch-Westfälische Elektrizitätswerke AG (following GEMSU the company was re-registered and became known by its initials)
RWI	Rheinisch-Westfälisches Institut für Wirtschaftsforschung, Essen
SED	Sozialistische Einheitspartei Deutschlands (communist-dominated East German governing party prior to unification)
SME	Social Market Economy
SPD	die Sozialdemokratische Partei Deutschlands (social democrats)
StRefG	Tax Reform Act (Steuerreformgesetz)
StWG	Act to Promote Economic Stability and Growth 1967 (Gesetz zur Förderung der Stabilität und des Wachstums der Wirtshaft)

SVR	Council of Economic Advisers (Sachverständigenrat zur Begutachtung der gesamtwirtschaflichen Entwicklung)
SZ	Süddeutsche Zeitung
TVG	Collective Bargaining Act 1949, as amended (Tarifvertragsgesetz)
UWG	Act against Unfair Competition 1977 (Gesetz gegen den unlauteren Wettbewerb)
VAG	Insurance Regulation Act (Versicherungsaufsichtsgesetz)
VEAG	Vereinte Energiewerke AG (established by three western utilities to take over electricity supply in the east)
VEB	Volkseigener Betrieb
VEBA	Vereinigte Elektrizitäts- und Bergwerks AG
VermBetG	Wealth Sharing Acts (Vermögensbeteiligungsgesetze)
VermBildG	Wealth Creation Acts (Vermögensbildungsgesetze)
VIAG	Vereinigte Industrie-Unternehmungen AG
VSt	Net worth tax (Vermögensteuer)
VVG	Insurance Contract Act (Gesetz über den Versicherungsvertrag)
WG	Housing Benefit (Wohngeld)
WSI	Wirtschafts- und Sozialwissenschaftliches Institut des Deutschen Gewerkschaftsbundes
ZDH	Central Association of German Handicraftworkers (Zentralverband des Deutschen Handwerks)

1

THE GERMAN ECONOMY
IN PERSPECTIVE

INTRODUCTION

All economies display short-term cyclical fluctuations around longer-run trends. The economic policies which influence the trends, and the policy response to each short-term cycle, are the result of inter-actions among groups of actors (or policy-makers). These actors therefore participate in a complex process of policy formu-lation which in turn determines the basic structural features of an economy. For example, the structure of the manufactur-ing industry will be related to such factors as the government's tax and anti-trust policies, although the companies in the manufacturing sector may make forceful representations to the government about the consequences of such policies. Changes in policy may then result. In addition, the banks and trade unions may also play creative roles because where and how the companies raise the funds for investment in capital equipment, decide how to train their labour (human capital) and settle the wage rates of their employees will affect the structure and organisation of the industry.

The study of a market economy also involves an examination of how markets function. It is therefore necessary in this opening chapter to isolate the market en-vironments in which the trends and cycles, as well as the policies and actors operate.

Future chapters will then deal with these features in greater depth. But any econ-omic perspective of Germany must also take into account the relatively late emerg-ence of political unity and constantly changing frontiers. The unification of the two German states in 1990 is only the latest example of these factors. Moreover, West Germany has been to the fore of moves to integrate the economies of the EC. Both EC 1993 and EMU were issues in which Germany inevitably played an important strategic role. Some brief com-parative remarks are therefore also con-tained in this chapter.

Why is this approach necessary? After all, it is well known that the West German economy passed through a period of reconstruction and rapid economic devel-opment after the Second World War. However, it is necessary to analyse this resurgence in the context of both the very long run and several discrete phases through which the economy has passed since the Second World War. It will be seen that there have been some changes, and some elements of continuity, in the various aspects of policy formulation. Developments in the East German econ-omy will be much more briefly con-sidered. This is because it was the west's policy and market framework into which the east was subsumed. Indeed, 'incorpor-ation' would be a better term than

1

'unification' to describe such a rapid process of transition (Buechtemann and Schupp 1992: 90). Far more space will therefore be accorded to the actual economics of this process. Last but not least, the contents of this chapter will provide a framework to examine the basic issue to which this book continually returns and with which it concludes: is it possible to say whether the 1992–3 fall in GNP reflected a long-run structural collapse or another cyclical downturn? In other words, did unification coincide with the inevitable emergence of deep-seated economic problems in the west?

UNITY AND FRONTIERS

Many German scholars are engaged in the study of '*the* German Question' – a shorthand term for the nation's chequered history. The convulsions and changes in the German nation's political, social and economic life have influenced the evolution of her institutions (Stingl 1977: 199). Her history can be summarised by the briefest of references to events since 1780 when the German nation consisted of a large geographical area of 1,789 territories. After the Napoleonic wars there were 36 states. Economic decision-making powers were decentralised and there was a north–south divide – features still readily discernible today. Political and cultural complexity began to fade during the early nineteenth century with unification, proceeding more rapidly, but not completely, under Bismarck. Hitler's corporate state by definition tolerated no political deviations. The western allies re-introduced decentralisation after the Second World War, while in the Russian sector a command economy took shape. German unification saw the principle of decentralisation re-introduced in the east.

Hence, the German question involves territorial rights. (See Mann (1974: 17) for a discussion of the proposition that Germany has no natural frontiers.) Changing frontiers have had profound effects on the performance of the German economy. In 1871, the annexed territories of Alsace and Lorraine were integrated into the second Reich and this secured many economic benefits (Henderson 1975: 159). After the First World War these territories reverted to French sovereignty. Saarland, Upper Silesia, the Rhineland and the Ruhr district were all occupied for parts of the inter-war period. Valuable industrial and mineral resources were thus lost or their output was disrupted. When the Nazis seized power, they annexed Austria, the Sudetenland and parts of Poland; the above French territories were also re-incorporated. This more than compensated for the industrial and mineral resources previously lost. However, territorial losses after the Second World War amounted to 25 per cent of the area covered by the third Reich, compared to losses of 13 per cent in 1919 (Henning 1974: 52 and 184). The Germans living in the former eastern territories were expelled. The Russians occupied what was to become East Germany and the western allies founded West Germany. Fairly shortly after the Federal Republic was established, the West Germans started to play a significant role in European economic affairs in general and, along with France, the formation of the EC in particular.

LONGER-RUN ECONOMIC TRENDS

It is first necessary to distinguish between long waves of economic development and longer-run trends within the German economy itself. Schumpeter identified three long waves of economic development which he termed Kondratieff cycles (Fels 1988: 23). (Kondratieff had earlier postulated the existence of such waves in economic activity.) Each wave lasted about fifty years and was caused by the impetus of basic innovations; the last such wave was interrupted by the First World War and there may well have been subsequent waves. Within the German economy, however, there have been longer term trends which are much more relevant to the present analysis. Whether these trends can be attributed to any particular model of economic development is of less significance here, although Braun (1990: 165–8) concisely examines the merits of such models in the context of post-war development.

More specifically, Abelshauser and Petzina (1981) have charted the long-run development of the German economy. Their analysis leads this author to suggest that Mann (1974: 16) could be paraphrased by saying that German long-run economic development has been characterised by a series of 'restless oscillations between extremes'. Over the last century or so there have been three phases of rapid economic expansion (four if one includes the early Nazi era). There have also been three periods of economic chaos, collapse and depression. The identity of the German economy was fashioned by all of these periods.

The first of the three notable periods of economic expansion occurred between 1871 and 1913. A hitherto tardy process of industrialisation was transformed during this period into an all-out effort which resulted in Germany becoming the leading industrial nation on the continent. This achievement was in spite of inflation, a badly bungled currency reform, and company collapses in the early 1870s (Henderson 1975: 162 and 170). It was 1876 before industrial output recovered its 1872 levels,

but German industrial output overtook that of France in the 1870s, caught up with Britain about 1900 and surpassed her substantially by 1910. Indeed, by 1910 the German economy was second only to that of the United States in terms of industrial production (Mann 1974: 335; Stolper *et al.* 1967: 34–5). Germany came to challenge Britain's supremacy in the markets of the world. Britain's international share in the output of manufactured goods decreased while Germany's relative share increased. Some observers were 'alarmed' at this invasion of what during the nineteenth century had become Britain's traditional markets (Henderson 1975: 173).

This first expansive phase in German industrial development was distinctive in several respects. The mechanical, electrical and chemical engineering industries became technical and export leaders. Cartelisation and protectionism were significant characteristics. The banks expanded with industry and became its capital market. New technical universities were established. Government ownership and investment played an important role at federal, state and local authority levels. The federal states remained autonomous in several fields, most notably education. They also retained, until as late as 1920, tax-raising powers. Finally, social insurance schemes were introduced. Bismarck saw these measures as an antidote to socialism and trade unionism. It was not until the First World War and the Weimar Republic that trade unionism and industrial democracy began to develop with government support, although employers in heavy industry still opposed collective bargaining (Owen Smith *et al.* 1989: 24 and 32).

The first economic collapse occurred during the period 1914–23. Germany was blockaded and chose to finance the war by an enormous increase in the internal borrowing requirement. Such borrowing was both long- and short-term in nature (Braun 1990: 30). It was based on the mistaken belief that the war would be short in duration (Marsh 1992: 95). (Tax revenue accounted for 6 per cent of government war expenditure; the equivalent proportion in Britain and the USA was 20 per cent – Henning 1974: 44.) The government borrowed from the public and the Reichsbank. The latter method created money because the government issued treasury bills which the Reichsbank discounted and used as a cover for increases in note issue. Cash in circulation rose sixfold during the First World War. The seeds of the post-war hyperinflation were therefore sown during the war and a large budget deficit emerged. After the war, the Allies made extortionate reparation demands which caused a balance of payments deficit and resulted in a disastrous fall in the exchange rate.

The government's borrowing requirement, including the need to purchase US dollars, was financed through the Reichsbank, again largely by discounting treasury bills and obtaining the equivalent amount in banknotes or claims upon the passive Reichsbank. In 1923, during the few months prior to the collapse of the currency, 300 paper mills and 150 printing works with 2,000 presses worked night and day in order to keep up with the demand for banknotes (Stolper et al. 1967: 100). The national debt on 15 November 1923 stood at 191.6 quintillion marks (191.6×10^{18} – Henning 1974: 70). The exchange rate to purchase one US$ was RM 100,000 in June 1923 but by November the rate was RM 4.2 trillion (4.2×10^{12}); in 1919 the inflation rate was 70 per cent but by 1923 it was 1.9 billion per cent (1.9×10^9 – ibid.: 66). The German public spent their money holdings as rapidly as possible as confidence

evaporated, that is to say the velocity of circulation rose rapidly. Higher taxes or lower government expenditure would have reduced the government's borrowing requirement. Alternatively, tighter credit controls on the private sector would have held back investment and encouraged savings. But the Reichsbank was the government's tool during both world wars. Little wonder, then, that the Allies formed an independent central bank and introduced a new currency after the Second World War. The Weimar hyperinflation was resolved by similar means. Historically, however, the efforts of the Weimar reformers were to be later dissipated by the Nazis, whereas the Allies' independent central bank proved to be the precursor of an institution which, for example, limited government borrowing on unification in 1990.

Not surprisingly, a currency reform was eventually introduced in November 1923, the basic mechanics of which were quite simple. A second note-issuing authority – the Deutsche Rentenbank – had been established during the previous month (Braun 1990: 44). It was independent of government and its capital took the form of unrealised paper claims on agricultural, industrial and commercial assets. This cosmetic exercise succeeded in restoring monetary confidence. Each Rentenmark issued by this new authority (on a strictly limited basis) equalled RM 1 trillion (1×10^{12}). This reform stabilised the currency almost immediately. Finally, the Reichsbank ceased to discount treasury bills. It gained independence from government in 1924 and began issuing RM at a value equivalent to the Rentenmark (ibid.). Although the Weimar hyperinflation was rapidly defeated, however, it is clear that it had a profound impact on German public opinion.

Partly because of the concern caused by

the Weimar inflation, and partly because unemployment reached 40 per cent of the labour force during the Great Depression (1929–32), the intervening period is known as the Golden Twenties. It represents the second period of expansion, just as the Great Depression is the second economic collapse.

German economic achievements after 1924 were quite remarkable – indeed, a new Germany was constructed (Mann 1974: 602; Stolper *et al.* 1967: 114). By 1929, Germany had the most modern merchant fleet, the fastest railways and an adequate system of roads. Hand in hand with modernisation went an increase in productivity and a concentration of economic power. Cartels and mergers were the order of the day. In the chemical, steel, electrical, rubber and cement industries very large enterprises dominated their markets. Germany became the most highly cartelised nation in the world; prices were kept artificially high in order to cover the costs of the least efficient member (Berghahn 1986: 21). Moreover, state subsidies were used to finance an enormous urban renewal programme. Cities vied with each other in the construction of housing, playgrounds, swimming pools, schools and hospitals. Electrical power cables spanned the countryside. In short, the infrastructure was completely reconstructed.

Hence, the dramatic rise in unemployment during the Great Depression, greater than the comparative rise elsewhere in the industrial world, must indicate the second collapse. When the depression struck Germany, real wages and unemployment had just begun to resume their pre-First World War levels. Matters were made worse by a banking crisis. The banks had borrowed heavily abroad, not least on a short-term basis from the USA. This capital was used to support industrial

and commercial reconstruction during the Golden Twenties, along with a much higher ratio of deposits to share capital. Borrowing short but lending long was risky business. Following the Wall Street crash, the borrowed funds were re-called which clearly left the banks badly exposed. The Great Slump and the American withdrawal of loan capital from her main direct investment base in Europe – Germany – seriously undermined the American presence (Berghahn 1986: 22). Total borrowing 1924–29 was RM 21 billion; almost as much flowed abroad to finance a current account deficit, reparations and overseas investment. Ironically, the expansion of exports during the same period resulted in their being greater than imports just prior to, and even during, the crisis.

When the Nazis seized power, the trade unions were among the early scapegoats for the economic malaise. Hitler confiscated their property. He also sent some of their leaders to concentration camps, while others fled into exile (Roll 1939: 106; Taft 1952: 298). It was for these reasons that the Allies, particularly the British, turned to the trade unions for assistance in the denazification process after the Second World War. In return, they were permitted to re-organise. The seeds for the re-emergence of industrial democracy were also sown at that stage (see Chapter 6 below).

German economic development reached a nadir after the Second World War. Hence, this is the third and most serious crisis; it lasted from 1945 to 1948. Initially, all the Allies were agreed that not only denazification, but also demilitarisation, administrative decentralisation, economic deconcentration and industrial decartelisation and disarmament were all policy imperatives (Berghahn 1986: 71; Carlin 1987: 13; Hardach 1980: 90–1; Stolper *et al.* 1967: 221–2). In practice, however, a clear distinction in policy implementation emerged. A centralised, command economy was installed in the Russian zone, whereas decentralisation was introduced by the western Allies. Moreover, dismantling was gradually abandoned in the western zones, not least because of protest strikes and the need to support the newly-elected Federal government in 1949. Even more significant was the American stipulation that all German cartel arrangements be declared null and void (Berghahn 1986: 101); on the other hand, the relatively little progress in deconcentration made by the western Allies was reversed during the first few years of the new Federal government's period of office – in spite of Erhard's efforts (see Chapter 8). Nonetheless, the decartelisation and deconcentration of trusts by the (western) occupying powers was undoubtedly one of the greatest experiments undertaken by political forces in a market economy, in spite of the reappearance of uniform market behaviour in industries previously characterised by the existence of strong cartels (Voigt 1962: 187 and 188).

At the end of the war, there was also a pressing monetary problem. The currency had collapsed in two distinct senses: it was no longer traded on the international exchanges, and Germany's unconditional surrender meant, among other things, that the central bank was abolished. In any case, the Reichsbank had again lost its independence. It had become a totally subservient tool of the Nazi regime. The following estimates indicate the implications of its subservience. From 1935 to 1945, currency in circulation rose from RM 5 billion to RM 50 billion; bank deposits increased from RM 30 billion to RM 150 billion (Backer 1971: 91). Backer (*ibid.*) also estimates that, without taking war claims of RM 350 billion into account,

government debt had risen from RM 15 billion in 1935 to RM 400 billion in 1945 – a period during which Germany's national real wealth had decreased by one-third.

Under these circumstances, there could be no confidence in the currency as a means of exchange and it was little wonder that a barter economy emerged. In fact between 1945 and the currency reform in 1948, the economic order was a bizarre mixture of white, black and barter economies (Hansson 1990: 8). In the white economy, the strict Nazi price and wage freeze was continued by the Allies. Of the three sub-spheres, the barter economy assumed greatest importance – an unmistakable signal that confidence had again evaporated in the currency. In other words, the monetary expansion was followed after the end of the war by a repudiation of the country's currency and a shift to money substitutes (Klopstock 1949: 277). But the shortages resulting from the hoarding of food and other goods, from allied coal expropriation and from the bomb-damaged housing and transport stocks, all caused black market prices to soar to about 150 times their legal level. Significantly, black markets accounted for only 10 per cent of the volume of trade, but they absorbed around 80 per cent of monetary circulation (Mendershausen 1974: 37). As will be shown in Figure 3.1 and the surrounding discussion, the Allies increased tax rates to the highest levels in German history. This too reduced the velocity of monetary circulation. The Weimar inflation had thus been open, whereas the post-1945 one was suppressed.

Two necessary (but not sufficient) conditions for economic recovery and reconstruction therefore existed: the re-establishment of a central bank and another currency reform. Both of these reforms required draconian implementation. The western Allies founded a central bank which would be governed by representatives of the federal states but also be independent of government in monetary policy matters (Hardach 1980: 153; Reuss 1963: 51); they also eliminated the huge monetary overhang and re-organised public and private debt (Abelshauser 1983: 49ff; Wallich 1955: 67ff). The bank was established in March 1948, followed in June by the currency reform which introduced the Deutsche Mark. These measures had the desired effect on the real economy in so far as dishoarding was concerned: goods appeared in the shops overnight. The Russians replied with a currency reform in their own zone, where the Ostmark was introduced (Mann 1974: 822). In effect, two separate German states now existed.

On examination, the necessary conditions for the introduction of the SME (see below) can be seen to possess immediate, medium and long term elements (Lösch 1990). The two big bang conditions of monetary reform were seen in the previous paragraph. A phased freeing of markets by the deregulation of prices and wages, along with fiscal reforms, were medium-term aims. Erhard began to institute these measures at the same time as the currency reform. Not least as a result of pressure from the USA, there was also to be a liberalisation of foreign trade (Abelshauser 1983: 151–3). Moreover, a relaxation of exchange controls was held to be necessary. However, full convertibility of the DM was not introduced until 1958 (MRDB 5/88: 16; Yeager 1976: 494–5). This thus transpired to be a longer-run objective, as were the competition, social-security and labour market elements of the SME. It will be useful to compare the SME and GEMSU in this context below.

Notice that the analysis of the last few paragraphs has been largely concerned with the post-war recovery in terms of the domestic economy – not least the resolution of the economy's internal debt problem. As a necessary prelude to the following paragraphs, it is equally important to note that West Germany's external debt problem was ultimately resolved at the London preliminary conference of 1951 and the tortuous main conference of 1952. A treaty was subsequently signed on 27 February 1953. The German delegation was led by Hermann J. Abs who represented Adenauer in this capacity. Abs was to become Germany's most important post-war banker (FT 8 February 1994). Nonetheless, the London debt treaty was probably the most complex issue in which he was involved. Whereas the position regarding Germany's pre-war debt was clarified, this agreement was only made possible by the USA's writing off two-thirds of the post-war foreign aid debt (Stolper *et al.* 1967: 282–3). Unlike the situation after the First World War, West Germany's gold and foreign-currency reserves were therefore left in a viable position (Abelshauser 1983: 158). The subsequent growth of these reserves will be traced in Chapter 4 (see particularly Figure 4.2). This growth implies that another of the necessary conditions for West Germany's restoration into the international trade community was fulfilled at the conference. Two further inferences can be drawn. First, the London debt treaty contributed to international confidence in the then young democracy of West Germany. Hence, along with the resolution of the internal debt problem and the establishment of a reputable banking system and currency, it laid a solid basis for the recovery of West German exports. Second, only following unification could the international debt obligations of the DDR be negotiated. Such a settlement was in fact reached at the London conference.

In West Germany, the third period of economic expansion (1949–59) now took place. It marked the zenith in German economic achievement. Average annual economic growth, in real terms, was more than double that achieved in 1871–1913 (Giersch 1971: 14). The processes of recovery and reconstruction can be accounted for, even though the roles played by good management and good luck are difficult to disentangle. For example, if potential output is defined as the long-run growth path of the economy, then West German super growth was due to the gap between existing and potential output after the war-induced shocks to the economy (Abelshauser 1983: ch. III(1)). Such a phenomenon may not have been confined to West Germany (Dumke 1990). In addition, demand side models which favour an explanation based on the growth of exports, labour supply and capital formation, as well as economic policies, cannot be discounted (*ibid*.: 486–7).

Although explanations of longer-run growth in West Germany are vital topics, which will taken up again, it is important to be clear at this stage on three features of the recovery which ended as early as 1950 (Abelshauser 1982). First, bomb damage to industry had been overestimated and a doubling of industrial production was achieved even before the currency reform. In other words, the index of industrial output stood at 25 per cent of its 1936 level in 1945; by 1948 it reached about 50 per cent of the 1936 volume (Siebert 1992a: 55). Second, in terms of its size, nature and timing, foreign aid as such was not a crucial instrument in priming the German economy (Abelshauser 1981: 566–8). Initially, Marshall Plan deliveries were primarily of foodstuffs. After 1949/50, imports were primarily raw materials. During the accounting years 1951/52,

36 per cent of the goods and services imported were foodstuffs, 52 per cent industrial raw materials and 12 per cent went on freight payments (Knapp 1981: 424). It is equally important to note, however, that the ERP-counterpart funds created a means of allaying public anxiety about government money creation because they were channelled *via* the Federal government's reconstruction and development bank – an institution destined to become one of the economy's largest banks (Abelshauser 1982: 49; Shonfield 1965: 276; Chapter 7 below). These funds were used to promote investment and therefore remove bottlenecks in basic material industries (Wallich 1955: 366). But there is no reason to classify this elaborate charade as foreign aid. This underestimates neither the role of GARIOA in preventing famine, disease and unrest, nor the invaluable EPU credits which facilitated West Germany's transition from a deficit country without foreign currency reserves in 1948 to the first large speculation in favour of a DM revaluation in 1957 (*ibid*.: 91 and 355); it simply implies that the Marshall plan dollar aid gained momentum after the traumatic phases of currency reform and economic liberalisation. Third, on the theory side, the concept of a 'free market' has been hopelessly confused with the 'social market economy'. Even more to the point, how the latter operated in practice is an area where misapprehensions are quite common. Here again valuable material for later discussion exists.

POST-SECOND WORLD WAR CYCLES

The main cyclical features of the West German economy in the post-Second World War era are illustrated in the three Figures which accompany this chapter. In

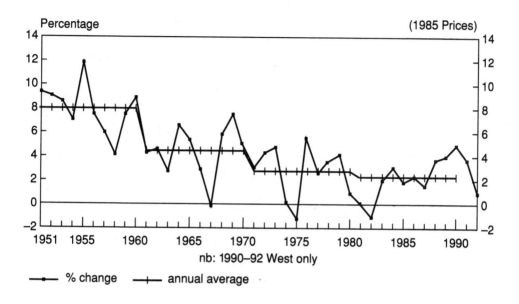

Figure 1.1 West German Gross National Product
Source: Dresdner Bank, *Statistische Reihen*

Figure 1.1, it can be seen that there were three major troughs in economic activity prior to GEMSU. They occurred in 1967, 1975 and 1982 and are indicated by the falls in real national income over the previous year. In all three cases, interest rates (not shown) had been relatively high in the preceding years. Indeed, in the latter two cases interest rates reached record post-war highs. Conversely, the peaks in the growth rates of real national income were partially a lagged response to a lowering of interest rates. This is a vital subject for the monetary policy chapter (see particularly Figure 4.4a). The post-wall boom and the beginning of the 1992–3 recession in the west are also detectable. An important caveat is that average annual growth rates in each of the four decades 1951–90 were 7.96, 4.45, 2.74 and 2.21 per cent respectively. These averages are included in Figure 1.1, thus illustrating the peaks and troughs in economic activity

during each of these time periods. Dumke (1990) shows how the re-construction phase of the 1950s marked a catching-up process, whereby the economy regained its output potential. The economy then resumed its normal growth path. This model tends to demonstrate that a *potential* for economic growth existed during the 1950s; the actual achievement of significant growth rates is attributable to structural factors such as the SME (Braun 1990: 168). Many other factors are examined in this book.

Donges (1980: 186) indicates that the trends in industrial production closely resemble those shown in Figure 1.1 for real national income: 10 per cent on average in the 1950s; 5.2 per cent in the 1960s; 2 per cent in the 1970s. Donges also points out that there is a close correspondence in these data to long-term cycles, the last one of which peaked in 1960. He adds: 'these developments should correct simplistic

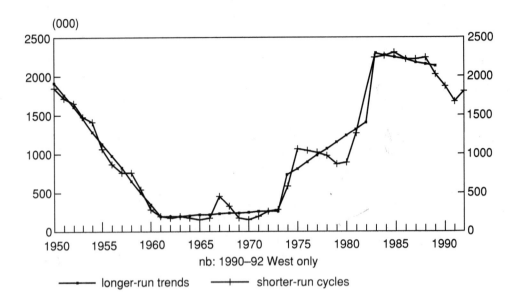

Figure 1.2 Unemployment in West Germany
Source: Plotted from Dresdner Bank, *Statistische Reihen*

notions about (economic) miracles in the Federal Republic'. However, the fluctuations in industrial production were more marked than GNRP in so far as there were falls over the previous years in 1967, 1974 and 1975 of 3.0, 2.7 and 6.5 respectively; since the Donges' article appeared, decreases also occurred in 1980–82 inclusive and in 1987. This book concludes (Figure 8.13) by posing the question: 'was the 1992–3 fall in industrial production just another recession in the west, or did it mark the beginning of a structural collapse?' In other words, did GEMSU coincide with the emergence of serious competitive shortcomings in the products of west German industry – a debate known as *Standort Deutschland*.

Perhaps the general behaviour of the labour market is even more instructive. Unemployment rose rapidly following the currency reform (Wallich 1955: 79). By 1950 it was nearing the two million mark.

Thereafter, as Figure 1.2 demonstrates, the following contrasting features were distinguishable. Initially, unemployment fell rapidly so that by 1960 it was at a very low level. Indeed, there were more unfilled vacancies (not shown) than unemployment. This situation continued until 1973, apart from the 1967 recession, as will be illustrated in the discussion around Figure 6.3. Unemployment then rose after the two crude oil price shocks of 1973 and 1979. It then remained at a plateau of two million until the western boom on unification. Very roughly, then, the 1950s and 1970s are mirror images: a steep fall compared to a steep rise in unemployment. Notice also the short-run cycles around the longer-run trends. Also note the initial continuation in declining unemployment following GEMSU; however, western unemployment began to rise again in 1992 (see also Figure 6.4).

A final perspective can be derived from

Figure 1.3 which, like Figure 1.1, is concerned with real national income. Consumption predictably shows a fairly stable rate of change, falling over the previous year only in the early 1980s. But note how the rate of change in exports is generally above that of consumption. Moreover, exports show only one major fall on the previous year – in 1975, although it must be added that in 1982 and 1986 they hardly changed in real terms. But in general the well-known phenomenon of export-led growth can be gauged from the impulses emanating from this injection. The invaluable impulse from the Korean boom, and the generally buoyant behaviour of exports during the period of reconstruction in the 1950s, are particularly noteworthy. The importance of exports to the German economy cannot be overstated. The *Economist* (20 February 1988: 79), for example, made this point clear with an incisive comment:

True, only 10 per cent of West Germany's exports go to the USA, compared with 40 per cent of Japan's, but exports account for a third of West Germany's GNP, against only 12 per cent of Japan's, so the dollar's decline has had just as severe an impact on West Germany as Japan.

Investment in plant and equipment, as would be expected, is a more volatile injection (investment in construction has been omitted from Figure 1.3). The 1967 and the oil-shock induced recessions of 1974 and the early 1980s are easily discernible; but the subsequent strong recoveries are equally evident. Finally, the post-GEMSU western recession can be seen from the fall in capital investment in the west. It can also be seen that western consumption and exports did not rise as vigorously in 1992. (Exports were also diverted to the east after GEMSU.)

All these fluctuations and trends reveal valuable material for future chapters. Fiscal and monetary policies, many general aspects of the labour market, as

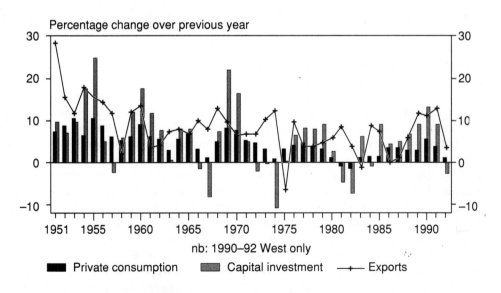

Figure 1.3 GNRP: Expenditure approach (West: 1985 prices)
Source: Plotted from Dresdner Bank, *Statistische Reihen*

well as the patterns of consumption, investment and foreign trade, are all areas germane to a consideration of German economic performance.

THE ACTORS

Six groups of actors who determine policy formulation have emerged from the above long-run phases of economic expansion and contraction from 1871 to 1959. They are: the Federal government, the Länder (or federal states), the Bundesbank (or federal bank), the banking sector, the company sector and the trade unions.

There is an elaborate system of power sharing between the Federal and Länder governments. The Länder governments are represented in the federal upper house (Bundesrat). Since elections at these two levels of government do not normally coincide and party popularity varies, it is possible for the party political complexion of the majorities in the two federal houses to differ. Should this occur, the Federal government's economic policies can be blocked in the upper house if a mutually acceptable compromise is not reached. Moreover, at both levels of government coalitions are usually necessary because no one party holds an absolute parliamentary majority. This leads to economic policies in the Federal and the sixteen Länder cabinets often being the subject of lengthy negotiation and compromise.

Both levels of government, and to a lesser extent local authorities, share the revenue from taxes on income from employment. Since 1980 the respective ratios have been 42.5:42.5:15. Corporate and investment tax revenue is shared equally between the Federal and Länder governments, whereas value-added tax revenue was divided 65:35 until 1993. As a result of the hard-fought solidarity agreement to fund the costs of unification, the ratio then became 58:42. In addition, all three levels of government autonomously levy a number of other taxes. On the expenditure side, there is a similar pattern of both shared and independent functions. Two critical areas – social security and education – are respectively the responsibility of the Federal and Länder governments. Understandably, defence is a federal matter, but the police fall within the purview of the Länder. Both levels of government are active participants in the economy in two other senses: they are business owners and dispensers of state aid.

This degree of Länder autonomy is a clear product of the historical factors noted above. Although allowed to re-emerge in the post-war era, its scope during the Bonn Republic was modified in the interest of economic planning. Legislation to be analysed in this book requires the two levels of government to draw up five-year fiscal plans, and jointly address such diverse questions as university expansion, regional planning and agricultural policy. Because of the appreciable regional disparity in economic structures, such a policy aim is more easily stated than achieved. This derives from the regional differences between the ability to raise tax revenue and expenditure demands, not least for subsidies. A complex equalisation scheme which required constitutional amendments was therefore introduced. Basically, this scheme stimulates revenue flows from the more prosperous Länder to the relatively underdeveloped regions. Since relatively impoverished Länder were added to the Federal Republic on unification, an already contentious policy area was further exacerbated. Above all, the extent to which the western Länder should contribute to the costs of unification became a major policy issue.

The establishment of an independent central bank is an even more obvious consequence of the preceding historical analysis. The Bank deutscher Länder, set up by the western Allies in 1948, was succeeded in 1957 by the Deutsche Bundesbank. By virtue of its founding statute (BBankG 1957), the Bundesbank ostensibly enjoys a virtual monopoly over monetary policy matters, hence the reason for including a whole chapter on this particular policy actor. It not only uses its instruments to control the degree of liquidity in the economy but also pronounces publicly on fiscal policy, particularly where budgetary deficits and the consequent borrowing requirements are concerned (MRDB 5/86: 22 and 25):

Against the background of historical experience with two major inflations, which were possible only because the central government had unlimited access to central bank finance, there was general agreement after the currency reform that the scope for central bank lending to the government should be kept within very narrow limits at all times . . . Central bank credit must not be provided to finance budget deficits . . . The fact that Bundesbank cash advances are meant to provide last resort very short-term liquidity assistance and are not primarily a source of cheap funds tends to be forgotten sometimes.

In taking such a firm view on price stability, the Bundesbank not only regards potential political interference in money creation with caution: 'it turned out to be difficult to make the general public – and especially management and labour – understand that . . . nominal income demands could not continue to rise, as they had been doing, at double-digit growth rates' (MRDB 5/88: 20). Its somewhat contradictory policy goals are price

stability and exchange rate control, with a growing post-war history of government involvement in the latter case. If anything, the Bundesbank's role in policy formulation increased further with unification and proposals for European monetary integration. In the latter case, the official Bundesbank view is that its constitution represents an ideal model for a federal banking system within the EC. It is little wonder, then, that even the German quality press frequently refers to the Bundesbank's governing council as *die Frankfurter Geldhüter*, or the currency guardians of Frankfurt. This eulogy may, however, be somewhat misconceived. Indeed, the extent of such an oversimplification will be clear from the arguments in Chapter 4. These arguments revolve around the precise contributions of monetary policy to price stability and recession.

The other major piece of banking legislation in the Bonn Republic (KWG 1963) placed the rest of the banking system at the other end of the legal spectrum when it comes to prudential control. Permitted activities, quantitative ceilings, ratios and other limits are the subject of regulation. Statutory amendments in 1976 and 1984 signified a quick response to the circumvention of particular banking regulations. To a certain extent this degree of regulation is the result of lessons learned during the inter-war banking crisis.

One traditional feature of German banking remains unchanged, however. Both commercial and investment banking are provided by the same institutions at branch level. This system of universal banking was historically developed to provide a capital market for industry. There are still very close links between these two sectors. (In spite of recent growth, the stock exchange remains relatively underdeveloped.) The universal banks have three categories of ownership:

private, public and cooperative. Each of these three segments possesses its own clearing system. Taken together with the recent growth in their insurance links and their specialist banking subsidiaries, the banks also provide sufficient material for a chapter in this book.

Many of the attributes of the company sector have also been highlighted above. The legal framework in which enterprises operated until after the Second World War was conducive to a high degree of cartelisation and large market shares. Post-war legislation (GWB 1957, as amended) may have reduced the number of cartels but it came too late to prevent a re-emergence of dominant enterprises in the major sectors, particularly chemical, electrical, motor vehicle and other mechanical engineering. As a result, German industry derives large economies of scale. It also enjoys a flourishing export market. Technical superiority, along with a related high level of R&D, also contribute to high productivity levels – as does the efficient vocational training system. Moreover, the large enterprises in Germany tend to be multinational in character. Hence, a number of issues pertaining to the company sector must be analysed in this book.

There is also the role of the company sector in terms of employment. German employers' associations are powerful organisations. They were established to enable employers to bargain collectively with the trade unions at regional and industry level. At the level of the enterprise, each large employer is required by statute to facilitate employee representation on the company's non-executive board, as well as according rights of co-determination and consultation to a series of works councils at plant, company and group level. These councils also have a statutory right to a flow of information from the employer. Although this system

of industrial democracy has firm historical roots in Germany, it was the Allies, particularly the British, who encouraged its re-emergence after the Second World War.

More generally, the Allies turned to the trade unions for assistance in the denazification process. Their revival was positively encouraged. But there were features other than the genesis of post-war industrial democracy at enterprise level. Above all, a non-sectarian basis was generally observed as the movement itself was re-built. The divisive religious and political affiliations of the many wings of the trade union movement which weakened their opposition to the rise of the Nazis were avoided. As a result of pressure from the British occupational government and trade union delegation, German proposals for an all-powerful central organisation were renounced in favour of a more traditional German type of union organisation (Hirsch-Weber 1959: 50; Schneider 1989: 240). The general principle is that each industry has its own trade union. This facilitates collective bargaining with the relevant employers' association at this level. There are some relatively minor exceptions on the trade union side, but these will be analysed below. It is important to emphasise here that trade unions are accepted as part of Germany's pluralistic democracy. The Christian Democrats (Germany's conservatives) have a strong trade union base. It follows that 'they do not instinctively dislike the important role played by the trade unions in running the country's industry' (*Economist*, 9 March 1991).

This complex policy-making process often results in a rather protracted decision-making interval. Unification is the classic case in point. The Federal government initially proposed to meet the costs by increasing its borrowing requirements. Tax increases were not a policy option in an election year (1990). The Länder in the west also agreed to increase borrowing for their contributions to the unity fund, but did not relish the prospect of the ex-DDR Länder immediately becoming full participants in the compensatory finance scheme (see Chapter 2). Both levels of government found it difficult to indulge in expenditure switching. Meanwhile, the Bundesbank viewed the increasing money supply with some concern and raised interest rates. Tax increases were eventually agreed, although the temporary income-tax surcharge of the Federal government met with opposition from the SPD majority in the Bundesrat. Eastern unemployment was rising rapidly but, for various reasons, the company sector and banks were rather reluctant to invest in the east. The trade unions were seeking a fairly rapid equalisation of pay rates in east and west. Each group of actors was therefore pursuing conflicting aims. When the inescapable conclusion was reached that for a decade transfers from west to east would total at least DM 150 billion per year, the need for a 'solidarity pact' concentrated the minds of the coalition and opposition at federal level, along with the trade unions, employers and the sixteen Länder. This was because the Bundesbank would not reduce its restrictive monetary policy until budget deficits and wage claims were reduced. But that had often been the initial situation in the west during the post-war era. Sooner or later, however, a consensus has emerged, especially during the phases of recovery and reconstruction (1945–59). Each group of actors generally seemed to contribute to the harmonious functioning of the economy – a somewhat nebulous concept summarised by the German term *Ordnungsfaktor*.

Because the actors are dispersed throughout the territory of the former Bonn Republic, there is also a high degree of decentralisation in this sense. Bonn itself, prior to unification, was the seat of the federal government and both houses of Parliament. Berlin, the new federal capital following unification, is to succeed Bonn in this respect, although the federal upper house is remaining in Bonn. Berlin is already the location of the Federal Cartel Office and the Federal Bank Supervisory Authority. The Bundesbank is remaining in Frankfurt am Main – a city which aspires to becoming, and in many senses already is, the federal financial centre. The largest stock exchange is located here. There are regional rivals in this respect – the next two largest exchanges being in Düsseldorf and Munich. These latter cities are also major banking and insurance centres but Frankfurt am Main houses the head offices of the major banks; if the Maastricht aspirations for EMU are attained, it will also probably become the seat of the envisaged European Central Bank. It is important to add, however, that the Länder have their own 'central' banks located in a major city within their territory – see Chapter 7 for further details. The law plays a major role in economic affairs so it should be noted that the Federal Constitutional Court sits in Karlsruhe, while the Federal Labour Court sits in Kassel. The federal employers' and industrial organisations are in Cologne and the main trade union federation is just up the road in Düsseldorf. In Chapter 6 it will also be seen that there are two further union organisations: the DAG in Hamburg and the DBB in Bonn. A similar degree of regional diversification applies to the location of industry. The attendant problems arising from this factor will be explored in Chapter 2. Suffice it to say at this stage that some local economies are almost entirely dependent on internationally famous companies. Some examples are Krupp/Essen, Bayer/Leverkusen, BASF/Ludwigshafen, Volkswagen/Wolfsburg and Opel/Rüsselheim.

Decision making with respect to the two main economic issues of the 1990s – unification and EMU – illustrates the competing influence of the six actors. There were three issues in particular which generated a fair degree of acrimony. First, the process of increasing VAT to 15 per cent and the introduction of income-tax surcharges to partially finance unification (Chapter 3). Second, the question of revenue sharing (Chapter 2). Third, restructuring the Bundesbank (Chapters 2 and 4).

WEST GERMANY AND MARKET FORMS

It has already been seen that the Social Market Economy (SME) was the underlying economic philosophy after the currency reform. Prior to the reform, there had been a fairly heated debate among the Germans themselves as to which form of economic and social organisation ought to be introduced. Nationalisation was advocated by the trade unions, social democrats, some Christian democrats and the communists, but British support for such measures had to be qualified as a result of opposition from the USA (Abelshauser 1981: 564; Carlin 1987: 16; Owen Smith 1983 : 12, 15 and 21). After all, there had been a long debate within the Catholic church about 'solidarism' which was often in open conflict with economic liberalism; the ethics of Protestantism were also modified along socialist lines by some philosophers (Genosko 1986; Riha 1985: 124–30). Indeed, as Hirsch-Weber demonstrated (1959: 60–1), the CDU had a strong press-ure group in favour of the socialisation clause in the Weimar constitution. Carlin (1987: 17–19) also explored the CDUs search for a new economic order but concluded (p.22) that organised labour saw Marshall Aid as being conditional upon abandoning these plans.

This tussle alone, to say nothing of other German perceptions, makes the SME a complex notion. It has two distinct aspects. First, its evolution as part of German economic thought and, second, its implementation as an allocative mechanism. An understanding of both aspects throws valuable light on many features of post-war economic policy. Indeed, Porstmann (1990) attributed the large difference in economic development between East and West Germany to the latter's receipt of Marshall Aid and the introduction of the SME.

Riha (1985: 218) helpfully defines the SME as the 'socially responsible free market economy'. In 1953, its ordo-liberal adherents formed a society in order to influence the actors in the policy-making process (*ibid*.: 229n). But as Riha also points out German economic science is, in its present form, the result of a process of development extending over 400 years; it always contained a sense of social purpose (*ibid*.: 222–4). More specifically, although the phrase 'social market economy' was coined by Müller-Armack, he acknowledged that this concept of 'a comprehensive order (which) went beyond the market' was inspired by the Freiburg School of economists (Müller-Armack 1978: 325). This school of thought was founded just prior to the Nazi *coup*. During the Nazi era itself, those members of the school who did not leave the country represented a kind of intellectual resistance movement, a stand which required a great deal of personal courage and independent thinking (Denton *et al.*

1968: 35; Wallich 1955: 114). The school's leading members were Professors Eucken and Böhm. Extracts from the works of other important members of the school – including Röpke – are contained in the first Peacock and Willgerodt volume (1989a).

On the theory side of the SME, it is necessary to emphasise four fundamental principles. The first is the definition of competition employed in the model; the second is the appropriate role for state intervention; the third is the place for anti-cyclical measures; while the fourth principle is concerned with the all-important ethical and political aspects of neo-classical liberalism (Denton *et al.* 1968: 41).

In defining competition, the Freiburg school conceived of two pure economic forms: the market or central control. Each of these two forms could be sub-divided, with competition representing the purest form of a market economy. Particular note must be taken of the working definition of 'competition' employed by the SME theorists. Böhm categorically rejected Anglo-Saxon models: 'what matters is not the degree to which perfect competition exists, but the opportunity for the free and untrammelled exercise of competitive energies' (quoted by Denton *ibid.*: 42). In fact, 'workable' competition was the somewhat more modest aim of the SME theorists (Peacock *et al.* 1980: paras 3.19 and 3.20). However, the market economy is prone to monopolisation which implies the need for state intervention in the form of anti-trust policies: 'even a market economy requires a framework within which to operate, and the creation of this framework is the role of the state' (Hallett 1973: 19). Indeed, Röpke was deeply concerned about the extent to which some thinkers apparently relied on market forces alone to secure

a thriving small business sector, or *Mittelstand* (Köster 1991: 52–3). According to the Freiburg hypothesis, therefore, open markets could be achieved by the removal of protective tariffs and state controls on private industry. But the reduction of quasi-monopolistic privileges granted by the state, and the banning of restrictive practices, were also essential elements of the model. The first and second principles can thus be summarised by saying that competition was the most promising means of achieving prosperity and anything which constrained competition was detrimental to society. However, active government intervention is viewed as a necessity in the SME model, otherwise dominant firms and collusive behaviour become major policy problems; in the Anglo-Saxon approach, the barriers to competition are seen as being erected by governments (Sawyer in Michie 1992: 331). Finally, it should be recalled that the theory of the SME is the present concern. Chapters 7 and 8 will be replete with examples of 'collusive behaviour and barriers to entry' (Steinherr 1991: 362 and 367).

With respect to stabilisation policy – the third principle – the initial search by the Freiburg School was for a built-in stabiliser. This was to be achieved by a strict control of the money supply. The influence of German monetary experience is plain to see. Given a stable monetary order, cyclical fluctuations would be significantly dampened by means of the signals to investors of an efficiently operating price mechanism. To ensure that monetary policy was not side-tracked by partisan pressures from its main objective of maintaining (price) stability, Eucken recommended that arrangements should be made for its automatic operation. His optimistic view that cyclical fluctuations could be avoided in such a simple manner was exposed when Schiller later incorporated Keynesian demand management policies into the SME framework. Eucken also favoured a progressive income tax as long as it did not interfere with capital formation incentives (Stolper and Roskamp 1979: 378). Whereas it must again be stressed that actual policy experience is the subject matter of subsequent chapters, an interesting relationship between the second and third principles of the SME can nonetheless be given at this stage. During the formative stages of postwar anti-trust policy, Karl Blessing – who was to become the first and tenacious president of the independent Bundesbank – represented West Germany's margarine industry in a series of exchanges with Erhard which resulted in a compromise on price-fixing cartels (Marsh 1992: 55 and 185). This is at once an excellent example of the juxtaposing of 'workable competition' in the product market and setting the sole goal of price stability for monetary policy.

It is when one considers the fourth and final principle of the SME's theoretical ramifications that the proverbial can of worms is opened. Although Müller-Armack (1978: 329) denied that the SME was a *Weltanschauung* like classical liberalism or socialism, he contended that the system provided by the SME produced greater personal responsibility and individual freedom. Erhard (1962: 186) undoubtedly had this in mind when he stressed the close links between economic and social policy. In his view, individuals would not display energy, effort and enterprise if an all-embracing social policy undermined incentive. Indeed, the more successful economic policy became, the fewer the social policy measures which would be necessary (Berghahn 1986: 159 and 205). Efficient production and personal freedom were the keystones of a

socially balanced order (Watrin 1979: 419). Within this central notion of order, however, the development of both freedom *and* social security were seen as historical tasks of equal significance (Müller-Armack 1978: 329). Hence, both a social security framework and the provision of an adequate social safety net are essential policy inferences of the fourth principle. It should be added that industrial democracy, along with trade union representation in more general economic affairs, are further strands in this complex fourth principle – to say nothing of the guarantee of a job appropriate to one's aspirations and abilities (Lampert and Bossert 1992: 85). This presumption of a 'democratic and *social* state' (writer's emphasis) is thus embodied in an almost peremptory manner in Articles 20(1) and 28 of the Basic Law (*ibid.*; Rosen and Windisch 1992: 307). Taken together, this social framework has resulted in the development of institutions and structures of state intervention which have reinforced the role of markets as an engine of accumulation and change (Eatwell in Michie 1992: 338; Figure 5.1 below). Nowhere is the fundamental difference between the German and Anglo-Saxon approach to markets more apparent.

The first federal chancellor (Adenauer 1966: 165) postulated an operationally meaningful test when he defined the SME as a renunciation of planning and the direction of production, labour and sales. Given his opposition to the Nazi and East German systems, that part of his proposition is understandable. But he added that the SME was a comprehensive economic policy combining monetary, trade, tariff, tax, investment and social policies, as well as other measures designed to ensure the welfare of the population as a whole, including provision for the needy. Chancellor Kohl (1987, before he became the first Chancellor of a unified Germany) gave an equally wide definition. More than anything else, he saw the value of the SME as lying in job creation, unemployment reduction, personal achievement (through tax relief), international competitiveness, environmental protection and social security. In arguing the significance of social welfare in the SME model, von Weizsäcker (1990: 11–12) points out that Germany's spending in this field is at the top of the EC and East European league tables. From a social and economic equity point of view, it must also be emphasised that a highly significant feature of German post-war fiscal and monetary policy was the notion of 'equalisation' (*Ausgleich*). Wallich (1955: 70 and 278) traces the emergence of this notion. Hence, expellees and refugees from eastern Europe, war victims, institutions which had their assets written off in the currency reform, economically weaker Länder and, following GEMSU, the new Länder were all beneficiaries from some form of financial compensation. The comprehensive nature of the 'social state' is thus beyond any doubt. Rather, addressing the degree of its comprehensiveness has become the principal social-policy issue (Lampert and Bossert 1992: ch. V; Chapter 5 below). In short, outside of Germany, one would be hard pressed to find such a positive attempt to mould all the elements of economic policy into a single concept (Denton *et al.* 1968: 41). It demonstrates the irrelevance of any *laissez-faire* considerations.

Most, if not all, of this theoretical framework can be found in the Peacock and Willgerodt volumes (1989a and 1989b). The economic, social and legal nature of the model, purporting to combine the fundamental objectives of efficiency, freedom and equity in an optimal manner, can be found in the extracts from Eucken (the economic and social system), Böhm (rule of law), Hensel (management/industrial democracy) and Müller-Armack which appear in the first volume, and the essay by Wiseman in the second. The necessary conditions are the absence of monopoly, the minimisation of government intervention and, as a minimal monetary position, an independent central bank which is obliged by law to preserve a stable currency (1989a: 56; Bernholz in 1989b: ch 10). A fully adequate monetary system required the re-establishment of the gold standard but a second-best solution is a system of flexible exchange rates, together with the abolition of foreign exchange controls (Röpke in 1989a: ch 5; 1989b: 208). Many post-war policy developments follow logically from this model. But as with all theoretical models, the theory does not always accord with the facts.

The implementation of the SME as an allocative mechanism has, in some way or other, affected all the markets with which this book is concerned. In the money market, and therefore to a certain extent in the financial market for bonds, the independent role of the Bundesbank has played a key role in the pursuit of price stability. However, at the very least between 1967 and 1982, fiscal policy makers in the form of the Federal and Länder governments were equally concerned with employment stability. Government intervention in various labour and product markets has certainly been a key and growing feature of the post-war economy in West Germany. This intervention has taken the forms of ownership, subsidies, regulation and anti-trust policy, although the latter was developed too late to prevent a resurgence of dominant firms in key industries. Moreover, subsidies, regulation and tax concessions in agriculture, energy, housing and transport have caused growing disquiet among German economists. The central argument has been that market failure is less of a problem than markets not being allowed to operate. Similarly, the banks' dominance of the capital market has implications for anti-trust policy. Finally, the generous social security system, along with industrial democracy and collective bargaining, all have implications for the labour market. This paragraph therefore outlines the principal issues to be addressed in this book.

EAST GERMANY AND THE COMMAND ECONOMY

It seems ironic that the powerful intellectual arguments put forward by the Freiburg School basically against the Nazi command economy were to continue to influence the economic debate in Germany until and even during the unification process. This particularly applies, of course, to the basic proposition that the market paradigm was one of two pure economic forms, the other being central planning.

East Germany faced a number of economic handicaps when compared to its western neighbour (Ardagh 1988: 326). Soviet dismantling after the war reduced her industrial capacity by an estimated 40 to 45 per cent, equal to twice the damage done by the war. When the transportation of these whole plants for re-assembly in the Soviet Union proved to be inefficient, the Russians substituted a policy of expropriating output. This latter policy accounted for 25 per cent of GNP between 1945 and 1953. Only from the 1960s onwards was East Germany integrated into Comecon, the eastern bloc's trading system (Flockton 1993: 1). As already shown above, West Germany's recovery had been completed by 1950.

By that year, the western Allies had completely abandoned their dismantling programme, mainly because of the cold war and trade union opposition. Reparation deliveries from West Germany had little economic impact and the British and Americans had begun to embark on a policy of reconstruction in their respective zones long before the establishment of the Bi-Zone on 1 January 1947 (Berghahn 1986: 76–7). Her integration into the west's trading system was fully completed shortly afterwards and by 1953 she had been a major beneficiary of the Korean war boom. Moreover, East Germany generally inherited a somewhat less industrialised part of pre-war Germany, although the southern part of the economy, together with the conurbation of Berlin, had significant industrial traditions. Her trade pattern became similar to West Germany's, with the traditional German products of chemicals, optical products and machinery being dominant (Stolper and Roskamp 1979: 400). Her mineral resources were largely limited to lignite (brown coal) and potash. As a result, 70 per cent of primary energy requirements were met from the highly pollutant lignite, the other 30 per cent coming from crude oil and natural gas principally imported from the Soviet Union. Nuclear energy latterly played a role in electricity generation but 80 per cent of demand was generated from lignite.

The implementation of the command economy in East Germany was in some respects a protracted affair. Three phases can be identified (Lipschitz and McDonald 1990: 70):

- strict central planning (1945–62)
- reform under Ulbricht (1963–70)
- recentralisation under Honecker (1971–89)

Immediately after the Second World War, the Soviet military authorities insisted on the expropriation of all Nazi and Junker estates located in their zone (*Bodenreform*). As just seen, dismantling of some industrial plants began; others passed into state control. The Ostmark was introduced at the same time as the DM in the west. Although small holdings were permitted, the collectivisation of agriculture continued throughout the period of communist rule so that by unification the number of farms had been reduced to about 4,000. This represented 90 per cent of all arable land in the east. (In strictly economic terms the size of the average holding compared well with the typical small-scale family holding in the west, although productivity was far lower.)

During the second half of the 1960s, the basic policy stance was characterised by an attempt to secure an optimal combination of state planning and independent decision making at enterprise level (Leptin and Meltzer 1978: 98). There was then a decisive change in economic policy at the beginning of the 1970s. Re-centralisation was introduced. Small and medium-sized businesses were nationalised in 1972, while in 1979/80 it was decided that the 'people's enterprises' (VEB) should be re-organised along product lines into a series of combines (Kombinate). The aim of this measure to introduce central coordination of research, production and sales within each combine. By 1988, this process had resulted in the establishment at the national level of 126 industrial combines, each of which consisted of between 20 and 40 enterprises with on average more than 20,000 employees. At the local level there were a further 95 combines with, on average, 2,000 employees (Cornelsen, 1990: 72). Finally, combines were established in other sectors such as construc-

tion. Lipschitz and McDonald (1990: 70n) report that the total of centrally-controlled combines was 173, while the locally-controlled total was 143; they accounted for about 60 per cent of establishments employing less than 500 employees. Given this type of economic system, it is not surprising that the only developed area in the service sector was in the public service.

On unification, 6 million of the 8.9 million employees worked in approximately 8,000 VEB. The 30 largest Kombinate employed one million persons, over 40 per cent of the industrial labour force in East Germany (*Die Zeit* 51/89). Private property was virtually non-existent. Because of excessive centralisation and widespread corruption, living standards had been deteriorating for some time. In spite of early warnings from economists, industrial profits had been channelled into the subsidisation of rents, fares, social services and culture (Leptin and Meltzer 1978: 151 and 182–3). In addition, a serious external balance problem was caused by the rise in crude oil prices during the 1970s. The DDR had followed the common international pattern of substituting oil for coal but along with other eastern European economies found it difficult to adjust to the rapid rise in oil import prices. Between 1960 and 1979 annual crude oil imports, mainly from the Soviet Union, rose from 2 million to 21 million tonnes; thereafter, imports stabilised at 23 million tonnes annually during the 1980s (Cornelsen 1990: 74–5). This was achieved by re-exploiting brown coal stocks for domestic use. Meanwhile, 50 per cent of oil imports were re-exported in either a refined or crude form to western economies.

When western banks demanded a reduction in the DDR's indebtedness in 1981/82, the pressure to increase exports and reduce imports was further increased.

Consequently, nearly all the growth in output during the 1980s was devoted to improving the current account. The result was an almost complete lack of capital investment and technical change. Product obsolescence was another consequence, as was low labour productivity. Industry was also overmanned. Outward migration to the west – the proximate cause of the construction of the Berlin Wall in 1961 – reached a peak after the re-opening of the Wall in 1989. It was only stemmed by the general expectations generated by German Economic, Social and Monetary Union (GEMSU). The term 'social' in both GEMSU and the SME were to prove particularly important: von Weizsäcker (1990: 12) argued that West Germany's generous social security provisions would have acted for several decades as a magnet for European migrants generally, had protective measures not been taken. He concluded that the only policy option is for other European states to emulate Germany's leading role in this field.

THE ECONOMICS OF UNIFICATION

A special report by the West German Council of Economic Advisers (SVR 1990) and the OECD in its annual *Economic Survey* (1990), both sounded the alarm bells about the economic implications of unification. In 1988, 52 per cent of East German households possessed a colour television set (in West Germany the proportion was 94 per cent). Only 9 per cent of households in the East had a telephone (West: 98 per cent). The dwelling space per inhabitant differed, too: in the East it was 27 m² compared to 35 m² in the West. But as the eastern housing stock was dilapidated, the difference in quality and living comfort was significantly greater. Similarly, there was widespread anecdotal evidence of inferior product quality and mismatches between goods supplied and demanded, indicating that the utility derived from consumption was substantially lower than the statistics suggested. There was also very severe environmental degradation along with unhealthy working conditions, which also adversely affected living standards.

Income per head in East Germany in 1990 was estimated at 55 per cent of that in West Germany. A sample survey by *Der Spiegel* (35/90: 40) revealed that 71 per cent of employed persons in East Germany earned less than DM 1,000 (net) per month, whereas the equivalent statistic for West Germany was 9 per cent; only one per cent of East Germans earned over DM 2,000, whereas the figure in the West was 52 per cent. Yet 53 per cent of employed East Germans thought their job was insecure, compared to only 7 per cent of West Germans. When GEMSU was introduced with generous, if unrealistic, exchange rates their worst fears were to be confirmed. In order to underwrite the exchange-rate decision, enormous financial transfers would have to flow from west to east (see the concluding section to Chapter 3). Without such transfers, the economic miracle expected to follow from the combination of democracy and the market would not be easily realised, even given a number of temporary exemptions from EC regulations (Boehmer-Christiansen *et al.* 1993: 358 and 371).

Such vast differences in real living standards and earnings reflected the significant differences in the relative capital stocks and labour productivity levels. The OECD (*ibid.*) estimated, on the then reasonable assumption that the East German level of productivity was 40 per cent of the West's, that it would take 15, 20 or 30 years for average productivity in the East to reach the western level, given that an annual respective 8.5, 6.75 or 5.25 per cent rate of productivity increase could be achieved in the East and assuming that the West's trend rate of a 2 per cent increase was maintained. Similarly, the calculations for the required increase to achieve equivalence in the capital stock were based on the equally reasonable assumption that the capital stock per worker in the East was not much more than a third of that in the West. In this case, with an annual depreciation rate of 8 per cent and an initial capital stock of DM 600 billion, the time periods were again 15, 20 and 30 years, given a respective increase in the order of 10.5, 8.5 and 7 per cent. The scenarios put forward by the Lipschitz and McDonald (1990: ch V) came to similar conclusions: if eastern labour productivity reached 80 per cent of the western level by 2001, unemployment (adjusted to incorporate part-time employees) would be 6 per cent and migration to the west would have ceased by 1994. The general budget deficit of east Germany would fall from DM 45 billion in 1992 to DM 7 billion in 2001. However, if only a 60 per cent relative productivity level were achieved, adjusted unemployment would remain high: a quarter of the labour force would still be unemployed in 1992, diminishing to 9 per cent in 2001. There would be appreciable migration – 207,000 in 1992 and still 90,000 in 2001. The general budget deficit would also be sizeable – DM 45 billion in 1992, and DM 29 billion in 2001. Such deficits had undermined post-war Federal governments in West Germany, as will be seen in the budgetary policy section of Chapter 3. Another big question mark hung over the future course of wage inflation and its effects on capital investment.

At a later stage, Hughes Hallet and Ma (1993) made three points of relevance here. First, they estimated that full convergence of productivity levels in east and west would take 30–40 years, with as little as 50 per cent of full convergence after 15 years. Second, this slow productivity catching up process would risk a Mezzogiorno problem in which investment and/or labour would have to be supported by continuing fiscal transfers – a phenomenon discussed in a wider context in Chapters 2 and 3. Third, the inflationary impact of unification would be limited by a tightening of monetary policy and this would cause spill-over effects in other ERM countries. Although the implications of this latter point are discussed in Chapter 4, it should be indicated here that experience following German unification demonstrated the limitations of the EMS, of which the ERM was a salient feature, of course (Chaffour *et al.* 1992: 271). West German economic and monetary policy-makers would necessarily be preoccupied with the unification and their dominance of the EC suggested that the EMU treaty negotiated at Maastricht would have been more attractive for the EC as a whole. Above all, EMU would probably have significantly dampened the rise of European, and hence German, short-term interest rates (*ibid.*: 264).

It was apparent at the outset, then, that the costs of unification were going to be enormous, especially when the required drastic reduction in pollution and the re-construction of the infrastructure are added to the re-building of industry. This writer consistently argued that the infrastructure and pollution-control costs would reach DM 1 trillion (1×10^{12}), an estimate similar to the considered views of von Dohnanyi (1990: 258), Porstmann (1990: 46) and *Time International* (9 October 1990). The Lipschitz and McDonald scenarios (1990: 77) assumed DM 1.0 to DM 1.3 trillion in net investment over the period 1991–2000 in the east, in order to achieve the 80 per cent of west German productivity levels referred to above. The key assumptions about the starting point in 1990 were that eastern productivity was 30 per cent of western levels and the capital stock in the east was DM 624 billion compared to DM 7.2 trillion in the west (*ibid.*: 72 and 76). By 2001, the relative capital stock would be DM 1.77 trillion compared to DM 10.25 trillion. This squares well with the RWI estimate of DM 1.5 trillion in net investment by 2000 in order to equalise productivity levels (quoted by von Dohnanyi (*ibid.*) – who personally estimated that an additional DM 1 trillion would be required for the modernisation of educational, scientific, sport, leisure and cultural facilities). The lower estimate by Lipschitz and McDonald (*ibid.*) of net investment to equalise productivity levels by the turn of the century was also DM 1.5 trillion.

Such costs would conventionally have to be funded by government borrowing, expenditure switching by government, tax increases, low interest loans, privatisation in both the East and the West and both foreign and domestic private investment. But it has already been demonstrated above that policy making is at the best of times a cumbersome affair in Germany. The Bundesbank's governing council would not permit too strong an increase in the money supply. They would have preferred an increase in taxes to cover the costs of unification. As late as May 1990, the Federal finance minister in the west (Waigel) was arguing that increased growth would compensate for extra spending needs. As already indicated, according to the Lipschitz and McDonald scenarios (*ibid.*: 84), budget deficits would only fall to more easily sustainable levels if the catching-up process of productivity succeeds in achieving at least the critical 80 per cent of western standards by 2001.

Viewed separately, the two parts of the economy faced a regional challenge: how best to ensure a rapid upward swing in the development of the eastern part of the economy, thus avoiding mass migration to the west (EC 1990a: 11).

The merger of the two German states therefore brought together countries with divergent economic systems, different trade orientations and a rift in terms of economic wealth (Welfens 1991). Transforming the East German system into a SME raised enormous internal and external adjustment problems during a period in which West Germany already faced the challenges of the EC 1993 project and EMU. Welfens (*ibid.*) goes on to show that German unification reinforced concentration and protectionist tendencies. Leibfritz (1990) posed three equally pertinent questions. First, what would be the consequences of the high costs of German unification on the western part of the economy? Second, to what extent was there a risk of inflation as demand grew but output declined in the east? Third, how long would the transitional period of high unemployment in the east last, and what were the medium-term prospects?

Given that a decision was made to incorporate the DDR into a highly successful market economy, one of the first things that East Germany required was an internationally convertible currency in which the domestic actors also had confidence. This is tantamount to saying that yet another currency reform was required. In other words, there would be no transitional phases. With GEMSU, which took place on 1 July 1990, the DM replaced the Ostmark and the Bundesbank's responsibility for monetary policy was extended to cover the former DDR. Fiscal policy – on both the revenue and expenditure sides – required reform and control respectively. Similarly the integration of other aspects of policy making was essential: regional, industrial and labour-market policies are paramount examples. Western models of independent collective bargaining, social security, price determination and property rights were further essential conditions for a viable union (EC 1990a: 52). Finally, East Germany had to be integrated into EC 1993 and EMU.

This section has therefore postulated the economic implications of integrating two highly dissimilar economies. It was clear at the outset that the costs of such a process would be high. Schrettl (1992: 147–9) correctly suggested that these costs were implicitly accepted by the west (the 'insurer') in return for a 'premium' consisting of the assets of the former GDR (the 'insuree'). But as Schrettl also emphasised (*ibid*.: 146), 'getting the DM' played a central role in the March 1990 campaign of the East German CDU and their political allies. Their western coalition partners effectively encouraged a Paretian promise: nobody would be worse off and many will be better off as a result of rapid monetary and economic union. Given the momentum produced by the campaign – along with the re-established free mobility between east and west with, at the time, financial inducements – it is easy to see why this undertaking was given. The reason was encapsulated by Collier (1991: 179) who helpfully quoted a Leipzig demonstration banner of February 1990: 'if the DM comes, we'll stay put; but if it doesn't, we'll come by foot'. The arrival of the DM was, of course, insufficient in itself to activate economic reconstruction. There was inevitable economic disillusionment. East Germans fairly rapidly grew impatient with democracy, while many west Germans jumped to the conclusion that everything in the east was inferior and their new fellow citizens

were no more than trainees in market economics (Henzler 1992: 24). In the east *Besserwisser* (know-all) became the pun *Besserwessie* – someone from the west who feels superior (*ibid*.). Many of the western managers transferred to acquisitions in the east arrived like 'colonialists', having reserved luxury-hotel accommodation and complete with their Mercedes or BMW (Ogger 1992: 136). Westerners, on the other hand, viewed the easterners as seeking the immediate implementation of western living standards without the necessary human and physical capital investment.

With GEMSU, then, the basis for a total transformation of East Germany was introduced. Inevitably, comparisons with the introduction of the SME into West Germany have been drawn. To complete this perspective of the German economy, therefore, the next section contains a comparison of these two economic watersheds.

THE SME, GEMSU AND EMU

Two difficulties are encountered when comparing the SME and GEMSU, both of which have been isolated by Lösch (1990). First there are no precedents for any transformation of a Soviet-socialist type of economy to a market economy, although it is somewhat misleading to add that no theory as to how such a process might be achieved exists (see, in particular, Propp (1990)). However, Lösch's principal point in this context must be accepted: is such a transformation attainable in one fell swoop? If not, then a piecemeal approach is clearly advisable. On examination, the introduction of the SME in West Germany can be seen to possess immediate, medium and long-run elements. By turning to the second comparative difficulty, these elements can all be seen.

The second comparative difficulty derives from the fact that the introduction of the SME by Erhard was accompanied by (or in some cases preceded by) a number of what may in retrospect be termed necessary conditions. Outstanding among such conditions must be the establishment, by the western Allies, of an independent central banking system, followed by their currency reform. These developments took place respectively in March and June 1948. They may be viewed as the first and second necessary conditions. The third element of the reform was instituted simultaneously with the currency reform: prices were largely deregulated and the majority of the control provisions were repealed. Fixed prices, and in some cases rationing, remained in force for staple foods, oil and petrol, fertiliser and iron and steel products; rents and lease payments also remained fixed. Another important part of the third element was money wage determination. The Nazis' wage freeze was not lifted until November 1948; once collective bargaining was again permitted, however, a new law on collective bargaining (das Tarifvertragsgesetz) came into force in April 1949 (Lösch 1990: 91). As a result of pressure from the United States, even before the currency reform, and therefore again before West Germany achieved sovereignty, a fourth transitional step was begun in 1948, namely the liberalisation of foreign trade (Abelshauser 1983: 151–3).

Before proceeding to the remaining conditions for the introduction of the SME, it is necessary to see why the third and fourth steps – price and wage deregulation, along with free trade – ran into difficulties. These steps were taken by Erhard himself and free trade in particular nearly brought the process to an abrupt halt. Not that Erhard was a dogmatic adherent of the ordo-liberal school – as his pragmatic approach to industrial policy demonstrated (Berghahn 1986: 151 and 158). However, output in 1948, which had stood at half of that achieved in 1938, expanded by 50 per cent in the second half of the year but prices also rose rapidly. Five months after the currency reform, in a move which coincided with the reintroduction of money-wage bargaining, the trade unions protested against the 15 per cent rise in prices by calling a one-day general strike (Siebert 1992a: 53; Stolper et al. 1967: 262 and 318). However, prices had only resumed the role of a meaningful economic indicator after the currency reform and the lifting of the price freeze half way through 1948. Hence, when output in 1949 rose by 23 per cent but prices fell the policy problem changed because unemployment rose rapidly. By the end of the first quarter of 1950 it reached 2 million or 12.2 per cent (Wallich 1955: 80–1). High unemployment was a serious political threat – it had facilitated Hitler's rise to power. Total employment had in fact hardly declined; the growth in unemployment was due to a growth in the labour force, mainly through refugees. Nevertheless, in the fifteen months from January 1949 to March 1950 bank credit increased by DM 8 billion, and the central bank became occupied with the worsening balance of payments position. But if it is doubtful that monetary policy strictly observed the SME code, fiscal policy seemed undoubtedly to breach it. In the ten quarters following the currency reform (July 1948 to December 1950) the combined budget of the Federal and Länder Governments was in surplus on only one occasion – the first quarter of 1950. There were thus deficits in 1948 when price inflation was a problem, followed by a surplus when unemployment was a problem. Moreover, there was a substantial DM 1 billion deficit in the second quarter of 1950 when the balance of payments deteriorated so badly that foreign currency reserves were completely exhausted. An important contributory factor to this enlarged deficit was the 25 per cent reduction in personal income tax rates enacted in April 1950 but made retroactive to January 1950 (*Annual Report*, US High Commission, 1950).

In addition, imports had risen more rapidly than exports as a result of import liberalisation. The external imbalance grew worse as a result of panic purchases of raw materials at the beginning of the Korean War in June 1950, added to which the reflationary expenditure programmes and tax cuts, which had been eventually decided upon during the winter of 1950, started to take effect at the same time as the outbreak of the Korean War. However, there was an international increase in output and this was reflected in West Germany by rapid increases in output and exports. The post-Korean boom drew German industry back into world markets at such prices that they were able to re-equip large sectors of run-down plant. It is nonetheless notable that the rise in exports was not initially sufficient to cover the rise in imports and the drain on foreign exchange continued. As a result import controls were re-introduced and West Germany took up special credits with the European Payments Union (Horn 1982: 13; Stolper *et al.* 1967: 266 and 274). Imports of food – in spite of the influx of refugees – were not responsible: German average daily calorific intake still stood significantly below pre-war levels. Raw material prices also began to fall after the Korean peak. Export surpluses emerged in 1952. Thus West Germany became independent of foreign aid in the year that the Marshall Plan came to an end (Knapp 1981: 424). Lösch (1990: 91) summarises this critical phase in the following manner:

During the course of the fourth step towards the market economy, therefore, Erhard was forced to slow down the pace of reform and to temporarily rescind some of the liberalisation measures already taken. The rapid relaxation of impediments to foreign trade had led immediately to a balance-of-payments deficit for West Germany in 1949 and 1950. For those two years, it was still possible to balance the current account thanks to the inflow of foreign exchange under the Marshall Plan. What precipitated the crisis, however, was the pronounced rise in raw material prices on the world markets at the end of 1950 in the wake of the Korean War. This sent West Germany's current account into the red. Even after it had taken up the US$320 million quota it was allowed by the European Payments Union, and had taken out an additional special loan of US$180 million, there was still not enough foreign exchange available to balance the books. The result was that the liberalisation achieved up to that time was drastically cut back in 1951: some import quotas were reintroduced, as also was the requirement to place 50 per cent of the equivalent value in DM of foreign exchange required for import on cash deposit; finally, a complete stop was put to the issuance of import licences for a time. It was not possible to continue with the liberalisation process until the Federal Republic's exports had risen strongly in the second half of 1951.

Apart from this setback, the liberalisation of foreign trade was accompanied by the fifth and final step, namely a relaxation of exchange controls. Starting in 1952, the DM was convertible for practical purposes at a uniform fixed exchange rate for the payment for goods and services.

However, capital convertibility was not introduced until much later (the end of 1958). With the help of these five reform measures, the West German economy was turned into a functioning, dynamic market economy within about four years. They were later followed by supplementary measures such as the Company Act, the Act Against Restraints on Competition, and increases in benefits and reforms in the field of social policy. Similarly, particular areas of economy were not deregulated until much later, or indeed have yet to be deregulated.

Hence, the introduction of a new Central Bank and currency reform by the Allies was a 'big bang'. The relaxation of price and wage controls, along with liberalisation of foreign trade, were medium-term measures. DM convertibility, along with social, labour market and competition legislation were all longer-run elements. Competition was seriously impaired by the time legislation reached the statute book and the economy displays even today fairly highly-regulated and significantly subsidised pockets.

Perhaps the establishment of the common-currency areas as part of GEMSU on the 1 July 1990 can be viewed in 'big bang' terms – even though this was a monetary union as opposed to a currency reform. After all, the introduction of the DM into the East, with monetary policy under a Bundesbank control, can certainly be viewed as analogous to the Allies establishing a central bank and introducing a currency reform back in 1948. But a monetary union – as will shortly be seen – also implies fixing exchange rates. Given that Ostmarks were converted at par or at 2:1 (see Chapter 4), there was to be a catastrophic increase in eastern industrial costs. This was in complete contrast to the early decision to *devalue* the DM in 1949, albeit at the instigation of the Allies (Marsh 1992: 165). However, the catalogue of other key elements contained in the GEMSU treaty are nearly all consistent with the immediate, medium- and long-term goals of the SME outlined above. There were two major exceptions, both of which were concerned with the abolition of central control in the East. First, the freedom of job choice and the introduction of a generally free-enterprise culture were key clauses in the treaty. Secondly, it followed that clearly-defined property rights, as well as the re-introduction of the private ownership of the means of production, were also embodied in the treaty. Both these and other fundamental differences led von Dohnanyi (1990: 157) and Siebert (1992a: 53) to argue that the 'currency reforms' of 1948 and 1990 cannot be compared. Their basic arguments are reviewed in this section and in Chapter 4. But here the notion of a 'big bang' is being examined.

Very generally, GEMSU resembled the introduction of the SME. For a transitional period the prices of a number of non-traded goods, in particular rents, were to remain under control. Otherwise, a market system with free price setting was to be established. This would involve the abolition of a wide range of subsidies on basic goods, plus the liberalisation of trade and capital movements. A similar banking system to West Germany's was to be introduced. Social security and tax systems, also resembling West Germany's, would be implemented. Finally, legislation in the areas of anti-trust, employment protection, employee participation and collective bargaining would be enacted.

GEMSU was therefore seen as a means of creating the correct investment opportunities for the introduction of a market economy. It was hoped that higher inflation in the West and socially unacceptable levels of unemployment in the East could be avoided. Moreover, this new environment was considered a necessary condition for inducing investment in new plant, new products and infrastructure. Finally, it was hoped that the market economy would remove the restrictions and constraints which in the past had adversely affected the level and evolution of productivity (OECD, *Economic Survey*, 1990: 52).

At this stage of the analysis, it will be helpful to distinguish between the initial 'big bang' nature of GEMSU and the comparatively tortuous nature of European integration. At the outset, it can be noted that, by virtue of the 'big bang', the aims of GEMSU were unambiguously spelt out, whereas EC 1993 may have been the ultimate goal of some EC members. Following Molle (1990: 12–13), the cumulative sequence of:

- a free-trade area (all internal tariff barriers removed)
- a customs union (common external tariffs)
- a common market (labour and capital mobility)

had been largely achieved by the time EC 1993 was finally implemented. However, economic and monetary union (vesting economic and monetary policy decision-making powers in supra-national authorities) was unacceptable to many policy makers in the member states.

GEMSU was a wide-ranging treaty which encapsulated the monetary, economic and social features necessary for the introduction of the SME. EC 1993 and EMU, on the other hand, are based on a phased process of European economic and monetary union. A social dimension to the process of European integration was added by the 'Social Charter', which was later embodied as a 'Chapter' in the Maastricht treaty. Hence, at the time of

GEMSU all three parts of the European process of integration were at various stages of implementation and negotiation. The degrees of enthusiasm among members ranged from a desire for rapid integration on all fronts to a cautious and even sceptical approach. For example, a convergence of economic policies and indicators was viewed, not least by the Bundesbank, as being an essential prior condition. Such convergence applied particularly to low rates of price inflation and low levels of public debt. Since GEMSU – rather like the crude-oil price shocks of 1973/4 and 1979/80 – seriously undermined the Bundesbank's stabilisation policies in this sense, it became even more sceptical about EMU. Following Maastricht, of course, there were numerous factors which disrupted the whole process of European integration. (Full political integration, incidentally, was on an even farther horizon. This again contrasts with GEMSU which was viewed by its signatories as a decisive first step to the introduction of a speedy and full political union.)

Before reviewing historical and institutional developments within the European Community, Schinasi (1989: 391) finds it useful to distinguish between three different meanings of forms of monetary integration, all of which were options facing the Community. The first form of monetary integration involves the fixing of exchange rates and most likely involves financing facilities to ease monetary and trade adjustments. In the literature this form has been called *currency union*. The second form of monetary integration involves the freedom of capital movements and the unification of financial institutions and markets to foster that freedom. In policy discussions surrounding EC 1993 this form of monetary integration was called *financial integration*: it is what the European Council had in mind when it enacted the Single European Act. This second form of integration does not require the first form of integration. In fact the two can be considered as independent policy choices. Their separate nature can be adduced from the turbulence in the ERM and concurrent tribulations in the German financial sector during the preparations for EC 1993 (see Chapters 4 and 7). The third form of monetary integration involves unification at the policy level and may or may not go beyond monetary policy. This form of integration has been called *monetary union*. In recent policy discussions this term has meant the coexistence of a currency union and the complete integration of financial markets. Currency union would be an essential prelude to the introduction of a common currency. The state of the ERM in 1992–3 therefore made the agonising over EMU something of a charade.

Seen in a broader context, then, the pursuit of EMU is still very relevant to safeguarding the achievements of the Common Market and ensuring the continued progress of European integration towards the goal of European union (Borchardt 1989: 54). The Single European Act, which was destined to become EC 1993, therefore sought to revive the goal of EMU by writing into the EEC Treaty a binding commitment on the part of the Member States to work progressively to bring it about. Acting on the instructions of the Heads of State or Government, a committee of advisers chaired by Jacques Delors, the President of the Commission, met to consider ways and means of achieving this objective. Their conclusions, known as the 'Delors Plan', were put before the Madrid European Council in June 1989. The plan envisaged the establishment of EMU in three stages. The first step was to bring the pound sterling, the drachma and the escudo into the exchange rate mechanism of the EMS by mid-1990 so that it covered all EC currencies. (Prior to exchange-rate turbulence which dramatically commenced in September 1992, only the drachma remained outside the ERM: significantly Greece still had a relatively high rate of inflation.) Economic policy in the member countries was also to be more closely co-ordinated than in the past. The second stage was to involve the adoption of new treaties gradually transferring national powers in the areas of fiscal, monetary and exchange-rate policy to the Community institutions. In the third and final stage, an independent central bank system would be set up, paving the way for the introduction of fixed exchange rates (or a single currency).

Prior to GEMSU's becoming politically feasible, stage one of the Delors' plan – all member countries in the ERM – had been largely accomplished. Stage two was being slowly introduced by virtue of the dominance of the DM and what the Bundesbank viewed as other members 'importing stability' from West German monetary policy. 'Stability' refers to the reduction in inflation and, at a later stage, interest rates which membership of the ERM endowed (see Chapter 4). In other words, the emphasis is on monetary stability. The rise in unemployment resulting from the deflationary transition was considered to be part of a necessary adjustment process. The simultaneous achievement of low rates of inflation and low levels of unemployment – the meaning of internal 'stability' in the Keynesian sense – was considered unachievable. Genuine long-run recovery required a prolonged period of price stability. Stage three evolved so as to be understood as meaning a single currency, thus removing the need for the ERM; in addition, proposals were drawn up by the central bankers of the EC for a European central bank which had much in common with the ethos of the Bundesbank. The Maastricht treaty, ironically concluded in February 1992 when the disastrous effects of GEMSU were palpably obvious, contained extremely rigorous conditions on economic and monetary integration. These conditions were convergence in inflation, exchange and long-term interest rates at levels achieved by the EC's best performers, along with PSBRs no greater than 3 per cent of GDP and debt/GDP ratios not exceeding 60 per cent. Not only did GEMSU threaten the likelihood of Germany's achieving these targets, but it effectively meant that only those economies with fairly equal living standards could realistically aspire to economic and monetary integration in the 1990s. Ireland, Spain, Portugal and Greece, with *per capita* incomes below DM 20,000 in 1991, would find that labour and capital investment would tend to flow to more affluent economies. Britain was on a borderline (DM 26,660) while West Germany's DM 31,990 was deflated to DM 27,510 when the east was included (*Die Welt* 23 November 1992). In fact, *Die Welt* (*ibid.*) graphically summed up this effect on the West German economy as 'relegation to the second division'. (The headline was also used – even more incredibly – in 1993 to illustrate the prospect of the French franc succeeding the DM as the anchor currency of the ERM – *ibid.* 17 June and Chapter 4 below.)

Before and even after GEMSU, therefore, it was at the very least conjectured that economic and monetary union between countries or regions with differing levels of development, economic structure and degrees of stability should be tackled in stages. In essence, this was the approach recommended in the Delors' report. If, however, the monetary union is implemented as a 'big bang' at the start of the unification process, it will be very difficult, for example, to make rapid corrections and counter adverse trends as they develop. In particular, it is no longer possible to use exchange rates to facilitate the process of adjustment, and there is by definition only *one* authority in monetary policy. For East Germany this meant there was no question of the exchange rate gradually finding its 'correct' level – instead, East Germany moved without any transitional period from a non-convertible currency to a strong currency with international convertibility. Given the problems in East Germany, there was no time for an alternative course. East German confidence had to be strengthened quickly to counter westward flowing emigrants. Exchange rate risks for potential investors had to be rapidly reduced to get the necessary capital flowing into East Germany. It must also be borne in mind that even prior to GEMSU there had been an accelerating decline in East German industrial production.

There was thus no policy option in terms of choosing the adjustment process. One cause of the decline in East German industrial production prior to GEMSU was the exodus of labour to the West. In the four months from October 1989 to January 1990 alone, more than 300,000 emigrated from East to West Germany, whereas in the first six months of 1990 this flow amounted to 200,000. The outflow fell back sharply following free elections and GEMSU. But this meant that the process of adjustment would fall on prices and employment. If migration had continued on the scale just indicated, however, the political, social and economic implications for both parts of Germany would have been incalculable. On the price front, commentators envisaged a rapid adjustment process in the East, with the West avoiding unacceptable inflationary pressure by re-routeing traded goods which would otherwise have been exported.

The rapid adjustment hypothesis is particularly interesting. A substantial proportion of profits from industry and other sources in the East had been earmarked under central planning for the purpose of subsidising rents, food, fares, culture, a huge housing programme and social services. Some of these non-traded goods were heavily subsidised. Hence, as these subsidies were removed the prices of these goods would rise. On the other hand, these price rises would be more than offset as the prices of many traded goods fell because western products became available, thereby removing extreme shortages. Hence both the price level and structure generally adjusted quite rapidly. Far from having an inflationary impact in its year of implementation, GEMSU as such probably had a disinflationary bias (Deutsche Bank *Bulletin* March 1990). The trend in retail prices – when measured over the average for 1989 – was indeed negative in 1990: there were monthly falls from May to December (MRDB 8/91: table VIII(10)). However, the east German price index began to rise quite steeply in 1991, largely because of the abolition of subsidies on energy, transport and housing. For example, at the beginning of the year western electricity tariffs were introduced; postal charges followed the same course in mid-1991 (BfG *Wirtschafts-blätter* 10/91). Moreover, only 10 per cent of eastern living accommodation was defined as being in an acceptable state of repair: rents were increased by stages to 'market levels' as from October 1991 (SZ 1 October 1991; Tomann 1992a). As a result of such adjustments, the east German index in November 1991 (July 1991/July 1990 = 100) was 22.2 per cent higher than in the same month of 1990 (MRDB 9/92:

ibid.). Ironically, the Bundesbank's governing council, always firm advocates of a rapid reduction in subsidies, saw this rapid rise in prices as a partial reason for their decision to raise short-term interest rates to post-war record heights. (Figures 3.10, 3.11, 4.2 and 4.4d illustrate these fluctuations, although it should also be emphasised that short-term interest rates and inflationary pressure were both increasing in the west prior to GEMSU. Following GEMSU, moreover, it was normally the rate of inflation in the west which influenced policy making at the Bundesbank.)

The employment adjustment process was even more problematical. This process can again be viewed in both structural and level terms. The level of unemployment was bound to rise because a significant proportion of industrial establishments in the east had to either close or at least drastically reduce their output. These establishments were uncompetitive in the sense that the quality of their products did not match the higher standards embodied in western products. In structural terms, it was expected that employment in the industrial sector would in any case contract. On the other hand, an expansion was expected in services such as commerce, banking and insurance. An expansion was also expected in the small-business sector and construction sections. But industrial output declined subsequent to the collapse of the Berlin wall in November 1989; it plummeted following GEMSU, so that by December 1990 it stood at only 50 per cent of the level achieved in December 1989 (MRDB 3/91 *ibid.*). (Recall that industrial output had *risen* by 50 per cent following the currency reform in 1948.) As Beyer and Nutzinger (1991:248–9) indicate the Wall had acted not just as a political boundary but also as an economic barrier. It had protected industry with an OM 4.4: DM 1 exchange rate. Because of the removal of subsidies on exports to eastern Europe, manufacturing output in the former DDR fell an additional 25 per cent between December 1990 and January 1991 (Akerlof *et al.* 1991: 31; Deutsche Bank *Bulletin* 7/91; Siebert 1991b: 305). This substantial rise in unemployment is considered in the discussion around Figure 6.4. (The official unemployment rate vastly understated the actual incidence of unemployment. Short-time working, job creation schemes, early retirements and withdrawals from the labour force all combined to make GEMSU a potential social disaster.)

In this crisis situation, emphasis soon shifted to the short run – not least because the long-run predictions of the catching-process requiring decades were confirmed by a number of further studies (*Guardian* 13 February 1992). Siebert (1991b: 304) pointed out that the determinant of short-run recovery was eliminating the inefficiency of existing firms. Market forces should be given their head – irrespective of the fact that they had not functioned freely in the SME (see Chapters 3, 5, 7 and 8). Indeed, estimates by Akerlof *et al.* (1991: 27) indicated that only 8 per cent of the Kombinate were economically viable. Two reasons were advanced for such a finding: demand for east German products fell, and firms could not *price* competitively and still cover short-run *costs* (*ibid.*: 15). Initially, loans and subsidies allowed products to be sold at prices *below* short run costs.

The price–cost squeeze emanated in the first instance from the GEMSU exchange rate of DM 1 = OM 1. Prior to GEMSU, average costs per DM earned by exports to non-communist block countries were OM 3.73 (*ibid.*: 17). After GEMSU the unadjusted average domestic resource costs of earning DM 1 from exports would thus

have been DM 3.73. But an adjusted post-GEMSU estimate of short-run variable costs gave a more meaningful indication of short-run viability. This meant adjusting pre-GEMSU resource costs by subtracting the 'enormous' taxes, profits and interest; the costs of imported inputs declined as a result of GEMSU and these were also subtracted from pre-GEMSU domestic resource costs (*ibid.*: 21–5). However, in the first 10 months of 1990 wages increased by 32 per cent more than was necessary to compensate for the post-GEMSU increases in income taxes and social-insurance contributions. This latter factor raised costs significantly, but overall short-run average variable costs fell by 50.6 per cent. Such a reduction in costs was probably reflected in price cuts by eastern firms.

When adjusted, the average post-GEMSU cost of exports was DM 1.84 for every DM 1 earned in revenue. Since a firm is only viable if its short-run average variable costs per DM earned are *less* than one, it meant that on average the Kombinate were unviable: they were making an 84 per cent loss on each item sold. Because there were significant differences between Kombinate and individual enterprises prior to GEMSU, only a single firm outside of energy had costs per DM earned of less than unity. Hardly surprisingly, that firm was the Meissen porcelain factory. (The Land of Saxony purchased this undertaking, beating off Japanese competition in the process.) In addition, the social costs of brown coal pollution were not included in these calculations (*ibid.*: 20). Even after GEMSU only the said 8 per cent of Kombinate were viable. They were subjected to a price squeeze on sales and a cost squeeze from domestic wage costs; moreover, demand for domestically produced consumption and investment goods declined sharply. A sharp increase in production costs had coincided with full exposure to world markets at a time when the rest of eastern Europe was going through profound political change and some major western economies were in recession.

Here again the contrast with economic conditions at the time of the 1948 currency reform can be readily seen. Whereas investment and technological change in East German industry had been in a time warp, it required only relatively modest investment in repairs to continue the processs of reactivating West German industry in 1948. The par conversion of the OM, dramatically overvalued East German output; the 1949 devaluation of the DM endowed West German exporters with an undervalued exchange rate. For a number of complex reasons, east German wage rates rose rapidly following GEMSU; collective bargaining had been illegal under Nazi and Allied rule. East Germany was being converted into a complex SME in the very short run; the domestic laws and regulations which implemented that system in West Germany took many years to evolve. The politically expedient fudges illustrated in this section resulted in GEMSU being a short-run disaster. The long-run economic imperative was to establish conditions which would induce investment in new plant and thereby equalise labour productivity costs. GEMSU was also a salutary reminder of the necessary conditions for a successful implementation of EC 1993, EMU and the Social Chapter.

Summarising, then, it can be said that the introduction of the SME consisted of five elements. The first two 'big bang' conditions were provided by the Allies. The third element – the introduction of a market economy – was much more problematical and only generous foreign exchange assistance (the fourth element)

pulled West Germany through. The Korean War also gave industry an enormous economic fillip. Thereafter, convertibility became a fairly easy fifth phase. In the longer run social, labour market and competition legislation completed the introduction of the SME. With GEMSU, on the other hand, East Germany received the initial two 'big bangs', convertibility and 'foreign exchange assistance', courtesy of her more affluent neighbour. Similarly, what had been long-run objectives under the SME regime were transferred to East Germany almost overnight. Yet another contrast is the tortuous introduction of EMU. It will be shown in Chapter 4, for example, that the strength of the DM inevitably meant that the Bundesbank would in effect lay most of the ground rules. But that process began in earnest as long ago as 1969.

CONCLUSIONS

Set against the backcloth of long-term economic developments in Germany, the economic problems posed by unification are far from being unique; a further dimension has simply been added to difficulties which have been inherent in the nation's long-term economic development. Such a generalisation is based on factors such as the rather mundane 'changing frontiers' argument, the jealously-guarded autonomy of the Länder, the traditional rivalry between north and south Germany, the apparent ability to recover from situations of economic collapse, experience of serious economic policy problems in both the fiscal and monetary fields and the ultimate introduction of the typically-German SME. Rutherford (1974: 23) wrote that 'German industry is little more than three generations old and it has been in and out of difficulties from the start.' That contention, along with other statements in this paragraph, seem to be a reasonable basis for including unification in this book only as a part of wider recent policy issues.

Much the same kind of thing can be said about Germany's role in European economic integration. The most striking comparative economic feature prior to unification was the similarity in land area, population, inhabitants per square kilometre, the labour force and employment in West Germany and the United Kingdom. France, for example, was much less similar. Unification transformed Germany into Europe's most populous nation, the long-term marketing implications of which are obvious. There are, however, a number of obstacles to European integration, even within the EC as it at present exists. From the German point of view, both EC 1993 and EMU represent challenges to the basic tenets of the SME. Consider first EC 1993 by comparing the implications for the British and German economies. As Woolcock et al. (1991) point out in their preface:

The British government's approach is characterised by a determination to ensure that the 1992 process does not reverse the Anglo-American deregulation revolution of the 1980s; Germany is equally determined to defend the national social consensus (rooted in a process of consultation between government, employers and unions) on which the Germans believe that their prosperity has been based.

The ascendancy of the Bundesbank in the ERM not only meant that its interest-rate policy determined the pattern of interest rates throughout the EC: its autonomy has far-reaching political implications as well. Kennedy (1991: 19) analyses the contrast between this notion of central-bank independence and the

systems which operate in Britain and the United States:

In Britain, the Chancellor of the Exchequer and the Prime Minister, both elected officials, enjoy decisive authority over the policies of the Bank of England. In the United States the Federal Reserve system is subject to Congressional review . . . The Bundesbank is comparatively unconstrained by such constitutional arrangements, and pursues its policies formally independent of the elected officials . . . In law and in fact, it is Germany's monetary sovereign.

Any EMU proposals, then, will inevitably have to confront the role of an EC central bank. Harden (1990) advisedly entitled his analysis of this question 'Eurofed or "Monster Bank"?' High interest rates in Germany would inevitably result from any high borrowing requirement to finance German unification. As will be shown in Chapters 4 and 7, the Bundesbank's governing council would not tolerate a rapid expansion of the money supply. Any consequent deflationary repercussions would be transmitted to other parts of the European monetary system.

In the short term, unification acted as a stimulus to otherwise hard-pressed economies. The impact of the massive surge in demand from the new eastern Länder could not be met solely by industry in the western Länder, even though it generated boom conditions there. The best indicator of this is (West) Germany's current account, which had been in handsome surplus for much of the post-war period. It deteriorated rapidly on unification and sank into deficit, although not to the extent of the longer-run British type. Initially, unemployment fell rapidly in the western part of the economy but rose substantially in the east. Unemployment later began to rise in the west too. In Britain this problem was also growing worse, although optimistic forecasters saw inflation and interest rates in the two economies converging because of increases in Germany but falls in Britain. It was even contended that the government's borrowing requirement in Britain was more under control. (As privatisation and North Sea oil revenues fell, the effects of the rapid reduction of income tax on more durable revenue sources became increasingly obvious.) But income per head in the former West Germany, France and Britain showed appreciable differences. For example, measured in 1989 prices and exchange rates, and using US$000 as units, the respective data were 19.7, 16.9 and 14.6. For that matter the growth of real income in Germany and France was higher. Nonetheless, for the first time in the post-war era, Germany in 1993 seemed likely to register an unfavourable combination of an above-average inflation rate, rising unemployment and a current account deficit. Zero or even negative growth was also predicted as a result of high interest rates squeezing domestic demand. The exchange rate was also driven upwards as a result of the strong DM and this made matters worse for exporters.

Hence, within two years of GEMSU the euphoria of unification was already giving way to a more realistic policy debate. In 1993, the solidarity pact sought to unite the actors and combine more rational approaches to monetary, fiscal, social and wage bargaining policies. It may have been imperfect (see Chapter 3) but it was an achievement for all that. There was certainly no comparison between, for example, the chaotic situation following the Wall Street crash (see above) and the determination to find socially acceptable solutions in 1993. In short, Germany started from a relatively strong base to fund a recovery in her eastern territories. But as Welfens (1991: 18) indicated, whereas she was likely to support any 'EC deepening', she would almost certainly block any comprehensive 'widening' – that is further enlargement of the EC. In the event, German politicians came to expect support for their social and monetary policies if Austria and the other Scandinavian countries were admitted to the EC before the critical stages in the implementation of the Maastricht treaty were reached. As a result of her experiences with GEMSU, it should be added, Germany's attitude to EMU hardened considerably. After Maastricht, she became apprehensive about the substitution of the ECU for the DM and the subordination of the Bundesbank to a new European central bank. Given those two powerful economic arguments, the British option to await developments looked a very tempting option for Germany too.

2

THE REGIONAL DIMENSION

(Written with David Lauder)

INTRODUCTION

In Germany, the Federal government and legislature, as well as the federal states (Länder) and thousands of local authorities collectively share legislative powers. As the EC (1990a: 41) pointed out even prior to unification, this system of government has repercussions at all levels of economic policy making, not least in terms of the need for binding budgetary rules on revenue sharing, taxation and borrowing powers. Germany's federal system of government therefore creates by its very nature a problem of power sharing between the Federal and Länder governments, a problem which has to be largely resolved by means of involving the Länder in the Federal legislature's upper house (the Bundesrat). In addition, the Länder have the powers of implementing Federal legislation (Bulmer 1989: 19).

Constitutionally, the revenue of the Länder must be regulated by the Federal government in such a way that there is uniformity of living standards throughout the economy; an additional requirement since the constitutional amendment in 1969 is that Federal legislation shall ensure a reasonable equalisation between financially strong and financially weak Länder (Basic Law, Sections 72 and 107). This requirement has given rise to a complex system of *fiscal equalisation*. In effect

– because of the involvement of the Bundesrat in the legislative process – the Constitution not only accords joint jurisdiction for regional policy to both Federal and Länder governments, it also makes them jointly responsible for *policy measures* in this area. Such a position almost invites disagreement where there are marked disparities between members of the federation. This is the case in Germany, especially since unification.

Following unification, the number of Länder was increased from eleven to sixteen. This thus posed further economic and political problems. These economic problems were inextricably linked with the nature of German federalism which in turn lies at the centre of the regional economic policy debate. The main argument here is that federalism has moulded the regional economic structures and that consequently the robustness of both regional solutions to economic problems and the fiscal equalisation system (described below) depend upon the robustness of federalism itself.

The suggestions for regional economic recovery and development put forward since the formation of the Bonn Republic were almost indistinguishable from the general solutions offered for the revitalisation of the east German economy as a whole: high levels of investment, improvement of the infrastructure and inducements to establish new industries – all to be achieved contemporaneously with the adjustment towards the SME. The impact of such policies on regional factors can be assessed by a consideration of regional economic differences, and by an analysis of the federal structure as it relates to both regional and fiscal policies. While it is extremely important not to confuse fiscal with regional policy, it will be seen that there is a very close connection between them.

What, then, is the difference between regional policy and fiscal equalisation? One can distinguish two broad types of regional policy: regional development policy and regional planning (Zimmermann 1985: 451). Regional development looks at how localities can best improve their economic conditions and takes little account of the overall scope of policies at the macro level. Here, no long-term targets for economic growth are required. Short-term growth and the raising of local income levels are the key indicators. Regional planning focuses upon overall standards of living and stability at the macro level and takes a long-term growth view based upon uniformity of living conditions. The main instruments of regional development are local subsidies, business incentives and local initiatives designed to create further incentives for local investment and job creation. The main instruments of regional planning are the establishment of government targets and the assessment of levels of disparities between different localities. Thus, regional development implies a bottom-up approach to economic decision-making, while regional planning depends upon a top-down approach with either a central decision-making authority or some tertiary form of decision-making authority containing representatives from different levels of government. German regional policy has in the past contained aspects of both approaches. Nonetheless, heavy central government involvement in regional planning has generally been something of an anathema to German policy makers. For this reason, regional policy employs a bottom-up approach.

To what extent does the system of fiscal equalisation differ from regional policy pure and simple? The granting of fiscal powers to lower levels of government brings attendant fiscal disparities. Even when localities achieve equality of revenue and expenditure, spill-over effects will ensure that inequality of fiscal strength results. Furthermore, the amelioration of these disparities must take place through either a) direct grants or b) equalisation. In the case of b) the mechanism can only be variable tax rates to a very limited extent, for in general uniform tax rates must apply to all localities. In the case of a) there is agreement that while direct grants may be justified on social welfare grounds, their application leads to allocative inefficiencies.

The central hypothesis of this chapter is therefore that regional disparities, as well as the policy measures designed to ameliorate regional imbalances, lie at the heart of the economics of German regional policy. It is necessary to show that the problems extant prior to unification were exacerbated by the sudden enlargement of the economy. These problems emanate from the unequal size and levels of prosperity of the Länder. Furthermore, the fiscal constitution, while quite separate from regional policy *per se*, has played a part in shaping regional disparities. While fiscal equalisation is not usually included within regional policy as strictly defined, this chapter will clearly illustrate that the strong interrelationship between regional disparities and fiscal equalisation justifies its inclusion within an analysis of the regional dimension of economic policy.

ECONOMIC GEOGRAPHY AND REGIONAL DEVELOPMENT

Figure 2.1 shows how the new Germany looks geographically. For much of what follows in this chapter, the reader unfamiliar with the geography of Germany may find this figure helpful. The area covered by five reconstituted Länder in the East was grafted on to the Länder in the West. A re-united Berlin acceded as a city-state, thus making sixteen Länder in all. This ostensibly resolved some regional problems but undoubtedly created others. The frontier corridor between the former two parts of Germany disappeared – only for a similar problem to re-emerge along the German/Polish border. This is because West German firms were reluctant to invest in both of these areas. The same was true of West Berlin, with the added problem that labour recruitment and retention presented difficulties for firms already located in the city (see the case study below).

The area of the unified Germany is often overestimated. It may be surprising to note, for example, that even the new Germany is of the order in size of some states in the USA. Moreover, the new Länder themselves comprise only 30 per cent of the total area of Germany (Sinn 1991: 3). Yet in a purely European context, the new Germany occupies a significant place in terms of population and location (Sinn and Sinn 1992: 22–3).

The flows of population into and out of an area obviously have a great bearing on development and a crucial factor for economic growth in East Germany was the historical migration of its workforce to the west – as will be seen in more depth in Chapter 6. Within West Germany, the patterns of population were complicated by patterns of internal migration and although it was primarily the southern states that had the highest net inflows, there were also many such districts in the north (Thieme 1991: 114–16). One example is north-west Lower Saxony. Following unification, western Germany again received a large inflow of eastern Germans, but this was merely the latest in a series of post-war migrations (see Chapter 6). During the 1980s the immigration of *Volksdeutsche* – emigrants of German origin from eastern countries – exceeded that of the flows of families joining southern European workers already in western Germany (Jones 1990: 224–5). As well as these flow factors, the distribution of population is instructive. For instance, like the west, the southern states in eastern Germany tend to contain higher populations than the north. The conurbations in the former GDR, accounting for 48 per cent of the population, are all, Berlin excepted, concentrated in the south. Thus some parts of Saxony have population densities of over 300 per km^2. The main urban population centres are located at the northern edges of the Mittelgebirge, in Thüringer-Becken, the Berlin area and the Baltic coast. In comparison to the west, the population densities of such areas are small, often under half the western level. On the other hand, the population distribution also differs spatially from the west as there is a sharper urban-rural division (Klemmer and Schrumpf 1990: 121).

The development of the regional economy in Germany has an even longer history. Regional imbalances existed during the nineteenth century and even earlier (Tipton 1976: 17). One factor in nineteenth century regional imbalances was the introduction of the customs union in 1834, which allowed the already wealthier states, Prussia and Saxony, to increase their export markets at the expense of foreign trading partners. At the same time, economic growth in the agricultural south was retarded (Robinson 1991: 66). However, for the purposes of the present analysis, the roots of the post-war regional divergence may be traced to the mid- to late-nineteenth century when industrialisation established an ever stronger footing and regional differences became sharper with regional specialisation. Naturally, the two world wars represented enormous discontinuities in regional economic development; yet despite the massive destruction (although the extent to which this damaged industry has often been greatly exaggerated), regions in the western Allied sector, which before the war had been generally the most industrialised, also managed to re-establish high levels of

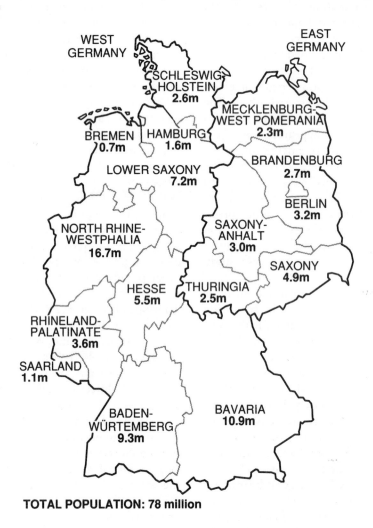

Figure 2.1 Unified Germany in 1990

Source: Author's compilation

industrial production in the new Bonn Republic.

Following the Second World War the most obviously economic backward regions were the areas to the west of the Rhine that suffered great destruction from allied bombing and the border regions which received the largest influx of refugees. The influx of refugees contributed to the early post-war reappearance of regional imbalances. In May 1949 the share of refugees as a proportion of their total populations in the three predominantly agricultural Länder, Schleswig-Holstein, Lower Saxony and Bavaria was respectively one-third, one-quarter and one-fifth. Against this, the overall proportion of refugees in the joint British/American (bizonal) Germany was one-sixth. The extent of this imbalance can be further illustrated as follows. If one adds the French zone, the three Länder constituted 38.8 per cent of the total labour force but 63.8 per cent of total unemployment (Heller 1950: 534).

Patterns of spatial economic imbalance continued into the early 1950s. In particular the frontier corridor between the two Germanies, as well as parts of Bavaria and what was to become the Saarland, were lagging well behind the rest of the country in terms of growth rates and employment. Later in the decade, they were followed by more northerly Länder. The persistence of such regional imbalances contributed to the evolution of regional policy.

EASTERN GERMANY: THE NORTH–SOUTH DIVIDE

As already mentioned, the acquisition of the new Länder means that regional disparities in Germany have been greatly accentuated. Yet this is, as previously stated, far from an unprecedented occurrence in the economic history of Ger-

many. The post-war economic development of West Germany was itself extremely uneven, leading to spatial disparities characterised by a 'north–south' divide. There is also a noticeable north–south division within eastern Germany.

Following unification, it was precisely those areas in eastern Germany with high population densities and concentration of industry which suffered the highest unemployment. Generally, there was far less regional diversification in industrial employment than in the west, which made particular areas still more prone to depression. The north–south divide in the former GDR was apparent in that the major centres of industrial concentration were located in the south and in the area around Berlin. Hence, mechanical engineering and vehicle production was found mainly around Chemnitz/Zwickau, Leipzig and Dresden (Saxony); as well as in Halle and Magdeburg (Saxony-Anhalt) and Berlin. Electrical engineering was mainly located in Berlin, Dresden and Chemnitz. The textile and light industries were also predominantly in the south.

For example, the Carl Zeiss optical works – reunited with its more prosperous western counterpart following unification – was located in Jena (Thuringia). Southern Brandenburg, on the other hand, possessed the disadvantages of having unviable brown coal, along with iron and steel, both of which were located near the Polish border at Cottbus and Eisenhüttenstadt respectively. The huge steel plant at Eisenhüttenstadt (intially Stalinstadt) was constructed at a land-locked location and fed by Soviet iron ore and Polish coal (*Guardian* 3 October 1992). (The plant shared the land-locked locational disadvantage with the Salzgitter plant built by the Nazis on domestic iron ore on the western side of what became the inner German border.) Following GEMSU it

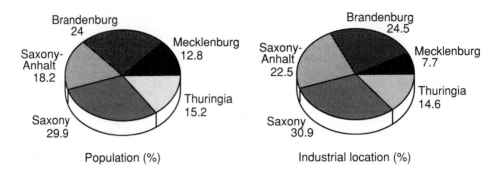

Figure 2.2 Location of population and industry in East Germany
Source: Klemmer (1990: 122)

was necessary to at least halve the labour force at Eisenhüttenstadt to 6,000. Frankfurt an der Oder (also in Brandenburg) had a slightly more viable industrial base than Cottbus and Eisenhüttenstadt, but was located right on the Polish border – an area which looked set to replace the former inner-German border as a relatively depressed region. Another industry which was bound to be particularly badly hit by GEMSU – shipbuilding – was on the northern coast of Mecklenburg-West Pomerania. Figure 2.2 shows the nature of the spatial correspondence between industrial production and population as it stood in 1988.

Saxony – with three of the biggest cities in the new Länder: Chemnitz, Leipzig and Dresden – is a good example of an area where radical change to the structure of the economy was required. However, these three cities form nodal points of a triangle of investment and modernisation of industry (Economist 14 September 1991). Saxony's infrastructure was also more extensive than elsewhere in the new Länder. This fact, along no doubt with recollections of Saxony's former industrial strength based on the abundance of raw materials located in the Erzgebirge mountains near the Czechoslovakian border,

attracted some well-established western companies back to the area. Thus Quelle (mail order), Siemens and AEG (electricals), and Volkswagen all initiated major investment projects (ibid.). Zwickau (where the infamous Trabant was produced) also provided evidence of change to the structure of the economy. A total of 75,000 were employed (as of 1990). Of these, 40 per cent were employed in the car industry, 14 per cent (largely female) in the textile industry and a further 12 per cent in electrical or electronic related industries (Heine and Walter 1990: 404). The figures clearly underline the vulnerability of such regions to competition from the more efficient western Länder. It remained an open question as to whether the location of a car plant (initially for the assembly of Polos) in Zwickau would significantly lessen the decline; in any case production levels at the plant will not reach significant levels until the mid-nineties (ibid.). Further, the technology for a later plant to produce Golfs was to be as advanced as any in the VW empire, and working methods were to stand comparison with Japan (Independent 2 October 1992). Jobs would therefore be reduced rather than created. Moreover, the Zwickau plant had to compete with

VW's low labour cost Spanish company (Seat) and its even lower labour cost acquisition in the Czech Republic (Skoda). (Following GEMSU, German trade unions decided that there must be a process of equalisation between eastern and western pay rates – see the policy section of Chapter 6.) Nonetheless, Saxony's unemployment rate was below that for eastern Germany as a whole (Figure 2.4b below). In another traditional location for motor-vehicle production – Eisenach in Thuringia – the labour force was also substantially reduced when the advanced Opel plant replaced the former Wartburg complex. Two regions with even more overriding problems of adapting to the new competition from the west were Halle and Cottbus. For ecological as well as economic reasons, these areas faced a massive overhaul and curtailment of their main industries (chemicals and energy).

It follows that the north consists primarily of agricultural production. More specifically, Mecklenburg-West Pomerania has been traditionally one of the most underdeveloped areas in the whole of Germany, whereas Saxony and Thuringia (in the south) may be areas where rapid economic recovery will be possible in the long term. The former Junker estates in Mecklenburg-West Pomerania became collective farms under the communists, while the port of Rostock has to compete with the larger and more modern facilities in nearby Hamburg. Similarly, shipbuilding in this and other coastal towns has to compete with the already hard-pressed, but much more efficient and subsidised, yards at Bremen, Hamburg and Kiel. The privatised shipyards in Rostock, Wismar and Stralsund were particularly badly hit (*Economist* 26 October 1991). Ultimately, some of the yards were taken over by Vulkan of Bremen, although the Land's

prime minister resigned in protest. A Norwegian yard – Kvaerner – purchased the Rostock facilities, but only after generous undertakings by the Treuhand to cover investment and losses (see Chapter 8). Of all the new Länder, Mecklenburg-West Pomerania has the highest unemployment (see Figure 2.4b below). Even agriculture in this northern area is handicapped by the fact that the soil around Magdeburg (Saxony-Anhalt) is more fertile. Indeed, the area to the west of Magdeburg (around the former inner-German border) is the traditional supplier of agricultural produce to the reinstated capital of Berlin – formerly Germany's most important industrial conurbation.

This north–south axis can be further illustrated by reference to the degree of urban development. The southern industrial area is typically urbanised, whereas agricultural villages predominate in the north. Having said this, it is necessary to re-emphasise that the east as a whole is more sparsely populated than the west. It should also be re-emphasised that around this north–south axis (in Saxony-Anhalt) lie the obsolete chemical plants which were a cause of widespread pollution. This is exemplified by the 'silver lake' near Bitterfeld in southern Saxony-Anhalt, so-called because of the high levels of lead, zinc and other toxic waste (*Economist* 11 January 1992). It is further exemplified by the environmentally enforced demolition of most of the former Nazi rubber and plastic plant at Buna (*Fortune* 21 September 1992; *Guardian* 20 November 1992). Moreover, the main pollutant in the east – lignite (brown coal) – was mined in this area. Even more of this fuel was mined in Saxony and Brandenburg, where it was the cause of proportionately more pollution. A final example is afforded by the aftermath of uranium mining begun near Zwickau to supply Soviet weapon and power requirements (Boehmer-Christiansen *et al.* 1993: 357 and 363). Although evidence of a severe deterioration of the cultural landscape was evident as early as the mid-1970s, surprise and horror was expressed in the west in the early 1990s when decisions had to be taken regarding, for example, the radioactive water and mud which had been accumulated over decades (*ibid.*: 363 and 366). Eliminating these environmental and ecological catastrophes required urgent attention, especially where the exhausted lunar-type landscape of former brown-coal workings had been filled with toxic chemical waste (DIW/IfW 1992: 15). It was October 1992 before the new Länder, Berlin and the Federal government reached agreement on the financing of pollution costs (*ibid.*). The high degree of reliance on brown coal as a source of primary energy was reduced more quickly (see the privatisation section in Chapter 8).

Eastern Germany is, if anything, even worse off than the western part of the country when it comes to raw-material endowment. The remaining copper and uranium deposits can no longer be economically exploited; hard coal deposits were exhausted by 1977; crude oil, natural gas and iron ore are largely unimportant. There are fairly abundant tin deposits but world prices are lower than domestic production costs. Even more abundant are brown coal and potash, but the notorious environmental damage caused by their exploitation and use present costly adaptation and substitution problems (see below).

The introduction of the market economy implied an extensive re-structuring of employment patterns. Further problems of integration are highlighted by the contrasting structures of production. This is in part reflected by the low level of GDP per head of working population in the former GDR. In 1990 this stood at 32.5 per cent of the western level (Roppel 1990: 379). Heine and Walter (1990: 403) provide a useful comparison of employment by sector of the economy which reveals that, for example, a much higher proportion, (amounting to one million in total), were employed in the primary sector in the GDR than the Federal Republic – a phenomenon also illustrated in Figure 2.3a. Indeed, in terms of type of employment, the clear need for the east to catch up with the west is illustrated in Figure 2.3b. Note the similarity of the structure of employment in West Germany as far back as 1967 with that of the GDR in 1988.

WESTERN GERMANY: THE NORTH–SOUTH DIVIDE

It is therefore clear that the united Germany will initially contain great regional and structural disparities in its eastern sector. The already apparent north–south regional division will be accentuated by a west–east division. Added to this is the fact that the West German economic development has itself been by no means even in terms of regions. In just under two decades the western part of the economy underwent a marked re-structuring of its industrial base which has had a significant impact on regional industrial location. The once prosperous north was overtaken by the south. Very generally, the southern part of former West Germany succeeded in attracting – or already possessed – the high growth, technologically-advanced industries. Bavaria, although still mainly rural, is now the principal centre of Germany's aerospace and other high-tech industries, especially around Munich. A good example is the relocation of Siemens, the electronic concern, from Berlin to

Bavaria. Baden-Württemberg – where the traditionally prosperous cities of Stuttgart and Mannheim are located – is the home of most of Daimler-Benz's motor vehicle production; Bosch is also located here. Both Baden-Württemberg and Bavaria exhibit a preponderance of small and medium-sized firms. It is significant that these two West German Länder played a large role in promoting technological development. Success then bred further success because they were perceived as booming areas by prospective investors (Sturm 1989b: 169). The southern area

also contains Frankfurt am Main (in Hesse), another area of marked economic expansion. Figure 2.4a demonstrates how these three Länder (Bavaria, Baden-Württemberg and Hesse) all enjoyed below-average unemployment rates. In spite of the fact that unemployment in the west fell somewhat, and indeed employment rose between 1989 and 1990, the relative position of the Länder in terms of unemployment remained the same (Bundesanstalt für Arbeit, *Presse Informationen*, 48/90; Figures 6.1 and 6.3 below). What has been said thus far about the

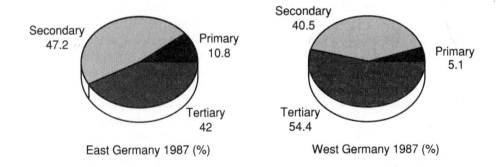

East Germany 1987 (%)   West Germany 1987 (%)

Figure 2.3a Industrial employment by sector (East and West)

Source: *Stat. Jahrbuch* 1989

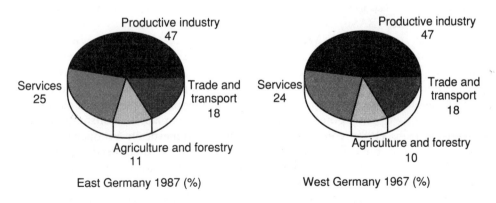

East Germany 1987 (%)   West Germany 1967 (%)

Figure 2.3b Employment by sector (East and West)

Source: Ifo (7/90: 15)

east–west and north–south divides is summarised in Figure 2.4b. Note, however, that the 1992–3 recession hit Baden-Württemberg with particular severity (FT *Survey* 29 April 1993).

There is a further Land that has below-average unemployment rates: the Rhineland-Palatinate. But there are a number of important differences between the generally more prosperous Länder of Bavaria, Baden-Württemberg and Hesse when compared to the Rhineland-Palatinate. The latter Land lacks the large industrial conurbations which are central to the economic expansion of the other three Länder. The Palatinate has therefore to rely more on the less viable economic activities of agriculture, including viniculture, and tourism – activities which supplement total output in the more prosperous three. (The Palatinate, along with Hesse, Baden-Württemberg and Bavaria have all been areas where small farms have historically predominated (Pfeffer 1989b: 201)). But 75 per cent of the direct transfer payments made to small farmers went to the industrially more advanced areas of Baden-Württemberg and Bavaria. Nonetheless, it indicated that the farm crisis in West Germany was regionally specific (*ibid.*). True, one of the economy's three large chemical combines (BASF) is located in Ludwigshafen opposite to Mannheim (Baden-Württemberg), on the Palatine bank of the Rhine. Otherwise, there is a tendency, notably in the Trier region, for the Palatinate to be a peripheral region.

Using his own and other studies, Schackmann-Fallis (1989) concludes that large companies are typically attracted by regional subsidies to such peripheral areas. Control remains vested in the company's head office in the conurbations, where these large companies are thus able to reduce their demand for labour in order to expand in other locations. Such a move enables companies to avoid the labour shortages and higher wage rates in the conurbations. For example, the motor vehicle companies have received financial and other inducements: as early as 1962 Opel (based near Frankfurt am Main) took advantage of redundancies in the coal industry to establish an assembly plant in Bochum (Ruhr). Similarly, Ford (Cologne) decided in 1966 to build an assembly plant in Saarlouis (Saarland) where manpower was readily available. Finally, Daimler-Benz (Stuttgart) assembles its Mercedes 100 Series in Bremen, having been persuaded to provide a purpose-built plant in the 1970s. The general level of skills within the labour force in these externally controlled plants tends to be lower than in the main plants, although their quantitative effects on employment and incomes tend to be equal to, or higher than, the local independent companies. Migration or commuting to the more prosperous regions are two further characteristics of peripheral areas. Many of these attributes also apply to Schleswig-Holstein. On the other hand, relative costs have risen in the conurbations. In such circumstances the critical question is: why has there not been more regional convergence instead of divergence (Wienert 1990a: 376)?

Several of the elements noted above apply to Lower Saxony. Somewhat paradoxically, the most prosperous areas of this region are situated close to the former inner-German border, above all the main Volkswagen plant at Wolfsburg. Virtually all the domestically-produced crude oil (a fraction of total needs), along with much of the modest natural gas reserves prior to unification, are located in this Land. Moving westwards, however, it soon becomes clear that rural problems are quite pronounced.

Percentage of the labour force

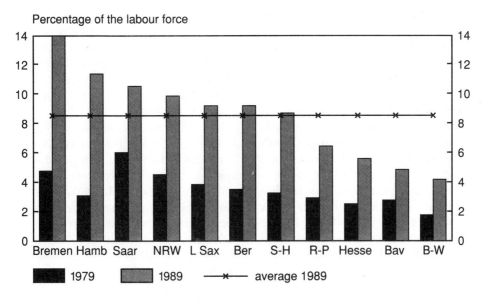

Figure 2.4a Unemployment by West German Länder (1979 and 1989)
Source: MRDB (8/89:37)

Percentage of the labour force

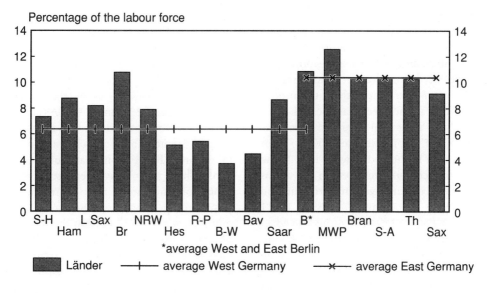

Figure 2.4b Unemployment by Länder (1991)
Source: IW *Zahlen* 1992: 2

Following the war, then, the 'southern' Länder in West Germany were primarily agricultural, the 'northern' Länder were industrialised. More recently, in contrast, the 'north' has been particularly prone to the problems of overreliance on old and declining industries; the 'south' has attracted expanding industries. In particular, industry in the Ruhr district (North Rhine-Westphalia) was based upon coal, iron and steel. Saarland, which possesses similar structural weaknesses, is another exception to the north–south divide: it lies well south of the Rhine–Main divide. However, the Land government and companies in North Rhine-Westphalia have been more successful in diversifying the industrial base of the Ruhr district, where the decline started as early as the second half of the 1950s. Once the power-house of Europe, and lying at the very heart of West Germany's spectacular post-Second World War success, the Ruhr district relied heavily upon its coal and steel industries. There followed the fairly familiar phases in the coal industry of subsidised expansion, gradual oil and (later) nuclear substitution and the consequent decline of the coal industry (Abelshauser 1984). In steel, international over-expansion also led to the need for drastic rationalisation. Since over 80 per cent of the total employment in coal and steel was located in the Ruhr, the structural changes have been remarkable. From the late 1950s to unification, 1.5 million jobs were lost. However, job creation resulted in an almost stable level of employment during most of the 1980s (Jochimsen 1989: 10–11; German Politics 1992). It should be added that another declining industry – shipbuilding – is located further north (Langer 1974: 278). From the late 1960s Hamburg, Bremen and Bremerhaven in particular were adversely affected by this decline, although the decline in Hamburg was cushioned by the establishment of part of the aerospace industry in the city. Bremen possessed no such cushion. On the contrary: with the near bankruptcy of Klöckner in 1992, the city state's other major industry – steel – ran into even greater difficulties.

In fact, the economic revival of Hamburg in the late 1980s and early 1990s is an important feature of regional development. One reason for this transformation was unification. In 1935, about one third of Hamburg's income came from its economic ties with what became East Germany (FT 26 October 1992). When, following the fall of the Berlin wall, this *Hinterland* was reopened imports into Hamburg soared, and the city's breweries, construction and food-processing companies all won new orders (*ibid.*). But the recovery even pre-dates unification. Compensation for the decline of the port, shipbuilding and, following the crude-oil price shocks, oil refining was found by encouraging high-tech and service industries to expand. For example, Hamburg shares much of the medical-technology industry with the fellow Hanseatic city of Lübeck. They are both, in this sense, further exceptions to the crude north–south argument, although unemployment in Hamburg remains above the western average (Figures 2.4a and 2.4b). As already shown, however, the other two Hanseatic cities – Bremen and Rostock – are indeed in decline. Rostock in particular could hardly have been less prepared for the shock of unification and overnight exposure to open markets. During the communist era, the city had been the recipient of scarce financial resources which enabled it to build up its port, shipbuilding and fishing industries (*Independent on Sunday* 3 January 1993). All three industries were decimated on unification.

Not surprisingly, then, Cheshire (1990:

316) includes the 'northern' conurbations of Hannover, Düsseldorf and Hamburg, along with some of the 'southern' cities already mentioned above, towards the top of his list of the 117 largest Functional Urban Regions – even though the data for more recent periods led Cheshire to revise downwards his earlier estimates for German cities (Cheshire *et al.* 1986). Significantly, however, the group of German cities with apparently more serious problems are in precisely those areas singled out for special mention in this respect – the Ruhr (Dortmund, Bochum and Duisburg), the capital of Saarland (Saarbrücken) and Bremen. They are all concentrated amongst the most deteriorating one-third of EC cities over the period 1971–88.

As can be seen in Figure 2.5, the resultant north–south disparities are more evident in terms of unemployment than per-capita income.

It can be seen that both measures diverge between Länder. In fact, during the first half of the 1980s north–south

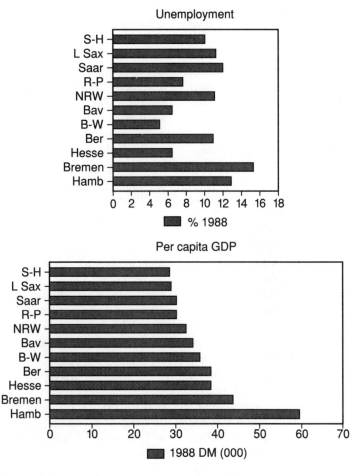

Figure 2.5 Unemployment and per capita GDP (West Germany: 1988)
Source: Calculated from *Stat. Jahrbücher* 1989/1990

differences in these terms widened, as have rates of growth. The city states excepted, there is also a fairly good correspondence between rankings, with Hesse, Baden-Württemberg and Bavaria having both high per-capita incomes and low rates of unemployment. But it is also important to note that high per-capita incomes are concentrated in urban areas. In 1988, Hamburg and Bremen were above Hesse, while Berlin was above Baden-Württemberg and well above the Rhineland-Palatinate; yet all three of the city states had unemployment rates above the national average (Figures 2.4 and 2.5). The urban–rural contrast is further highlighted by the measure of per-capita gross value added (Thieme 1991: 102). However, owing to the regional interdependence of many firms, per-capita income measures are less reliable and can be subject to misinterpretation (ibid.: 101).

One indication of the policy makers' growing disquiet was a special programme which targeted unemployment in 1979 (Schmid and Peters 1982). It was aimed particularly at North-Rhine Westphalia and the Saarland. It consisted, first, of encouraging vocational training; second, hiring inducements to employers who provided jobs for the unskilled and long-term unemployed were financed; finally, work was created in the social services and environmental improvements. Wage subsidies of up to 100 per cent were offered to employers who provided jobs in these three ways. Quantitatively, most jobs were created in the vocational training category, with an unsurprising if regrettable bias towards young males (ibid.: 106–7). The same situation obtained in the case of the relatively less successful hiring inducements which in any case displayed large drop-out rates. In fact, only the social services created (a relatively negligible number of) jobs for females – and

part-time work was included in this category. Moreover, there was an appreciable variation in take-up rates as between districts (ibid.: 110). This all points to the need to discuss labour market adjustment in a special section in Chapter 6. There are two policy conclusions here. First, relative regional decline was discernible in Germany prior to unification. It was therefore exercising the minds of policy makers. Second, provided additional permanent jobs can be created, and given the extremely high economic and social costs of unemployment, it might be worthwhile to pay a fairly high price in employment creation measures (ibid.: 114).

More generally, the pattern of change in West Germany as a whole was one of employment increasing in the services and decreasing in manufacturing, along with the extension of industrial employment to rural areas and decreasing urban industrial employment. The latter is partly connected with changing patterns in the division of labour, with administrative and management functions still being carried out in the urban areas and productive and storage facilities transferring to rural locations.

Some of the changes mentioned can now be further highlighted by focusing on developments in two regions: Berlin and North Rhine-Westphalia. In order to emphasise the long-term nature of regional development problems, the present tense is often used in these case studies.

BERLIN

Berlin's case is unique when it comes to discussion of regional problems. Prior to its becoming the federal capital of a united Germany, it was a divided city. The eastern part of the city was the capital of the former GDR; the western part was de facto an eleventh Land of West Germany.

It was not only peripheral in the sense defined above, but it was physically separated from the rest of West Germany. Now situated in a central European location between west and east, this region is of great significance economically (and in the future also politically) for it will play a great part in the hoped-for economic recovery of the east. At the same time, and depending upon opinion, the prospect of Berlin becoming a centre of high economic growth is either regarded as a spur to recovery in east Europe or as potentially detrimental to other regions in Germany. The latter view is based on the argument that as an area of intensive expansion, Berlin would suck in resources from outside. Further objections to allowing Berlin to grow too quickly rest with the fact that the prosperity of West Germany was built up without the presence of one central growth node.

Certainly there are a number of factors which may in any case deter investment. There is a lack of productive industry. Typically for an urban area are the pollution and traffic problems. Added to this are other factors which may make it difficult to attract labour. One is the acute housing shortage with rents soaring in both east and west Berlin. As with other agglomerations, costs are likely to soar, especially in the centre, so that the main areas of development may be located in the surrounding residential areas, as has happened in Hamburg. Such development could, however, come into conflict with the historical growth of the city, which has spread out along axes from the centre, as manifested by the transport networks. Improvement to the infrastructure, especially of east Berlin, will require massive investment – the transport network from west–east will need to be almost entirely reconstructed.

Given the isolation and consequent high transportation costs, it was only through support from the Federal government that the city survived as an economic unit. The passing of the Berlin Development Act (*Berlinerförderungsgesetz*) was an early attempt to halt the economic decline of the city (Burtenshaw 1974: 156). It allowed lower taxation (30 per cent less) and a tax free wage supplement. Costs of travel and removal to Berlin were paid out of funds. Depreciation allowances and capital grants were available. Goods produced in Berlin and sold in West Germany enjoyed reduced VAT. There were also tax-free investment grants, and low interest long-term credits. In 1983, more than 50 per cent of Berlin's budget was financed by Federal Government (FT 30 September 1983). Despite the incentives, in the decade from 1961 only 168 new companies established themselves in Berlin. Since the VAT deductions given to manufacturers in Berlin as well as their West German customers favoured capital-intensive large volume production using mainly unskilled labour, there was a great lack of specialised high-tech industry. Thus, most of the new companies relied upon high-volume, low-technology production (*ibid.*). (The chemical and pharmaceutical industries may, perhaps, be exceptions.) Hence the encouragement of high-technology small- to medium-sized companies using skilled workforces in the early 1980s. However, Berlin failed to become a high-tech silicon valley. The tax reform of 1988 meant a cut in Berlin aid; it also affected aid for the high-technology industry which Berlin was lacking (*Die Zeit* 11 March 1988).

In some ways the pattern of economic development in Berlin seems to be following a similar course to some of the *Förderungsgebiete* (whose significance is described further below) in West Germany: a transfer of productive resources from the central urban area to the peripheral areas and a reduction of manufacturing and an increase in service industries. This begs the question as to what extent one could expect the model of West German regional development to be repeated in the new Länder. A clearer answer to this will naturally depend upon analysing interregional differences (see the regional comparisons above). Nonetheless, if the pattern of West German development is repeated, a greater dispersion of productive industries can be expected to occur.

It was therefore not surprising that Berlin and Brandenburg agreed to merge on a phased basis during the 1990s (FAZ 7 December 1992). After all, much of the substantial aid previously available to Berlin was to be discontinued by 1994 (as was that to the former inner-border area). The gradual reduction of subsidies commenced in July 1991, and the average VAT deduction of 4.2 per cent for purchases of products made in Berlin will be removed by that date (*Die Welt* 2 May 1991). Similarly, tax subsidies amounting to at least 5 DM billion were cut. As greater investment aid is given to east Germany, excluding Berlin, firms may in fact find it appropriate to relocate outside the city. This is likely to speed the above mentioned spatial transfer of resources away from the inner-city region (with the urban area increasingly becoming an administrative centre), especially since preferential treatment for capital-intensive, productive industries will no longer apply. The reduction in assistance is also affecting wages and living costs. By 1995 the 8 per cent tax break formerly available to Berliners will no longer apply. Transport costs will rise as subsidies are cut (*Economist* 9 November 1991).

The effects on future employment are difficult to assess in the long term. Three years after the Wall came down, there were still disparities within the city itself. Unemployment in east Berlin is three times that of the western part (*ibid.*). The city has long suffered from a shortage of a skilled labour force. A long standing problem in west Berlin has been how to find jobs for the large number of refugees who have settled there from eastern and southern Europe while at the same time striving to maintain or improve living conditions for the indigenous population. Between the early 1960s and 1983, 800,000 left Berlin and 650,000, mainly Turks but nearly all foreigners, arrived. Like many large conurbations, Berlin suffers from an acute birth deficit and, as a result, possesses an over-aged population (*Der Spiegel* 24/91). A survey by the DIW found that the present number of deaths exceeds the birth rate by about 10,000 a year (DIW 27/90: 369).

In view of this, and the need for development, immigration of workers into the region will be necessary. According to the DIW analysis, it is expected that the number of job places will be reduced in the western part of the city. In general terms east Berlin will (in the short-term at least) suffer job losses on a similar scale to the rest of the former GDR. Such a development would also endanger the main industries, primarily machine, electronic and electrical engineering and this could amount to about a third of all jobs 'by the year 2000' (*ibid.*: 367). On the other hand, a slight expansion of small industry is 'realistic'. Overall, a slight increase in employment may be expected in the long-term (*ibid.*: 369). Figure 2.6 shows the DIW projection of employment in Berlin up to the year 2010.

East Berlin nonetheless offers great potential for commercial relocation. There is a high proportion of east Berliners with a high school or university education. Some

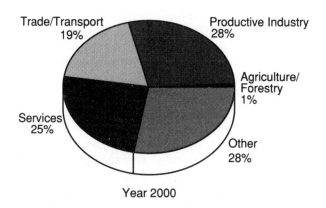

Year 2000

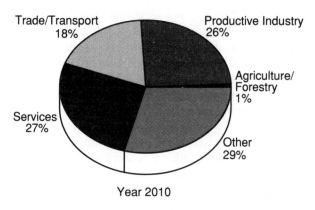

Year 2010

Figure 2.6 Berlin: employment by sector
Source: DIW (27/90: 366)

firms are returning to Berlin. A good example is the relocation of Lufthansa to the city where it was founded. The airline made substantial investments in the redevelopment of the old airport in the east (Schönefeld) (FT 14 May 1991). Other new developments were also taking place (*Wirtschaftswoche* 16/90). That was until the post-unification boom in the west faded dramatically. Thereafter, like the rest of the former GDR east Berlin was trying to attract new investment at the time of a major recession in the west. It was in such conditions that Mercedes-Benz drastically modified its DM 1 billion

plans to build a new truck plant in Ahrensdorf, near east Berlin.

THE RUHR AND NORTH RHINE-WESTPHALIA

North Rhine-Westphalia (NRW) was created in 1946 when the British Occupation Authorities set up a Land parliament in Düsseldorf. With the onset of the Cold War the American and British authorities recognised the region's importance as a steel and coal area and any thoughts of de-industrialisation (as espoused by the Morgenthau Plan) were shelved. The French government for reasons of security wished to establish the Ruhr as a separate unit, economically integrated into France. Later, they wished to see it come under international jurisdiction. However, the British view was that a much larger economic unit would effectively dilute the power of the Ruhr region. The British view prevailed and NRW was therefore formed from the northern Rhine province of Prussia, Westphalia and Lippe-Detmold (Bade and Kunzmann 1991: 94).

Wehling (1991: 328) has distinguished four main regional sub-divisions of economic development within the Ruhr: the southern zone; the Hellweg; the core coal-mining zone; and the northern and western fringe development zone. These zones can also be regarded as indicative of the differentiated nature of responses according to need in the four zones employed by the regional planning authority for the Ruhr. The zones mentioned have experienced a divergent economic development. The core coal mining zone contains the Emscher valley and has had the most serious problems. The Hellweg zone follows an ancient west–east line of trade stretching back to the eleventh century. It contains areas of high density urban settlement including the cities of Duisburg, Essen, Mülheim, Bochum and Dortmund.

The post-war economic recovery of the region proceeded rapidly. This is hardly surprising, since the Ruhr was Europe's largest coal and steel producer. The formation of the European Coal and Steel Community in 1951 abolished tariff barriers and other forms of trade discrimination. Transport costs subsequently came down and by 1956 coal production had reached its highest level – as can be seen from Figure 2.7. The decline of this sector can be traced to 1957 when there was a world-wide surplus of oil. During the 1960s diversification of energy demand into alternative and cheaper sources, particularly oil and natural gas, led to a decline in production. Also, exhausted pits entailed the gradual northern migration to deeper and therefore more costly depths of mines. The Ruhr region reacted by undergoing an extensive restructuring process. In 1969 twenty-six local coal companies merged to form Ruhrkohle AG. In the 1970s the external shocks of the oil crises and increasing competition from low-cost producers accelerated the decline of the steel industry. Thus steel production peaked in 1974 and thereafter fell rapidly (see Figure 2.8). This was an indication of the more general downturn in industrial production. The consequential fall in the demand for steel was unexpected (Wienert 1990b: 207). It came at a time when European steel companies were reacting to Japanese competition by introducing costly technological change (ibid.). Further major industries of the Ruhr, textiles and clothing, suffered similar decline.

Some theorists have explained the declining growth of old industrial areas such as the Ruhr in terms of Kondratieff cycles and the exclusion of new technological transfer owing to an outmoded technological base (Butzin 1991: 188–9). Support for this hypothesis would point to the 'long-waves' of industrial growth and decline of about 50 years which can be traced back to the nineteenth century. Such cycles for Germany were first identified by Josef A. Schumpeter. Wehling (1991) also supports the cyclical hypothesis, describing growth and spatial patterns of decline in terms of historical development. If correct, then the growth and decline of the Ruhr industry can be seen as the latest cycle, and so one would expect the 1990s to be a

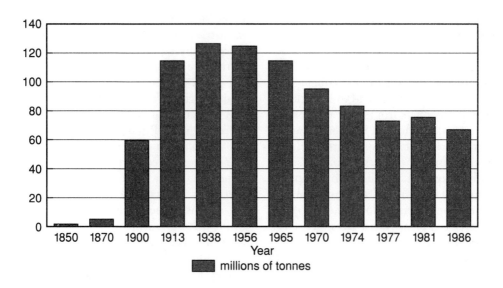

Figure 2.7 Ruhr coal production
Source: Minshull (1990: 171)

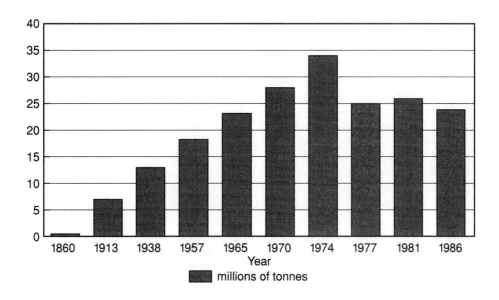

Figure 2.8 Ruhr steel production
Source: Minshull (1990: 171)

period of growth for the Ruhr and other problem areas in Germany. In other words, decline and recovery are functionally related to time (Wienert 1990a: 389). The theory does not of course take account of both shocks and competition in identical products from other regions and economies. Unification is a good example of a shock, while competition clearly emanates from the far east. More pessimistically, regional inability to adapt to change has been seen as a deep-seated process of deindustrialisation (*ibid*.: 375).

Other explanations have revolved around the under utilisation of specifically-trained employees and insufficient R&D (Butzin 1991: 192). Growth of professional services in the Ruhr has declined, while in contrast NRW as a whole has almost one-third of about fifty technological bodies throughout west Germany with an interest in industry (Fiorelli 1991: 101). Bertelsmann, the world's largest media concern is based in Gütersloh and the computer group Nixdorf (now part of Siemens) is in Paderborn; both of these are rather remote towns in NRW (FT 1 July 1988). The establishment of a 'technological park' in Dortmund is a further indication of the importance attributed to the evolution away from dependence on coal and steel to high-tech industry. Significantly, two other factors have contributed to the Ruhr's inability to recover fully from economic decline – the lack of a suitable highly-trained workforce and significant population loss, particularly in the Emscher zone, initiated by the collapse of the region's coal and steel industries (Butzin 1991: 194). During the period 1961–88 the Ruhr witnessed a 550,832 or 9 per cent population reduction (Wehling 1991: 327). The skill-shortage problem is itself connected with the lack of technologically-related industry in the area. Most of the available training tends to be orientated to skills based on older industries which are less in demand. Accompanying this is the slow economic growth (between 1983 and 1988 it was 1.4 per cent against an average of 2.2 per cent for the whole country). In 1950 NRW accounted for 42 per cent of West Germany's GDP but only 29 per cent in 1988 (*Economist* 21 May 1988).

Yet another concern for future economic growth in the area is the fact that there is a shortage of new development areas. This is due to the spatial dispersion of the old mines which, incidentally, have caused considerable ecological damage. The Ruhr District Land Office estimated that approximately 80 per cent of the land was contaminated. There was also strong dissatisfaction with the poor form of urban development and bad environmental conditions (*ibid*.). The importance of providing the appropriate conditions in order to attract a workforce into the region is highlighted by the successful example of the Ruhr town of Mülheim. The town administration successfully restructured employment in the region. The local mine was closed at a cost of 5500 jobs, but 80,000 m^2 of industrial development area was purchased and an active policy of resettlement followed which led eventually to the creation of 4500 jobs centred around the canalised area of the Ruhr (*Die Zeit* 4 May 1979). The main aim of recent regional policy, in the face of the reluctance of new enterprises to establish themselves, has been to prevent the closure of existing industry plus the provision of suitable development land. Diversification of production and a shift away from over-dependence on traditional export markets has also been attempted.

Starting in the 1970s, special conferences have been held to discuss the particular problems of the Ruhr region.

One example was the 'Rau Plan' to revitalise the area. The plan involved the investment of DM 5 billion and was named after the prime minister of NRW, Johannes Rau. Essentially the problem of the Ruhr was one of industrial transformation and of ways of restructuring the local economy to adapt to this process. In particular, the policies aimed at creating more service-related jobs, as well as measures to improve the quality of life for the inhabitants (FT 16 May 1979). As already indicated in this section, the policies were only partially successful; attracting high-tech firms, and other industries which do not depend upon proximity to raw materials, has proved difficult because of quality-of-life factors which deter labour immigration – even though this is to some extent based on perception and prejudice rather than reality. Nevertheless, in the Ruhr there has been an enforced switch away from jobs in iron, steel and coal; in 1987 only 30 per cent of the labour force was so employed against 80 per cent in 1950 (FT 1 July 1988). There was much resistance to plant closures which has slowed industrial transformation. As unemployment increased during the early 1980s, the once prosperous NRW needed ever more urgently to find ways of attracting new investment. The steel firms which underwent massive rationalisation were nearly all large enterprises so it was vital that the region should attract small to medium-sized companies.

By way of contrast, Bavaria and Baden-Württemberg have succeeded in attracting small and medium-sized firms, along with the electronics and aerospace industries. As already indicated, many industrial giants are also located in these two Länder, as are some important banks (*The Banker*, March 1991: 27–9). The largest concentration of German millionaires lives around Baden-Baden and the second biggest around the Starnberger See, some 30 miles south-west of Munich (*ibid.*). This is all well summarised in the following manner by Bade and Kunzmann (1991: 95):

The (Ruhr) actors involved in the concerted public-private support for the dominating industries . . . do not act independently . . . the indigenous regional tradition may become a heavy burden rather than an asset for the future if technological changes occur or international market competition becomes tight. The large coal, steel and energy complexes (Thyssen, Krupp, VEBA, RWE, VEW, Hoesch, Mannesmann) . . . dominated industrial development for decades. Heavily subsidised by the public sector . . . the large corporations had to be forced to innovate and diversify . . . [this has created] a socio-political environment that has been less favourable for small and medium-sized firms outside the traditional industrial sector . . . Baden-Württemberg is known as a modern industrial region where innovative, flexible small and medium-sized industries have contributed to . . . economic wealth . . . However, the dominance of one powerful industry, the Daimler-Benz Corporation, is continuously growing.

Yet as Sturm demonstrates (1992: 28), NRW was one of three Länder which played an important role in the industrial-policy debate of the 1980s, the other two being Berlin and Baden-Württemberg. Berlin's policy, as would be expected from what was said above, was determined by its location and the degree of federal support it received. Baden-Württemberg set its stall out to become the model for high-tech development in a commercial manner. NRW, however, involved the trade unions in the formulation and implementation of policy, the nature of which was to be socially acceptable (*ibid.*: 29; *German Politics* 1992). True, the area has manifestly coped far better with the attendant problems of transformation than peripheral areas of Europe such as the Mezzogiorno in southern Italy. At its worst, unemployment in the Ruhr was still under that of other old industrial areas in Europe such as north-east England and northern Spain. Several reasons for this may be posited. The Ruhr is located in what is still a potentially economically powerful Land, even though per-capita income in NRW has dropped below the average (Minshull 1990: 177); in addition, the Land enjoys representation on account of the Federal system – unlike peripheral regions in Britain; and the area does not suffer from the geographical and economic isolation of areas like the Mezzogiorno – one possible scenario put forward for eastern Germany (Hughes Hallet and Ma 1993; Siebert 1991b: 328). In any case, industrial development can succeed as it has in Wales and parts of Spain (Henzler 1992: 29). Although regional aid affected 40 per cent of the Ruhr district's population (Fiorelli 1991: 97), basic regional strategies have been initiated; again this is lacking in many peripheral regions of Europe. Examples of the strategies have included creation of inner-city recreational sites; the development of housing; and the conversion of industrial wasteland to green-belts.

Despite the above advantages, the Ruhr continued to suffer from the characteristic problems of an old industrial area into the 1990s. It has been estimated that during the decade a further 30,000 mining jobs along with another 40,000 in ancillary industries will be lost (FT 6 December 1991). It is doubtful that unification will assist old industrial areas like the Ruhr – in the short term at least – even though the opening up of Europe and unification may provide gravitational vitality in the sense that more workers could be attracted into the region from east Europe. But at the end of the 1980s, unemployment in the Ruhr region had reached 15 per cent. Following unification, moreover, the Federal government was obliged to consider the repercussions in east Germany of assisting the Ruhr. More specifically, the shedding of jobs in Eisenhüttenstadt had been a far less protracted affair than in the Ruhr. Relatively few jobs would be saved by the building of a high technology mini-mill in the east. Hence, the decision not to close the Duisburg-Rheinhausen plant in 1988 proved to be only a temporary reprieve. In addition to the long-term decline in steel demand and the need to consider Eisenhüttenstadt, cheap imports from eastern Europe and subsidised output in other parts of the EC doomed the plant to closure in 1993.

INFRASTRUCTURE, TRADE AND ENVIRONMENTAL POLLUTION

Stark contrasts in the infrastructure between west and east will have to be overcome in order to promote regional specialisation and trade. Although East Germany, like other eastern block countries, traded the vast bulk of its goods with other Council for Mutual Economic Assistance (Comecon) countries, it nevertheless had a far higher proportion of east–west trade than other such countries. For freight transport, the former GDR relied heavily upon rail. Like most of its public transport system, its railway system is obsolete. While there is higher rail line density in the east than west, with 131 km per 1000 km^2 as opposed to 124 in the west, only 3,475 km of its 14,024 km rail network is electrified, compared with 11,669 km out of 27,284 km in western

Germany (Button 1991: 5). Moreover, the creation of an integrated transport network in Germany will be hampered in that the main rail arteries in both parts of Germany run from north to south. Furthermore, the public transport system in the former GDR suffers from inadequate rolling stock and the road network is in a very poor state of repair.

The heavily subsidised low fares of the public transport system in East Germany led to levels of demand with which the system could not cope, both at a national and regional level. Nevertheless, as in the west, car travel had increased in comparison to other forms of travel during the last ten years. Based on the assumption (amongst others) that transport preferences were similar in the GDR to those of the Federal Republic, the IfW produced regional projections of transport flows and usage up to the year 2010; of particular interest were predictions with regard to long-distance passenger transport which state that east–west traffic flow will increase substantially while north–south flow will decrease (Kowalski and Rothengatter 1991: 223).

The unification of Germany and the opening up of the east offers the prospect for some regions to improve their position through trade. Thus, Hamburg can recover its former hinterlands, while Kassel, near the former inner-German border, has re-established its position on the crossroads between east and west. Yet efficient trade depends upon mobility and of course adequate levels of production. In highly industrial areas such as the Ruhr congestion is a problem, as investment in the infrastructure has failed to keep pace with increased demand, particularly on the roads. Any increase in investment is threatened by the implied need for greater investment in the infrastructure of the east, and by the estimated increases

in transport costs during the 1990s. Consequently, increases in trade between west and east are only expected in the long term, while in the short term trade actually diminished, with east German exports particularly affected by the currency reform, large productivity differentials and projected pay equalisation (see Chapters 1 and 6).

One survey showed that 81 per cent of western managers believed that the most urgent improvements required to the eastern infrastructure were in the field of telecommunications; 50 per cent also believed that road transport improvements were important (Städler 1991: 4). Illustrative of the need for improving telecommunications was the observation that in Brandenburg only every nineteenth person has a telephone (SZ 2 March 1991).

The strong ecological awareness within the former West Germany was bound to add to the already difficult economic problems of the former GDR. This awareness is reflected in a number of regulations limiting emissions from industry: for example, the technical directives for pure air and the Act against emissions (*Immisionsschutzgesetz*). With the aim of integrating environmental and regional policy, programmes of investment were set up in the Saarland, North Rhine-Westphalia and areas within the coastal belt (Oßenbrügge 1991: 368). Initially, such regional policy was aimed at the improvement of infrastructure; now it is aimed primarily at 'environmental improvement'. One question of importance is whether such regulations will be imposed rigidly in east Germany. The reliance on the highly polluting production of brown coal for domestic as well as industrial energy supply (particularly in the chemical industry) are cases in point. It is accepted that its production will be reduced and that power stations will have to eschew their dependence on it. Thus in the future there is likely to be a greater dependence on nuclear energy – itself – a subject of some controversy. The interim-East Government under Hans Modrow estimated that demand for brown coal should drop from 300 million to 180 million tonnes per year. It is intended eventually to phase out production altogether. As just implied, it was not only the energy industry that was likely to be affected by the need for environmental improvement. The chemical industry was also a major polluter. As a consequence of the need for less environmentally harmful means of production, it is extremely likely that employment in this industry will be considerably reduced.

Yet environmental measures need not always lead to job losses. Oßenbrügge (1991: 362) points out that there has been a shift away from research into the job destroying effect of environmental policies to their potential to create jobs. One rationale for this is the growing consumer demand for environmentally 'friendly' goods. Comparing expenditure on environmental protection at Federal, Land and local-authority level, Oßenbrügge notes (ibid.: 363) the high proportion of expenditure by local authorities. The promotion of environmental technologies in deprived areas can therefore be viewed as promoting regional growth. But the contrary opinion has also been expressed (ibid.: 368). However, Oßenbrügge (ibid.) adds a number of important riders to such doubts: environmental protection may be used as an effective economic tool. Moreover, it is perhaps significant for the new Länder that many studies have shown that regions already plagued by environmental problems, especially the heavily-industrialised agglomeration areas, are attractive locations for all types of enterprises in the environmental industry.

Given this situation, it is only a small step further to recommend an environmental regional policy for old- and heavily-industrialised regions, because they offer intensive environmental problems, a skilled labour force, existing investment in environmental improvement, and little productive investment in their traditional industries.

THE SIGNIFICANCE OF FEDERALISM AND THE FISCAL CONSTITUTION

A crucial point of change, bearing both on Federal-Länder relationships, and the ability of the Federal Government to grant aid to the regions, came in 1967 with the Stability and Growth Act (StWG). Before the introduction of this Act, macroeconomic policy had been primarily concerned with the maintenance of price stability through the application of monetary rather than Keynesian-type fiscal policy instruments. (As will be seen in the next two chapters, budgetary policy had been confined mainly to a housekeeping role and the Bundesbank was able to pursue an independent domestic monetary policy.) In the face of the recession of 1967 the limitations of purely monetary policy to cope with lower sectoral growth led to the impulse towards creating more efficient and flexible instruments of policy. Although this reform was primarily concerned with fiscal and macroeconomic policy, there were also important implications for the coordination of policy between different levels of government.

An interest-free anticyclical reserve fund (Konjunkturausgleichsrücklage) was established at the central bank which was to be used to slow-down growth or stimulate the economy as required. In effect, the fund represented a withdrawal of capital from market circulation. In times of recession funds could be distributed from Federal to Länder governments which required help. Contributions to the fund by these governments were set at a maximum of 3 per cent of the total tax revenue from the previous year. In addition, the Federal government could raise taxes by up to 10 per cent to meet additional reserve requirements, but only when there was a disturbance in the overall equilibrium. As the Federal government could make the funds conditional upon the Land complying with wider aims of macroeconomic equilibrium, they represented a useful means of controlling state policy. Similarly, in times of expansion, the Federal government could issue decrees to the lower levels of government to restrict their borrowing, and repay funds to the Bundesbank, thereby preventing overloading of the capital market (Knott 1981: 20). It should be noted that the Federal government cannot put the above measures into effect without the approval of the Bundesrat. While the act seems at first to impinge upon the ability of Länder to independently frame their fiscal administration, as provided by Section 109(1) of the Basic Law, it is in fact compatible with Section 109(4) which requires that the Federal and Länder authorities should take account of the overall economic equilibrium. Further constitutional sanction is given in 109(4) which allows the Bundesrat to enact legislation of the above type to avert disturbances to macroeconomic equilibrium. In summary, the StWG provided the Federal government with a significant role in fiscal policy, and allowed for restrictions to be placed on budgetary policy in times of severe economic recession.

One weakness of the above legislation has been the difficulty in creating unambiguous guidelines on occasions when 'macroeconomic imbalance' has occurred,

and therefore under what conditions budgetary restrictions should be applied (EC 1990a: 43). In an effort to clarify matters, in 1989 the Federal Constitutional Court published a number of guide-lines concerning Federal borrowing requirements. On the whole, these guide-lines reinforced the idea that borrowing could only be allowed to exceed specified limits when such borrowing would help to reduce the risk of severe macroeconomic imbalances. In view of the events since the Court's decision, particularly the growing budget deficits resulting from unification, the guide-lines have taken on a new significance: they give further constitutional sanction to the Federal deficit financing required to assist the new Länder. With the above reforms in place, Section 115 of the Basic Law, which placed restrictions on deficit financing, was changed to legalise for the first time credit financing up to the officially designated level of investment expenditures, or beyond in the event of economic necessity (Knott 1981: 21)

The policy initiated by the StWG could not be effective unless the Länder played a role complementary to that of the Federal government. Therefore, as a direct consequence of the StWG a Fiscal Planning Council (FPC) was established to coordinate policy between Federal and Länder governments. Including members from all levels of government, the FPC draws up economic plans and produces economic projections. The FPC meets three times a year, the timing following the budgetary year. As the council contains representatives from many different quarters including the political parties and the Bundesbank, agreement is often difficult to achieve. Yet the fact that there are so many conflicting interests makes the role of a coordinating body if anything more indispensable. Undoubtedly the most important role of the FPC is to coordinate budgetary policy between the Länder and the Federal government. Under the terms of the Federal budgetary legislation, the FPC is chaired by a representative of the Federal Minister of Finance. The ability of the FPC to set budgets is limited in so far as the constitution allocates such authority to the Federal government and Länder. The FPC accordingly must change policy through persuasion, but its high-powered membership ensures it a great influence over budgetary policy.

It is possible to better appreciate the role of the FPC by looking at some important developments since its inception. The basis of the consultative role of the FPC was not properly established until 1977. In that year the nature of the FPCs consultative role was decided, along with the frequency of meetings and details regulating the statistical data upon which the different levels of government could base their policy (BMF 1983: 111). Henceforth, the FPC was able to contribute to drawing up draft budgets for subsequent fiscal years as well as the continuation of medium-term fiscal planning. In 1982 the FPC confirmed its original view that a clearer division of budgetary competence between Federal government, Länder and local authorities was necessary along with a stricter control of budgetary deficits. In that regard, the FPC stipulated that rates of growth of expenditure should not exceed those of GNP. Furthermore, tax reductions leading to cuts in expenditure should take account of overall macroeconomic policy, as laid down by the Basic Law (109[2]). In this respect at least, the FPC had been successful: between 1981 and 1989 expenditure as a percentage of nominal gross national product of all three levels of government had fallen from 35.1 per cent to 30.9 per cent (MRDB 7/90: 40). More recently, in the face of

increases in overall expenditure as a result of unification, the FPC has urged central, regional and local authorities to limit their expenditure expansion to 3 per cent of GNP (*ibid.*). Thus, the FPC has played an important role in seeing that the fiscal policy of the Länder and local authorities should complement rather than contradict Federal economic policy. On the other hand, it is fair to say that the significance of the FPC in setting macroeconomic policy has diminished since its inception.

By virtue of further fiscal reforms passed in 1969, the Länder Revenue-Sharing Act (*Länderfinanzausgleichsgesetz*) and the Budget Basic Rules Act (*Haushaltsgrundsätzegesetz*), grew from the Basic Law requirement that uniform living standards throughout the Federal Republic should be promoted. These measures can also be regarded as building upon the foundations of the StWG. They had the further purposes of allowing fiscal assistance programmes to promote macroeconomic stability, and improve coordination of budgetary policy between Federal and Länder governments. In this respect, they required constitutional amendments. As they are of fundamental importance to regional economic structure, the 1969 reforms, in particular in relation to revenue sharing, are dealt with in more detail below. But there was a marked shift to supply-side macroeconomic policies in 1982. The application of measures legalised by the StWG do not therefore play a central role in the policy debate today. Nevertheless, the StWG was vitally important in laying the basis for further changes to the fiscal-policy constitution and for altering the basis of regional policy.

FEDERALISM AND LEGISLATIVE COMPETENCE

A number of elements go to make up the fiscal constitution in Germany, all of which are related to the federal political structure. Above all, the complexity of the Federal political system is often underestimated by non-German writers. For instance, it is possible to take models based on different definitions of 'levels of government'. The Basic Law describes a two-level model in which local municipalities are subsumed within the Länder. In terms of administrative structures, a five-level model is also possible (Mäding 1989: 116). For the purposes of the following analysis, a division into three levels, corresponding to Federal government, Land and local authority (*Gemeinde*), is sufficient.

The federal system, to some extent a result of the influence of the Americans after the war as well as the traumatic experience of a central dictatorship under Hitler, implies that in practice the Federal governments' abilities to pass binding economic legislation are curtailed. Thus, the occupying authorities insisted that a system of checks and balances should curtail central authority. Accordingly, before unification, the Federal government and legislature, as well as the Länder governments and around 8,800 local authorities (*Gemeinden*), all shared fiscal policy responsibility. The basic structure, as laid down by the Basic Law, has been left largely unaltered by the unity treaty, although the revenue sharing amongst the Länder had to be reorganised (see the discussion surrounding Table 2.2 below). Nonetheless, integrating East Germany was no easy matter.

Historically, of course, federalism was familiar to the east Germans and initially the GDR constitution had officially recognised the existence of the five Länder in East Germany. But the process of centralisation had caused the system to be abandoned, with the result that in 1952 the country was reorganised into administrative districts with the Länder becoming no more than historical appendages (RWI-*Mitteilungen* 1990 1/2: 120). Thus the restructuring of Land level economic administration in former East Germany was not straightforward. It has been pointed out that various alternative administrative boundaries in East Germany could be drawn. Any re-drawing of territorial boundaries in East Germany would need to pay particular attention to the following considerations (Blaschke 1990):

- natural divisions (mountains, rivers etc.)
- historical development of boundaries
- the regional economic structure
- customs and cultures
- attachment of local populace to territorial institutions
- effective administrative functioning

Any plan embodying the above criteria would also apply to a wider reorganisation of German federalism (*German Politics* 1992). For instance, the long-term existence of three city states would be difficult to justify on any grounds other than pure nostalgia. Moreover, Baden-Württemberg and Saxony-Anhalt were 'artificial' in the sense that they were formed after the Second World War from historically and culturally somewhat diverse groupings. Finally, the post-war emergence of North Rhine-Westphalia was discussed in the case study above.

But the latent rivalry between the Länder, and their attempt to resist any centralisation, was brought into sharp relief when the Bundesbank governing council was reorganised following unification. (The council's functions are discussed at the beginning of Chapter 4.) It was eventually agreed (in mid-1992) that there should be only nine Länder representatives as opposed to the hitherto separate representation of each western Land. The resultant amalgamation of some Länder for this purpose is illustrated in Figure 2.9. It will be seen that – not surprisingly in view of what has been said about their economic importance – Baden-Württemberg, Bavaria, Hesse and North Rhine-Westphalia retained their own central-bank representatives. Also fairly predictable was the requirement that the Rhineland-Palatinate and Saarland should share central-bank representation. A northern conglomerate was comprised of Hamburg, Schleswig-Holstein and Mecklenburg-West Pomerania. Two critical masses were chosen for central Germany: first, Bremen, Lower Saxony and Saxony-Anhalt; second, Berlin and Brandenburg (which later declared their intention of becoming a single Land). Significantly, one of the most difficult questions to resolve was whether the east's most viable Land from an economic standpoint – Saxony – should obtain its own seat on the council. It was ultimately decided, however, that Saxony and Thuringia should share representation, although the local branch's offices would be located in Leipzig (Saxony). From the point of view of ameliorating the substantial problems of reorganising the system of revenue sharing, the Bundesbank scheme as a whole had much to commend it – see the discussion around Figures 2.10–2.13b inclusive, as well as Table 2.2.

Nonetheless, the Basic Law lays down the constitutional relationships between the Federal government, the Länder and the local authorities and, given German federal traditions, will continue to do so. It determines also the areas of legislative competence for each level of government.

In 1969 there were several amendments to the basic law which altered not only the balance of jurisdiction but also the financial and fiscal relationships between the levels of government. Reforms to the fiscal constitution (Article X of the Basic Law) lay at the centre of many of the amendments.

The budgetary reform of 1969 can be introduced by referring briefly to its historical background. It became apparent as far back as 1949 that budgetary reform was needed. Legislation at that time was still based on the budgetary regulations of 1922. Moreover, the Länder made little real use of their Basic Law budgetary rights. Although the Saarland (in 1958) and West Berlin (in 1966) passed their own budgetary regulations, this did not materially affect the influence of the 1922 regulations (BMF 1990: 15). Final bills to change the budgetary regulations which required constitutional change were placed before the Bundestag along with the other fiscal reforms in 1968. The Budget Basic Rules Act (*Haushaltsgrundsätzegesetz*) was finally passed by the Bundesrat, along with Federal budgetary regulations (*Bundeshaushaltsordnung*), in 1969. Hence, constitutional amendments which reformed budgetary arrangements followed twenty years after the founding of the Bonn Republic. Under the reform, principles of budgetary authority were to apply equally to the Federal and Länder governments. The Act required the Länder to apply their own legislation and consequently between 1970 and 1972 (1978 for Berlin) a series of budgetary regulations were passed.

The Budget Basic Rules Act provided a further instrument for maintaining macroeconomic stability as defined by the StWG (Arnold and Geske 1988: 47). Thus, the emphasis was put on ensuring that the Federal and Länder governments' budgets would take account of overall economic objectives. By means of Federal legislation, requiring the consent of the Bundesrat, Section 109(3) thus explicitly allows the establishment of budgetary principles 'applicable to both the Federation and the Länder'. The Act could be regarded as a compromise between the need to protect Länder sovereignty by preventing Federal encroachment upon their legislative authority, and the need to obtain some overall basis for cooperation between these two levels of government when framing budgetary policy. The Act

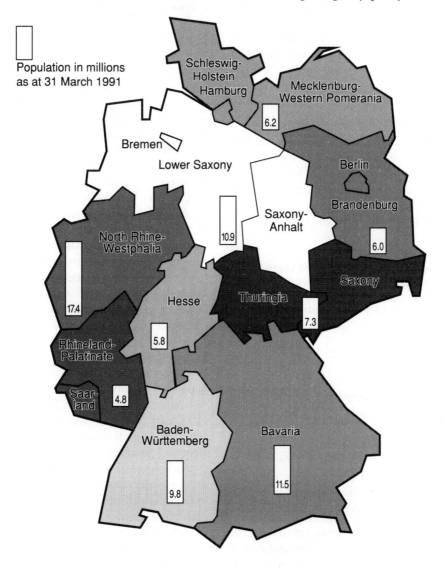

Figure 2.9 The nine areas represented on the re-organised Bundesbank Council
(effective from 1 November 1992)

Source: MRDB (8/92: 51)

may be split into two sections (BMF 1990: 17). The first part contained the necessary common basis for Federal and Länder legislation and required legislation to be enacted at both levels. The second part dealt directly with Land and Federal legislation. It required budgetary planning and accounting at the level of the Land to be compatible with that at the Federal level. Borrowing had to be limited to the levels of expenditure set aside for investment purposes.

Summarising, then, the main elements of the fiscal constitution are:

- the StWG (see above), which led to the establishment of the FPC and an anti-cyclical fund
- the reform of budgetary authority between the Federal government and the Länder, discussed in this section
- the system of fiscal equalisation

FISCAL EQUALISATION AND LEGISLATIVE COMPETENCE

This system may be divided into three areas:

- the division of legal competence between the levels of government which determines the balance of policy-making authority between the Federal government and the Länder
- the vertical and horizontal distribution of tax revenue
- the system of revenue sharing which lies at the heart of fiscal equalisation and which is mainly related to the horizontal distribution of tax revenue

The division of legal competence between the different levels of government lies at the core of the federal system. As will be seen in greater detail in the next chapter, taxes are either an exclusive responsibility of a particular level of government or a joint responsibility (Figures 3.4–3.7). Section 106 of the Basic Law deals with the apportionment of taxes as well as the basis for tax revenue distribution. Federal and Länder governments have independent responsibility for fiscal administration (Section 109[1]), and their joint responsibility for preserving overall economic stability was recognised in 1967 with the StWG. Revenue- and power-sharing with the Länder has in the past limited the Federal government's ability to act independently in order to attain macroeconomic policy objectives. As already indicated, the Länder and local authorities have independent budgetary authority. Accordingly, prior to unification, 85 per cent of total public funds were disbursed by these two levels of government (FAZ 19 February 1991). This gives a clear indication of how important the distribution of tax revenue at the lower levels of government is – not only for regional policy, but also for budgetary policy as a whole.

The distribution of legislative authority between the three levels of government is closely tied to the notion of a separation of powers, under which three main areas may be identified: administration; legislation; jurisdiction or legislative competence. Section 30 of the Basic Law allocates the duty of the administration of federal laws to the Länder. Section 70 allocates legal competence to the Länder in so far as it does not already rest with the Federal government. Legislative competence itself is put into four different categories: exclusive, concurrent (or competing), basic principles and skeleton legislation (laying out guide-lines). Section 71 defines exclusive legislation as referring to those matters within the exclusive legislative powers of the Federal government, except where Federal law allows the Länder to pass legislation on such matters. Examples of exclusive legislation are foreign policy, national security, transportation, the postal service, telecommunications, immigration, social security, and, significantly for the financial and budgetary reforms to be described, macroeconomic policy. Matters defined by Section 72 as concurrent are those for which the Länder may legislate, but only where the Federal government chooses not to exercise its right to do so. Examples are the court system, police, education and cultural and health policies. The Federal government is deemed to have such a right if the Länder cannot effectively regulate a matter or when failure to legislate would endanger the overall economic unity of the country as a whole. Section 75 deals with skeleton legislation which gives the Federal government the right to pass provisions in areas such as regional planning, land distribution and protection of the countryside.

A good example of the Federal government exercising its right to legislate was in the field of higher education: in 1969 central control over the principles of higher education passed to the Federal government (Section 75[1a]). Matters relating to the construction of institutions of higher education became by Section 91a a joint objective of the Federal government and the Länder. The principal body charged with financial planning for education is the BLK (Federal-Länder Commission for Educational Planning and Promotion of Research). Usually covering a period four years ahead, the 1981 plan of the BLK stipulated a 20 per cent reduction in the Federal overall share of 50 per cent in the financing of higher education building (Kloss 1985: 273). However, expenditure was once more increased in the years between 1985 and 1988. As education was seen as one area where the Länder had almost exclusive control, this particular amendment to the Basic Law created a

significant amount of opposition from the Länder governments. Section 91b, which allowed for cooperation between the Federal government and the Länder on matters relating to educational planning and research, meant that the Federal government could contribute to the financing of the comprehensive schools (*Gesamtschulen*). These schools were regarded as experimental and therefore came under the terms of this Section.

Section 104 of the Basic Law states that the Federal and Länder governments are separately responsible for expenditure arising from roles allocated to them under the constitution. In other words, the granting of legislative authority for one particular area is linked with fiscal responsibility for that area. As a consequence of this, Section 109(1) stipulates that the Federal government and the Länder are independent of one another in their fiscal administration (Arnold and Geske 1988: 46).

There has been a great deal of controversy over the issue of how much the Federal government should be allowed to impinge upon the fiscal authority of the Länder (*ibid.*: 30). An amendment of the Basic Law (Section 104(4)) allows the Federal government to grant the Länder and local authorities financial assistance for direct investments whenever this investment is necessary to prevent the overall disturbance of the economic equilibrium. On the one hand, the Länder have seen in this a potential means for the Federal government to threaten their independence by tying financial aid to policy measures stipulated from Bonn. On the other hand, the Federal government could point out that often financial assistance, and in particular investment designed to promote growth or correct a budgetary imbalance, is linked not just to regional needs but has a bearing on the overall health of the economy. The Federal government can therefore control the type and purposes of investment within a Land. However, financial planning originates in the Länder. In other words, the Federal government can exercise control by refusing to finance particular projects rather than by directly outlining projects from their inception.

FISCAL EQUALISATION: THE DISTRIBUTION OF REVENUE

The distribution of tax revenue between Federal and Länder governments has continually been a matter of some dispute, with many Länder complaining that they received an unfair share of revenue. Matters have been exacerbated by the addition of the five new Länder. The original post-war constitution gave the Länder legal control over revenue from income and corporation taxes. In 1955 the Federal government was for the first time given some share in this revenue (Shonfield 1965: 268). As there are no means of determining the exact level of consumption in each of the Länder, the number of inhabitants is used as a proxy upon which to base shares of VAT revenue. The problem is that this assumes uniform consumption patterns in all Länder, a questionable assumption, especially when comparing eastern with western Länder. Nonetheless, it is on this basis that revenue will be divided between the east and west – thus meaning that the weaker revenue raising power of the east will be ameliorated at the expense of the west. The western Länder have argued that until 1994 such revenue should be distributed according to the ability to raise revenue. Furthermore, the discord between Federal and Länder governments has been further intensified by the increased demands which the growing east German budget

deficit has made on Länder finances. Tensions have also been heightened by the increase in tax revenue going to the central government. Since 1982 the combined Länder budgets have declined by DM 93.4 billion against an increase in the central budget of DM 46.5 billion. The Länder governments see this as a threat to their independence which could conceivably have serious implications for the stability of the federal system itself (FT 11 December 1991).

The dispute over tax sharing following unification was closely associated with the problems caused by the increasing costs of financing the new Länder. An example of this was provided by the development of these Länders' share in VAT receipts. Initially, a compromise agreement allocated 55 per cent of the west German share of per-capita VAT to east Germany, rising to 70 per cent by 1994 and not reaching the west German levels until 1995. However, in the face of the threatened bankruptcy of many east German Länder authorities, it was decided in February 1991 to grant the new Länder a full share of this revenue immediately. This reflected the fact that public sector debt in the new Länder had risen much more sharply than originally expected. At the same time the old Länder feared that this would cause an intolerable burden on their own finances. While the necessity for more investment was widely recognised, the Federal Finance Minister (Theo Waigel) argued that any spending over the DM 35 billion of public funds which had thus been made available would be unwise (SZ 2/3 March 1991).

Fiscal equalisation (explained in more detail below) was actually based on the constitutional reforms of 1969. The relevant Sections of the Basic Law are 106 and 107. Section 106 deals with the *vertical* distribution of tax revenue between the Federal government, the Länder and the local authorities. The revenue from the high-yielding income taxes is shared on a proportionate basis and these ratios are analysed in more depth in Chapter 3. Basically, shares in these *joint* taxes vary according to the type of tax being considered. In addition, the Federal and Länder governments raise revenue from taxes to which they have *exclusive* access. Note, however, that Section 106(3) stipulates that the Federal and Länder governments have an equal claim to revenues in such a way as to *promote uniform living standards throughout the country*. By 106(4), the allocation of the turnover tax (a joint tax) between the Federal and the Länder governments depends on the relative disparities between expenditure and revenue at these two budgetary levels. Whenever budgetary developments at the Federal level create relative disparities, the allocation of the revenue from the turnover tax must be revised. Disparities may also be reduced by means of grants-in-aid from the Federal government. Under 106(5) the local authorities are entitled to receive from the Länder a share of another joint tax, income tax, on the basis of the number of income tax payers within a local authority area. The actual distribution of taxes at the local level is controlled by Länder legislation, and the Federal government can only influence this indirectly (Arnold and Geske 1988: 51). Finally, the Länder have a responsibility for granting compensatory payments to local authorities in their area which encounter special problems (106[8]).

Section 107(1) deals with the *horizontal* allocation of tax revenue. It stipulates that the Länder are to receive their share of Land taxes as well as income and corporation tax to the extent that the taxes are collected by the revenue authorities within their area. Section 107(2) forms the constitutional basis for (horizontal) *fiscal equalisation* between the Länder. Fiscal equalisation is to take place between financially strong and financially weak Länder. Again, the details of this are explained below.

In particular, *horizontal* equalisation is the procedure by which tax revenue is distributed between the Länder. As previously indicated, it is based on Section 107(2) of the Basic Law which aims to achieve a reasonable equalisation between Länder, taking into account their relative financial strengths. Another feature of the horizontal redistribution of taxes is the principle, as stated in Section 107(1), that the revenue from income and corporation taxes shall accrue to the Länder to the extent that the taxes are collected by the revenue authorities within their respective territories. Without some means of correction, this would imply that some states would receive much higher revenues than others, and regional differences would thereby be aggravated. Thus, horizontal equalisation acts to correct tax distribution in favour of those Länder whose tax revenue-raising power (*Finanzkraft*) is lowest.

Horizontal equalisation, which is of particular relevance to the distribution of turnover tax, is carried out by a two-step procedure. In the *first step*, under the terms of the Basic Law (107[1]), up to 25 per cent of a Land's total revenue from turnover tax may be allocated to those Länder whose total share of per-capita tax revenue, excluding VAT, is less than average. This redistribution aims to raise the tax power indicator for all Länder to at least 92 per cent of the average. The other 75 per cent of turnover tax is allocated according to the number of inhabitants in a Land. In the *second stage*, 'revenue-weak' Länder get additional help from the other Länder if their tax-power indicator lies below 95 per cent of that of the average for all Länder. As already mentioned, the tax-power indicator relates tax revenues in relation to the particular problems and burdens of the Länder, and takes account of demographic factors. Hence, there is a transfer of revenue from stronger to weaker tax-revenue Länder and therefore a convergence of tax revenue to at least 95 per cent of the average (EC 1990a: 45). Note that from 1956 Berlin did not take part in fiscal equalisation as it received alternative assistance directly from the Federal government.

Crucial to *vertical* fiscal equalisation arrangements is the fact that they occur between the three levels of government; in other words revenue equalisation occurs from the Federal government to Land, and then from Land to local authority. In this sense they are closely tied to the horizontal distribution of taxes as well as the distribution of legal competence already described. *Vertical* revenue sharing occurs through the two per cent of Federal VAT receipts reserved for grants-in-aid (*Bundesergänzungszuweisungen*). These grants are allocated to Länder which are still considered as falling below national norms. The revenue is then passed on by such Länder to selected local authorities. Selectivity in these cases is used to offset disparities between localities with high tax revenues and those with low revenues. Vertical equalisation is based upon Section 107(2) of the Basic Law which allows grants to be made to financially weaker Länder from Federal funds. The extent of the grants-in-aid had been raised by 0.5 per cent by an amendment in 1986, following complaints by the Länder that their share was insufficient. The amendment was to have had effect from 1988 until 1993 but this was, significantly, before unification.

THE FRAMEWORK OF FISCAL EQUALISATION

As already pointed out, the 1969 Acts concerning fiscal equalisation were a logical development of the stabilisation measures first introduced in 1967. It is thus within the framework of protecting *macroeconomic stability* that the Federal government is permitted to grant regional aid to the states (GG: Section 104). The Basic Law confirms the view that regional aid for the new Länder can be regarded as a means for creating a preferential bias in their favour – thereby reducing economic disparities between west and east (MRDB 3/91: 21). As for regional policy as a whole, it became, as already shown, a joint Federal and Länder responsibility.

The Fiscal Equalisation Act (*Finanzausgleichsgesetz*) is based not on determining the financial requirements of the Länder, but on their tax-raising ability. However, if Länder are still considered to be weak after financial transfers have been made the Federal government may make direct grant payments to such states. But recall that taxes are collected by the Federal government and then distributed to the Länder which in turn distribute a share of their income-tax revenue to the local authorities (Knott 1981: 29). In addition, a system of horizontal and vertical revenue sharing aims at ensuring a reasonable degree of convergence of living standards between regions. In the following description of horizontal equalisation, one must distinguish between turnover taxes, which are largely distributed on a per-capita basis, and income and corporate taxation which are distributed on a local revenue basis.

Two major factors are considered when calculating the contributions or receipts which should accrue to a Land through equalisation: the fiscal commitments

(*Finanzbedarf*) of a Land and its fiscal strength (*Finanzkraft*). Its fiscal strength is measured in terms of tax revenue. Whether a Land is entitled to receipts (*Ausgleichsberechtigt*) or must be a contributor (*Ausgleichspflichtigt*) is determined by the fiscal-power indicator (*Finanzkraftmeßzahl*) in relation to the equalisation indicator (*Ausgleichsmeßzahl*). When the first indicator exceeds the second then the Land is a net contributor and vice-versa. The fiscal-power indicator is determined by the sum of all tax revenue which a Land and local authorities are entitled to receive, while the equalisation indicator is simply a measure of what transfers a Land and local authority require according to the equalisation rules. As both indicators depend to some extent upon measures of number of inhabitants at the local authority level, a complex sliding scale has been established to give more weight to those local authorities with larger populations.

The calculation of the fiscal-power indicator has always been a matter of great dispute. This is because of the controversy over which Land and local authority taxes should be counted and, further, to what extent local-authority taxes should be included within the measurement (Peffekoven 1987: 194). Moreover, the local authorities are, as mentioned above, entitled to a share of joint taxes and for this reason they have an influence on the calculation of the fiscal-power indicator. In order to arrive annually at the fiscal-power indicator, the following sources of a Land's revenue are included (*ibid.*; Chapter 3 below):

- its share of joint taxes
- its share of the trade tax
- with minor exceptions, its share of exclusive Länder taxes

- half of any grants provided under the Federal Mining Act

A further problem, also connected to the redistribution of local authority tax revenue, has revolved around the principle that tax revenues should go to the Länder where they were collected. This has given the city states – Bremen and Hamburg – and other Länder with financial centres (Frankfurt am Main in Hesse, for example) a higher share of revenue than other Länder. In particular, the revenue from employees' income tax (which is collected at the place of work), and the revenue from corporation tax (which is collected at the headquarters of an enterprise) tend to be concentrated in the conurbations, thus giving them an artificially high tax-power indicator (Peffekoven 1987: 186). In the case of the income tax levied on employees, an attempted solution was a ruling of 1970 which allocated tax revenue according to the domicile of an employee (*Wohnsitzprinzip*). In 1985 the effect of this was a DM 3 billion redistribution of revenue. Hamburg and Bremen lost revenue (DM 1.4 billion), while Schleswig-Holstein and Lower Saxony gained (DM 0.8 billion and DM 1 billion respectively) (*ibid.*).

The determination of the fiscal commitments of a Land have been even more problematic (*ibid.*: 200). Objective means for determining such commitments have been lacking. Based on the idea that obligations are the same regardless of location or the affluence of an area, fiscal commitments have been calculated on the basis of the population of each Land. The resulting benchmark is the equalisation indicator, which is determined by multiplying the tax revenue per inhabitant for taxes to be counted for equalisation purposes by the total population of each Land. The use of this measurement also presents difficulties, however, particularly as to whether more weight should be given to the tax contributions per head or to the total population. The regulations make allowances for areas with a high population by allocating a weighting of 135 to the tax revenue per inhabitant in the city states of Bremen and Hamburg. Similarly tax revenue received by the local authorities is given a weighting of 100 to 135 according to the size of the locality, with an additional weighting of between 2 and 6 for local authorities with more than 500,000 inhabitants (*ibid*.: 201). Hamburg and Bremen have nevertheless complained that this is insufficient, pointing to the higher costs experienced in conurbations. Their argument is that for services such as the police and the maintenance of the judicial system, as well other important expenditure items such as health, education, public transport and environmental protection, the burden of costs tends to be higher in conurbations.

The purpose of equalisation, then, is to prevent the inequitable distribution of revenue between the different levels of government (Federal, Land and local authority) that would result if the constitutional distribution of tax receipts were to be applied without adjustment. Moreover, the constitutional principles themselves were drawn up with economic and regional considerations in mind. The largest revenue raisers – income taxes (50 per cent of total revenue) and turnover taxes (a further 25 per cent) – are joint taxes. Thus, in 1989 tax revenue which accrued exclusively to (as opposed to jointly to) either the Federal or Länder governments amounted to DM 90.8 billion, or 17 per cent of the total tax revenue of the Federal Republic; local authorities received DM 40.9 billion, or 8 per cent of total tax revenue (Figure 3.4 below). But the revenue raised by the different levels

of government from exclusive taxes varies, as will be seen in greater detail in Chapter 3, particularly Figures 3.5–3.7. The critical point here, however, is that indirect taxes such as expenditure taxes on mineral oil are imposed at the place of production – and this particular tax is the highest revenue raiser of all the exclusive taxes. Hence, Hamburg, where many oil refineries are located, would enjoy an inordinately high tax revenue were it not for the fact that all revenues from this tax are exclusive to the Federal government. The revenue from tax on mineral oil varies from 16 per cent of the national average in Schleswig-Holstein to 1664 per cent in Hamburg (Peffekoven 1987: 184).

Another crucial question revolves around whether the financially weaker Länder should be assisted by means of horizontal revenue sharing amongst the Länder or through direct payments from the Federal government. The two are in fact interrelated, for by raising payments through horizontal equalisation, the tax power indicator is raised, which in turn is likely to reduce the amount of direct payments. Over the years since its inception in 1967, funds used for vertical equalisation have risen sharply in relation to those for horizontal equalisation. Peffekoven (*ibid*.: 213) explained this rise by reference to the dependence of grants-in-aid upon GDP, which has risen far more than differences in tax power indicators which largely determine the extent of horizontal equalisation. By 1991, the sum involved in vertical equalisation had reached DM 3.5 billion; this compared to a horizontal equalisation of DM 3.9 billion, plus a further DM 400 million from the first step (BfG *Standpunkt* 5/91).

The implications of unification for fiscal equalisation are, as in so many other cases, best seen in the context of the pre-unification evolution of the system. Figure

2.10 shows how the pre- and post-equalisation indicator of tax power in the western Länder in 1985 converged from a range of over 28 to within 10 percentage points. Such evidence tends to point to the success of revenue equalisation. Although prior to unification the funds used for equalisation were by nationwide standards comparatively small (0.3 per cent of GDP for horizontal revenue sharing), for some Länder they formed a significant share of their finances. Following unification, however, the integration of the new Länder into the system (from 1995) changed the amounts involved quite significantly. One estimate was that the total amount involved would rise from DM 6 billion to DM 30 billion, while the Länder's share in this amount would rise to DM 21 billion (*Handelsblatt* 21 January 1993). Perhaps not surprisingly, the Finance Minister of Bavaria thought this proposal was totally unacceptable, whereas his opposite number in Bremen regretted that his own Land and Saarland would have to wait until the new scheme was introduced before some assistance with their debt problem could be expected (*ibid*.). Yet the prime ministers of all sixteen Länder later agreed that DM 60 billion would have to flow east in the shared revenue arrangement (*Economist* 6 March 1993). Moreover, there had been a significant shift in the structure of net contributors and recipients. North Rhine-Westphalia became a net recipient in 1987, while Bavaria would have become a contributor had some areas within this Land not been exempted (*Ausgleichsfreie Zonen*). By 1989 Bavaria had in fact become a slight net contributor. A look at the situation in 1985, revealed that, in line with the regional disparities discussed above, Baden-Württemberg was by far the highest net contributor, while Lower Saxony, Bremen and Schleswig-Holstein

were the highest recipients. This latter factor is illustrated in Figure 2.11, along with an indication of how receipts and contributions changed between 1985 and 1989. By 1989 Baden-Württemberg was still a large contributor but Hesse had assumed the position of largest contributor.

Revisions to the revenue sharing provisions were made as a result of a ruling from the Federal Constitutional Court in 1986 (BMF 1988: 32). The ruling had followed complaints, in particular from Saarland and Schleswig-Holstein, that the distribution of revenue was inequitable. Lower Saxony, for instance, had received a large revenue from oil and gas yet was one of the main beneficiaries from revenue equalisation. In 1982, 22 per cent of the revenue from oil and gas produced in this Land was returned under the revenue sharing rules, while total revenue received amounted to DM 1.5 billion – far higher than any other state (*Die Zeit* 2/82). Yet both Saarland and Schleswig-Holstein had particular charges to meet. Hence, the 1987 changes resulted in the full inclusion of revenue from crude oil and natural gas exploitation, although Lower Saxony, Hamburg and Bremen received larger allowances for their port facilities.

Income and corporation taxes account for half of total tax revenue (Figure 3.4). They therefore represent the area in which the highest redistribution of revenue is necessary. In terms of receipts per inhabitant, Hamburg was in first place followed by Hesse, Bremen and Baden-Württemberg (BfG *Wirtschaftsblätter* January 1989). If revenue equalisation had been applied immediately to a unified Germany, there would have been a large revenue transfer from western to eastern Länder. It is for this reason that an immediate German-wide application of the rules for determining fiscal equalisation

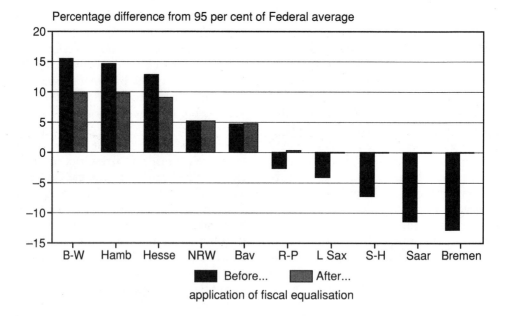

Figure 2.10 Tax Power Indicator (West German Länder)
Source: Peffekoven (1987: 213)

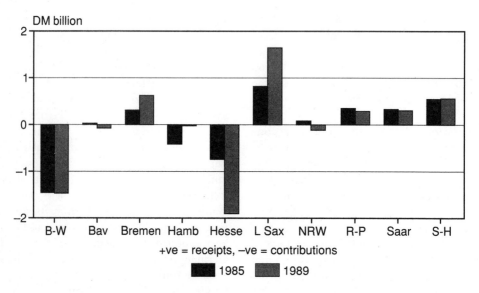

Figure 2.11 Revenue Equalisation: changes between 1985 and 1989 (West German Länder)
Source: MRDB (4/90: 27)

was successfully resisted by the Länder which were recipients prior to unification. Heavy demands would otherwise have been placed on the weaker western Länder if there had been an immediate revision of the system. After all, it was with a view to protecting these weaker Länder that horizontal equalisation had been put into effect. Such reasoning resulted in an extension of this type of funding to the eastern Länder being rejected, at least until 1995 (Geske 1991: 35). In any case, as Milbradt (1991: 60) points out, the relevant Section in the Basic Law (107[2]) laid down prerequisites which would have effectively excluded the new Länder. These were that the provisions applied only to compatibility of living-standards within West Germany. Roppel (1990: 16) estimated the effects of the immediate application of the fiscal equalisation system and the results are contained in Figure 2.12a. It can be seen that of the six recipient states before unification only Bremen would remain a net beneficiary.

The calculation embodied in Figure 2.12a was based on 1989 data. By 1991, DM 4 billion was redistributed (BMF *Finanzbericht* 1993: 131–2). Baden-Württemberg, Hesse and Hamburg – in that order of significance – contributed DM 4 billion, while Lower Saxony, the Rheinland-Palatinate and Schleswig-Holstein received DM 3 billion of that amount in horizontal equalisation (BfG *Standpunkt* 5/92). Yet if the existing method had been applied to the whole of Germany, all six of these old Länder would have become contributors. Bremen and Saarland – in that order – received the remaining DM 1 billion. They would have remained net beneficiaries had the unmodified scheme been applied to all Germany, but on vastly inferior terms. (Bavaria and North Rhine-Westphalia just about broke even in 1991 – also see

Figures 2.10 and 2.11). Similarly, the revenue-raising powers in all the Länder, again using the pre-1990 system, are estimated for 1995 in Figure 2.12b. The degree of revenue reduction in the western Länder is also apparent.

Moreover, it soon became plain in the post-GEMSU era that the degree of fiscal discord would increase as the deadline for a nation-wide scheme became more imminent. Contrary to expectations in mid-1990, when the undertaking to integrate the new Länder in the fiscal equalisation scheme was made, the catching-up process in the east proved to be a protracted affair. In consequence, predictions of tax revenue in the new Länder by 1 January 1995 – the date when full integration was planned – were continuously down graded. For instance, one estimate at the Länder level was that average tax revenue by that date would rise to only DM 3,000 per head in the east compared to DM 4,600 in the west; at the local-authority level, the situation was even worse – DM 700 per head compared to DM 1700 (*ibid.*). There was also an important structural difference on the expenditure side. Personnel costs in the new Länder represented 12 per cent of total expenditure, compared to 40 per cent in the western Länder (*ibid.*). It is little wonder, then, that Land politicians in Berlin and Brandenburg conjectured that their views on fiscal equalisation would carry more weight if the two Länder were to unite during the 1990s (FAZ 7 December 1992). Finally, the 1993 solidarity agreement contained modifications to the revenue-sharing arrangements. These modifications are considered in the section on the effects of unification below.

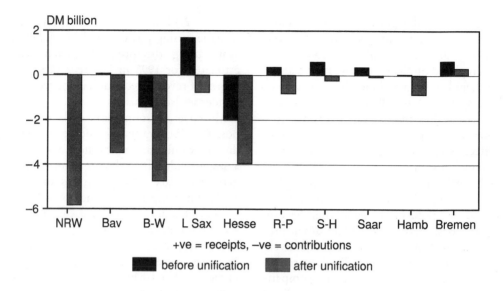

Figure 2.12a Fiscal Equalisation: model (West German Länder)

Source: Roppel (1990: 17)

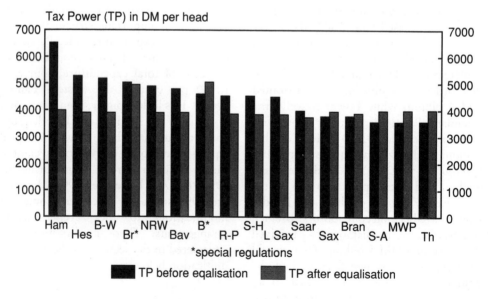

Figure 2.12b Pre-GEMSU Equalisation in 1995

Source: BfG *Standpunkt* 5/92

THE POST-WAR EVOLUTION OF REGIONAL POLICY

As already emphasised, the development of regional policy in West Germany cannot be described without reference to the Federal structure. Generally, this has implied a gradually larger involvement of the Federal government in regional policy and a steady extension of areas eligible for assistance. Such spatial imbalances in economic growth can be linked to the comparatively late formation of a unified state as well as the existence of particular areas enjoying export-led growth. It has also been seen that most of the regional imbalances which re-appeared soon after the war in fact originated in the nineteenth century. The clear necessity for policies to counter regional imbalances led in 1951 to the establishment of the first Regional Development Programme, which primarily was aimed at assisting economic development in the deprived rural areas (Mayhew 1969: 73). In 1953 this was supplemented by aid to an extensive zone along the inner-German border known as the 'frontier corridor' (*Zonenrandgebiet*), a belt of land 40 km wide and stretching from the Baltic zone in the north to the south-eastern corner of Bavaria; Berlin was also included (Wild 1979: 134). Moreover, the *Landkreise* with very poor levels of agricultural production must be added to those regions already mentioned. These areas were collectively designated as development areas (*Fördergebiete*) in the late 1950s. Eligibility for classification as a development area depended upon the levels of per-capita income and employment structures.

Despite the disparities, *ad hoc* subsidies and tax concessions designed to counteract the reluctance of West German firms to invest in such areas were eventually seen as being no longer a policy impera-

tive. These policies were replaced by more coherent policies of regional planning. Yet this did not happen until the late 1960s. Many of the regional policies before this time were found to be ineffective in combating regional backwardness. In 1965 larger financial budgets were provided under the terms of the Regional Development Act (*Raumordnungsgesetz*). Bavaria, Lower Saxony and North Rhine-Westphalia were allowed to designate their own development areas (*Landesausbaugebiete*). The emphasis, as with much of subsequent regional policy, was put on the provision of favourable terms for industrial redevelopment together with improvements to the infrastructure of the designated areas.

An amendment to the Basic Law in 1969 granted the Federal Government joint responsibility with the Länder to promote the 'improvement of regional economic structures' (Section 91a). Some of the implications of this have already been discussed above. It was under this provision that some of the direct investment in the new Länder was later to be made (also see the section on investment programmes below). In the same year greater provision was made for development areas in that from then on they were split into twenty-one 'Regional Action Areas'. Regional policy, including the designation of development areas and the determination of eligibility criteria for the receipt of regional subsidies, became 'joint tasks' of the Federal and Länder governments (Spahn 1978: 30). The concept of growth centres as areas of agglomeration was also adopted and eventually no less than 312 such areas were classified as development nodes or Federal Development Centres. Three grades of assistance were established, with most assistance going to areas considered most in need. This greater centralised control of regional policy can be regarded as official recognition that Land administration alone was insufficient to counteract regional imbalances, something which the weaker states such as Schleswig-Holstein, North Rhine-Westphalia and Saarland had already tacitly accepted when they requested Federal grants-in-aid to ameliorate their particular economic problems. It is worth noting that at one stage development areas amounted to 66 per cent of the total area of the Federal Republic and 45 per cent of the population. Partly as a result of EC directives (see below), this figure has fallen since 1989 to 27 per cent of the total population. Yet if the same rules were to apply to the whole of post-unification Germany, it would mean that a large proportion of the remaining western development areas would lose their development status.

A further development of considerable importance which came in 1975 was the Federal Regional Planning Programme (*Bundesraumordnungsprogramm*). The main aim of this was to coordinate regional policies between the Länder so as to promote uniform development across the country. From the 1970s onwards, however, it is not possible to isolate German regional policy from the fiscal system and, indeed, overall economic policy. In turn, the fiscal system is largely moulded by the federal structure of the country. Other radical changes to the framework of regional policy have taken place. As will be explained in more detail below, the pure form of German regional policy, as understood in terms of subsidies to areas defined as requiring assistance, has, to some extent been supplanted by the emergence of regional policy in the EC. Finally, since unification, assistance schemes must now take account of the requirements of the new Länder. For instance, regional assistance to the former inner-German border and

Berlin was transferred to the new Länder (MRDB 7/90: 40). The inclusion of the new Länder means considerable adjustment will be required not only to the tax structure (see above) but also to Federal and regional structures. Unlike in pre-unification West Germany, no long history of development in regional policy existed in the former GDR and regional considerations played a subordinate role in economic planning (Klemmer and Schrumpf 1990: 119). Following unification the restructuring process was to be a two-way affair. Examples were the transfer payments from west to east, labour mobility from east to west and the opening up of markets for both east and west.

REGIONAL POLICY: THE EUROPEAN DIMENSION

With further developments of EC integration, most notably through EC 1993, it is increasingly clear that German regional policy can no longer be examined in isolation (*German Politics* 1992). The following section therefore looks at the European dimension of regional policy. The nature and development of EC regional policy is examined along with the implications for national and Land-level policy. In order to understand the context of EC regional policy in Germany it is firstly important not to exaggerate the scope of regional aid from the EC. It is still far smaller than similar national aid, and EC regional funds are themselves still dwarfed by the European Agricultural Guidance Guarantee and Fund (EAGGF).

Structural Funds from the EC (The European Regional Development Fund (ERDF) and the European Social Fund) are categorised by certain 'objectives' which regions must fulfil in order to be eligible. Over 70 per cent of funds are allocated to the most underdeveloped

Objective 1 regions which exclude German Regions (Portugal, Greece, Ireland, the Mezzogiorno, central Spanish regions and Northern Ireland). By contrast, Germany occupies a large part of the most affluent European 'Central Axis'. Between 1975 and 1988 the total amount of ERDF funds going to Germany amounted to DM 1.8 billion (Deutscher Bundestag *Drucksache* XII/895: 18). Hence, European disparities prior to unification were far wider than purely German disparities and it comes as no surprise that the share of ERDF going to Germany was small. It was around 3 per cent, although even after the accession of Spain and Portugal it remained remarkably constant (Krieger-Boden 1987). For Germany, most aid has come through Objective 2 (areas of industrial decline) and Objective 5b (Development of Rural Areas). However, the significance of EC aid for Germany increased after unification. The new Länder have been included in the Objective 1 category. Between 1991 and 1993 the new Länder were expected to receive DM 3 billion from the ERDF (Deutscher Bundestag *ibid.*: 20).

The definitions of most underdeveloped regions are based on EC averages and the calculation of an index based on standard regional variables such as per capita GDP and unemployment rates. From this a list is compiled of regions in order of relative affluence. The production of comparable data applicable to all EC Member States was certainly an improvement from the situation when only national data of little comparability was available. Yet the main problem remains that of how to dissect the EC into units of comparable administrative structure. How, for example, is one to compare a German Land with a county in England? The implications of a community-wide average for the 'richer' Member States are of particular import-ance as any possible widening of the EC through the accession of the East European states would have a negative effect on overall German shares of structural funds.

To what extent does EC regional assistance infringe upon purely national regional policy? Although the Treaty of Rome contains a statement on the desirability of convergence of living standards within the EC, the true beginning of EC regional policy was marked by the establishment of the European Regional Development Fund in 1975. Aid at this time had to be linked with and supplementary to national regional development funds. Significantly, EC regional policy has long been perceived as falling under the umbrella of competition policy and as a countervailing force to any free-market imperfections which might lead to disparities. It is now almost a truism to assert that greater economic integration can have very uneven spatial consequences. In Germany, as much as in other areas of Europe, it is likely to be regions with the largest export-led growth potential which benefit most from further economic integration. Regional policy from an EC perspective can thus be regarded as complementary in its ultimate aims to other policy areas, most particularly to those pertaining to competition policy. As part of regional policy in the EC, the Commission intervenes to prevent unfair competition. Within the EC Commission, the Competition Directorate (DG IV) has thirty senior officials five of whom control regional aid as well as infringements of competition such as monopolies (Budd 1987: 47). Until 1979, a largely interventionist approach had been followed to procure regional aid on a country-to-country basis, the amounts being determined by national quotas. Thus there was then less interference with purely national-level regional policy. During the recessions of the 1970s, the Commission expressed great concern over the increasing competition for EC aid initiated by the larger number of eligible regions (Krieger-Boden 1987). In order to control aid funds, a more stringent regional categorisation was established. This has necessarily involved more EC involvement in the shaping of national regional policy. Following reforms made to the ERDF in 1984, quotas were abolished and coordinated schemes of assistance agreed between Member States and the EC were instigated.

From 1979, aid was no longer linked to purely national policy but could also include programmes designed to counteract the effects of other EC policy. This has entailed considering projects not necessarily confined within national borders, as well as national projects perceived as benefiting wider EC interests. A good example of the latter was the National Programme of 1988 which involved aid from the ERDF going in particular to development areas in Lower Saxony, Schleswig-Holstein, Bavaria, Rhineland-Palatinate and the Saarland (Deutscher Bundestag ibid.: 18). As well as the ERDF, the EC also supports regional convergence through the European Investment Bank. Investments from this bank have also been significant for the new Länder (see below).

Greater coordination of EC regional policy between member states inevitably has meant less ability for nations to control their own policy and as the scope of regional policy increases, so Member States find it increasingly important to satisfy EC criteria for the granting of aid. The procurement of EC regional aid for the new Länder mentioned above was a notable example of a regional policy measure which was taken after negotia-tions between the German government and the EC Commission. Articles 92 to 94 as well as Article 130 (a–e) of the Treaty of Rome describe the central aims of EC regional policy. Thus, in order to attract EC funding, local projects must also have demonstrative benefits at a non-local level. In other words, such projects must not be to the detriment of other problem areas nor distort overall European competition. This deepening of EC level regional policy has specific implications for the workings of the German federal structure. The integration process by its very nature involves a transfer of authority from the national state to EC level and a major concern of the Länder must be that this could effectively threaten the bottom-up approach to policy formulation which was defined in the Introduction to this chapter. Regional or local decisions would per force be increasingly taken in Brussels. Greater co-ordination of policy between Member States could be at the expense of more local decision making. More specifically, policy decisions taken by the joint-task Improvement of the Regional Economic Structure became more subject to control from Brussels. This included decisions as to which areas should be accorded development status (Eser 1991b: 42). The influence of the EC has not necessarily been to limit these areas. Rather, it uses different criteria for the designation of development areas (Eser 1989: 46). Thus, as already hinted above, the EC gives more weight to declining industrial areas than does the joint-task system in Germany, while the latter is more likely to accord under-populated areas development status (ibid.: 152). In an attempt to counteract this threat to their decison-making authority the Länder governments have demanded greater legislative powers within the federal system (Guardian 13 March 1992). Moreover, Länder representatives have sought a leading role within German EC delegations when regional matters are at stake. The alternative would be for the Federal government to unilaterally represent German regional interests in Brussels. How does this all work out in practice?

Having to concur with EC regulations entails, among other things, ensuring that the 'additionality' principle is upheld (funds are not to be used as substitutes for national aid), that the project contributes to EC competition and uniformity, and that the funds are used only for purposes clearly stated in an Action Programme (Eser 1991b: 43). National programmes are submitted to the EC Committee for Regional Policy which consists of representatives of Member States. The Committee then advises the Commission on the implementation of regional policy measures (Eser 1989: 31). Again, the critical issue is the influence of the Länder on the formulation of EC policy. It is certainly not the case that the Länder are completely excluded. Indeed, the Commission is aware of the need to consult localities as represented by regional governments or local authorities. In this sense, the Länder have an important influence on the determination of economic and structural policy. In other words, although they are not directly represented in the EC organisation and so have no direct influence on the Council of Ministers, they have other means of influencing EC guide-lines. The Länder send Bundesrat representatives to act as mediators between the EC and Germany. They also have offices in Brussels and Länder representatives attend meetings of the EC Commission. Consent from the Länder is required before the ratification of treaties. Ultimately, however, the Länder are not in the position to change EC legislation but merely to delay it (Eser

1991b: 19). Yet in the face of increasing centralisation, they have placed increased emphasis on the role of their offices in Brussels. In essence, while national regional policy as a whole remains far from being an area of direct EC control, there are certain scenarios which could lead to an erosion of policy-making authority at *both* a national and local level.

THE EFFECTS OF UNIFICATION

As it was vital for the former GDR to attract sufficiently high levels of investment, if it was not be confirmed as an economic backwater of the new Germany, one must ask what part regional factors play in investment decisions. Indeed, the implementation of successful investment programmes would play a large part in ameliorating the obvious disparities between east and west Germany. Despite the relatively high costs of factors of production (Heine and Walter 1990: 402), the main conurbations will provide more favourable conditions for investment than remote areas. First, they provide a differentiated labour market; second, they retain a more extensive infrastructure. Thus factors such as the cost effectiveness of the storage and transportation of goods to the market, access to service industries, and better communications explain why economic growth takes place around such central 'nodes'.

Potentially serious consequences for an effective economic policy in the unified Germany are implied by what has just been said. On the one hand, the Federal government must consider the most effective means for maintaining the health of the economy as a whole. On the other hand, such policies are not necessarily compatible with the aim of ameliorating regional differences, both within the former GDR and within western Germany. Initially, financial assistance seemed to come mainly from the private sector, with the Federal government playing only a complementary role (Gebhardt *et al.* 1989: 324). However, the Unity treaty allowed for a series of new programmes as well as the continuation of existing Federal programmes of regional assistance. Such programmes will be described below.

It is tempting to analyse the prospects for investment by a comparison with the currency reform of 1948 and the results of the counter-part funds produced by Marshall Aid. Such an analysis would, however, be misleading for the conditions of post-war West Germany were very different from that of the new Länder. First, the inclusion of the new Länder requires the transformation of economic systems. Second, the industrial base of post-war Germany was in a healthy enough state to provide a basis for later recovery. Third, the technological base was more up-to-date than in the new Länder. Fourth, the infrastructure of the new Länder was far inferior to that of the west. One must recall, however, that the infrastructure in many western European countries was successfully reconstructed after the war. From this point of view, therefore, the task was not completely formidable. Finally, the West German economic recovery benefited from the various administrative and legal structures then in existence. In the new Länder such structures had to be constructed from scratch along West German lines. Virtually the rest of this book will be devoted to demonstrating the economic implications of these structures.

Threatened bankruptcies to the traditional industries in eastern Germany would have only hastened the onset of economic polarisation between east and west Germany. Yet investors in western Germany seemed to regard the east as more of a lucrative market for their own goods than as a potential location for productive industry (Akerlof *et al.* 1991: 37). The establishment of distribution networks within eastern Germany was likely to sharpen this trend. The penetration of west German products into the east exceeded all forecasts (Chaffour *et al.* 1992: 254). A phrase was coined in the east to express the disillusionment with such a trend: 'instead of more development in the west, rebuild the east!' (Boehmer-Christiansen *et al.* 1993: 359). It was argued with some justification that it was difficult to estimate with any certainty the future pattern of expenditure, but prospects for private investment were improved by a series of tax concessions granted to the new Länder retroactively from January 1991. Thus the Tax Amendment Act of the GDR (March 1990) allowed for general reductions in income tax, corporation tax and property tax rates. Top rate income tax was lowered to 60 per cent, and 50 per cent for corporation tax; special depreciation allowances were also made (MRDB 7/91: 19 and 25). GEMSU then provided for the adoption of major elements of the west German tax system which brought substantial tax relief to many residents and enterprises in the former GDR (*ibid.*).

Nevertheless, the ability of the east to attract investment was still hampered by the difficulties of attracting the workforce to an area with generally low quality housing and services. On the other hand, social security provision and the incremental introduction of wage levels comparable to the west were particularly important factors in preventing the further exodus of employees from the east to the west. More will be said about the costs of introducing the generous western social security system in Chapter 5 – although it must be added that many parts of this system were already being revised prior to unification. Similarly, the arguments for equalising pay rates are rehearsed in Chapter 6. However, there was also a balance to be maintained between preventing the emigration of workers from east to west through quickly closing the earnings gap, and the detrimental effects this was likely to have on investment. In order to achieve this, efficient and rapid capital transfers from west to east were required. But such objectives were difficult to achieve alongside the maintenance of 'macroeconomic stability', the constitutional importance of which has been a recurring theme in this chapter. Interest rates, as well as the creation of favourable tax structures, had vital roles to play in such capital transfers, as did the removal of the administered price regime so characteristic of a command economy (Leibfritz and Thanner 1990: 8). But the Bundesbank's basic objective in using interest rates is to ensure price stability (Chapter 4 below). Moreover, the Federal government had other competing goals when it came to the reform of tax structures (see Chapter 3).

As indicated, estimates of the extent of the capital transfer required were extremely hazardous and subject to revision. Nevertheless, based on available data from East Germany, and with the previously-mentioned provisos, Filip-Köhn and Ludwig (1990: 2) calculated a total sum of DM 200 billion based on 1988 prices; indeed, they went further, forming an input–output table based on various factors and directed at flows between the two former states. These calculations indicated that a real transfer of DM 200 billion was a resource limitation in the sense that a larger amount would undermine the western part of the economy. In addition,

it was necessary to invest heavily in the infrastructure of east Germany in order to attract further investment to the area. The DIW (17/90) looked at the 1988 levels of fixed investment in the GDR and pointed out that more investment was required – particularly in construction and related industries. Industries which provided materials and services for various other vital industries also needed investment assistance. (Mechanical and electrical engineering, vehicles and plant manufacturing were all classified as 'vital' industries.) Locational factors are also of significance. A peripheral location is prone to the following disadvantages (Schackmann-Fallis 1989: 249):

- poorer quality of jobs
- lower levels of pay
- poor facilities

In 1990, a telephone poll of 501 west German enterprises by the Ifo-Institut revealed that over half already had some financial interest in the former GDR (Brander 1990). Many enterprises were involved in the building and construction industry. But many were interested in the establishment of delivery or supply networks in the new Länder. However, significant for the prospects of investment was the low figure (6 per cent) who experienced no difficulties or restrictions to their investment plans. Many regarded the legal position regarding ownership of property as a major stumbling block to investment. A statute enacted soon after unification allowed property expropriated after 1949 to revert to its original owner. The uncertainty generated inhibited investment to such an extent that compensation was substituted for restitution. Note, however, that lower compensation may be an incentive to seek restitution in the courts (Siebert 1991b: 299). On the other hand, long-term legal disputes for restitution would have ensued (Sinn 1991: 29). Nevertheless, an encouragingly high proportion of companies covered in the Ifo-Institut survey (78 per cent) had either invested or planned to do so in the near future.

As already suggested, it was the weaker states in western Germany that would suffer most from the transfer of capital mentioned above, although in a European context disparities within West Germany were comparatively moderate. Even before unification there had been an increasing divergence in the Länder levels of debt per head between the northern and southern Länder with the northern Länder levels increasing far more than the southern. Figure 2.13a compares the growth of this concept of debt during the years 1975, 1980 and 1987. It is evident that the city states of Bremen and Hamburg were running into deeper difficulties; also note again how Saarland was a significant exception to the north–south generalisation. In terms of overall debt as a percentage of expenditure, again the worst off in the west were Bremen (16.8 per cent), Saarland (15.2 per cent) and Hamburg (13.3 per cent); the Land with the least debt was Bavaria with 4.1 per cent (SZ 1 October 1991). (The situation was still worse for some of the new Länder: Brandenburg (26.5 per cent), Mecklenburg-West Pomerania (19.3 per cent) and Thuringia (18 per cent). There was then a significant degree of overlap with the weaker western Länder: Berlin (16 per cent), Saxony (15.9 per cent) and Saxony-Anhalt (14.8 per cent) (*ibid.*). Moreover, the substantial aid previously available to Berlin and the inner-border corridor was to be discontinued by 1994. The granting of the full West German share of VAT receipts to the new Länder had resulted in reduction of revenue to the western Länder amounting to around DM 5 billion (BfG *Wirtschaftsblätter* May 1991). Expected tax revenue from the new Länder has been estimated as a 'meagre' DM 12.8 billion (Milbradt 1991: 60). But because the new Länder started from scratch, their accumulated debt was insignificant compared to the problems in the west (Figure 2.13b refers).

It was feared that the reduction of tax revenue at Land level would have detrimental effects on planned investment and financial help at the local-authority level, particularly if the Länder were required to observe a maximum net budget deficit. Although it made no economic difference whether the new Länder were helped by inclusion in the fiscal equalisation system or through the availability of credit, it made a great difference to the old Länder which were already at the limit of their borrowing powers. A drastic reduction in their expenditure patterns was politically unacceptable. Generally, the old Länder would have preferred payments to be made directly rather than by raising the new Länder's allocation of turnover tax. The reason was that the latter depend upon per-capita incomes while the former have more the nature of direct subsidies which could be allocated for particular purposes. Krupp (1991) concluded that the cost burden of unification fell too heavily on the western Länder as opposed to the Federal government. This point also seemed to be taken at the Federal level: from 1995 an additional allowance of DM 15 billion was made for the introduction of the new equalisation system (BfG *Standpunkt* 5/92). Moreover, after much controversy, a solidarity pact to partially finance the costs of unification was agreed in 1993. The agreement was made between the Federal ruling and opposition parties, along with the prime ministers of the sixteen Länder. Significantly, the western Länder achieved a higher share of VAT

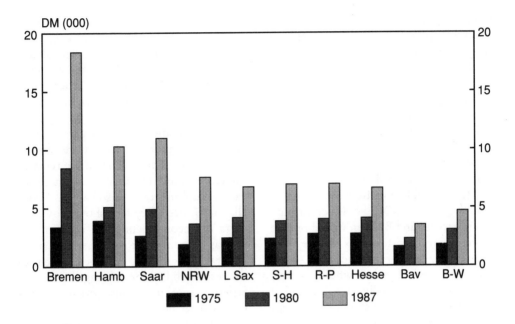

Figure 2.13a Per capita debt in West German Länder (1975, 1980 and 1987)
Source: BfG *Wirtsbl.* (January/February 1989: 6)

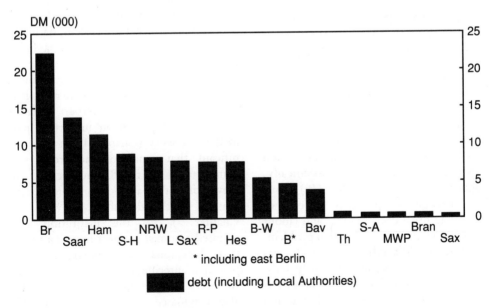

Figure 2.13b Per capita debt in the Länder (1991)
Source: BMF *Finanzbericht* 1993: 130

revenue to fend off what they regarded as unbearable pressures on their spending plans. If total savings of DM 9.2 billion on the Federal expenditure side were not collectively identified and achieved, however, the Länder were required to forfeit the corresponding amount from their VAT revenue (FT 15 March 1993). For the rest, the solidarity pact contained specific provisions for the adjustment of fiscal equalisation. Baden-Württemberg and Hesse would contribute less; Bavaria, Hamburg and NRW would contribute more; Saarland and Bremen would receive supplementary assistance to resolve their exceptionally desperate budgetary positions; the new Länder would receive DM 60 billion annually (FAZ 1 and 2 March 1993). One crucial issue was swept under the carpet: if the Länder's revenues and commitments remain unmatched, will the Länder ultimately be permitted to increase their own revenues (*Economist* 20 March 1993)?

CONCLUDING REMARKS: REGIONAL INVESTMENT PROGRAMMES IN GERMANY

Much of the economic restructuring in the new Länder represented an attempt to prevent the area from becoming a terminally disaffected German Mezzogiorno. Siebert (1991b: 328) saw this as 'two opposite scenarios' – full integration or permanent poverty. More specifically, Hughes Hallet and Ma (1993: 416) define the Mezzogiorno problem as one of continuing fiscal transfers east and labour migration west. To avoid such a problem, convergence in productivity levels was necessary. However, as previously indicated, regional problems are by no means new in Germany. The critical question was whether there was any difference in kind when it came to the post-wall

era. Investment programmes designed to ameliorate regional differences originated in the late 1960s when the regional disparities already described became more apparent. In this sense the programmes implemented to promote economic activity in the new Länder can be regarded as a continuation on a larger scale of policy prescriptions which were already in existence. These concluding remarks therefore draw together the strands of various arguments in this chapter. Above all, it is necessary to show how the costs of reconstructing the economy in the east were met. It will be seen that the Federal government assumed much of the responsibility for meeting these costs. Strictly speaking, this situation was intended to pertain only until the fiscal equalisation scheme was reorganised. In reality, it probably forged a more highly centralised system. In any case, the two recessions in the west which followed the first two oil shocks, along with the prolonged period of relatively high unemployment concentrated in certain Länder, probably meant that the system, dating as it did from 1969, was due for a fairly fundamental restructuring.

Tracing the development of investment further back to the post-war period, it is true to say that the counterpart funds of Marshall Aid played an important part in that recovery (Chapter 1). It was significant that much of the credit was administered by the Reconstruction and Development Loan Corporation (Kreditanstalt für Wiederaufbau (KfW) – see Chapter 7), for this institution later counted amongst its most important roles that of regional development. It is the principal intermediary for the European Recovery Programme (ERP) fund which also originated from the Marshall Aid Programme. Like another public fund established about the same time, the

Equalisation of Burdens or *Lastenausgleichsfonds*, it played an important part in investment in East Germany. The KfW became a banker's bank and therefore a source of additional funds, supplementing those of the commercial banks. As it received interest on its loans and eventual repayment, it was able to build up substantial assets. Moreover, the KfW provided an efficient means of distributing industrial capital (Shonfield 1965: 277). As this example illustrates, mechanisms for the vital re-structuring of the east German economy were therefore established well before unification. The involvement of the KfW in offering private investors favourable credit terms alongside its support of government schemes of regional redevelopment, suggests that the larger-scale regional problems posed by unification were not as daunting as in those eastern European states which remained independent.

Hence, it is not surprising to note that the investment programmes geared towards assisting the new Länder have much in common with previous regional programmes: low interest credit, incentive allowances to attract new workers, favourable terms of repayment and improvement of the infrastructure. For example the KfW provided low-interest loans for investment in the commercial and industrial sectors. This programme extended favourable loans to large as well as small and medium-sized firms at a nominal interest rate of 7.5 per cent with a repayment period of ten years and not more than two redemption free years (MRDB 3/91: 24). A credit ceiling of DM 10 billion was applied. Such assistance may be supplementary to loans made directly from the ERP fund as such (see the next paragraph). The programmes were also extended to larger companies by the establishment in March 1991 of the investment loan programme of the KfW for the new Länder (*ibid.*: 17). Similar loans for small and medium-sized industrial and commercial businesses are also provided by the supplementary programmes of the Deutsche Ausgleichsbank (German Equalisation Bank – see Chapter 7) and the promotional measures of the ERP. In 1993, the principal publication of the Bundesbank described these developments as follows (MRDB 5/93: 55–6):

In the last three years, the volume of business [of 'promotional banks'] has skyrocketed as a result of the expansion of promotional measures in eastern Germany . . . promised subsidised loans in both 1991 and 1992 [rose to] DM 50 billion, i.e. more than twice as much as in 1989.

Loans from the Deutsche Ausgleichsbank were to assist industry and independent professions (*Freie Berufe* – see the definition of the *Mittelstand* in Chapter 8). Moreover, assistance was provided for the establishment of industrial sites and the re-settlement of labour, as well as the development of new products. Individuals, medium-sized enterprises and undertakings owned by local authorities were also entitled to apply for environmental-protection loans. In addition, ERP loans, which aimed at creating a more balanced mix of enterprise size, were made available to medium and small firms. This promotional policy aimed to reduce operating costs by means of government lending and guarantee schemes. For this purpose, the ERP fund was reactivated in February 1990. Loans were offered at favourable rates of interest and repayment. Indeed, these loans were granted on more favourable terms than comparable assistance to the old Länder. The interest rate was on average 2.5 per cent below the market rate, and the beneficiary is shielded from interest rate

Table 2.1 ERP Promotional Schemes in the new Länder (as at 8 March 1991)

Type of programme	Number of applications (000)	Application volume DM billion	Number of loan commitments (000)	Volume of loan commitments DM billion
Modernisation	24.32	4.43	23.27	3.02
Establishment of businesses	46.57	4.30	35.34	3.10
Environmental protection	0.45	0.40	0.33	0.18
Tourism	6.91[1]	0.93	6.37	0.61
Total	78.26	10.06	65.31	6.91[2]

Source: MRDB (4/91: 17)

Notes: [1] Including about 5,900 new establishments
[2] Previous payout volume: DM 3.02 billion

changes. The maturity period of loans was 15 years for machinery and equipment and up to 20 years for industrial or commercial buildings. There may also be up to five redemption-free years. The sources of such credit will be institutions throughout Germany. In order to comply with the principle of proportionate financing, the borrower must additionally raise finance from alternative sources. Table 2.1 shows the extent of take-up and how this borrowing was initially utilised. Eligible recipients of the fund were firms in the former GDR, as well as foreign firms willing to undertake joint-ventures in the east. Additionally, there was assistance for private investors in the former GDR. Again, favourable conditions were applied: for example, the first three years of the loan will be interest-free. The annual volume of ERP loan programmes almost tripled between 1989 and 1993; annual planned expenditure in 1993 was DM 14.25 billion (MRDB 5/93: 45–6). Finally, the European Investment Bank, which gives financial help to less developed areas throughout the EC, also contributed to the economic development in the former GDR. It aims to promote a balanced economic development in the EC.

In May 1990, following agreement between government officials at both the Länder and Federal level, a German Unity Fund was established (*Fonds Deutsche Einheit*). Amounting to some DM 115 billion, the fund was created as a transitional arrangement over the subsequent four years, pending the inclusion of the new Länder in the revenue-sharing system analysed above. (Such an undertaking was embodied in the unity treaty and, along with the closely related objective of securing a consolidation of the public budgets, it represented the biggest fiscal challenge of the 1990s – BfG *Standpunkt* 5/92.) As can be seen in Table 2.2, DM 95 billion of this sum was to be financed by borrowing, the resultant debt being shared equally by, on the one hand, the Federal government and, on the other, the western Länder and local authorities. The other DM 20 billion was to come from Federal government budgetary savings (Geske 1991: 35). Servicing the debt over a thirty-year period would cost DM 23.6 billion during 1990–4 and an annuity of DM 9.5 billion thereafter (Lipschitz and

Table 2.2 The German Unity Fund (DM billion)

Item	1990	1991	1992	1993	1994	Total 1990 to 1994
Expenditure on assistance to the former GDR financed by	22	35	28	20	10	115
Borrowing by the Fund	20	31	24	15	5	95
Allocations by the Federal Government	2	4	4	5	5	20
Payments to meet debt service commitments	–	2.0	5.1	7.5	9.0	23.6[1]
To be paid by the Federal Government	–	1.0.	2.6	3.8	4.5	11.8
by the Länder Governments	–	0.6	1.5	2.3	2.7	7.1
by the Local Authorities	–	0.4	1.0	1.5	1.8	4.7

Source: MRDB (7/90: 20)

Note: [1] Debt service payments will have to be made for another 15 to 25 years, depending on interest rate movements

McDonald 1990: 29). The Federal government assumed responsibility for half the 1990–4 servicing costs.

The envisaged split between the Federal and Länder governments was the subject of heated debate. By meeting a larger share of this off-budget item than the old Länder, the Federal government may conceivably have increased its influence in the east. Of more importance, was the fact that the slow recovery in the east indicated that either the revenue-sharing scheme would require fundamental reform, or the new Länder would become sizeable net beneficiaries in 1995. Hence, it is not just the size and financing of this fund which were of interest. Its various implications for the future of fiscal (and regional) policy were of even greater significance. Ultimately, the solidarity pact of 1993 contained an agreement whereby the eastern Länder would receive revenue from the western ones, which in turn would receive a higher share of VAT receipts. Nonetheless, the prime minister of Saxony

– whose yearly spending of DM 26 billion was two thirds higher than revenue – estimated that the richer parts of the east would still require ten years to catch up with the wealth levels and public amenities in the poorer parts of the west (*Economist* 20 March 1993).

A further scheme of financial assistance, also agreed in the unity treaty, was subsumed under the Basic Law scheme for the 'improvement of regional economic structures'. For a transitional period of five years the new Länder were granted special status as an area requiring regional aid. Improvement grants have been made under this scheme, particularly for 'economy-related' infrastructure investment. This allows a reduction in investment or acquisition costs. Further grants were made to local authorities for the improvement of schools, hospitals and homes for elderly persons. In addition, there were further investment schemes designed to assist at the local authority level, including one for the modernisation and refurbishing of the housing-stock. For this purpose, DM 10 billion was made available.

A series of measures taken by new organisations were of equal importance to schemes funded by existing institutions. An example is the *Gemeinschaftswerk Aufschwung-Ost* (Upswing East). Established at the beginning of March 1991, this was a programme amounting to some DM 24 billion (DM 12 billion in both 1991 and 1992) to provide economic assistance to the new states (BMF *Finanzbericht* 1992: 32). Of this, DM 5 billion was to be allocated for the replacement and overhaul of rundown machinery. It was directed at locally-owned enterprises. The programme also envisaged expenditure totalling DM 5.5 billion on job creation measures (*ibid.*). Its distribution not surprisingly linked in well with what was said about the north–south structure of the former GDR's economy at the beginning of the section on regional comparisons. It probably also reveals something about the changed development status of Berlin which was described above in the section on that city state. Hence, the distribution was as follows:

- Saxony DM 1.5 billion
- Saxony-Anhalt DM 902 million
- Thuringia DM 817 million
- Brandenburg DM 804 million
- Mecklenburg-West Pomerania DM 598 million
- Berlin DM 390 million

An additional DM 6.3 billion was to be provided for the improvement of the transport infrastructure, particularly the public transport system and the road network. Further sums were allocated to housing (see also immediately below): included in this was assistance for the renovation of housing stock and privatisation of state-owned flats.

Two further areas vital for regional development – housing and agriculture – also received attention. The involvement of the KfW programmes was likewise extended to the building trade, where an extensive programme of modernisation and construction of dwellings in the new Länder got under way. Sums amounting to DM 10 billion over the period 1990–3 were allocated for this purpose. It was estimated that this will be enough to cover at least 300,000 dwellings (*ibid.*). In October 1989, an identical development had taken place in West Germany. Similar terms and conditions were applied to the programme in the east. The latter funds came from the Federal budget, whereas the source of the DM 10 billion mentioned previously was the KfW. Housing modernisation, however, was yet another area where costs had been underestimated. In 1993, therefore, the solidarity agreement which was designed to partially fund the costs of unification raised the KfW's borrowing limit from DM 30 billion to DM 60 billion for the purpose of financing housing modernisation in the east.

The eastern German agricultural sector gave rise to concern both from a German perspective and that of the EC. While the inclusion of the former GDR within the EC added an area of arable land equivalent to the combined area of Bavaria, Lower Saxony and Baden-Württemberg, it was estimated that agricultural production per man-hour was only 50 per cent of the west German level. Accordingly, agricultural production in east Germany was far less efficient, and the price of production therefore higher, than in any other region of the EC (Balz 1990). Moreover, the efforts to curb agricultural surpluses within the EC received a positive setback: the agricultural sector of the new Länder came under the auspices of the CAP market regulatory rules and production was concentrated where the most stringent price support rules apply (Döhrn 1990). To support the agricultural sector, the government made purchases of goods which farmers were unable to sell on the open market. This support-buying process is carried out along similar lines to the EC model (*ibid.*: 21). Note that these acute agricultural problems exacerbated the extremely serious problems in the west – see the subsidies section of Chapter 8.

When one adds to the above programmes those which are designed to support the infrastructure in the new Länder, the diversity of investment programmes initiated during 1991 becomes clear. Examples already seen were programmes of the *Gemeinschaftswerk Aufschwung-Ost* to improve the transport infrastructure and housing as well as the housing modernisation loans provided by the KfW. In addition, infrastructure investment received particularly favourable treatment under the terms of the joint Federal and Länder scheme for Improving the Regional Economic Structure (MRDB 3/91: 21). As already emphasised, improvements to the infrastructure were major prerequisites of long-term economic recovery in the new Länder. It was argued that in the face of the increasingly onerous burden of public debt, the costs of investment in the infrastructure should be provided by private sources (Dresdner Bank *Trends* 9/91: 4). Moreover, despite the interventionist nature of the state in German economic policy making illustrated in this chapter, the potential extra pressures on Federal and Länder finances made it increasingly likely that private sources would have to be found. As the Deutsche Bundesbank pointed out, state measures to regenerate the economy should be regarded as purely supplementary to private measures (MRDB 3/91: 22). Some of the shadow budgets introduced to transfer financial resources to the east have already been analysed – see Tables 2.1 and 2.2, for example. Further examples and analyses will appear in each subsequent chapter. There was, as indicated, a finite limit to these fiscal arrangements. Not only had they to be refinanced, they needed to be supplemented by private investment. This is an excellent note on which to conclude this chapter.

3

FISCAL POLICY

INTRODUCTION

Fiscal policy can be divided into two parts corresponding to the revenue side and the expenditure side. Revenue is mainly derived by the various levels of government from taxation. Public-sector enterprises may also be expected to make positive contributions, although in some cases this has proved to be an over-optimistic expectation. As will be shown in Chapter 5, the largest item on the expenditure side is social-policy spending. Other large expenditure items include education and defence. Policy interest, however, has been increasingly focused on the general level of government expenditure, along with the size of the budget deficit. Subsidies have been the object of particular attention. In both Chapter 8 and in the section on budgetary policy below, it will be emphasised that subsidies in the west were particularly at odds with the supply-side (free market) economics pursued after 1982 and with the problems associated with unification.

As already demonstrated in Chapter 1, such an extent of government intervention is inconsistent with the received theory of the SME. A recurrent theme of this chapter will be the extent to which fiscal policy failed in practice to conform with this theoretical framework. It will be found that not only government spending, but also high marginal tax rates have been perceived as problematical by taxpayers. After all, there is a need within the SME model for low marginal rates to stimulate effort and risk taking, although some progression in the tax system is necessary in order to achieve the social equity goal of this model. Not that these two elements – neutrality and equity – are unique characteristics of the SME, albeit that this is the model which must be tested here: a common problem of all tax systems is modifying income inequalities by means of a progressive tax system but avoiding very high marginal rates which may undermine risk taking. (Only the effect of tax rates on risk taking is relevant here. In the next chapter, the equally important role played by interest rates will be considered.)

Above all, it is in this sense that unification, and meeting its attendant costs by increasing government spending and taxation, hardly represented a new phenomenon. In principle, it was just another redistribution problem. Moreover, Germany has historically been a good example of how a sizeable part of the national income is re-distributed by government in accordance with equity rather than market considerations (Mendershausen 1974: 78). If unification further constrained the reform of fiscal policy, however, membership of the EC in some ways proved to be a stimulus.

In order to show that unification simply exacerbated existing fiscal problems, the following hypotheses on the pre-unification position need to be validated:

- tax rates were considered to be unacceptably high and the structure was in need of reform
- reducing expenditure had proved to be an intractable problem
- by German post-war standards, there was already a serious public-sector debt problem

REFORMING THE STRUCTURE OF TAXATION

Taxes are levied on incomes, capital and expenditure. The two general categories of income taxes are employment and corporate taxation. In addition, as will be seen in Chapter 5, both employers and employees contribute to various social insurance funds. Not surprisingly, value added tax is the major expenditure tax. Two factors make the structure of taxation in Germany complex. First, as already seen in Chapter 2, there are elaborate revenue-sharing arrangements between the various levels of government. (This factor also complicates the expenditure side.) Second, there is a large number of taxes, as will be shown in the next section. Even at this stage, however, it is instructive to note that *Wirtschaftswoche* (10/91: 20) listed 30 taxes. By far the largest revenue earner was the tax on employees' income (DM 181.3 billion in 1990). Total tax revenue in 1990 was DM 549.5 billion (MRDB 2/93: table VIII[1]). Hence one third of total tax revenue was derived from taxes on employees' income. Rank 30 in the *Wirtschaftswoche* list was occupied by the tax on licensed premises in certain Länder (DM 11 million in 1990). Several minor taxes on sugar, salt, tea and lightbulbs/

fluorescent tubes were abolished on 1 January 1993, although the coffee tax remained in force. Individual churchgoers may also elect to have a 'church tax' (*die Kirchensteuer*) deducted from their income. This voluntary 'tax' is authorised by Article 140 of the basic law (GG), which in turn refers to Article 137(6) of the Weimar constitution. On unification, it was introduced into east Germany. Its average rate was 3 per cent in 1991, when it raised DM 15.6 billion for the Catholic and Evangelical churches (iwd2 40/92). More detail on tax revenue and its distribution will be given in Figures 3.4–3.7 below. Initially, however, an overview of the tax structure will be given.

Income tax (ESt) is levied on the total income of an individual, subject, of course, to allowances being deducted in order to arrive at taxable income. For collection purposes, income tax is divided into:

- assessed tax on total income
- taxes on employees' income (LSt) deducted at source from salaries, wages, pensions, etc.
- capital yields tax of 25 per cent, deducted at source from dividends, interest, etc. received from limited companies
- directors' fees tax deducted at source from fees received by non-executive directors from overseas

Corporate tax takes two main forms. First, there is a national corporation tax (KSt) which is not levied on partnerships or small businesses. These latter type of enterprises are assessed for ESt. The tax yield of the KSt on retained and distributed profits differs. Second, there is a local trade tax (GewSt) which is generally payable by business enterprises, irrespective of their legal status. The liberal professions are presently the main exceptions.

Hence, for collection purposes, corporate tax was divided into:

- a KSt of 50 per cent on retained profits
- a KSt of 36 per cent on distributed profits
- a local GewSt of up to 20 per cent of profits and capital values, deductible from KSt liabilities

Shareholders are entitled to include the corporation and capital-yield taxes for crediting against their total income tax liability. Such a provision – introduced in 1977 – prevents double taxation. Consequently, Germany's system of corporate taxation favours the distribution of profits. When German companies complain about high taxation, therefore, they are referring to retained profits (Härtel in Cowling and Tomann 1990: 350–1). Although the amendment of corporate taxation was, prior to being subordinated to the fiscal imperatives of unification, the subject of lively debate, no significant consideration was given to changing the distributional bias of profits taxation. It is noteworthy that this system is diametrically opposed to the principles underlying the systems in the UK and the USA. Yet paradoxically Britain's biggest 115 companies distribute at least twice and sometimes three times as much in dividends as the Germans (*Guardian* 20 June 1990). This higher dividend/earnings ratio may have more to do with firms in the UK (and USA) being driven by short-term profit considerations in order to avoid hostile takeover bids, an essential question for the sections on corporate finance, ownership and control, and mergers and acquisitions in Chapters 7 and 8. An even more surprising paradox will also be demonstrated in Chapter 8 (Figure 8.2). West German firms relied heavily on internal financing from retained profits. The expected effect of the system's bias in favour of distri-bution, namely a greater reliance on loans or equity finance, does not therefore seem to have materialised (Härtel *ibid.*: 352).

A major reform of taxation on personal incomes was introduced on 1 January 1990. Its implementation in West Germany at the beginning of unification year was coincidental: increasingly high marginal income tax rates had been a problem throughout the post-war period. This factor was the cause of a number of reforms, culminating in the 1990 amendments to the tax structure. There was a second important reason for the tax reforms during the 1970s and 1980s. As one of the world's most powerful economies, West Germany was expected to provide a stimulus to international economic growth. The Bonn and Louvre accords are two cases in point: they will be dealt with in a little more depth below. Since the gross annual cost of the 1990 tax-reform package in terms of the reduction in revenue was DM 40 billion, its implementation in unification year, given the enormous consequential increase in expenditure demands, posed a serious policy dilemma: either there would be an enormous increase in government borrowing, or the tax reform plans would have to be modified. There has tended to be a basic conflict of this description throughout the post-war era.

The dramatic economic changes in the period 1946–58 were analysed in general terms in Chapter 1. More specifically, Figure 3.1 plots the income tax schedules during this period – a period which was sequentially characterised by inflation, currency reform, liberalisation of markets and, ultimately, the introduction of full foreign-exchange convertibility. Notice first of all the swingeing increases in taxes introduced by the Allies in 1946. Even though this diagram shows average tax rates (taxation/taxable income at current prices), the relatively high position of the 1946 schedule can be easily seen. Reuss (1963: 83) reports that marginal income tax rates (the change in taxation relative to the change in taxable income) were raised to a maximum of 95 per cent. Although these rates were the highest in German history, they were designed to reduce the huge monetary overhang which had been one of the legacies of the Nazi regime (Denton *et al.* 1968: 187–8). In 1948, the Allies feared that if they allowed the drastic tax cuts sought by the Economic Council chaired by Erhard, budget deficits and consequential inflationary pressure might vitiate their currency reform. (As will be seen below, the Council therefore introduced tax privileges which are still problematical.) The first amendment under the new German jurisdiction (still subject to reluctant Allied approval) resulted in a decrease of 15 percentage points in the top rate (Reuss *ibid.*). By 1953, 80 per cent was the maximum marginal rate on taxable incomes between DM 250,000 and DM 350,000, with an overall maximum of 70 per cent on incomes over DM 500,000 – a product of the staggered marginal system in operation at that time (*ibid.*: 83–5). In 1955, the maximum rate was 63.45 per cent with an overall maximum of 55 per cent.

Wallich (1955: 104–5) termed the 1953 changes as 'the little tax reform' and reports that the debate about the 1955 measures was 'distinctly muted'. By way of contrast, the 1958 reform was 'major' (Denton *et al.* 1968: 194). A new proportional 'entry stage' was also introduced, whereby a flat rate of 20 per cent was payable up to DM 8,000 (single person) or DM 16,000 (married person). Thereafter the rates were calculated so as to rise continuously with even the smallest rise in income, with two separate formulae being used in a progressive zone. The

reduction in the upper proportional rate to 53 per cent, also introduced in 1958, cannot be gauged from Figure 3.1. This is because in average terms the new rate was payable on incomes over DM 1 million! Although some of the essential features of the 1958 reform are not completely clear in Figure 3.1, the 'low' position of the 1958 curve relative to preceding tax regimes can be seen at a glance. In other words, the virtue of Figure 3.1 is that it demonstrates the continual process of adjustment during the period 1946–58; the actual amount of tax payable on a given income is indicated for each of the amendments to the tax structure which took place during the period. For example, the 1958 schedule in the figure shows the entry rate of DM 4,261 which was applicable to a married person (allowance of DM 3,360) with one child (additional allowance of DM 900). It then shows how the average rate rose, given this unlikely case of a taxpayer entitled only to these basic allowances. Nonetheless, marginal rates of tax and the effects of inflation are not apparent in the figure. These difficulties can be resolved by plotting income margins along the horizontal axis and by using a constant price level – as can be seen by comparing Figures 3.1 and 3.2.

Summarising, it can be said that the 1958 reform introduced an initial formula which resulted in a constant marginal rate of 20 per cent but a gradually rising average rate. This rising average rate is due to the fact that tax-free allowances decline as a percentage of total income as income rises. In this sense, all tax regimes are progressive. Moreover, higher-income groups tend to avail themselves more of tax-free allowances which makes the income tax system bear more heavily on lower-income groups – a paradoxical result when the social objectives of taxation are borne in mind (Denton *et al.* 1968:

191). Conversely, if the tax-free allowances available to lower-income groups are raised, a certain proportion will be removed from the tax system altogether, whereas the absolute value of the tax relief is greater for higher-income earners because they are taxed at higher marginal tax rates. Emphasis in the present analysis, however, is on marginal rates.

In the 1958 model, following the application of a constant marginal rate of 20 per cent up to a total taxable income of DM 8,009 for a single person, the marginal rate increases. The degree of progression was governed by two formulae, the first being applied to total taxable incomes between DM 8,010 and DM 23,999. Thereafter, the second formula was applied until total income reached a level of over DM 110,000. At this latter point, the upper constant marginal rate was applied. Let T be the tax payable and Y the taxable income, then:

$$T = 0.2 \, (Y - \text{tax-free allowances})$$

In the progressive zone the two equations were:

$$T = 0.2 \, (\text{tax threshold} -$$
$$\text{tax-free allowances})$$
$$+ aY + bY^2$$
$$T = A + cY + dY^2 - eY^3$$

(Where A, a, b, c, d and e are all constants)

Finally, the upper proportional zone also displayed a constant marginal rate (53 per cent) but an average rate that rose to a given finite income:

$$T = 0.53Y - \text{a constant}$$

(The equations are based on the German original source of Figure 3.1, page 163. The log function introduced in 1954 can be found in the same series of reports, 1955: 164. The 1981 formula-based schedule is analysed in OECD 1981b: 40–1.)

The next major reform, enacted in 1964, can be seen in Figure 3.2. The first function for 1965 shows how the proportional entry stage was lowered from 20 to 19 per cent and the curve of progression was smoothed out. The top rate of 53 per cent can be clearly seen, as can the effect of the 3 per cent surcharge of 1965. In 1975, the bottom rate of tax was raised from 19 to 22 per cent, payable on taxable income to DM 16,000 for a single person – double the 1958 point. (The 22 per cent level in the lower proportional zone can be clearly seen in Figure 3.2 but see Owen Smith 1983: 87, for a graph of the DM 16,000 entry into the progressive zone. Figure 3.2 is based on a constant-price assumption, although note the 1981 entry into the progressive zone – DM 18,000.) In 1975 the progressive range began at this point (DM 16,000) with a rate of 30.8 per cent, rising to the previous top rate of 56 per cent. However, the step increase which featured this jump from 22 to 30.8 per cent was removed in 1979, thus resuming its pre-1975 exponential rise but from DM 18,000 (Figure 3.2). In real terms, and this is the main point about Figure 3.2, the shape and position of the marginal rate curve changed very little between 1965 and 1981. Changes in the tax structure in 1975, 1979 and 1981 compensated for inflation but left unchanged in real terms the starting point of the progressive region (OECD *Economic Survey* 1982: 42). A similar change in the tax structure – not shown in the figure – took place in 1978 (*ibid.*).

In turning to Figure 3.3, the reader will be able to combine the approaches of the two previous figures. First, it can be seen that there were further reforms of marginal tax rates in 1986, 1988 and 1990, with

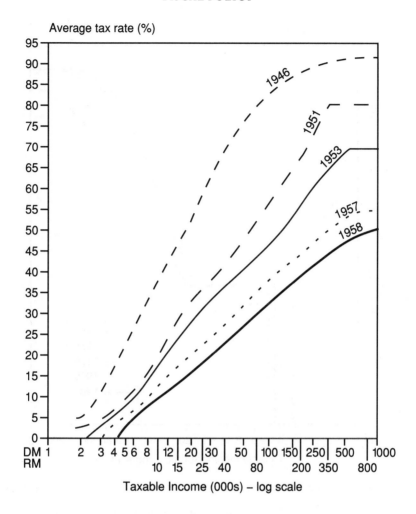

Average tax rate (%)

Taxable Income (000s) – log scale

Figure 3.1 Income Tax on taxable income: 1946–58 (at current prices)

Source: BMF, *Vorbemerkungen zum Haushaltsplan* 1959: 169 (reproduced in Reuss 1963: 87)

the 1990 function becoming a straight line. It can also be seen that the amount of tax actually paid by the tax payers indicated on the horizontal axis (the average rate of tax) fell in 1990 when compared to 1986. Clearly, then, the 1990 reforms are significant for several reasons which can be summarised as follows:

- the annual minimum rate on taxable income was reduced three percentage points to 19 per cent
- the annual maximum tax rate was reduced by the same amount to 53 per cent
- the tax threshold for single persons was increased by DM 1,080 to DM 5,616; children's allowances were increased by DM 540 to DM 3,024 per

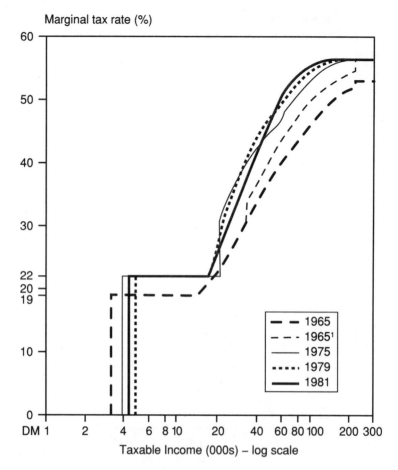

Marginal tax rate (%)

Taxable Income (000s) – log scale

– –	1965
– – ·	1965[1]
——	1975
·····	1979
——	1981

[1] Including surtax of 3 per cent on incomes over DM 16 020 from 1965–1974

Figure 3.2 Marginal tax rates at constant prices: 1965–81

Source: SVR, *Jahresgutachten* 1981/82 (reproduced in OECD Economic Survey (Germany) 1982: 43)

year; in addition, children's educational allowances were increased
- most important of all, the gradient of
the marginal rate function between the
lowest and highest threshold was converted from an exponential to a linear
function (also see Figure 3.3)

By way of contrast, the reform of
both the level and structure of corporate
taxation was being actively considered at
the time of unification, although the 50
per cent level of corporation tax was intro-

duced concomitant to the reforms analysed in the previous paragraph. Prior to 1
January 1990, the level had been 56 per
cent. Yet the Deutsche Bank *Bulletin*
(December 1989: 4) estimated that corporation and trade taxes combined meant a
marginal rate of almost 60 per cent even
after the tax cuts of 1990:

Even those who claim that West German
corporate taxation is on the whole average
in international terms admit that the
'psychology of high tax rates' counts

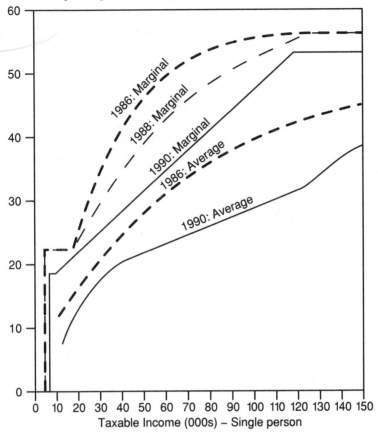

Average/marginal tax rate (%)

1986: Marginal

1988: Marginal

1990: Marginal

1986: Average

1990: Average

Taxable Income (000s) – Single person

20 40 60 80 100 120 140 160 180 200 220 240 260 280 300
Taxable Income (000s) – Married person, without children

Figure 3.3 Tax reforms: 1986–90 (at current prices)
Sources: Der Spiegel 42/87; 18; Dresdner Bank, *Wirtschaftsberichte* April 1987: 12

against West Germany as a corporate location.

(*ibid.*)

Certainly the West German business community became acutely concerned about EC 1993 and the real or imagined threat posed by high tax rates in Germany. For example, the chief executive of IBM Deutschland estimated that his company paid 54 per cent tax on distributed profits compared to the 26 per cent paid by IBM England (*Der Spiegel* 6/88). His interviewers asked how the figure of 54 per cent was arrived at, given the 36 per cent corporation tax rate on distributed profits. The reason was that trade and capital-yield taxes had been included. Had profits not been remitted to the parent company, the rate would have been 70 per cent. His interviewers countered that this assumed the most pessimistic scenario imaginable, and quoted an estimate (made by Professor Littmann) of an average corporate tax rate of 34 per cent; the interviewee pointed out that this average value was deflated by the inclusion of companies which recorded losses. Ironically enough, IBM was to record large international losses in the early 1990s. Such was the substance of this aspect of the cost debate surrounding West Germany's future viability as a competitive industrial location (*Standort Deutschland*).

Differing estimates of the corporate tax burden are not unusual. Indeed, different methods of calculation yield a variation from 20 to 70 per cent of net income; even using the same methodology produces the estimates of 20, 34 and 54 per cent made respectively by the SVR, Professor Littmann and IW (Deutsche Bank *ibid.*). Consider also the IfW comparative research on undistributed profits reported in the OECD's *Economic Survey* (Germany – 1989: 90). The data are net of tax allowances and since these differ significantly as between countries, the results are misleading. Such a data base is selective because 'profits' would be more meaningful if defined as total revenue minus total costs. However, no business enterprise, least of all a German company, would release such data to the general researcher. Nearly 25 per cent of the tax in the IfW model comprises local taxation; since the study also assumes the pre-1990 rate of corporation tax of 56 per cent on the remaining 75 per cent of profits, the tax burden is about 70 per cent. The MRDB (8/89: 44–5), on the other hand, reported an average rate of corporation tax for 1983 of 43 per cent. This ratio was, however, 'higher than the actual burden since the profit on which it is based has already been reduced as a result of several tax concessions, such as special depreciation allowances'.

Along with the contention that wage costs were also adversely affecting international competitiveness (see Chapter 6), there is at least something in the view that the corporate community was crying wolf. Quite apart from the positive locational factors emanating from the high efficiency of German labour brought out by the IBM interviewee quoted above, there is the fairly spectacular array of standard or itemised deductions for business expenses implied by his interviewers. There are also other allowances. For example, all trade insurance premia are deductible, as are uninsured pension commitments and employee welfare funds. Accelerated depreciation allowances are widely available (see Chapter 2). In any case, the post-tax profits of large companies in particular had been booming prior to unification (*Der Spiegel* 13/89). Yet the vast majority of medium and small businesses, which comprise 90 per cent of the total number of companies, are subject to income tax rather than corporation tax. It is therefore the top rate of income tax which is the relevant policy consideration in this case. The minority FDP partners in the Federal coalition government advocated a radical reduction of marginal tax rates, not least to favour small businesses faced with EC 1993 (*Wirtschaftswoche* 26/89: 41).

In fact EC 1993 concentrated the policy makers' minds wonderfully when it came to corporate tax reform (Härtel in Cowling and Tomann 1990). The trade tax is the general element of company taxation which received particular attention. The Federal government established a commission to examine the alternatives. Partially unrelated to company profitability, it can bear more heavily in a recession (Flockton 1990: 59). But its complete abolition is constitutionally difficult: it is the main source of income for local authorities. Their autonomy would therefore be adversely affected. An alternative source of income for local authorities would be an even greater degree of revenue sharing – already a problem area as seen in Chapter 2. A removal of the capital-tax element, and a concomitant widening of the taxable income base, therefore seemed to be the most favoured line of reform (OECD *Economic Survey*, 1989: 91). Reform of this tax would not be new: in some cases (until 1979) the trade tax had also contained a pay roll tax. When the pay roll element was abolished, the local authorities' income tax revenue share, details of which are given below, was raised by one percentage point to 15 per cent.

The tax on working capital (*die Gewerbekapitalsteuer*) was duly scrapped on 1 January 1993. Small businesses also received some relief from the GewSt and there was an increase in the threshold at which the wealth tax (*die Vermögensteuer*) on companies became payable. This latter tax is unrelated to sales. The conservative-liberal Federal coalition reduced its rate on coming into office and subsequently agonised over its reform (*Die Zeit* 37/91). More significantly, the *Standort-sicherungsgesetz* received the approval of the Federal cabinet late in 1992. Scheduled to come into force on 1 January 1994, it reduced the rate of the KSt on retained profits to 44 per cent while the rate on distributed profits was reduced to 30 per cent. Similarly, businesses not eligible to pay KSt, received a reduction in their ESt to 44 per cent (SZ 10 December 1992). (The top rate for personal income remained 53 per cent.) In all these amendments, depreciation allowances were also reduced so that the fiscal effect was neutral. As a result of the amendments' fiscal neutrality, the likely effect on investment was uncertain (Dresdner Bank *Trends* June 1993).

West Germany's membership of the EC ultimately stimulated a reform of VAT. Proposals for such a reform can be traced back to 1953 when they formed part of a package recommended by a panel of advisers to the BMF (Denton *et al.* 1968: 190). In the same report, the panel had dealt with the tax system as a whole. The 1958 reform of income tax discussed above was based on one of their recommendations. However, the government did not accept their recommendation for an overall reduction in corporate tax and introduced the two-tier system which favoured distributed profits. The financial requirements remaining after the re-shaping of income and corporate tax, the report stated, would have to be met by indirect taxation. No increase in these taxes was envisaged: quite the contrary because as a result of the drastic increase of the turnover tax in 1951, the Federal government's revenue from this source was already as great as income and corporate taxation combined. As will be seen below, achieving budget surpluses was the principal policy objective of the time.

In the report to the BMF (see the previous paragraph), the stated aim was rather the reform of the turnover tax to encourage competition and prevent concentration. No one in Germany doubted that the cumulative indirect tax system of the time encouraged vertical integration and price distortions; it was thus alien to the competitive order. Hence, the cumulative turnover tax, which was levied like a 'cascade' at each stage of the productive and marketing processes, should, the report contended, be replaced by a non-cumulative turnover tax, or 'value-added tax'. Ultimately, a bill containing proposals for a value-added tax appeared in 1963 and the final measure reached the statute book in 1967. Consequently, the normal rate of value-added tax was to be 10 per cent as from January 1968, but it was raised to 11 per cent to help balance the budget. A special rate of 5 per cent was also introduced by the 1967 legislation.

It is appropriate to look at the EC side of things in a little more depth. Articles 95 and 96 of the EEC Treaty respectively outlaw taxing imported products more highly than their domestically produced competitors; similarly, repayments of tax on exports may not exceed the taxes actually paid on the product in question. Calculation of the taxes so included is extremely difficult under a cumulative tax system and this gave rise to claims and counter-claims among member states that exports were being given hidden subsidies by overestimating the refundable taxes. Concomitant to the German reforms of the 1960s, therefore, efforts were being made at the EC level to introduce a neutral and transparent turnover tax system. In 1967, two VAT directives introduced such a tax and this replaced all other turnover taxes in member states. France and Germany were the first members to comply – in 1968. Other members followed later, the last one being Italy in 1973. New members are required to introduce the tax within three years of their accession.

VAT rates differ widely within the EC. To achieve fiscal harmonisation with EC 1993, the Commission proposed that two VAT rates should be applied: a standard and a reduced rate. Since the recommendation for the former was between 14 and 20 per cent, and the latter between 4 and 9 per cent, Germany was particularly well placed to conform: her rates since 1983 had been 14 and 7 per cent respectively. Moreover, she remained in such a position when the proposed minimum standard rate was increased to 15 per cent because the Federal Minister of Finance (Theo Waigel) announced in June 1991 his intention to seek parliamentary approval for a new German rate of this amount as from the beginning of 1993. (It will be shown that this increase in VAT revenue will also assist in financing unification.) The minimum standard rate, finally agreed as late as October 1992 by the EC Council of Ministers, applied to both VAT and the special excise taxes on mineral oil, alcohol and tobacco (MRDB 10/92: 19; BfG *Standpunkt* 7/92). The German reduced rate remained unchanged (OECD *Economic Survey* 1992: 103n). Britain was the only member country to retain a zero band for goods such as food, books and newspapers; pressure to scrap the zero rating on transport was expected to begin as early as 1994 (*Guardian* 1 April 1992). British zero rating on domestic energy was to be abolished from 1994, although the British secured a reprieve for the sale of duty-free goods until 1999.

As would probably be expected, Germany's system of excise duties is as incongruous as that of any other Member State. It is for this reason that even less progress has been made in harmonising excise-duty structures than VAT structures. Germany, along with other wine producers, imposes no duty on still wine; this is in contrast to the UK, Denmark and Ireland where duty on this item is very high. These three states also charge a relatively high duty on spirits, whereas Germany is nearer the median in this frequency distribution and there is also only a small amount of duty payable on sparkling wines and beer. Petrol and tobacco, of course, bear fairly heavy duty. More surprisingly, especially as it ran contrary to the EC specific proposal to abandon such duties on the grounds of collection costs, duty in Germany was also payable on tea, coffee, sugar, salt and light bulbs. These duties were levied by the Federal government and were known as *Bagatellsteuern*, or taxes of little significance. In 1991, they raised only DM

517 million out of a total tax revenue of DM 662 billion (*Handelsblatt* 29 April 1992; MRDB 2/93: table VIII(1)). With the exception of the tax levied on coffee, they were ultimately abolished as from the end of 1992. Four *Bagatellsteuern* were retained by the Länder and local authorities, however (*Handelsblatt ibid.*).

The effect of GEMSU in 1990 on the structure of German taxes was allied to the effect of EC 1993. An inevitable increase in taxation to meet the costs of unification was not proposed by the Federal government until February 1991. As well as the increases in unemployment and pension contributions to be examined in Chapter 5, a one-year surcharge of 7.5 per cent on income and corporation tax was proposed to run from 1 July 1991. The SPD majority in the Bundesrat sought to modify the bill so that only taxpayers with annual earnings of more than DM 60,000 would be affected until March 1994. Also affected were excise duties on petrol and tobacco, as well as motor vehicle and insurance taxes. The ultimate compromise was to agree the implementation of the foregoing measures but to postpone any immediate modification of the local trade tax. The tax was not to be levied in the east until at least 1993, but would remain in the west (FT 17 June 1991). As a result of these tax increases, the total tax burden on individuals was expected to rise to over 45 per cent of GNP by 1994 – a historic peak (IDS *European Report* 355). From January 1995, as a result of the solidarity pact agreement, there was to be a further surcharge on income tax of 7.5 per cent. (The wealth tax was also to be increased.) These higher income taxes were to compensate for the higher share of VAT conceded to the western Länder. These changes will be considered in a wider budgetary policy context below.

THE INCIDENCE OF TAXATION

All tax reforms are, of course, undertaken with a view to introducing changes in this context. As shown in the last section, the reforms in post-war West Germany covered all forms of taxation with varying degrees of success. For example, the general structure of the personal income tax schedule remained unchanged during the period 1958–89. The basic policy problems were concerned, first, with where taxation at the lower proportional rate should commence and what that rate should be; second, the progressive zone rose with such an initial steepness from the lower rate that the marginal rates bore heavily on tax payers propelled into this zone by rising real incomes; third, the upper proportional zone was varied over the period. The 1990 reform marked a highly significant phase in the attempts by policy makers to address all three problems, especially the second one.

It was indeed this second problem which grew more serious as the period progressed. As the original German source of Figure 3.1 makes clear (p.165), the 1958 reform of the tax schedule, plus the increase in allowances, meant that approximately 75 per cent of the reductions in tax liability benefited individuals in the lower proportional zone. Including persons no longer eligible for taxation, this zone now contained 95 per cent of all pre-reform tax payers, representing some 80 per cent of taxable income which provided 50 per cent of income tax revenue. Hence, the remaining 20 per cent of taxable income in the variable marginal rate and upper proportional zones provided the other 50 per cent of income tax revenue. (Only 0.1 per cent of taxpayers included in these latter data earned more than DM 100,000, representing 4 per cent of taxable income.)

Only a decade later – in 1968 – the proportion of taxpayers in the variable marginal rate zone had more than trebled to 15.5 per cent (OECD source of Figure 3.2). By 1974 this proportion had reached almost 42 per cent, although the reforms of 1975 and 1979 had the effect of reducing it to 35 per cent in 1980. Even so, in 1980 taxpayers in the variable marginal rate portion of the schedule paid 78 per cent of total personal income tax revenue, while the 15 per cent of tax payers with marginal rates of over 35 per cent provided half that total (*ibid*.). The Dresdner Bank (*Wirtschaftsberichte*, April 1987: 12) estimated that by 1985 two-thirds of all tax payers had moved into the variable marginal rate zone. This bank attributed the move into this zone by more and more nominal incomes to inflation, whereas the OECD source above preferred to associate the move with rising real incomes. There is probably a significant input from both sources, although real wages (net of taxes and social insurance contributions) fell for the six successive years to 1986 (OECD *ibid*. 1987: 15).

The position in the mid-1980s can be seen as a major driving force behind the reforms depicted in Figure 3.3. The Dresdner Bank data outlined above, and reported in more depth by this writer elsewhere (1989: 62), indicated an average tax rate on employees' income in 1985 of 18.8 per cent plus a further 14.9 per cent for social security contributions. Moreover, the marginal rate of these two items reached over 60 per cent. The Deutsche Bank (*Bulletin* April 1987: 14) referred to the 1990 reform as meeting 'the decades-old demand to eliminate the disproportionately sharp rise in tax rates on middle-bracket incomes'. Two powerful examples (see also Figure 3.3) are, first,

that the marginal rate for a married couple earning DM 60,000 fell from approximately 32 to 25 per cent; secondly, on DM 80,000 it fell from roughly 38 per cent to about 28 per cent. In absolute terms, of course, the fall in the upper proportional rate brought even bigger windfalls: DM 12,000 to single persons earning more than DM 120,000 (married couples DM 21,000 if earnings exceeded DM 260,000 – *Der Spiegel* 3/90: 88). In addition, there had already been adjustments towards levelling off the tax scale in the progression zone in both 1986 and 1988 (MRDB 8/90: 43). The OECD (*ibid*. 1985: 30) predicted in 1985, however, that these two latter adjustments to the schedules would merely compensate for inflation since 1982. The 1990 reform can thus be seen as going some considerable way towards meeting the SME model's requirements – only to be undermined by subsequent developments. There was thus a perceptible increase in the incidence of personal taxation, especially if social-insurance contributions are included. Between 1970 and 1985, for example, total deductions from each DM 1000 of pay rose on average from DM 220 to DM 310 (TVF 18 February 1993). The 1990 reform brought this amount down to DM 299, but inflation of pay rates, the 7.5 per cent 'solidarity' surcharge of 1991–2 (see below) and increased social-insurance contributions (see Chapter 5) caused the average deduction to rise to DM 323 and DM 335 in 1991 and 1992 respectively.

As already implied several times above, allowances give rise to difficulties in calculating the actual incidence of taxation. Reasonably straightforward from the operational point of view is the 1958 'splitting' of the income of married couples which is still in operation: unless they opt to be assessed separately, their combined income is halved, and the tax on this sum is doubled. On the other hand, this system possesses a number of discriminatory features, particularly in terms of the costs of child raising, single-parent families and married women whose husbands have a high tax liability (Spahn et al. 1992).

Tax allowances as such are classified as follows:

- a basic tax-free allowance (der Grundfreibetrag)
- an initial deduction (der Vorwegeabzug)
- a child allowance (der Kinderfreibetrag)
- allowances for prudential expenditure (die Sonderausgaben)
- a ceiling to allowances (der Höchstbetrag)

Hence, whether one considers a single or married person there is a basic allowance. As well as an additional basic allowance for children, all employees receive a lump sum allowance (DM 2,000 in 1990). Interestingly, the Federal Constitutional Court (BVG) ruled in 1990 that the government must ensure that the level of income deemed necessary for a decent existence for families with children is entirely free from tax (IDS European Report 355). As a result, family tax allowances and benefits were significantly improved in 1992 (OECD Economic Survey 1992: 34). Claims for improved basic and child allowances could be backdated to 1986, together with a supplementary allowance for 1983–5 (also see Table 5.5 below). The BVG also required the tax exemption limit for low incomes to be lifted. In addition, employees may deduct social and many private insurance contributions and premia ('prudential expenditure'), thereby lowering taxable income. Regular payments on a savings contract with a building savings bank are also an appreciable

deduction in the category – see the section on housing finance in Chapter 7. The effort-inducement aspect of the SME can be seen from other employee-related outgoings such as travel, trade union membership and running a second home, all of which are classified as 'normal' expenses. Then there are a number of exemptions such as unemployment and redundancy pay. Premia payments for overtime, as well as Christmas, marriage, long service and SAYE bonuses are also exempted to pre-set limits. Finally, there is a category of 'extraordinary' expenses. Social policy preconceptions in this area have led to educational and single-parent allowances, the latter being in addition to the basic single-person household allowance. As a result, a typical employee in 1980 earned DM 33,607 gross. However, income tax deductions amounted to DM 10,902, leaving a net taxable income of DM 22,705 (OECD Economic Survey, 1982: 42).

Total taxation as a proportion of GNP lay well within the range 20 to 25 per cent during the post-war period, but this apparent stability is misleading. The relative contribution of indirect taxes to government revenues has diminished (OECD ibid. 1985: 27). Social security contributions have risen fastest, and receipts from the direct tax on employees' incomes also increased rapidly relative to other direct taxes. Perhaps the relative tax rates reveal the basic problem: in 1989, the effective social security contribution rate was 32.5 per cent; the average effective personal income tax rate was 20.1 per cent; the standard rate of VAT was 14 per cent (OECD ibid. 1990: 120). This latter source shows that, as a proportion of GNP, direct and indirect taxes contributed very similar amounts to general government receipts: 12.5 and 12.3 per cent respectively in 1989. Social security contributions on the other hand amounted to 16.9 per cent of GNP. It is this latter feature of Germany's tax system which pulls her to the middle of the EC's tax league – on other tax ratings she has a lower incidence (MRDB 8/89: 41).

The increasing incidence of direct tax and social insurance contributions on the employed population has been a policy issue for many years (Owen Smith 1983: 82–5). It is becoming increasingly difficult to estimate the direct tax element because the tax on employees' income is only a special type of income tax which overlaps increasingly with assessed income tax (MRDB *ibid.*: 44). A growing number of employed persons are assessed for income tax because their total income exceeds the limits of DM 24,000 for single and DM 48,000 for married persons. These limits date from 1948 and 1973 respectively.

Nevertheless, there has been a conspicuous growth in income tax on employees compared to assessed and corporate income taxes. As a percentage of GNP the former grew from 1.7 per cent in 1950 to 8 per cent in 1989; over the same period the average of the latter taxes amounted to 3.5 per cent (BMA *Statistisches Taschenbuch* 1990: table 1.23). The same source can be used to calculate even more telling statistics (tables 1.13 and 1.15). Expressed as a proportion of average gross income per employee in employment, the average deduction for income tax and social-insurance contributions rose from 12.5 per cent (1950) to 33.9 per cent (1989). Social-insurance contributions, which are examined in depth in Chapter 5, almost doubled during this period, rising on average from 7.9 per cent to 15 per cent as a proportion of average gross income per employee in employment. The fall in average real disposable ('net') wages in the 1980s was mainly the consequence of these trends (*ibid.*). The amendment of the income-tax schedule in

1990 (Figure 3.3 above) caused total statutory deductions from pay to fall for the first time during the period 1950–90 (*ibid.* 1992). This average decrease of −1.4 per cent in 1990 was followed in 1991, however, by an increase of both tax rates and social-insurance contributions. As a result, total statutory deductions rose on average by 13.2 per cent and they again represented a third of average gross income per employee in employment (*ibid.*). Meeting the costs of unification would probably increase this proportion still further.

During the 1970s and 1980s direct taxes on income as a whole rose from 14 to 17 per cent of total income from employment and public service pensions, plus corporate and property origins (MRDB 8/82 and 8/89). The effect of the various tax reforms can be clearly seen in these sources. The 1975 reductions induced a temporary one percentage point decrease but by 1977 the ratio reached a new peak of over 18 per cent. By 1981 it was back down to 17 per cent, while the 1986 and 1988 adjustments brought down another upward trend. Until unification, it was expected that the major reform of 1990 would bring about a resumption of the 16 per cent figure last achieved in the mid-1970s. Quite apart from this two decade exercise of running fast in order to stand still, there was a significant difference between both decades in terms of the relative behaviour of the tax and social insurance ratios. The average ratio of tax to GNP in the 1970s was half a percentage point higher than in the 1980s, when it was 24 per cent. (The average ratio for 1970–5 was much the same as 1965–9 – MRDB 8/76: 16.) However, when social insurance contributions are included, the average for the 1970s is 38 per cent, compared to 39.5 per cent for the 1980s.

THE ALLOCATION OF TAX REVENUE

'Allocation' in this context is an important fiscal issue not just because there are competing demands on the expenditure side, but also from the three levels of government (Federal, Länder and local authorities) in terms of securing a guaranteed share of tax revenue. As seen in both Chapters 1 and 2, the attempts to resolve this latter problem go to the very heart of German fiscal policy. The 'provisional' regulations of 1949, based on the 1922 model, were eventually replaced by a constitutionally guaranteed revenue-sharing model. The Federal government's share in this arrangement has declined, although it remains in gross terms the largest single recipient of tax revenue.

Until 1980, the yield from employees' and assessed income taxes was allocated on the basis of a 43 per cent share each for the Federal and Länder governments, with the remaining 14 per cent going to the local authorities. Following the abolition of the pay-roll element of the trade tax in 1980, the ratios became 42.5:42.5:15, but the Federal and Länder governments each receive a 7 per cent share of the trade tax. Since 1970, the yield from corporation and investment income taxes has been divided equally between the Federal government and the Länder. Although both VAT and the turnover tax on imports are also shared between the Federal and Länder governments, the Federal share gradually declined from 70 per cent in 1970 to 65 per cent in 1986. To assist the Länder in meeting their share of the transfers to the east, the solidarity pact agreement in 1993 specified that their share of VAT receipts should rise (see the budgetary policy section below). Hence, the Federal government's share fell to 58 per cent of total receipts. In addition, the Federal govern-ment re-distributes a given proportion of its share to the financially weaker Länder. Since 1987 this amounts to 2 per cent of its share in turnover tax revenue. The payment to the EC out of this latter tax yield is also deducted from the Federal government's share. The EC also receives a share of customs duties.

Even prior to unification, therefore, the Federal net share in total tax revenue had been falling. In 1970, this share amounted to 53 per cent; by 1989 it had declined to 45.9 per cent. On unification, the financially weaker Länder in the west were faced with the daunting prospect of becoming net contributors to the revenue sharing mechanism and also seeing the eastern Länder receive an equal share in turnover tax revenue. The unity treaty envisaged a phased introduction of turnover tax sharing by the new Länder, from 55 per cent on unification but culminating in an equal share by 1995. The dire financial situation in the east resulted in equal shares being introduced in 1991. Although the western Länder contributed to the German Unity Fund, the question of eastern participation in the revenue sharing arrangement remained unresolved. It was the Federal government which was obliged to take the initiative: in 1991 about 25 per cent of the federal budget of DM 410 billion represented unification costs. This represented expenditure over a broad front, including investment inducements, infrastructure improvements, financial assistance to the eastern Länder and local authorities and employment creation.

As well as the shared tax yields, there are a number of taxes exclusively levied by each level of government. For example, the Federal government (the largest recipient of such revenue) enjoys exclusive rights to the proceeds from the taxes on mineral oils, tobacco, insurance and spirits. Petrol tax was increased 14 times between 1950 and 1991; diesel tax was raised on ten occasions (*Die Zeit* 28/91). A 25 per cent average increase in mineral-oil tax in 1991 was introduced within the framework of the Solidarity Act (*das Solidaritätsgesetz*) to contribute towards the costs of unification (OECD *Economic Survey* 1992: 102n). Note that reference was made to an *average* increase. There are fairly wide differentials between unleaded and leaded petrol, and between petrol and diesel. The Länder, on the other hand, do not have a perfectly uniform tax system, although they all levy taxes on motor vehicles, property and beer; there is also an inheritance tax at this level. It will have already been gathered that the trade tax is by far the most important source of revenue for local authorities: this tax accounts for 7 per cent of total tax revenue. There is also a tax on land and buildings at this level.

It is shared tax revenue, however, which still brings in the lion's share, amounting to 75 per cent of the total tax yield. This is demonstrated in Figure 3.4 where shared taxes on income and expenditure amounted to almost DM 400 billion in 1989 – the last full fiscal year prior to unification. A generally accurate picture of the subsequent position can be gleaned from the figure, but the reader should bear the following factors in mind. In 1989, GNRP rose by 4 per cent, thus increasing tax revenue. In 1990, the major tax reform predictably affected revenue, while in 1991 the unification surcharges also created an abnormal revenue impulse. Finally, GEMSU generated a continuing debate about relative shares in tax revenue and the financing of transfer payments. Part of this debate was reported in Chapter 2. Its culmination was marked by the solidarity pact, to which the analysis returns below. Nonetheless, the relative

magnitude of independently levied taxes can also be gauged from Figure 3.4: the rank order being Federal, local authorities and the Länder. (The 7 per cent share of the trade tax has been added to the shares of both the Federal and Länder governments, but 14 per cent deducted from the local authorities' tax revenue.)

The breakdown of the Federal government's tax revenue can be seen in Figure 3.5. As would be expected from the above emphasis on the increasing importance of personal income tax as a revenue raiser, just over a third of revenue emanates from this source. It is even more important to the Länder (50 per cent) and the local authorities (just over 40 per cent) – see Figures 3.6 and 3.7 respectively. Even though the Federal government received 65 per cent of the revenue on turnover taxes, they did not proportionately produce a very much higher share of total taxes when compared to the Länder. (Recall that both the EC and the Länder are entitled to part of the VAT revenue flow nominally accorded to the Federal level. Also recall that one of the effects of the solidarity pact agreement in 1993 was to reduce the Federal share of VAT receipts to 58 per cent.)

Hence, the taxes increased by the Federal government to assist in financing unification were either the large revenue earners or, with one exception, taxes levied exclusively at the Federal level. As well as the 7.5 per cent surcharges on income and corporation taxes, therefore, mineral oil, tobacco and insurance taxes were raised. These latter three taxes are included in Figure 3.5, although insurance taxation (DM 4.19 billion in 1989) is included in the 'Other' category in this figure, as is the DM 2.65 billion share of the trade tax. Only a relatively small change was made to the taxes exclusively levied by the Länder as a result of the unification

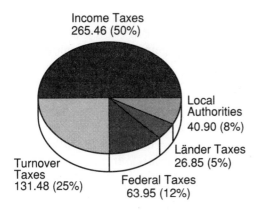

Figure 3.4 Total Tax Revenue 1989
(DM billion)

Source: MRDB Tables VII (5/6)

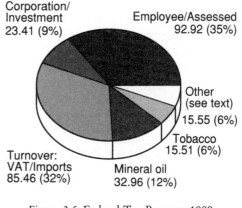

Figure 3.5 Federal Tax Revenue 1989
(DM billion)

Source: Figure 3.4

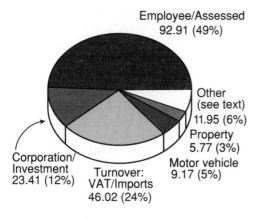

Figure 3.6 Länder Tax Revenue 1989
(DM billion)

Source: Figure 3.4

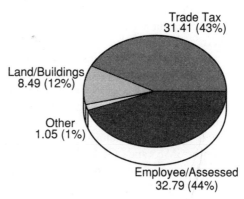

Figure 3.7 Local Authorities' Tax Revenue
1989
(DM billion)

Source: Figure 3.4

tax increases, namely the tax on diesel-powered motor vehicles, but there has in any case been a move away from independent taxation in favour of a jointly-levied tax base. In 1970, the independently levied taxes still accounted for 35 per cent of total tax revenue.

Finally, Figure 3.7 shows the importance of the trade tax to the local authorities: it generates more revenue than the

corporation tax and the same amount as assessed income tax. The latter two generated DM 30 billion and DM 36 billion in 1989, while the gross amount of the trade tax was also DM 36 billion. After allowing for the Federal and Länder share of DM 5.3 billion, it still left over DM 31 billion for the local authorities. It is by far the most important local tax, and as such it represents the backbone of the fiscal autonomy constitutionally guaranteed to the local authorities. On the other hand, it has already been seen that it also represents the largest tax problem for German businesses. Resolving this dilemma – it should be re-emphasised – is probably the biggest problem confronting the German policy makers.

BUDGETARY POLICY

The general government budgetary position reveals very little about the disaggregated levels of the four critical variables in public finance, namely revenue, expenditure, borrowing and debt. Indeed, it has already been seen in Chapter 2 that a principal budgetary problem is co-ordinating the fiscal policy of the three levels of government. Similarly, it will be seen in Chapter 5 that the social-insurance funds, including the finances of the Federal Labour Office (BA), are also part of the general budgetary arrangements. The importance of these latter items can be gauged from the inclusion of 'social' in both SME and GEMSU. National accounts include the revenue and expenditure of the three levels of government and the social-insurance funds. Even this general-government budget, which will shortly be analysed in depth, yielded an estimated average deficit balance between revenue and expenditure of DM 100 billion in the early 1990s (Heilemann 1991b: 300). Yet in 1989 it had produced a surplus of DM 4 billion. This deterioration took place in spite of even higher tax revenue in 1991 and 1992 than anticipated (Dresdner Bank *Trends* December 1991). In addition, however, several shadow budgets are included in the public-sector accounts. Some of them were analysed in Chapter 2 where it was seen that two of these funds emanate from the post-war refugee Equalisation of

Burdens programme (*Lastenausgleich* – LAG) and the ERP. They had become relatively insignificant prior to unification (MRDB 8/92: 24–6). Two completely new special funds were respectively set up under the GEMSU and unification treaties. The first was the German Unity Fund (Table 2.2) and the second was the Debt Management Fund (*Kreditabwicklungsfonds* – see below). It was also seen in Chapter 2 that the Upswing East project was adopted in March 1991.

Hence, the general public-sector accounts are quite complex, even when one omits public enterprises. But such enterprises account for a significant amount of total public-sector debt. Using the term 'public enterprise' in its widest sense, therefore, one is bound first of all to refer to the Treuhandanstalt – an eastern privatisation agency established prior to GEMSU (see Chapter 8). Its deficits were expected to reach DM 55 billion before it had fully discharged its functions (BMF *Beteiligungen* . . . 1990: 8). By September 1992, in fact, the Treuhand's debt had reached DM 73 billion (MRDB 3/93: table VIII(10)). Its borrowing powers were extended as part of the solidarity pact in 1993. The financial needs of its enterprises, which will outlast the Treuhand's planned existence, could reach an estimated DM 400 billion by the year 2000, net of asset sales (Flockton and Esser 1992). Because the Federal government was its guarantor, however, the Treuhand possessed a triple-A credit rating. In 1991, its financial deficit, that is the difference between its revenue and expenditure, was DM 20 billion; between 1992 and 1994 this deficit was expected to rise to DM 30 billion annually, all of which would have to be borrowed (FT 12 November 1992). As a result, the three levels of government, the shadow budgets and the Treuhand had a collective borrowing requirement provisionally estimated at DM 150 billion in 1992 – 5 per cent of GDP; in 1989, the borrowing requirement was DM 27 billion (BfG *Standpunkt* 1/93).

Moreover, the railways in both the west and the east, along with the Federal post office, were also all in deficit. These financial problems, along with constitutional constraints, prevented the expeditious privatisation of the railways and post office (see Chapter 8). By adding the shadow-budget and public-enterprise deficits to the general-government deficit, Heilemann (1991b: 300) estimated a total public-sector deficit for 1991 of DM 150 billion, or 6 per cent of GNP; he suggested that the magnitudes of the deficits were reaching the tolerable limits for a democratic society. (The post-GEMSU growth in the components of this total deficit are also illustrated in Figure 7.4c). This public-sector deficit corresponds to the amount which must be borrowed by government, its agencies and its enterprises. Since reference is here being made to the public sector as a whole, it is convenient to conceptualise this exigency as the German public sector borrowing requirement (PSBR). Such a flow of new debt, when added to the stock of accumulated debt, indicates the level of national debt, which must be serviced by reimbursing and paying interest to lenders. The PSBR is therefore a critical indicator of unification costs. Consider in particular the following comparison. German public-sector borrowing in 1992, expressed as a percentage of GDP, may well have exceeded the borrowing requirement in the USA and Japan (*Economist* 20 March 1993). Yet the USA was still inflicted with the legacy of Reaganomic profligate deficit spending.

Summarising the argument thus far, it can be said that the deficits of the Federal and Länder governments, along with the local authorities, represent the tip of the iceberg. The borrowing requirement of these three levels of government was provisionally estimated at DM 71 billion in 1992 (MRDB 5/93: 44–5). By 1993, the recession in the west, and industrial collapse in the east, were reducing tax revenue but increasing unemployment benefits. The Federal government was forced continually to revise its budget deficit estimates. In addition, the other deficit items noted above – the shadow budgets, the Treuhand, the railways, the post office – meant an additional borrowing requirement of DM 118 billion, a sum which also included the borrowing by the Federal government's special-purpose banks (*ibid.*; and see Chapters 2 and 7 for a review of the special-purpose banks). In 1993, the annual German PSBR was expected to reach DM 231 billion, or over 8 per cent of GDP (FT 26 May 1993). It can also be shown that the West German PSBR historically caused policy strains. Budgetary policy therefore requires closer examination.

Initially, the trends in the general-government budgets will be traced. It has already been indicated that the general-government budget in this context consists of the accounts of the Federal and Länder governments, local authorities and social-insurance funds. Figures 3.8a, 3.8b and 3.8c contain detail on the trends in these budgets. It will be noted from the source that the data for the diagrams were obtained from national accounts. This basis was preferred because they are compared to GNP itself in Figure 3.8c. Financial statistics (or flow of funds analysis) show larger absolute magnitudes but the same trends (also see MRDB table VIII [1]). When the shadow budgets are added to the three levels of government, however, the emphasis is on financial statistics because the problem is one of financing the deficit. The same is true when public enterprises are included.

In Figure 3.8a, it can be seen that the federal budget balance – that is federal revenue minus federal expenditure – nearly always makes a significant contribution to the general budgetary balance. There have been three distinct phases in the post-war period. Surpluses in both balances in the 1950s gave way to more mixed experience in the 1960s and the very early 1970s; from 1972, with the exception of 1973, there was a continuous series of Federal deficits. The general budget balance also slipped seriously into the red after 1973, with the exception of 1989. Of particular note is the behaviour of deficits and surpluses between 1967 and 1970. It will shortly be shown that this was the heyday of Keynesian economics: reflation by deficit spending during a recession and deflation by running surpluses during the subsequent recovery.

Now compare Figures 3.8a and 3.8b, noting the shorter time period covered in 3.8b. Take first of all the Keynesian heyday of 1967–70. All three of the individual balances under consideration were in deficit in 1967 and 1968. In 1969 and 1970 it can be seen that the Federal-government and social-insurance balances were in surplus, whereas the Länder and local authorities were still running deficits. It can be concluded that it was the Federal government which made the most constructive contribution to the Keynesian reduction in government spending when the economy had recovered in 1969–70. Note also that the social-insurance balance was positive in 22 out of the 30 years included in Figure 3.8b. These surpluses made particularly substantial contributions to the general balance in 1989 and 1990. Yet the policy makers' consternation about the perceived future course of the social-insurance funds will be a recurring theme

in Chapter 5. It will be seen that this trepidation preceded unification, although this event was clearly associated with still further significant social-policy problems. Prior to the recession which began in 1992, the strong expansion of employment was expected to go on contributing to a social-insurance surplus until 1994 (Fritzsche *et al.* 1991: 22). Thereafter, demographic trends would undermine the historically sound financial basis of this budgetary item (Chapters 5 and 6 above).

Figure 3.8c, like Figure 3.8a, contains only the general and federal balances. It is therefore possible to cover the period 1950–90 again. Above all, Figure 3.8c gives a good relative picture in that the budget balances are expressed as a ratio to GNP. In this sense, the surpluses of the 1950s are somewhat larger than the deficits from the mid-1970s, with the oscillations of the 1960s and early 1970s still apparent. Note how the budgetary position was improving in 1989 just prior to unification – tax revenue rose markedly as a result of high economic growth and reference has also been made to the strong finances of the social insurance funds. Apart from 1989, however, there was not a substantial improvement in the Federal position after 1982. Yet this was another watershed year – as will shortly be shown. Supply-side economics was espoused by the incoming Christian-liberal coalition at Federal level. This economic philosophy requires a minimum amount of government intervention in economic affairs, with economic agents being left to order their affairs in free markets.

A number of further inferences can be drawn from Figure 3.9 which is again based on a ratio, this time public debt and its principal components as a percentage of GNP. The experience of the three levels of government analysed thus far are plotted in these new terms. But an important point has to be made about the data included in the general stock of debt. They include not only the three levels of government, but also the ERP and LAG Funds mentioned in the first paragraph of this section. The German Unity and Debt Management funds – also mentioned in the first paragraph of this section – are included in the general debt data for 1990 and 1991 (MRDB 3/93: table VIII(9)). In 1991, the debt of the eastern Länder and local authorities was added for the first time. Hence, the definition of general accumulated debt was extended so as to include the government and shadow budgetary debt incurred as a result of unification. At the end of the first six months of 1992 – not plotted in Figure 3.9 – total general debt in absolute terms was estimated at DM 1.2 trillion (= 1.2×10^{12}) (*ibid.*). But recall that the social-insurance funds, and more particularly government agencies and enterprises, all had separate accounts (*ibid.*: table VIII). Since unification, accumulated debt had already risen 30 per cent (iwd2 11/92). (The total social budget, also including the new Länder, reached DM 1 trillion in 1992 – see Figure 5.2b.)

It is plain from Figure 3.9, however, that the ratio of the stock of general accumulated debt to GNP climbed steeply after 1975: from 25 per cent to 42 per cent at the end of 1990. The steepest rises were incurred during the recessions following the two crude oil price shocks (the mid-1970s and early 1980s). It is particularly important to note, however, that the absolute level of accumulated debt rose annually during the period 1950–91. Where the debt/GNP ratios display a fall in Figure 3.9, it is mainly due to a relatively strong growth in GNP, although debt has generally grown fastest during recessions. Note also that in 1991 the GNP of the new Länder has also been included. The debt/GNP ratio thus declined to 42 per cent. It will be shown in Table 3.1 below that the ratio for West Germany had already reached 41.1 per cent in 1989. By 1992, the debt/GNP ratio in the west reached 45.6 per cent because the numerator for the west included most of the debt, but the denominator did not include the east's GNP; if the east's GNP was added to the denominator, however, the debt/GNP ratio fell to 42 per cent (also see Table 3.1). Once again, it can be adduced from Figure 3.9 that the Federal government played a dominant role in a rising trend: in 1991 it was responsible for half the total debt. The Länder also became sizeable contributors. Indeed, the Länder's behaviour is particularly notable because of the decline and subsequent stability of their debt/GNP pattern during the 1950s, 1960s and early 1970s respectively. The local authorities show the opposite trend: a gradual rise and then a tapering off in their debt/GNP ratio. It was the threat of a 50 to 55 per cent ratio of general accumulated debt to GNP by the mid-1990s (as a result of unification) which forced the Federal government to increase several taxes during and after 1991. As already implied, the precise ratio would clearly depend on the factors which affect the denominator and the numerator. Among other things, these factors respectively consist of economic growth and the extent to which the increase in government expenditure could be contained (Fritzsche *et al.* 1991: 22).

The critical budgetary problem is thus the extent of the gap between revenue and expenditure. It will be shown below that the surpluses of the 1950s contributed, along with an undervalued exchange rate, to the international speculation which plagued German monetary policy from 1960. On the other hand, deficit financing became a problem from 1975. The

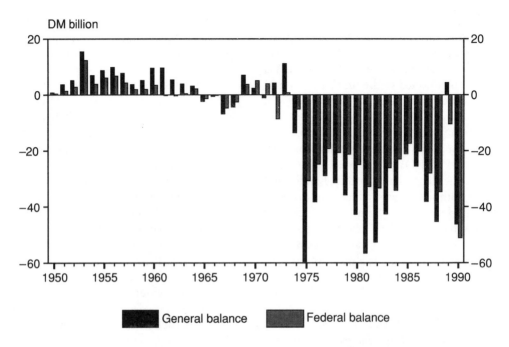

Figure 3.8a General and Federal Government Budgets
Source: OECD National Accounts (Vol. II)

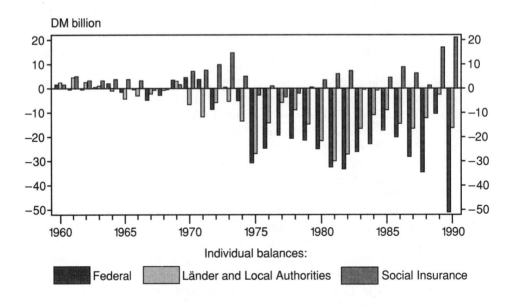

Figure 3.8b General Government Budgets' Components
Source: Plotted from OECD National Accounts (Vol. II)

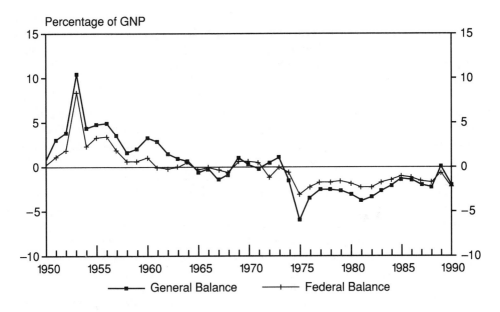

Figure 3.8c Budget Balances as a percentage of GNP

Source: Plotted from OECD National Accounts (Vol. II)

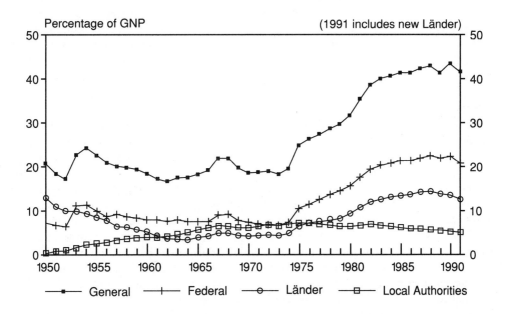

Figure 3.9 Public Debt as a percentage of GNP

Source: Plotted from Dresdner Bank, *Statistische Reihen*

consequent borrowing requirement by the three levels of government was always a matter of keen policy interest, with particular emphasis on the contribution of the Federal government to any indebtedness. The minority FDP coalition partners in various post-war governments at Federal level have been particularly vigilant in this respect. For example, they brought down the Erhard government in 1966 when it was discovered that the federal borrowing requirement in 1967 was likely to exceed DM 4 billion – a post-war record at the time. Similarly, although the FDP saw the assumption of the Economics portfolio in 1974 as a means of controlling SPD 'excesses', they deserted the Schmidt regime in 1982 when a decade of deficits culminated in another post war record at the federal level of DM 33 billion (Hellwig and Neumann 1987: 112–13; Riemer 1983: 9). Even this sum paled into insignificance when predictions for the first united-German budget in 1991 anticipated a federal deficit of DM 66 billion, with a possible PSBR of DM 200 billion or 7 per cent of GNP. Again, the FDP objected strongly with threats of resignation.

There are a number of budgetary options if spending demands unexpectedly increase. (The rise in unemployment in the 1970s and 1980s, or unification are good examples of such unexpected increases.) These options are not mutually exclusive, so they may therefore be pursued concurrently.

First, the government can increase its long- and short-term borrowing, although the bitter experience of German governments' unsophisticated forays into this field in the past – see Chapter 1 – have resulted in such policies incurring constitutional constraints and electoral unpopularity. The next option is to increase taxation. It has already been seen above that this was done as a means of partially financing unification. However, successive West German governments have tried to reduce the direct tax burden, again as seen above. Then there is reducing or switching expenditure. Subsidy reductions in the west, for example, were advocated, under the threat of resignation, by the FDP Federal Minister of Economics (Möllemann) at the time of unification. (His eventual resignation in early 1993 was precipitated by a matter unrelated to subsidies.) Very little inroad was made. Hence, the seemingly intractable problem of subsidies is analysed in Chapter 8 where the topic is related to privatisation and deregulation. This is because yet another policy option is selling off government assets by privatisation in order to raise revenue. Finally, where a particular policy cannot be achieved by purely budgetary means, a government may give tax incentives or introduce regulatory frameworks. These closely allied policy options are thus vitally significant areas when studying German economic affairs. As Stolper and Roskamp (1979: 384 and 387) point out both Germans and their critics have, for reasons which are not entirely clear, played down the importance of fiscal measures and other direct intervention by the state; they add that the price mechanism was skilfully modified in this sense in order to influence market decisions. A good perspective of German budgetary policy can therefore be gained by examining post-war experience by using this rather wider definition.

There were three eras of budgetary policy, although each of them were linked by transitional phases. First, during the 1950s, the 'housekeeping' era under Fritz Schäffer (the Federal Finance Minister) was typified by a determination to balance revenue and expenditure. Fortuitously, budget surpluses were achieved but the Federal Minister of Economics (Ludwig

Erhard) judiciously utilised subsidies and tax concessions to stimulate recovery and remove bottlenecks. Second, there was a gradual movement to Keynesian aggregate demand policy during the 1960s, culminating in Karl Schiller's 'magic square' approach in 1967. As the 1970s evolved, the failure to clamp down on public spending once growth had recommenced, along with a growing international perception that West Germany – and Japan – should act as locomotives to pull the world out of recession, caused increasing disillusionment with demand management. Third, improving the productivity of the supply side of the economy, accompanied by a withdrawal of government, became the policy ethos. This process was espoused by the Kohl government from 1982. Initially, the Federal finance ministry was headed by Gerhard Stoltenberg who was later replaced by Theo Waigel.

An essential starting point is the Erhard liberalisation of markets which accompanied the Allies currency reform in 1948. While radical, the Erhard package was far from a complete liberalisation (Hansson 1990: 28; Wallich 1955: 16). Wide sections of the economy such as housing, farming, transport and coal were not regulated by market forces alone; capital formation was not integrated into the market economy at all (Abelshauser 1982: 49). Shonfield (1965: 274–5) lucidly describes the schizophrenic approach to economic policy which characterised the early years of the Bonn Republic:

While the Ministry of Finance was busy keeping house, and conscientiously disregarding the effect this exercise might have on the rest of the economy, the Ministry of Economics was most actively intervening wherever opportunities for more production, aided by strategically placed subsidies or tax concessions, presented themselves.

More will be said about the Finance Ministry in a moment. Of immediate relevance here is the fact that the tax concessions directed at stimulating capital formation forced saving by encouraging the ploughing back of profits (Mendershausen 1974: 75–6; Stolper and Roskamp 1979: 388; Wallich 1955: 161–2). In order to remove bottlenecks by financing investment in vital industries (mainly coal, steel and electricity), the Investment Aid Act, 1952 placed a levy on the rest of industry. As already seen in Chapter 1, Marshall Aid counterpart funds were also used to remove medium- and long-term economic bottlenecks. Moreover, government funds financed over half of Germany's current investment programme in 1949, even though deficit financing was prohibited both constitutionally and by the Allies (Heller 1950: 538 and 542–3). In short, Erhard's role in economic recovery – not least his pragmatic approach to industrial and competition policy – was a far cry from the neo-liberal philosophy frequently attributed to his administration (Berghahn 1986: 151 and 158).

To illuminate further the back drop to this period of budgetary policy, it is necessary to remove another common misunderstanding. Bomb damage to industry – as opposed to transport and housing – was relatively negligible. Germany's productive capacity was certainly in disarray, but her post-war industrial potential was roughly equivalent to that which had existed in 1938. Wartime destruction had simply cancelled out the additions to capacity (Dyas and Thanheiser 1976: 43). Indeed, reconstruction with technically more advanced capital equipment meant that Germany had a more superior capital stock after the war than before hostilities had commenced (Abelshauser 1982: 35; Vogl 1973: 4). Generally speaking, bomber raids obliterated housing and commercial premises in city centres but left industrial capacity on the outskirts intact (Manchester 1969: 522 and 525; Mellor 1978: 142). Destruction of plant was only 10 per cent for metallurgy; 10–15 per cent chemicals; 15–20 per cent engineering and 20 per cent textiles (Grosser 1974: 91). In this sense alone Germany did not start from zero in 1948; further, good luck and economic policy had prepared the German economy to take advantage of the impetus provided by the Korean boom. Between 1951 and 1958 economic expansion was sparked off by the demand for exports and domestic investment (Stolper and Roskamp 1979: 380, 393 and 397). When Marshall Aid came to an end in 1952, West Germany had begun to produce export surpluses (Knapp 1981: 424). These real-economy factors have to be added to what has been said about government intervention in the previous paragraph. Some of them meant that an industrial recovery began even before the currency reform. It was further stimulated by government intervention thereafter.

Consequently, the Finance Minister could indulge in what has already been described as 'housekeeping'. Schäffer ran the federal budget with a surplus until he left the ministry in 1957 – a year prior to the major tax reform analysed around Figure 3.1 above. Although only part of the general-government budgetary picture, these surpluses were deposited at the Bundesbank and became known as the 'Julius Tower' – a historical reference to the fortress in Spandau where Prussian kings had stored their war treasures. The term had somewhat pejorative overtones, given the high tax rates at the time (see Figure 3.1 above). The surpluses themselves were partly the result of an under-estimate of revenue, but mainly came about as a result of an overestimate of future defence commitments. They represented a source of forced savings – in addition to the ploughed back profits referred to immediately above. Hence, they unintentionally skimmed off internal demand, and probably served as an additional incentive to West German industrialists to seek further overseas markets after the Korean boom; they probably also helped to damp down the boom of 1955–6 illustrated in Figure 1.1 (Denton et al. 1968: 226). In addition, the budget surpluses eliminated the inflationary potential caused by the trade surpluses arising from export earnings. Schäffer's financial orthodoxy must mean that these anti-cyclical features of his budgetary policy were accidental: he simply regarded his policies as consistent with Article 110(1) of the basic law (GG) which required him to balance the budget. He did not wish to be a party to any repetition of the disastrous polices which produced the economic collapses described in Chapter 1 (Hartrich 1980: 165). However, as will be seen in Chapter 4, his very success in stabilising West German prices aggravated the balance of payments problem of subsequent years (Stolper and Roskamp 1979: 399).

What Schäffer saw as the pillaging of his Tower began even before he left for the Justice Ministry in 1957. Significantly, agricultural subsidies were increased by the 'Green Plan' and there were marked improvements in pensions (Denton et al. 1968: 226; Shonfield 1965: 285). But it was in 1960 that the next phase in budgetary policy really began. There are two basic features which need to be stressed. First, there was a new determination to use fiscal policy alongside monetary policy for anti-cyclical purposes. Second, expenditure by all three levels of government increased more rapidly than revenue, thus creating budgetary deficits and endangering price stability after 1963. Erhard's seeming inability to prevent public expenditure and public income from moving apart brought down his government in 1966, although his government had initiated detailed financial planning in 1964 (Korff 1983: 60). Moreover, it was at this juncture the phrase 'deficit spending' was used for the first time (Knott 1981: 19).

The 'Grand Coalition' of Christian and social democrats which replaced the Erhard administration set about pruning public expenditure and raising revenue. These efforts to balance the budget ironically coincided with the first postwar recession of 1967. Such a situation demanded a U-turn. Public investment was therefore increased and special depreciation allowances were introduced. A reform of budgetary policy which would give policy makers more flexibility was required – a process which had begun under Erhard (Denton et al. 1968: 228).

Hence, the final break with what might be termed fiscal orthodoxy came in 1967. It was replaced by Keynesian demand management in the sense that fiscal policy was formally assigned a role for the purposes of stabilisation and counter-cyclical intervention. An Act to Promote Economic Stability and Growth (StWG) reached the statute book in that year. The original Erhard plans were transformed into the more ambitious mode of the new Federal Economics Minister Schiller. A 'magic square' of macroeconomic policy goals replaced the former 'magic triangle' – economic growth being added to high employment, price stability and balance of payments equilibrium (Bendix 1978: 58–9; Spahn 1978: 61). This Act provided the government with a wide range of instruments with which to counter cyclical movements. More especially, it linked the budgetary arrangements of the three levels of government more closely together – thus potentially creating, it was thought, a greater degree of coherence in the formulation of the Federal budget (Denton et al. 1968: 229).

The magnitude of the changes stimulated by the StWG can be gauged from the number of subsequent changes made to Section X (Articles 104a–115) of the GG which is the Section concerned with fiscal policy. For example, as it proposed to change the budgetary relationship between the Federal government and the Länder, the StWG required an amendment to Article 109. An authorisation was inserted into this Article for the Federal and Länder governments to maintain an anti-cyclical reserve fund at the Bundesbank, a fund which was to be changed in size in the opposite direction of changes in the level of economic activity. Finally, the Article was also amended in 1969 by the Budgetary Principles Act (HGrG) which required these two levels of government to cooperate in fiscal policy implementation and planning. The federal authorities can only proceed with any Article 109 measure after receiving the consent of both houses of the Federal parliament, thereby ensuring that the representatives of the Länder in the federal upper house are involved. Both houses must also approve another StWG measure, namely the variation in either direction of income and corporation taxes by up to 10 per cent, as well as the introduction of investment premia, all as counter-cyclical measures. In order to accommodate the changes in budgetary policy required by the HGrG, the Federal government changed its budgetary regulations in 1969 by the Federal Budget Act (BHO); the Länder followed suit over the following few years. Such a battery of measures meant (EC 1990a: 44):

- pursuing a budgetary policy consistent with macroeconomic equilibrium
- planning revenues and expenditures in the medium term, also bearing macroeconomic needs in mind
- implementing a comparable and homogeneous system of budgetary procedures
- guaranteeing the co-ordination and compatibility of measures implemented at the three levels of government (with the Länder maintaining the right to coordinate the role of local authorities in their respective areas)

Another constitutional amendment to Article 115 was introduced as a result of the StWG and HGrG. This provided all levels of government, subject to federal legislative authorisation, with a legal basis for deficit spending. The general rule is that borrowing to finance a deficit in any one year must not exceed investment expenditure provided for in the budget, unless it is necessary to avert a macroeconomic imbalance. Subsequently, 'investment expenditure' has been defined as the sum of government gross fixed capital formation (national accounts definition), investment-related subsidies to public enterprises and subsidies which aim at fostering investment in the private sector. In 1989, following a fairly heated political debate during the intervening two decades, the Federal Constitutional Court (BVG) published some general rules designed to clarify the federal borrowing requirement in the context of the term 'macroeconomic imbalance' (EC 1990a: 43):

- the PSBR is only allowed to exceed investment expenditure if there is (the risk of) a severe macroeconomic disequilibrium

- exceeding borrowing requirements must be justified by the need to reduce the (risk of severe) macroeconomic imbalances
- the limit of Article 115 is a maximum limit and a simultaneous application of Article 109 (public bodies have to make allowance for the needs of macroeconomic equilibrium) might require smaller budget deficits in periods of favourable economic performance or a risk of overheating

As well as these far reaching constitutional changes, the StWG established a Business Cycle Council while the HGrG established a Finance Planning Council. The latter is composed of the federal and Länder finance ministers, the federal Economics Minister, representatives of the local authorities and, frequently, representatives of the Bundesbank. It is chaired by the federal Finance Minister. Its terms of reference require it to meet at specified intervals throughout the year in order to make annual and five-yearly joint budgetary plans. The Business Cycle Council consists of the Economics ministers from the Federal government and Länder, plus again local authority and Bundesbank representatives. It is more concerned with the short-term economic impact of fiscal policy, but because the finance ministers dominate budgetary policy it has been somewhat over shadowed by the Finance Planning Council; the concern over federal finance subsequent to the Act has also meant that the Federal government preferred to take a longer view. There was also a Concerted Action Council set up under the StWG. It was composed of government, employers and trade unions but, for reasons to be explored in Chapter 6, it broke down in 1976.

There are some other institutions which

issue pronouncements on economic trends and policies. The most important is arguably the Council of Economic Advisers (SVR), set up by statute a few weeks before Erhard became chancellor in 1963. Schiller had more in common with the SVR than Erhard and he joined them in quantifying the four policy goals of the StWG – goals which also appeared in the act which established the SVR (Wallich 1968). The SVR prepares an annual report and other analyses of economic activity, all of which contribute to the general debate about economic policy (Knott 1981: 19). A similar function is carried out both collectively and individually by the five independent economic research institutes (DIW, HWWA, Ifo, IfW and RWI – plus their joint working party). In 1992, an east German institute was established in Halle, although it did not initially contribute to the joint reports of the other five institutes. Members of the SVR and the research institutes also serve on the councils of academic advisers (wissenschafliche Beiräte) in the various Federal ministries, the most important of which are the councils which advise the Ministers of Economics and Finance. The national employers' and trade union bodies also possess their own economic research institutes (IW and WSI respectively). An important non-market orientated group of academics (*Memorandumgruppe*), which attempts in particular to influence trade union policy, publishes a rival report to the SVRs. A valuable source of labour market analyses is the Federal Labour Office's research institute (IAB). Hence, official projections must compete with the wealth of information generated by these multifarious bodies. As can be imagined, a continual debate on economic policy is conducted by all these actors and agencies. The 1992/3 SVR report was, for example, thought in some quarters to constitute a

good case for independent economic advice (FT 17 November 1992). On the other hand, the amount of economic advice, unaccompanied by action on the part of the policy makers, was subjected to some criticism (SZ 17/18 November 1992).

How did these manifest changes work out in practice? The first thing to note is that the share of general government current revenue in national income rose considerably in the 1960s and early 1970s (from 35.1 per cent in 1960 to 42.3 per cent in 1973 – OECD *Economic Survey* 1985: 27); the revenue share then rose more slowly to 1980 (44.5), stabilising thereafter (44.7 in 1989 – *ibid*. 1990: 120). Second, the deficit spending during the 1967 recession was handled in a text book manner, with surpluses re-emerging in 1969–70; thereafter, deficits and public debt rose during the 1970s and early 1980s to levels unprecedented in post-war West Germany as policy makers struggled to deal with an unfavourable external environment (Lipschitz and McDonald 1990: 167). Excluding the Bundesbank transfers which – as will be shown later – is the relevant concept when trying to assess the stance and economic impact of budgetary policy, the budget balance remained practically unchanged until 1988 when the debt/GDP ratio reached record heights (EC 1990a: 17). Expenditure was therefore outstripping revenue. In short, unification did not present an entirely new budgetary scenario, but before passing on to unification, the Schmidt and early Kohl eras must be examined. It was during these two regimes that the tax, expenditure and debt problems exacerbated by unification came to the fore.

To stimulate the lagging economy, the Federal government passed four special budget programmes during 1974 to 1975. At a micro level, for that matter, the government stimulus in 1967 applied to the coal industry was analogous to that given in 1974–6 to the construction industry and the inner-German border areas, particularly Volkswagen (Knott 1981: 18). But by 1976, due to opposition from many sides, it had retreated from using the budget for stabilisation policy. It cut investment grants to the Länder, passed no additional stimulus programmes (despite continued high unemployment), and turned instead to tax and (the Bundesbank's) monetary instruments (*ibid.*: 15). The change in the SVRs fiscal impulse – as measured by their definition of the difference between the actual and a 'neutral' budget – was negative in both 1976 and 1977 (Franz 1990: 19). This cautious policy generated a heated debate; Knott (*ibid.*) sees it as leading to the strict monetary policy to defend the DM despite a current account deficit in 1979. Franz (*ibid.*: 20) sees both oil price shocks as being accompanied by restrictive monetary policy as a response to a previous overly expansive policy. (See Figures 1.1, 1.2 and 1.3 for an indication of these trends.) Giersch *et al.* (1992: 154) summarise the post-housekeeping era of budgetary policy in the following manner:

If we look back over the whole drama of macroeconomic policy in the period 1960–73, an element of tragedy can hardly be dismissed: an impressive apparatus of policy counselling had been established and, at least in the eyes of the public, the door to a new era of demand management had been opened when the sharp and frightful recession of 1966/67 was overcome, seemingly through the magic tools of fiscal and monetary policy. Just as this optimistic belief in the power of government as a macroeconomic manager reached its peak, an irresistible wave of inflation flooded through the channels of the Bretton Woods system. Soon it

became clear that under pegged exchange rates a relatively open economy like that of West Germany could not remain an island of stability, and the hopes pinned on the macroeconomic power of government were badly disappointed.

This excellent summary has much to commend it, even though a few factors which resulted in an overvalued DM exchange rate seem to have been overlooked. For example, the very success of the housekeeping era in building up budget surpluses ironically contributed, along with retained profits, to the forced savings which led to exporters seeking larger markets. The consequent export surpluses in turn contributed to international instability as speculators anticipated a revaluation of the DM's nominal exchange rate. Moreover, the real exchange rate of the DM was arguably undervalued as an immediate consequence of the 1949 devaluation (see the trade sections of Chapter 8). Equally, the West German policy of counteracting the appreciation of the DM, in the search for continuing export-led growth, meant that the DM was undervalued over the bulk of the post-war period (Peacock *et al.* 1980: para 3.8). In short, it will be seen in Chapter 4 that speculation in favour of the DM was inevitable. It built up a remarkable head of steam in the period cited in the above quotation (1960–73). Another issue would be to query whether 'Keynesianism' was confined to the shorter period 1967–73. The tax changes in 1975 were designed to be reflationary and those in 1979 were introduced as a result of the Bonn G5 summit in 1978. The latter were seen by the Federal government as 'measures to stimulate demand and improve economic growth'. Further, both of these Schmidt tax reforms are seen by Lipschitz and McDonald (1990: 167) as 'prime examples of Keynesian policies'. The critical point here is that the 'locomotive theory' led West Germany into introducing expansionary fiscal policies in order to bring about an international economic recovery – just prior to the second oil price shock.

But this version of Keynesian economics was fundamentally flawed. Keynes put forward a short-run model which was designed to reflate aggregate demand in a depressed *national* economy. Locomotive theorists applied this notion to the industrial market economies as a whole. Differing budget deficits, saving propensities, rates of technological change and, affecting all these factors, defence-spending commitments rendered the Keynesian model inapplicable. These factors were responsible for the large West German and Japanese export surpluses. In any case, the now influential monetarist opponents of the locomotive strategy differed from this (misconceived version of) Keynesianism in both diagnosis and policy prescription (Giersch *et al.* 1992: 241). Both oil shocks also caused domestic inflationary pressure to rise. West Germany herself entered an extremely difficult phase in her post-war economic development. At the end of the 1970s a whole series of policy issues thus came to the fore: foreign competition, inflation, unemployment and both budgetary and current account deficits.

As a result, the Schmidt government found itself confronted by a policy dilemma. Reflation increased inflationary pressure while deflation increased unemployment. Improving the supply side of the economy became the vogue policy approach. This brought Kohl to power in 1982. Kohl's U-turn (*die Wende*) was based on the notion that budgetary policy required consolidation. A priority would be the reduction of the deficit and expenditure; there would also be a privatisation programme. Tax changes would follow: the progressive nature of personal taxation, the tax burden and special exemptions would be targeted. As shown above (Figure 3.3 and the section on the incidence of taxation) there was nothing really new in these tax goals. Indeed, the out-going Schmidt government had introduced major reforms in 1974 and 1979; as a post-war government it also needed little convincing that budgetary deficits generated apprehension throughout the economy. Indeed, Schmidt's search for budgetary consolidation began in 1980; it was his FDP Economics minister (Lambsdorff) who caused the coalition to be dissolved in 1982 with his 'blueprint' (Hellwig and Neumann 1987: 112–13):

[This document] called for a clear turn-round, asking in particular for a more determined policy in such matters as fiscal consolidation, industrial deregulation, and the degeneration of the 'social net' of the welfare state into a 'social hammock'.

Because of the gradual shift in emphasis, however, it is not possible to be absolutely precise about the paradigm shift by West German policy makers and advisers from a policy emphasising the role of aggregate demand to a supply-side orientated approach. Indeed, Helmstädter (1988: 415) argues that 'the continuity of thought on German economic policy can be demonstrated . . . (by) the SVRs 1986–87 Report'. Hence, fiscal policy's role in the offensive strategy against unemployment consists essentially of the removal of distortions in economic incentives – in other words removing the heavy tax burden, high marginal rates of taxation and subsidies. Monetary policy's task, on the other hand, is to protect the value of money by expanding the money supply in line with the growth in productive capacity at approximately stable prices. As the above quotation from Giersch *et al.* (1992: 154) made clear, however, aggregate demand and fiscal policy were perceived as having a far more important role during the period 1960–73. In fact, the SVR was unable to see the gradual shift in its own views on what governments could achieve in this respect; moreover, Giersch himself was convinced that arriving at some ground rules to make wage bargaining consistent with stabilisation was a protracted process (Riemer 1983: 165 and 171). Significantly, Helmstädter (*ibid*.: 413) also quotes from the SVR's 1976–7 Report in which the Council insisted that demand management should be supplemented by a 'supply-oriented policy'. This was shortly after the failure of Concerted Action – an attempt at incomes policy more fully reviewed in Chapter 6. Suffice it to say here that its failure marked for many the end of Keynesian 'full employment' aspirations. However, this emphasis on incomes policy revealed an attempt by the SVR and Federal government to resolve the macroeconomic distributive problem by simultaneously achieving high levels of employment and low rates of inflation. It was therefore a fundamentally different approach from the sole emphasis on price stability by the Bundesbank.

Admittedly, it would be extremely easy to exaggerate the extent to which policy makers and their advisers espoused either Keynesianism or the Friedmanite monetarist counterrevolution (Riemer 1983: 80). An effort was made to integrate the SME into the Keynesian framework, and this was coupled with a preference for private rather than public expenditure (*ibid*.: 269 and 280). There was a profound debate about whether the Freiburg SME model and Keynesianism could be reconciled. The chosen target monetary aggregate, an attention to the short-term

countercyclical requirements of the economy and a continued emphasis on the behaviour of the wage bargainers all indicated no fundamental change in monetary policy (*ibid*.: 234–8). It will also be seen immediately below and in Chapter 8 that the degree of government involvement in economic affairs did not fundamentally change in the supply-side era. The truth is that the West German brand of Keynesianism was not suddenly superseded by Friedmanism in the early 1970s, nor was there whole-hearted support for the supply-side revolution in the 1980s. This lack of a clear-cut macroeconomic approach exacerbated the problems generated by unification. Moreover, new policy problems emerged in both the 1970s and 1980s because the system of managed exchange rates generated at least as many problems as the Bretton Woods system of the 1950s and 1960s. As in other market economies, the need to resolve the 'distributive struggle' between the wage bargainers remained a prime policy problem.

If there was a clear paradigm shift, it was in the advice given by the SVR. Much to the chagrin of the Erhard government, the Council initially supported Schiller's search for a synthesis between the SME and Keynesian aggregate demand management. In the 1960s, the Bundesbank was identified by the Council as an institution which demanded monetary and fiscal orthodoxy but disregarded the costs of forgone growth (*ibid*.: 148). There was to be a combination of fiscal, incomes and exchange-rate policies which would offer an innovative expansion of the state's economic steering capacity (*ibid*.: 99). It was the unexpected phenomenon of stagflation, preceded by a profits explosion and then a profits squeeze, which caused this new policy framework to be called into question. Hence, by the time the 1975 recession had made the 1966–7 affair appear comparatively trivial, the SVR had moved nearer to the Bundesbank's philosophy that employment creation required above all else expectations of low inflation (Paprotzki 1991: 227). In its 1975 Report, the SVR thus stated (Riemer *ibid.*: 190):

The more profit margins shrank, and the more slender the prospects for businesses to pass on increasing costs in spite of accelerating inflation, the more the propensity to invest was undermined . . .

Moreover, the economic environment in which the implementation of the Kohl policies took place, however, was far more favourable than those experienced by the Schmidt government (Owen Smith 1989a). Price inflation and interest rates decreased markedly, culminating in a fall of the price level over the previous year in 1986. The rapid decline in crude oil prices was the principal cause. Even as prices and interest rates increased again, the trade balance, economic growth and investment reached high levels – in the case of the trade balance, record levels. An indication of the behaviour of these variables has already been gleaned from Figures 1.1 and 1.3, while the discussion around Figures 8.8 and 8.9 will explore the reasons for the record trade balance. In short, as early as 1986, the recovery under Kohl was longer lived than the protracted recession following the second oil shock (OECD *Economic Survey* 1986: 61). Only unemployment remained obstinately high, although it had reached a plateau and therefore differed from the rapid rises under Schmidt (Figure 1.2). Moreover, while the transfer of profits from the Bundesbank were of minor importance in the 1970s, they increased appreciably after 1982; transfer payments and public investment both fell, thereby decreasing expenditure and the fiscal impulse (Franz 1990:

27; Hellwig and Neumann 1987: 134). However, several measures were taken to stimulate private investment: general investment premia, special depreciation allowances and subsidies for housing construction (Franz, *ibid.*).

Little wonder, then, that the Louvre G7 agreement resulted in some of the tax cuts planned for 1990 being brought forward to 1988 (OECD *ibid.* 1987: 19). The German and Japanese governments were again urged to stimulate domestic demand in order to bring about an international recovery. Although fiscal policy had been tightened 1982–6, however, the total public-sector deficit had already begun to rise again in 1987, a rise steeper than the 1978–80 'locomotive' one induced by the Bonn summit. This rise coincided with a fall in the Bundesbank's profits, but the fiscal impulse of budgetary policy was again positive. Moreover, observers had become even more critical about government economic intervention. Hellwig and Neumann (1987: 114 and 127–9) complained that 'the Kohl government had simply done nothing in such matters as deregulation or government subsidisation of lame-duck and eternal "infant" industries . . . [and] structural rigidities in the labour market'. Nearly every OECD *Economic Survey* after 1984 contained a critical account of such matters, and the EC (1990a) devoted a chapter to 'Regulations, subsidies and the need for a forward-looking supply-side policy'. The *Economist* (20 February 1988 and 8 June 1990) probably summarised the common view:

West Germany's economy is riddled with rigidities: tightly regulated labour markets, generous unemployment benefits, and regulations which cover everything from shop-opening hours to the composition of beer . . . cutting subsidies will not be easy . . . the coalition government has achieved [very little] in the last nine years.

Trapp (1987) effectively echoed these views when he considered the 'loco-motive' theory which characterised the Bonn and Louvre accords, although the inflationary pressure and current account deficits which West Germany experienced at the end of the 1970s are attributed to the reflationary measures taken as a result of the former agreement. Evidence to be presented in Chapter 4 would favour an explanation of this deterioration in econ-omic conditions based more on the effects of the second oil shock. Similarly, the dis-inflationary effect of the third oil shock on the West German economy was a major contribution to the fall in prices in 1986, while the record trade surpluses in the second half of the 1980s inevitably led to the Louvre requests from deficit econo-mies for domestic reflation on the part of Germany and Japan. Trapp (*ibid.*: 242) explicitly concedes the salutary effects of the third oil shock, having correctly postulated an alternative strategy of protectionism on the part of 'weak' coun-tries (*ibid.*: 237). Nonetheless, it is easy to see from Trapp's fairly representative and trenchant opposition to Keynesian dom-estic reflation why Louvre led to some coordinated intervention in the foreign exchange, but very little change in fiscal and interest-rate policy. Indeed, it is ironic that the economies (the USA and the UK) which introduced more labour market flexibility and deregulation – the policy prescriptions favoured by Trapp – con-tinued to build up serious trade problems. The employment growth achieved by the USA in the 1970s and 1980s receives approbation but the UK is not considered (*ibid.*: 243).

After unification, budgetary policy-makers and advisers became increasingly concerned with meeting the costs of trans-fers to the east. Both the increase in VAT from 1993 and the solidarity pact have been mentioned above, but a little more detail about the controversies surrounding their introduction will illustrate the main thrust of budgetary policy in the early 1990s. Leading members of the Federal coalition government had argued prior to the 1991 election that no tax increases would be necessary to finance unification. A package of such measures, including a temporary 7.5 per cent income tax sur-charge, was however introduced in July 1992 (OECD *Economic Survey* 1992: 102n). The SPD Länder in the west were particularly opposed to the increase in VAT proposed by the coalition. They would have preferred to see a further in-crease in the German Unity Fund. Most of the costs of this off-budget item were financed by the Federal government. Since the SPD held the majority in the Bundesrat, it was February 1992 before the VAT increase was approved, mainly because the SPD Brandenburg voted with Berlin. The eastern Länder were anxious to secure a settlement so that the conse-quent increase in tax revenue in 1993 could be anticipated. Increasing VAT rates to finance part of the public transfers necessary after unification was, however, inconsistent with the envisaged rules on EMU fiscal harmonisation (Chauffour *et al.* 1992: 263). Moreover, the increases in indirect taxation probably had a far stronger inflationary impact than the increases in direct tax (*ibid.*: 264; Figure 3.11 below). Although the impact of tax rises was relatively less damaging to growth, their inflationary cost was 'enor-mous' compared to their benefits (*ibid.*). Chauffour *et al.* (*ibid.*: 271) conclude that in this sense the fiscal policy adopted to finance unification had precisely the inflationary effects that monetary policy was seeking to avoid. (Inflationary pressure and short-term interest rates were already increasing prior to GEMSU – *ibid*. 257).

In many respects, however, the solidarity pact of 1993 better represented the complex process of compromise involved in reaching agreement on financing the costs of unification. By this stage, these costs were expected to reach DM 110 billion per year from 1995 (FAZ 2 March 1993). This sum included DM 60 billion for the revised revenue sharing arrangements and DM 40 billion to service the accumulated debt of the new Länder. Tolls for the use of motorways, higher mineral oil taxes, a 'solidarity surcharge' and cuts in social spending were all discussed. The road and oil taxes were intended to meet the burgeoning debts of the railways prior to privatisation. Ultimately, an income tax surcharge of 7.5 per cent from January 1995 was agreed. This avoided the need for a tax hike during the super election year of 1994 when a total of 16 elections were due at federal, Länder and local authority level. But the decision to use a tax surcharge followed months of disagreement. A proposal that the surcharge should be borne by the 70 per cent of the working population who contributed to unemployment insurance was considered inequitable by the 'social' wing of the CDU, the SPD and the SVR. This would have left *Beamte* and the self-employed contributing far less to the costs of unification. Moreover, the SPD successfully opposed cuts in social spending. Something was nevertheless being done about the public sector borrowing. Combined with the unions forgoing real pay increases in the west it left the Bundesbank with few excuses for maintaining its relatively high interest rates.

CONCLUSION: UNIFICATION AND FISCAL POLICY

Prior to unification, or more accurately GEMSU, the principal areas of subsidisation which received increasingly strident criticism in the west were: agriculture, coal mining, housing, the railways, steel, shipbuilding and power generation. Many of these sectors, together with some aspects of the labour market and financial services, were also targeted for adverse comment by the Deregulation Commission appointed by the Kohl government in 1987 (*Deregulierungskommission* 1991). Along with privatisation, the problems of subsidisation and deregulation will be considered in Chapter 8. In addition, housing finance is considered in Chapter 7. It simply needs to be emphasised here that they represent some of the major issues in the sphere of government intervention which still remained unresolved at the time of unification. Moreover, budget deficits were already a fairly intractable policy problem, and the reform of the tax structure was only half complete. The hypotheses postulated at the beginning of this chapter have thus been substantiated, and from a budgetary policy point of view unification could not have come at a worse time.

Clearly, then, unification did not pose an entirely new fiscal policy challenge in terms of the already existing predilection for government intervention and history of deficit spending. The difficulties lay elsewhere. Given the huge costs of modernising the eastern economy (already seen in Chapter 1), the obvious needs were for expenditure switching and raising additional revenue to meet these costs. This involved challenging vested interests in the west. For example, the Bavarian farmer with an uneconomic small farm and the

Ruhr miner working in a sheltered industry both faced the prospect of subsidy cutting. Moreover, federal-coalition politicians fought the first all-German election on a platform of 'no tax increases to finance unification'. Kohl categorically rejected this policy; Waigel said such a policy prescription would undermine economic growth and the vital propensity to invest; Lambsdorff was still concerned with subsidies and saw their reduction as an alternative to increasing taxes, the latter not being a serious policy option (*Die Zeit* 9/91; *Die Welt* 2 March 1993). Particularly in view of GEMSU's generous exchange rate, there could not have been a more inauspicious start to economic union between two such dissimilar economies. As already shown above, tax increases were ultimately introduced. Whereas they were an essential contribution to meeting the costs of unification, they frustrated the process of reforming the incidence and structure of taxation for the rest of the 1990s. Increases in indirect taxation were also inflationary.

Because of the delay in coming to grips with the enormous costs of unification, public transfers to the east were the cause of a serious deterioration in public finances. Three observations can be made with a high degree of certainty. First, public transfers took the general form of social benefits, investment in the infrastructure and the provision of liquidity to firms. They were thus far more extensive than transfer payments in the normal sense, namely unemployment and other social-policy benefits. Secondly, however, the proportion of transfer payments in 1991 was probably as high as 60 per cent of total public transfers (Tietz 1991: 224). An alternative way of viewing this distribution of transfers would be to point out that in 1991 they funded one-third of private consumption in east Germany

(MRDB 3/92: 20). Another estimate further exposes this aspect of transfers. Public investment in the infrastructure was DM 30 billion in 1991 and DM 36 billion in 1992, almost one and a half times as much *per capita* as in the old Länder (Dresdner Bank *Trends* February 1992). But total public net transfers to the east in the 1992 were estimated in the same source as lying between DM 125 billion and DM 145 billion; it was thus shown that these transfers were still largely used for consumption purposes in 1992. Note the wide band of DM 20 billion in the estimate of the magnitude of transfers. This leads nicely to the third and most frustrating aspect of the debate. The quantification of public transfers was made difficult by statistical shortcomings and methodological differences (MRDB 7/91: 30 and 3/92: 16):

- tax receipts of the Federal government emanating from east Germany can be deducted from gross receipts in order to arrive at net transfers
- net transfers comprise all the services and loans supplied to the east from public budgets in the west
- but the funds provided by the Federal post office and railways, as well as the Treuhand, were not included by the Bundesbank (*ibid.*)
- the burgeoning deficits of the Treuhand in particular could not in any case be assessed precisely
- the sum total of transfers must not be equated with the cost to west German budgets because costs associated with partition had been terminated or were being phased out

Total public net transfers on this basis in 1990 had probably reached DM 67 billion, whereas they may have been as high as DM 140 billion in 1991 and DM 180 billion in 1992 (Deutsche Bank *Bulletin*

July 1991; MRDB 3/92: 16). Because it was drawn up earlier, and on a different basis, the AdwF estimate for 1991 was DM 97.5 billion (Tietz 1991: 224–5). However, total GNP in the unified Germany in 1991 was DM 2,826.6 billion, while the east's contribution to that total was estimated at DM 195.4 billion (BMWi *Wirtschaft* . . . 1992: 33). Hence, the estimated percentage of the east's GNP represented by public net transfers lay between 50 and 70 per cent, with the larger proportion probably being nearer the mark. Indeed, in mid-1991 there was even one estimate that 90 per cent of east German GNP consisted of transfers from the west (IDS *European Report* 355). The numerator in this case was presumably gross transfers as defined above. Nonetheless, the unavoidable conclusion is that public net transfers were of an appreciable magnitude. Public budgets in the west, particularly at the federal level, were inevitably placed under great strain. Belated tax increases and inadequate expenditure switching meant a steep rise in the PSBR.

But the distribution of public transfers must also be considered in a little more depth. In view of the collapse of economic activity in the east, especially in manufacturing, their consumption bias is understandable. However, extensive public aid in the form of investment subsidies and special tax write-offs were again on offer in 1993 (Dresdner Bank *ibid.*). The Federal government alone offered more than forty such promotional schemes (MRDB 8/92: 21). Low interest loans were available from the special purpose banks to be discussed in Chapter 7, although examples of this form of assistance were given in Chapter 2. This form of assistance was defined by the Bundesbank as 'interest subsidies' (MRDB *ibid.*). Yet private investment remained totally

inadequate. Some disaggregated data will be presented in Table 8.2, but a general indication can be obtained from the relevant economic aggregates. A note of caution is in order: the ratio of gross domestic fixed capital formation to GNP in 1991 was 42 per cent in the east, compared to 21 per cent in the west (calculated from BMWi *ibid.*: 34). But this was due more to the post-GEMSU decline of 45 per cent in the east's GNP than to an expansion in investment (Pilz and Ortwein 1992: 27). If the same investment indicator is divided by the number of employees in employment, a totally different estimate is yielded. In 1991, the east's ratio was DM 11,878 per employee compared to DM 21,777 in the west. Per industrial employee in the east, investment was under half of that in the west: £50,000 compared to £110,000 (IDS *ibid.*). Assuming, however, a rise in private investment in the east from DM 52.5 billion in 1991 to DM 73 billion in 1992, it was estimated that this investment gap was slowly being eliminated (Dresdner Bank *ibid.*). Unsettled property claims, bureaucracy and insufficient infrastructure remained the main obstacles to investment (*ibid.*; chapters 1, 2 and 8). Yet the policy debate continued to focus mainly on the convergence of minimum nominal pay rates by 1994, agreed in 1991 (ch. 6). The AdwF, in their Autumn report for 1992, argued that these agreements should be renegotiated, adding that this process of equalisation should be postponed until productivity in the east attained western levels. It will be shown in Chapter 6 that some employers' associations rescinded the agreements in 1993.

Consider next the important nature of the German Unity Fund, Debt Processing Fund, the ERP special-asset fund and the LAG fund. These four shadow budgets incurred a financial deficit of DM 36 billion in 1991 (Pilz and Ortwein 1992: 160).

By far the largest part of this deficit (DM 31 billion) was incurred by the German Unity Fund. By also including the deficits of the three levels of government, Pilz and Ortwein (*ibid.*) show that the total deficit rose to DM 135 billion. The Unity and Debt Processing Funds were established with the express purpose of meeting some of the costs of unification, whereas the ERP fund started life as the depository for the Marshall Aid counterpart funds and the LAG fund was designed to assist in the process of integrating expellees, refugees and war victims into the west (Chapters 1 and 6; MRDB 5/93: 43–4). Marshall Aid was preceded by GARIOA, while the LAG was preceded by the Immediate Relief scheme (Wallich 1955: 276–9 and 355–6). It will be shown in Chapter 7 that these two funds were also used to form two special-purpose banks (the KfW and Deutsche Ausgleichsbank). Both funds are correctly viewed by the Federal government as assets: they possess a portfolio of DM assets which could be disposed of to finance government expenditure, rather like issuing national debt to finance such expenditure. In this sense, the German Unity Fund also operated as a substitute for the direct issuance of national debt. It is little wonder that Shonfield (1965: 278) emphasises how the Germans accepted the KfW without fuss. It was an ideal alternative to direct government involvement, whereas in the Anglo-Saxon world it would probably have caused a furious ideological debate. This writer is convinced that, had the Germans enjoyed the tax revenue from British North Sea oil and gas, they would have formed a permanent special asset (fund) out of the immediate reach of politicians and the German equivalent of the Treasury. As it is, one can only guess about the purposes to which this revenue was put.

The Debt Processing Fund (*Kreditab-wicklungsfonds*) performed a fundamentally different role. Indeed 'processing' – or 'management' – are euphemistic translations of *Abwicklung* which means 'to wind up'. Hence, this fund acted as a debtor for the 'equalisation' of claims arising from the currency conversion under GEMSU and public-sector debts of the former DDR. ('Equalisation' (*Ausgleich*) in this context is another euphemistic translation. It refers to balancing assets and liabilities; a direct analogy may be drawn with the German judicial practice (*das Vergleichsverfahren*) of writing down debts to a level which will keep an enterprise commercially viable.) A similar equalisation of claims fund – *Ausgleichs-forderungen* – had arisen from the 1948 currency reform (Wallich 1955: 70). After all, the reform threw the banks' balance sheets into even greater disarray than writing off the Nazi government's debt. Hence, the Bundesbank still shows DM 8.6 billion of this 'equalisation' fund on the asset side of its balance sheet (MRDB table III[1]). Estimates of the accumulated debt of the Debt Processing Fund were DM 26 billion in 1991 but DM 70 billion in 1992 (iwd2 11/92). Yet the financial deficit of the fund in 1991 was posted as only DM 1 billion (Pilz and Ortwein *ibid.*). This is the fundamental difference from the funds outlined in the previous paragraph. The Debt Processing Fund cannot be regarded as a 'special asset' (*das Sondervermögen*). In effect, the Federal government either issued treasury discount paper through the Bundesbank or borrowers' notes to domestic and foreign banks (MRDB 3/93: table VIII(7)). Such securities added to the total (accumulated) national debt without, however, providing the government with revenue from which goods and services could be purchased.

Large financial deficits and a significant accumulation of public-sector debt will therefore characterise at least the first half of the 1990s. Public debt could reach over 50 per cent of GNP by 1995 – a level regarded as critical in some quarters. As already indicated, however, an element of crystal-ball gazing is implied by the assumptions made about the magnitudes of national debt and GNP. Three sources illustrate the assumptions about the numerator and denominator used in calculating the estimated ratios. They are the *Economist* (4 April 1992), the FT (2 September 1992) and the OECD (*Economic Survey* 1992: 42–3). They respectively estimated that national debt in 1995 would be DM 1.8 trillion, DM 2 trillion and DM 1.9 trillion. These estimates, as a proportion of GNP, represented 51.4 per cent in the case of the *Economist*, but 50 per cent in the other two cases. The FT was referring to three levels of government in unified Germany, plus the German Unity, Debt Processing and ERP funds. The Treuhand was added by both the *Economist* and OECD, the latter also including DM 62 billion for the accumulated debt of the east German housing stocks. Surprisingly, the debts of the federal railways and post office were excluded in all three cases, presumably on the grounds that by 1995 they may be partially privatised (see Chapter 8). Nonetheless, all three definitions of national debt did not strictly correspond to the full extent of Germany's public-sector debt in the chosen base year of 1991.

Although the actual development of debt in the 1990s was uncertain, a number of important policy issues were closely related to the assumptions and dispositions involved in its assessment. The first thing to note is that it is possible to calculate the implied percentage growth in GNP by 1995, given that the united-German GNP in 1991 was DM 2.826 trillion. The *Economist*, whose data were

from the IfW, in effect predicted a 4.4 per cent average annual growth rate, the OECD 6.1 per cent and the FT 7.2 per cent. Allowing for the 1992/93 recession, the *Economist* possibly made the most realistic estimate. (The average annual rate of economic growth achieved since 1980, for example, was 5.4 per cent). The assumption that the budget deficits which led to an increase in debt would have produced economic expansion is, however, at heart a Keynesian concept. Financing the deficit itself is less important than the role of the budget deficits in managing aggregate demand. Moreover, even an annual growth rate of 4.4 per cent became increasingly unlikely given the depth of the recession engineered by the Bundesbank's policymakers (see Figure 8.13). (Short-term interest rates and inflationary pressure had both been increasing since 1989 – Figures 4.2 and 4.4b). This, of course, reveals the basic policy stance of the Bundesbank: the size of the numerators in the debt/GNP and budget deficit/ GNP ratios is of paramount policy importance. High public deficits were axiomatically assumed to be inflationary. The consequent decline in the denominator as a result of deflationary monetary policy was a transient phase. Finally, the OECD estimated that the annual cost of servicing the national debt of DM 1.9 trillion would be about DM 150 billion, which meant 3.9 per cent of the implied GNP in 1995.

Compared to other industrialised market economies, however, a national debt ratio of 50 per cent by 1995 would still be quite tolerable for Germany herself. Table 3.1 contains data which facilitate such a comparison. It will be seen that there are data for three years: 1980, 1989 and 1992. This period thus respectively covers the mid-year of the recession caused by the second oil shock, the year prior to GEMSU and a post-unification shock year. Data for 19 market economies are reported. Notice the wide dispersion of the ratios: in 1992 Luxembourg's ratio was 6.4 per cent, whereas Belgium's was 132.9 per cent. Although these two economies differ in size, note that the debt/GNP ratios do not seem to have played a role in their trade and monetary unions. Only three economies could demonstrate a secular reduction in the ratio: Luxembourg, Norway, and the UK. (North Sea oil and gas tax revenue, privatisation and council-house sales affected the course of national debt in the UK; Norway enjoyed similar tax revenue. There was a sharp increase in the UK's PSBR from 1993.) Although Germany's ratio deteriorated during the supply-side era, by 1989 the Bundesbank was able to show that it was well below the weighted average for the G7 industrial economies (MRDB 8/91: 35). This average was 58.6 per cent, even though Germany's ratio was reported as being 43.4 per cent in the Bundesbank's data.

There is also another relativity of some note in Table 3.1. In 1992 Ireland and Italy, as well as Belgium, had ratios of over 100 per cent. Greece's ratio was 87.1 per cent. The ratios of Canada and the Netherlands were 79.1 per cent, while the ratios of Denmark, Japan and the USA all lay above the 60 per cent mark. Hence, all these economies had worse ratios than the 50 per cent forecast for Germany in 1995. It was probably historical factors which started the alarm bells ringing within Germany itself. But would 50 per cent be intolerable *per se*? Indeed, was the 50 per cent alarm bell almost a red herring? Japan is Germany's most important trade rival, but Japan was 10 percentage points above this 'critical' watershed. The Netherlands and Belgium are often seen as members of the fast stream towards European (or

Table 3.1 National Debt as a percentage of GNP/GDP

Country	1980	1989	1992
Germany[1]	32.5	41.1	42.0
Austria	37.2	56.6	52.6
Belgium	79.9	130.7	132.9
Canada	44.7	69.6	79.1
Denmark	33.5	58.0	61.6
Finland	13.8	15.0	27.7
France	37.3	46.6	48.5
Greece	27.7	76.1	87.1
Ireland	78.0	125.1	108.8
Italy	58.5	98.8	107.8
Japan	52.0	70.2	60.9
Luxembourg	13.8	8.5	6.4
Netherlands	45.9	79.7	79.1
Norway	55.9	43.1	45.8
Portugal	37.1	71.2	62.7
Spain	18.5	43.2	48.0
Sweden	44.8	47.7	50.3
UK	54.6	37.4	38.5
USA	37.9	54.0	60.5

Source: BMF *Finanzbericht* 1992: 302 and 1993: 313 (author's translation)

Note: [1] 1980 and 1989: West Germany only

DM!) monetary union, although sight must not be lost of the fact that the EC was authorised under the Maastricht treaty to grant exemptions from both the 60 per cent debt/GNP and the 3 per cent PSBR/GNP ratios (Chauffour *et al.* 1992: 263). In the last analysis, assuming the treaty or its equivalent were introduced during the 1990s, Germany would no doubt qualify for such exemptions on the grounds that unification was an atypical occurrence (*ibid.*). This would be particularly likely when the Federal government inherited the Treuhand and other debts in 1995. While this exception would probably be permitted under EMU's fiscal harmonisation rules, however, the method by which part of the deficit is financed would have to be changed: that component of public transfers financed by indirect taxes would be disallowed (*ibid.*). Moreover, the mounting German deficits in 1993 were also caused by recession in the western part of the economy. However, there are also several of Germany's important trading partners in an 'over 55 per cent' list which could be derived from Table 3.1. Is it suggested that they too are heading for economic instability as a result of their national debt ratios? Finally, the prediction for the united-German gross debt/GNP ratio in 1993 – only three years before the Maastricht 'final assessment' on EMU – was 44 per cent (see the source of Table 3.1). Even if the treaty's EMU provisions are not implemented, it is pertinent to ask whether there is a really intractable debt problem. In short, there were far more important economic indicators for Germany herself. Above all, her future competitive position was related to factors which were a far cry from her national debt ratio – see, for example the trade section in Chapter 8.

The argument thus far has been confined to the assumption of a debt/GNP ratio of about 50 per cent in 1995. Sight must not be lost of the fact that a continued rise in tax revenue and expenditure switching will be necessary to achieve that goal. Moreover, only the post-unification implications for Germany have been considered. In the debate on the international costs of German unification, it was hypothesised that a significantly higher debt/GNP ratio would ultimately affect bond yields in Germany and, consequently, long-term interest rates generally. Such a chain reaction would be initiated by the complex interaction of several variables. This is because the principal determinants of long-term interest rates in Germany are:

- the domestic inflation rate
- domestic monetary policy
- bond yields in important bond markets abroad
- the DM/US$ exchange rate
- the public-sector budget deficit in Germany

It can be said immediately that the debate about the likely future course of bond yields generally focused on an annual minimum PSBR of DM 150 billion. This was equivalent to 5.3 per cent of the united-German GNP in 1991. Similarly, the maximum assumed PSBR was DM 200 billion, or 7.1 per cent of the united-German GNP in 1991. This latter PSBR would produce a national debt of DM 2 trillion in 1995, the DM 1 trillion mark having already been reached around the time of GEMSU.

Figures 3.10 and 3.11 encompass the variables referred to in the previous paragraph. The first thing to note – because of its effect in the bond market – is the decline and subsequent recovery in the DM/US$ exchange rate during 1990 and the first half of 1991 (Figure 3.10). There is generally a lagged pattern of a falling US$ (appreciating DM) leading to an increase in demand for German bonds, thus depressing the average annual yields on newly issued bonds. This process reflects comparative rates of return in international bond markets. Similarly, the Bundesbank's short-term interest rates, which are analysed in the next chapter, are a good proxy for the stance in monetary policy. These rates were increased in response to both the rise in average annual yields on newly issued bonds and the increase in inflationary pressure (see Figures 3.10 and 3.11, but note that bond yields are proxied here by the nominal rate of return on all newly issued bonds; in Figure 7.6a the yield on all bonds in

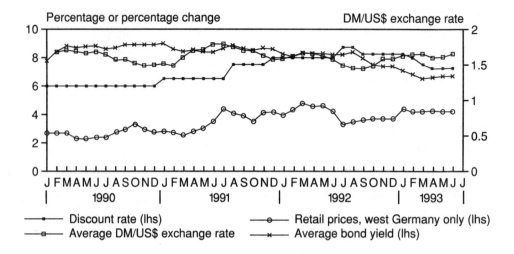

Figure 3.10 Inflation, Interest and Exchange Rates
Source: MRDB VI1/VII6/IX7/X9

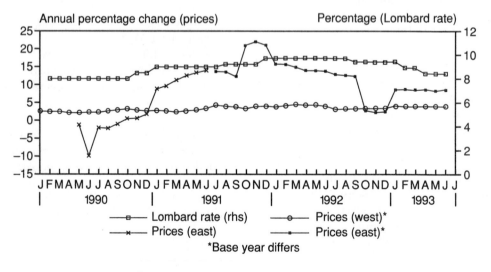

Figure 3.11 Price Inflation and Interest Rates
Source: MRDB VI1/IX7/IX10

circulation is considered more appropriate). Inflation in the west was typically considered by the Bundesbank policymakers to be the more critical indicator, although it will be shown in the next chapter that they probably overreacted on this basis. Following GEMSU, on the other hand, long-term interest rates were initially affected by market expectations of long-term inflation (Chauffour *et al.* 1992: 257). It can also be seen from Figure 3.11 that the removal of subsidies in the east seriously exacerbated the upward pressure on prices. Finally, the inflationary pressure emanating from the increase in VAT in January 1993 can be seen in both figures.

Because of the importance of the PSBR in these linkages, it is apposite to consider its implications in a little more depth. Since the analysis is about to turn to monetary policy, it is also appropriate to recall that the Bundesbank has consistently viewed deficit spending with a great deal of apprehension. After referring to a PSBR equivalent to about 5.5 per cent of the united-German GNP, the Bundesbank stated that 'deficits of such an order can be considered tolerable in the exceptional situation that arose as a result of German unification' (MRDB 7/91: 30). If maintained over an extended period, however, they would pose risks to domestic and external stability. Even more specifically (MRDB 8/92: 28):

Continued massive subsidisation of capital investment in united Germany gives cause for concern in terms of anti-inflation policy and monetary policy . . . the east German economy is being virtually insulated from interest rate effects.

Given the 'massive' tax concessions and subsidies introduced by Erhard during the recovery and reconstruction of the West German economy, there are elements of a double standard at work here. More examples of double standards will be given in Chapter 8 when, for example, privatisation is discussed. One aspect of the debate is nonetheless beyond doubt: the probity of the Bundesbank's approach to inflationary pressure, even if it meant generating a recession in west Germany and internationally, was a parameter of modern economic affairs.

The Bundesbank would not be prepared to finance budget deficits by central bank credit. As will be seen in the next chapter, public authority securities are used in the main by the Bundesbank policymakers to manage the money market. However, if the deficit is financed principally by long-term bonds, any increase in bond yields would almost certainly be matched by increases in the Bundesbank's short-term rates. There was indeed every intention to fund a major part of the deficit in this way and public bond sales soared in 1990–1 (see Figures 7.4d and 7.8a). Since there is a correlation in Germany between the trends in government borrowing and bond yields, increases in short-term interest rates were on the cards (see, for example, Figures 4.2 and 4.4b, but also note again that increasing interest rates and inflation preceded the fall of the Berlin wall). There was, in fact, an appreciable period when short-term rates were higher than long-term ones (Figure 3.10). In addition, the interest payments by the Federal government alone – set to increase at 1990 rates by over 70 per cent to DM 61 billion by 1994 – would clearly rise even further if bond yields increased in the meantime. There were two mitigating factors: in 1990, personal savings were running at a record DM 200 billion and, at the turn of 1990/91, German domestic bonds were particularly attractive to foreign investors again. Such foreign purchases fluctuate wildly – the previous high influx had been during the period of extremely low interest rates, and low-cost government borrowing, in 1986. As a prelude to what will be said around Figures 4.4b, 4.4c and 4.6b, and to put the Bundesbank's views on government borrowing into a wider perspective, it is also important to note that the market for bonds is Germany's dominant securities market (see Chapter 7). For these and other reasons, it requires sophisticated handling (Bayerische Landesbank, *Money and Capital Markets*, May/June 1991):

Between the autumn of 1990 and February 1991, a falling dollar caused foreign investors to pile into German bonds . . . the dollar's recovery (subsequently) prompted foreigners to dump German securities on a large scale. In contrast to similarly abrupt reversals in the past, however, the latest sell-off did not push up bond rates. On the contrary, the average yield dropped to 8.42 per cent, although the market had to absorb the securities dumped by foreigners. In January . . . [it had been] 9.17 per cent . . . foreign investors are still playing a prominent role [but] can be expected to provide the bond market with relief whenever the DM appreciates against the dollar and major European currencies.

It will be seen in the *Finanzplatz Deutschland* section of Chapter 7, however, that German bonds soon regained their attractiveness for foreigners.

At the domestic level, the Bundesbank set out to curb what it saw as the profligacy of government. During the GEMSU negotiations, it adopted its usual firm stance over budgetary policy. Above all, this stance was typified by its insistence that borrowing to fund unification should be minimised. More preferably, existing spending plans should be pruned; as a last resort taxes should be raised. Put in a slightly wider context, this meant that

strict spending controls were necessary, and that East Germany's tax system should be speedily brought into line with the West's as soon as possible. Experience following GEMSU was to stiffen further the resolve of the Bundesbank that EMU would have to evolve on the basis of economic convergence and an unambiguously anti-inflationary monetary policy conducted by an independent central bank.

Other firm budgetary guide-lines were drawn up by the Bundesbank for GEMSU (MRDB 7/90). Above all, meeting budget deficits by means of direct recourse to lending by the State Bank was ruled out by GEMSU. Under the East German regime recourse to this bank (in its capacity as central bank) had been possible. At the same time, the public authorities in the GDR were obliged to deposit their liquid funds with the Bundesbank (pursuant to section 17 of the Bundesbank Act), and to issue government paper primarily through the Deutsche Bundesbank, or otherwise in consultation with it. In addition, the borrowing authorisations for the public authorities of the GDR were limited by GEMSU to DM 10 billion for the second half of 1990 and DM 14 billion for 1991. It is also interesting to note the views of the Bundesbank on some of the other aspects of public borrowing analysed above. First, the German Unity Fund was established, thus shifting the borrowing needed for substantial financial assistance to the GDR to a new special fund of the Federal Government, with the debt service burdens (distributed over a fairly long period) being shouldered by the Federal and Länder Governments. Next, the total net borrowing requirements of the central, Länder and local authorities in the Federal Republic (including the German Unity and the ERP Special Funds), together with the GDR, were estimated at just over DM 80 billion in 1990 and about DM 100 billion in 1991; this would correspond to about 3.5 per cent of the common nominal national product 1991. From the outset, the ERP Special Fund played a crucial role in promoting economic activity in eastern Germany (MRDB 8/92: 24). Between 1990 and 1992, ERP lending programmes tripled, reaching DM 13.28 billion in 1992 (*ibid.*: 25). Net new borrowing for this fund alone was over DM 10 billion in 1992. This meant that the fund developed into an off-budget deficit item, whereas prior to its unification-related expansion it had been principally a revolving fund.

This general increase in the PSBR was attributed mainly to the initially small tax-raising powers of the GDR, the 'start-up finance' for the pension and unemployment insurance funds, and the structural adjustment measures in the GDR. Most of the expenditure of the GDR budget to be financed by borrowing was to serve consumption purposes. It was recognised that it would not be possible, at least for the time being, to apply the basic principle of budget legislation – that is, to limit borrowing normally to the amount of capital expenditure. How some of this all turned out in practice was discussed above. The decision to re-unite was obviously a political one, but it can be concluded that the Bundesbank took a very firm line over GEMSU.

The strong growth in public-sector deficits had a vigorous expansionary impact on business activity in western Germany and (*via* increasing imports) in the other western nations, too (MRDB 6/91: 25). These increasing imports, caused mainly by the lack of appropriate capacity in the east, in turn caused a current-account deficit in January 1991, followed by a trade deficit in April. It was not just this enormous shift in demand within Germany itself which brought about this

untypical current-account deficit, but also the cyclical downturn in foreign demand. There was no reflection on the competitiveness of German industry (*ibid.* – but see the trade sections of Chapter 8). Nonetheless, the weakening DM was raising inflationary pressure and the Bundesbank policymakers would not view such developments with equanimity.

At the international level, the united-German PSBR, along with her unusually high rates of price and wage inflation, were expected to place the bond markets under strain. Since 1979 the DM had dominated the ERM because shadowing the Bundesbank's interest-rate policy was considered to be the best method of ensuring low inflation. But the west German annual inflation rate of 4.8 per cent in March 1992 meant that seven of the ten member countries had lower inflation rates; moreover, Germany's PSBR was about 6 per cent of GNP (*Economist* 2 May 1992). Consequently, the Bundesbank's council raised interest rates to record levels. This had the effect of reassuring the bond markets that inflation would be reduced, and German yields on public bonds outstanding fell to an average annual of 6.33 per cent by mid-March 1993 – the lowest level since 1988 (MRDB 6/93: 25–6). Borrowed long-term funds were thus markedly cheaper than their multi-year average. In real terms, this rate of return was just 2.5 per cent, a level previously known only in the early 1960s and the mid-1970s; it is also worth noting that the real rate of interest on the same basis had not been negative for forty years (*ibid.*). Short-term interest rate policy also kept long-term government bond yields lower than in other ERM member countries. In the meantime, however, high short-term interest rates in Germany had driven some ERM members out of the system and the widening of the permitted fluctuation band for most of those who remained meant floating exchange rates in all but name. The general view was that a lower German PSBR would have enabled the Bundesbank's council to cut interest rates earlier. (An alternative would have been to revalue the DM. This would have dampened inflationary pressure in Germany by lowering import prices. Indeed, as early as Autumn 1990 there had been a surge in inflation due to a rise in imported crude oil prices. But other ERM members did not find a realignment an acceptable policy option.)

Yet a high German PSBR, together with the need for the Germans to refinance the outstanding debt, had been expected to have a more direct effect on the bond markets. For example, Holtham (*Guardian* 18 November 1991) assumed that the German PSBR in 1991 would be 9 per cent of GNP, or DM 254.34 billion. Such a ratio was twice as high as the most profligate time of the Reagan era. German predictions of a decline to 3 per cent of GNP by 1995 were not accepted, since this implied only interest payments on outstanding debt would have to be met by that date. (Recall that a PSBR of more than 3 per cent of GDP would not have met the Maastricht treaty goal.) Wage inflation in the east was held to be a significant determinant of the borrowing requirement. This was because the income of the unemployed, pensioners and *Beamte* (see Chapter 6) were indexed to the general wage level. Moreover, the higher the rate

of wage inflation in the east, the longer it would be necessary to maintain investment subsidies. On 'reasonable assumptions', therefore, 'the debt/GNP ratio would exceed 60 per cent within five years adding perhaps 0.75 to 1 per cent to German bond yields'. Notice that such a debt/GNP ratio would require special exemption for Germany from the second stage of the Maastricht common-currency agreement, again assuming that the treaty's implementation is a realistic proposition.

In short, it would seem that the Bundesbank's determination to act against wage and price inflation, along with a lower PSBR due to higher tax revenue, meant lower post-unification bond yields than might otherwise have been expected. The Bundesbank increasingly preferred a lowering of government expenditure because it feared the effect of tax increases on wage inflation. Significantly, its president in 1993 co-authored a book entitled *State Debts – Endless?*. The basic message was that interest rates would have been much lower if public borrowing and spending had been genuinely curbed (*Guardian* 29 April 1993). High interest-rate levels had been maintained in order to attract foreign capital and compensate for the growing current account deficit. These arguments echo what was said following the first two crude oil price shocks. More generally, they demonstrate why the next chapter is exclusively concerned with monetary policy.

4

MONETARY POLICY

INTRODUCTION

One of the clearest inferences which may be drawn from Chapter 1 is the need for a German institution which would contribute to monetary stability. Not only have there been a number of currency crises during the development of the economy, but an important theoretical aspect of the SME entailed the creation of an independent central bank which would control the money supply so as to create a built-in economic stabiliser. In 1948, the western Allies established a central bank in each Land. The policies of these Länder central banks were coordinated at the federal level by the Bank deutscher Länder (BdL). The BdL was given considerable legal autonomy and a substantial degree of operational independence from the later-established Federal government (Hardach 1980: 153). Indeed, the BdL had also asserted its domestic independence from Allied influence over interest-rate policy as early as June 1948; on the other hand, the decision by the Bonn cabinet in 1949 to devalue the DM by 25 per cent was overruled by the Allies who invoked a 20 per cent devaluation (Marsh 1992: 165). When the more unified Deutsche Bundesbank (BBk) became the new West German central bank in 1958, it confirmed this independent trend. But whereas the BdL had been owned by the Länder central banks, ownership of the BBk passed to the Federal government (*ibid.*: 19; Paprotzki 1991: 207). The BBks profits must have been particularly welcome to the Federal government as its budget deficits rose steeply in 1992–3. In April 1992 the profit transfer was DM 14.5 billion, while in the same month in 1993 it amounted to DM 13 billion (MRDB 5/93: 9).

It follows, therefore, that the main statutory base for monetary policy is the Deutsche Bundesbank Act (BBankG 1957). Notice that this means that the Bundesbank was established by a federal statute. Article 88 of the Basic Law, which came into force in 1949, simply required the Federal government to establish a 'note issuing and currency bank as the Federal Bank'. As things transpired, the BBk thus replaced the BdL – the decentralised, two-tier institution created by the Allies in 1948. Its policy makers continued to enjoy the BdL's discount and minimum reserve powers, the latter being a new feature when they were introduced in 1948. There is thus *no* constitutional provision for such a body with these powers, in spite of the fairly widely held view to the contrary. Given the fairly wide public support which the Bank seems to enjoy, however, it is doubtful whether the legislators could successfully challenge its present powers. On the other hand, should EMU materialise, politicians would be reluctant to concede further powers – most notably influence over the foreign currency exchange rates with external trading blocs. After GEMSU, this is bound to give the Bundesbank's policy-makers even further doubts about surrendering its powers to the proposed European Central Bank System (ECBS).

As was seen in the previous chapter, a decade after the Bundesbank was established the StWG involved its policymakers in an innovative series of stabilisation measures. At least in theory, this gave the Federal government some say in monetary policy matters, as did the EMS when the Schmidt government entered this system as a founding member in 1979. Indeed, Vaubel in discussing the Hellwig and Neumann paper (1987: 141), agrees with the SVR's hypothesis that 'the EMS hung like a millstone around the DM's neck'. However, it will be shown below that the very opposite view is taken by other observers. In this latter scenario, the Bundesbank, because of the DM's strength, is perceived as dominating monetary affairs within the EC. Finally, it will also be seen that the External Trade and Payments Act (AWG 1961) has played an historical role in the efforts to control speculative capital inflows.

In short, there are thus two ostensibly contradictory hypotheses to be examined in this chapter:

- an independent central bank has dictated the course of monetary policy
- exchange-rate considerations have involved the Federal government in monetary policy matters

In order to examine these hypotheses, it is necessary to isolate how domestic monetary policy is related to the international monetary system. Basically, the success of West German exporters resulted in an inflow of foreign-currency earnings which was associated with relative low inflation. As the strength of the DM increased, speculative short-term capital inflows were also attracted. The strength of the DM also encouraged its use as an international trading and reserve currency. West Germany's economic and monetary prowess therefore became an important international influence whenever the stimulation of trade and stabilisation of exchange rates were considered. The independent Bundesbank policymakers have historically reacted by implementing measures designed to mitigate any domestic monetary instability arising from export earnings, capital inflows and international treaties negotiated by politicians. In addition, they have adopted an extremely firm stance against domestic inflation. In short, the Bundesbank's policymakers seek to maintain confidence in *both* the external and internal value of the DM. They would prefer to concentrate on domestic monetary policy objectives, but they have been unable to prevent politicians negotiating international monetary treaties. They have been even more powerless in the face of international currency speculation. Matters came to a head in mid-1993 when the serious domestic recession demanded a reduction in interest rates but international speculators required higher interest rates to compensate for the unusually high rate of inflation in Germany, along with a weakening DM on the foreign exchanges. Hence, the ostensible contradiction in the two introductory hypotheses is resolved – at least as far as the argument here is concerned. Its policy implications are, however, quite manifold. This is why there is a need to analyse the operational details and return to the policy stance of the Bundesbank in the concluding sections.

The first section thus contains a general

overview of the methods by which the independent Bundesbank's policymakers conduct monetary policy, and the factors which affect their goal of 'safeguarding the currency'. This is followed by a slightly more detailed analysis of the relevant markets. Next, with domestic monetary policy principally in mind, the trends in the key monetary indicators are traced. International monetary trends are then considered, including the role of the DM/US$ exchange rate, the EMS and the proposals for EMU. Because GEMSU represents a treaty which embodied both a new exchange-rate regime and the DM, it is considered in a section which follows the outline of EMU, but which also compares the monetary aspects of the SME and GEMSU first introduced in Chapter 1. Finally, during the course of the implementation of monetary policy, there have been various conflicts between Bundesbank policymakers and politicians, not least over GEMSU, the EMS and EMU. These are therefore considered in a final section.

DECISION MAKING, GOALS AND INSTRUMENTS

Policy decisions are made by the Central Bank Council (*der Zentralbankrat*). The implementation of the Council's decisions and day to day administration of the Bundesbank's business are the responsibility of its Directorate which is comprised of the President, the Vice President and up to eight other directors (*das Bundesbankdirektorium*). Until unification, each of the eleven western Länder had its own central bank whose function was to deal with transactions arising within its own area (*die Landeszentralbanken*). The Council was composed of the Directorate, the eleven Presidents of the Länder offices of the Bundesbank and non-voting mem-

bers of the Federal government. Because the Council would have become, in the opinion of some policy makers, more 'unwieldy' if the five new Länder had been represented, a compromise was reached whereby the number of Länder representatives was reduced to nine and the maximum total for the Directorate to eight. The regional implications of this reorganisation have already been reviewed in the discussion around Figure 2.9. This modification was not implemented until November 1992 and, since it represented a greater degree of centralisation, it was opposed by some Länder – as will be shown below. Members of the Directorate are nominated by the Federal government and appointed by the President of the Federal Republic. Until the post-unification changes, the Presidents of the Länder central banks were nominated by the Bundesrat, which in practice meant following a nomination by the affected Land. Since unification, the various groups of affected Länder are expected to cooperate when a new Council nomination is necessary. Under both the new and the former schemes, the nominee is/was also appointed by the Federal President. Under the BdLs regime, the presidents of the autonomous Länder central banks elected their own Directorate at the federal level (Sturm 1990: 257). However, the power to appoint the BBks president and the other members of its directorate passed to the Federal government when the BBk was established (Marsh 1992: 19).

A brief introduction to the areas in which decision making is necessary now seems appropriate. Central banking throughout the market economies is concerned with the same basic functions. Hence the Bundesbank is, first, the sole bank note-issuing authority. Second, it acts as the bankers' bank by supervising inter-bank dealings in the reserves it requires each bank to hold at the Bundesbank, thereby governing credit creation in the economy. Third, as seen in Chapter 1, it acts as the principal banker to government, although the post-war central bank has been able to place strict restrictions on the state's access to central bank credit, and therefore the latter's ability to create additions to the stock of money in the economy. Finally, the Bundesbank is the custodian of the country's foreign exchange reserves – a role which has been a major source of monetary policy problems in the post-war era.

The fundamental features of the Bundesbank's *modus operandi* can best be seen by highlighting the crucial phrases in its founding statute (BBk 1982: 93 and 97–8; 1989: 111 – writer's emphases):

Section 3. Functions

The Deutsche Bundesbank shall regulate the amount of money in circulation and of credit supplied to the economy, *using the monetary powers conferred* on it by this Act, with the *aim of safeguarding the currency*, and shall provide for the execution by banks of domestic and external payments.

Section 12. Relations between the Bank and the Federal Government

Without prejudice to the performance of its functions, the Deutsche Bundesbank shall be required to support the general economic policy of the Federal government. In exercising the powers conferred on it by this Act, it *shall be independent* of instructions from the Federal government.

Section 13. Co-operation

(1) The Deutsche Bundesbank *shall advise* the Federal government on monetary policy matters of major importance and provide it with information on request.
(2) The members of the Federal government *shall be entitled* to attend meetings of the Central Bank Council. They shall not enjoy voting rights, but may propose motions. At their request, a decision shall be *deferred for up to two weeks*.
(3) The Federal government *shall invite* the President of the Deutsche Bundesbank to attend its discussions on important monetary policy matters.

In contrast to the Bank of England, therefore, the Bundesbank attained independence because its monetary responsibilities, relationship to the Federal government and its organisational structure are codified in the BBankG (Paprotzki 1991: 207–8). Hence, although the Bundesbank is owned by the Federal government, and in the 1980s contributed an appreciable stream of profits to Federal government's total revenue, there is no similarity with the Bank of England as far as its subservience to the British Treasury is concerned. Moreover, even though the Bundesbank is not responsible for the prudential regulation of the banking system – again in contrast to the Bank of England – Germany's central bank is a far larger organisation. (Prudential regulation is reviewed in Chapter 7.)

Two further inferences may be drawn from the above excerpts from the BBankG. First, the seventeen appointed Council members carry exclusive responsibility for the determination of monetary policy. Their renewable period of office is normally eight years, which is twice the length of the legislature's session (*ibid.*: 209). The elected politicians in the Federal government formulate their economic policies – particularly fiscal policy – within a clearly constrained arena: where they create public debt, the Bundesbank's policymakers may well take remedial action. Second, Section 3 of the BBankG ('safeguarding the currency') is taken very seriously by members of the Council. In other words, their long-run regional and national interests are invariably perceived as being synonymous with the stability of the DM and the control of inflation. Somewhat paradoxically, retaining the stability of the DM has been increasingly threatened by international speculative short-term capital flows attracted by the Bundesbank's Council's strict adherence to its monetary code. Ironically, the genesis of these flows more or less coincides with the year when the Bundesbank succeeded the BdL. But the flows became larger over time, with the exchange rate against the US dollar and the protection of parities within the ERM proving particularly problematical. More will be said about exchange-rate policy below. For now it is sufficient to note that the Bundesbank's Directorate, especially the President, have a vital role to play in international diplomacy when it comes to exchange-rate problems. In general terms, it can be said that the Länder central banks' presidents are more concerned with domestic monetary affairs.

On the domestic front, 'stabilisation crises' have been induced by the Council's monetary policy (Riemer 1983). The first such crisis occurred in 1966 when the goal of economic growth was subordinated to monetary stability; Schiller's new approach to fiscal policy and, even more so, an export boom, brought about a rapid recovery (*ibid*.: 118 and 147). (Schiller's 'Keynesian revolution' was evaluated in the budgetary policy section of Chapter 3.) The second crisis occurred in 1973 when what was described as a 'drastic curtailment of the money supply' succeeded the Keynesian framework of cost containment and DM revaluations (*ibid*.: 74, 202 and 208). (As already shown in Chapter 3, the SVR shared the Bundesbank's policymakers conversion to monetarism.) Keynesian economists argued that

implementing such draconian measures at the beginning of 1973 exacerbated the crisis which, without economic policy restrictions, lay ahead (*ibid*.: 238). When world markets sagged in late 1974, a recession in 1975 thus became inevitable (*ibid*.: 239–40). A strong US dollar and domestic inflation caused an even longer credit squeeze which culminated in a postwar record period of high interest rates in 1980–1 (see the discussion around Figures 4.4a–d below). Finally, the post-wall boom was brought to an abrupt end by record interest rates (see, for example, Figures 4.2 and 8.13). Ostensibly, however, the goals of the Bundesbank's policymakers go beyond 'safeguarding the currency'. Consider the following reply by the then Bundesbank's president, Helmut Schlesinger, when he was asked about the conditions for a decrease in short-term rates (*Fortune* 16 November 1992):

For us, the development of the money supply is important. Development of credit demand is important. At the moment, we have no clear deceleration of the strong growth we have had. And we look certainly at price developments, cost developments, and the tendencies as far as wages are concerned. And we look into the real economy, what is going on in production and employment, the demand for goods. This is not so strong at the moment. And we are also looking at the exchange rate of the D-mark; the rise in its value in the last few months is diminishing the danger of inflation. The rise helps suppress home-grown price increases. All of this together is important.

In other words, the goal which receives priority from the Bundesbank policymakers is 'safeguarding the currency'. As will be seen shortly in a little more depth, political controversy has been aroused by the rigorous manner in which this goal has been pursued. At this stage, it is sufficient to note that full employment and equilibrium in the balance of payments were also initially considered as additional goals for inclusion in the BBankG (Sturm 1990: 261). Because of the conflict between these latter two goals and monetary stability, this proposal was not instituted. The Bundesbank therefore concentrates on monetary policy and price stability, leaving fiscal and economic policy to the government. In 1973 (significantly a period of high interest rates), there were unsuccessful attempts by the SPD and DGB to add the goals of the StWG to the BBankG (*ibid.* and Chapter 3 above). Note that concentrating on price stability implies the need to take external as well as domestic sources of inflation into account. A depreciation (or fall) of the DM on the foreign exchanges – especially against the US\$ – means that import prices rise adding to inflationary pressure. On the other hand, reducing monetary growth raises domestic interest rates and the foreign exchange rate of the DM appreciates (or rises); as a result the growth in interest-sensitive spending and net exports is reduced which leads to lower inflation and growth rates (Kahn and Jacobson 1989: 22 and 24).

It is now necessary to summarise, and then define in a little more depth, the Bundesbank's instruments. The analysis can then return to the operation of the money market and the implementation of monetary policy. The Bank endeavours to influence monetary demand by influencing two basic sets of indicators, namely bank liquidity and short-term interest rates. To a certain extent, the 'traditional' instruments available to the Bundesbank to control bank liquidity have become less effective. However, the instruments are:

- minimum reserves
- rediscount quotas
- open market operations with non-banks

These instruments also affect interest rates, since they change the relationship between supply and demand in the money market. In this sense, short-term interest rates would act as an indicator of the direction in which the Bundesbank is seeking *on its own initiative* to change the level of liquidity in the banking system. In other words, the reserves of the banks held at the Bundesbank are varied unilaterally by the central bank. Since these reserves are a critically important component of the money supply, varying their amount by means of the above instruments would enable the Bundesbank policymakers to control the *size* of the money stock. These instruments have, however, become less effective. The limited use of the minimum reserve instrument will be discussed very shortly. The rediscount quotas place an absolute ceiling on the extent to which the banks may borrow from the Bundesbank, or 'seek refinancing' as it is technically known. In this case, the banks achieve refinancing by selling eligible bills to the Bundesbank at its lowest interest rate (the discount rate – see below). It was originally intended that there would normally be a fairly substantial margin between this method of refinancing and their quotas. But in recent years these quotas have been generally fully exhausted. They have also risen quite dramatically: from DM 22.3 billion in 1977 to DM 63.9 billion in 1985; in 1990 – partly to accommodate the east German banks – they peaked at DM 84.6 billion, falling back to DM 64.6 billion in 1993 (Issing 1988: 6; MRDB: table III (2)). In such a situation the banks have had to find alternative methods of refinancing in order to maintain their central bank balances. Finally, open market operations with nonbanks have not been extensively utilised. Moreover, there has been very little dealing in money-market paper between the banks and nonbanks – or, for that matter, between the banks. In other words, trading in such paper nearly always involves the Bundesbank.

Some instruments of interest rate policy also exert an influence on bank liquidity in that the cost of converting liquid reserves into central-bank money is raised or lowered. In this case the Bundesbank policymakers announce the various rates at which the banks may change their reserves at the central bank. This is the converse of acting directly on bank liquidity since it is the demand side of the money market which is influenced. Hence, the relevant indicator in this case is the monetary base (or 'high-powered money'). Interest rate instruments are:

- the discount rate
- the Lombard rate
- the special rate
- open market operations in money-market paper

The latter comprises the treasury bills (*Schatzwechsel*) and 'funds' of the public authorities and their agencies, a full analysis of which appeared at the beginning of the budgetary policy section in the previous chapter. There are in addition treasury 'bonds' (*U-Schätze*) which are discounted like treasury bills, but to avoid confusion with long-term fixed-interest bonds they are best regarded as bills. Since 1985 the Bundesbank has enhanced the flexibility of its ongoing money-market management by introducing new methods of open market operations. As a next step, it is important to see why.

There are several types of money-market paper and types of transactions used in open market operations:

- financing paper
- mobilisation paper
- liquidity paper
- 'quick' tenders
- repurchase agreements

Financing paper, as its title implies, provides short-term financing for part of the public-sector borrowing requirement. It is important to distinguish between, on the one hand, paper issued under this heading which is subject to the Bundesbank's money-market management (and which may therefore be used for refinancing) and, on the other hand, paper which will not be repurchased by the Bundesbank until it reaches maturity ('N paper'). Moreover, the purchase of 'N paper' by the banks is not normally permitted and financing paper may be issued by various public authorities only in consultation with the Bundesbank. Because they create public debt, the Bank has tended to place strict limits on these issues, although the Debt Processing Fund (see Chapter 3: *ibid.*) has been permitted to use the vehicle relatively intensively.

In effect, the other four types of paper are issued on the initiative of the Bundesbank itself. This practice delineates the Bank from other central banks, since it places a constraint on the supply of short-term securities. Mobilisation paper thus derives from the 1948 currency reform and is created on the basis of the DM 8 billion equalisation claims on the Federal government held by the Bundesbank. Liquidity paper originated in the further DM 8 billion allocated by the StWG; it may be used when the full amount of mobilisation paper has been created. However, the annual average of both types of paper between 1986 and 1990 was about DM 5 billion (MRDB: table II[1b]).

Again, unification resulted in an increased issue, but only liquidity paper now appears in the Bank's liabilities (*ibid.*: table III[2]). If they are issued for money-market management purposes, they may be sold only to non-residents and the Federal post office. Clearly, then, open market operations lacked both flexibility and products. A special type of paper was therefore created for money-market management, an idea which was eventually developed into the 'quick tender' arrangement used since the end of 1988. Under this arrangement the Bundesbank has established an intervention rate at which it offers the banks short-term treasury bills, normally with a maturity of three days. Another major development – the repurchase agreement – dates from mid-1979. Securities eligible for use as a collateral for Lombard loans (see below) may be offered by the banks provided they agree to repurchase them, initially within one or two months. From October 1992, these repurchase agreements were modified so that they were of one-month or two-week maturities. The interest rate in all such cases is the repurchase – or *repo* – rate. Although supplemented in 1983, the critical change in open market techniques was undoubtedly the decision to detach the repo rate from the banks refinancing method by the Lombard facility in 1985 (MRDB 7/91: 34–5; Figure 4.2). It has become the key central bank interest rate. These repurchase agreements rocketed from a value of DM 33 billion in 1986 to DM 108 billion in 1989; they continued to rise following unification, reaching DM 150 billion in 1993 (MRDB: table III[1]).

The Bundesbank has emphasised that its instruments do not include ceilings on either bank lending or the interest rates payable for bank deposits and credit; interest on securities is also uncontrolled (BBk 1989: 44). All such interest rate con-

trols were abolished in 1967. It will be shown below, however, that its periods of high central-bank rates have been deflationary. Equally important for the German banking system is the more permanent and conceivably restrictive effect of minimum reserves requirements (MRRs), although in practice the banks may have simply used them as working balances. After all, they have only to fulfil these requirements on average each month. They thus hold hardly any other central bank balances and excess balances are generally very low; indeed, some banks appear occasionally not to meet their requirements – in spite of the 30-day fine of three percentage points above the Lombard rate (MRDB: table V [1]). Since May 1986, MRRs have been differentiated by the *type* of liability subject to these requirements. An increasing *graduated scale* according to amount was retained only for sight deposits. The ratio for the highest point applies to the liabilities to non-residents. When the targeting of central bank money (CBM) is discussed below, it will be seen that this and other changes in the pattern of MRRs created difficulties. Between 1987 and 1993, moreover, MRRs were not changed and there has been a decline in their levels since 1973 (BBk 1989: 64; MRDB table V[1]). On 1 March 1993 the MRRs on both time liabilities and savings deposits were reduced to only two per cent. On the other hand, no change was made to the relatively high graduated scale on sight liabilities, a scale which culminated in a 12.1 per cent rate. Moreover, although DM 32 billion in bank deposits were thus released for lending, the Bundesbank largely neutralised the effect on liquidity by issuing DM 25 billion in short-term paper to non-banks (*Economist* 13 February 1993; FT 5 February 1993). It will be necessary to return to the effects of MRRs on

Germany's ability to offer internationally competitive financial services in the *Finanzplatz Deutschland* section of Chapter 7. The important point here is that MRRs have become relatively unimportant as an instrument of monetary control. Of far greater significance in this respect are the relatively newer instruments for conducting open market operations, particularly the repo rate.

All the central bank's instruments and the system in which they operate can now be viewed in a little more depth. By way of introduction, Figure 4.1 is offered as a summary of this system.

The first thing to note is the pride of place accorded to the Bank's central goal of price stability. Indeed, the medium-term target inflation rate of the Bundesbank policymaker's is a mere two per cent per annum. During the four decades 1950–90, they were ostensibly deflected only by the crude-oil price shocks of the 1970s which had the effect of pulling up the 40-year annual average to 3 per cent (see the discussion surrounding Figures 4.4 below). Doubt has, however, been cast on the assumption that this relative price stability is attributable to the Bundesbank's policymakers (Ramser and Riese 1989: 110–11). Moreover, monetary policy has not been costless in terms of the unemployment created and forgone economic growth, and its incidence was probably misdirected in that it had relatively little impact on wage and price leaders (Riemer 1983: 88). As already indicated, the dynamic export sector made major contributions to recoveries from the recessions created by the Bundesbank's Council. In any case, the Council itself succumbed in 1967 (under pressure from Schiller), and in 1974–5, by adapting its monetary policy to the reflationary needs of the domestic economy (*ibid.*: 237). A similar step-by-step reduction of interest

rates was made in the early 1980s and, under even more notable pressure, in 1993 (see Figure 4.4d below). Finally, West Germany's attractiveness as a financial centre has been severely undermined by the Council's controls (see the account of Schiller's resignation over the *Bardepot* measures below and the section on *Finanzplatz Deutschland* in Chapter 7).

Figure 4.1 next notes the three sources of inflation introduced earlier in this section, namely public-sector budgetary deficits, wage inflation and exchange-rate gyrations. All three of these variables are closely observed by the Bank's Council. The Figure then proceeds to show that although the Bank's instruments operate within the money market by influencing the money stock, there will be consequential effects in the capital and foreign exchange markets. Hence, all three markets will be analysed immediately below. It will then be possible to examine the role of the instruments in monetary policy determination. In addition, the Bundesbank became the first institution where policy makers practised monetary targeting when controlling the money stock took on a new importance in the 1970s. However, it will be shown that defining the monetary aggregate to be targeted and then controlling its growth was not an easy task. This is in any case apparent from the complex processes sketched in Figure 4.1. Above all, it will be found that the pure Friedmanite model of controlling the money supply and introducing flexible exchange rates was eschewed by the Bank's policymakers.

THE MARKETS

How do the Bundesbank policy makers intervene in the money market? First consider open market operations – a technique which has developed into the

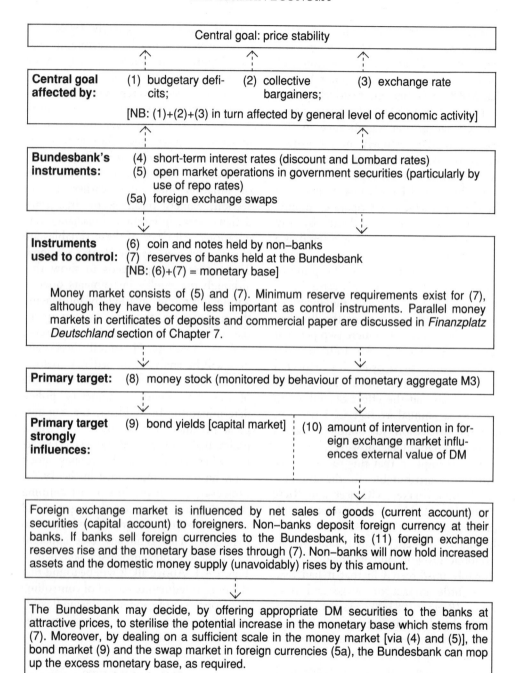

Figure 4.1 The Bundesbank's central goal, indicators, instruments, targets and markets

Sources: Based on McKinnon 1979: 239; Frenkel's comments on Obstfeld 1983: 201; Tew 1989 (also see preface)

Bundesbank's most significant method of managing the money market. By selling (buying) government securities to (from) banks and nonbanks the Bundesbank can reduce (increase) the liquidity of the banking system. As already indicated, these transactions also tend to increase (reduce) interest rates if nonbanks are involved. Far more frequently, the banks are involved in open market operations. In this case the money market is influenced at the rates of interest determined by the Bundesbank's Council. Second, when banks are short of liquid assets, any eligible bills they possess may be rediscounted – in effect sold – to the Bundesbank. Hence, the discount rate determines the 'charge' made by the Bundesbank when it purchases securities. There is a limit placed on the extent to which banks may rediscount bills; this limit is known as the rediscount quota. Hence, the *actual* level of liquidity is raised to the extent that bills are sold to the Bundesbank, whereas the *potential* level of liquidity was for many years controlled by the quota. Third, when a bank has exhausted its rediscount quota, it may resort to borrowing from the Bundesbank using eligible collateral. This is where the Lombard rate is used – a penalty interest rate normally set above the discount rate. Fourth, there are the minimum reserve requirements whereby banks are required to deposit, interest free, a given proportion of their funds at the Bundesbank. The requirements vary according to the type of deposits held by the banks. Failure on the part of any bank to comply with these requirements by the end of a month results in the Bundesbank imposing its special rate on the amount by which the reserves fell short of the requirement. This rate is normally three percentage points above the Lombard rate and it is imposed for a period of 30 days.

During two periods of severe credit rationing in 1973–4 and 1981–2 a special Lombard rate was introduced. It varied from half a percentage point to four percentage points above the normal facility (MRDB: table VI (1)). Initially (in May 1973), the Bundesbank decided to grant no more Lombard facilities for a time. 'But to ease excessive tensions in the money market' the special Lombard facility was introduced from November 1973 (BBk 1982: 47). This new facility could be suspended at any time – in which case the loans had to be repaid the following day. Normal Lombard loans were made available again in July 1974. Following further strict conditions in 1979–80, the Bank again introduced special Lombard conditions between February 1981 and May 1982.

The wholesale money market therefore functions in a narrow and wide sense. The narrowly defined market is concerned with inter-bank dealings in central bank balances. In the wide sense one takes the dealings in money-market paper into account.

Taking the narrow definition first, it is necessary to distinguish between overnight money and longer-term funds. Overnight, or day-to-day, money plays a crucial role because it is used to determine the banks' minimum reserve requirements. These are expressed as a daily average which must be met over the period of each calendar month. But the banks' balances at the Bundesbank often fluctuate quite sharply due to unforeseen foreign-exchange and public-sector cash transactions. The rate on overnight money in the inter-bank market – the call-money rate – would also be subject to marked gyrations if the Bundesbank did not offer adequate refinancing. (In Figure 4.2, the call-money rate is known as the 'day-to-day rate'). The first method of achieving this level of refinancing is by granting discount credit, although the quantity of such borrowing is limited by the discount quotas which in recent years have been generally fully utilised. The second method is the Lombard facility by which the banks may obtain additional liquidity at a penalty rate. While there are no explicit ceilings on Lombard credit, the Bundesbank discourages the use of Lombard credit in large amounts or over long periods.

Longer-term funds – usually with one or three months time horizons – generally enable the banks to redress foreseeable liquidity disequilibria, such as shortages on the part of private-sector customers on major tax payment dates. (Likewise, all three levels of government may experience cash shortages when they are awaiting tax payments). Since discount credit is restricted to a maximum period of up to three months, the discount rate would be the operative instrument in these cases if access to discount credit were not limited by the discount quota. This limitation on recourse to discount credit, and the consequent need for the banks to seek additional means of refinancing, results in the rate for three-month funds lying above the discount rate. Its precise level is determined by the Bundesbank's monetary-policy stance.

Hence, the Bundesbank sets out to achieve its monetary- and credit-policy objectives by controlling the unsatisfied demand for central bank balances and the refinancing terms for the funds the banks themselves require. In this sense, the wholesale money market consists of bank deposits at the Bundesbank. Minimum requirements are set by the Bank and the system is geared to maintain them. Monetary-policy options are used by the Bank not just to control the demand for money by the banks at its rates of interest but also to iron out any distortions created

by retail operations, particularly by intervention in the foreign exchange market (see below). Another large retail variable is the seasonal tax revenues which decrease bank liquidity when they are credited to the Federal and Länder accounts at the Bundesbank.

In the wide sense, it was stated above, the wholesale money market consists of dealing in money-market paper. Although the Bundesbank also deals with foreign investors and public institutions, especially the Federal Post Office and the ERP Special Fund, money-market regulation is confined to dealing between the Bundesbank and the banks. Since the deregulation of interest rates in 1967, the Bundesbank and the Federal Finance Ministry have unsuccessfully attempted to extend participation in the non-regulatory part of the money market to the non-banks, either directly or through the medium of the banks. Hence, the Bundesbank sets the selling rate for this type of money-market paper. Much of the paper is created, on the other hand, by the Federal and Länder governments, as well as the Federal Railways and Post Office. This paper, issued in conjunction with the Bundesbank, enables these authorities to meet short-term financial requirements. In other words, some of the public sector borrowing requirement is met in this way. Since almost all the paper issued in this manner, however, has not been included in the Bundesbank's market-regulating arrangements, the banks have in recent years not been permitted to hold paper of this category. Otherwise, in the view of the Bundesbank, there was a danger of the money supply being increased if the banks presented such paper for refinancing.

Because there are potential limitations on the Bundesbank's ability to conduct open market operations and therefore control bank liquidity, a second source of money-market paper is in effect the Bundesbank itself. As already shown, it has developed several means of creating such paper. First, under Section 42 of its founding statute it may request the Federal government to convert into treasury bills all or part of the DM 8 billion equalisation claim which it holds on the Federal government as a result of the 1948 currency reform. The Act knows this as 'mobilisation paper'. Second, the StWG (1967) added clause 42a to the Bundesbank's founding statute which increases the amount of mobilisation paper available by a further DM 8 billion. This is liquidity paper. Additionally, the Bundesbank has established an intervention rate at which it offers short-term treasury bills, usually with a maturity of three days – known above as the 'quick tender' or treasury bill selling rate. As it is now used, it has become one of two new methods of money-market management, the other being a repurchase rate. Thus the call money rate is bounded from above by the Lombard rate and, until mid-1991, from below by the 'quick tender' rate offered by the Bundesbank on short-term treasury bill transactions; the call money rate, in turn, follows the repurchase rate (MRDB 7/91: 34–5). Such an approach has increased the relative significance of managing liquidity in the money market by means of open market operations. It has detached the banks' refinancing from the Lombard facility. Variations in the Lombard and discount rates, which used to be key Bundesbank interest rates, now *follow* preparatory liquidity policy measures. This entirely new approach to monetary control is illustrated in Figure 4.2. (The *rise* in interest rates following unification is also apparent; the general *variability* of interest rates will prove to be the basic feature of the section on key monetary variables below.) The

Bundesbank described this new approach as follows (BBk 1989: 106):

. . . the discount and Lombard windows can take on a sort of 'buffer function' which offsets the monthly deficits or surpluses in central bank balances, in so far as these are not neutralised . . . by the central bank. Since the money market has been managed more flexibly, this 'buffer function' has lost significance because fluctuations in the banks' central bank money requirements are largely offset through fine-tuning measures by the Bundesbank . . .

Note that reference has been made solely to the internal management of the money market. Interest-rate variations have, however, critical external repercussions. Repo-rate changes initiate international speculation as to possible movements in the Lombard 'ceiling' and the discount 'floor'. During a period of rising interest rates, an upward movement in the Lombard rate will almost certainly herald a general international movement in the same direction. Conversely, a reduction in the discount rate not only indicates lower interest rates in the wider German economy, but also more generally declining rates internationally. Although the ERM brought this speculation into sharp relief, the growing international role of the DM has for many years meant that such speculation is more general in nature.

The credit and capital markets are dominated by the German banks. This is because, as will be seen in Chapter 7, the central characteristic of the German banking system is its universal nature. In short, the banks all deal in every type of business – both long- and short-term. For various reasons – also to be explored in Chapter 7 – the share market is somewhat underdeveloped; the bond market is thus by far the most important securities market in

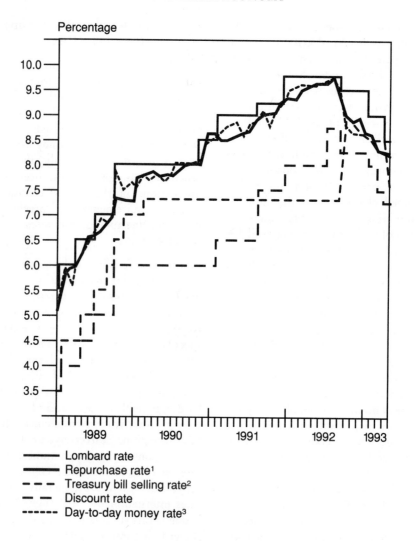

Figure 4.2 Interest Rates of the Bundesbank and the day-to-day Money Rate

Sources: Report of the BBk 1990: 41; 1991: 42; 1992: 53 and MRDB Table VI(2)

Notes: [1] Average rate during month applied to securities repurchase agreements with one-month or, from October 1992, with two-week maturities; uniform allotment rate (fixed-rate tender) or weighted allotment rate ('US-style' variable-rate tenders).
[2] Normally for 3 days.
[3] Monthly averages.

Germany. The banks are by far the largest issuers and investors in this market. They act as intermediaries in issues of securities by nonbanks, whether they are bonds or shares. For this reason, a Central Capital Market Committee was established by the most important issue banks in 1957. An observer from the Bundesbank is present at all of its deliberations; a representative of the Federal government is also sometimes in attendance. Under the StWG, statutory orders which place various limitations on public-sector bond issues may be made by the Federal government. Any such orders are valid for up to one year and can only be made with the approval of the Bundesrat. A Federal Act which has had a much more controversial history – the External Trade and Payments Act (AWG 1961) – sought to impose restrictions on the purchase of foreign securities by German nationals and the sale of domestic securities to non-residents. It will be shown below that Federal Finance and Economics Minister Schiller resigned over the exercise of these powers; moreover, there are limitations on their unilateral use under the EC treaty (Article 73).

Two difficulties are encountered when referring to the bond market. First, it is an oversimplification to refer to the long-term rate of interest: the structure of long-term rates is related to the varying terms over which funds are invested. Second, it is at the short end of the bond market where the direct impact of monetary and liquidity policy is most pronounced – because it is here where the substitutional links are quite significant. Nonetheless, contrary to Germany's historical experience, there are nowadays marked nominal interest-rate fluctuations in the bond market; the impact of foreign purchases on this variability was mentioned towards the end of Chapter 3, but the domestic banks have also had an influence by switching to

bond purchases when the demand for capital has been low (MRDB 4/78: 15). The largest gyrations coincided with the high rates in the money market (1973–4 and 1980–2). The fact that long-term rates fell below short-term rates following unification, and also remained relatively low by international standards, were both seen by Bundesbank policymakers as a vote of confidence in their anti-inflationary stance as far as short-term rates were concerned (Figures 3.10 and 3.11 above; MRDB 2/93: 9). Such confidence could not be disappointed because (MRDB *ibid.*):

. . . if fears arise that it will not be possible to reduce the rate of price rises to an acceptable level, setbacks in the capital market might well be the upshot. This would hit borrowers harder than any easing of short-term interest rates, *for longer-term funds account for 83 per cent of all bank lending*, and short-term loans for only 17 per cent thereof (writer's emphasis).

Superficially at least this means that short-term interest rates have a relatively negligible internal effect. It will be seen below, however, that an exaggerated importance may have been accorded to the 'acceptable level' of price rises. It will also be shown that the relatively high short-term rates caused a substitution of higher yielding bank deposits for bonds. This made the control of the money supply more difficult.

Externally, high short-term interest rates in Germany have international effects via the foreign-exchange market. Above all, these high rates make the DM even more attractive to international speculators. Short-term capital movements into DM securities may therefore be reduced if short-term interest rates in other economies are kept above German levels. With fixed exchange rates, however, the German money supply is affected not only by the domestic demand for money, but also by the inflows of foreign currency which are exchanged for DMs. There are thus two consequences to be examined below. First, what effect do these inflows have on the foreign-currency reserves, especially if the exchange rates of the DM are changed? Second, how can the Bundesbank policymakers prevent the domestic money supply increasing, given that this will cause inflationary pressure to increase? (If the Bundesbank's policymakers were able to permit the money supply to rise sufficiently, interest rates would fall and capital outflows would occur.) The alternative would have been to implement a system of flexible exchange rates, but among other things international treaties have not permitted such a development. Although comparatively little will be added about the policy implications of the foreign-exchange market at this stage, it will be necessary to return to the critically important nature of this topic when the phenomenon of imported inflation is considered below. Consider for now simply its main features.

First, the banks also play a dominating role in the German forex market, acting as both dealers and intermediaries. This dominance means that the Bundesbank's policymakers must for the following reason always pay close attention to bank lending. To the extent that German exporters deposit their significantly high export earnings at their banks, they will receive DM credit balances. These export earnings will be in foreign currencies which the banks may present to the Bundesbank for conversion into DMs and crediting to their central-bank balances. To the extent that the Bundesbank does not require the banks to purchase its

securities, the banks will be able to increase their lending by an amount equivalent to the rise in their central-bank balances. The money supply thus rises by some multiple of the increase in bank lending.

Foreign exchange dealing therefore requires full convertibility at a given rate of exchange between currencies. This was introduced in West Germany, along with most other European countries, in 1958. (The UK was the major exception – Gallant 1988: 10.) Under the Bretton Woods fixed-exchange rate regime, which collapsed in 1971, the DM gained in international strength and importance. Two DM revaluations – in 1961 and 1969 – were required. In 1972, under the 'snake in the tunnel' arrangement, the DM and various other European exchange rates were managed in their relationship to each other and to the US dollar. The fixed parities against the US dollar were required as a result of the Smithsonian agreement. After 1973, the 'snake' was floated against the dollar and the 'tunnel', along with the Smithsonian parities, both disappeared. From 1979, the EMS – which incorporated an exchange-rate mechanism – was in operation. Given that the DM was committed to all these systems, the Bundesbank's policymakers became actively involved in their administration – see below. During the regime of fixed exchange rates, demand for the DM increased in the forex markets and the West German banks became increasingly engaged in international money-market dealing and lending. Their nominal short-term foreign assets grew from DM 2 billion at the end of 1958 to DM 15.5 billion in 1968 (BBk 1982: 39). From December 1968, this data series is not fully comparable due to a change in valuation, but the increase in the banks' short-term foreign assets continued to grow between 1969 (DM 17.4 billion) and 1973 (DM 26.2 billion); with the advent of a floating exchange rate against the US dollar, there was an even more dramatic increase: DM 73 billion in 1981 and DM 265 billion in 1993 (MRDB: table X(7)). When the relatively low West German inflation rate, along with the revaluation of the DM, are taken into account, the growth in the real value of these holdings dramatically demonstrates the important international position of Germany's banks.

Second, the growth in the banks' short-term foreign assets from 1958–68 was the result of changes in the Bundesbank's policy stance. Fixed exchange rates and full convertibility led the Bundesbank to encourage the banks to acquire interest-bearing assets to counterbalance large inflows of funds from abroad. Increasing amounts of short-term foreign assets were also acquired by the banks. Relatively little mobilisation paper was sold to the banks, especially following the 1967 domestic recession when domestic liquidity was increased. Although no more mobilisation and liquidity paper was sold to the banks after 1975, part of the massive inflows of liquidity from abroad in 1978 was absorbed by the Bundesbank selling non-returnable money-market paper to the banks. This paper was repurchased prematurely in 1980 to counterbalance the outflows of foreign exchange (BBk 1989: 67).

Third, the advent of floating exchange rates did not absolve the Bundesbank from intervention in the foreign exchange markets. In the policy section below, it will be shown that in many ways this is the most significant aspect of the Bundesbank's history. To understand the background, it is necessary to appreciate that the Bundesbank built up enormous foreign exchange reserves in the period prior

to floating (see Figure 4.3). Speculation in favour of a revaluation of the DM and export surpluses meant that the Bundesbank – the only official holder of foreign currency reserves in West Germany – purchased large amounts of foreign currency in order to maintain the various fixed parities. The largest holding was in US dollars. (Gold reserves are valued at their original acquisition price of DM 13.7 billion dollars). Central bank money grew as the Bundesbank purchased these foreign currency inflows for DMs. Indeed, the Bundesbank itself attributed the creation of central bank money 'largely (to) the "monetisation" of foreign assets' (BBk 1982: 22). Nor could it withdraw from intervention in the foreign exchange market after the advent of floating exchange rates in 1973. Somewhat euphemistically, the Bundesbank added it still had to pursue a policy of smoothing out short-term fluctuations in the DM/US$ exchange rate in order to 'maintain orderly market conditions' (*ibid*.: 40). Moreover, the intervention commitments under the European monetary arrangements have added an additional dimension to the Bundesbank's international commitments. The big difference between the period towards the end of the fixed exchange rate regime and 1989–90 was that foreign holdings, including mobilisation and liquidity paper, rose quite steeply during the latter period. The consequent decline in the Bundesbank's foreign currency reserves can be seen in Figure 4.3.

Bocklemann, in discussing Obstfeld's paper (1983), nicely draws together the relative position of the changes in the methods of intervention in the money and the foreign-exchange markets:

In recent years the Bundesbank has refined its methods of supplying or withdrawing reserves from the system, and

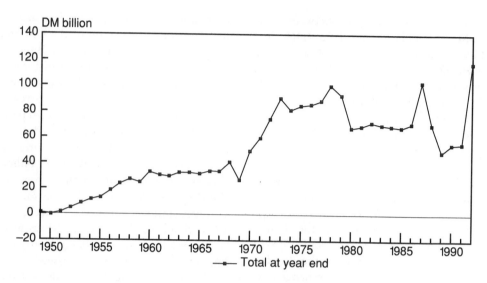

Figure 4.3 Foreign Currency Reserves
Source: MRDB Table X(6a)

correspondingly less use has had to be made of the relatively cumbersome methods of increasing or lowering reserve requirements or changing rediscount quotas. Outright interventions in the foreign-exchange market as a means of adjusting the reserve position of banks are not among these new methods; swap transactions and repurchase agreements involving foreign exchange have, however, been used in this way.

THE TRENDS IN KEY MONETARY INDICATORS

With the aid of Figures of 4.4a, 4.4b, 4.4c and 4.4d, the behaviour of the key monetary indicators will now be analysed. For many reasons, all of which will become clear as the analysis proceeds, it will be necessary to concentrate mainly on the time-period since 1970. As in so many other cases examined in this book, it will be shown that a series of dramatic econ-

omic events culminated in GEMSU. The variables requiring analysis are:

- interest rates
- the supply of money
- the rate of inflation
- the DM/US$ exchange rate

The obvious starting point in the context of this chapter is the behaviour of the Bundesbank's interest-rate policy. As early as 1962, Opie observed that there had been a greater degree of interest-rate volatility in West Germany than any other European country: between 1948 and 1961 the discount rate had changed twenty-three times. However, the greatest degree of post-war variability in this set of instruments came in the 1970s and 1980s (MRDB 4/78, 1/83 and 7/91). Moreover, the highest West German levels were reached in the 1970s and very early 1980s (Owen Smith 1983: 116–18); indeed, in 1973–4 and 1981–2 Lombard loans were not generally available to the banks and 'special' Lombard rates were introduced (MRDB Tables VI[1 and 2]). Figure 4.4a therefore plots the course of nominal interest rates during these two decades. When the factors involved in the level and variability of these rates have been discussed, it will be possible to consider the implied level of real interest rates by including price inflation in Figure 4.4b. (As already shown in Figures 3.10, 3.11 and 4.2, there was another sharp increase in short-term nominal interest rates following GEMSU. Hence, as well as unification, other factors must be borne in mind when considering both the level and variability of the interest-rate instruments. They will be analysed in no particular order of importance, but rather by developing the argument using Figures 4.4a–d).

The first factor was the use of short-term interest rates to achieve monetary targets as from December 1974. Figure 4.4a shows that, predictably, the growth of the money supply is inversely related to interest rates in the money market. (Monthly values of this variable are expressed in the figure as annual averages). The closing of the Lombard window in 1973–4 and 1981–2 are graphic illustrations of the growth in the monetary target variable being low when interest rates are high. Until 1987, the target was central bank money (CBM). This consists of cash in circulation plus the banks' minimum reserves requirements (MRRs). The Bundesbank attributed its choice of this aggregate to the availability of information and data, as well as the CBMs income velocity of circulation being historically fairly stable in comparison to the behaviour of other monetary aggregates. From January 1988 the target has been M3. The aggregate M3 consists of currency in circulation, plus the three types of bank deposits in Germany: sight deposits of domestic nonbanks with domestic banks;

time deposits of the same nature, along with funds borrowed for less than four years; and the savings deposits of non-banks at statutory notice, again held at domestic banks (BBk 1989: 84; MRDB 2/88: 9). These two measures of the money stock have therefore been plotted as appropriate in Figure 4.4a.

Since the banks' MRRs vary according to the type of deposit, CBM is a weighted average of the components of the broader aggregate M3 (Trehan 1988: 31–2). But the pattern of these weights on MRRs had changed since 1974, the base year for defining this element of CBM for targeting purposes. In addition, since 1978 the banks have been permitted to deduct their holdings of domestic legal tender from MRRs. These holdings doubled as a proportion of the total requirement between 1978 and 1991 (MRDB: Table IV[2a]). Indeed, currency in circulation rose from the mid-1970s; it grew particularly strongly in the second half of the 1980s (BBk 1989: 17–18). After the monetary target was overshot in 1987, the Bundesbank believed that its monetary stance would be clearer if it changed to M3 as a basis for monetary targeting; its reasoning ran as follows (*ibid.*: 93):

. . . owing to the smaller share of currency in [M3] (about 11 per cent), its response to interest and exchange rate swings and to the random fluctuations in the demand for DM banknotes at home and abroad is less pronounced than that of the CBM.

Because of its vital policy relevance, especially during the 1970s when 'monetarism' was in vogue, this section will be concluded by returning to the Bundesbank's experience with monetary targeting.

The second factor which increased the variability and levels of interest rates was the DM/US$ exchange rate. Following the introduction of floating in March

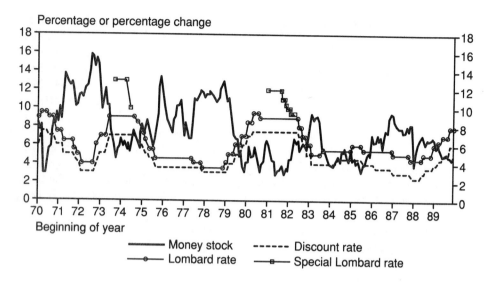

Figure 4.4a Key Monetary Indicators (money stock and interest rates)
Source: MRDB Table VI (1)/*Beihefte Reihe* 4 and 5

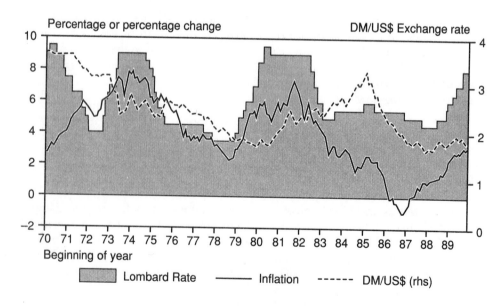

Figure 4.4b Key Monetary Indicators (interest, inflation and DM/US$ exchange rates)
Source: As Figure 4.4a

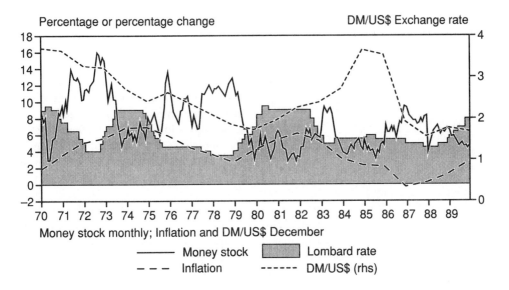

Figure 4.4c Key Monetary Indicators
(money stock, interest, inflation and exchange rates)

Source: As Figure 4.4a

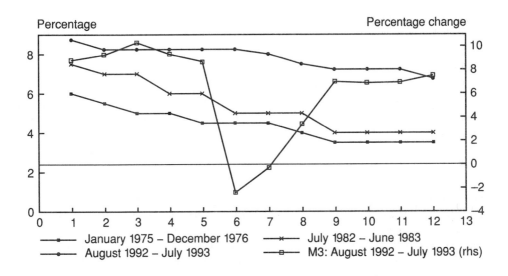

Figure 4.4d Discount Rate decreases (1975–6; 1982–3; 1992–3) and M3 (1992–3)

Source: MRDB Table VI (1)/*Beiheft* 4

1973, the external scope for interest-rate policy was widened, although this scope was somewhat narrowed again by (BBk 1989: 55):

- the European 'snake'
- the establishment of the EMS in 1979
- the increasing integration of financial markets
- the consequent greater global inter-dependence of interest rates

The course of the monthly average of the middle spot DM/US$ exchange rate is shown in Figure 4.4b. Note how the DM appreciated during the 1970s, particularly after the final collapse of the fixed exchange rate regime in 1973. In January 1970 the rate was DM 3.69 to the US$; in the same month in 1973 it was DM 3.20, and by 1980 DM 1.72. Thereafter the DM began to depreciate until early 1985, reaching a trough value (the right hand scale has not been inverted) of DM 3.31 to the US$ in March 1985. The subsequent appreciation was halted, among other things, by unification.

There are two further, if closely related, reasons for the periodic high levels of interest rates and their high degree of variability since 1970. The first is the rate of inflation, while the second reason is the higher rate of increase in labour costs. The latter will be analysed in Chapter 6. Suffice it to say here that the growth of money wage rates has always been closely observed by the Bundesbank's policy-makers (see Figure 4.1).

Consider for now the rate of domestic inflation. Because Germany produces a negligible amount of crude oil, the three oil price shocks which occurred in 1973, 1979–81 and 1986 were bound to critically affect the West German economy. In 1973, the international price of a barrel of oil (customarily quoted in US$) more than trebled; between 1979 and 1981 it nearly

doubled again. By 1981, the dollar price of imported oil was twenty times higher than in 1970, but because the DM/US$ exchange rate appreciated throughout the 1970s and there was a relatively small growth (in volume terms) in crude-oil imports, the import bill expressed in DM rose eightfold (*Die Zeit* 1/79 and 42/88). Nonetheless, this was still sufficient to have a marked impact on the domestic price level, of course, as can be seen from the two peaks in Figure 4.4b. In this figure the monthly percentage changes in the all-items index have been expressed as annual averages (1985 = 100). Inflation in 1973–4 – at 7 per cent – was at its highest since 1951 when exceptional circumstances also prevailed (see below). In 1981 the second peak was nearly 6.5 per cent. During these two periods, then, interest rates were held at high levels mainly because of inflation-ary pressures in the economy.

The third oil price shock was in the opposite direction. By 1986, the average annual price of a barrel of oil (US$ 15.35) was under half the level it had been in 1981. Moreover, it has just been seen that the depreciation in the DM/US$ exchange rate peaked in early 1985. Import prices in 1986 were on average 19 per cent lower than in 1985; the Bundesbank president at the time (Pöhl) was quite euphoric about the level of monetary stability 'achieved' (Kennedy 1991: 66). There were consist-ent monthly falls in the price level over the previous year – see Figure 4.4b. This was again reminiscent of the early 1950s. Unlike the early 1950s, however, there was a sustained period of low interest rates: between early 1986 and the end of 1987 the average discount rate was 3 per cent. It fell at one point to the record low of 2.5 per cent (see Figure 4.4a).

By way of a conclusion to this over-view, the four variables have been drawn together in Figure 4.4c. The central feature must be the fluctuations in the growth of the money supply, especially given the Bundesbank's monetary targeting during most of the period covered. There are compelling reasons for including the first half of the 1970s in the figure. Monetary targeting began in 1975 as a result of rapid monetary growth, increasing inflationary pressure and rising unemployment; externally, the same factors, plus accelerating raw material prices, had led to a final collapse of fixed exchange rates by 1973 (Kahn and Jacobson 1989: 28 and 30). Hence, the nature of these targets deserves further attention. (A definition of their composition was given above.)

The formulation of the money-supply targets has been undertaken in a variety of ways. Table 4.1, which illustrates these different formulations, has significantly become a mandatory feature of German monetary policy studies. Initially, a year on year single target of 8 per cent was used; after only the first year of operation, however, an annual average was introduced – again of 8 per cent. During this period (1975 to 1978) the target was overshot. Following the move to a year on year *range*, the target was achieved between 1979 and 1985. Another new feature of the move to a target range was that the growth in the money stock was now measured over the fourth quarter of the previous year. But the target range was overshot between 1986 and 1988. The formulation in 1989 was changed to 'about 5 per cent'; there was then a return to a range in 1990 and 1991. During the latter half of 1989, apart from August, the growth rate was below the target. (In August the unrounded out-turn for the year as a whole was recorded: 5.2 per cent.) The interesting feature of 1990 was that not even GEMSU prevented the achievement of the target, though the money stock was increased by 15 per cent

to accommodate monetary union (MRDB 7/91: 15). Indeed, as from January 1991, the targeting of M3 covers the whole of the DM currency area. As a result, the absolute amount of M3 increased from DM 1.2 to DM 1.4 billion, but because the demand for money in eastern Germany had fallen, the Central Bank Council decided at its first July (1991) meeting to reduce the target range from 4–6 to 3–5 per cent (*ibid.*). In spite of the regular mid-year review of monetary growth targets, this was the first occasion on which a revision had taken place (Kahn and Jacobson 1989: 21). On the other hand, the targets had gradually declined from their introduction in 1975, reaching 3–5 per cent in 1985; moreover, the revised range for 1991 was identical to the 1985 values (Table 4.1). Given, among other things, the vastly different productive potential between the two parts of Germany, the 1991 revision was probably inevitable (Reichert 1991). Note also that under EMU it would be necessary for the proposed ECBS to consider the EC-wide productive potential in order to determine a monetary growth target. Alternatively, a wider DM bloc of countries – often regarded as a more viable form of monetary union – would take into account the productive potential of all member states. (The importance of the productive potential to the Bundesbank's monetary targets is discussed below.)

As can be seen from Table 4.1, however, the revised target for 1991 was not achieved. For that matter, Table 4.1 also shows that the 1992 target range was higher but still exceeded by an appreciable margin. There were four reasons for the target range being exceeded in 1992, but then being considerably undershot in early 1993 (see Figure 4.4d, which also compares the noteworthy resemblance between the decreases in the discount rate

Table 4.1 The Monetary Targets and their implementation
(per cent)

Year	Target: growth of the central bank money stock or the money stock M3[1]			Actual growth (rounded figures)		
	In the course of the year[2] (%)	As an annual average (%)	More precise definition during the year	In the course of the year[2] (%)	As an annual average (%)	Target achieved
1975	about 8	–	–	10	–	no
1976	–	8	–	–	9	no
1977	–	8	–	–	9	no
1978	–	8	–	–	11	no
1979	6–9	–	lower limit	6	–	yes
1980	5–8	–	lower limit	5	–	yes
1981	4–7	–	lower half	4	–	yes
1982	4–7	–	upper half	6	–	yes
1983	4–7	–	upper half	7	–	yes
1984	4–6	–	–	5	–	yes
1985	3–5	–	–	5	–	yes
1986	3.5–5.5	–	–	8	–	no
1987	3–6	–	–	8	–	no
1988	3–6	–	–	7	–	no
1989	about 5	–	–	5	–	yes
1990	4–6	–	–	6	–	yes
1991	3–5	–	see note 3	5	–	no
1992	3.5–5.5	–	–	9	–	no
1993	4.5–6.5	–	–	–	–	–

Sources: BBk 1989: 96; *Report* of the BBk 1990: 50; MRDB 12/91 and 2/93; BfG *Standpunkt* 8/92

Notes: [1] As from 1988: money stock M3
[2] Between fourth quarter of the previous year and fourth quarter of the current year; 1975: December 1974 to December 1975
[3] Target revised downwards half way through year from 4–6 per cent

in the 1970s, the 1980s and the 1990s – a subject shortly to be examined in a little more depth). The first reason for the large increase in M3 during 1992 was the rise in one of its components, namely the sharp growth in cash holdings of DM. These holdings increased particularly, but not exclusively, in Eastern Europe. Large amounts of cash were also being taken over the border to Luxembourg where securities which would not be subject to the pending German investment tax were purchased (FT 14 December 1992; also see the account of the international expan-sion of German banking in the 'general aspects' section of Chapter 7). Second, an important counterpart of M3 – bank loans – started to expand rapidly (MRDB 2/92: 9). This was the direct result of an increase in bank deposits, particularly time deposits, as savers switched from the lower interest bearing long-term securi-ties. Bank deposits, it will be recalled, are a part of M3, whereas the longer term secur-ities are not included.

Third, as a former Federal Chancellor (Helmut Schmidt) pointed out, the high short-term rates also attracted considerable amounts of foreign liquidity to Germany (FT 9 October 1992). (Given the circumstances of his departure from office in 1982, he understandably also referred to the large amount of public debt being created by the Kohl government, especially by subsidies and tax allowances in areas from defence to agriculture – *ibid*.) Foreign currency reserves were also bolstered as DM were sold on the forex markets during the various ERM crises in 1992–3. As a result of the *quasi* fixed (or managed) exchange rate of the DM, the short-term capital inflows would have provided the impetus to the rise in the money supply, just as the more flexible dollar exchange rate may have contributed to the relatively slower growth of M3 in the USA (compare the Bayerische LB *Review* August 1992, but also see the *Economist* 10 October 1992). On the other hand, the reason may simply be related to the greater involvement of nonbanks in the ownership of treasury bills in the USA – a situation studiously avoided by the Bundesbank. This means that initially US bank deposits can be transferred from the US importer to the exporter. Where the exporter is German, the dollar deposit may be exchanged via a German bank for DM at the Bundesbank. If so, the Bundesbank, acting as a nonbank in the USA, may purchase US treasury bills with the increase in its dollar reserves. There is thus no change in the US bank's central-bank balances and also no change in the US money supply. (West Germany was a significant holder of US debt – Gowland 1991: 35.) Conversely, the rise in the German bank's central-bank balances will increase the money supply if the Bundesbank permits bank lending to increase.

The fourth explanation for the wayward behaviour of M3 relates to its decay at the beginning of 1993. Clearly, the Bundesbank Council's record interest rates had caused M3 to shrink under the pressure of recession. Moreover, pay settlements in the west had been moderated, mainly as a result of the unions' contribution to the solidarity pact. Hence, the abrupt end to the growth in the money supply and, more important, the behaviour of the wage bargainers led to an easing of interest rates in February 1993 (Figure 4.4d). It will be seen in the trade-union policy section of Chapter 6 that a key pay settlement and an interest-rate reduction fell on precisely the same day. Budget deficits, however, were still perceived by the Council as a problem (Chapter 3). These deficits were partially the result of recession, but proposals to reduce social-policy benefits were made at the end of June 1993 (see the conclusion to Chapter 5). Short-run interest rates were duly decreased on 1 July. Meanwhile, the high short-term interest rates had contributed to the strength of the DM and, as a result, other economies, notably within the ERM, had also been obliged to retain high rates – just as they were facing a major slowdown in growth (Chauffour *et al*. 1992: 251). An admirable perspective on the factors discussed in the previous few paragraphs was provided by Sievert (1992: 8–9):

. . . contrary to everyone's expectations, including economists, [we simultaneously achieved] almost an additional DM 400 billion in government transfers and an increase in inflation from a good 2.5 per cent (1989) to currently a bare 3.5 per cent . . . yet we are running the customary risk of eagerly managing the economy, which faces unprecedented exigencies and an undesirable recession . . . [with] above all a monetary target which we have set too low, using a monetary aggregate whose indicative qualities are temporarily – not permanently – impaired . . . We determine the monetary policy for the whole of Europe. These countries can reasonably expect that we resolve German [monetary] stability problems without displaying inappropriate zeal.

It is of particular interest to note that Professor Sievert subsequently joined the Bundesbank's Council. He was described as possessing 'orthodox credentials' and as someone who had 'helped to design the monetary steering formulae that are still used by the Bundesbank' (*Economist* 12 June 1993). Moreover, inflationary pressure existed in West Germany well before GEMSU and it would in any case have persisted in 1990 (Chauffour *et al.* 1992: 257). Hence, unification did not seem to be responsible for more than a very small share of the 1990 increase in short-term interest rates (*ibid.*). Indeed, West German inflation since the mid-1980s had been due to domestic causes – see especially the medium-term weakening of the dollar exchange rate in Figures 3.10 and 4.4b. Given further hikes in taxation and social-insurance contributions, predictions for 1993 and 1994 indicated that inflation in the west would still be respectively 4 per cent and 3 per cent over the previous year; this was despite a resumption of falling real wages, cuts in unemployment benefits and a reduction of real motor-fuel prices (BfG *Standpunkt* 7/93; Dresdner Bank *Trends* June 1993; WestLB *Economic Analyses*). Admittedly, a strengthening of the dollar against the DM in mid-1993, along with an upturn in bond yields, also made the Bundesbank's policy makers even more cautious about reducing short-term interest rates. Nonetheless, the recession, moderate pay settlements, the Federal government's attempts to cut its deficit, and indications that real GNP in the west would be lower at the end of 1993 and 1994 than in the previous

year, all indicated that domestic factors brought about the 1993 reductions in interest rates (*ibid.*). For example, the reductions on 1 July caused the DM/US$ exchange rate to rise to DM 1.7115 from an overnight DM 1.7075. It remained to be seen, however, whether in the medium term the dollar would emulate its climb of the first half of the 1980s. That would have been good news for German exporters, but would be considered inflationary at the Bundesbank. Irrespective of the tensions within the ERM, the Bundesbank's policymakers were thus not prepared to induce further downward movements in interest rates by lowering the discount rate at the end of July. Finally, West German inflation following the first two crude-oil price shocks, and therefore during the first two periods covered in Figure 4.4d, was as much as three percentage points higher than during the post-GEMSU period (see Figures 4.4b and 4.4c). (Bundesbank and other policymakers seemed to concentrate on west German inflation even after GEMSU.)

Figure 4.4d thus clearly demonstrates this consistent use of short-term interest rates during the periods of relatively high inflation – a policy prescription already discussed above (Figures 3.11 and 4.4b). The chosen proxy is the discount rate. As already shown, this is the relevant rate during periods of falling interest rates. In any case, the Lombard window was closed during the relevant periods in the 1970s and 1980s, so the Lombard rate would have been misleading in this context (Figure 4.4a). Similarly, the repo and 'quick-tender' rates did not exist during the first two recessions. Their fine-tuning role may also cause misleading fluctuations in their behaviour; this applies particularly to the repo rate after mid-1991 (Figure 4.2). Above all, however, note the use of the interest-rate approach to monetary control. Is was seen in the first section that this was one of two sets of instruments, the other being the direct control of bank liquidity and therefore the monetary base. By using an operational interest-rate target, the Bundesbank policy makers have thus focused on the demand for money rather than the orthodox monetarist policy of controlling the supply of money (Witschi 1992: 3). After all, Friedman had advocated the reduction of monetary-policy instruments to quantity-orientated open market operations and the introduction of high minimum reserve requirements (Paprotzki 1991: 56). On the other hand, MRRs became increasingly identified as a major factor undermining the competitiveness of German banking – see the *Finanzplatz Deutschland* section of Chapter 7. Another departure from the Friedmanite model was the absence of flexible DM exchange rates (Paprotzki *ibid.*). As already seen, however, exchange-rate treaties made by politicians, especially the EMS, constrained the discretion of the Bundesbank's Council in this respect. The introduction of monetary targeting in 1974 should not therefore be confused with the received theory of monetary control at that time. Perhaps the most apt metaphor is that it was a case of *Hamlet* without the prince.

Nonetheless, the theoretical correctness of a policy based on the growth of the money supply was not the issue at stake (Riemer 1983: 213). Indeed, during the period 1971–3 monetary control was seen by Bundesbank officials as in a state of near-collapse. Freer capital movements were making it impossible for the Bundesbank to control either money creation or interest rates. Schiller had taken the term 'market' in the SME quite seriously. He therefore abandoned interest-rate controls and preferred free exchange rates as

opposed to capital restrictions (*ibid.*: 223 and 229). Following his resignation, capital controls were introduced (see below). But the liberalisation of West German banking meant that the close relationships between monetary policy, the free liquid reserves of the banks and lending activity all broke down. If the banks could not obtain central-bank money, they continued their lending activities by the easy access West German banks had to the Euromarkets and inter-bank assets (*ibid.*: 230; also see the section on *Finanzplatz Deutschland* in Chapter 7). The Bundesbank's policy makers thus made a substantial departure from attempting to directly control bank liquidity because this method of monetary control had been undermined. It has been shown that CBM was regarded by the Bundesbank policy makers as being more easily controllable. This is only true, of course, if the banks use additional CBM to increase their lending. If they rely on funds from other sources to increase their lending, however, the control problem still remains. Since these additional funds from other sources would be reflected by a corresponding increase in MRRs, monetary *creation* by the central bank is not the same as the measured amount of CBM (Riemer *ibid.*: 213 and 230).

The Bundesbank policy makers base their predictions of the required growth in the money stock on their estimates of the growth in the productive potential, although they may well have underestimated the post-wall productive potential. As a result, the target ranges for M3 in 1991 and 1992 would have been set on the low side. Far less doubtful, however, is the contention that they would prefer to treat the productive potential as a real variable which determines the increase in the demand for money. Since 1984, however, an allowance for 'unavoidable' inflation has been included in the calculations. This is because aggregate demand really determines capacity utilisation, irrespective of the productive potential; and aggregate demand is a nominal variable which (like the money stock itself) can only be measured in current prices. Price increases may therefore already be in the pipeline. Such unavoidable inflation 'can only be eliminated by degrees' (BBk 1989: 97). However, Trehan (1988) arrived at the real value of monetary aggregates by using the GNP deflator in order to convert nominal to real values. His subsequent estimations indicated a stable relationship between, on the one hand, the real value of output and, on the other hand, both CBM and M3. Interest rates also had a stable relationship with CBM. No such stable, long-run relationship existed for M1 and M2 – thus suggesting that both CBM and M3 possessed the characteristics required for a target variable. These findings accorded with the official Bundesbank position on the relative nominal stability of CBM and M3 (BBk 1989: 90):

Both aggregates show in the long run a rather stable positive correlation with the growth of the nominal overall production potential and a negative correlation with interest movements.

Conversely, both M1 and M2 tended to exaggerate the effects of interest-rate movements (*ibid.*: 85–6). Kahn and Jacobson (1989: 23 and 27) also attributed the general success of the Bundesbank's Council in achieving its targets to the choice of aggregate, although they made the prophetic caveat that M3 could develop the distortions which afflicted CBM, or even entirely new distortions. As already shown in the early discussion surrounding Figure 4.4d, it transpired that these 'new distortions' consisted principally of the DM's widespread use in

Eastern Europe and the inversion of the bond yield curve.

There have been times (for example, 1978 and 1986–7) when a deviation from monetary targets was accepted by the Bundesbank as being even propitious. On both occasions, the appreciation of the DM/US$ exchange rate was basically responsible (MRDB 1/83: 13; 7/91: 32). In 1978, the year of the Bonn summit, the Bundesbank's monetary stance was relaxed. Similarly, in 1986–7 monetary policy was subordinated to some extent to the external constraint following the Plaza and Louvre accords. In both cases the monetary targets were overshot. These exceptions would be seen by the Bundesbank as vindicating its view that its general approach to monetary targeting has been pragmatic, but its overall record favourable (BBk 1989: 103). Emminger told the Treasury and Civil Service Committee of the House of Commons that the 1978 overshoot of the money supply target by three percentage points was 'tolerable' under the circumstances (*Evidence II* 1982–3: 237). However, the international agreements just mentioned were not consistent with domestic price stability. For example, the 1987 Louvre accord to stabilise the dollar involved reducing interest rates, at least in the short run. Yet a recovery of inflationary pressure at this juncture really called for a tightening of monetary policy (Kahn and Jacobson 1989: 20).

In short, protecting the domestic purchasing power of the currency, and attaining exchange rate stability, are often incompatible goals (Kennedy 1991: 57; Trehan 1988: 41–2). Restrictive monetary policy measures could only be used effectively if the higher interest rates they generated remained below those of other major countries; in practice, this meant that the Bundesbank's control of the money supply was possible only if foreign interest rates were also rising (Hennings 1982: 488). Moreover, periods of reductions in monetary growth, such as the one introduced to halt the DM's depreciation in 1979–82, generally preceded falling inflation; but periods of monetary expansion, such as the one prompted by the DM's appreciation and internal recession in 1974–9, generally preceded inflation. By the same token, sharply decreasing monetary growth, as in 1973–4 and 1979–81, preceded periods of rapidly rising unemployment; and the effect of monetary policy on unemployment is asymmetric: periods of decreasing monetary growth increased unemployment, whereas increased monetary growth did not reduce unemployment (also see Figure 1.2). Kahn and Jacobson (1989: 31) summarise the arguments of this paragraph:

The sharp increase in unemployment, especially after 1981, reflected the Bundesbank's determination to maintain restrained monetary growth in the face of an inflationary shock. As inflation rose, the Bundesbank kept a tight grip on monetary growth. Adding to the Bundesbank's resolve were a depreciating DM and a Federal government budget deficit [also see Figures 3.8 and 3.9 – writer]. The combined effect of the oil shock and tight monetary policy sent West Germany into a recession that lasted from 1980 to 1982.

Although this section has been mainly confined to the internal conduct of monetary policy, it has been constantly necessary to show how the question of external balance represented an important policy constraint. The DM/US$ exchange rate and the crude-oil price shocks are basic illustrations of this point. In short, an important aspect of the German economy is its open nature. The next section is therefore concerned with wider balance of payments issues.

MONETARY ASPECTS OF THE BALANCE OF PAYMENTS

It is salutary to note the effect of West Germany's relatively low inflation rate on her real exchange rate. This can be done by means of Figure 4.5, in which the nominal and real exchange rates are compared. Note that the nominal exchange rate is expressed as a weighted geometric mean against eighteen other industrialised countries; the real exchange rate is the same measure, except for an added allowance for differential inflation rates. The general appreciation of the DM nominal exchange rate since floating can readily be seen; the DM's international strength and therefore its attraction to investors and speculators derives from this general upward trend. Equally, the economy's competitive strength can be gauged from the performance of the real exchange rate. At first glance it appears that the real exchange rate has remained fairly constant. Given the first two crude-oil price shocks and the other economic circumstances attending the three periods of high interest rates considered in Figure 4.4d, even stability would be a remarkable achievement. On closer examination, however, there was something of a deterioration in West Germany's competitive position in the 1970s. Similarly, there was an improvement in the 1980s. Even unification did not cause a loss of competitiveness in the early 1990s.

Movements in the terms of trade also illustrate the turning point of 1980. They deteriorated on average by −9.2 per cent between 1973 and 1980, which contrasts with a gain of 10.5 per cent between 1980 and 1986; the gains in the terms of trade during the period 1962–73 (12.3 per cent)

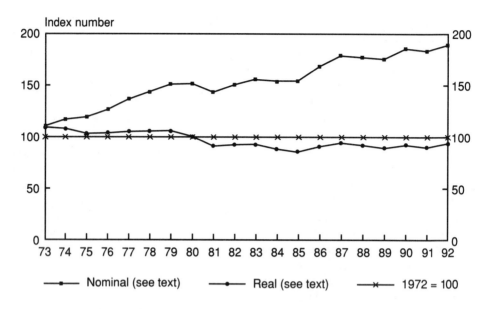

Index number

Figure 4.5 Nominal and Real Exchange Rates
Source: MRDB *Stat Beihefte Reihe* 3: III(2)

had been even greater (OECD *Economic Survey* 1987: 40). Note that this latter period culminates in the final abandonment of fixed exchange rates against the dollar. Were West German exporters given an 'artificial' competitive advantage by the 'reluctance' of the monetary authorities to revalue (Donges 1980: 187)? If so, can this be attributed to the Machiavellian conspiracy between the Bundesbank and German exporters? There are three reasons why such a malevolent view of history should be discounted. First and foremost, it will be shown in the trade section of Chapter 8 that German goods possessed real trade advantages. Second, it is by no means certain that the Bundesbank's policy makers unilaterally achieved the relative price stability which contributed to the gains in both the real exchange rate and the terms of trade. Third, the real gains of the 1980s, in contrast to the deterio-

ration during the 1970s, were not predicted by those who thought that the introduction of flexible exchange rates would remove the 'artificial' advantage by means of a sequence of real revaluations. (During the 1980s, export surpluses soared to unprecedented levels and it became fashionable to see the 1990s as Germany's Armageddon – see the trade section of Chapter 8.) It will be helpful to trace the nominal counterparts of these trends.

Figures 4.6a, 4.6b and 4.6c contain a number of perspectives on the balance of payments. Figure 4.6a compares the current and capital balances. The oscillations in these two balances during the 1970s and 1980s are particularly plain. There is also an indication that there were some fluctuations in the second half of the 1960s when the capital outflows were reversed at the end of the decade but current account surpluses started to mount in magnitude. Although relatively rare, the current account deficits grew secularly worse: DM 1.6 billion in 1962, DM 6.2 billion in 1965 and, during the three successive years 1979, 1980 and 1981, a trough of DM 25 billion was reached in 1980. (The reader will recall that the first two oil shocks occurred during the periods 1973–75 and 1979–81. They were respectively accompanied by current account surpluses and deficits, and by a relatively strong US$ during the first shock but a weak US$ in the second case.) There then followed a very substantial improvement throughout the rest of the 1980s, although the unification shock produced an all-German deficit of nearly DM 33 billion in 1991, and nearly DM 40 billion in 1992.

From an accountancy point of view, the current and capital accounts (including foreign currency reserves) must balance. Hence, the improvement on the current account during the 1980s was matched by increasing net capital outflows (Figure 4.6a). Similarly, the current account deficit in 1991 was accompanied by clearly diminished but nevertheless still high long-term capital outflows. In consequence, the 'compensatory financing' was on the whole focused on the short-term imports of funds – predominantly by the banks (MRDB 3/92: 33). Within the capital account itself, therefore, long-term flows tend to be more autonomous than the 'accommodating' short-term flows. A further means of 'adjustment' lies in the flow of foreign currency reserves which varies with exchange and interest rates. Many important economic implications are, however, concealed by these accountancy conventions. Consider first capital flows.

As can be seen in Figure 4.6b, it is indeed important to distinguish between long and short-term capital flows. A relatively minor short-term inflow in 1960 brought about the DM revaluation of 1961. During the 1950s, sales of services to NATO forces stationed in West Germany, in spite of her becoming a net donor on a growing scale, were added to export surpluses and resulted in an inflow of foreign exchange. The long-term capital outflows were the result of external debt repayments and purchases of foreign securities, whereas the short-term transactions by government, banks and non-banks fluctuated wildly (Yeager 1976: 487). A distinction drawn between these two components of the capital account also reveals that there were concurrent short-term speculative inflows and long-term outflows in 1968–70. There was a consequent revaluation of the DM in 1969. The introduction of a withholding tax on domestic investment income conversely caused an outflow of short-term capital in 1988–9. This outflow was so large that the tax was repealed half way through 1989. (In June 1991, the Constitutional Court ruled that by January 1993 the Federal government would have to introduce an alternative to the voluntary declaration of investment income for tax purposes. The major policy problem was devising a method which did not result in a further panic short-term outflow. The method devised consisted of a flat rate tax of 25 per cent on residents' interest income, deductible from final tax liability, but with a tenfold increase in savers' tax allowances – BBk *Report* 1991: 39.) An important long-term change took place in direct investment: from 1980 the stock of German investment abroad has been (increasingly) greater than foreign investment in Germany, thereby implying a net capital outflow annually. Whether this outflow will be gradually reversed by unification is an intriguing question, but there is up to a four-year lag in data reporting in this area. Finally, the fluctuations in foreign purchases of bonds were seen at the end of

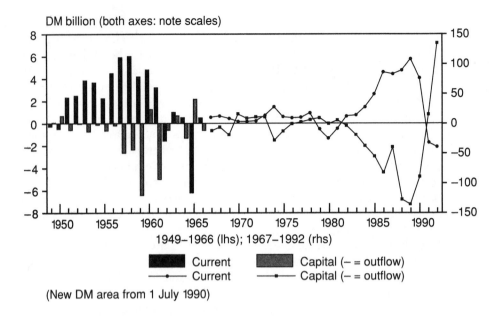

Figure 4.6a Current and Capital Balances

Sources: MRDB *Stat. Beihefte Reihe* 3: 1. See also the note on New DM area

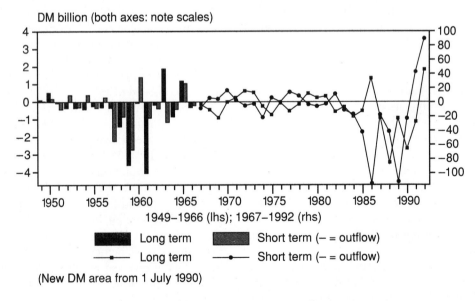

Figure 4.6b Capital Account Balances

Source: Plotted from MRDB *Stat. Beihefte Reihe* 3: 1

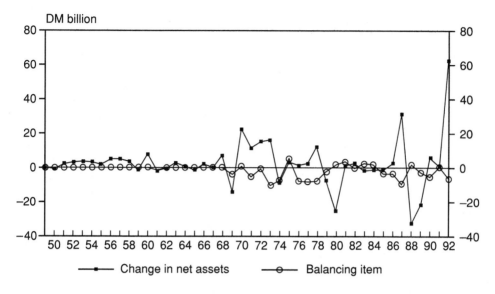

—■— Change in net assets   —○— Balancing item

Figure 4.6c Bundesbank's External Balance
Source: MRDB: Table X (1)

Chapter 3 to be an increasingly important factor on the long-term capital account. The net result of the record DM 60 billion inflow in 1986 is particularly clear in Figure 4.6b. It stands in marked contrast to the short-term outflows to foreign banks in the same year.

Not surprisingly, the annual changes in the Bundesbank's foreign currency reserves, or net external asset position, reflect these oscillations (Figure 4.6c). It is immediately obvious that one cannot refer to any clear trend. Indeed, the second largest annual increase in foreign currency reserves was in 1987 (DM 32 billion), while the largest decrease (DM 32.5 billion) occurred in the following year. The large inflow in 1987 is attributable to the stock market crash and the subsequent weakness of the dollar. Not surprisingly, the largest increase (DM 62 billion) occurred in the ERM's crisis year of 1992. (The magnitudes were even larger in 1993 prior to substantial widening of

the bands for fluctuations.) There were also large changes in 1970 and 1980. Their magnitudes were DM 23 billion and −DM 26 billion respectively. For the period as a whole (1949–92), the median was only DM 2 billion. Of these 44 observations, 36 lie between −DM 15 billion and DM 15 billion, with a standard deviation of DM 14 billion. This apparent stability generally stems, however, from the period prior to 1968. The subsequent variation is evident from Figure 4.6c. Significantly, there was also an isolated peak in 1960.

In other words, the variation observable in Figure 4.6c is largely attributable to exchange-rate fluctuations. This can be seen from the balancing item which is the counterpart of changes in the Bundesbank's external position that are not attributable to current and capital transactions with non-residents. Hence, the balancing item indicates the changes in the DM value of the Bundesbank's assets and liabilities denominated in foreign currencies owing to the valuation adjustment at the end of the year (MRDB table X[1]). For example, the only such adjustments during the 1960s, given the fixed-exchange rate regime, took place at the time of the two DM revaluations in 1961 and 1969. In 1961, over half of the fall in reserves was accounted for by a revaluation. In 1969, DM 4 billion of the DM 14 billion decline in reserves was represented by a revaluation. Thereafter, the Bundesbank generally accumulated foreign reserves until 1978, usually at a more rapid rate than their revaluations. After a sizeable outflow in 1980, the weak dollar contributed to a number of revaluations which kept the reserves fairly constant for the first half of the 1980s. The reasons for subsequent oscillations have already been discussed. A president of the Bundesbank (Karl Otto Pöhl) quantified the value of these oscillations as follows (*Der Spiegel* 4/88):

If the DM/US$ exchange rate declines by one Pfennig (= DM 0.01), the foreign currency reserves of the Bundesbank decline by DM 500 million.

Finally, Figure 4.7 demonstrates how under the fixed exchange rate regime, the foreign currency reserves of the Bundesbank gradually rose. The only exceptions, of course, are the revaluations in the DM/US$ exchange rate in 1961 and 1969. These revaluations had the effect of reducing the relatively negligible degree of inflationary pressure. In any case, during the 1960s sterilisation – discussed below – was a feasible short-run strategy in the case of West Germany (Obstfeld 1982). Moreover, although the Allies initially set the dollar exchange rate at DM 3.33 in May 1949, it was arbitrarily devalued to DM 4.20 in September. This rate was to prove highly advantageous to West German exporters. Investment and productivity also rose rapidly, and conse-

quently the rises in nominal wage rates were not inflationary; indeed, the relative price stability in West Germany during the 1950s and 1960s may be more attributable to these factors than to monetary policy (Ramser and Riese 1989: 111). Externally, the DM/US$ fixed exchange rate, along with convertibility, pegged West Germany's price level to that of the USA – the latter being quite stable from 1951 to the mid-1960s (McKinnon 1979: 257). On the other hand, during the 1950s the inflow of foreign exchange shown in Figure 4.7 derived mainly from positive current account balances; but from 1960 short-term (speculative) capital also became a problem. The Bundesbank in particular feared that excessive liquidity entering the economy in this way would cause domestic prices to rise. It therefore became known as 'imported inflation', although the term was often extended to cover the more nebulous concept of contact with trading partners whose inflation rate was higher. (The wage and price leaders in the domestic economy were also generally found in the dynamic export sector – Riemer 1983: 88). Even before 1960, the money supply expanded rapidly and the low inflation rate may be partly an indication of the success in combating imported inflation (Yeager 1976: 489–90).

At the time of the first revaluation (1961), the exchange rate against US$1 was reduced by DM 0.20 to DM 4.00 (an increase in export prices of 5 per cent, but a decrease in import prices of 4.76 per cent). Initially, this measure seemed to be successful: in 1962, the trade balance was halved, the current account balance was −DM 1.6 billion and short-term capital was flowing out of the economy. But, as will be seen in more depth in Chapter 8, the trade surplus soon recovered its spectacular growth; the only notable exceptions occurred in 1965 and 1980, when the current account was consequently in deficit (Figure 8.9). However, France and Italy – two of West Germany's 'new' EC trading partners – deflated their economies as early as 1963–4 to counteract their trade deficits with Germany (Denton *et al.* 1968: 172 and 357). Significantly, the Bundesbank blamed this on an *ex ante* lack of monetary discipline, while the trading partners blamed the Bundesbank's one-sided pursuit of monetary stability. Even at this early stage, however, some form of international action was commonly considered to be the only tenable long-term solution. Meanwhile, the 1965 current account deficit meant that the Bundesbank for the first time since 1960 could raise interest rates to control domestic inflation without undue anxiety about imported inflation from capital inflows. Until this juncture these inflows during the 1960s would have exacerbated the problem of large foreign exchange

inflows from current-account surpluses. Reliance had therefore been placed on measures such as taxing the capital earnings of non-residents. The Bundesbank's zealous use of this short respite in which it could use the interest-rate instrument caused a domestic recession in 1967. But by 1968 both current-account surpluses and capital inflows were again a problem.

The percentage changes resulting from the second revaluation in 1969 were nearly double their 1961 values: the DM/US$ rate was reduced to DM 3.66, thereby increasing export prices by 9.3 per cent, but reducing import prices by 8.5 per cent. As can be seen in Figure 4.7, this latter revaluation in particular still did not obviate the need for foreign-currency purchases by the Bundesbank. By the spring of 1971, an international monetary crisis caused several countries, notably West Germany to sever temporarily their rigid link to the dollar. Later in the year the Smithsonian agreement resulted in a

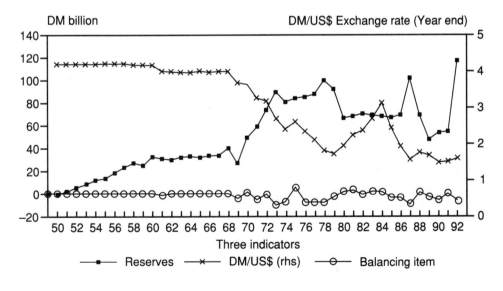

Figure 4.7 Bundesbank's External Position

Source: Stat. Beihefte Reihe 3 and 5

transient reprieve for fixed exchange rates, although with wider bands. Yet in the meantime, the DM/US$ rate had fallen even further (to DM 3.27). Following the formal adoption of floating exchange rates in 1973, there were phases of appreciation and depreciation in this exchange rate (a phenomenon also discussed in the previous section). The dollar was noticeably supported in 1978 and 1987 – the times when West Germany, along with Japan, led international efforts to stabilise the dollar. The Bundesbank reviewed the experience under floating exchange rates as follows (MRDB 5/88: 20):

In particular, the rate for the dollar tended to display swings whose implications for business activity could not be ignored. Whenever excessive appreciations of the DM rate threatened seriously to disturb domestic economic trends – as in 1978 and 1986–87 – the Bundesbank of necessity tolerated the overshooting of its monetary targets in order to mitigate the upward pressure by keeping interest rates down and buying foreign exchange, in order to bolster domestic demand.

In addition, the expectation of an appreciation in the DM can also attract long-term capital flows into the bond market (see the Conclusion to Chapter 3).

But the international changes in the position of the DM are not confined to its crucial role in supporting the international rate of the dollar in a regime of floating exchange rates. It also came to be used more frequently in international trade, financing and reserve transactions. The global interdependence of the money and financial markets saw the rise of the 'Euro-market' offering special conditions for international banking, especially in Luxembourg. In the course of these developments, the DM developed into a major international reserve and investment currency (ibid.: 21). In addition, the DM became a major intervention currency, as well as being used for international transactions. It began to play a key role in the EMS since other central banks in the system endeavour to stabilise their own exchange rates by buying and selling DMs, a role on which this analysis will concentrate in a moment. At this point, however, it must be stressed that the Bundesbank opposed the creation of these obligations because of the 'considerable problems' they pose for an economy; it attributes the development of the DM as a second reserve currency to 'the markets' (ibid.: 22). One must re-emphasise, however, that politicians formulated the Bonn, Plaza and Louvre accords; similarly, the EMS is primarily a political creation, albeit that the Bundesbank is represented as part of the German delegation at international monetary conferences (Sturm 1990: 278). Every international monetary agreement to which West Germany was a party thus sooner or later reflected the influence of the Bundesbank's Council. Since GEMSU involved negotiations between the representatives of two sovereign states, it was also primarily a political step. It will be shown below, however, that the Bundesbank president resigned because of, among other things, the lack of consultation with Bundesbank policymakers over GEMSU. GEMSU also probably further stiffened the resolve of the Bundesbank's Council as to the conditions necessary for EMU. After all, it was envisaged that EMU would replace the EMS as it had developed: EC member states wanted to abandon a fixed-exchange rate system in which monetary decisions were taken by one dominant country (Chauffour et al. 1992: 251). Macroeconomic aggregates would be defined on a European scale and the German inflation rate, for example, would have less of an impact on European monetary policy (*ibid*.: 263 and 272). Subsequent sections of this chapter are therefore concerned with such matters.

It is first necessary to briefly review the development of the EMS. Planning for EMU was started as early as the summit conference held at The Hague in 1969, followed by a Council recommendation in 1971 that an autonomous EC exchange rate system should be established to take coordinated action and keep the fluctuations of the US$ within narrower margins. 'The snake in the tunnel' system commenced in 1972, a system whereby unlimited obligatory intervention by central banks in the currencies of participating countries was intended to keep their various exchange rates against the dollar within a margin of 4.6 per cent, narrowed the following year to 2.25 per cent. There were changes in membership and revaluations before a stable arrangement between seven EC and associate countries was established in 1975; the DM was notably revalued twice in 1973 and consequently its relative value increased by 8.5 per cent during the year (MRDB 1/76: 25–6).

The EMS as such came into force in March 1979 and succeeded the 'snake' arrangement. The most notable change was the introduction of the ECU as the common numeraire and reserve asset. Moreover, if a participating currency is revalued against the ECU, the bilateral central exchange rates of this currency against all other basket currencies are changed uniformly. By the tenth anniversary of the founding of the EMS (in 1989) there had been a total of eleven realignments, resulting in an average weighted revaluation of the DM against other EMS currencies of 38 per cent; however, much of the turbulence occurred during the first four years, 1979 to 1983 (MRDB 11/89: 30–1). Smeets (1990) found that the EMS,

during the second part of its history in particular, became a DM zone as far as monetary policy and price stability were concerned. He expressed doubt, however, on whether there were any long-term interest rate linkages between Germany and other members. Until the exceptional 1992–3 period, therefore, the Bundesbank's short-term interest rates became the undisputed floor (or anchor) to the rates of other currencies in the ERM. This was because international investors would always prefer to hold DMs if interest rates were identical. It followed that the authorities in all the other ERM economies had to offer an interest-rate premium to compensate international investors for the greater erosion of other ERM currencies by relatively higher inflation rates and the risk of devaluation.

The Bundesbank viewed this process as one of countries with weak currencies 'importing (monetary) stability' (MRDB 11/89: 33). The rationale behind this argument started from the premise that revaluations of the DM within the EMS helped to offset the differences between more stable prices in West Germany and higher rates of inflation in most of its partner countries. In these higher inflation countries, monetary policy in particular was oriented towards achieving stable nominal exchange rates against the DM. This would lead towards price and cost convergence, although the Bundesbank significantly saw fiscal policies in countries running relatively large budget deficits as being particularly inconsistent with the requirements of a system of fixed (albeit in principle adjustable) exchange rates. Continuing discrepancies in cost and price structures could also result from differing underlying conditions. In short, all EC countries should be members of the narrower band of permissible fluctuation of exchange rates and they should all use as a target variable the most stable currency within the EC (*ibid*.: 35).

By 16 September 1992 ('Black Wednesday') all EC members apart from Greece were in the ERM, most of them having implemented the narrow band. At that juncture, the British government abortively sought by means of increasing interest rates to prevent sterling falling through the floor of its (wide) band value. The Bundesbank's Council, on the other hand, predictably saw a further realignment as being the only solution. Clearly, the forex markets also preferred to think that a realignment was a necessity. In any case, earlier in the week the Italian lira had been devalued, Belgium and the Netherlands supported a realignment and the Bundesbank's Council had been prepared to reduce interest rates by only 0.25 of a percentage point. Other currencies within the ERM were also under pressure. Suspending the ERM membership of sterling and the lira, along with the devaluation of other members' currencies in 1992 and 1993, demonstrated that realignments had in fact been necessary.

Even the DM came under some pressure in early 1993. In contrast to the recessions in the 1970s and 1980s, interest rates in France and inflation in all the G7 countries fell below German levels. Rather like previous recessions, moreover, the US dollar also began to strengthen. *Die Welt* (17 June 1993) saw this as further evidence of Germany's 'relegation to the second division' and the French franc was seen as a supplementary or even replacement ERM anchor. (No mention was made of the depleted French foreign currency reserves. Moreover, just over a year earlier Britain was thought to be about to 'slip into the ERM driving seat' (*The Times* 11 May 1992). At least the latter article mentioned the tremendous costs which resulted from the high interest rates which

endowed this transitional comparative advantage, namely driving up unemployment and bankruptcies.) The folly of the suggestion that the French franc should replace the DM as the ERM anchor was exposed when the Bundesbank Council felt unable to cut German short-term interest rates in both mid- and late-July 1993. The franc had slumped perilously near its ERM floor on the first occasion and the ERM was fatally undermined on the second occasion. France had been in the classic position of devaluing or increasing nominal interest rates which would endanger any fragile recovery. (Real interest rates were already high.)

This central role played by the Bundesbank's policymakers led Marsh (1992) to subtitle his book *The Bank that Rules Europe*. Similarly, Kennedy (1991) added *Germany's Central Bank in the International Monetary System*. Yet the Bank's Council have tended to regard international monetary obligations as an inevitable but serious distraction from their goal of pursuing internal monetary stability. Since the EMU clauses of the Maastricht treaty envisaged the substitution of the ECU for the DM, and the subordination of the Bank to the European Central Bank Council (ECBC), members of the Bundesbank's own Council were bound to have misgivings. Such doubts were probably shared by the majority of the German public, not least because these radical proposals came hot on the heels of GEMSU. Moreover, they were to be implemented by 1999 at the latest, only a decade after the fall of the Berlin wall. On the other hand, the EMS system meant that German monetary policy had a sharper impact than an EMU system based on EC-wide considerations (Chauffour *et al.* 1992: 264 and 268). Interest-rate growth following unification would have been less steep under EMU and therefore less growth inhibiting, not least in Germany itself (*ibid*.: 266).

Although this present book is generally concerned with past trends, therefore, a brief consideration of the implications of the Maastricht treaty for German policy-makers is in order. After all, politicians in most EC member states are adamant that a single European currency will eventually emerge. Whether that single currency would transpire to be the DM or ECU, and if it initially involved only a minority of EC members, the Bundesbank's Council would have identical expectations to those it expressed on the Maastricht form of EMU. Legislative developments in those ERM countries which were really serious about EMU certainly demonstrated that the introduction of an independent central bank was not an obstacle. With an independent ECBC, there would be one currency, one internal set of interest rates and, it follows, no longer any internal exchange rates. However, the principal remaining questions would concern the policy making roles remaining for politicians. Would they have any influence over exchange rates with the external trading blocs? Or, more unlikely, would a flexible exchange-rate regime be introduced? Moreover, would fiscal policy be severely curtailed as an instrument of domestic demand management? If so, would price stability be the only goal of the ECBC, especially bearing in mind that its members' periods of office would probably significantly exceed those of politicians and would not coincide with the differing electoral cycles in member countries? In such circumstances, unemployment levels and growth would be subordinated to minimising inflation. Notice that all of these basic economic-policy problems had not been resolved by the German system – indeed, this is the principal inference to be drawn from

Chapters 3 and 4 of this book. For its part, the Bundesbank's Council is bound to insist that all the robust Maastricht convergence criteria are met before it considers voluntarily relinquishing its statutory powers – irrespective of the final form and membership of EMU. Quite apart from the British and Danish opt-out clauses, several of the poorer member states would not be ready to move to the third stage when the situation is due for review in 1996 – unless they heavily deflate their economies, or accept further drastic currency realignments. A two-speed EC therefore seemed inevitable, a situation which would ironically be exacerbated by the envisaged accession of Austria, Sweden, Finland and, possibly, Norway. (Also see the discussion around Table 3.1.)

It can nonetheless be observed that exchange rate stability became a target of the Bundesbank's Council. If West Germany had fully exploited its competitive position (which was the result of its more stable price level) it would probably have led to an even greater number of devaluations and deflation among its trading partners. (See the trade sections in Chapter 8.) Hence, there has been an increasingly pronounced tendency to insist on a process of convergence within the EC. Even before unification, revaluations of the DM within the EMS were seen as a less preferable policy option. Indeed, following GEMSU, the dominance of the DM was viewed with disquiet within the EC. Initially, it was thought, the costs of unification would be partially transmitted to other members *via* increases in the Bundesbank's interest rates. Ultimately, a reconstructed eastern Germany would contribute to an even more powerful DM. The idea of a single currency, which lies at the heart of EMU, was intended by definition to abolish completely the need for any exchange rate policy within the EC.

The ideal single currency would therefore be the ECU and the dominance of the DM would be a thing of the past. It also follows that the Bundesbank would have to be satisfied that any Euro central bank would have the power to maintain an independent stance on price stability.

The exchange rate of the DM against the US$ is another matter. How could the ECU replace the DM here? Revaluing the Bundesbank's own foreign exchange reserves became a major monetary-policy problem during the 1970s and 1980s (Figures 4.6c and 4.7 above). Revaluing the international holdings of DM would be an even more major exercise, as GEMSU indicated (see Table 4.2 below). Moreover, although the DM is an emergent trading and reserve currency, the dollar still accounts for the lion's share of these international currency obligations. Speculative movement between these two currencies, together with more general trends in international interest rates, always gave more than pause for thought at the Bundesbank. Could the ECU withstand such speculative pressure, especially if it assumed the DM's international obligations? One is reminded of Britain's problems in managing the Sterling Area. Meanwhile, capital movements have become the single most important influence on exchange rates. For example, the British chancellor at the time of the 1976 sterling crisis pointed out that new information technology has produced a single global capital market which is open twenty-four hours per day (Healey 1989: 413). By 1988, short-term speculative funds were up to fifty times the amount needed to finance the whole of world trade. The trend towards the freeing of capital movements had an increasing impact. There had been, for example, a perverse rise in the US$ in the first half of the 1980s, even though the current account and federal budgets were both in deficit. Given that such important 'fundamentals' were awry, a fall in the dollar would have seemed more probable. The 1987 stock-market crash, however, caused a high degree of dollar sales. Similarly, the abortive attempts by the British authorities to peg sterling's exchange rate on Black Wednesday (16 September 1992) had extremely high intervention costs on the forex markets and speculators made millions of pounds. In theory, extremely high real interest rates in the UK could have prevented the speculation, although the economy was already in a deep recession. Because of sterling's degree of overvaluation, however, last-minute increases in interest rates could not obviate an ultimate devaluation. The world's monetary system was arguably out of control. As can be seen from Figures 4.6c and 4.7, these events all influenced the amount of intervention by the Bundesbank. It should be added, however, that an appreciating DM provides the Bundesbank with a shield against inflation because it reduces the international demand for German products and also reduces the price of imports. Since unification placed additional strains on the demand side, the Bundesbank might well have preferred a further appreciation for this reason. But prior to unification there was another currency reform when the weak OM was converted overnight into DM. There was more than a hint that this policy would produce identical results to the introduction of the DM in 1948. The next section therefore compares both the 1948 and the 1990 currency reforms.

THE CURRENCY REFORMS OF 1948 AND 1990

The Allied 1948 currency reform was seen in Chapter 1 as the 'big bang' which preceded the introduction of the relatively more gradualist economic and social reforms of the SME. Only a military dictatorship could have imposed such a draconian measure. As with the re-introduction of a central banking system, however, there was no alternative. The money supply during the Second World War had increased ten fold, whereas output stood at half of its 1938 level. Hence, the aim of the currency reform was to reduce the amount of money in circulation until it reached the level of current output. A re-organisation of the structure of public and private debt was also essential, as was the need in the real economy to bring about dishoarding given the acute shortages which existed at the time.

In order to eliminate the excess money supply, individuals and firms were required to register all currency holdings and bank deposits. These were scaled down in DM terms to ten per cent of their RM value. One half of the new DM amount (i.e. 5 per cent of the original value) was made available to its owners as quickly as possible. Of the remaining 5 per cent, 1 per cent was made freely available at a later stage, while 0.5 per cent was set aside for investment purposes in a blocked account. Because the release of the remaining 3.5 per cent was later seen as a threat to the reform, it was cancelled. Hence, the net effect was to reduce the original RM holdings and bank deposits to 6.5 per cent of their original value. It was little wonder that this was a source of much bitterness and social distress (Wallich 1955: 69).

Cash requirements during the conversion were met by a *per capita* allowance of DM 60, of which DM 40 was paid on Sunday, 20 June 1948, and a further DM 20 two months later. These allowances were made at the rate of 1:1 against the RM, but amounts over RM 60 received the 10:1 rate of RM for DM. Employers were able to maintain wage and other outflows by virtue of an allowance of DM 60 per employee. Wages, rents, insurance and pensions were paid at par but savings were devalued to 10 per cent of their original RM levels. Public authorities received the equivalent of one month's revenue, their previously-held funds being cancelled in entirety. Here again, the 'big bang' nature of the 1948 Currency Reform can easily be seen: a shock treatment had been preferred as opposed to a gradualist approach.

Debt also had to be re-structured. Obviously, short-term obligations could not be met at a 100 per cent rate by those whose nominal holdings had been scaled down to 6.5 per cent of their original levels. This type of debt was therefore reduced to 10 per cent of its original level. Long-term debtors (mortgagors of property which had escaped war damage in particular) found that their windfall profits from the extinction of their debts was expropriated and paid into a fund from which war-damage payments were paid at a later stage.

As far as the banks were concerned, the Currency Reform was nothing short of catastrophic. Their deposit liabilities were reduced by over 90 per cent overnight but their assets (mainly RM securities) almost vanished. To re-build their balance sheets, the banks received new government obligations which restored their assets to the level of their liabilities plus a modest capital allowance. In addition to these compensatory claims (*Ausgleichsforderungen*), the banks were granted reserves to restore their liquidity – 15 per cent of demand deposits and 7.5 per cent of time and savings deposits (Wallich 1955: 70).

A liquidity crisis was therefore deliberately engineered by the instigators of the Currency Reform. It had the desired effect in the real economy of forcing the dishoarding of food and consumer goods which were known to be held in large quantities by farmers, middlemen and manufacturers throughout the economy. Black market prices collapsed overnight. Cigarettes ceased to be an alternative form of tender and the price of a packet of twenty fell from RM 100 to DM 8. As Wallich (*ibid*.: 71) puts it:

. . . [the Currency Reform] transformed the German scene from one day to the next. On June 21, 1948, goods reappeared in the stores, money resumed its normal function, black and gray markets reverted to a minor role, foraging trips to the country ceased, labour productivity increased, and output took off on its great upward surge. The spirit of the country changed overnight. The gray, hungry, dead-looking figures wandering about the streets in their everlasting search for food came to life as, pocketing their 40 DMs, they went on a first spending spree. That there were dark spots in this bright picture will become apparent from the further unfolding of the tale. The dominant fact, however, was the great success of the reform in getting the German economy back into operation.

This quotation implies that the contrasts between the 1948 currency reform and the introduction of the DM into East Germany in 1990 were quite manifold. First, the amount and type of planning which went into GEMSU was far less detailed. Second, the basic aim of GEMSU was totally different in that its purpose was the incorporation of a command economy into an established and affluent market economy. Third, no Western-style banking system existed in the East, although the principal implications of this factor will be considered in Chapter 7. Finally, it has been emphasised on several

occasions that an undervalued DM exchange rate gave a fillip to West German exports in the 1950s and 1960s (see, for example, the discussion around Figure 4.7 above and the trade sections in Chapter 8). The GEMSU exchange rates were dictated by political considerations. As a result, East German assets were hopelessly overvalued and the intrinsic exchange rate was highly uncompetitive (on the disastrous effects of the conversion of exchange rates see the SME, GEMSU and EMU section of Chapter 1). Notice also that the conversion of assets (or stocks) was particularly critical. The conversion of flows, at least as regards money wages, was about correct, since wages in the East were only up to one half of western levels. It was the subsequent plans for the equalisation of eastern and western wage rates which was a more difficult question – see Chapter 6 below. For the moment, however, consider some of the monetary contrasts between the establishment of the SME and GEMSU.

To begin with, the English-speaking western Allies had three years to plan the 1948 Currency Reform, although it was not until the events leading up to the final breach with the Soviet Union (the 1947 London conference and the beginning of the Berlin blockade in 1948) that they decided – ultimately supported by France – to go it alone (Hardach 1980: 105–6; Stolper *et al.* 1967: 242). The new money was printed in the United States and shipped to their zonal port of Bremerhaven before being despatched under heavily-armed guard to the three western zones for distribution. With GEMSU the notes were printed in West Germany and transported to the East. However, the period for planning was considerably shorter than in 1948. The Berlin Wall was opened on 9 November 1989, free elections were held in the East on 18 March

1990, the GEMSU treaty was signed on 18 May 1990 and implemented on 1 July 1990. The political imperatives of stemming the mass migration from East to West and achieving unification transcended economic considerations. This period of rapid monetary, economic, social and political integration not only contrasts with the immediate, medium- and long-term aims of the SME, it also contrasts with the slow process of European integration – a topic already considered in Chapter 1.

GEMSU was a leap into the unknown, with unforeseen human costs as well as opportunities. The East German economy, as Professor Schiller wrote in the *Financial Times* (2 July 1990), was to be exposed to the full brunt of national and international competition. Convertibility, which was a long-term aim in 1948, was introduced with immediate effect. Although balance of payments problems therefore disappeared, there was every possibility that consumer demand in the East would be concentrated on foreign and West German goods. In effect, the aim of GEMSU was to convert a centrally-planned economy to a SME, involving a shift to economic specialisation and the entry of modern technology. This would almost certainly create unemployment unless and until inflows of new capital were attracted and new employment opportunities were then created. In other words, there was no hoarding as in 1948; the condition of the real economy was totally different. Schiller (*ibid.*) nevertheless predicted that the great and (more or less) unprecedented experiment of GEMSU would be successful. In a different kind of way from 1948, therefore, GEMSU was designed in part to provide a 'big bang' or shock treatment for East Germany. The contents of this paragraph make clear why von Dohnanyi

(1990: 159) argued that the economic circumstances obtaining in 1948 were immeasurably more favourable than those of 1990.

Arriving at the rates of conversion from the Ostmark to the DM was not an easy process, yet it was essential for the transition to a single currency area. Further, much uncertainty was caused by the many alternative exchange rates being used: 1:1 for the first tranche of the Travel-Currency Fund; 1:3 for visitors in the GDR; 1:4 for the internal GDR conversion of trade-related payments; 1:5 for the second tranche of the Travel-Currency Fund, and 'black-market' rates oscillating between 1:6 to 1:10. As the Bundesbank suggested (MRDB 7/90: 14), the ideal treaty would strike a balance between the major economic, social and political decision-making criteria. It was, after all, equally vital to minimise the inflationary risks of the currency conversion, to safeguard as far as possible the competitiveness of GDR enterprises, to contain the budgetary pressures and to make the monetary union socially acceptable to the residents of both the GDR and the Federal Republic. In order to satisfy these – at least partly conflicting – requirements, a distinction had to be made from the outset between flow and stock variables.

Stocks in this context were in the main defined as monetary assets and liabilities. Flows were wages, pensions, rents and capital services. For stocks a once and for all conversion rate was necessary. As far as flows were concerned, the main problem was that of wages because the inferior economic performance of East German enterprises required adjustment of their input and output prices to vastly revised market conditions. Instead of wages being fixed by government decree, the newly-created bargaining framework would use the initial conversion rate purely as a signal. As the OECD pointed out (*Economic Survey* July 1990: 55), a vastly different relative wage structure would eventually emerge across skills, sectors and firms, in particular as between those companies competing internationally and those in sheltered sectors.

Even given all the problems posed by comparing economic data from different economic systems, labour productivity in the East German economy was estimated on average at about 40 per cent of the West German level. The relatively low gross average wage in German Ostmarks was roughly in line with this performance differential, although the differences in the respective price systems and in tax burdens made it difficult to compare wages in the East with those in West Germany. However, in view of the sharply distorted price and cost pattern in the East, as compared with the West, there were in principle two ways of achieving an appropriate wage differential immediately after the currency conversion. One option was to eliminate the worst price distortions, particularly the massive government subsidies for major consumer goods, *prior* to the currency conversion. This would have generated a price surge, especially for food, and the general view was that considerable compensatory payments in the Ostmark would have been required for wages, salaries and pensions. Moreover, there might have been an additional demand for pay increases upon the conversion, as a result of higher social security contributions. The resulting higher gross wage level could not have been converted at a rate of 1:1, however, because this would have entailed a considerable further weakening of the already low competitiveness of GDR enterprises. The Bundesbank in an advisory report requested by the Federal Government therefore recommended that the flow variables should be converted at the rate of 2:1 *after* the elimination of price distortions and a compensatory increase in incomes, both of which should be effected *before* the currency conversion. Starting from this initial level, which was broadly in line with productivity, further adjustments of wages and salaries in keeping with market conditions and a correction of the excessively flat wage structure could have been effected after the conversion (MRDB July 7/90: 14).

In the course of the intra-German Treaty negotiations, however, a second option was chosen, namely that of converting wages and salaries at the rate of 1:1 on the basis of the 'pay agreements applicable on May 1'; this was not least because the proposals for implementing a comprehensive price reform prior to the currency conversion were dwindling. Nonetheless, converting wages at 1:1, but removing state subsidies for basic products, would clearly affect living standards. This would be before any re-adjustment of the wage structure as envisaged by the OECD (*Economic Survey* 1990: 52). Such a re-adjustment process would be accompanied by 'transitional' unemployment.

Given that stocks are concerned with monetary assets and liabilities, the problem of equating these two sides of the banks' balance sheets in terms of the new currency presented enormous difficulties. It will be recalled that this problem had also been met in 1948. On the liability side, savers in the East would like to have seen a 1:1 conversion rate for all their savings. (About 80 per cent of East German savers possessed 5000 Ostmarks or less in their accounts). On the asset side, such a conversion rate would have been devastating if applied to the outstanding debts of East Germany's industrial groups with the East German banking system. These debts had come

Table 4.2 The conversion of Ostmark to Deutsche Mark – GEMSU 1990

Assets	OM billion	DM billion	Liabilities	OM billion	DM billion
Lending to domestic borrowers			Deposits from domestic non-banks		
Total	397.4	180.7	Total	249.9	156.6
of which			of which		
Enterprises	231.7	115.8	Enterprises	57.0	27.8
Housing sector	102.6	51.3	Individuals	182.1	123.4
External assets	45.0	36.3	External liabilities	152.5	55.6
			of which		
			Provisions for external liabilities (*Richtungs-koeffizienten*)[1]	96.4	–
Participations	1.1	1.1	Currency in circulation (excluding cash holdings of banks)	13.6	6.8
			Accumulated profits/ reserve funds/ guarantee funds	23.4	23.4
Other assets	3.1	1.5	Other liabilities	7.2	3.6
Total	446.6	219.6	Total	446.6	246.0
Balancing item	–	26.4	Balancing item	–	–
Total	446.6	246.0	Total	446.6	246.6

Source: MRDB 7/90: 15

Notes: [1] These are actually liabilities of the banking sector to the government which might also be shown in the first Liabilities item. In this table they are shown in connection with the external liabilities of the GDR because the item may also be regarded as a kind of 'valued adjustment' for the external liabilities, which are otherwise put at too low a value in Ostmark
[2] (Basis: Consolidated balance sheet of the banking system of the GDR at 31 May 1990)

about as a result of government prescription; they had therefore to be reduced dramatically so as not to weaken their competitiveness through excessive debt service. The significance of these debts, along with lending to the housing sector, can be gauged from Table 4.2.

As in 1948, reducing the banks' assets by a greater proportion than their liabilities would have resulted in the banks requiring interest-bearing equal-isation claims on the government to close the balance sheet gap created by such an approach. Ultimately, however, financial assets and liabilities were generally converted at the rate of 2:1, thus halving the liabilities of government, enterprises, the housing sector and individuals in nominal terms – a far more favourable exchange rate than most of the array of rates quoted above.

In two respects, this was essentially a

paper exercise. First, the value placed on the banks' assets had to be an arbitrary one. In the real economy many of the industrial enterprises and many parts of the housing stock were in a parlous state. Second, some of the banks' liabilities were converted at the rate of 1:1 because a social element was taken into account: East German residents were permitted, on a *per capita* basis, to convert the following amounts of their savings. Persons up to 14 years, up to 2000 Ostmarks; persons between 15 and 58 years, up to 4000 Ostmarks; persons over 59 years, up to 6000 Ostmarks. Similarly, although currency in circulation was converted at 2:1 in Table 4.2, it seems that approximately DM 13.6 billion was made available for this purpose on 1 July 1990 (= 1:1). (In all, DM 25 billion in notes was transported to the East.) Certainly, the first four weekly Bundesbank returns showed a total expansion of DM 15.2 billion. Although this represented only a 10 per cent increase in this particular monetary aggregate, and the Bundesbank's target variable is in any case M3, it was necessary to introduce an Equalisation Fund to compensate for the shortfall in the banks' assets resulting from both of these 1:1 conversions of liabilities. (In 1948, the banks had also found their balance sheets thrown into disarray. They were also permitted to make equalisation claims to bring their assets up to the level of their greatly reduced liabilities (Wallich 1955: 70).)

Although there was no cash conversion and no *per capita* allowance of the new currency – as there had been in 1948 – savers thus experienced windfall gains. Hence, the proportion of the savings converted at 1:1 which were retained in the savers' accounts was important from an inflationary (gain in purchasing power) point of view. Some sense of proportion is

required here. For example, the 4000 Ostmarks converted at 1:1 would not purchase a car, but assuming the price structure of consumer durables adjusted rapidly, this sum would purchase a washing machine, refrigerator or colour television set imported from the West. Not surprisingly, therefore, just as DM currency was transported across the border to the savings and cooperative banks for 1 July, so were goods (*Time International* 30 July 1990: 17):

The logistic marvel of supplying thousands of East German shops with Western products was brought off so smoothly and quietly that hardly anyone noticed. In the days before July 1, thousands of West German trucks rolled through the frontier posts, like so many military convoys, ferrying in goods most East Germans had only dreamed of. Used-car lots sprang up in small towns and along country roads hardly changed since the end of World War II.

This latter effect on the real economy has to be compared and contrasted with the dishoarding effect of the 1948 Currency Reform. The quotation from Wallich above was used to illustrate the dishoarding which took place at that time.

Even more important than the choice of exchange rate for conversion was the need for the Bundesbank to obtain control of the banking process in East Germany. Otherwise it could quite conceivably be called upon to create DMs to finance the public and corporate deficits. Moreover, if special claims against the Federal government to replace devalued assets were going to be issued to the banking system (as in 1948), a Western-style system would be required in East Germany. The new banks in the East could then be issued with securities which could be discounted at the Bundesbank. Unlike the situation in

1948, however, East Germany did not possess a functioning banking system with proper banks. There was no experience with operating a system with discount and Lombard rates, or any of the other refinancing arrangements examined above. In short, money and capital markets did not exist in East Germany.

Yet to enable the Bundesbank to carry out its monetary policy role, it was essential for it to control the money and credit creation process in the eastern part of the extended currency area. It will be recalled that, under its founding statute, the Bundesbank is empowered to act on monetary policy matters independently of instructions from the Federal government. This factor, along with its statutory duty of safeguarding the currency, led to its monetary policy powers and duties being extended to East Germany under the GEMSU treaty. Conversely, the State Bank in East Germany had been part of the centralised control apparatus. Hence, business with domestic enterprises was carried out by this institution. Similarly, although savings accounts were concentrated in the savings and cooperative banks, these funds were passed on to the State Bank. In April 1990, however, the Deutsche Kreditbank took over the business with domestic enterprises. The two largest West German banks (the Deutsche and the Dresdner) in turn took large shares in the Deutsche Kreditbank.

As from 1 July 1990 the Bundesbank granted the GDR banks what were known as refinancing quotas which, in contrast to traditional rediscount credit, could be utilised temporarily not only on the basis of trade bills but also on the basis of bank promissory notes. These refinancing loans were settled at the Bundesbank's discount rate. Over and above the refinancing quotas allocated to them, the banks in the GDR (like those in the Federal Republic)

have access to Lombard loans at the Lombard rate. Initially, GDR banks were permitted to submit bank promissory notes as collateral for this credit, too. In addition, the Bundesbank declared bank claims on the Equalisation Fund of the GDR to be eligible as collateral for Lombard loans. The volume of refinancing quotas granted, at a total of DM 25 billion, was relatively high compared with the rediscount quotas of banks in the Federal Republic (about DM 59 billion). As soon as the prerequisites were met, the refinancing quotas were to be reduced accordingly and converted into 'normal' rediscount quotas, for which only blue-chip trade bills can be used as collateral. Moreover, as soon as the balance sheet patterns of banks in the GDR had approximated to those of banks in the old Länder, the Bundesbank applied the criteria 'traditionally' used in the Federal Republic (MRDB 7/90: 18). This process began as early as Autumn 1990 when the Bundesbank countered the high degree of liquidity in East German banks by a greater degree of Lombard lending; in February 1991 these banks were admitted to the securities repurchase scheme and from 1 July their refinancing quotas were lowered to DM 18 billion (MRDB 7/91: 20–1). Moreover, the use of bank promissory notes was limited. In short, the Bundesbank was determined to model central banking practice in the new Länder on its existing practice – and as soon as possible (but see Sinn and Sinn 1992: 69 and 117).

THE COURSE OF MONETARY POLICY

The basic feature of monetary policy formulation to be explored here is the interaction between the Bundesbank and politicians. It was seen above that the mechanics for cooperation were laid down in the BBankG. But both before and, more particularly, after the enactment of this statute, there have been both domestic and international monetary events about which the Bundesbank and politicians have disagreed. At the heart of these differences lay, first, the perceived conflict between pursuing, on the one hand, the goal of price stability and, on the other hand, concentrating more on the level of economic activity and therefore employment. The second reason for conflict emanated from the differing views about internal and external balance. 'Imported inflation' is included under this second general heading.

One advantage enjoyed by the Bundesbank's president, his deputy and fellow directors is that their usual term of appointment (eight years) is double the elected tenure of the Federal and Länder governments. In addition, of course, Finance ministers and even Chancellors may not survive the full length of a parliament. Hence, there were only six central bank Presidents between 1948 and 1991 – and precisely the same number of Chancellors. However, some Chancellors served for a relatively short period. Each President has stood his ground against political, industrial and even financial opposition.

The first President (of the BdL) was Dr Wilhelm Vocke. Hartrich (1980: 165) refers to the common objectives of Erhard, Schäffer and Vocke. It is certainly true to say that Erhard's theoretical market approach and Schäffer's 'Julius Tower' lend a lot of credence to this view. Moreover, Vocke retrospectively mounted a campaign of staunch opposition to lax monetary policy when called by the British in 1948 from a Nazi-enforced (fully remunerated) retirement; he subsequently pursued the single-goal career of promoting monetary stability

(*ibid.*: 168; Marsh 1992: 48 and 123). Much the same as Schäffer, however, he received support from the generally advantageous economic climate of the time. Although he was contemptuous about Schäffer's – and Adenauer's – abilities, he ultimately won Schäffer's support for his policies; he also won the argument on the need to maintain the central bank's independence (Marsh *ibid.*: 48, 166–7 and 177–9). Not only did Vocke wish to see no increase in prices, he also wished to encourage high savings to finance investment (Shonfield 1965: 286). Restrictive monetary policies at the time of high unemployment, and then at the time of the Korean crisis, were pursued in both cases until prices were actually falling: −6.4 per cent in 1950 and −1.8 per cent in 1953 (Denton *et al.* 1968: 170). Similarly, there was a credit squeeze in 1955–6; on this occasion, there was a vitriolic attack from Chancellor Adenauer in what became known as the 'Fallbeil speech'. It is significant that Adenauer made the speech before industrialists (BDI) and complained about the effects on small businesses: he was supported by both the industrialists and the banks who were collectively arraigned against Vocke, Schäffer and Erhard (Sturm 1990: 265–6). Moreover, Adenauer openly criticised 'his' ministers (Schäffer and Erhard) for having publicly praised this restrictive monetary stance without prior cabinet approval, although 'he finally gave up his tactically motivated opposition' (Giersch *et al.* 1992: 66; also see Marsh 1992: 179). At the 1957 Federal elections, however, Adenauer secured an absolute majority, including the highest number of post-war seats for his wing of the Christian democrats. This is generally accepted as the electoral verdict on the remarkable progress of the real economy, for which Erhard must receive due acknowledgement. It must, however, be re-emphasised that Erhard's policies were at once pragmatic and interventionist (see the budgetary-policy section of Chapter 3). Moreover, Adenauer and Erhard appointed Dr Karl Blessing, instead of Vocke, to head the newly-established Bundesbank (Marsh *ibid.*). Blessing, like Vocke, had been dismissed by the Nazis, although, also like Vocke, prior to his dismissal he had cooperated in the implementation of Nazi policy (*ibid.*: 120). Unlike Vocke, however, Blessing moved to the corporate sector during the war; nonetheless, after the war he became an equally dedicated proponent of monetary-policy rectitude (*ibid.*: 54–5; Hartrich 1980: 169).

Paradoxically, the very success of Vocke's (and Schäffer's) policies meant that the comparatively low West German price level and her undervalued exchange rate contributed in no small measure to large export surpluses and imported inflation (also see Figures 4.6 and 4.7, along with the surrounding discussion). Indeed, when the Bundesbank took over as the central bank in 1958, full convertibility had almost been reached and short-term capital inflows would exacerbate the problem. The danger of imported inflation explains the ambivalent policy pursued by the Bundesbank from 1957 to 1959. Interest rates were lowered to discourage the inflow, but encourage the outflow, of hot money; at the same time minimum reserve and open market policies were used to restrict bank liquidity at home (Denton *et al.* 1968: 171). By 1959, it seemed that this policy was succeeding: the balance of payments was in deficit for the first time since 1950; in 1960, however, another domestic boom was accompanied by a large inflow of capital (Figures 4.6b and 4.6c). Notwithstanding the potential domestic inflationary impact, the Bundesbank's Council astonishingly lowered

interest rates and its minimum reserve requirements in late 1960 and early 1961; however, the government ultimately revalued the DM in March 1961 – a controversial move first recommended in 1957, but an election was now imminent and it seemed less controversial than other policy options (Denton *et al.* 1968: 172; Yeager 1976: 500). Note, however, that a manipulation of interest rates for electoral reasons – not unknown in Britain – was not within the politicians' gift. On the other hand, it is significant that Erhard did not consult the Bundesbank's Council about the size of the 1961 revaluation (Marsh 1992: 183). Most commentators saw the revaluation as being too little and too late and the exchange rate pressures moved to other European countries during the period 1962–7 (Kennedy 1991: 59).

Blessing and Erhard found themselves in disagreement about the upward trend in interest rates prior to the recession which began in the second half of 1966. Along with a looming budget deficit, the recession brought about Erhard's resignation in December 1966 (Chapter 3 above; Sturm 1990: 267). He therefore resigned before Germany's first post-war year of recession (1967). The recession forced the Bundesbank's Council to act. By mid-1967 the discount rate was back to its mid-1966 level of 3 per cent, but Blessing continued to serve until the end of 1969 – a year of revaluation. This altercation between Erhard and Blessing will be compared with similar policy disagreements below.

It is extremely instructive to note for now that the 1969 revaluation was even more controversial than its 1961 counterpart. In the face of capital inflows and a rising money supply during 1968, Blessing was in favour of this method of reducing imported inflation – as was the SVR and Federal Economics Minister Schiller

(SPD). Chancellor Kiesinger (CDU), Finance Minister Strauß (CSU) and German industrialists were against the step (Giersch *et al.* 1992: 149). As well as allowing it to become an electoral issue, Schiller (and the SVR) thought that an important economic principle was at stake. They saw flexible exchange rates, the free international movement of capital and the control of the money supply for stabilisation policy as all being essential to the successful operation of free market forces (Hallett 1973: 80; Spahn 1978: 71; Wallich 1968: 358 and 369). As already seen in Chapter 3, however, Schiller saw fiscal policy as a valuable aid for boosting confidence during recessions; in Chapter 6 it will be shown that he also persuaded the wage bargainers to participate in a national forum. This combination of aggregate-demand management to avoid unemployment but stimulate growth, an incomes policy in the interests of equity and a free exchange rate represented the most ambitious policy scenario ever implemented in Germany. In the 1969 Federal elections Schiller's policies were supported and the Grand Coalition with the Christian Democrats was dissolved. The day following the election, the outgoing government was forced in the face of an enormous capital inflow to accede to the Bundesbank's recommendation that the DM be permitted to float temporarily. Predictably, the DM appreciated and this pressure alone forced the new government to revalue and return to a fixed exchange rate (Yeager 1976: 509–10).

From the beginning of 1970, Schiller found himself increasingly at odds with the new President of the Bundesbank (Dr Karl Klasen). Curiously enough, Klasen was brought in from the Deutsche Bank and took up his appointment as the highest-ranking banker sympathetic to the SPD; Blessing, on the other hand, had

been associated with the CDU – a factor which cemented his close relationship with Erhard until 1966. The Bundesbank explained that its high interest-rate policy of 1970 was necessary to reduce both the private long-term capital outflows of 1968 and 1969 and the inflationary boom conditions. Because interest rates were falling elsewhere, the consequent interest-rate differential reversed the capital flows, but with an element of overkill. With balance of payments considerations in mind, therefore, the Bundesbank gradually reduced its interest rates, with the discount rate eventually reaching 3 per cent in 1972 (Figures 1.1, 1.3, 4.4a, 4.4b and 4.6b; Yeager 1976: 510–11). Once again, the Bundesbank policymakers depended on reserve requirements to control the banks' domestic liquidity, thus implementing an aspect of monetarism which they ironically no longer used following the introduction of monetary targets. However, the legacy of the relatively high interest rates in Germany had caused a continued rise in foreign currency reserves, heavy borrowing abroad by domestic nonbanks, speculative capital inflows and an appreciation of the DM exchange rate. This situation is succinctly described by Yeager (*ibid.*) as the classic dilemma of trying to restrict both domestic and foreign sources of funds in a non-reserve currency country with fixed exchange rates and full convertibility.

Even in 1972, the doubts about the future of the Smithsonian parities far outweighed the low German interest rates and speculative inflows continued at an increasing rate. This prompted the Bundesbank to successfully advocate measures which were widely interpreted as an abandonment of West Germany's opposition to capital controls: Klasen had persuaded the Cabinet to introduce physical controls in spite of Schiller's opposition to what he believed to be an unwarrantable constraint on market forces. Earlier in the year Schiller had reluctantly gone along with the introduction of the *Bardepot* (cash deposit) measures whereby the government could impose reserve requirements of up to 100 per cent on certain foreign loans. Even tighter exchange controls requiring foreigners to seek Bundesbank approval before purchasing domestic bonds – the statutory base for which was the ill-fated AWG – transpired to be the last straw for Schiller. In any case, he disagreed with his colleagues on budgetary questions, namely the nature and timing of medium-term financial planning for 1973 and cuts in current expenditure (Marsh 1992: 190–1). He consequently resigned in early July 1972 and was replaced as Economics and Finance Minister by Helmut Schmidt – a minister who believed that '5 per cent inflation was better than 5 per cent unemployment'.

Exchange controls are a double-edged weapon. They leave the central bank freer to use interest rates for internal objectives, but they also prove a powerful stimulus to expand the Euro-market as a means for international transactions. This stimulus was also fuelled by the DM's strength and was already causing Luxembourg to grow as a financial centre at the expense of the more tightly regulated Frankfurt. Nonetheless, dollars continued to flow into the Bundesbank's foreign exchange reserves. Even before Schiller's resignation it had been necessary to call an early Federal election for the Autumn because of defections in the lower house to the opposition. For electoral reasons, therefore, the Federal government felt that after two floats followed by revaluations (all within a three-year period) the idea of a further revaluation was politically unacceptable. Consequently, by August

1972 the money supply was 13 per cent above what it had been a year earlier (Yeager *ibid*.: 515). In this sense, Schiller was vindicated. He had been in favour of a joint European float against the dollar – or the Snake arrangement referred to above. In effect, this would have led to a higher value for the DM against the dollar and speculative inflows would have fallen markedly. As it was, by the end of 1972 the money supply had continued to expand rapidly and the increasing rate of price inflation had reached 5.5 per cent (Yeager *ibid*.). Schmidt, who had supported the Bundesbank's policymakers' capital controls, was forced by events in 1973 to bow to the inevitable and introduce floating exchange rates (Marsh *ibid*.).

The policy alternative was for the Bundesbank to be much more ruthless in 'sterilising' the dollar inflows – by requiring the banks to purchase central bank assets instead of increasing their lending. As Tew (1988: 236) has shown, however, there will still be an unavoidable increase in the money supply because the banks' liabilities will increase by the amount to which nonbanks pay the proceeds from foreign-exchange sales into their bank accounts. The only avoidable element is by preventing the banks from increasing their lending by – as already indicated – requiring them to purchase central-bank assets instead. Under Emminger, the Bundesbank was initially unsuccessful in sterilising the avoidable element. Indeed, Obstfeld (1983: 184–5) found that the Bundesbank had attempted to use sterilisation over the period 1975–81, although he also estimated that this sterilisation had significant but short-lived effects. The two discussants of his paper were rather sceptical about the relevance of his model (*ibid*.: 193 and 201). Their observations were that foreign-exchange intervention was 'just part of the overall calculation which forms the basis of controlling the money market' and 'if sterilisation was ineffective why did the Bundesbank sterilise?' Moreover, Kennedy (1991: 85) suggested that it was easier for economies with appreciating currencies to sterilise foreign-exchange intervention and maintain their preferred domestic policy course because they can sell the domestic currency for a period and sterilise with comfort; depreciators, on the other hand, run out of reserves and credit-worthiness quickly.

Klasen forced Schiller's resignation by his insistence that the DM should not be allowed to appreciate further against the dollar. His view, in effect, was that the DM must remain competitive, whereas Schiller was arguing that it was under-valued. However, within two years (1974) several factors had resulted in Klasen allowing the DM to appreciate, quite apart from the formal abandonment of fixed exchange rates. Above all, the first oil price shock caused a new determination to control the money supply in the interests of price stability. Moreover, it was shown above that the Snake was already domi-nated by the DM and therefore by the Bundesbank. Adjustments in partner countries were targeted on the DM exchange rate. Klasen now became unpopular with the government, although he remained on good terms with Chancellor Schmidt. His argument was that low inflation was in the long-term interests of the economy. In other words, he had shifted from targeting the DM/US$ exchange rate to targeting the domestic money supply and inflation.

The policies of those who subsequently headed the Bundesbank became, if anything, even more unpopular. Their backgrounds differed, yet there was a consistent thread running through policy formulation under their stewardship.

Consider first their backgrounds. Dr Otmar Emminger replaced Klasen in 1977. He had served on the Directorate of both the BdL and the BBk since 1953. Although he was aligned to the Christian Democrats (without being an actual party member), Schiller had secured Emminger's appointment as Klasen's deputy in 1969. Because of his vast inter-national experience, he was known as 'West Germany's secret foreign minister'. Herr Karl Otto Pöhl, an SPD member and a person with long experience in various government ministries, became his deputy. Pöhl became president in 1980, although Emminger (at the age of 68) still retained an office at the Bundesbank and continued to express his views in a variety of ways. Emminger's former tutee and long-standing colleague at the BdL and BBk – Dr Helmut Schlesinger – became vice-president in 1980. From 1980, Pöhl moved in international circles with con-siderable aplomb, whereas Schlesinger assumed responsibility for money-market management. Schlesinger, like Emminger before him, became president too late in life (in 1991 when he was 66) to remain very long in the Bundesbank's most senior position (also see Marsh 1992: 43). His deputy was Dr Hans Tietmeyer who, like Pöhl, had worked as a Federal ministerial adviser but during Christian Democrat administrations.

The most prolonged period of policy difference commenced in 1979 and culmi-nated in Chancellor Schmidt's resignation in 1982. For example, the discount rate was 3 per cent at the beginning of 1979; by mid-1980, it was 7.5 per cent. This had been a reaction to the second oil-price shock and the depreciation of the DM/US$ exchange rate. It was thus contended that a strong DM was an international necessity and this was tantamount to con-ceding that the DM was now an international reserve and trading currency. Emminger had opposed such a development, whereas in Pöhl's view it was unavoidable. Allowing the money supply to expand as a result of the Bonn summit in 1978 was also seen retrospectively with regret by the Bundesbank's Council. From 1979, there were not only bitter public criticisms from parts of the SPD; the banks and industry also expressed dissatisfaction with the Bundesbank's policy stance, especially when the special Lombard rates were introduced in 1981. Chancellor Schmidt blamed high interest rates in the USA and high energy prices; but by 1981 the neo-liberal approach of Reagan and Thatcher had succeeded the coordinated demand-management approach advocated by Schmidt and the French (Kennedy 1991: 41–2). (In the late 1970s, Schmidt had not informed the Bundesbank about his EMS plans until it was too late to prevent the mechanism from being introduced). Large budget and current account deficits prompted Pöhl to remark that 'a deficit country cannot afford a policy of low interest rates' (*ibid.*). When Pöhl himself resigned (see below) the *Financial Times* (17 May 1991) paid tribute to his personality and commented as follows:

As Chancellor Schmidt's 'Sherpa' to the London summit of the G7 industrial countries in 1977, Mr Pöhl was responsible for inserting into the final communiqué a famous phrase: 'inflation does not reduce unemployment. On the contrary, it is one of its major causes' . . . the Bundesbank disliked the establishment of the EMS, has fretted against its constraints and has repeatedly insisted that monetary policy must be framed with domestic monetary policy objectives in mind . . . By raising the desirability of a two-speed move to EMU, by insisting on conver-

gence of inflationary performance, by rejecting outright the premature creation of a European monetary institution that might prejudice the Bundesbank's own role in European monetary affairs and by insisting that any replacement must match the Bundesbank in independence and commitment to low inflation, Mr Pöhl has immeasurably improved the quality of the debate and increased the chances of a fruitful outcome.

Another rift over monetary policy between the USA and the Bundesbank caused the international stock exchange crash in 1987 – five years after the West German government had switched to the Thatcher/Reagan supply-side economics. US Treasury Secretary James Baker asserted that the Bundesbank was undermining international agreements on exchange rates and an internationally agreed strategy for coordinating economic policy by the G7; he threatened to allow the dollar to go on falling against the DM (Kennedy 1991: 56). This remark caused the 1987 crash, but Baker later blamed the 'obstinate monetarism of the little clique headed by Helmut Schlesinger'; he also accused Schlesinger of spying inflation around every corner (*Independent on Sunday* 28 July 1991).

Pöhl held strong views on both GEMSU and EMU. Chancellor Kohl did not inform him about the plans for speedy monetary union between the two Germanies. Less than a year after GEMSU, Pöhl said (FT 20 March 1991):

We introduced the DM [into East Germany] with practically no preparation or possibility of adjustment, and, I would add, at the wrong exchange rate . . . [the result] is a disaster: eastern Germany is completely uncompetitive.

He was equally blunt about the implications of unification for the size of the Bundesbank's Council. Chancellor Kohl found himself trying to mediate between Pöhl and the Council member for North-Rhine Westphalia (Professor Reimut Jochimsen). The latter wanted the new Länder to be admitted as full members with a resultant increase in the Council's size. Pöhl viewed it as an opportunity to reduce the size of the built-in majority of the Länder on the Council.

In part, he viewed his plans for a reduced Council size as a preparation for how the European Central Bank Council (ECBC) would be composed. More importantly, he had laid out the following plan for such a body (Pöhl 1990: 8–9):

Members of the ECBC who are bound by instructions from their governments would represent national interests. Therefore the principle of 'one man, one vote' in this body can only be implemented if the members of the ECBC are really independent, not only in their capacity as council members but in their domestic functions as well . . . Even under a federative system, *monetary policy must remain indivisible* [Pöhl's emphasis – writer], the 'monopoly of monetary creation' must be retained. In the European Central Bank System, therefore, it will not be possible for the national central banks to have any autonomous policy powers of their own: they will only be the operational arm of the European central bank.

Although Pöhl found himself on the opposite side of the fence to Tietmeyer over GEMSU (the latter had played a central role by advising Kohl on German monetary union), the two were in agreement about convergence and the required fiscal stance for EMU. There would have to be a convergence over a two year period in price stability, low budget deficits and successful application of exchange rates

within the narrow band as well as little or no difference in interest rates.

However, Pöhl found himself increasingly at odds with government and resigned in 1991 – half way through his second term. Pöhl's appointment to that second term had in any case been opposed by the Federal Finance Minister (Theo Waigel) when Waigel was a more junior minister. It was the first time that a Bundesbank President had resigned; as shown above, it had usually been the politicians who had been forced into such a step. Consider, for example, a scholarly deduction made by Riemer (1983: 61):

. . . the political establishment has always sought to increase welfare only when it has proven compatible with stability. No public figure would dare to challenge the fundamental duties and operating methods of the Bundesbank without risking a short-lived career in Bonn. Just as Keynesianism tried to supplement the market without replacing it, the Keynesian Revolution in West Germany tried to combine the pursuit of stability with the pursuit of other goals.

Three deductions can in turn be made at this point. First, the Bundesbank's policy makers precipitated the resignation of Schiller even though his favoured method of resolving the problem of imported inflation was far more SME orientated than Keynesian in nature. Indeed, the policy prescription put forward by the Bank's Council was interventionist and doomed to failure if capital controls were to be abolished. Second, Schmidt's ideas on EMU, together with his view that public-sector spending was inevitable during a recession, were incompatible with the orthodox view of achieving (monetary) stability. This latter transgression also contributed to Erhard's resignation, Blessing later admitting that he had to use 'brute force to put things in order' (Marsh 1992: 187). Third, Kohl's 'unilateral' negotiation of the GEMSU treaty was seen by the Bundesbank's policymakers as an unacceptable act of largesse.

Schlesinger (1991) made it even clearer that the experience of GEMSU had made the Bundesbank much more cautious about EMU. He emphasised that both arrangements were not just simply a case of monetary union but also economic union. The greater the difference between economies, the slower the progress to monetary union should be. Only those economies which could withstand the shock of introducing a single currency (because of prior economic convergence) should attempt monetary union. Otherwise, the exchange rate would not be available to a country that has not succeeded in developing at the same pace as other countries. A depreciation in the exchange rate would avoid cost adjustment via higher unemployment, given that wage rates are not flexible. He was equally adamant that the Eurofed would have to be fully independent from the monetary-policy influence of EC finance ministers.

The changes in the Bundesbank's directorate in October 1993 confirmed the above observations, especially that experience of GEMSU would probably strengthen the opposition of the Bank's policymakers to a fully-fledged EMU. Tietmeyer was confirmed as Schlesinger's successor. His term of office was coincidentally due to expire in 1999 – the planned year for EMU. Although described as 'a well-established, authoritative international figure, and a stout proponent of monetary rigour', he was also reported as being more concerned about the depth of the German recession 'than many others in the Bundesbank' (FT 18 June 1993; *Independent on Sunday*

20 June 1993). The new vice-president was Johann Wilhelm Gaddum who, like Tietmeyer, was a close associate of Kohl. However, Gaddum had previously been the directorate member most immediately involved with the transformation of the former East German monetary system; he was also described as 'a hawkish member of the directorate known for his opposition to EMU' (*ibid.*). Finally, Otmar Issing – a member of the directorate, and at one time thought to be an alternative candidate for the vice-presidency – also made it clear that radical economic changes were required in Europe. Increased public expenditure to boost weak economies reflected obsolete ideas which had been proven not to yield permanent benefits (FT 10 June 1993). Moreover, European labour markets were especially inflexible because the differential between earned income and unemployment pay was too narrow (*ibid.*).

CONCLUSION

Whenever there has been a conflict between monetary policy and other policies which affect price stability, the Bundesbank's policy makers seem to have deliberately opted for a deflationary course of action. Such a policy stance has caused permanent animosity between former colleagues: Klasen and Schiller, as well as Schmidt and Pöhl, represent classic cases. Domestically, both the government and wage bargainers have thus found their policy options limited. Internationally, the Bundesbank found exchange-rate policy rather more problematical. It has also been cautious about international agreements which may impinge on its autonomy.

For example, the Bundesbank initially opposed the EMS. Former Federal Chancellor Schmidt has claimed that he threatened to amend the BBankG if the Bundesbank did not agree to the EMS, although the Bank has not agreed to this version of events (Kennedy 1991: 81 and 122). Ultimately, some discretion over exchange-rate policy was accorded to the Bank. But the formal alignment of EMS currencies remains a political decision with the Bundesbank acting as adviser to the Federal government. Even more important are the terms and conditions for EMU laid down by the Bundesbank. There is some debate about whether any future Eurofed bank should enjoy complete autonomy over exchange-rate parities (*ibid*.: 123). The obvious alternative was to give EC finance ministers the powers to determine exchange-rate arrangements with the dollar and the yen. Similarly, the brakes were applied by the Bundesbank to the proposals for a Franco-German Economic Council as soon as they were made public (*ibid*.: 92–3).

Moreover – even though this was somewhat ostrich like – Emminger attempted to prevent the DM becoming an international reserve currency. In 1979 he was still attempting to prevent the Federal Republic becoming 'a dumping ground for the unloved dollar which would expose it to imported inflation' (*ibid*.: 81–2). Although not doctrinally opposed to 'tolerable' revisions of the monetary target, he saw a finite limit to intervention in the foreign-exchange market; at some stage a change in exchange rates may become necessary (Treasury and Civil Service Committee *Evidence II*, 25/10/82: 237). All this supports the Obstfeld (1983: 163–4) contention that the traditional case for flexible exchange rates had been far too sanguine. If internal balance demands a fall in interest rates, the accompanying exchange rate depreciation causes domestic inflation to accelerate.

GEMSU was thus a dramatic example of political decisions which affect price stability. Given the Bundesbank's response to previous such threats, it could be anticipated that the growth of the money supply would be controlled so as to, if deemed necessary, engineer a recession. After all, 1967, 1974 and 1980–1 have been shown to be similar cases.

5

SOCIAL POLICY

(Written with Hsueh-Fang Lin)

INTRODUCTION

Welfare states have developed rapidly in western Europe, but a common model has not been fully established. Each welfare system has its own peculiar policy problems. For example, the British and Swedish systems have been criticised for placing excessive strains on the economy (Friedman 1980: 100). It was Bismarck, however, who established the forerunner of all social-insurance systems. His system was subsequently developed during the Weimar Republic and under the Nazis. In the post-war era, social policy became an integral part of the SME. It will be shown below that there is a valuable conceptual framework – the social budget – which illustrates the formal incorporation of the welfare state (*Sozialstaat*) into German policymaking. It will also be shown that other policy developments, notably *Allfinanz* and *Finanzplatz Deutschland* (Chapter 7), are of a more recent and less rudimentary nature. The crucially important policy debate over *Standort Deutschland* (Chapter 8) has been misleadingly associated by some observers solely with the debate over the future of the welfare state. While obviously related in some ways, the two debates are in fact concerned with a number of independent issues.

Subsidies have historically played a very important policy role in the financing of social policy from Bismarck's time. They have amounted to nearly one third of the total expenditure on social insurance. For instance, in 1989 a subsidy of DM 38 billion had to be found for the retirement-pension insurance fund (Bellermann 1990: 70; IW *Zahlen* 1991: 57). Following unification, the financial problems were particularly acute, even though important parts of the system had been generally reformed as recently as 1989. For example, in 1992 the biggest recipient from the federal budget was the Federal Ministry of Labour and Social Affairs. It received a record DM 92.8 billion, up 5.3 per cent on 1991 and well above the 3 per cent increase in the budget overall. The main reasons for the increase were higher government subsidies for pensions arising from reforms which came into force from January 1992 and the government's determination to bring the social-welfare system up to a uniform level throughout the country: it was felt that inequities in this field should be eliminated as soon as possible. The Labour Ministry's expenditure on the eastern German states alone amounted to about DM 21.6 billion, up nearly 18 per cent on 1991 (FRG Embassy *Report* 7/91). In short, there have always been financial problems connected with social policy: unification simply exacerbated existing problems.

Apart from the contributions which became payable by the employed population in the east, the costs of converting and integrating the eastern system were therefore met mainly out of funds supplied by western Germany. The difference in living standards in the two parts of the united Germany have already been emphasised in Chapter 1. But quite apart from relative poverty and hardship in the east, unification also meant that two different social welfare systems had to be merged. Nonetheless, from a long-term point of view, the development of social policy in Germany can be regarded as a comparative success. But there has been a need for almost continuous reform. This is because the implementation of social policy depends on the economic climate, the age structure of the population, and the level of unemployment. In this sense, too, unification poses yet another challenge for policymakers.

THE EVOLUTION OF SOCIAL POLICY

Between 1850 and 1880, the number of industrial workers in Germany rose from 0.8 to 6.0 million (Alber 1989: 45). Bismarck hoped that by means of a system of statutory social insurance he could reconcile the employee to the emergent industrial order, undermine the power of liberals and weaken the opposition powers enjoyed by the social democrats. In particular, the German government feared that the growth of the urban population posed a potentially revolutionary situation.

Bismarck's social-insurance proposals were only accepted by the German parliament after several heated debates. Eventually, health insurance was established in 1883, accident insurance in 1884 and retirement-pension and disable-ment insurance in 1889. Initially, these social-insurance measures applied only to manual employees. In 1911 the National Regulations were extended to include white-collar employees and they remain the basis of the system of insurance-based benefits. Bismarck's social legislation, although successful, was still limited. Alber (1989: 49–50) notes that the main legacy of Bismarck social policy by 1913 was the concentration of expenditure on education and cultural development (RM 1.3 billion, or about 46 per cent of the total social expenditure). Social insurance was second but with only RM 53 million. Total social expenditure was about RM 2.7 billion. Social expenditure was 37 per cent of total public expenditure, or 5 per cent of the GNP. Bismarck had thus constructed a basic social-insurance system which was a good foundation for the development of German social policy and, indeed, a model for other countries.

It was well into the period of the Weimar Republic before the next important social policy development took place. In 1927, a far-reaching unemployment insurance scheme was introduced. As a result of this Act, the National Employment Placement and Unemployment Insurance Office was established. It operated as an independent self-governing body responsible for the administration of the placement and the new compulsory, contributory unemployment insurance system. The Nazis placed the Office under direct control but in 1952 a Federal Office with the same title was placed under the tripartite control of employers, trade unions and government (at local, Länder and Federal levels). The 1927 Act was in 1969 incorporated into the Employment Promotion Act (AFG) which, with amendments, provides the legal basis for unemployment insurance. The 1969 Act also established the Federal Labour Office

(Bundesanstalt für Arbeit – BA). The 1927 scheme was jointly financed by deduction of the employee's contribution at source of income, and by an employer's contribution. However, the Great Depression undermined this and other social-insurance schemes. Expenditure on social policy as a whole declined from RM 15.8 billion in 1930 to RM 12 billion in 1932. Social insurance expenditure, including unemployment insurance, declined from RM 10 billion to RM 8.5 billion (Alber 1989: 54).

During the Nazi period the Weimar unemployment-insurance scheme was abolished. From 1934 the statutory regulation of social insurance reflected the Nazi philosophy. Social policy in the Third Reich was defined as the 'security and maintenance of the German nation'. From December 1937 the right to opt out of the retirement-insurance scheme was introduced, thereby making the scheme voluntary. One year later an old-age welfare scheme was introduced in the handicraft trades. The insured population could therefore join either a private insurance scheme or remain in the statutory scheme. Child benefits were implemented as from September 1936. In 1941 the 26-week limit on sick pay was abolished. Subsequently, there was no time limit. Pensioners were eligible for health insurance and their contributions were paid by the Land government. A widows' retirement pension scheme was also started (Hentschel 1983: 144). The Nazi policy followed the general guideline of: 'we must be in possession of one united healthy nation so that we can make our way in the world' (Lampert 1985: 89).

After the Second World War, West Germany took and adapted some ideas for the social-insurance system from the British Beveridge plan (Alber 1989: 58), but as the SME developed, West Germany reconstructed her traditional social-insurance system. Social-insurance contributions have increased in line with growing social-policy expectations. There has also typically been a high degree of political consensus that a high level of spending on social security in its widest sense is desirable, although the economic climate has played a critical role in determining the actual level of expenditure. From 1949 the West German system of health, retirement-pension, accident and unemployment insurance was revised several times. First, the aim of the insurance-based benefits was no longer simply to meet bare needs but rather to ensure that a consistent standard of living was maintained in times of adversity. Second, the scope of the benefits became much wider, and, third, where the insurance system was inadequate to meet foreseeable contingencies, direct Länder aid became payable. Viewed against this backcloth, the German social policy system performs three functions (Lampert and Bossert 1992: 61):

- Members of society are protected against risks which are related to loss of income and unplanned expenditure arising from illness, accident, age, unemployment and death
- Members of the labour force are protected against the inevitable effects of economic development and related technological change by unemployment benefits, short-time working and redundancy payments, retraining and further training
- Lower-paid members of society receive transfer payments designed to moderate the differences in income and wealth distribution by means of housing, child and parental benefits, as well as saving and share-purchase incentives

The social state in post-war Germany developed both quantitatively and qualitatively into a vastly superior system compared with the pre-war systems (*ibid.*). Initially, the rebuilding of the housing stock, compensation for refugees and war pensions received priority. Not just policy formulation as such, but also the means of financing social expenditure – especially pension and health insurance – became an increasingly important aspect of social policy. The development of social policy is summarised in Figure 5.1. Above all, the wide scope of West German social policy in the post-Second World War era should be noted. Certain features of this policy framework will be considered in Chapter 6, notably the items entered under the headings Labour Market and Establishment and Company Policy. The important features for subsequent analysis in this chapter are social insurance, social security and social welfare. What follows is initially concerned with West Germany with respect to these three sub-divisions of social policy. The transplantation of the developed western social-policy system into East Germany is then considered.

THE STRUCTURE OF SOCIAL POLICY

It is somewhat difficult to translate the German terms used in a social-policy context. However, the structure of social policy in Germany can be defined for the purpose of analysis as falling into mainly three areas: social insurance, the provision of social security (*Versorgung*) and social welfare (*Fürsorge*) (Lampert 1985: 144). Cumulatively, all three categories provide an estimate of the social budget – a most important accounting concept in German social policy. Lampert (*ibid.*: 150) usefully describes the social budget as an attempt to assign expenditure and revenue to the relevant institutions, functions, types and sources of finance (cf. BMWi *Leistung in Zahlen* 1989: 92).

Figures 5.2a to 5.2d present various analyses of the expenditure side of the social budget. In Figure 5.2a it can be seen that the total social budget in the west was 29.4 per cent of GNP in 1990. Thereafter the effects of unification, and the associated transfers, are clear. As a proportion of the GNP in the west, the social budget in the old Länder was 29.8 per cent in 1992 – a negligible change over 1990 (KND 45/93). In the east, the decline in GNP and the enormous transfers meant that the ratio of the eastern social budget to the new Länder's GNP was 70.5 per cent (*ibid.*). In 1992, the total social budget exceeded DM 1 trillion for the first time (Figure 5.2b). By way of comparison, it is interesting to note that the national debt exceeded this magnitude prior to unification (see, however, the discussion around Table 3.1). Figure 5.2c shows that social-budget expenditure per head initially declined in 1991, but then rose strongly in 1992.

Figure 5.2a also shows that the social budget in 1975 reached a pre-unification peak. It is instructive to note that this peak was due to the following factors. On the revenue side, there was a shortfall in income from contributions. Transfer payments were therefore necessary. Owing to the inflationary sharp rise in wages in 1974, pensions were lagging distinctly behind the increase in wages and salaries. This is because the pension adjustment factor at that time was calculated each year as an annual average over the previous three-year period. By advancing the adjustment date, however, the level of pensions relative to wages and salaries was not only corrected in the short run but in fact raised with lasting effect, especially since wages and salaries grew more slowly from 1975 onwards (MRDB 11/77: 32).

Sphere of Social Policy	1881–1918	1918–1933	1933–1945	1949–1993
Employee Protection	1891: Employee Protection Act 1901: Child Protection Act	1918: Regulation of Industrial Employees' Working Hours 1927: Maternity Leave Act	1935: Maternity Benefit Act 1938: Youth Protection Act	1951: Employment Protection Act 1952: Maternity Protection Act 1960 Act to Protect Employed Young Persons 1963: Federal Holidays Act 1971: Pupils', Students' and Kindergarten Children's Accident Insurance
Social Insurance	1883: Employees' Health Insurance Act 1884: Accident Insurance Act 1889: Invalidity and Retirement Insurance Act 1911: National Insurance Regulations	1923: National Miner's Guild Act 1927: Unemployment Insurance and Employment Exchange Act	1938: Act for Retirement Provision in German Handicraft Trades	1957: Act to Reform Retirement Pensions 1957: Retirement Provisions in Agriculture 1965–1968: Retirement Pension Reform 1972: Health Insurance in Agriculture 1972: Retirement Pension Reform 1984: Early Retirement Act 1984: Hospital Reform Act 1982: Health Insurance Reform 1992: Retirement Pension Reform 1993: Health Service Reform
Labour Market Policy		1918: Collective Bargaining Regulation 1920: Establishment of a National Office for Employment Exchanges (Regulations) 1922: Employment Exchange Act 1923: Regulation of Arbitration System	1933: Employment Trustees' Act 1934: Act to Regulate National Employment 1934: Act to control the Deployment of the Labour Force	1949: Collective Bargaining Act 1952: Establishment of Minimum Working Conditions Act 1969: Employment Promotion Act 1985–1986: Work Promotion Act
Establishment and Company Constitution Policy	1916: Auxiliary Service Act	1920: Works Council Act 1922: Representation of Works Councillors Executive Boards Act		1951: Codetermination (Coal, Iron and Steel) Act 1952: Company Constitution Act 1955: Personnel Representation (Public Service) Act 1972: Company Constitution Act 1976: Codetermination Act
Social Welfare and Social Assistance		1922: Youth Welfare Act 1924: Principles of Public Welfare Activities		1961: Federal Social Assistance Act 1961: Youth Welfare Act 1974: Disabled Persons Act
Family Policy			1935: Regulations to Provide Child Benefits to large Families	1954: Child Benefits Act 1979: Maternity Leave 1985–1986: Child–Rearing Assistance 1991: Maternity Leave
Housing Policy				1950: House Building Act 1952: House Building Incentives Act 1964–1965: Rent Rebate Act
Wealth-Formation Policy				1959: Savings Incentives Act 1961: Act to Promote Asset Creation
Vocational Training Policy				1969: Vocational Training Act 1971: Federal Vocational and Education Promotion Act 1981: Vocational Training Promotion Act

Figure 5.1 Schematic expression of Basic Social Policy Acts

Sources: Lampert 1985: 98–101. *Informationen zur politischen Bildung* 215/87: 31. Bellermann 1990: 42–3. KrV 1992b: 195

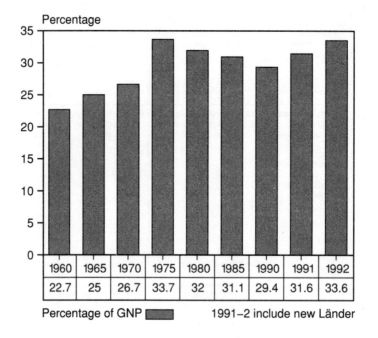

	1960	1965	1970	1975	1980	1985	1990	1991	1992
	22.7	25	26.7	33.7	32	31.1	29.4	31.6	33.6

Percentage of GNP ▓▓▓▓   1991–2 include new Länder

Figure 5.2a Ratio of Social Budget to GNP

Sources: IW Zahlen 1991: 48; KND 45/93

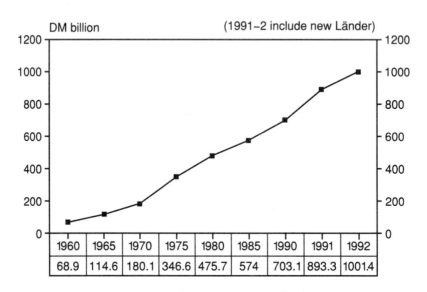

	1960	1965	1970	1975	1980	1985	1990	1991	1992
	68.9	114.6	180.1	346.6	475.7	574	703.1	893.3	1001.4

Figure 5.2b Total expenditure on Social Policy

Sources: Plotted from Figure 5.2a sources

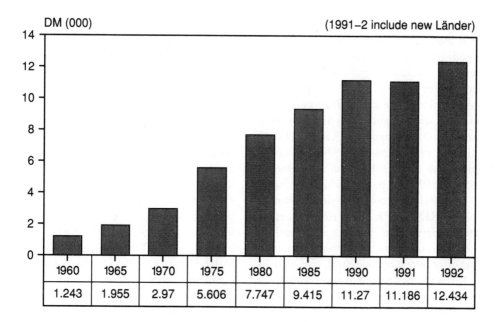

DM (000)   (1991–2 include new Länder)

1960	1965	1970	1975	1980	1985	1990	1991	1992
1.243	1.955	2.97	5.606	7.747	9.415	11.27	11.186	12.434

Figure 5.2c Social Budget: expenditure per head

Sources: Plotted from Figure 5.2a sources

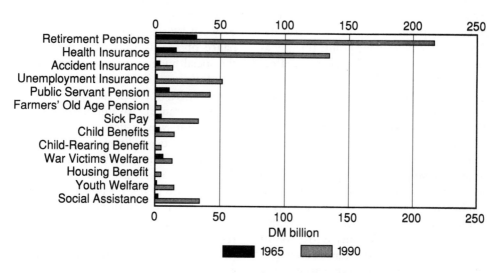

Figure 5.2d Social Budget: comparison of expenditure 1965 and 1990

Source: IW *Zahlen* 1991: 48

In addition, during the first half of the 1970s the finances of the BA were characterised by a sharp rise in expenditure. Spending reached a high level during the recession of 1974–5 and did not decline significantly in the succeeding years, despite the improvement in the economic situation. On average the BA spent DM 15 billion a year between 1974 and 1978 against less than DM 2.5 billion between 1965 and 1969, a period which included the (less serious) economic slow-down of 1967 (MRDB 4/79: 15). An important factor, apart from the higher spending on traditional items (unemployment and short-time working benefits), was that in the 1970s the BA had to assume additional functions, particularly in the field of vocational training. This was due to the Employment Promotion Act which was approved in 1969 (*ibid.*). The growing financial problems in the recession year of 1975 were reflected not only in mounting deficits (as in the case of the Federal, Länder, and local authorities) but also in an increasing contribution ratio. The share of social-insurance contributions in the gross GNP rose in that year by 0.6 of a percentage point, while the tax ratio declined by 1.2 percentage points (mainly as a result of the tax cuts which became effective at that time [MRDB 3/80: 20]).

As already indicated, total expenditure on social policy during the period 1960–92, as well as expenditure per head, are shown in Figures 5.2b and 5.2c. The exceptionally strong expansion of social-policy expenditure in the pre-unification period was to some extent due to demographic factors. Over the period as a whole, however, average demographic developments were conducive to a robust growth in the social-insurance funds (see Figure 3.8b). Thus the population grew by 7.82 million (or over 14 per cent), excluding the inflow of foreigners. The

proportion of persons covered by social insurance increased continuously as a result of the extension of the insurance liability or eligibility. Less significantly, the proportion of self-employed persons, who are covered by statutory social insurance to a lesser extent than employees, tended to decrease (MRDB 11/75: 23). Finally, successive policy decisions to extend general coverage had an even more decisive influence than the growth of the insured population. Within thirty years, therefore, social-policy expenditure increased strongly from DM 68.9 billion in 1960 to DM 703 billion in 1990 and the expenditure per head increased from DM 1,243 in 1960 to DM 11,270 in 1990 (see Figures 5.2b and 5.2c). The effects of unification are also illustrated in these two figures. There was a rise over 1991 of 12.1 per cent in total social-budget expenditure and an increase of 11.2 per cent in social-policy expenditure per head.

The retirement-pension and health insurance schemes account for the largest increases in expenditure – as shown in Figure 5.2d which illustrates the rise in various items of social-policy expenditure between 1965 and 1990. In fact, the dominance of social-insurance expenditure in the social budget can be gauged from the first four items in Figure 5.2d (retirement-pension, health, accident and unemployment insurance). An important aspect of unification was reflected by the steep growth of expenditure on these social insurance items in 1992. Collectively, expenditure increased over 1991 by 14.4 per cent, or DM 79.5 billion (KND 45/93). In other words, this collective growth rate was greater than the 12.1 per cent registered by the social budget as a whole (Figure 5.2b). This rapid expansion of social-insurance expenditure was primarily due to the financing of labour-market policies out of the unemployment-

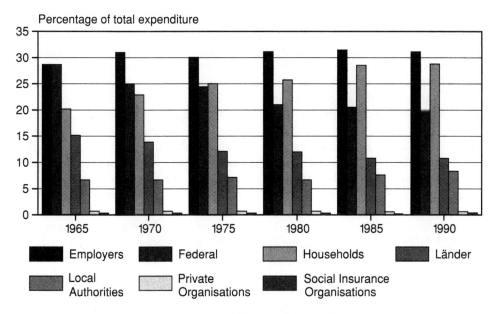

Percentage of total expenditure

Figure 5.3 Sources of Finance of the Social Budget

Source: As Figure 5.2d

insurance fund and the integration of the east's retirement-pension scheme into the western statutory-pension fund.

The revenue side of the social budget is analysed in Figure 5.3. The variety of sources of finance is immediately evident. There are no fewer than seven sources, in the following order: employers, the Federal government, private households, Länder governments, local authorities, private organisations, and social-insurance companies. In this social network, employers contribute on behalf of their employees and, as demonstrated in Figure 5.3, they are almost always the largest single contributor to the social budget. Their share in the total social budget grew from 28.6 per cent in 1965 to 31.2 per cent in 1990. The Federal government, which contributes both for its own employees and makes transfer payments, accounted for 28.6 per cent in 1965 but only 19.8 per cent in 1990 – a reduction of nearly

9 percentage points. Households contribute to the social-insurance funds and part of their income tax is used to finance the social network; this source of revenue rose from 20.1 per cent in 1965 to 28.7 per cent in 1990. The Länder and local authorities finance some of the social-security and social-welfare schemes. Their combined contribution fell from 21.8 per cent in 1965 to 19.1 per cent in 1990 (IW *Zahlen*: 48).

In 1992, social-insurance contributions by employers and employees accounted for 64.9 per cent of total social-budget revenue (KND 45/93). More specifically, the three levels of government contributed 38.7 per cent of total social-budget revenue; employers contributed 31.2 per cent and private households 29.5 per cent. Charities supplied the remaining 0.6 per cent to the social budget. Although the budget showed a surplus of DM 16.2 billion in 1992, this sum was well down on the DM 33.5 billion posted as a surplus in 1991. Above all, however, these data demonstrate the incidence of funding considerable financial transfers to east Germany. Very roughly, the three parties – government, employers and private households – contributed equal amounts.

By referring again to Figure 5.3, the reader will also appreciate that social-policy expenditure is a highly significant part of total government expenditure. Figures 5.4a and 5.4b illustrate the general pattern of this expenditure.

Figure 5.4a shows that the total social-policy expenditure of Federal, Länder, local authorities and social-insurance funds was 47 per cent of total government expenditure in 1987. Figure 5.4b indicates that the proportion of social-policy expenditure by the Federal government was nearly 30 per cent of total expenditure in 1989. Alber (1989: 331) points out that government expenditure can be defined in three different ways. In the first instance, a very broad definition would include expenditure by the three levels of government and social-insurance funds, plus indirect taxes paid by government and any change in its indebtedness. The second category (shown in Figure 5.4a) is expenditure by the three levels of governments and the social-insurance funds. Finally, one could consult simply the accounts of the three levels of government. Alber (*ibid*.) reports that, in 1983, these three methods produced ratios to GNP of 52, 49 and 34 per cent respectively.

It was seen above that social insurance can be categorised under four subheadings: retirement-pension, health, accident and unemployment insurances. (More accurately, unemployment insurance should be translated as 'employment promotion' insurance. It will be shown, however, that rising unemployment in both the west and the east has forced the policymakers to concentrate on the provision of unemployment benefits.) This part of the social-policy system is financed through a system of contributions. Insurance funds were intended to be self financing and contribution driven – even after an escalation in costs when a demographic shift and rising unemployment accompanied unification. Social-insurance contributions are calculated as a percentage of gross earnings, subject to ceilings. With the exception of accident insurance – which is paid by the employer – the contributions are paid equally by employee and employer with no distinction in statutory pension rates between manual and white-collar employees. Until 1992, however, contributions to the general (mainly manual-worker) health insurance scheme were on average higher than the white-collar scheme. To assist in the financing of German unity in general, and high unemployment benefit outgoings in particular, social-insurance contribution rates were temporarily restructured from 1 April 1991, with a partial reduction from 1 January 1992. Overall unemployment-insurance contributions rose again in 1993, while pension and average health-insurance contributions respectively peaked in the mid- and late-1980s. In addition, the monthly income ceiling to which unemployment contributions were payable was increased by DM 400 to DM 7,200. Partially financing unification by increasing the rate and ceiling of unemployment-insurance contributions was inequitable. This was because the self employed and established public servants (*Beamte*: see Chapter 6) do not contribute to the unemployment-insurance fund. For that matter, *Beamte* enjoy a non-contributory pension scheme. As a result, a more general social levy was advocated. Ultimately, as part of the

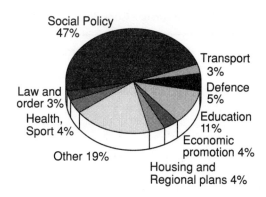

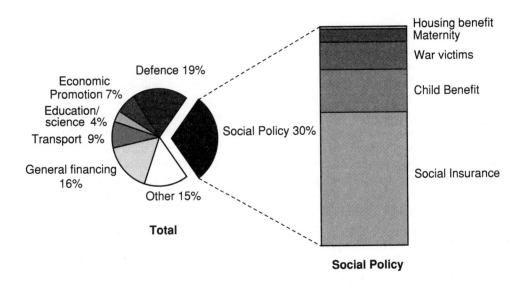

Figure 5.4a Expenditure of Federal, Länder, Local Authorities and Social Insurance Funds: 1987
Source: Stat. Jahrbuch 1990: 443

Figure 5.4b Federal expenditure: 1989
Source: BMF 1990: Chronik der Finanz- und Währungspolitik 1989: 19

1993 solidarity agreement, a six-month pay freeze was imposed on the *Beamte* and general tax increases from 1995 were announced (see Chapter 3). Notwithstanding this point, Table 5.1 contains an overview of social-insurance contri-

butions. A measure of the policy significance of contributions is that it will be necessary to refer back to this Table as the analysis proceeds. Also recall that social insurance accounts for the biggest proportion of the social budget: almost three

Table 5.1 Statutory Social Insurance Contributions from January 1993

Scheme	Contribution rate as percentage of earnings			Contribution ceiling monthly (DM)[2]	
	Employer	Employee	Total	West	East
Health Insurance	6.30	6.30	12.6[1]	5,400	3,975
Retirement Pension	8.75	8.75	17.5[3]	7,200	5,300
Unemployment Insurance					
from 1 January 1992	3.25	3.25	6.5	7,200	5,300
Accident Insurance (average rate)	1.5				

Sources: BMA *Statistisches Taschenbuch* 1992: 7.7 and 7.8; Schneider 1992: 328

Notes: [1] Average rate, 1992: figure varies between schemes. For example in 1992 the AOK rates lay between 9 and 16 per cent; the salaried employees' scheme rate was 12 per cent. In eastern Germany a standard health insurance contribution of 12.8 per cent was set until local funds established their own rates
[2] In eastern Germany the employer is liable for all contributions on earnings up to DM 450 monthly; the starting threshold for contributions is earnings of DM 450 per month, compared to DM 610 monthly in the west. All ceilings increased from 1 January 1994
[3] From 1 January 1994 total contribution rate 19.2 per cent

quarters of the total social budget is spent on insurance items.

The Federal Ministry of Labour and Social Affairs (Bundesministerium für Arbeit und Sozialordnung – BMA) is responsible for social-insurance legislation. But the various schemes are run by independent self-governing institutions. Health-insurance matters are administered by a wide variety of health-service offices (*Krankenkassen*) (BMA *Übersicht* . . . 1991: 489–95). Retirement-pension business is transacted by an equally wide variety of insurance offices (*Versicherungsanstalten*) (*ibid.*). Accident insurance is administered by occupational and industrial cooperatives (*ibid.*). It will be seen below that the variation in all these three types of social-insurance schemes derives from the occupational spectrum of coverage. With the exception of the white-collar health-insurance funds (*Ersatzkrankenkassen*), which are run by elected representatives of the insured persons only, all the self-governing bodies mentioned thus far are controlled by the parity rep-

resentation of employers and employees (*ibid.*). Unemployment-insurance administration, which will be seen to cover an assortment of labour-market matters, is the responsibility of the BA. There is a hierarchical structure of control from the Federal level, through the Länder, and then down to the local level. All these bodies consist of governors on a tripartite board drawn from government, employers' associations and the trade unions.

The previous paragraph demonstrates the far-reaching nature of the social-insurance system, and the democratic means by which it is controlled. In addition, a new social-insurance regulation was introduced as from 1 July 1991. From this date, everyone in employment is required to have a social insurance pass (*Sozialversicherungsausweis*) (IDS European Report 355). This pass is issued by the social-insurance authorities, and it is endorsed with the employee's name and his/her social insurance number.

Social security consists of child and housing benefits, war victims' compensation and the support of certain training schemes (Lampert 1985: 145). These items are financed from taxes, rather than from contributions (Bellermann 1990: 90). In other words, there is an important element of income redistribution, or transfer payments, used to provide these social services. (However, about 90 per cent of health-insurance expenditure is financed from contributions; in this case, there is an even higher redistribution element). Social welfare is intended to act as a social safety net for the relief of poverty. It is therefore best regarded as a last resort. The financing of social-welfare projects is undertaken by public authorities (usually at the local level), and by private charities. Payment is made by either direct grant, or in kind by the provision of a service.

RETIREMENT-PENSION INSURANCE: THE GENERAL PRINCIPLES

As already seen, statutory retirement-pension insurance has existed for more than one hundred years. There are three areas of retirement pension insurance: the non-contributory scheme enjoyed by established public servants (*Beamte* – see Chapter 6) and the compulsory contributory schemes applicable to employees in both the private and public sectors. Voluntary insurance can be taken up by all other German nationals not in these categories, including those working abroad. Prior to unification, there were nearly 33 million employees and other persons in the statutory retirement-pension scheme (*Statistisches Jahrbuch* 1991: 465).

During the post-war period, the retirement pension insurance system became more generous as economic prosperity increased. Major reforms were introduced in 1957, 1972 and 1992. The 1992 revision derived from a major reform of

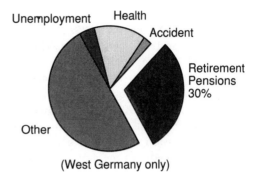

Figure 5.5 Retirement Pensions as a proportion of the Social Budget: 1990

Source: IW Zahlen 1991: 48

retirement-pension insurance which took place in 1989. This package of measures therefore reached the statute book just prior to unification with its attendant increase in population. They remained in operation until the end of 1991, when they were modified in order to incorporate this new addition to the insured population. Retirement-pension insurance is the most costly element of the social insurance system in Germany. As can be seen from Figure 5.5, it accounts on average for 30 per cent of the social budget.

An important decision was made in 1957 which resulted in pensions being dynamised from that year. They were reviewed every year and adjusted so as to ensure that the amount payable reflects increases in the income of insured persons and is therefore also related to changes in purchasing power. The basis of this adjustment was calculated each year as an annual average of the previous three-year period. In short, the goal of the 1957 reform was that the pension recipient would not become, relative to wage and salary earners, increasingly worse off. The pension of an insured person was therefore increased if the average income of the employed population rose. As a result of dynamisation, retirement pensions rose rapidly: by 1989 they were 639.3 per cent higher than in 1957 (IW *Zahlen* 1991: 52). The 1957 reform initially distinguished between manual workers and salaried employees for pension entitlement purposes (Schmidt 1990b: 131). However, further amendments resulted in the provision of a pension equal to 60 per cent of net final earned income for all insured persons who had contributed for 45 insurance years and who had reached the age of 65 years (BMA 1990: 43).

The watershed reform in retirement-pension insurance was reached, however, in 1972. First, the minimum age for recipients of retirement pensions was reduced to 63 years, thus introducing a 'flexible retirement age'. Second, each pension was set at a basic minimum level which was determined by the number of contribution years (Boss in Giersch 1983: 281). As a result of the minimum-income regulation, persons with a contribution record of more than 25 years became entitled to a pension calculated on a minimum level of earnings which was equal to 75 per cent of the annual gross average earnings of insured persons (*allgemeine Bemessungsgrundlage* or general-measurement datum). Prior to 1972, for example, an insured person with a 25-year contribution record, but receiving only 50 per cent of the annual gross average earnings of insured persons, would have received a pension calculated on that basis; after 1972 this 50 per cent was automatically raised to 75 per cent of the general-measurement datum for pension-calculation purposes. (An example is given in and around Table 5.2, but it is necessary to emphasise here that the general-measurement datum must not be confused with average gross earnings in the economy as a whole.) Insured persons with a minimum of five years, and up to 24 years, received a proportionately lower pension because they failed to fulfil the minimum 25-year contribution period criterion.

On 1 May 1984 the Early Retirement Act came into force. Some trade unions saw this policy development as a move by the Labour and Social Affairs Minister Norbert Blüm to undermine their campaign for a 35-hour week since both measures were designed to reduce unemployment. The Act applied to all employees who were already over 58, or who reached that age before the provisions of the Act were due to expire in 1988. (The provisions of the Act were later extended to 1992.) During this period any eligible employee could apply for early retirement on a pension of 65 per cent of former gross earnings which, the government calculated, was the equivalent of 70 per cent of net earnings to most employees (BMA *Sozialpolitische Informationen* 24 April 1984). Provided the pension was at least 65 per cent of former gross earnings, and provided the employer recruited an unemployed person to replace the employee taking early retirement, the employer could claim a subsidy of 35 per cent of the pension payable from the government. This would then apply until the employee reached a statutory retirement age – usually 63 – and for this period the employer and employee would continue to pay social-insurance contributions and the pension was included in taxable income. Following usual West German practice, an early retirement agreement – like any other agreement – could only be reached by the appropriate trade union and employers' association; alternatively, an individual employee and employer could reach an early retirement agreement, but company agreements were not possible. Agreements were reached in the construction, textile and catering industries. According to a government estimate, there were one million employees between the ages of 58 and 64; about 600,000 of them were expected to take early retirement (*ibid.*). Probably 200,000 eligible employees took advantage of the Act, only half of whom were subsidised because the resulting vacancy had been filled by an unemployed person (Seifert 1991: 507). The total employment effect of the Act – 100,000 jobs created for unemployed persons – was therefore of limited significance (Neifer-Dichmann 1991: 519–20). From 1989, these early-retirement provisions were extended to incorporate part-time working instead of complete retirement (Bellermann 1990: 64). Earlier models of early retirement had contained such a measure: the retirement shock of boredom or loneliness could thereby be averted (Franz 1984: 635). In all cases, contributions to the statutory retirement-pension and health insurance schemes remained payable by the former employee and employer, and a retirement pension became payable at the normal retirement age (BMA 1991: 87). These early-retirement payments were therefore regarded as compensation for forgone earnings.

As a result of the 1992 reform, the compulsory age of retirement remained 65 years, and retirement from the age of 63 years was still possible. However, a critical change to the regulations was that for retirement at 63, the minimum-contribution period became 35 years instead of the 25 years required by the 1972 revision. Until 2001, a female/disabled employee with a minimum of 15 years' contributions may retire with a part-pension at the age of 60. But flexible-retirement provisions will be gradually abolished from 2001. By 2006, males will be eligible for a full retirement-pension only on reaching the age of 65. Similarly, by 2012 females will also not be eligible

for retirement benefits until they reach the age of 65. Even where insured persons have contributed for the maximum 45 years, they will not receive a pension until they have attained their 65th birthday (BMA 1990: 18). Exceptions will be made where insured persons who are at least 63 years of age are prepared to accept a reduction of 0.3 per cent in their monthly pension entitlement (IW 1991: 16). Alternatively, insured persons who do not retire until they have reached the age of 65 will receive a monthly additional amount equal to 0.5 per cent of their pension entitlement (BfG *Wirtschaftsblätter* 3/90).

There are further exemptions to the normal retirement age which have been in operation for some years. They will continue to operate after 2001. Most notably, the following two conditions are regarded as sufficient grounds for claiming benefits before the insured person reaches his/her 65th birthday:

- the ill health of an insured person
- where family dependants of an insured person survive his/her premature death

In the event of ill health, any pension granted by reason of reduced earning capacity is required to replace the income of the insured. There are two conditions to be observed when assessing the pension as a result of disablement. First, a minimum of five contribution years must have been attained. Second, a contribution level which is between one seventh and one half the insured's income is also a necessary condition – the precise level being determined by the extent of the disability. In the event of the premature death of the insured, his/her benefits pass to the bereaved. These benefits take the form of a widower's/widow's pension and, where applicable, a pension for the surviving children. Orphans would also be entitled to benefits in these circumstances. These benefits amount to a maximum of 60 per cent of the net final earnings of the insured person and are based on the number of contribution years. There are also different minimum-contribution periods; for example, a miner could receive a pension at the age of 60, or after a minimum contribution period of 25 years (BfA 1989: 29–30).

Another important change resulting from the reform of 1992 was to specify a new insured group, namely mothers who have withdrawn from the labour force in order to raise children. This meant that a woman having a child after 1 January 1992, would not be required to contribute for a period of three years, as opposed to one year during the period 1986–91. A related provision made it possible for the father – rather than the mother – to assume the responsibility for raising a child and to claim the three-year exemption (BfG: *Wirtschaftsblätter* 3/90).

Finally, the basis of calculating pension entitlement was amended. From 1992, the dynamised element in pension calculations was based on the actual increase in average annual net earnings over the previous year, instead of the average increase in annual gross earnings over a three-year period used since the 1957 reform. Consequently, pensions will be dynamised on an annual basis from 1992. Also from 1992, the aim was that the average statutory retirement pension would be in the region of 70 per cent of the *net* annual average earnings of insured persons, the latter becoming the general-measurement datum. In other words, after 45 contribution years an insured person on average earnings at retirement would receive a pension equivalent to 70 per cent of the average net earnings of all insured persons; this could be regarded as the 'standard pension' (Schmähl 1992: 41).

Summarising, it can be said that the retirement-pension scheme is a good example of why the term 'social' appears in both SME and GEMSU. The scheme is mandatory and an element of personal income redistribution is implied. Consider the four fundamental principles of the scheme. First, there should not be a substantial deterioration in living standards as a result of a retirement decision on the part of a duly eligible insured person. Second, the pension should be related to current nominal wage rates. Third, as a corollary, the real value of the pension should be maintained, provided real wages do not decline. Finally, there should be some flexibility in the statutory age of retirement, although the likely future upward trend in costs necessitated a fairly substantial reduction in pension entitlement. As an illustration of these features, the analysis now turns to methods of calculation.

In terms of the 1992 reform, the calculation of pension rights is based on the following factors (BMA *Sozialpolitische Informationen* 7 May 1991):

$$(Ep \times Zf) \times Raf \times aRW$$

where:

- *Ep* is an individual assessment (*persönliche Bemessungsgrundlage* or personal measurement datum) which is related to the length and level of an insured person's contribution record compared to average gross earnings over the same period. (A person on average earnings in any one contribution year becomes entitled to an *Ep* of one)
- *Zf* becomes operative from 2001 and is a factor which reflects a reduction/

Table 5.2 Calculation of Ep (personal pension entitlement)

Year	Annual earnings (1) DM	Annual gross average earnings of insured persons (2) DM	Payment points $Ep = (1)/(2)$
1955	3,388	4,548	0.7449
1956	4,117	4,844	0.8499
1957	4,640	5,043	0.9201
1958	5,437	5,330	1.0201
1959	6,000	5,602	1.0710
1960 to 1983			31.2390
1984	62,400	34,292	1.8197
1985	64,800	35,286	1.8364
1986	67,200	36,627	1.8347
1987	68,400	37,726	1.8131
1988	72,000	38,896	1.8511
1989[1]	73,200	40,063	1.8271
1990[1]	75,600	41,986	1.8006
1991[1]	78,000	43,917	1.7760
		Total Ep:	50.4037

Source: Based on BMA-*Rentenreform* '92 1990: 137
Notes: For further details on calculation method see Rosen and Windish (1992: 375ff)
[1] Author's estimate for illustrative purposes

increase in pension entitlement due to early/late retirement

- *Raf* is a weighting factor dependent upon the type of pension. (For example, a normal retirement pension receives a weight of 1.0 but occupational incapacity is weighted 0.6667)
- *aRW* is a general assessment (*allgemeine Bemessungsgrundlage* or general measurement datum) which is laid down annually by statutory instrument. (In 1991 = DM 38.40)

For example, Mr L. is 63 years of age on 14 July 1992 and he decides to retire with effect from 1 August and claim his retirement-pension benefits (BMA 1990: 137). His contribution period amounts to 35 years. His pension can be calculated for the contribution years 1955–91 as shown in Table 5.2. From Table 5.2, it can be seen that Mr L.'s Ep is 50.40; since he is retiring before 2001, *Zf* is not applicable; *Raf* is 1.0 for this type of pension; from 1992 *aRW* was calculated annually and was therefore as stated above (DM 38.40). Therefore, Mr L.'s pension per month is:

$$50.40 \times 1.0 \times 38.40 = DM\ 1,935.36$$

Thus Mr L. would receive 70 per cent of the net annual general measurement datum (in 1991 = DM 33,149 – IW *Zahlen* 1992: 97).

But it is important to add that he would in all probability receive a supplementary pension from his employer. This is because benefits received under the statutory scheme are supplemented by various occupational schemes. About 70 per cent of employers organise such schemes, partly via insurance companies and pension funds, and partly within companies' own balance sheets. Thus employees' contributions may be a significant source of corporate funds. For example, provisions for this purpose in public limited companies in manufacturing amounted to 13 per cent of total financial liabilities in 1982, double the figure of a decade earlier (BEQB 1984: 369; Chapter 7). The resultant supplement from this second tier of pension arrangements may be between 10 and 20 per cent of final earnings – in addition to the 40 to 50 per cent of final earnings which can be expected from the state scheme. Some occupational schemes are non-contributory and represent a large non-statutory indirect labour cost for employers (IDS *European Report* 335; also see Table 6.3). In addition, 2.7 million salaried employees in the public service were covered by nearly thirty supplementary funds (MRDB 8/78: 21).

THE ORGANISATION AND FINANCE OF RETIREMENT-PENSION INSURANCE

Retirement-pension insurance policy is implemented as follows (BMA *Übersicht* . . . 1991: 491):

- there are eighteen regional Insurance Fund Offices (*Landesversicherungsanstalten*) for *Handwerker* (see Chapter 8) and manual workers
- a Federal Insurance Office (*Bundesversicherungsanstalt*) assumes direct responsibility for salaried employees
- the Federal Miners' Insurance Office (*Bundesknappschaftskasse*) is responsible for miners' retirement pensions
- two special funds exist for merchant seamen (*Seekasse*) and employees of the Federal Railways

- nineteen regional agricultural funds are administered by the *Landwirtschaftliche Alterskassen*
- established public servants (*Beamte* – see Chapter 6) enjoy a special non-contributory pension scheme
- employees of the various pension funds administer their own pension affairs

Supervision and administration can therefore be at the regional or national level. As already indicated, however, each fund is an independent self-governing organisation. The executive committees of the pension-fund offices are composed of equal numbers of elected representatives from the trade unions and employers' associations. Every six years, lists of candidates are drawn up by the eligible institutions and elections (*Sozialversicherungswahlen*) are then held (*ibid.*: 494).

Half of the contribution rate for retirement-pension insurance is paid by the employee and the other half by the employer (Table 5.1). In addition to contributions, the retirement-pension insurance fund is also subsidised from the Federal Government. For example, from 1986 the Bonn Government paid contributions for women who were rearing children. Moreover, women born before 1921, could claim retirement-pension benefits from the Federal Government. Such practices were set to continue after the 1992 reform (*Der Spiegel* 47/88: 23). The Federal subsidy, which amounts to 20 per cent of total retirement-pension expenditure, was in line with the subsidy envisaged by the Social Democrats in both 1972 and 1990 – that is at the time of their own and the Christian Democrat reforms respectively (*ibid.*). There is another important cost aspect of retirement-pension insurance. In 1989, the potential cost of unemployment to the retirement-pension insurance fund reached a total of DM 12.5 billion (*Die Zeit* 14/90). In order to compensate for this shortfall, the loss of contributions from the unemployed to the retirement-pension insurance fund was contributed by the BA (DM 9.5 billion) and the Federal government (DM 3 billion).

The pension contribution rate was fixed in 1989 at 18.7 per cent of earnings. It was expected that this rate would be maintained until 1996. However, following unification, it was reduced to 17.7 per cent (Commerzbank *Economic Trends* 3/91). In 1993 there was a ceiling contribution rate of 17.5 per cent of DM 7,200 a month (West Germany), shared equally between employer and employee. For earnings above DM 7,200 the contributions therefore remain at 17.5 per cent of DM 7,200. On the other hand, the calculation of pension entitlement is based on earnings (see Table 5.2). In the Miners' Insurance scheme, contributions were fixed at 24 per cent of earnings in 1983; employees contribute 9 per cent of earnings and employers 15 per cent. As employment in this industry declined, the ratio of employees to pension recipients fell to 1:4. Federal subsidies to their pension fund accordingly rose to two-thirds of total revenue. More generally, the 1992 revisions will result in increased contributions by 2010; this will assist in offsetting what would otherwise have been a deficit of DM 106 billion in the retirement-pension fund by that date. These increased contributions will add another DM 49 billion to revenue. A further reduction in the protracted deficit – of DM 43 billion – was to be achieved by lower increases in pensions and modifications to pension entitlements (BfG *Wirtschaftsblätter* 3/90).

Policy makers found it difficult to estimate the future costs of pension insurance

in 1989 when the legislation for the 1992 reform was considered. An indication that the contribution rate might increase to 21.4 per cent in 2010 was given (Bellermann 1990: 73). The reason for the uncertainty was that the long-term planning of retirement-pension insurance depends, as will be seen, on attempting to predict developments in the structure of the population. Note also that the rate of growth in earnings will, because of the dynamised element in retirement pensions, determine the rate of growth in pension entitlement.

RETIREMENT-PENSION INSURANCE PROBLEMS

For many years in the post-war period, the problems in the statutory health-insurance scheme concealed those of statutory retirement-pension insurance. Consequently, the cost/benefit structure of the retirement-pension insurance system was not strictly controlled. Insurance systems are dependent upon the economic climate and changes in social policy. Moreover, if further increases in contributions are politically unacceptable, a problem of indebtedness eventually emerges if the number of retired persons receiving pensions increases relative to the number of contributors in the labour force. Germany will be in such a position by the next century. Based on trends prior to unification, it was estimated that large deficits would only be avoided if contributions were increased to 35 per cent of earnings – nearly double the rate of the time (Bellermann 1990: 72). (The demographic situation following unification was equally onerous – see Figures 5.16 and 5.17.)

Following the reform of 1957, pensions began to increase quite strongly – in both nominal and real terms. Pensions in general increased by 617 per cent between 1957 and 1989, whereas prices for a two-pensioner household rose by 187 per cent. Viewed generally, the growth in pensions during this period favoured manual workers: the average manual worker's monthly pension rose by 855 per cent, but that of the average salaried employee increased by 655 per cent. Moreover, the distribution between males and females was unequal. As a percentage of average expenditure for a two-person pensioner household in 1981, the average manual female worker received 49 per cent; the average for males was 87 per cent. But for salaried employees the respective averages were 77 and 124 per cent. By 1989, the averages were 48, 68, 72 and 101 per cent. Again, it can be seen that males received higher average pensions than females, and on this basis salaried employees received more generous pensions than manual workers. The reasons for the relatively low pensions of females are related to their generally lower number of contribution years and their lower average earnings when compared to males. This is due mainly, of course, to the females' general propensity to withdraw from the labour market in order to raise children. Methods of compensating for this discriminatory effect on pension eligibility are still at a somewhat rudimentary stage. Note, however, the general decline in pensioner-purchasing power during the 1980s (BMA *Statistisches Taschenbuch*; IW *Zahlen* various).

As will also be seen when the analysis turns to the social-policy implications of unification, the future trend in the costs of retirement pensions is difficult to estimate. Both domestic and international economic developments will play a major role in determining the extent to which increasing costs can be absorbed. Costs in the west will almost certainly increase strongly

from the beginning of the next century because of the increase in the number of pensioners. Indeed, the expenditure pattern was already becoming unsustainable by the late 1980s as a result of the presage of change in the population structure and, more particularly at that stage, past improvements in the pension provisions. This was the background to the 1989 statute which introduced the 1992 amendments to statutory pension entitlement. The nature of these demographic changes can readily be seen from Figure 5.6.

In 1987 persons between 60 and 65 years of age made up 5.4 per cent of the population, with those over 65 years accounting for a further 15.3 per cent. However, by 2030 the proportion of persons of retirement age is predicted to rise rapidly, so that those between 60 and 65 years will constitute 8.9 per cent of the population, while the proportion over 65 years will reach 27.4 per cent (*Sozialpolitische Informationen* 3/88: 21). The ratio between the bulk of the labour force (20–60 years of age) and those over 60 is therefore expected to change from 2.8:1 to 1.3:1 during the period 1987–2030 (Boss in Giersch 1983: 279; Figure 5.6). Moreover, increased life expectancy will also increase the financial burden on the labour force from 2010 at an increasing rate; from 1985 to 1995 alone average life expectancy is forecast to rise by two years (*Der Spiegel* 42/89: 25). Hence, it is predicted that the proportion of the population of pension age will be even more dramatic between 2030 and 2040. In 1985, there were 37 persons of pensionable age out of every 100 of working age. By 2025, this ratio will almost double (to 70 out of every 100); by 2040 it will be 80 pensioners in every 100. There were 328 pensioners per 1000 contribution payers in 1986, compared to the expected 826 per 1000 in 2030 (Zohlnhöfer 1990b: 315).

In order to illustrate this critical point, Figures 5.7a, 5.7b, 5.7c present various analyses of the population structure in 1910, 1989 and 2030. It will be gathered from Figure 5.7a that the total population of Germany was 64.6 million in 1910. It is evident that the distribution of the population was 'normal' in so far as young persons represented the biggest proportion of the population. As Wallich (1955: 264) indicates, 'the population pyramid of a healthy and growing nation' resembles a Christmas tree: broad at the bottom, tapering off smoothly towards the top, its two sides (male and female) symmetrical. Figure 5.7a conforms to this pattern. Figure 5.7b applies to West Germany only. First, it shows that the total population in 1989 was 62.06 million. Second, the effects of two world wars and economic developments can be seen. Wallich (*ibid.*), in continuing his analogy to a conifer describes Germany's post-war tree as a 'stunted storm-whipped plant'. There are 9.96 million persons in the age range 0–15 in Figure 5.7b, while there are

12 26 million over 60. Moreover, Figure 5.7c illustrates how the West's population structure for 2030 is predicted to resemble a mushroom rather than a Christmas tree. The total population will be 40.0 million in 2030 and the proportion of those between 0 and 30 years will have declined strongly. Hence, contributions alone will not support the retirement-pension insurance scheme in the future. Therefore, any cost involved in subsidising the retirement-pension scheme is, in this sense, a factor completely separate from the costs of unification. The same is true of eradicating the inequalities in the pensions of males and females (*Statistisches Jahrbuch* 1990: 53).

However, instead of the customary seasonal deficit, a surplus of DM 1.5 billion was recorded in the first quarter of 1991, compared to a deficit of just under DM 0.5 billion in the corresponding period of the previous year. In the later part of the year, the receipts of the pension insurance funds in the old Länder profited from increasing employment and

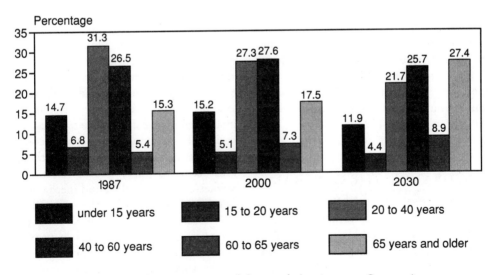

Figure 5.6 The age structure of the population (western Germany)

Source: Informationen zur politischen Bildung 3/88: 21

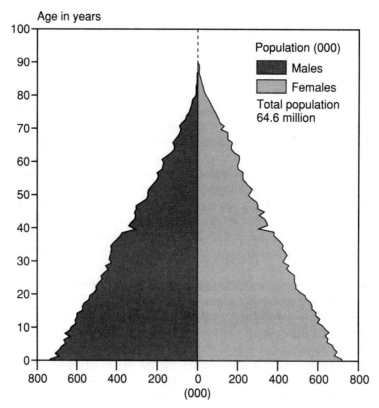

Figure 5.7a Population structure: 1910

Source: Informationen zur politischen Bildung 3/88: 7

higher wages and salaries; but the growth in revenue was restrained by the fact that the contribution rate was lowered from 18.7 to 17.7 per cent in April 1991. Expenditure by contrast began to grow more vigorously; contributions were therefore raised to 19.2 per cent in January 1994.

STATUTORY-HEALTH INSURANCE: THE GENERAL PRINCIPLES

There are a number of principles which characterise the health service. The 'solidarity principle' of statutory health insurance means that not only do the healthy provide financial support for the sick, but also the same treatment is available irrespective of income and family size and age. Note once again, therefore, that redistributive elements are inherent in the system. More specifically, high income earners subsidise those on low incomes, while single persons and small families subsidise large families. The notion of any equivalence between contributions and benefits is alien to the scheme. This seems to imply a clear rejection of market-orientated allocation mechanisms. These are replaced by the principle of free access to medical care. Also note that statutory health insurance provides pharmaceuticals and medical services rather than direct financial grants for medical care. For this purpose, the services provided are secured by contracting

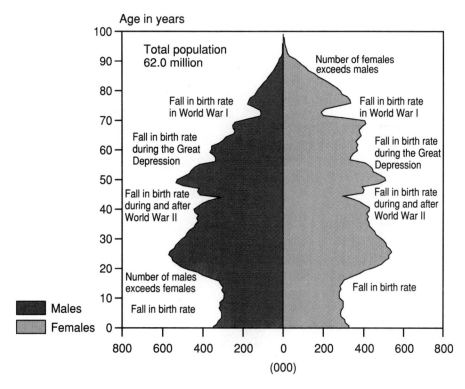

Age in years

Total population
62.0 million

Number of females
exceeds males

Fall in birth rate
in World War I

Fall in birth rate
in World War I

Fall in birth rate
during the Great
Depression

Fall in birth rate
during the Great
Depression

Fall in birth rate
during and after
World War II

Fall in birth rate
during and after
World War II

Number of males
exceeds females

Fall in birth rate

Males

Females

Fall in birth rate

(000)

Figure 5.7b Population structure: 1989
Source: Stat. Jahrbuch 1990: 53

a wide range of highly-qualified persons and in many cases supplying an equally diverse range of buildings and equipment. As will shortly be seen, these services are free of charge to the patient, but the fees charged by the suppliers of the services are the subject of negotiation with the health offices.

Decision taking in the health-care market depends not only on the patient but also on the provider of medical services. It is the latter who controls the supply of health-care accessories; the doctor, for example, controls the supply of costly pharmaceuticals (Murswieck 1990: 157). Similarly, it is the suppliers who decide which treatment, drug or medical aid the patient receives or how long he/she

remains in hospital. In the case of outpatient treatment, there is a low cost to the insured person for the use of these services. Consequently, there is no reason to limit demand. As a rule, the patients are not aware of the price of treatment, and they are thus not well enough informed about costs. Furthermore, the doctor will probably comply with most requests since he can thereby increase his income and avoid the risk of a patient transferring to another doctor (Deutsche Bank *Bulletin* 10/88: 20).

It is necessary to distinguish between compulsory statutory health insurance on taking up employment, voluntary health insurance within the statutory system and private insurance. Statutory and voluntary

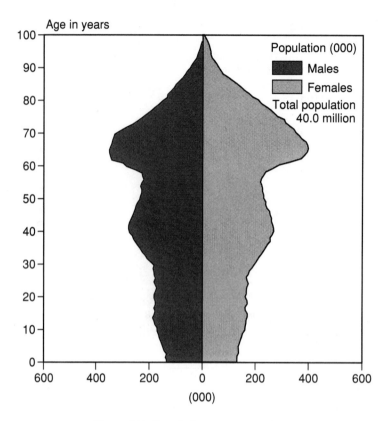

Figure 5.7c Population structure: 2030

Source: As Figure 5.7a

health insurance cover the insured and the members of his/her family. It accounts for around 90 per cent of the population (*Statistisches Jahrbuch* 1991: 69). The remaining 10 per cent are insured privately. There are two basic differences from the statutory system. First, the premium payable in the case of private health insurance is based on the medical history of the insured, his/her age on entering the scheme and on the sex of the person. Second, a premium is payable in respect of each member of the insured's family in the private health insurance system. Compulsory statutory insurance also applies to those in receipt of unemployment benefits, those receiving statutory pensions, students, and the self-employed, including artists and writers (BMA 1991: 87). The contributions of the unemployed and pensioners are met out of state funds. According to one estimate (*Die Zeit* 14/90) the Federal Government had to forgo health-insurance contributions from the unemployed which would have totalled DM 3.3 billion in 1989. Instead, the BA contributed DM 5.5 billion to the health-insurance fund on behalf of the unemployed.

Demand for health insurance normally varies according to age: it is particularly high at birth, during early childhood, and in old age, especially advanced old age. In other words, changes in the population

Table 5.3 Health Care expenditure

Age group (years)	Hospital expenditure per capita		Out-patient expenditure per capita	
	Males	Females	Males	Females
0–4	130	47	58	57
5–14	53	44	48	48
15–24	75	60	55	68
25–34	72	70	66	82
35–44	81	82	81	90
45–54	114	127	90	105
55–64	193	153	92	121
65–74	267	241	118	125
75 and over	391	372	133	138
Total	1376	1196	741	834

Source: Deutsche Bank Bulletin 1988: 19
Note: Index numbers; hospital care per male patient aged between 15 and 64 years is 100

structure affect the demand side of the health market (Murswieck 1990: 158). The relatively large number of births during the period 1965–75 caused financial strains on the system; subsequently, the growing percentage of older persons means expenditure on health care will increase early in the next century. In Figure 5.7b the relevant age groups were respectively clustered around the ages of 20 and 45. The former group were the result of the high birth rates between 1965 and 1975. Both groups will cause financial strains in the health-care sector when they are over 60. This has also been seen to be a significant problem area in the retirement-pension insurance. Table 5.3 shows the expenditure on health care for both males and females corresponding to various age groups.

Consequently, the number of patients grew very fast as a result of these demographic trends. Average *per capita* expenditure by the health-insurance funds during the years 1985–89, for example, rose by 4 per cent per annum for pensioners, whereas it increased by only 2 per cent for insured persons still at work (MRDB 1991: 28). The financial burden on the insurance funds increased, not least because hospitals were permitted to offset losses due to unplanned expenditure by claiming reimbursement from the insurance funds. Indeed, hospitals simply reported all their costs to the health insurance offices and they were reimbursed in full (*das Selbstkostendeckungsprinzip*). During the period 1985–8, more than 12 million patients were treated by 3,100 hospitals and the average patient cost per department was DM 4,245 (BMA 1989: 66). Hospital expenditure represented the biggest part of total outlay in the statutory health-insurance scheme. It was 24 per cent of statutory health-insurance expenditure in 1970, but by 1990 this expenditure item had increased to 32 per cent (IW *Zahlen* 1991: 50). There was one formal reform before 1989, namely the Hospital Reform Act (1984). The dual system of hospital financing, whereby the capital cost was borne by the public authorities and current operating and treatment costs by the patients and/or the health insur-

219

ance, was relaxed: hospitals and health insurance offices were subsequently able to conclude investment contracts and in particular rationalisation investments (MRDB 1/85: 30). The funds for hospital building and improvement were raised by the Länder Authorities alone (the previous system of mixed financing by the Federal and Länder Authorities was therefore abolished); the Länder Authorities' powers with respect to hospital planning were extended correspondingly. Furthermore, any costs that were not covered by health-care costs as calculated in advance were no longer reimbursed retroactively (*ibid.*). Hospitals which operated particularly efficiently could retain any profits, while loss-making hospitals were expected to rationalise their activities.

Because the insured do not meet the full cost of health care, the health-insurance funds assume the responsibility for paying the balances. For example, in 1987 the cost of prescribed drugs and medicines was DM 18.9 billion; this cost increased a further DM 1 billion in 1988 (BMA 1989: 24). On average, each German was prescribed one item daily. However, the number of prescriptions issued varied by doctor. The expenditure on drugs and medicines by country is compared in Figure 5.8.

It can be seen in Figure 5.8 that between 1975 and 1983 the expenditure on drugs and medicines in West Germany was just under France. Yet some caution is required when comparing these expenditure patterns. In France, high expenditure is caused mainly by large quantities, whereas high expenditure in Germany was more related to high drug prices. Although not shown in the figure, there was also an increase in expenditure in the first half of the 1970s. Spending on pharmaceuticals, the third largest expenditure item in statutory health insurance,

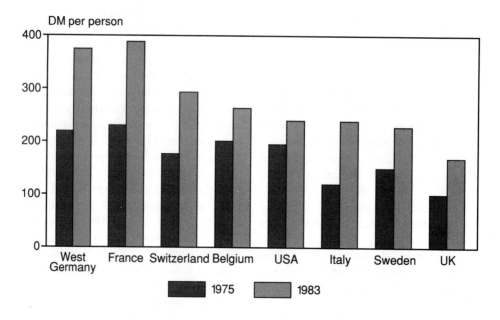

Figure 5.8 Expenditure on pharmaceuticals

Source: BMA: *Gesundheitsreform'89*: 27

fluctuated particularly wildly at the end of the 1970s; after a sharp increase in 1980 and 1981, expenditure went up only slightly in 1982 but its rise accelerated again from 1983. A saving of DM 930 million was expected as a result of the flexible contribution operative from 1991, the effect of which reduced the price of patent medicines by an average of 20 per cent (*Sozialpolitische Nachrichten* 37/91: 17–18).

When considered as a part of the services' sector, the proportionate growth in statutory-health insurance has displayed rapid development. There has been an increase in the number of patients by reason of everyday habits. For example, the number of alcohol-related diseases affecting persons over 15 years of age increased threefold between 1950 and 1970; in the same period the number of road accidents increased by the same margin (Alber 1989: 205). Deaths from heart disease, moreover, increased from 15 per cent of total deaths in 1927 to 50 per cent in 1986 (Tietz 1991: 425). Over the same period the incidence of fatalities from cancer doubled, although infectious diseases caused 20 per cent of all deaths in 1927, while in 1986 they were responsible for only 0.7 per cent (*ibid.*). Additionally, cases of blood pressure, diabetes and rheumatism – which have a far smaller effect on the death rate – have also increased (*ibid.*). Modern-day illnesses and chronic sickness, which often require lengthy and expensive treatment, are thus increasingly common. At the same time, progress in medical technology has made possible new but also expensive therapies, organ transplantations being an obvious example. There is also a strong probability that consumer demand will increase as contributions increase. Moreover, as wealth increases, so does the demand for health services: more importance is attached to good health – which increasingly is understood as an integral part of total well-being.

A reform of the health-insurance system was introduced in 1989 – as was also seen to be the case with retirement-pension legislation. But the debate on health-care reform had been a much more protracted and controversial affair. Moreover, with unification, further reform was needed. On the other hand, the 1989 reform set out to stimulate what the policy makers viewed as a more rational allocation of resources.

The main point of the 1989 reform was to counteract the cost explosion in the health-care sector. As already shown, costs are functionally related to the structure of the population and increasingly sophisticated methods of treatment. Figure 5.9a depicts the growth of health insurance in the social budget during the period 1960–90. It can be seen that health-insurance expenditure amounted to DM 135 billion in 1990. As shown in Figure 5.2b, the total social budget in 1990 was DM 703 billion in 1990. Hence, health insurance expenditure in 1990 accounted for 19 per cent of the social budget. Although the health system in West Germany was undoubtedly one of the best in the world, then, it was also very costly. Expenditure had increased by a factor of nearly six from 1970 to 1990. Figure 5.9b demonstrates the health insurance expenditure during the period 1970–90.

Even more specifically, the development of the expenditure side of statutory health insurance has been characterised from the beginning of the 1970s by alternating periods of exceedingly sharp rises and periods of only moderate expansion. The spate of expenditure increases experienced in the first half of the 1970s (with growth rates of up to 25 per cent a year – which admittedly also owed something to inflation), and the increases in

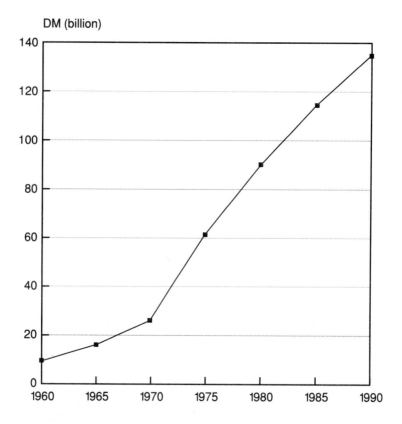

DM (billion)

Figure 5.9a Health Insurance in the Social Budget
Source: IW *Zahlen* 1991: 48

contribution rates which it necessitated (8.1 to 11.4 per cent 1971–7), put the policy makers under growing pressure to slow down the pace of cost increases. In 1984 the expenditure of the statutory health insurance institutions increased more rapidly than that of the other public authorities, after having grown at a pace similar to that of overall public spending between 1980 and 1983. The share of health insurance in total public expenditure climbed to approximately 12.5 per cent in 1984 (MRDB 1/85: 28). Since 1970 health insurance expenditure has increased by a factor of five but GNP by a factor of three and one half (IW 1991: 14).

Figure 5.10 shows the increase of health

insurance expenditure during the period 1960–87. It can be seen that, relative to the growth of major economic indicators, the trend in health-sector expenditure was problematical. It was 3.2 per cent of GNP in 1960; by 1987 it had reached 6.3 per cent. During the same period, prices rose by 152 per cent while average monthly earnings increased by 524 per cent. Meanwhile, health-insurance expenditure rose by 1,304 per cent. It was against this background that in 1988 an Act to reform the health insurance system reached the statute book. During the first full year of its operation (1989) the ratio of health expenditure to GNP fell back to 5.8 per cent.

The 1989 reform – known as the 'Blüm

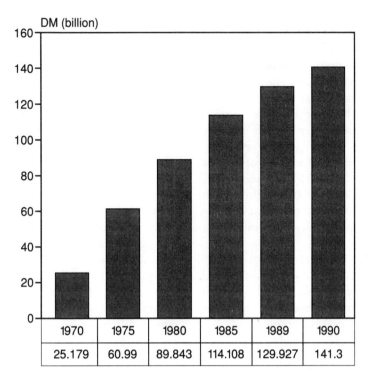

Figure 5.9b Expenditure on Statutory Health Insurance
Source: IW *Zahlen* 1991: 50

model' because the Federal Minister of Labour and Social Policy assumed parliamentary responsibility for the measure – therefore set out (BMA 1989: 10–11; OECD *Economic Survey* 1989: 94–5) to:

- contain the costs of statutory health insurance but at the same time ensure a continuation in the availability of treatment
- provide adequate resources to meet the health-care aims outlined in the introductory paragraph
- set contribution rates consistent with the economic climate

Prior to the appearance of the proposals for the 1989 Act, an increasingly vociferous lobby which advocated a more market-orientated system of health-

resource allocation had emerged. The containment of the cost increases emanating from the age structure and the application of developments in medical knowledge was only a short-run aim. Their principal aim was to devise a system which would ensure a more optimal allocation of resources. The argument of these observers runs along the following lines (Deutsche Bank *Bulletin* 10/88). Flexible prices and competition provide suitable incentives when dealing with scarce resources without – as with other systems of allocation – encroaching on the individual's freedom of choice. Only under these conditions is it possible for economic growth to thrive and to make the optimum provision for the population. This all shows that the problems of the statutory health insurance cannot be resolved satisfactorily by state intervention. Instead of increasing regulation in the health sector, it would be better to try more market in this sector. Not only would this provide more efficient solutions, but should also be in line with the basic principle of a market economy, that is to limit collective regulations as far as possible in favour of the individual's freedom of choice. The reforms of health insurance envisaged the development of a higher degree of public awareness, cost consciousness, collective responsibility and more self-determination.

There was, on the other hand, a general view that the country could afford its high standard of health care. The drive to cut costs came mainly from the employers who, as well as contributing for their

employees, meet the costs of the first six weeks of sick pay. The total cost of this latter item was over DM 33 billion in 1990 (IW *Zahlen* 1991: 48). It represented the sum of either 80 per cent of sick employees' gross earnings or 100 per cent of their net earnings, whichever was the lesser. Hence, Blüm's proposals had two main elements. The first element was to significantly increase the proportion of direct costs met by the patient. Most notable here was an effort to cut the relatively high costs of drugs in Germany. This was to be achieved by supplementing the arrangement whereby the funds operated a series of fixed upper limits to the refund per drug (*Festbeträge*). Where patients wanted more expensive branded drugs, they had to pay the whole difference between the drugs they

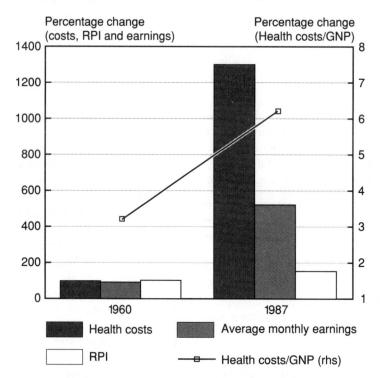

Figure 5.10 Relative increase of Health-Insurance costs

Sources: BMA: *Gesundheitsreform'89*: 8; IW Zahlen 1984: 33, 1989: 8; Bundesarbeitsblatt 7–8/91: 114

required and the upper limit determined by the funds. This practice was to continue until 70 per cent of the drug market was covered. In addition, however, (from July 1992) the patient was required to pay 10 per cent of each item prescribed – up to a maximum of DM 15. Prior to this there was a flat charge of DM 3 per item. Another part of the first element was to set limits to various other items of expenditure. Included here were dentures, dental bridges, hearing aids, contact lenses and wheel chairs. Here again, patients were required to make contributions if they wanted non-standard – and therefore more expensive – materials and models.

The second element was to introduce a patient contribution to institutional costs. To this end, the costs of patient transportation were cut by 30 per cent, and those of recuperation by 10 per cent. (All German employees are periodically entitled to the latter on a paid-leave basis.) These savings were respectively achieved by requiring the patient to pay the first DM 20 of any travel costs and DM 10 per day for any stay at a spa. Both items had previously been funded in full by the local insurance office. Because the length of an average stay in hospital was the longest in Europe, the daily charge to the patient was doubled to DM 10. Where the patient's stay in hospital exceeded fourteen days, however, the costs were met in full by the appropriate insurance office. (Hospitals received a fixed daily fee for most services, irrespective of the treatment required. There was therefore an incentive to maximise the periods of in-patient treatment.) Half the total DM 14 billion savings in 1989 went towards a reduction in contributions in 1991. The rest went towards improvements in the care of the chronic sick, which was one of the weakest points in the system. There was no insurance to cover chronic sickness and patients had to rely on either self-finance or state supplementary benefits. (See the Conclusion to this chapter.)

It is perhaps indicative of the policy problems which remained if it is noted that a Federal ministry exclusively responsible for the health service emerged in January 1991. Its first ministerial head (Gerda Hasselfeldt) resigned in favour of her CSU colleague Horst Seehofer in April 1992. Seehofer thought that the 1989 measures ought to have included incentives to encourage more out-patient care, an opinion shared by his predecessor (Dietzel 1991: 54; FAZ 14 July 1992). Moreover, in record time, he saw a Bill through parliament, securing agreement not only with his coalition partners but also with the SPD. Hence, from January 1993, his measures were estimated to be capable of realising savings of DM 11.4 billion per year – about twice the deficit incurred in 1992. Prescription charges of DM 3 (minimum) to DM 7 (maximum) were introduced. Dentists' fees were reduced by 10 per cent compared to 1992 and the costs of dental care deemed 'inessential' by the authorities was to be met privately. The number of doctors who could be registered in the state-funded scheme was limited. Relatively strict guidelines were placed on what could be prescribed. The daily cost of the first 14 days stay in hospital was raised to DM 11 (1993) and DM 12 (1994) in the west; in the east the respective charges were DM 8 and DM 9. Last, but by no means least, the methods used by the hospitals to recover costs were to be fundamentally revised on a staged basis by 1995. The *Selbstkostendeckungsprinzip* was abolished with immediate effect (TVF 13 August 1992). Until 1995, increases in reimbursement costs were to be limited to the rise in contribution income. From 1995, differentiated lump sums were to be payable according to the type of treatment (*ibid.*). Private investment and incentives were to be introduced. It will have been gathered that the incidence of cost cutting fell mainly on the supply side. Doctors, dentists, hospitals and the pharmaceutical industry financed DM 8.2 billion of such costs, while patients met the remaining DM 3.2 billion (KrV 1992b: 196; Pfaff *et al.* 1992: 216). Whether this will be the last word in health-service reform is open to some doubt (Pfaff *et al. ibid.*). There is less doubt, however, about the effects on the pharmaceutical industry. As the government restricted both the range and price of drugs which could be supplied, doctors could either recommend a direct purchase over the pharmacist's counter, or prescribe cheaper copies. Hence, drugs, traditionally the non-cyclical buffer cushioning German chemical companies' profits, seemed drained of their power to protect profitability (FT 16 March 1993). There was nonetheless an almost immediate improvement in the financial position of the health-insurance offices. They posted a surplus of DM 1 billion in the first quarter of 1993, compared with a deficit of DM 3.5 billion a year earlier (MRDB 6/93: 46).

Reducing costs in the health sector by adopting a firm line on drug prices, doctors' and dentists' pay and the hospitals' pricing system, did not mean that Seehofer succeeded in taking the heat out of an even more controversial, if less costly, issue. This was the system whereby employers meet their employees' sick-pay costs from the first day of absence. By introducing a waiting period, some members of the Federal government argued, financial resources would be released to fund nursing-care reforms *Pflegeversicherung*. Germany was the only country in the EC where there was no time interval between an employee reporting sick and becoming entitled to paid sick leave (*Karenztage*). In Belgium and Denmark, employees did not receive payment for the first day's absence; in the Netherlands the interval was two days, whereas in the remaining Member States it was three days (FAZ 27 May 1993). In Germany, the issue was seen, on the one hand, as yet another factor responsible for high labour costs (see Table 6.3 and the section on *Standort Deutschland* in Chapter 8). On the other hand, identical sick-pay conditions for white-collar and manual employees was confirmed in the 1969 Act; unlike other characteristics of the West German welfare state, the sick-pay scheme was directly attributable to a lengthy strike in 1956–7 (see the section on trade union policy in Chapter 6). Some members of the CDU and CSU supported the SPD and trade unions in their opposition to the proposed introduction of a one or two-day interval; the opponents in the CDU/CSU saw no relationship between sick-pay schemes and nursing care (FAZ 22 April 1993). Strike action was predicted by the DGB and the DAG threatened to take the Federal government to the Constitutional Court (*ibid.*). Because sick pay was guaranteed by collective agreements, the employers preferred a system whereby sick pay was lower than normal pay (*Handelsblatt* 26 May 1992). A possible compromise may eventually be the abolition of one or two statutory holidays. (The provision of nursing care for the old and infirm is discussed in the Conclusion at the end of this chapter.)

THE ORGANISATION AND FINANCE OF HEALTH INSURANCE

The task of balancing income and expenditure is assigned to the various statutory health-insurance funds. These funds are independent organisations, although their contribution levels are subject to approval by the Federal Ministry of Labour and Social Affairs. Nonetheless, contribution rates vary from fund to fund and normal practice is to refer to the average contribution rate of all funds. The range of rates in 1991 was from 8 to 15 per cent of gross earnings (*Bundesarbeitsblatt* 10/91: 131).

The most important insurance fund operates at the local level throughout Germany, although there is a co-ordinating office in Bonn. Each local office is therefore known as the 'general district' insurance fund (AOK). Certificates for treatment, reimbursement of costs incurred in receiving treatment and the determination of fees payable are among each AOK's duties. There are about 17 million AOK contributors – mainly manual workers. The next largest fund – the substitute or *Ersatzkrankenkasse* – has about 11 million members, most of whom are salaried staffs. Over 1,000 companies have their own funds, accounting for a further 5 million members. The handicraft trades' fund has two million members and, rather like the pension-insurance schemes, there are relatively small funds for miners (1 million), farmers (0.75 million) and the merchant navy (*Bundesarbeitsblatt* 6/91: 129).

The prices of, and conditions on which, health-care services are supplied are established in negotiations between representatives of the health-insurance funds and the suppliers of services. For example, the AOK will negotiate the fee level for treatment received by its insured members with representatives of the association of local medical practitioners (*Kassenärztliche Vereinigung*). The contracts negotiated with medical practitioners contain an undertaking that the insured will receive equal, sufficient and appropriate treatment. In return, the funds pay an

agreed general fee to the association, which then distributes it among its membership according to an agreed formula. Similarly, hospital staff also have a series of local associations, and so on. Hospital representatives negotiate the fees chargeable by their institutions with the local funds. In all cases the work of the local associations is coordinated by a federal-wide organisation, usually situated in Bonn. It is important to add that the pharmaceutical companies negotiate their prices with the funds on a direct basis.

Thus, the principle of free service at the point of treatment means that both doctors and patients can pass on the costs of statutory health insurance. Since negotiations between representatives of the health-insurance funds and the suppliers of services determine the prices at which benefits are supplied, there is no direct incentive to economise, provided that the funds themselves can be certain of subsidisation. The system has, in this sense, a tendency to waste resources and suppliers are in a monopoly position (Murswieck 1990: 157). (Payments of doctors' and dentists' fees account for one-quarter of all health-insurance expenditure (IW *Zahlen* 1991: 50).)

An Act to Contain the Expansion of Health Insurance (1977), established a Concerted Action Group in the health sector. Its members are the health-insurance institutions, the suppliers of health-care products, representatives of health-care staff and the Federal, Länder and local authorities. The group's terms of reference require it to formulate economic bench marks and make recommendations as to appropriate revisions of overall remuneration and maximum prices for medical supplies. In addition, the group is expected to submit proposals for the rationalisation and greater efficiency of health care (MRDB 1/85: 30).

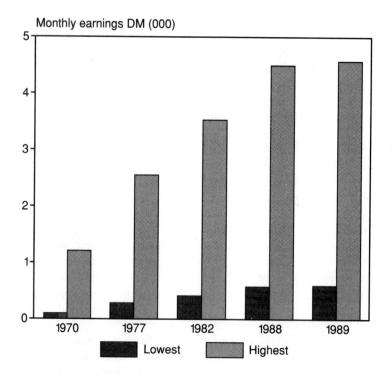

Monthly earnings DM (000)

Lowest **Highest**

Figure 5.11 Threshold/Ceiling: Health-Insurance Contributions
Source: BMA: *Gesundheitsreform'89*: 119

There are various contribution levels within the statutory scheme. They are related to monthly earnings, with both a minimum and maximum amount. In 1989, the minimum (or threshold) earnings level was DM 595, while the maximum level of earnings (or ceiling) was DM 4,575 . The difference between the 1970 and 1989 contribution levels demonstrates the effects of increasing nominal incomes and the rate of economic growth: the minimum increased from DM 98 to DM 595 and the earnings ceiling rose from DM 1,200 to DM 4,575 (BMA 1989: 119). Figure 5.11 illustrates these minimum and maximum contribution limits during the period 1970–89. As from January 1993 the limits in western Germany were DM 610 and DM 5,400. Employees with earnings above the upper limit may opt to join a private scheme (Commerzbank *Economic Trends* 3/91: 15). Statutory health insurance is partially financed by these contributions. They have gradually risen, on average, from 8.2 per cent of earnings in 1970 to 12.2 per cent in 1991 (West), but 12.8 in the East (MRDB 6/91: 26). Total contributions received by all the health insurance funds in 1990 amounted to DM 147 billion, of which the AOK (see above) received DM 65 billion and company funds DM 17 billion (*Bundesarbeitsblatt* 6/91: 129). The contribution system is the same as other forms of social insurance, namely one half is paid by the employee and the other half by the employer. However, students, pensioners and other persons in receipt of small incomes, as well as farmers, contribute at a reduced rate.

HEALTH-INSURANCE PROBLEMS

Health-insurance finances have been influenced by the structure of the labour force and the population; of equal financial importance are the human and physical capital resources employed in the health sector. There have been a number of reforms aimed at controlling rising costs, culminating in the 1989 and 1992 Acts – the former being another example of a reform measure which reached the statute book just prior to unification. Although this latter event clearly posed yet further cost problems, it is important to note that the fundamental economic problem has not changed. This basic problem is technically known as one of 'moral hazard': in this context it refers to a person being insured in such a manner that the personal cost of obtaining treatment (contribution rates plus fixed charges) is less than the cost to the insurance fund of such treatment (Knappe 1983: 324). Murswieck (1990: 161) adds that health-insurance policy has developed in a piecemeal fashion and has therefore lacked a precise overall framework.

On present predictions, the number of small children will decline sharply after the year 2000. However, as noted above, the high birth rate 1965–75 had important cost implications for health care – just as it will for retirement insurance in the next century. This burden alone, it is estimated, will cause a rise in statutory health-insurance contribution rates from 12.2 per cent in 1991 to just under 13 per cent in the year 2000 and to over 15 per cent by 2030 (Deutsche Bank *Bulletin* 10/88: 18). The high burden of contributions may be not only a threat to the international competitiveness of German companies, it also possibly lowers the motivation of employees and encourages absenteeism and moonlighting (*ibid.*).

EMPLOYMENT PROMOTION (UNEMPLOYMENT INSURANCE)

As already seen in Figure 1.2, unemployment rose sharply during the first two oil price shocks in 1973 and 1979. Unemployment had reached over two million by 1983, and the rate of unemployment was over 9 per cent (Alber 1989: 177). By 1990, there were around 28 million people in gainful employment and 2 million unemployed – a rate of 7 per cent (von Weizsäcker 1990: 26; Chapter 6). As early as 1969 the Employment Promotion Act (AFG) established active labour market intervention measures, including employment research. The objective was to assist the unemployed in finding employment, or to obtain training for work which matched their existing skills and potential.

The AFG therefore empowers the BA to provide (Grochla and Gaugler 1990: 2222):

- vocational counselling
- information on employment opportunities
- measures which provide vocational training
- re-training or further training
- grants for the maintenance or creation of jobs
- unemployment and short-time working benefits
- payment for employees in cases of bankruptcy

Since the beginning of the employment crisis in West Germany in 1974, the major share of the Labour Office's expenditure has been on unemployment benefits. Hence the original intention of the Employment Promotion Act has been frustrated: the Act was intended not to concentrate on the effects of unemployment, but rather its prevention and reduction. Nevertheless, finance was provided for employment creation, vocational counselling and securing employment. Measures taken by the BA under the Employment Promotion Act are supplemented by financial grants paid under the Act to Promote Education and Training (BAFÖG) (Grochla and Gaugler 1990: 2222). The actual size of these Federal subsidies is determined by the degree of liquidity in the BA's finances (Soltwedel in Giersch 1983: 337). The promotion of vocational training for under-privileged young people, and the facilities laid down in the Federal Aid Act for assisting unemployed young people, are incorporated in the Employment Promotion Act. These latter items are also financed by the BA. Sixth-formers and students are entitled to unemployment benefit and unemployment assistance. They must however prove that they are not doing any work in addition to their studies. If they do work, they are liable to make an unemployment-insurance contribution (MRDB 1/89: 16). The general guideline of the BA is that the unemployed should be able to maintain their living standards and have time to train and search for new jobs through the provision of unemployment insurance.

Employers are also required to contribute to the unemployment insurance fund. The unemployed claim benefits from this fund. As well as unemployment-insurance expenditure, the cost of labour offices (including premises, staff salaries and superannuation) have to be met from the fund; the cost of vocational guidance and schemes to reduce unemployment are also charges on this fund. Until the Federal government introduced spending cuts in 1993, unemployment benefit for an unmarried person was 63 per cent of net earnings, but 68 per cent for persons with at least one child. These benefits were

Table 5.4 Unemployment Benefits

Contribution days	Age (years)	Benefit (days)
180		78
240		104
360		165
480		208
600		260
720		312
840	42	364
960	42	416
1080	42	468
1200	44	520
1320	44	572
1440	49	624
1560	49	676
1680	54	728
1800	54	780
1920	54	832

Source: AFG 1991: 106

reduced by 3 and 1 percentage points respectively from 1 January 1994. Since social-insurance contributions were increased from the same date, the net earnings received when still in employment would have been reduced. Inflation also had to be taken into account. The real respective reductions in benefits were therefore about 10 and 4.5 per cent (BA *Presse Informationen* 7/94). The duration of benefit is basically limited to between 6 and 32 months according to the age and contribution record of the unemployed person. It is necessary to show that unemployment is involuntary, otherwise a waiting period of between 2 and 12 weeks will be enforced. Unemployment benefit (*Arbeitslosengeld*) is paid only if the unemployed person has been in employment and paid contributions for at least 12 months in the preceding three years. To obtain unemployment benefit a claimant must attend in person at a labour exchange for registration and when called for interview. The claimant must also be capable of, and be available for, work.

Table 5.4 summarises unemployment-insurance benefits. The regulations on eligibility for, and duration of, unemployment benefit, are governed by the number of days and, in some cases, the age of the claimant. Age is not relevant until the claimant has attained his/her 42nd birthday. Until this age is reached, unemployment benefit is related to the contribution period: the minimum period is 180 days, for which the claimant receives 78 days benefit; for a contribution period of over 720 days, the benefit received is limited to a maximum of 312 days. Between the ages of 42 and 54 there are various limits. For example, at the age of 42, between 840 and 1,080 days' contributions will qualify a claimant for between 364 and a maximum of 468 days' benefits. Similarly, the increments between 1,680 and 1,920 days govern the amount payable to a claimant aged 54 years (from 728 to 832 days). Age is again irrelevant for persons exceeding the age of 55: 832 days is the maximum benefit payable, irrespective of the contribution period. Similarly, 78 days benefit is a minimum entitlement, provided 180 days contributions have been paid. As already pointed out, an unemployed person must apply for a retirement pension on reaching the age of 60.

If there is no entitlement to unemployment benefit, either because insufficient contributions have been paid or because the maximum period of eligibility has expired, unemployment assistance is payable. This allowance is subject to a means test, and is less than unemployment benefit. It amounted to 58 per cent of net earnings for persons with at least one child, 56 per cent otherwise. From 1 January 1994 these benefits were reduced to 57 and 53 per cent of former net earnings respectively (BMA 1991: 338; IW 1991: 30; *Bundesarbeitsblatt* 1/94). Recipients of unemployment assistance are entitled to the same help in respect of training schemes and in securing employment as those in receipt of unemployment benefit. Those not eligible for unemployment assistance may seek social assistance (see below). Note that unemployment benefits are funded from insurance contributions, whereas the cost of unemployment assistance is a charge on the Federal budget. (Both are paid at the local branches of the BA.)

Short-time working benefits are also payable out of the unemployment-insurance fund. These benefits are paid to employees but an application must be made by the employer to the appropriate local labour offices. The employer must show that there is an unavoidable economic cause, and that it will be possible to protect jobs if this benefit is paid. At least 10 per cent of total working time at the employer's premises, and a third of all his employees must be affected by the economic downturn, which must also last for at least four weeks. Note that these benefits are payable only where the cause is economic. In 1984, during a metal workers strike, both the BA and Blüm resisted claims for benefits arising from short-time working caused by the strike (Owen Smith *et al.* 1989: 205). The central issue was whether locked-out employees outside the districts involved in the conflict were entitled to benefits. Several social courts ruled that the law permitted such payments. However, in spite of bitter opposition from the unions, an Act to Safeguard the Neutrality of the BA during Industrial Disputes was passed in 1986. The Act confirmed that within a district where a dispute is in progress, benefits would be paid only to claimants who would not directly profit from any eventual settlement. It also stipulated strict conditions for claimants outside the affected district who were in similar jobs and subject to the same type of collective agreement as the parties to the dispute (BMA *Sozialpolitische Informationen* 7/86). The probability of consequential pay claims similar in type and scope was the critical test. Compensation for short-time working was, like unemployment benefit, reduced on 1 January 1994 to 60 per cent for childless persons, or 67 per cent for persons with at least one child. The compensation paid by the BA in the event of bad weather preventing work in the construction industry was also reduced to these percentages. Moreover, the period during which these benefits were payable was reduced from November–March to December–February and they were to be abolished completely at the end of February 1996. In addition, however, the construction industry received grants and loans if it can be shown that short-time working has been avoided (Bellermann 1990: 76–7; Lampert 1985: 207). Finally, all employees can claim compensation from the BA for loss of earnings if their employer becomes involved in bankruptcy proceedings.

There are also numerous training schemes supported by the BA. They come under the general headings of specific and general training, re-training and further training. Training grants for the acquisition specific and general skills are made available through BAFÖG. (Students in higher education receive loans from the same source.) BAFÖG grants and loans are reduced where trainees or students are living with their parents. Allowances for re-training and further training amount to 65 per cent of previous net earnings for unmarried persons, 73 per cent for the married. In addition, certain other expenses (such as travel costs) are payable. Two alternative qualifying conditions apply: a person must not have completed a course of specific training, or if a person

wishes to train for another job. Candidates must have either contributed to the unemployment-insurance fund, or have been in receipt of unemployment assistance. Assimilation payments are made by the BA for previously unemployed persons and difficult placements.

Faced with persistently high unemployment and a growing share of long-term unemployed, the thrust of labour-market policy progressively changed from temporary income support to measures enhancing employment chances for job-seekers. In the period prior to unification, reflecting a more 'active labour market policy', the overall growth of outlays rose much faster than total government spending. Total labour-market related expenditure amounted to 2.3 per cent of GNP, ranking third of the seven major OECD countries (OECD *Economic Survey* 1989: 95). Aiming at promoting economic adjustment and easing the associated costs for workers, existing labour-market schemes were improved in the late 1980s. Vocational assistance schemes were extended, with spending increasing by 75 per cent between 1985 and 1988. Similarly, insurance cover and benefits were also increased, with the maximum entitlement period being prolonged at the end of 1984 from 12 to 32 months. In addition, the rapidly-rising number of German immigrants (see Chapter 6) led to significantly increasing payments of unemployment benefits and to higher costs for language and vocational training courses.

As a result of these measures, and the introduction of an early retirement scheme in 1984, outlays were estimated in 1988 to have been some DM 6 billion more than projected on the assumption of no policy change from 1985. Although the contribution rate was raised in 1987, increased revenue and reserves were not large enough to finance the DM 5.25 billion deficit in 1988. This meant that the Federal Government, in accordance with its statutory obligations, had to transfer DM 1 billion to the fund. For 1989, a further rise in the deficit was feared, although a rapid economic recovery caused a fall in unemployment and the deficit fell to DM 2 billion (IW *Zahlen* 1991: 61). Moreover, in order to stem this trend and limit the implied upward drift in the tax wedge between wage costs and take-home pay, it was decided to stabilise vocational assistance at the level reached in 1988, and to concentrate on hardship cases (with savings estimated at DM 1.75 billion). Hence, all in all, for 1989 a further – though smaller – deficit was registered, which had to be covered completely by Government transfers. With the actual labour market situation being more favourable than expected, the envisaged outlays of the BA were thus significantly lower in 1989. Against this relatively sound financial background, the Government announced new measures to assist the long-term unemployed, the financial costs of the scheme being fixed at DM 1.75 billion and distributed over the years 1989 to 1992. Most of these additional outlays – DM 1.5 billion – were to be payments of wage-cost subsidies to employers hiring people who had been registered as unemployed for at least one year. It was estimated that about 60,000 long-term unemployed would benefit from this scheme (OECD *Economic Survey* 1989: 95–6). The deficit of the BA in western Germany fell again in 1990 – this time to DM 0.7 billion. (Revenue was DM 40.7 billion, while expenditure was held at DM 41.4 billion – *Statitisches Jahrbuch* 1991: 470). However, this was yet another example of ultimately successful budgetary consolidation prior to the shock of unification on the BA's finances (see below).

Die Zeit (14/90) reported the total cost of unemployment in 1989 as DM 58.7 billion: there were 2.04 million unemployed who did not pay social-insurance contributions or income tax. Figure 5.12 illustrates the trend in employment promotion (unemployment insurance) expenditure from the social budget between 1960 and 1990. Figure 5.12 also shows that total employment promotion spending in the social budget rose from DM 1,206 million in 1960 to DM 49,270 million in 1990. It increased as a proportion of the social budget by nearly 5.2 percentage points, and as a percentage of GNP it rose from 0.4 to 2.03. Prior to the second oil shock, the OECD (1979: 188) had summarised the reasons for this dynamism of unemployment benefits as follows:

- the total amount of unemployment
- the proportion of unemployment insured
- the structure of unemployment (age, occupation, duration etc.)
- the level of unemployment benefits
- the duration of benefits

All of these factors combined to produce a steep rise in this expenditure item in the 1970s and 1980s. Soltwedel (in Giersch 1983: 335) suggests, however, that this rise in expenditure could have been checked by the introduction of a different type of incentive scheme.

Figure 5.13 demonstrates the relative growth revenue and expenditure of the BA in the 1980s and early 1990s. Total revenue in 1980 was DM 19,050 million, but in 1991 this total, including the new Länder, reached DM 70,190 million. Joint total contributions were 3 per cent of earnings in 1980, 4.3 per cent in 1990 and 6.5 per cent from January 1993. (As with retirement-pension and health insurance, there is a contributions ceiling: after the January 1993 increases, for example, it was

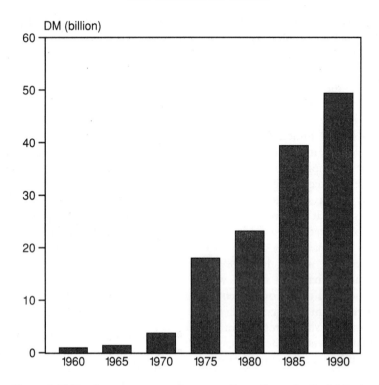

Figure 5.12 Employment-promotion expenditure (from the Social Budget[1])

Source: IW Zahlen 1992: 92

Note: [1] Series differs from Figure 5.13

set at earnings over DM 7,200 monthly.) The growth in expenditure was mainly due to the trend of unemployment benefits, which by 1991 accounted for almost one third of the finances of the BA. For example, this expenditure increased sharply in 1982 (by DM 5 billion to DM 18 billion), when the number of unemployed persons rose by over 0.5 million (MRDB 3/86: 25). Moreover, short-time working allowances rose sharply after unification (OECD *Economic Survey* 1992: 69). Indeed, the dramatic increase in the BA's expenditure resulted in an equally dramatic increase in the Federal government's subsidy. Because of the BA's deficit in 1991, for example, the federal subsidy reached DM 22.8 billion (Pilz and Ortwein 1992: 211).

Figure 5.14 illustrates the overall expenditure pattern of the BA under different headings. The expenditure of the Federal Labour Office on unemployment-benefit payments is, however, only one part of public-sector payments for jobless persons. Spending on unemployment assistance, which comes direct from the Federal budget, rose sharply in the period 1981–85, in contrast to the trend of unemployment benefits. The number of recipients of unemployment assistance went up from an average of 170,000 in 1981 to about 620,000 in 1985. Notice also that active labour market policies also collectively account for a fairly high level of expenditure. In this context, the expenditure headings of vocational training, rehabilitation and research are all relevant.

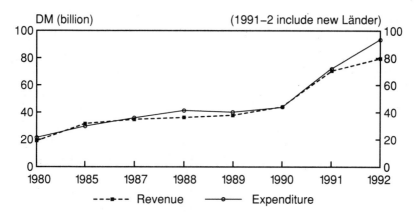

Figure 5.13 Revenue and expenditure of the Federal Labour Office[1]

Sources: IW *Zahlen* 1992: 104; MRDB VIII (14)

Note: Compare Figure 5.12

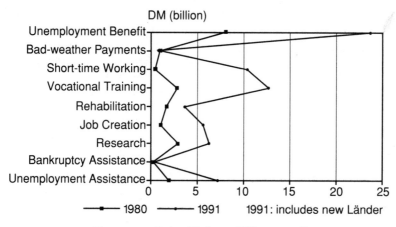

Figure 5.14 Federal Labour Office expenditure

Source: IW *Zahlen* 1992: 104

Finally, the expenditure of the BA on short-time working benefits responds to changes in economic activity (MRDB 3/86: 26).

The administration of unemployment insurance is the responsibility of the BA in Nuremberg with, after unification, 38 Länder and 161 local labour offices (*Der Personalrat* 1990: 205). These three levels are under the executive control of representatives drawn from the appropriate level of government, the employers' associations and trade unions. Members are not elected, as is normally the case in social-insurance bodies, but appointed as a result of nominations.

PROBLEMS OF THE UNEMPLOYMENT-INSURANCE SYSTEM

There has been a debate on the 'new poverty' in Germany over the past few years. In 1983 the duration of unemployment was on average over seven months; 50 per cent of beneficiaries had been unemployed for longer than half a year and one third had been unemployed over one year. One seventh of beneficiaries remained unemployed for longer than two years. Unemployment benefit at the time was payable for a maximum duration of 12 months (Alber 1989: 179). (From 1984, the maximum period was increased to 32 months.) Among the long-term unemployed, one fifth of households were under the subsistence level; the high-risk group was households with four or more persons. The 1984 amendments to the Employment Promotion Act were only partially successful in ameliorating the increase in unemployment. Although unemployment benefits are related to income, the unemployed are increasingly reliant on social assistance (SZ 3/7/91). There will be hidden unemployment where unemployed persons rely on social assistance. Social assistance payments for the unemployed totalled DM 3.5 billion in 1989. Under the Employment Promotion Act, the average unemployed person receives DM 700 monthly. On average, during the period 1985–9, social assistance for the unemployed was DM 3.4 billion (*ibid.*).

The highest-risk groups in terms of unemployment are females and foreigners. For example, the rate of unemployment for foreigners in 1989 was 12.2 per cent and for females it was 9.4 per cent; the overall average was 7.9 per cent (IW *Zahlen* 1991: 15). It has been suggested that the labour market should be adjusted to suit the changing conditions of more of the workforce by means of shortening working hours (Riedmüller and Rodenstein 1989: 91). Employers preferred to see more general flexibility. These problems are examined in Chapter 6.

ACCIDENT-INSURANCE SCHEME

The accident insurance system is administered by the Occupational/Industrial Cooperative Associations which are responsible either for particular companies or regions. As well as cooperative associations, statutory accident insurance can also be the responsibility of a wide variety of other institutions. In detail, the Federal government, the Länder, the local authorities, associations of local authorities, the BA and the Federal Mines Office are involved. Their functions include retraining, rehabilitation, preventive measures, inspection and workplace monitoring of working conditions. These functions are carried out on a day-to-day basis in conjunction with the factory inspectorate. The insurers are autonomous organisations run by a delegate assembly and an executive committee consisting of elected representatives of the insured and the employers (Grochla and Gaugler 1990: 2221).

Membership of the statutory-accident insurance scheme is compulsory for all employees, regardless of their occupation, the length of their employment and their pay. Self-employed farmers are also covered. If the self-employed are not liable for compulsory insurance, they can opt for voluntary membership. In addition, compulsory insurance coverage is provided for the unemployed, rescue workers, holders of honorary positions, children whilst attending nursery school, school children, students, overseas-aid workers, prisoners, and those undergoing rehabilitation. Accident insurance is financed solely from employers' contributions (see Table 5.1). Contributions are assessed on the aggregate income of a company's employees and the level of accident risk within the company. Thus those industries with a higher level of risk pay higher contributions. Individual companies may have to pay higher or lower premiums according to the number of insured accidents which have occurred and the costs involved. The premium is adjusted annually in accordance with average wage/salary increases (the dynamic principle). Rates vary between 0.7 per cent and 7 per cent of pay. In April 1991, the contribution rate was on average approximately 1.5 per cent (IDS *European Report* 355: VII).

The budget for accident insurance was DM 10,019 million in 1980 and DM 13,316 million in 1990. Since 1963 accident rates have fallen. This decrease in the number of accidents was a testimony to the success of both the factory inspectorate and industry itself. The number of vocational accidents decreased from approximately 2.3 million in 1960 to 1.3 million in 1990 (IW 1991: 25). However, the expenditure on accident insurance increased from DM 1,789 million in 1960 to DM 14,234 million in 1989, but as a proportion of total social-policy expenditure it fell from approximately 2.5 per cent to 1.8 per cent (*ibid*.: 27; IW *Zahlen* 1991: 58).

Accident insurance becomes payable from the day the injury occurs. The size of care grants varies according to the degree of injury. Normally, however, the grants are between DM 436 and DM 1,747 per month and, like retirement pensions, they are dynamised. Accident insurance covers not only the cost of sickness and rehabilitation, but also injury benefits which are payable for the working disabled provided the insured person is not unemployed or not in receipt of maternity benefit. After the seventh week of sickness the recipients of injury benefits are entitled to 80 per cent of previous earnings (or maximum of net earnings) for a maximum period of 78 weeks in every three years. Vocational benefits are another important aspect of accident insurance. They are payable to the employer for re-training and wage costs. During the period of retraining the insured receives the transitional benefit from the seventh to thirteenth week. This benefit amounts to 80 per cent of previous earnings for insured persons with a dependent married partner or at least one child. The benefit is reduced to 70 per cent for others, or for persons who have not been gainfully employed for more than three years.

The question of whether a person covered by accident insurance is entitled to a pension arises after the thirteenth week of absence. At that stage the issue is whether the vocational injury has led to a permanent loss in earning ability amounting to 20 per cent or more. For total loss of earning capacity an insured person receives benefits equal to two-thirds of previous annual earnings which is equivalent to a full pension. For a partial loss of earning capacity, benefits are set at a proportional rate. In the case of an entitlement to 50 per cent of a full pension, for example, an additional 10 per cent of the pension is payable for each child up to 18 years (Bellermann 1990: 64). If the insured person dies, a death grant (*Sterbegeld*) equal to one month's earnings is payable (or a minimum DM 400). Widows' pensions are paid at a maximum rate of 30 per cent of annual earnings of the deceased until the widow's death or remarriage. If the widow is over the age of 45, then the pension is at least two-fifths of the insured's annual earnings. In addition, an allowance of one-fifth of annual earnings is payable until any child reaches the age of 18; orphans receive thirty per cent (Lampert 1985: 168).

It is essential to note that retirement on the grounds of ill health became an important policy issue in the two decades prior to unification. The probability of a male *manual* worker reaching the normal retirement age decreased so that by 1988 45 per cent of all new retirees in this category had been forced to retire on health grounds (*Die Zeit* 4/90). Overall, the proportion of males retiring on health grounds was 39 per cent, compared to 30 per cent of all new male retirees availing themselves of early retirement schemes. Only 18 per cent retired on reaching the normal retirement age, the remaining 13 per cent being unemployed. Hence the average retirement age for male manual workers fell from 61.7 to 58.6; for male salaried employees the equivalent reduction was from 63.3 to 60.8 years (*ibid.*). (Because of their withdrawal from the labour market to raise children, many females did not have sufficient contribution years to claim early retirement; almost half of them therefore worked until reaching the normal retirement age of 65.)

There are two major problems associated with accident insurance. First, the prevention and reporting of accidents. Second, the extent of occupational disease. There is also a significant difference in the incidence of accidents between economic booms and recessions. In a recession there are always fewer accidents. The recognition and classification of occupational disease is a problem area, too. At the moment the legislators have recognised only 59 diseases (Bellermann 1990: 65). Thus, if there is a new disease which cannot be treated through accident insurance because it fails to come under any recognised classification, the insured must meet the high cost of the industrial injury themselves.

PROVISION OF SOCIAL SECURITY AND SOCIAL WELFARE

The notion of social security, which is an integral part of social policy, was initially postulated by Gerhard Mackenroth in 1952 (Riedmüller and Rodenstein 1989: 289). He emphasised the needs of the family and young people. The relevant provisions must be distinguished from the social-insurance system. Eligibility for social security is not related to income or social circumstances. Rather, the aim of social security is to maintain the living standards of claimants. The following are examples of social security:

- war victims (this type of assistance was introduced for the first time in eastern Germany)
- child benefits
- promotion of education and vocational training
- housing benefit

There are other areas under this system such as tax allowances which are calculated under the social-security regulations. However, social security in general is financed from taxation rather than by contributions. Half of the benefits are financed by the Federal authorities, the other half by the Länder. Expenditure on social security accounts for approximately one tenth of the social budget.

Families or individuals who have difficulty in paying rent for their accommodation, or in a limited number of cases difficulties in meeting mortgage repayments, qualify for housing benefit. Other outgoings on accommodation also qualify. In practice, although benefit may be paid to needy house owners, more than 95 per cent of recipients are in rented accommodation. Payment is made by postal warrant sent from the offices of the local authorities. These and other housing subsidies are examined in Chapter 7.

Child benefits have accounted for an increasingly important part of social security, peaking in 1981 at DM 19.2 billion (BMWi *Leistung in Zahlen* 1989: 95). Since 1955 eligibility has been widened as far as family size is concerned; family income was again taken into account from 1983. This can be clearly seen from Table 5.5. BA data on child benefits (*Presse Informationen* 26/91) showed that in east Germany they amounted in 1991 to DM 325 million for approximately 2.3 million children; 750,000 claimants had a single child, 570,000 had two children and 180,000 more than two children. As a result of the revisions introduced in the Child Benefit Act, Employment Exchanges made additional payments amounting to almost DM 100 million in July and August 1991. But it must be emphasised that these payments symbolised a fundamental change in social-security regulations in the east – a change which would result in eastern females losing some of the advantages they had enjoyed relative to their western counterparts. In the GDR direct financial transfers had much less weight in the spectrum of social-policy measures compared to indirect forms such as price subsidies, especially for rent, food and social services (Rudolph *et al.* 1990: 36). Further, leave of absence for family reasons was treated as the equivalent of working time for the purpose of calculating pension eligibility (*ibid.*).

Another contrast in the incidence of child-rearing costs between the two former Germanies was to be found in the general approach to maternity/paternity leave. Given the demographic time bomb illustrated in Figure 5.7c above, there are two absolutely critical economic and social-policy issues: the birth rate should

desirably be increased, and discriminatory behaviour towards females is socially unacceptable as well as unenlightened in terms of the future supply of labour and should therefore cease. In July 1985 the government gave its approval to a bill to be introduced into the Bundestag. The consequent Act outlined provisions for a new federally financed child-rearing benefit (*Erziehungsgeld*) which replaced the existing scheme of maternity benefit from 1 January 1986. Under this scheme mothers or fathers who were bringing up a child and who were not economically active on a full-time basis were entitled to a monthly child-rearing benefit of DM 600 for the first eighteen months after the child's birth (BMA 1991: 353). If both parents were working, either of them could take parental leave during this period in order to qualify for the benefit. However, after the birth of a child, an East German mother (or grandmother, or – rarely – the father) had the right to parental leave with 60 to 90 per cent of net income for one year (Rudolph *et al.* 1990: 39). Meanwhile the person's job was guaranteed. Long periods of paid leave were provided for parents with three or more children, and for single parents who needed to care for a sick child up to the age of fourteen. This was replaced by the western regulation of five days per year per child up to the age of eight. Perhaps even more significantly, the gap in living standards between East and West was considerably smaller for families than for single persons, although the additional credits payable to young parents were generally insufficient to support a family attempting to live on one income (*ibid.*: 36 and 39–40). Nonetheless, these different provisions do not seem to have dramatically affected the population structure in favour of the former GDR (see Figures 5.16 and 5.17 below).

Table 5.5 The introduction and growth of Child Benefits

Period	*Monthly benefit (DM) for*				
	first child (3)	*second child* (1) (2) (3)	*third child* (2) (3)	*fourth child* (2) (3)	*fifth and each additional child* (2) (3)
1 01 1955 to 30 09 1957	–	–	25	25	25
1 10 1957 to 28 02 1959	–	–	30	30	30
1 03 1959 to 30 03 1961	–	–	40	40	40
1 04 1961 to 31 12 1963	–	25	40	40	40
1 01 1964 to 31 08 1970	–	25	50	60	70
1 09 1970 to 31 12 1974	–	25	60	60	70
1 01 1975 to 31 12 1977	50	70	120	120	120
1 01 1978 to 31 12 1978	50	80	150	150	150
1 01 1979 to 30 06 1979	50	80	200	200	200
1 07 1979 to 31 01 1981	50	100	200	200	200
1 02 1981 to 31 12 1981	50	120	240	240	240
1 01 1982 to 30 06 1990	50	100	220	240	240
1 07 1990 to 31 12 1991 (4)	50	130	220	240	240
from 1 01 1992	70	130	220	240	240

Notes: (1) Paid only to persons whose monthly income did not exceed (DM):
        until 31 12 1964: 600
        until 31 08 1970: 650
        until 31 12 1971: 1,100
        until 31 12 1972: 1,250
        until 31 12 1973: 1,400
        until 31 12 1974: 1,530
        From 1 1 1975 to 31 12 1982 there was no upper income limit

(2) From 1 1 1983, the benefit payable was incrementally reduced to the basic payments of DM 70 for the second child and DM 140 for each additional child if the net income exceeded specified bands. From 1 January 1994 the DM 140 was halved to DM 70 for the third child if joint parental income exceeded DM 100,000 per annum, or DM 75,000 for single-parent families (BA *Presse Informationen* 2/94)

(3) From 1 1 1986, beneficiaries whose joint income was too low to qualify (in whole or in part) for the child income-tax allowance, could claim a supplementary benefit as follows:

Period	child tax allowance (per annum) (DM)	monthly supplement up to (DM)
1 1 1986 to 31 12 1989	2,484	46
1 1 1990 to 31 12 1991	3,024	48
from 1 1 1992	4,104	65

(4) Introduced into the new Länder from 1 1 1991

Source: BMA *Statistisches Taschenbuch* 1992: 8.18 (author's translation)

Under the Act to Promote Education and Training (BAFÖG) school pupils entering the upper level of secondary education at the age of 16 may apply for a long-term loan if they are not living with their parents. (Pupils at this level would be preparing to enter some form of higher education after reaching the minimum age of 18 – Münch 1991: 26.) Students in higher education may also apply for this form of financial assistance. All applicants must be German or EC citizens.

Social welfare, on the other hand, is characterised by an emphasis on personal need. It may be analysed under two main headings. First, social assistance – which is the largest expenditure heading. Second, youth welfare – which since 1991 includes child welfare (Bellermann 1990: 96 and 107–9; Frerich 1987: 35).

Since the beginning of the 1970s, expenditure on social assistance has risen more rapidly than spending in virtually any other area of government activity. From 1970 to 1981 it rose by four and a half times, while total social-budget expenditure nearly tripled and the gross national product rather more than doubled (MRDB 4/83: 34). Moreover, total expenditure on social assistance almost doubled during the 1980s. Expenditure by the bodies responsible for paying social assistance increased from DM 3.34 billion in 1970 to almost DM 15 billion in 1981, an average annual increase of 14.5 per cent (*ibid.*). By 1989, it had reached almost DM 29 billion (IW *Zahlen*: 1991). Expenditure within the framework of social assistance is extremely heterogeneous and can be roughly divided into two major groups (Frerich 1987: 204):

- subsistence assistance – the classical form of benefit intended to guarantee every person living in the Federal Republic of Germany the socio-cultural minimum needed for existence; spending under this heading accounts for only about one-third of total social-assistance expenditure
- assistance given in particular circumstances which accounts for the other two-thirds of expenditure on social assistance. The circumstances themselves are heterogeneous. They include, for example, such varying needs as establishing and then maintaining minimum living standards, assistance for the aged and sick, plus care and reintegration of the handicapped

There were many factors which determined this rapid expansion of expenditure on social assistance, and they cannot always be clearly distinguished one from another. The number of persons receiving social assistance and the circumstances facing them both play a major role. In the case of assistance granted to persons living in institutions, improvements in benefits and the general rise in costs also have to be taken into account. Significantly, perhaps, the total annual number of beneficiaries increased from 1.5 million in 1970 to 3.6 million in 1989 (IW *Zahlen* 1991: 61); however, the BDA (*Arbeitsmarkt* 1/92) was critical of the fact that it will be 1994 before average data on the duration of entitlement become available. There are also many forms of payment included under this amorphous heading, although unemployment assistance accounted for almost a third of total expenditure prior to unification; supplementary benefits paid to persons whose pensions fell below the subsistence level represented a further 15 per cent (*Die Zeit* 7/90). Figure 5.15

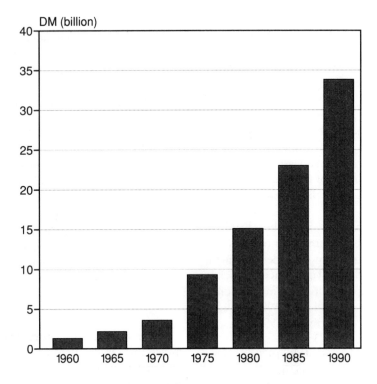

Figure 5.15 Social-assistance expenditure
Source: IW *Zahlen* 1992: 92

therefore concentrates on the growth of total expenditure on social assistance.

SOCIAL POLICY AND UNIFICATION

The social-policy system in East Germany was governed by the SED principle of the Unity of Economic and Social Policy. This principle implied that social benefits were determined without reference to the economic resources actually available. The insurance system was not divided into retirement pension insurance, health insurance and unemployment insurance as in West Germany. Employees, who constituted 91 per cent of the employed population, were covered by the social insurance scheme administered by the

Confederation of Trades Unions (FDGB – Freier Deutscher Gewerkschaftsbund). Members of cooperatives (7 per cent of the employed population) and the self-employed (2 per cent) belonged to the East German state-administered insurance system. Employees paid compulsory social-insurance contributions amounting to 10 per cent of standard earnings to a ceiling of OM 600; employers paid 12.5 per cent (Akerlof *et al.* 1991: 57). Total contributions were therefore 22.5 per cent of earnings, as opposed to the evenly-divided 36.5 per cent in West Germany – a difference of 14 percentage points (*ibid.*). Contributions were not deducted from premia and bonuses, unlike the system in West Germany. Social-policy benefits for employees consisted mainly of retirement

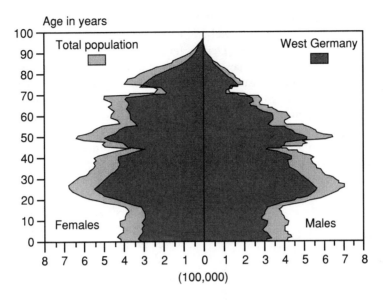

Figure 5.16 The population structure in East and West: 1990

Source: Stat. Jahrbuch 1991

pensions (44 per cent) and health insurance (35 per cent). The total expenditure on social policy was OM 35 billion in 1989. The social-policy system was on the verge of collapse as a result of the uncontrolled spiralling of costs, which could only be met from public funds (European Parliament 1990a: 62). In addition, a large number of people were leaving the country.

Between 1950 and 1985, the GDR population decreased from 18.4 million to 16.7 million. This might be regarded as a substantial amount in absolute terms, but it is surprisingly little when the migration loss of 3.1 million is taken into account (see Chapter 6). Despite its declining total population, East Germany possessed a younger population in the late 1980s than the population of West Germany. This was the result of different population trends and their implications for the age composition of the population (Ott *et al.* 1991: 9). Hence, the pressure on retire-

ment insurance from the east was somewhat less than the impact on the other aspects of social policy. It would be wrong, however, to overestimate the differences in the structure of the two populations on unification. As a proportion of the total population, the principal differences were to be found in the 0–15 age group (four percentage points larger in the east) and the over 65 age group (two percentage points smaller in the east) (IW *Zahlen* 1992: 11). This close resemblance between the two population structures is demonstrated in two slightly different ways in Figures 5.16 and 5.17.

The social-union aspects of GEMSU were confirmed in the first section of the Unification Treaty. A comprehensive system of social insurance was to be based on the improvement of eastern standards until they achieved western levels. Determination provisions for a Social-Policy Union were contained in sections 17–25 of the Unification Treaty. These sections adopted the social-insurance systems, social security scheme and social welfare measures of West Germany (*Der Personalrat* 7–8/90: 203). The organisations of retirement pension insurance, health insurance and unemployment insurance (employment promotion) were amalgamated on 1 January 1991. The enabling Act stipulated that the revenue and expenditure accounts should be divided into the separate branches of the insurance system.

THE SOCIAL BUDGET AFTER UNIFICATION

The financial problems of the social-policy funds in the new Länder owed a great deal to the introduction of the West German system. This was because the level of many social benefits became linked to wage movements and there was a rapid catching-up process of east German wages. Moreover, the increase in wage rates outpaced the improvement in productivity. It led to the heavy shedding of labour and a marked increase in unemployment and related benefits. Sharp wage increases thus affected social-policy expenditure, while the decline in employment caused contributions to dwindle. The finances of the social-policy funds were progressively weakened and the social-policy system (mainly retirement pensions, unemployment or short-time working benefits) necessitated transfer

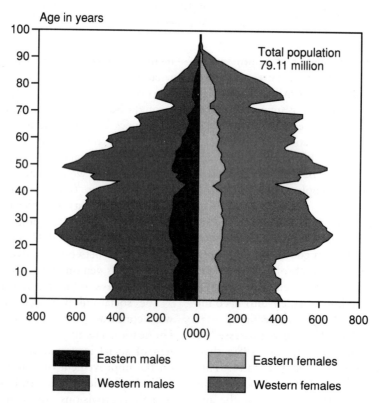

Figure 5.17 Population structure: 1990

Source: Stat. Jahrbuch 1991: 67

244

payments from west to east estimated at DM 7 billion in 1990. In 1991, transfer payments to the social-policy system in the east were DM 40 billion, of which the retirement-pension insurance fund received DM 11 billion, health insurance DM 2 billion and unemployment insurance DM 27 billion (Siebert 1991b: 319–20). These transfer payments in 1991 represented 34 per cent of total transfers (DM 117 billion) against 15 per cent of total transfers in 1990 (DM 45 billion). The costs of converting the eastern system were therefore a significant burden to western Germany. Yet it has been shown that the western retirement-pension and health insurance schemes were overhauled prior to unification, reforms which themselves had been cost driven.

Financing the costs of conversion was problematical, in that it is not customary in the western German system to finance social-insurance deficits from borrowing. To the extent that the fund managers are unable to draw on reserves, the level of which is limited by the current system of contributions and Federal government grants, existing social-policy legislation requires an increase in contributions when expenditure exceeds revenue in the long term (MRDB 11/91: 30). In April 1991, for example, BA contribution rates were raised by 2.5 percentage points in order to cover heavy expenditure in eastern Germany (see Table 5.1).

RETIREMENT-PENSION INSURANCE

Following unification, then, retirement-pension insurance was restructured in eastern Germany. Although the model used was along the lines of the western system, the financial accounts were kept separate between the two parts of the economy. However, there was to be a phased harmonisation of the payments from the statutory pension-insurance funds in western and eastern Germany (Schmähl 1992: 41). Following substantial increases in eastern retirement-pension entitlements on 1 January 1991, the 1992 Reform was extended to the east by the Pension Transference Act passed by the Federal Parliament in the summer of 1991. At the beginning of 1992, the financial systems of the retirement pension insurance funds were unified, so that any deficits incurred in eastern Germany were to be financed from reserves accumulated in western Germany.

The Transference Act meant that the retirement-pension legislation of West Germany became applicable in the new Länder. Hence, the more generous western retirement-pension scheme was introduced into eastern Germany. This improved the provision for surviving dependants and conditions governing the entitlement to occupational-disability pensions. On the other hand, East German retirement-pension legislation had included some more favourable provisions, in particular for insured females (above all, a minimum pension and longer benefit periods for raising children). These advantages were gradually dismantled. However, under the Transference Act, special and supplementary pension payments granted by the former DDR authorities (especially to members of the public service) were reduced if payments could not be justified. Alternatively, where pensions were left intact, the resultant expenditure was to be refunded by the Federal and Länder Governments as the successors of the previous employers (MRDB 11/91: 36). On balance, the harmonisation of pension legislation entailed substantial additional expenditure, which was estimated by the retirement pension insurance funds to amount to an annual DM 10 billion between 1992 and 1995. However, even without this extra burden, the funds' finances would have deteriorated in 1992. As well as the fall in receipts which accompanied the sharp deterioration in the eastern labour market, the reduction in contribution rates which became effective in April 1991 had an impact over a full year; moreover, the number of insured people in the west would probably not increase as vigorously as it had done in the years prior to unification. In line with wage movements in eastern Germany, pensions were raised by just over 11.5 per cent at the beginning of 1991; a further increase was likely to follow in mid-1992. Overall, the pension insurance funds in the united Germany were expected to incur a deficit of about DM 10 billion in 1992. Compared with 1991, their position would therefore deteriorate by about DM 20 billion (MRDB 11/91: 36).

Even with supplementary pension schemes, average pensions in the GDR were only OM 480 after at least 15 years of compulsory contributions. Under the Unification Treaty, pensions were indexed to earnings in the east. With 45 years of insurable employment at around average earnings, pension entitlement was set, as in West Germany, at 70 per cent of average net annual earnings (von Maydell 1990: 392). Low pensions were raised to a minimum of DM 495 per month by means of supplementary benefits (Doetsch 1990: 379). Pensions were increased by 15 per cent from 1 January 1991. Hence, although in June 1990, the standard monthly retirement pension per retired person in the east was OM 470, it had risen to DM 773 by January 1991. Retirement pensions were increased by a further 15 per cent in 1992 (IW 1991: 23; Pilz and Ortwein 1992: 130). Employers and employees each contributed 9.35 per cent of gross pay up to the ceiling, as in

western Germany. Company pensions covered by the 1974 West German legislation were to be introduced on a phased basis from 1991 (IDS *European Report* 348: 15). A contribution ceiling of DM 2,700 per month was set on 1 July 1990, but it was changed to DM 5,300 starting from 1 January 1993 (see Table 5.1).

An early retirement pension system was introduced in East Germany in February 1990. Under this system, persons who lost their jobs during the five-year period prior to reaching retirement age were entitled to a pension which was the equivalent of 70 per cent of net wages, or a minimum of OM 500. To be eligible, females had to have paid contributions for 20 years and males for 25 years (European Parliament 1990a: 60). Following GEMSU, east German males aged at least 57, and females aged at least 55, who became unemployed could retire on a state early-retirement pension of 65 per cent of previous net pay for a period of three years for men, five years for women. In 1991, a common age limit of 57 was introduced for both sexes. Claims made before 1 April 1991 entitled the beneficiary to an early pension for the first 312 days. Eligible earnings for pension calculation purposes were not permitted to exceed the contribution ceiling. Claims would be refused where there were skill shortages. Initially, they were limited in 1990 to the end of 1991 but were extended indefinitely at the beginning of 1992 (IDS *European Report* 348: 15). From 1 April 1992 employees aged 58 or over were able to retire early on 75 per cent of their former gross pay, rising to 80 per cent for employees with at least 20 years' service. This provision was agreed as an implicit trade-off against further working-time cuts below the then current 38 hour week. Under the deal the employers have the option of terminating the early retirement agreement with three months' notice as a possible response to a union claim for shorter hours (IDS *European Report* 359: 6).

In addition to the unfavourable labour market situation, which depressed contribution receipts, administrative difficulties associated with the levying of contributions initially also played a part. The relevant procedures had to be reorganised: since the beginning of 1991 the contributions have no longer been levied by the tax offices, but rather (as in the west) by the appropriate health insurance institution. As a result, the difficulties were overcome and the inflow of contributions reached levels consistent with the number of employed persons. Finally, however, it must be noted that the policy makers are faced with a dilemma. Each new intervention in the retirement-pension system undermines public confidence in the viability of the system; but such interventions are rendered necessary if that viability is to be maintained (von Maydell 1990: 393).

HEALTH INSURANCE

The health insurance system of former East Germany was controlled by the central government. There was high subsidisation. For example, in 1989 the Government subsidised health insurance by approximately OM 18.4 billion, one half of total social expenditure. There were over 600,000 employees in the health sector before unification, although migration to the west jeopardised healthcare standards after the Berlin wall fell (Tietz 1991: 428). However, in 1989, there were only 389 doctors and 473 dentists in private practice (*ibid.*). (There were 70,000 doctors, and 30,000 dentists in private practice in the west – *ibid.*: 430). The total number of doctors in the east in 1989

was 40,840 compared to 188,225 in the west; the respective numbers of dentists were 12,288 and 40,805 (*Statistisches Jahrbuch* 1991: 450). From January 1991, the health-insurance system of the former East Germany was replaced by the health-insurance scheme of West Germany. Administration is now through the various health insurance funds. AOK took over fourteen areas of eastern Germany and the other funds were also able to develop their own system.

The Statutory Health Insurance Act, passed as a result of the Unification Treaty, meant that eastern Germany had to adopt not only the structure of the western system but also the financial principles of that system:

- finance depends mainly on contributions
- half of the contribution is paid by employers
- sick pay is largely financed by employers
- a contribution-free system for pensioners
- recompense from pension to health insurance funds for pensioners' health-insurance contributions

Hence, with the implementation of sick-pay schemes, the employer became financially responsible for the first six weeks of work incapacity. The West German health insurance system, in which statutory local funds are financed by equal employer and employee contributions, was introduced in eastern Germany from 1 January 1991. A standard total contribution rate of 12.8 per cent was introduced for all schemes in 1991. Also from 1 January 1993, the contribution ceiling in health insurance was DM 3,975 in eastern Germany (see Table 5.1). The system of outpatients' departments and ambulance services in eastern Germany was kept for a transitional phase for five years. After the five-year period these institutions were to be integrated into the western system. Following unification, east Germans were free to choose their own doctor. Doctors' and dentists' fees were set at 45 per cent of western levels.

Qualitatively, the doctors in the two parts of Germany differed significantly. Doctors in the east may have been twenty years behind western standards. A special regulation applied to the finances of hospital departments and ambulance equipment in eastern Germany meant that investment was financed from federal budgets of these organisations, rather than from contributions (*Der Personalrat* 7–8/90: 206). The growth in expenditure on health insurance in eastern Germany was expected to accelerate mainly because of the inevitable delays initially encountered in introducing the new system. Soaring labour costs in the hospital sector also made themselves felt. Although surpluses were probable in the initial stage in 1991, these were not expected to last for long (MRDB 11/91:37). The German Health Institution in Düsseldorf estimated that new investment in hospitals should be set at DM 30 billion in the east to reach the quality of western Germany, of which DM 17.5 billion was for new construction costs (*Wirtschaftswoche* 27/91: 17). In 1991, there was an estimated increase of 8.6 per cent in the total costs of hospitals, doctors, pharmaceuticals and allied areas, as opposed to a planned increase of contribution income of 5.6 per cent; a deficit of approximately DM 1.8 billion therefore arose in the first quarter of 1991 (*ibid.*). Underlying the deficit crisis in eastern Germany was the fear that the deficit in the health sector would increase between DM 2 billion and DM 4 billion in 1991 – 20 per cent of contribution income (*ibid.*). As a result of

the 1993 Health Service reform alone, an allowance for hospital maintenance costs of DM 330 million from 1994 was made (KrV 1992b: 196).

UNEMPLOYMENT

East Germany's opportunity to be covered by a well-operating employment policy and to join a financially well-equipped unemployment insurance scheme was unique. It was a means of avoiding the most difficult social pressures which resulted from job and earnings losses (Hoene 1991: 21).

The introduction of a uniform system of employment promotion was in accordance with the Employment Promotion Act of West Germany. Hence, an active labour market policy was intended – especially for females and disabled persons. As in western Germany, contribution rates for employer and employee were 2.25 per cent of gross income up to the contribution ceiling. However, liability to contributions begins at a lower level than in western Germany. Rates of unemployment benefit were set at 63 per cent of previous net wages for single persons, but 68 per cent for married persons; in both cases there was a minimum of DM 495 per month for claims submitted before 31 December 1991 (IDS *European Report* 348: 15). A special provision for short-time working applied until 30 June 1991, under which employees received state short-time benefit. This applied even if there was no guarantee that their jobs could be saved, in contrast to the western German provisions. The state met the social-insurance contributions of all affected employees (*ibid.*). The BA is organised into regions which have 38 Employment Offices. Within the region there are 161 branch-offices (*Der Personalrat* 7–8/90: 205).

The guaranteed work system operated

in East Germany prior to unification was phased out – although numerous schemes were put in its place. As companies began to modernise, they became over-manned and commenced dismissing employees; in addition, previously hidden under-employment was transformed into open unemployment, despite the fact that employees became protected by western German unfair dismissal regulations (European Parliament 1990a: 64). Early retirement, migration, and special employment schemes reduced east German unemployment somewhat, but the rate of unemployment was still forecast to rise from 3 per cent in 1990 to 17.5 per cent in 1991 (IDS *European Report* 348: 12). From March 1990, job hunters were for the first time able to register for unemployment benefit at about 200 specially-created employment offices. (At a time when the number of unemployed was estimated to be 80,000, 79,000 jobs were advertised as vacant – European Parliament 1990a: 64.) In particular, females constituted over half the unemployed of eastern Germany in 1991 (BA *Presse Informationen* 34/91). Although the unemployment-insurance contribution rate was increased from 4.3 per cent to 6.8 per cent in April 1991, the BA estimated that the east German finances were in deficit to the tune of DM 1 billion.

The costs of the BA rose substantially after unification. In 1989, total expenditure was DM 40 billion (IW *Zahlen*: 60). By 1991 the sum was DM 71 billion and by 1992 the Office's estimate was DM 85 billion (*Presse Informationen* 77/91). In 1991, the federal-wide expenditure was DM 5.6 billion for job creation measures as such, and DM 12.7 billion for vocational training and DM 3.6 billion for rehabilitation (IW *Zahlen* 1992: 104). By far the largest item, DM 43.7 billion, was for maintaining living standards by means of

unemployment benefit, allowances while undergoing training and payments to those taking early retirement. In addition, the BA's administration costs were DM 4.9 billion in 1991. Much of the additional expenditure was concentrated on various measures in the east: in 1991 a total of DM 30 billion was spent on training, job creation and unemployment benefits; by 1992, about half of the Office's total expenditure of DM 94 billion was flowing to the east (BA *Presse Informationen* 34/91 and 14/92). Revenue raised in the east, on the other hand, was only 4 per cent of that raised in the west.

Consequently, the unemployment rate posed a major challenge for Germany. In 1991 the first job-information centre in the new Länder opened in Magdeburg (capital of Saxony-Anhalt), an area particularly affected by the pace of economic change. It was hoped another ten such centres would be in operation by 1992. They were established by the BA as part of a crash programme to improve employment levels throughout eastern Germany. The centres were equipped with information news, job magazines, films, slides and audio tapes to inform job-seekers of all ages not just about employment opportunities but also training and educational programmes. A fleet of vans acted as mobile job centres to widen the availability of the service. Eventually all 38 Employment Exchanges in the new Länder will have their own information centre. The Labour Office in 1991 received enquiries from at least 550,000 east German employees who were suitable for employment. Of these, 280,000 were placed on advanced vocational training and job creation schemes (BA *Presse Informationen* 1991).

Overall spending by the BA was therefore set to increase by about one-fifth. Admittedly, revenue was anticipated to grow vigorously again. However, at the beginning of 1992 the contribution rate was lowered – by a 0.5 percentage point to 6.3 per cent (as was envisaged at the time of its increase). A deficit of the order of DM 5 billion (east and west) was probable in 1992. It could be financed by running down the reserves of the BA, which were due to be supplemented in 1991 by an additional payment from the Federal Government (MRDB 11/91: 37). As shown in Table 5.1, however, it was decided in 1993 to increase the total contribution rate to 6.5 per cent and the monthly ceiling to DM 7,200. Consequently, the western unemployment fund had a surplus of DM 4 billion at the end of the first quarter of 1993, although this was DM 2 billion lower than the previous year (MRDB 6/93: 44). The deficits in the eastern fund in the first two quarters were DM 8.5 billion and DM 5.5 billion respectively (ibid.: 43).

In addition, expenditure on active labour market policies (ABM) in the east rose by 80 per cent in the first quarter of 1993; until 1992 these policies had been a charge on the Upswing East shadow budget. Early in 1993, the BA announced that the planned DM 9.9 billion for ABM programmes had been fully committed. Although DM 7.8 billion of this amount was earmarked for the east, the absence of support for further programmes was considered a 'political catastrophe' (FAZ 27 February 1993). In addition, new retraining schemes were similarly threatened (ibid. 2 March 1993). These difficulties had arisen from cuts of DM 7 billion in the proposed DM 94 billion budget for 1993; among other things, the resultant budget of DM 87 billion had assumed that unemployment in the west would not exceed two million (ibid. 11 January 1993). By July 1993, however, total unemployment in the old Länder had increased over July

1992 by 27 per cent to reach 2.3 million (BA Presse Informationen 67/93). There was also a further increase in the east: from 1.10 million in June to 1.17 million in July. In the first half of 1993 the BA consequently received DM 1.9 billion less in contribution income, but paid DM 7.7 billion out in unemployment benefits alone (ibid. 51/93). As a result the budget was supplemented by a further DM 16 billion, thus topping DM 100 billion for the first time.

ACCIDENT INSURANCE

Accident insurance in eastern Germany was introduced at the beginning of 1991. (As with other social-insurance rights, the accident insurance eligibility of a migrant employee may be transferred to the west under the Pension Insurance Act [Section 20]). As in the western system, the provisions of accident insurance apply if there is an accident at work, or in the event of occupational disease. Benefits are payable as follows (Marburger 1990: 203):

- sick pay or pension in the event of an accident
- orphan or widower/widow pension
- transitional pension
- partner and child pensions
- chronic sickness, blind and other special benefits

SOCIAL SECURITY AND SOCIAL WELFARE

The Unification Treaty required that social security would in future be based on the principle of the equality of provision in east and west. Until the end of 1990, the Federal government absorbed the cost of eastern child benefits: DM 50 for the first child, DM 100 for the second child and DM 150 for each additional child; supplements between DM 45 and DM 65 were also paid (BMA *Stat Taschenbuch* 1992: 10.16). From 1991, eastern beneficiaries were integrated into the more benevolent western system (see Table 5.5). Because the population structure in the two parts of Germany did not differ a great deal, the structure of child benefits was almost identical (BA *Presse Informationen* 26/91). However, where supplementary child benefits related to income were payable, the differences between east and west were more striking. Every second recipient of benefit in the east was entitled to a supplement, compared to every twelfth recipient in the west (BA *ibid.*). Similarly, every twelfth eastern recipient with two or more children was subject to a reduction in benefit by reason of income. In the west every third beneficiary in this category suffered such a reduction. The addition of the east to this form of social security caused a jump in the total costs of child benefits from DM 12 billion (1990) to over DM 16 billion in 1991 (BMA *ibid.*: 8.17). Where the child is older than 16 years of age, the family could apply for an extension of payment provided it is certified that the child is still in full-time education (BMA *Sozialpolitische Nachrichten* 36/90). Before unification, women in eastern Germany were entitled to 20 weeks paid leave following the birth of a baby but this was reduced to eight weeks after unification. By the end of 1993, the western system of disablement certification was to be phased in (*ibid.*).

Eastern Germany also took over the Social Assistance Act of western Germany with effect from 1 January 1991. Living standards in eastern Germany were thereafter secured through social maintenance payments (*Der Personalrat* 7–8/90: 207). Normally, the amount of assistance payable is DM 400 per month for someone who has earned under DM 447.

Adjustments in benefit levels are made according to circumstances. Those unfit for work or the elderly receive up to 20 per cent more (BMA *Sozialpolitische Nachrichten* 36/90). In 1990, the following reasons were given for claiming social assistance in eastern Germany (*Wirtschaft und Statistik* 9/91: 636):

- 67.4 per cent for unemployment
- 17.4 per cent for insufficient income
- 3.6 per cent for insufficient insurance or assistance
- 2.7 per cent for ill health
- 8.9 per cent for other reasons

CONCLUSION

In the final analysis, deficits in the social-insurance funds are bound to lead to rising contributions. In the area of the statutory retirement-pension insurance funds, for instance, new medium-term forecasts (based on the Federal Government's projection of economic activity) have come to the following conclusion. The fluctuation reserve will probably have shrunk almost to the statutory minimum of one month's expenditure by the end of 1993 and consequently an increase in the contribution rate currently at 17.5 per cent to not more than 18.7 per cent will be necessary in 1996. This is mainly due to the additional spending caused by unification. In the longer term, growing demographic burdens may well lead to further increases in the pension-insurance contribution (MRDB 11/91: 38). Allied to this, one must also allow for increases in health-insurance costs and, in the wider social policy field, an increasing demand for social assistance. This is not only because of greater longevity as such, but also because the individual and the family have traditionally been responsible for providing domestic and institutional care for the chronically sick and elderly. The social security and welfare systems only gave help when the financial strain on individuals and families became unendurable. However, the growing trend towards single-parent and single-generation households is causing a fundamental change in the nature of the problem.

Moreover, in 1992, the number of Germans over the age of 60 increased by 3.8 million and the number of people in this age group in need of care rose by 250,000. In the population as a whole, the number of people in need of care was estimated at 1.65 million, about two per cent of the population of 79.2 million. Of the 1.65 million, 400,000 were regarded as immobile, often bed-ridden and needing round-the-clock care, while 1.25 million were regarded as mobile – a group where the nature and level of care needed varied greatly and many of those affected could remain at home, requiring only some form of general nursing (BMA 8/91: 3). As shown above, the Health Insurance Reform Act of 1989 was not sufficient in itself to contain the growth of expenditure by the mid-1990s. This resulted in the 1993 Act. Perhaps further revisions in the health service will follow. Contributions to the BA, on the other hand, could be reduced as the labour market situation in eastern Germany improves; the trends in employment in the new Länder will, among other things, depend on the wage policy stance of management and labour (MRDB 11/91: 38). Nonetheless, the deficits incurred by the BA after unification resulted in emergency assistance from the Federal government and calls for a revision of the contribution-based method of financing some of the BA's activities.

The question of making provision for nursing care (*Pflegeversicherung*) for the elderly and chronically sick was at the centre of the social-policy debate in the early 1990s. Various solutions to the problem were conceivable. Blüm proposed a provision whereby insurance to provide nursing care should be supplementary to the statutory health-insurance scheme. In this case, the costs of nursing-care insurance would be met from contributions levied on employers and employees. The contribution ceiling for nursing-care insurance would be DM 5,100 per month – identical to health insurance at that time. It has been estimated that a nursing-care insurance scheme would raise DM 13 billion from total contributions. However, the amount required in 1991 may have been DM 25 billion. Differences arose between Blüm and the FDP. The FDP proposed that care insurance should be privately organised (SZ 4 July 1991). The employers initially supported this private-insurance model because they were opposed to a further joint-contribution scheme. The Federal cabinet ultimately made it clear (in 1993) that they were determined to introduce a system of nursing-care insurance, thus adding a fifth social-insurance scheme to Germany's social-policy network. It was the financing of the new scheme which caused social conflict – see the reference to *Karenztage* at the end of the section on the general principles of health insurance.

In short, any social-policy option involving a contribution system would increase the burden of social policy charges to a growing extent in the long run – since the number of old people, and thus the number of pensions and the frequency of cases in which care is needed, are both likely to rise. This means that if the contribution system continues intact, but the costs are not fully covered, the burden of financing the necessary subsidy would be shifted to taxpayers or, via higher government borrowing, into the future. In any case, to fully cover the costs by contributions would probably result in an unacceptably high cost burden to the diminishing number of contributors in the insured population. On the other hand, cost reductions on the supply side can quite conceivably cause a long-run deterioration in the quality of service – thus leading to disenchantment on the part of the contributors. This is why, for example, some observers advocate the introduction of more competition among those supplying health care. Nonetheless, the unions generally supported the 1993 Health Reform Act but bitterly opposed giving up holiday pay to finance the new nursing-care insurance scheme. Only the FDP and employers were undivided in their opposition to a contributory scheme.

An increase in overall social-policy contributions would raise the non-wage element of labour costs. It might also involve the risk of triggering off compensatory wage claims, with the associated adverse consequences for price stability if monetary policy were not tightened. (It was shown in Chapter 4 that the Bundesbank would almost certainly react to any threat to price stability by raising interest rates.) Higher social policy contributions may also reduce corporate profits and this could undermine enterprises' capacity to invest. Moreover, as will be shown in the next chapter, western German enterprises already have the highest supplementary labour costs of all major industrialised countries. Another question that has to be asked is: how far can charges on wages and salaries be increased without having serious effects on employees' willingness to work and propensity to save? This means that, for various reasons, increasingly higher social-insurance contributions weaken economic growth and

thus, in the final analysis, also the financial basis of social-policy benefits in general (MRDB 11/91: 39).

In macroeconomic terms, a solution based on the cost-cover principle might induce individuals to accept a greater proportion of total costs as an alternative to ever-increasing contributions. Dissaving, increasing family commitment to provide care and seeking private insurance are all possible methods of reducing, if not eliminating, the cost/contribution spiral. Admittedly, in this case, a transitional solution (which would probably require transfer payments or a contribution system) would have to be found for a fairly long period of time for those who are unable to build up a sufficient capital stock or who are already in need of care. On the other hand, an equally powerful argument would contend that the remarkable degree of social consensus in West Germany owed a great deal to the stress placed on the adjective 'social' in the term SME. GEMSU followed suit, and raised expectations in the east by the identical inclusion of the term. As the Federal budget deficit increased in 1993 under the joint impact of unification and recession, however, the debate switched to the means by which the deficit could be reduced. (The Bundesbank's policymakers saw this as a necessary condition prior to the reduction in short-term interest rates which in turn would ameliorate the recession.) Reductions in unemployment benefits, increases in statutory-pension contributions, a pay freeze for senior public servants and means-tested child benefits were therefore proposed. Was this a passing phase or the beginning of a new social order?

6

THE LABOUR MARKET

INTRODUCTION

The developments to be examined in this chapter are concerned with the quantitative and qualitative aspects of the labour market. Put another way, the analysis will concentrate mainly on supply-side factors, although some aspects of the derived demand for labour will also be explored. On the supply side, the analysis is initially concerned with those factors which determine the size of the labour force. (The more problematical question of 'efficiency' forms the basis of the final section.) Next, the development of vocational training is considered. This is followed by an account of the evolution of collective bargaining. Some caution is necessary here: minimum wage rates and other conditions of employment are settled at the regional level. The actors at this (first) level are the trade unions and employers' associations. These general conditions are then implemented, often with some enhancement, at the establishment or company level. The actors at this second level are the relevant works councils and individual employer. Policy making in the labour market is therefore a complex process.

There is a further fundamental difference between the two levels of collective bargaining. It will be shown that there is free collective bargaining at the first

level. Section 9 (3) of the Basic Law and the Collective Bargaining Act were formulated with this in mind. By way of contrast, there is a detailed statutory framework operating at the second level. This has resulted in a form of industrial democracy which both the German and French governments wanted to see as part of EC 1993, but which the British Conservative administration saw as being inimical to their own legal reforms of employment law during the 1980s. On the other hand, both the system of industrial democracy, and the system of collective bargaining, were exported intact to the new Länder.

The basic hypothesis to be explored in this chapter is that in spite of the advanced system of vocational training and relatively co-operative industrial relations, the bargainers found it difficult to find a mutually acceptable solution which would reconcile their high labour costs to the levels of unemployment which resulted from the first two oil price shocks. Note yet again that this fundamental problem preceded the problems of unification.

LABOUR MARKET TRENDS

Several indicators are relevant here, the first of which is total population. Since this variable is functionally related to the rates of fertility, mortality and migration, it determines the size of both current and future flows onto the labour market. Fertility and mortality rates have already been examined in Chapter 5 – see Figures 5.7a, 5.7b and 5.7c. Migration will be considered in more detail below. At this stage it is necessary only to point out that migratory flows into West Germany compensated for some of the labour shortages which would otherwise have occurred as a result of factors noted in and around Figure 5.7b.

But another important feature is the proportion of the total population in employment – the general method in Germany of measuring 'activity rates'. The vital trends in this respect are threefold in character. First, the proportion of employed persons in the total population averaged about 45 per cent in the period 1950–89; it grew during the 1950s, declined during the 1960s and 1970s, recovered during the 1980s and, even before unification, was predicted to reach 50 per cent between 1995 and 2000 (IW *Zahlen* 1991: 1). Second, the activity rates of males was lower in 1989 than in 1950; even with a predicted recovery to 60 per cent by the period 1995–2000, this rate will still be lower than the 65 per cent recorded during the 1950s. Third, there has been a more than equivalent rise in female activity rates: by 1995–2000 this rate is predicted to reach 40 per cent. However, western German female activity rates remain low by international standards (see below). On the other hand, in 1987, the East German activity rates of females were marginally higher than those of East German males. Expressed as a proportion of the population of working age, the female rate was 84 per cent compared to 82 per cent for males; the equivalent ratios in West Germany in 1987 were 53 per cent for females but 77 per cent for males (*Die Zeit* 12/90). The more plentiful

provision of crèche and Kindergarten facilities, along with a right to accommodation for single-parent females, allowed women to more easily combine family and working life in East Germany. Consequently, females constituted 50 per cent of the East German labour force as early as 1975, whereas the equivalent proportion in the west as late as 1990 was only about 40 per cent (Rudolph *et al.* 1990: 34).

Some of the trends to which reference has just been made can be illustrated by considering actual employment data. Figure 6.1 presents such an analysis. The employed labour force is the sum of employees and the self employed. It also includes the armed forces but these are relatively small in number. More significantly, the activity rates referred to above traditionally include the unemployed and attention will shortly be focused on this latter group. Concentrating on the line plots in Figure 6.1 for the moment, it can be seen that the lower line records the movement in the number of employees in employment. The vertical distance between the two lines therefore gives an indication of the number of self-employed, and there is some convergence of the lines: perhaps not surprisingly, then, the general trend for self employment to fall in industrial countries is reflected in the figure. This is one reason why the grid lines are displayed. Another reason is to bring out more clearly the substantial rise of seven million in the number of employees in the 1950s. The subsequent trend increase of four million from 1960 to 1989 is much more gradual and it is interspersed with a series of falls during the recessions of 1967, 1975 and the early 1980s. Indeed, the number of employees in 1970 and 1983 was almost identical. (The effects of the 1992–3 recession are not, of course, captured by annualised data which end in December 1992.) But the number of

Figure 6.1 Employment and unemployment: West Germany, 1950–92
Sources: BMA: *Stat. Taschenbuch* 1990; MRDB 4/93

persons in the total labour force (that is employed and unemployed) displayed a different trend. There was a strong growth in this latter method of measuring labour supply during the 1980s as the influence of the strong birth rates in 1965–75 made itself felt (see Figure 5.7b). This stood in marked contrast to the slow and cyclical growth of the labour force in the two previous decades (MRDB 8/89: 32):

. . . the labour force began to grow at a faster pace towards the end of the 1970s – a tendency which has persisted up to the present. In 1989, for example, an estimated 2.5 million more persons are in the labour force than in 1979; in the preceding ten years from 1970 to 1979 the increase ranged only between 300,000 and 400,000, and from the beginning to the end of the 1960s it was only about 200,000.

A number of implications of these labour force trends for the subsequent analysis of unemployment and migration can be pointed out at this stage. There was

a labour shortage during the 1960s and early 1970s, a shortage exacerbated by the introduction of compulsory military or community service in 1956 and its extension in the early 1960s. Consequently, the policy makers encouraged the inward migration of labour. West German birth rates were high between 1965 and 1975 and this caused a flow onto the labour market in the 1980s when there was already high unemployment. The policy stance on migration was duly modified. In 1990, compulsory military or community service was reduced to 12 or 15 months respectively.

A comparison of the sectoral deployment of employees in both East and West Germany appears in Figures 6.2a and 6.2b. These figures are essentially more detailed than the trends already indicated in Figures 2.3a and 2.3b. Above all, a comparison of the deployment of males and females is included in each figure. Both more men and women were employed in agriculture and industry in East Germany.

Conversely, more men and women were employed in the service sector in West Germany. These factors show the degree of adjustment which became necessary following GEMSU: East German industry would have to become less labour intensive and there would have to be an expansion in the service sector.

Trends in the incidence of regional unemployment in West Germany were considered in Figure 2.4a, but the federal unemployment data in Figure 6.1 are reproduced on a larger vertical scale in Figure 6.3. Associated measures (short-time working and unfilled vacancies) have

also been plotted in Figure 6.3. The steep fall in unemployment during the 1950s is immediately apparent. But note that the magnitude of this fall (1.3 million) is far less than the seven million jobs created during the same period (Figure 6.1). With the exception of the 1967 recession, there then followed a period of excess demand for labour in the sense that unfilled vacancies exceeded unemployment between 1960 and 1973. Expressed as a ratio, there were often three unfilled vacancies to every person registered as unemployed; the ratio reached 4.4:1 in 1965 and 5.3:1 in 1970. Significantly, the Berlin wall

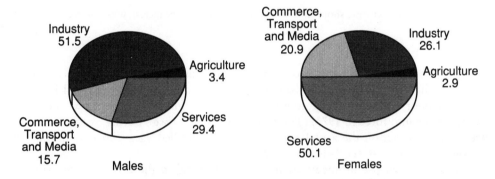

Figure 6.2a Employment by sector: West Germany, 1987
(percentage of the employed labour force)

Source: Die Zeit 12/90

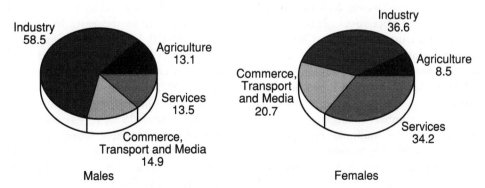

Figure 6.2b Employment by sector: East Germany, 1987
(percentage of the employed labour force)

Source: Die Zeit 12/90

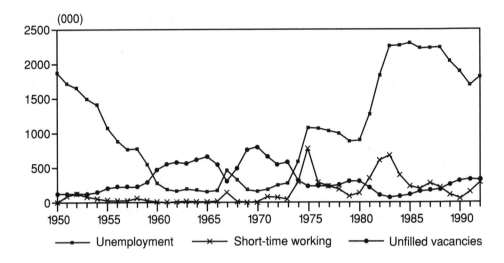

Figure 6.3 Unemployment, short-time working and unfilled vacancies: West Germany, 1950–92

Source: As Figure 6.1

brought the flow of migrants from the East to a halt in 1961, while a ban on further labour recruitment in southern Europe came into force in 1973. (The ban had a small impact on the actual number of foreign workers – see below.) There followed a sudden rise in unemployment during 1974 – the time of the first oil price shock. In 1975, unemployment doubled again to over one million; there was then only a relatively small remission before the dramatic rise to over 2.25 million after the second oil price shock. It remained at that level during most of the 1980s, nearing two million again only as a result of the pre-GEMSU boom. The post-GEMSU boom brought unemployment down below the two million mark. By 1991, the number of registered unemployed was 1.7 million. However, in December 1992 the number returned to two million as the post-GEMSU recession made an impact on unemployment. By January 1944 total German unemployment had reached 4 million. Note that there seemed to be a ratchet effect in

operation after the oil price shocks. Some explanation for this will be sought below. Finally, note how short-time working rose during each recession, while unfilled vacancies rose during each recovery.

Turning to the post-GEMSU situation by means of Figure 6.4, the differing fortunes of the western and eastern labour markets can readily be seen. The boom conditions already existing in the west were given further fuel by the demand for western goods in the east. In 1988 and 1989, GNRP had been growing at the highest rates for a decade (3.7 and 3.8 per cent respectively). In 1990 and the first half of 1991, this rate rose to 4.5 per cent. As a result, unemployment continued to fall. In January 1990, it was still 8.4 per cent of the dependent labour force, defined as all employees but excluding members of the armed forces. By April 1992, this ratio was 5.6 per cent – quite an improvement when related to the ratchet effects of the 1970s and 1980s. As economic growth slowed markedly in the

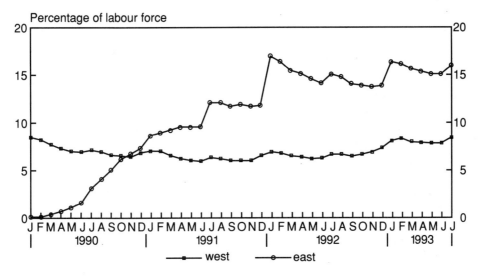

Percentage of labour force

Figure 6.4 Unemployment in West and East Germany: 1990–3
Sources: MRDB Tables IX (3 and 10)

second half of 1992, however, unemployment began to rise.

The stark contrast with experience in the east is vividly displayed in Figure 6.4. The collapse of eastern industry caused unemployment to rocket from negligible levels to 12 per cent of the dependent civilian labour force by mid-1991. From January 1992, unemployment was expressed as a ratio to the total civilian labour force. Even so, there was an increase in unemployment of 300,000 over December 1991; as can be seen in Figure 6.4, this increased unemployment to 17 per cent of the new labour force definition (BA *Presse Informationen* 15/92). This latter upturn in unemployment was associated with the termination of the special provisions whereby short-time benefits were payable to persons who had already permanently lost their jobs (MRDB 2/92: 8). In consequence, the number of employees on 'short-time' fell by over 500,000, and the (admittedly erratic) unfilled vacancies indicator rose by only 4,000 (BA *ibid.*). In addition, over

100,000 employees availed themselves of the 'transitional retirement' arrangements outlined in Chapter 5 (MRDB *ibid.*: 35). The take up of these arrangements in only one month was thus identical to the number who took early retirement over a period of four years under the 1984 Act (see also Chapter 5). Precisely one year earlier (January 1991), most of the subsidies which enabled eastern German companies to continue exporting to the rest of eastern Europe had been withdrawn (Akerlof *et al.* 1991: 31). This latter measure, along with further subsidy withdrawals in mid-1991, also caused monthly increases in unemployment of 100,000 and 200,000 respectively. Finally, it will be seen in the section on training that a number of schemes provided temporary employment in the east. These schemes thus reduced headline unemployment.

MIGRATION

This has been an extremely important labour-market and social-policy issue throughout the post-war period. During the late 1940s ethnic German expellees from the former eastern territories of the Third Reich migrated into West Germany; they were joined by political refugees from East Germany and this latter flow continued until the building of the Berlin wall. During the ensuing period, until at least the early 1980s, the largest migrant group came from what may be loosely described as southern Europe. Towards the end of the 1980s, ethnic German immigrants (*Aussiedler*) from the then Soviet Union and other eastern European countries began to arrive in West Germany in significant numbers; there was also a renewed inflow from East Germany (*Übersiedler*) before and after unification. There were thus three broadly discrete periods during which a wave of migrants had an important impact on the labour market: 1945–61, 1962–85 and a third wave commencing in the late 1980s. (Non-Germans seeking political asylum under article 16[2] of the GG – whose inflow reached a peak in 1992–3 – are excluded from the following analysis.)

At the end of the Second World War there were large-scale population movements. While the collapse of the Third Reich released for resettlement in their own countries the eight million forced labourers brought to Germany by 1945, an almost identical number of German nationals expelled from former eastern territories of the Reich flooded into western Germany. A further four million expellees fled to the Russian zone, although about 3.5 million inhabitants of that zone later fled to West Germany as political refugees. The inflow of expellees into Western Germany came to an end in the late 1940s. (Their arrival coincided with the return of four million German ex-POWs – Henning 1974: 196.) About

3.6 million political refugees from East Germany continued to flow into West Germany between 1950 and the building of the Berlin Wall in 1961, with a peak occurring around the mid-1950s but the annual number falling below 200,000 in only 1959 (Stolper *et al.* 1967: 337). After 1961, the flow soon dwindled to a complete halt. By 1965, there were almost certainly 14 million expellees and refugees in West Germany – over 22 per cent of the total population; the real figure was probably 10–12 per cent higher because of non-registration (Mellor 1978: 189). Approximately 6.5 million (4.7 million expellees and 1.8 million refugees) were of working age on arrival (Henning 1974: 196). Notice the resemblance between this number and the rapid growth in the number of employees noted above in the discussion of Figure 6.1. For the purpose of analysis, both expellees and refugees are treated here as a homogeneous first wave of post-war migrants.

As mentioned in Chapter 2, well over 50 per cent of the expellees arriving in the western zones settled in the three rural Länder closest to their points of origin: Schleswig-Holstein, Lower Saxony and Bavaria. Gravitation to these areas was prompted by the housing and food shortages in the cities – shortages which had also caused the former populations of those cities to drift to the countryside (Stolper *et al.* 1967: 233). Hence, in 1951, significant proportions of the total populations in these three Länder were accounted for by expellees, as well as some refugees (Wallich 1955: 273). However, with the rebuilding of the bombed towns, and with industry reviving under the stimulus of the Korean crisis, there was already a strong current back to the urban areas as early as 1950. Many of the newcomers in the over-crowded northern rural areas sought employment in the

Rhine and Ruhr industrial districts, which also became a focus for the refugees arriving from East Germany (Mellor 1978: 193). In 1954, it was estimated privately that some four million expellees had moved into the industrial areas, but as a result of resettlement programmes, and of private migrations, an equal number remained in less optimal areas (Wallich 1955: 275–6).

There were thus two longer-term advantages of this first wave of post-war migrants. First, there was an elastic supply of labour with respect to the growth in aggregate demand. In his now classic study, Kindleberger (1967: 27–37) sees this as being the single most important factor in Germany's post-war recovery. Without this substantial flow of population, then, the rapid rate of expansion in output achieved in the Ruhr and other industrial areas would not have been possible. This leads on to the second point, which applies both to this flow from the east and to the later flow from southern Europe: there was an exceptionally high degree of labour mobility. After all, the migrants were under great pressure to succeed (Mann 1974: 860). In the case of the first wave, the expellees intensified competition wherever they went and local firms found themselves faced with immigrants who brought new techniques and ideas (Wallich 1955: 283). Competition for jobs in the industrial centres tended to depress wage levels somewhat, especially since uprooted natives of Western Germany were also seeking work. But the depressant effect on wages was not all that strong. This was because of the housing shortage and the consequent maldistribution of manpower. In other words, the demand for labour was high in the industrial conurbations and unemployment was at its worst in the rural areas (*ibid.*: 284).

Rivalry for housing sometimes devel-oped between the newcomers and the bombed-out members of the local population, although the newcomers generally tended to be more badly housed. This rivalry, and the bitterness felt by the immigrants, only gradually subsided during the 1950s – a trend partially due to the integration of second-generation immigrants and the enormous output of housing (Stolper *et al.* 1967: 311). In any case income per head rose rapidly during the 1950s and the excess supply of labour fell rapidly. There is thus an important inference to be drawn at this stage, namely that the smooth integration of a sizeable flow of migrants, albeit that in this case they were of the same nationality, is more likely to occur during periods of economic expansion.

There was another important characteristic of the refugees from East Germany. Qualitatively, the migrants of working age either tended to possess above average skill levels, or they had at least completed their schooling. For that matter, the expellees were also a highly select group (Mellor 1978: 149). Among them were two million Sudeten Germans, an alert people with an excellent educational background. Other groups, too, were especially well qualified in various respects. They had all been through a brief but ruthless process of natural selection: many of their weaker colleagues had not survived the rigours of expulsion and the long trek to safety (Wallich 1955: 282–3).

Any country of immigration greatly benefits from the fact that the costs of child rearing and the education embodied in the immigrants has been borne in the country of origin (Blitz 1977: 479). Furthermore, the typical age and sex composition of immigrants is such that they seek employment to a proportionately greater extent than the native population. It has already been seen that their mobility and education were positive assets but the first wave were also native German speakers. In short, West Germany derived a large added value from these inflows (Ergun 1975: 187). For example, among the refugees from East Germany were skilled workers, doctors, technicians, and scientists (Stolper *et al.* 1967: 338). After the building of the Berlin Wall, First Secretary Ulbricht claimed that the loss sustained by East Germany because of migration was the equivalent of DM 30 billion or DM 10,000 per person – presumably at 1962 prices (Blitz 1977: 481; Stolper *et al.* 1967: 310). Blitz also reports that 60 per cent of the 2.5 million refugees who reached West Germany by 1957 were of working age. This represented an East German outlay on education and child rearing of DM 22.5 billion. Extrapolated to 1961, this figure reached DM 28.5 billion. Output added in West Germany was probably in the order of DM 36 billion.

However, four types of costs are imposed on the receiving country. First, additional capital equipment had to be supplied, although the high and expanding level of aggregate demand – to which the migrants also contributed – was in itself an investment incentive. The growing share of profits in the national income, along with various other investment incentives introduced by government, were also conducive to a high level of capital accumulation. Moreover, without migration there may well have been a serious labour-shortage constraint due to the numbers killed or badly wounded in the war. Having said all this, however, the capital absorbed by the migrants would have been quite high: when they numbered between 3.4 and 4 million, Wallich (1955: 285) estimated a non-agricultural *per capita* requirement of DM 12,000.

A second cost imposed by an influx of migrants was the additional strain placed on the infra-structure. Since much of the infra-structure lay in ruins when the bulk of the expellees arrived, they further exacerbated the shortages which already existed. Such were the degrees of devastation and recovery, however, it would be very difficult to disentangle the later costs and benefits of the migrants. Third, there was an increase in the tax burden attributable to the expellees. In 1950, it was estimated that they received about 40 per cent of the various social security benefits, more than twice their share of the population (*ibid.*). But the social security system was generally extended from the second half of the 1950s onwards, while initially the tax burden fell (Chapters 3 and 5). At the very least it can be said that the degree of economic recovery and expansion therefore concealed the problem. The fourth and final problem was the balance of payments cost. On the one hand, further food had to be imported because of shortages which existed before the expellees began to arrive. Nonetheless, Wallich (*ibid.*) attributes to the expellees extra food imports with a foreign-exchange cost of US$450 million annually. On the other hand, many of the industries in which the expellees were employed were export-intensive; and they evidently did not prevent the achievement of equilibrium during the 1950s.

An alternative source of labour was required once the Berlin wall effectively stemmed migration from the east (Giersch 1970: 18). There was an excess demand for labour (Figure 6.3). Further, the number of hours supplied by the indigenous labour force had begun to fall (Blitz 1977: 483); and compulsory military service was increased from 12 to 18 months (Völker 1973: 64). Hence, recruitment of foreign labour commenced in southern Europe and a second inflow of migrants began.

('Southern Europe' is broadly defined so as to include the whole of Turkey). There are a number of similarities to the earlier inflow of migrants from East Germany. First, during the 1970s this second inflow of migrants reached on average an annual rate equivalent to the inflow of persons of working age during the 1950s; second, the ban on further recruitment in 1973 came after roughly the same period as the stemming of the earlier inflow by the Berlin wall; third the growth in the number of foreign workers, and later their families, was dramatic – in 1961, barely 12 inhabitants out of 1,000 was a foreigner but by 1973 it was 64 and by 1980 it was 72; finally, another similarity to the inflow during the 1950s was therefore that the second inflow reached about the proportion of the population (Federal Labour Office 1974: 5 and 70; also *Presse Informationen* 14/81).

Throughout the 1960s, the most important sending country was Italy, although by the end of the decade Yugoslavia, Turkey and Greece had also become major sending countries. The absolute number of Italians decreased after 1972 while the number of Turks, Yugoslavs and Greeks continued to rise, although returning migrants to Greece exceeded emigration by 1974 (Xideas 1986: 55). Hence, between 1973 and 1980 the number of both Turks and Yugoslavs exceeded that of the Italians.

An important policy change took place between the end of the 1967 recession and the recruitment ban of 1973 (Federal Labour Office 1974: 6–7). This change consisted of a gradual move from a continuous, administratively enforced *rotation* of unaccompanied employees on fixed-term contracts to immigration for an indefinite period with the possibility of employees being joined by their families – the *integration* principle (Feix 1973;

Schiller 1975: 338). A comparison of the troughs in economic activity which were reached in 1967 and 1975 brings out the effects of this policy change. In both recessions, the index of industrial production decreased. There was a consequent rise in unemployment. But whereas the proportion of foreign employees in the labour force fell by 1.1 percentage points in 1967 over 1966, the fall in 1975 over 1973 was 0.8 percentage points; in absolute numbers the falls were from 1.313 million to 0.991 million between October 1966 and September 1967 and from 2.6 million to 2.3 million in an eighteen-month period following the recruitment ban in 1973 (Federal Labour Office 1974: 5; Schiller 1975: 350n). Hence, a smaller proportion of foreigners returned home during the second recession (MRDB 12/74: 5). Further, there was every indication that second-wave migrant employees were being joined by their families and 'temporary migration' was becoming 'permanent settlement' (Martin 1981: 34). In 1979, the *total* number of foreigners therefore exceeded 4 million; a decade later there were 4.85 million, or 7.8 per cent of the total population. No really important change had occurred by 1989 in both trends and composition when analysed by national origin: the Turks (at 33 per cent of the foreign population) remained the largest group, next came the Yugoslavs (13 per cent), followed by the Italians (11 per cent) and Greeks (6 per cent). Following unification, several minority groups who had settled in the east – notably Vietnamese – were added to the total number of migrants. Including the inflow from other parts of the EC and wider-Europe, along with other smaller minority groups, the *total* number of foreigners residing in Germany in 1992 reached 6.25 million (DAAD *Letter* December 1992). The relative rankings of the Turks, 'Yugoslavs',

Italians and Greeks, however, remained roughly the same as in 1989. But the fourth group (at 279,000) became the Poles. As a result, the proportion of foreigners in the total population was at least two and a half times greater than in Britain, but a half of the Swiss proportion (*Independent on Sunday* 6 June 1993).

As already indicated in Figure 6.3, unemployment remained at relatively high levels between 1975 and 1980. However, the number of second-wave migrant employees was over two million in both years. They were reluctant to leave – not least because unemployment benefits had been improved since 1967. At first, however, they had also been reluctant to register as unemployed during the 1974–75 recession; fear of accelerating unemployment resulting in loss of residence rights may have been partly responsible for low-registration rates (Paine 1977: 219). In addition, some motor-vehicle manufacturers granted fairly generous severance payments to any employees prepared to leave and the offer was accepted by several thousand foreign workers. But instead of leaving the country, they took up employment in other sectors (Schiller 1975: 343–4).

As the recession became more firmly entrenched, and after existing savings and other assets had been used up, economic pressure forced immigrants to register as unemployed (Paine 1977: 219). Hence, the number of foreigners registered as unemployed increased from 16,000 in 1973 to 133,000 in 1975 (OECD *Economic Survey* 1980: 15). Between 1976 and 1979 an annual number of 81,500 foreigners were unemployed. Expressed as a percentage of foreign workers, unemployment among foreigners rose to 8.2 per cent in 1981, compared to 5.5 per cent for total unemployment; thereafter, the foreign worker ratio was well into double digits for the

rest of the 1980s, even though the total ratio remained below double digits (IW *Zahlen* 1991: 15).

In many senses there was an inexorable substitution of foreign workers from southern Europe for indigenous German employees (Federal Labour Office 1974: 15–16). For example, between 1961 and 1973 about 3 million German workers moved to white-collar jobs. About half the manual jobs consequently vacated were refilled by foreign workers. Martin and Miller (1980: 319 and 325) predicted that competition would come later when foreigners attempted upward mobility or recession limited the number of jobs available. Hence, only a minority of the migrants from southern Europe, in contrast to the earlier inflow from the East, were skilled workers. Those migrants who arrived in possession of skills, however, were much more likely to settle permanently in West Germany; the cost to Turkey and Yugoslavia of such permanent emigration was particularly significant (Böhning 1975: 270 and 272–3; Ergun 1975: 195–6; Martin 1981: 40). Moreover, two-thirds of the migrants from Turkey had been educated to primary school level, a rather high percentage for a country where almost half the population was illiterate (Ergun 1975: 196). Xideas (1986: 73) found 70 per cent of Greek immigrants had received a primary school education, although emigrants were of a lower educational standard than the Greek population as a whole; he therefore concludes that Greek migrants were inevitably destined to 'accept low status jobs'. Nonetheless, at the peak of Greek emigration, 80 per cent of newly qualified apprentices emigrated within six months of qualifying (*ibid.*: 87). More generally, Blitz (1977: 501) demonstrates that, for the period 1957–73, West Germany benefited greatly from immigration because the costs of child rearing and education had been borne abroad. Because of her superior factor and training endowments, it would have taken West Germany only a fraction of the time and cost invested in human capital to convert this inexperienced second inflow into semi-skilled workers; however many of them returned home untrained (Böhning 1975: 272). Instead, they were used on unskilled and non-industrial work (Berger and Mohr 1975: 78). Moreover, as Martin (1981: 34) contends, the private costs to employers of hiring these unskilled workers may have been lower than the social ones, although it was not only the foreigners who caused the deficiencies in the social structure: social demands for education, housing and child care were already high in the conurbations to which the migrants were attracted and to which they later brought their families (Blitz 1977: 500–1; Schiller 1975: 352; BMA *Sozialbericht* 1973: 19–20). Nonetheless, the inflow of young and mobile foreign workers may have reduced employment opportunities for females and older workers; they may also have obstructed technological progress because capital intensity increased after the building of the Berlin wall (Giersch 1970: 18; Schiller 1975: 337 and 342).

Thus far, only the costs and benefits of migration to the receiving country have been analysed. At the level of the individual migrant, such an approach assumes that the decision to migrate is determined by a comparison of the net present value of future earnings in the sending and receiving country. A clear example of this decision-making process can be gleaned by anticipating an important feature of the third wave of migrants. East Germans who migrated or commuted to western Germany after the collapse of East Germany appeared to earn a comparable return to their education as native West Germans (Krueger and Pischke 1992: 36). Since this rate of return was far higher in the west, migrants and commuters from the east almost doubled their income (*ibid.*: 35; OECD *Economic Survey* 1992: 24). East Germans were highly educated and the human capital stock was therefore considerably increased. On the other hand, only about one half of the commuters indicated that income gain was the main incentive for commuting, suggesting that joblessness was a significant 'push' factor; a further 40 per cent expressed a clear preference for alternative employment in the eastern Länder (OECD *ibid.*).

Maldonado (1976: 8–9) estimated a classical model which predicts that labour will migrate from regions with surplus labour and low wages to regions where there is an excess demand for labour and relatively high wage rates; in addition, she also estimated the chain effects of cumulative migration as earlier migrants provide potential migrants with information and assistance. Non-material aspirations such as a better education for the migrant's children also enter the equation (Feix 1973: 40–64). Although Zell (1977) criticised both Maldonado's data and model, her findings on the determinants of Puerto Rican migration to the USA seem to be similar to those factors which affected migration from both Turkey and Greece to West Germany (Ergun 1975: 144–9 and 213; Xideas 1986: 78–84). In all three cases, the presence in the home country of higher unemployment, lower wages and lower social-policy provision were seen as inducements to migrate. Such migration was possible because not enough Germans were willing, at the wages offered, to undertake the low-paid manual jobs (Berger and Mohr 1975: 118). Franz (1981: 599–601) also modelled and tested the employment and real-wage inducements specified in this paragraph, while Xideas (1986) additionally estimated Keynesian and Marxian models of migration. Burda (1993: 454 and 456) supplemented his analysis of east-west migration within Germany by postulating that uncertainty accounted for the relatively small flow even in the face of low employment prospects. But the huge savings remitted home by second-wave migrants were not generally utilised in the industrialisation of their own countries: those workers who returned home found they had financed, at best, a re-equipped peasant holding or a small holiday hotel (Berger and Mohr 1975: 78; Blitz 1977: 498–9; Ergun 1975: 181–6; Xideas 1986: 89).

In 1983, the Return Migration Assistance Act marked the first substantial policy decision on migration by the newly-elected conservative-liberal coalition (Jones 1990: 225). This Act was directed towards the bulk of the foreign population who originated from non-EC countries. Financial inducements to permanently leave with their families were offered to foreign employees who were either unemployed or who were on short-time; the unemployment pre-condition was waived in the case of Turkish and Portuguese workers and they were offered other inducements (ibid.). Both sets of measures were operative for six months as from January 1984 and departures increased 42 per cent over the previous year. There has, nonetheless, been a significant qualification (ibid.):

On closer inspection, however, it is also apparent that the decline was most noticeable amongst the western Mediterranean nationalities (Italians, Spanish and Portuguese), and rather slower amongst the populations from the eastern Balkan/Mediterranean countries (Greeks, Yugoslavs, Turks).

A more important characteristic of migration in the 1980s, it was said above, was the inflow of Eastern and other ethnic Germans towards the end of the decade. Almost 344,000 East Germans migrated to the West in 1989, with a marked concentration in November following the opening of the Berlin wall (Lipschitz and McDonald 1990: 131; OECD Economic Survey 1990: 63). In the period January 1989 to January 1992, roughly 870,000 East Germans – equivalent to 5 per cent of the population or 10 per cent of the labour force – migrated to West Germany (Burda 1993: 452). In addition, there was an inflow of over 377,000 ethnic Germans in 1989, most of whom came from Poland (250,000) and the former Soviet Union (98,000) (Wirtschaftswoche 16/90). In 1988, the inflow of ethnic Germans had been well over 202,000 (BfG:Wirtshaftsblätter 12/89: 5). Hence, over half the total of nearly one million ethnic Germans who entered West Germany in the 1980s did so during the last two years of the decade; the influx during the 1980s was, in turn, half the total of 2 million who came to West Germany in the period 1950–89 (Lipschitz and McDonald ibid.). Between 2.5 and 3.0 million were expected to arrive before the end of the century (IDS European Report 335). The inflow appeared to have peaked in 1990 when nearly 400,000 arrived; very roughly, Poland, the former Soviet Union and Romania sent equal proportions (BA 1993: 887–8). In 1991 and 1992, the respective inflows amounted to 222,000 and 231,000, the bulk of whom not surprisingly came from the former Soviet Union (BA ibid.; IW Zahlen 1992: 13). On the other hand, the OECD (ibid.) predicted that the migratory flows between eastern and western Germany would become more balanced. Various reasons were given for this prediction. The major ones were the abolition of special assistance for East Germans following

GEMSU, the high relative cost of housing in the west and the expectation that eastern Germany would become the most dynamic region of a unified economy. The largest flows did indeed precede GEMSU, and the flow seemed to stabilise at a monthly rate of 12–15,000 in early 1992 (Burda 1993: 452). However, this was a significant rate when compared to other regions in Germany and other countries (*ibid*.). Another significant finding was that the unemployment rate in east Germany would exceed 25 per cent until 1995, and would still be 14 per cent in 2000 despite a net migration of 1.8 million east Germans to the western part of the country (Chauffour *et al*. 1992: 253).

Not surprisingly, the benefits of this third wave of migrants were similar to those associated with the first wave (*Economist* 23 September 1989; IDS *ibid*.). Perhaps above all, the age composition of the new arrivals meant that only 10 per cent of the total inflow for both groups were over 60; 25 per cent were under 18, while a further half were between 18 and 44. Taken in isolation, only 6 per cent of the ethnic Germans were aged between 60 and 65; similarly, only 3 per cent were under 20, with nearly two-thirds being between 20 and 45 (BA 1993: 884). This was bound to at least ease the medium-term demographic problems referred to in Chapter 5 (see Figure 5.7c in particular). Many of them were qualified to fill the 300,000 unfilled vacancies for skilled workers, and others were capable of filling unfilled vacancies for apprentices; they were also seen as mobile, fitter than the indigenous labour force and a boost to domestic demand. However, at least one of the costs of integrating some of the ethnic Germans differed from the first wave: they had lost touch with the German language and the Federal Labour Office estimated the cost of language

tuition at DM 3 billion. They also required far more training than the migrants from the former DDR.

Moreover, it was feasible for those living in the former inner-border region to commute from east to west; commuting also became possible in the area surrounding the former West Berlin. These practices soon became widespread. In 1991, for example, it was expected that the number of commuters would rise to 300,000, while the number of east Germans seeking to settle permanently in the west would fall to 200,000 (*Wirtschaftswoche* 16/91). In fact, the number of commuters in 1991 exceeded 500,000, 33 per cent of whom worked in west Berlin; by mid-1992 the proportion of commuters working in west Berlin had risen to 37 per cent (BA *Presse Informationen* 43/93; OECD *Economic Survey* 1992: 24). These commuters are highly mobile: the average daily commuting distance is 50 kilometres and 44 per cent commute for weekly or longer periods (OECD *ibid*.). They are typically young (on average 31, compared to the west German average of 38) and skilled (69 per cent) manual employees; however, the downgrading of their occupational levels meant that half of them were not employed in their own trades (*ibid*.).

From an economic point of view, therefore, the Berlin wall was undoubtedly used as an instrument to segment the German labour market (Schrettl 1992: 145). Substantial differences in living standards between East and West Germany had resulted in large migratory flows from east to west during the 1950s. The East German regime found itself confronted with the options of either building the Wall or offering West German wage levels. The re-opening of the Wall, rather than GEMSU, restored a unified labour market. One effect of GEMSU, as just shown, was to markedly slow down the haemorrhaging of the East German labour pool. The unification of the labour market in turn had an impact on trade union wage policy. It will be seen in the section on trade union policy that a rational stance was to insist on the fairly rapid equalisation of wage rates in the two parts of the newly unsegmented labour market. It would hardly be rational, however, to demand that a process of wage cutting in the west should produce equalisation. Instead, the terms of GEMSU almost axiomatically meant that eastern pay levels should be brought up to western standards.

TRAINING

Although training and skills are not in themselves an infallible protection against unemployment, the acquisition of suitable vocational skills is one of the most decisive factors determining an individual's prospects on the labour market. In an industrialised society, the acquisition of skills is also of crucial significance in terms of the development and growth of the economy as a whole – hence the use of the term 'human capital formation'. A European comparison by Saunders and Marsden (1981: 296) demonstrated that formal vocational training among manual males was most fully developed in West Germany. Moreover, Porter (1990: 369) correctly viewed Germany's 'well-developed and distinctive' apprenticeship system as an extremely valuable factor endowment. This system must, therefore, be described.

The basis of the German vocational training scheme is the 'dual system'. In its normal usage, the term applies to the initial training provided on a joint basis by firms and educational establishments. However, important supplementary training opportunities exist. Indeed,

the flexibility of vocational training can be measured in this latter respect. New jobs emerge as technology changes; conversely, other jobs become redundant (Fels 1988: 23). The need for retraining and further training is an inevitable consequence. In contrast to the system of initial training in the dual system, however, further training is organised in a multifaceted system (Mahnkopf 1992: 68).

Although each Land possesses a largely autonomously determined system of education, the dual system is more or less uniform throughout the economy. Figure 6.5 demonstrates that the system is fed from all three levels of secondary education. Using the plural terms for this level of education, it can be seen that virtually all *Hauptschulen* pupils, most *Realschulen* pupils and some pupils from the *Gymnasien* (grammar schools which exist in most Länder) enter either directly into the system, or via the technical colleges (*Berufsschulen*). It should be noted that the majority of *Haupt-* and *Realschulen* pupils are typically trained in manual skills, whereas dual-system *Gymnasien* pupils tend to enter professions like banking and finance. A more general overview of the whole system may be gained by reference to the scheme's seven main characteristics:

- After leaving compulsory schooling (*Haupt-* or *Realschule*, followed where necessary by one year at a *Berufsschule*) at the age of 16, training for the qualified school leaver is organised on a contractual basis. The practical in-firm training is combined with compulsory part-time education between the ages of 16 and 18 in 'vocational schools' or technical colleges (*Berufsschulen*)
- Private firms are responsible for the in-firm training which, however, is regulated, guided and controlled since

1969 by Federal legislation (Vocational Training Act – *Berufsbildungsgesetz* – BBiG, as amended – see below). The chambers of industry and commerce conduct examinations

- About 73 per cent of vocational costs are met by the firms themselves, including some help from the state in special cases. In addition, the state provides vocational education which accounts for the remaining 27 per cent of the total costs of the dual system. But see below for a further discussion of the incidence of costs

- An apprenticeship lasts approximately 2 or 3 years, depending upon the candidate's educational qualifications and his or her progress. At the end of the apprenticeship, there is an official written examination and the candidate prepares a piece of practical work (*Gesellenstuck*). An apprentice who passes these examinations receives a certificate and becomes a qualified *Facharbeiter* (skilled worker)

- At a minimum age of 25 the *Facharbeiter* may enrol for a *Meister* course, which again will conclude with a written and practical examination, usually set by the Land government. Possession of the *Meisterbrief* (foreman's certificate) awarded to successful candidates usually gives the *Meister* a great deal of kudos and supervisory powers. However, in some small firms a foreman may not possess a certificate, while in large firms there may be an excess supply of *Meister*

- As already seen in Chapter 5, adults may avail themselves of courses in retraining, occupational rehabilitation and further training

- The universities are also providers of vocational training, although they are normally excluded from consideration of the educational aspects of the wider system (Münch 1991: 25). Porter (1990: 369) considered German university education to be less effective in the social sciences and management than in science and technology. He pointed to the highly theoretical nature of these 'less effective' subjects. Lumley (1992: 285–6), on the other hand, insisted that there was a subtle blend of theory and practice in a German university's business education. Suffice it to say that the vocational orientation of most university courses causes occasional protest from some students. This demand is articulated in some variant of 'academic instead of vocational studies' (*Bildung statt Ausbildung*). Perhaps these protests may be regarded as the afterglow of attempted university reform in the 1960s (Hallett 1973: 107–19 and 143–5). Finally, numerous other higher educational institutions unambiguously provide vocational-training courses which require full-time attendance (Münch 1991: 28)

Hence, vocational training in Germany has historically been the responsibility of institutions in both the public and private sectors. The state plays an important role by providing a wide range of educational and training institutions, and by regulating the large number of occupations for which an apprenticeship must be served. There have been over 400 such occupations since the 1969 Act (*ibid.*: 88). Qualified persons in these occupations are located in virtually every sector of the economy. Most notably, the *Handwerker* ('handicrafts' – see Chapter 8) sector in the west supplied nearly 500,000 training places in 1991. The number of places in industry and commerce was only 250,000 higher (IW *Zahlen* 1992: 128).

Apprenticeships in the *Handwerker* sector must be served, for example, in hairdressing and baking. Only persons possessing a *Meister* qualification are permitted to own a *Handwerker* business. In commerce, occupations such as sales persons and bank clerks are in the 'top ten' trades attracting apprentices (*ibid.*: 130). A fairly constant proportion (53 per cent) of the 16–19 year-old age group were in 'dual system' apprenticeships in the 1970s and 1980s (Casey 1986: 78n; Sadowski 1981: 234).

There is a very high level of general support for sustaining a high volume of vocational training; it is seen as being essential to maintain an internationally competitive advantage (Casey 1986: 71). But as Münch (1991: 33) indicates, employers advocate the minimisation of legal regulation, while the trade unions would like to see in-firm training integrated more closely into the state education system with a consequent tighter network of legal regulations. The policy debate in the 1970s and 1980s reflected these different approaches. In effect, the principal policy issues were concerned with the incidence and implications of training costs. Underinvestment in human

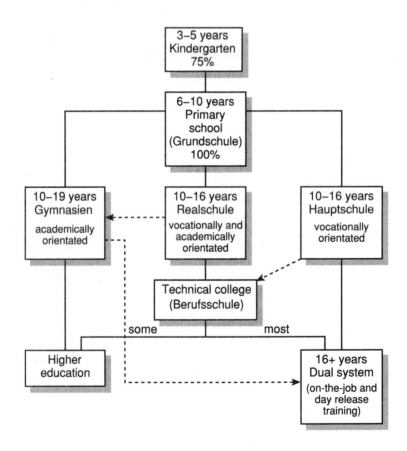

Figure 6.5 Basic structure of the Education System in Germany

Source: Independent 4 June 1991

capital, one argument ran, would occur in a system which relied on the voluntary participation of firms; this leads to firms using the system as a means of attracting and selecting their own future estimated supply of skilled labour (Sadowski 1981: 237). The result is that firms supplying training places later compete for skilled labour with firms that have not supplied such places; there is thus no reason to suppose that firms will train the number of apprentices justified by their self-interest as a group. Moreover, this 'voluntary' system could well result in trainees selecting jobs already in excess supply. The result is that future labour productivity rates and income tax yields are lower, and any consequent unemployment and retraining costs are borne by society as a whole (*ibid.*: 238 and 240).

Three different collective methods of compensating for the market failure of the 'voluntary' system were postulated: a system of state subsidies; a levy-grant system administered by the state; a levy-grant system administered by the relevant collective bargainers. Legislation permitting the two levy-grant systems was contained in the Act to Promote Training Places 1976 (*Ausbildungsplatzförderungsgesetz*) (Münch 1991: 32). Hence, if the overall supply of apprenticeships did not exceed demand by 12.5 per cent on a given day each year, this Act empowered the Federal government to impose a maximum levy of 0.25 per cent of the payroll on all firms whose payrolls exceeded DM 400,000.

However, in 1980, the Act was declared unconstitutional by the Federal Constitutional Court on the grounds that the *Bundesrat* had not consented to the Act (*ibid.*). This constitutional point made no contribution to a resolution of the market failure hypothesis, of course. Of more significance is the fact that Germany's collective bargaining system is for the most part industry specific (see below). The relatively minor levy-grant schemes of this nature operating in Germany seem to indicate that they are more efficient than the more general levy-grant system embodied in the 1976 Act – both in terms of targeting and incidence (Sadowski 1981: 243–7). (The remaining amendments to the 1969 Act contained in the 1976 statute were reenacted in the Act to Promote Vocational Training, 1982 [*Berufsbildungförderungsgesetz*].)

Because of their relatively low pay when expressed as a proportion of the skilled rate, the costs of training are probably borne to a greater extent by German trainees than is the case in France and the UK; however, not all the costs of training are recouped by the German employer during the apprenticeship itself (Casey 1986: 65–6). Moreover, it may well be the case that larger industrial and commercial enterprises invest substantially more in the training of each apprentice than smaller enterprises (*ibid.*). Since retention rates are not particularly high, therefore, there is an inequitable sharing of costs, or a free rider problem. On qualification, trainees – particularly in the handicraft sector – are sometimes not offered permanent employment contracts: hence, the peculiar German problem of unemployment among 20–25 year-olds being higher than among teenagers (*ibid.*: 73–5).

During the 1980s, the demographic factors already illustrated in Figures 5.6 and 5.7b, along with a structural change in the demand for higher education, played significant roles in the training market. Initially, demand for industrial training places grew strongly, reaching a federal-wide peak of 764,000 in 1984; this compared to a supply of 727,000 places (*Die Zeit* 17/90; MRDB 8/89: 33). Partly as a result of the decline in birth rates which commenced in the mid-1960s, however, the demand for places then began a secular decline: it sank significantly below the supply of places in 1988. Prior to unification in 1989, federal-wide demand was just over 600,000, compared to a potential supply of about 670,000. Perhaps even more significantly, there was a relatively large excess supply of training places in Bavaria and Baden-Württemberg; in Bremen and Hamburg, on the other hand, there was still a minor excess demand for training places (Casey 1991: 207; Figures 6.4 and 6.5 above). Moreover, there is yet another market-failure problem implied by the changed structure of education. In 1979, over 670,000 more young persons were in the dual system than in higher education; by 1989, this gap was only 45,000 (BMA *Statistisches Taschenbuch* 1990: 2.9 – the 1989 data were 1.553 million and 1.508 respectively). From the policy point of view, the change in the demand for places in higher education could have an impact on unemployment: graduates seem increasingly to be qualified in fields where there is already an excess demand for (further) training places. These elements persisted after unification. Above all, the supply of places in the west outstripped demand, whereas under half the persons between 16 and 19 in the east were in training (IW *Zahlen* 1992: 129; iwd 4/93). Females were particularly badly affected. In addition to the factors analysed in this paragraph, account must also be taken of studies which show that the supply of apprenticeships depends on business cycle conditions (Casey 1986: 69).

There have been other changes in the apprenticeship system. The average age of an apprentice in 1987 was 18.5 years, one year higher than at the end of the 1970s and two years higher than at the beginning of that decade (Casey 1991: 208). A growing proportion of young persons were re-maining at school in order to matriculate. Instead of going immediately to university, however, these more highly-qualified persons were increasingly taking up apprenticeships in commerce, insurance and banking. Moreover, whereas 70 per cent of school leavers eventually enter an apprenticeship, half of them do not do so immediately. The proportion of females in apprenticeships also increased in the 1980s; in 1979 this proportion was 38 per cent, but by 1989 it was 44 per cent (BMA *Statistisches Taschenbuch* 1990: 2.9). There was also an indication that they were beginning to move into previously male-dominated occupations (Casey 1991: 211–12). The average length of the apprenticeship has been a more controversial issue. In the interests of increasing the future supply of skilled labour, the employers would like to see an increase in the number of occupations which require only a two-year apprenticeship; the trade unions, on the other hand, would prefer to see these apprenticeships phased out where they still exist, their reasoning being that such training is too firm-specific and narrow (*ibid.*: 216–17).

The declared educational policy of the former East German state was to give everyone access to a good education and resulted in a well-trained labour force (Hoene 1991: 21). In 1988, 90 per cent of all employees possessed an occupational qualification. The proportion of trained females – 87 per cent of employed women – was higher than in the equivalent West German statistic of 65 per cent (Rudolph *et al.* 1990: 34). As in the west, large proportions of females were to be found in 'typically female' trades, although women had increased their share of technical training to a greater extent than in the west (*ibid.*: 34). However, there were several fields in both male and female employment where there was an urgent need to catch up. Modern accounting methods, finance, banking, insurance and marketing had all been underrated and more and more neglected (*ibid*.). In other cases, the lack of modern equipment and technology resulted in a lower level of advanced technical skills. The very limited use of computers, for example, caused a shortage of skills in this critically important industry. Hence the retraining of 170,000 persons undertaken in 1990, with an increase in 1991 to 300,000 persons.

The experience gained in the Ruhr and Saar during the steel crisis of the mid-1980s was applied to the crash-retraining programmes in the east (Wächter and Stengelhofen 1992: 30). The employment contracts of redundant employees were not terminated but rather transferred to new institutions (*ibid*.). Three such institutions were created: temporary-employment schemes (*Auffanggesellschaften*); emergency-employment schemes (*die Beschäftigungsgesellschaften*) and retraining schemes (*die Qualifizierungsgesellschaften*). As practised to a limited extent in the west, an emergency employment scheme could be established where the specific purposes were providing training and creating jobs in the public sector for unemployed persons (OECD *Economic Survey* 1992: 68). Such a scheme was not permitted to compete directly with the private sector, although trainees received the relevant contract rate of pay which was subsidised by the Federal Labour Office. In the east, on the other hand, emergency-employment schemes were typically comprised of units established from non-viable parts of the *Treuhandanstalt* firms discussed in Chapter 8 (*ibid*.: 83–4). A fairly major policy debate addressed the extent to which these schemes improved the quality of training. They were frequently seen as a selective employment subsidy designed to keep

headline unemployment to a minimum (*ibid*.; Flockton 1992). Moreover, the unions criticised the system because retrainees received only 68 per cent of their former earnings, compared to 90 per cent if unemployed (Wächter and Stengelhofen 1992: 31). The unions argued that the *Treuhandanstalt* should finance the schemes, whereas the *Treuhandanstalt* argued that this would prolong the process of transforming its companies into privately owned enterprises. There was thus a clear implication for the adjustment process in the labour market. This process is analysed in the concluding sector of this chapter.

THE GROWTH OF COLLECTIVE BARGAINING

Against the oscillating economic background of expansion and chaos seen as early as Chapter 1 above, the long-term growth of German collective bargaining has displayed four basic features:

- the degree of disunity within the trade union movement
- the strong bargaining power of employers
- the interventionist role played by the State and the courts
- significant developments in industrial democracy, or 'codetermination'

Because the present analysis is principally concerned with what occurred after the Second World War, it must be emphasised that a number of fundamental changes in these four long-term features took place in the post-war period. Above all, trade unions became an important actor in West German economic and social affairs. It will also be seen that, following unification, the unions rapidly assumed the same critical role in the east. The following sections therefore concentrate on these post-war changes, rather than the pre-war evolution of the collective bargaining system.

Nonetheless, it is important to note that the oscillating economic background was one of the factors which affected trade union growth. State opposition was another historical factor which constrained union activity. Following the repeal of the Anti-Socialist Act in 1890, which had driven the movement underground, trade union membership doubled within a decade. By 1913 total membership had doubled again to reach 3 million, or 10 per cent of the labour force. In 1922 unionisation stood at 9 million, or 30 per cent. It then hovered around the 4–5 million mark until the Nazis seized power and banned the movement. Following the Second World War trade unionisation reached over 40 per cent of the labour force. (Data extracted from: Kendall 1975; Roll 1939; Taft 1952.)

Consider the period 1871–1945 in a little more depth. In spite of determined opposition from both the state and employers during the Imperial era, the German trade unions, although weakened by internal division, found themselves ultimately catapulted into significant positions of social and political influence after the 1918 revolution (Grebing 1969). However, the unions became part of the state apparatus during the Weimar Republic. The divisions within the movement grew worse. These divisions were based on both political and religious differences. Rank and file revolutionary fervour was transformed into disillusionment as time elapsed. The decline of revolutionary fervour can be gauged from the trend in strikes. These fell from about 5,000 in number in 1922 to under 500 in 1931 – a figure which resulted in Germany being top and bottom respectively of the trend in the number of strikes when com-

pared to France, Sweden, the UK and the USA. In 1924 over 36 million working days were lost – the highest in German history (Hopkins 1953: 219–20; Taft 1952: 293–4). There was opposition from the national union organisations to the extension of the works council principle. They feared that the councils would either become the tools of management or, alternatively, revolutionary weapons along the lines of 1918. The experiences with works councils and, for that matter, the compulsory arbitration and conciliation machinery were to influence trade union policy when the movement was re-established in the late 1940s (Owen Smith et al. 1989: 32 and 232).

During the post-war occupation, the trade unions were involved in the restructuring of German industry. This was because of their resistance to the Nazis. Nevertheless, trade union bargaining power was rather narrowly circumscribed until the Allies imposed currency reform in 1948. Initially, trade unions were allowed to organise only at plant and local levels. Trade union demands for economic democracy and socialisation after the Second World War echoed those of the post-First World War period. There was an even larger majority of German political opinion which was anti-capitalist and there was widespread support for public ownership. British support for such measures had to be qualified as a result of American opposition. German proposals along these lines were continually turned down (Anthes et al. 1972: 80–4). In 1949, however, the Christian Democrats (CDU/CSU) appointed a neo-liberal Economics Minister (Professor Erhard) and they dropped their nationalisation proposals in favour of the SME. Ten years later the Social Democrats (SPD) and, to a certain extent, the trade unions were to do the same.

The wage freeze inherited by the Allies rendered collective bargaining over money wages of secondary importance in trade union policy until the relaxation of the freeze in November 1948. The re-emergence of this bargaining function, along with the mounting conviction that their political influence was waning, were two factors behind trade union attempts to avoid the divisions of the pre-Hitler period. An emphasis was placed on the non-religious and neutral party-political nature of the new organisations. This left them to pursue their own independent social and economic objectives. By far the most important step in this respect was the founding in the British zone of the DGB (*Deutscher Gewerkschaftsbund*) – the equivalent of the British TUC or North American AFL-CIO. Hans Böckler, who was to lead this organisation, favoured a powerful centre with regional and occupational branches. The occupations would be grouped according to whether they were manual workers, white-collar employers or *Beamte* (a classification of some employees in the public sector – see the next section). Böckler's proposals were vetoed by the British occupation authorities who saw the proposed organisations as being potentially too powerful (Hirsch-Weber 1959: 50). Moreover, a British trade union delegation had advocated a small number of unions, each one of which would enjoy bargaining autonomy for the industrial affairs of their members (*ibid.*). In 1947, the revised constitution for the DGB was approved and 15 industrial affiliates were established in the British zone. Each affiliate accepted the philosophy of 'one union for each plant'. Following, first, the linking with unions in the American and French zones, as well as, second, the failure to agree terms for an amalgamation with the Communist-dominated unions in

the Russian zone and, third, the elections to the Bonn Parliament in August 1949, the DGB became the new Federal Republic's trade union federation with Böckler as its chairman. Its headquarters are in Düsseldorf where its Ruhr power base after the Second World War was also situated. A sixteenth union was formed when Textiles and Clothing split from Leather. Note that the DGB's affiliates negotiate with the appropriate employers' associations – usually at the regional level.

As early as 1945 proposals for a white-collar union (DAG – *Deutsche Angestellten-Gewerkschaft*) were drawn up in Hamburg (still the location of its headquarters). These proposals were approved by the British military authorities in 1946. The DAG was as anxious as the DGB to avoid disunity, although it could not accept the industrial union principle. Several conferences between the DGB and DAG culminated in 1948 with an offer from the DGB to accord exclusive organisational rights in white-collar intensive sectors such as banking and commerce to the DAG. For its part the DAG insisted that it must have the right to organise all white-collar workers, irrespective of their industrial location. Agreement could not be reached, with the result that the DGB unions and the DAG established inter-zonal organisations and subsequently became competitors for membership. However, both organisations stress their non-religious and party-political neutral philosophies. They both also emphasise that they exist to promote the social, economic and cultural interests of their members. However, where they share organisational rights, they sign separate agreements – see below.

A less serious threat to unity was the formation of a break-away Christian trade union movement in 1955. It was renamed the Federation of Christian Trade Unions (*Christlicher Gewerkschaftsbund Deutschlands* – CGB) in 1959. Its establishment was opposed by prominent Christian trade unionists who wanted to avoid a divided movement. The breakaway from the DGB was partly caused by what some Christian trade unionists regarded as an anti-CDU campaign by the DGB during the 1953 federal elections, although this party's vote increased. Other reasons advanced were the debate over the nature of defence contributions at the 1954 DGB Congress and a controversial speech at the same congress on the political role of the unions. Support for the CGB dwindled even further during the 1960s (Limmer 1966: 105–6).

These developments were reflected by a fall in the proportion of the labour force in trade unions. Prior to the re-emergence of the large industrial undertakings, the proportion of the labour force organised in West Germany reached 50 per cent in 1951 – a much higher proportion than Weimar in approximately half the land area. But by 1960 it had fallen to 40 per cent. The decline continued until 1970 but during the 1970s there was a revival and the figure now stands at over 40 per cent again. (Grosser 1974: 308–9; Kendall 1975: 109 and 112; Kerr 1954: 546; Limmer 1966: 130; Schuster 1973: 61; Taft 1952: 301).

The role of employers' associations is also extremely important in German collective bargaining. However, during the denazification programme employers had not been allowed to organise. It was 1950 before the Confederation of German Employers' Associations (BDA) was formed. It differed from its Weimar predecessor (which had been abolished by the Nazis) in that it included in membership not just employers' associations from industry, but also from banking, transport, insurance, commerce, handicrafts and agriculture (Bunn 1960: 653). The most notable exceptions are the iron and steel employers and Volkswagen, the latter having traditionally negotiated its own agreements direct. Public sector employers are also unaffiliated. There are 47 vertically organised national associations affiliated to the BDA (for example, Engineering Employers and Agriculture and Forestry Employers); in addition there are 11 horizontally organised state (Länder) associations in membership; through these direct members' associations, a further 750 employers' associations (usually regional vertical or local horizontal) are indirectly members of the BDA and generally a firm is a member of both the appropriate vertical and the local association (Berghahn and Karsten 1987: 11–13). Each vertical regional association is responsible for negotiating legally-binding agreements with the appropriate trade union. As a result of all these factors, the employers are a strongly united and disciplined body whose bargaining is centrally co-ordinated through the BDA. The BDA is more interventionist than the DGB. For example, between 1975 and 1984 it successfully coordinated regional and industry-level negotiations so that the 40-hour week and 30 days' annual holiday became federal-wide standards (Bosch 1990: 614).

One is bound to conclude that the employers are far better organised than the employees. A BDA memorandum in 1954 recommended that each bargaining unit should establish strike protection funds; at the same time the BDA should establish its own permanent co-ordinating committee. In 1956 the Ruhr coal owners were invited by their employers' association to create a DM 6 million 'solidarity fund'. In 1961 'Solidarity between Employers' was extended to include not engaging workers on strike at other firms; not enticing customers of strike-bound firms; or, conversely, not transferring orders to strike-free firms. Guidelines were issued in 1965; in 1970 they were supplemented so as to include unofficial strike action. (Aaron and Wedderburn 1972: 44, 193 and 280; Adams and Rummel 1977: 5; Grosser 1974: 304–5; Hopkins: 1953: 210). Moreover, the BDA is opposed to any restriction of private property ownership and it found an ally in the CDU after the latter had been converted to the SME. Under the strong leadership of Adenauer, the CDU government of the 1950s built up a strong working relationship with the BDA and, more particularly, its sister organisation (the Federation of German Industry: BDI). The relative political stature of the BDA increased in the 1960s and 1970s, particularly under Dr Schleyer who for a short time before his assassination in 1977 was president of both the BDA and the BDI (*Die Zeit* 24/77 and 36/77). However, some chinks in the armour later began to appear, not least as a result of the agreement to equalise east/west wage rates (see below). For example, Opel, the German subsidiary of General Motors, did not affiliate its Eisenach plant in east Germany (*Economist* 23 January 1993). Moreover, IBM's financial problems caused the company to disaffiliate from its employers' association in 1992, although this caused a rise in trade unionisation at the enterprise (*ibid.*).

The 1949 Constitution of the Federal Republic differs from the Weimar Constitution in an important respect: there was no attempt to enshrine the concepts of industrial democracy and specific collective bargaining rights, much less public ownership, in this new order. Under Section 9(3) of the Basic Law, the unfettered right to form a trade union is guaranteed and the state is strictly prohibited from intervening in industrial conflicts. It is thus left to the collective bargainers to autonomously determine money wages (*Tarifautonomie*) in a spirit of co-operation (*Mitwirkung*) and codetermination (*Mitbestimmung*) (Bendix 1978: 26–7). As a result there was no codified collective bargaining law and a general code has been formulated from rulings made by the courts (usually by the Federal Labour Court or the Federal Constitutional Court). In fact the judiciary have demonstrated that they are not bound by the text of the Constitution and that they have the power to create law if they wish (Aaron and Wedderburn 1972: 195). The founding of the Federal Republic also gave the Federal Labour Court the opportunity to begin anew without the burdens of precedent (*ibid.*: 268).

In other words, freedom of speech, assembly and association are respectively granted in general terms by Sections 5, 8 and 9 of the Basic Law, but the courts have asserted the right to rule on these concepts when applied to collective bargaining. Hence a strike is not legal unless supported by a trade union which *ipso facto* renders unofficial strikes, and probably sympathetic strikes, illegal (Kendall 1975: 125). A political strike is similarly unlawful – the only exceptions being first, a short token stoppage and, second, a possible right under Section 20(4) of the Basic Law to resist anybody who attempts to overthrow the constitutionally established order (Aaron and Wedderburn 1972: 328–30; Bendix 1978: 40–1). Peaceful picketing may be justified under the constitutional right of freedom of speech, but all employees who want to work must have free and secure access to the premises of an employer. Case law prohibits both force and mass picketing. However, whether groups of workers may pass a picket line, and whether insults hurled by a picket threaten secure access, are uncertain areas (Aaron and Wedderburn 1972: 274).

If the negotiation of new agreements results in a dispute of interests, the parties are considered to be at liberty to pursue sanctions, provided such sanctions are 'socially adequate'. The labour courts work from the premise that since all industrial disputes cause economic disruption, strikes are undesirable (ibid: 195 and 267; Bendix 1978: 37; Kendall 1975: 116; Rajewsky 1970: 67). All other means of resolving a conflict must have been explored before a strike is called. This in turn requires both parties to avoid industrial sanctions during the currency of an agreement – the so-called relative 'peace obligation', a concept which originated in Germany (Aaron and Wedderburn 1972: 169–70; *Die Zeit* 46/80).

Labour courts therefore play a crucial role in the Federal Republic. They operate at local, state and federal level and are composed of professional judges and lay wing members. In addition, the Big Senate, also at federal level, makes rulings on subjects of fundamental importance – such as cases on the holding of strike ballots and lockouts. The labour courts will hear cases brought as a result of either individual or collective disputes of rights. In the former case an employer/employee relationship is usually involved, although rival work groups may also take their disputes to the court. When the court arbitrates on collective disputes it does so either on the basis of a collective agreement or on the basis of the employer/ works council relationship (Ramm 1971). It is the latter which forms the core of industrial democracy. Before considering either of these critical bargaining relationships, however, it is necessary to examine the present-day German trade union movement in more depth.

THE STRUCTURE OF TRADE UNIONS

Following the affiliation of the police union in March 1978, the DGB had 17 affiliates with a then record total of 7.75 million members. The number of DGB unions returned to 16 when the smallest union (Arts and Media) merged with the printers in the late 1980s. In consequence, the IG Medien was formed. The affiliated unions are listed in their 1989 rank order (with 1950 data for comparison) in Table 6.1.

The difficulties involved in defining an 'industry' for the purposes of trade union organisation, and the consequent need for a DGB inter-union demarcation disputes procedure, will be clear from the titles of the unions (DGB *Geschäftsbericht* 1975– 7: 436; Taft 1952: 304). For example, when the police union was formed in the early 1950s it was prevented from becoming a DGB affiliate because the ÖTV claimed that it was the strongest and most suitable union for all public sector employees. On the other hand, the HBV voluntarily withdrew from organising a group of members and recommended that they join the more appropriate, and newly formed, IG Medien (FAZ 23 February 1993). Moreover, in order to secure greater organisational strength the IGC and IGBE planned to merge in 1993 (*Economist* 23 January 1993).

The 16 unions which affiliated to the DGB on its federal-wide foundation have subsequently had a diverse experience in terms of membership. Perhaps surprisingly, in view of the high level of cultural activity in every German city, plus the growth in television and film acting, the Arts union had almost the same member-

Table 6.1 DGB Affiliated Unions

Union	Membership			
	31 December 1989		31 December 1950	
	Number	*Rank*	*Number*	*Rank*
Metal Workers Union (IGM)	2,679,237	1	1,352,010	1
Public Services, Transport and Omnibus Crews (ÖTV)	1,234,546	2	726,004	2
Chemicals, Paper and Ceramics (IGC)	664,618	3	409,998	5
Post Office Workers (DPG)	472,145	4	190,500	9
Construction, Quarrying and Building Materials (BSE)	460,559	5	405,536	7
Commerce, Banks and Insurance (HBV)	407,326	6	63,600	14
Coal Mining and Power (IGBE)	331,106	7	580,661	3
Railway Workers (GdED)	319,641	8	426,059	4
Food, Drink and Catering Industries (NGG)	271,291	9	256,186	8
Textiles and Clothing (GTB)	250,783	10	409,924	6
Education and Science (GEW)	188,910	11	61,037	15
IG Medien	182,150	12	–	–
Police (GdP)	161,310	13	–	–
Printing and Paper Manufacture (IGD)	–	–	133,074	11
Timber and Plastics (GHK)	149,098	14	189,661	10
Leather (GL)	44,583	15	100,412	13
Market Gardening, Agriculture and Forestry (GGLF)	43,817	16	103,404	12
Arts (GK)	–	–	41,924	16
Totals	7,861,120		5,449,990	

Sources: DGB *Geschäftsbericht* 1950–1: 797; IW *Zahlen* 1991: 116 (author's translation)

ship at the end of 1978 as it had at the end of the DGB's first year in 1950. In fact its membership generally declined until 1970; following the decision to amalgamate with the printers, its membership declined to barely 30,000 in 1988. One reason may have been competition from the DAG. Less surprising on grounds of changes in the economic structure is the fact that membership in mining, rail, textiles, timber, leather and agriculture had secularly declined during the period covered by Table 6.1 (1950–89). Membership in metal, the public services, chemicals, the Post Office, construction, commerce, food and education had, on the other hand, increased. However, this overview of the period 1950–89 conceals the effect of cyclical fluctuations and other influences on sectoral trade-union membership. For example, during the shorter period 1978–89, metal membership remained static; commerce improved its overall ranking from 8 to 6 while education stagnated at rank 11 (IW *Zahlen* 1990: 117; Table 6.1).

Following unification, the western trade unions became key actors in the integration of the new Länder; indeed, this process presented a challenge second only to the reconstruction period following the demise of the Nazi regime in 1945 (Fichter 1993: 21). They made significant recruitment strides in the east. The rapid and extensive restructuring in the new Länder prevented the collection of precise data but the estimated eastern DGB membership at the end of 1990 was 3.3 million, compared to 7.9 million in the west (FRG Embassy London *Report* 2/92). Eastern membership in IG Metall was about 700,000, with the same number in ÖTV. Fichter (*ibid.*: 35) shows that in 1991 the DGB had an affiliated membership of 11.8 million: western membership had fallen to 7.6 million, while eastern membership had risen to 4.2 million. Hence, 36 per cent of the total DGB membership was located in the east, while total eastern manual and white-collar employment was 30 per cent of the western level (BMW *Wirtschaft . . .* 1992: 13). In fact, two unions (GEW and GGLF) had a larger absolute membership in the east, and in the HBV the relationship was almost 50:50 (Fichter *ibid*: 34). IGM spent DM 20 million in building a base in the east, although due to its large total membership only 27 per cent (990,553) of its members were located in the new Länder (*ibid.*; *Guardian* 21 March 1991). Nonetheless, it seemed that, in general, the unions with the highest rates of organisation in the west (IGBE, IGC, GdED, GL, IG Medien, GdP and DPG) showed a lower level of absolute membership increase in the east when compared to the unions with low rates of membership in the west (GEW, GGLF, HBV and ÖTV) (Fichter *ibid.*).

In 1992, total DGB affiliation fell by nearly 800,000 (FRG Embassy *ibid*. 6/93). Not surprisingly, rapidly rising unemployment caused most of this decline to be concentrated in the east. The three largest unions (IGM, ÖTV and IGC) accounted for 56 per cent of the total DGB affiliated membership, whereas the GGLF and GL contributed only 1.4 per cent. The western unions were surprised at the degree of support they enjoyed among the labour force in the east, especially given the legacy of Stalinist unions there. A possible reason was the pressure for active labour market policies which the DGB brought to bear on the Federal government (FT 10 April 1991). Trade unions, perhaps predictably in view of their established postwar role in the west, thus emerged in the east as a critical agent in economic and social affairs.

At a more general (or aggregated) level, Schnabel (1989: 134–5) has shown that *total* trade-union membership in West Germany exhibited a steady, albeit slow, increase until 1965 – with the exception of 1959. (The concept of *total* membership will be discussed below – Table 6.2.) Three years of decline in unionisation (1966–8) were followed by a period of rapid expansion (interrupted only in 1975) which reached its peak in 1981 with a membership of 9.34 million. In 1984, total membership was 3.5 per cent lower than in 1981. As will shortly be shown (Table 6.2), total membership in 1989 was 9.46 million, compared to 9.11 million in 1986 (Schnabel 1989: 135).

A secular expansion or contraction of membership is not the only relevant factor when estimating a trade union's potential bargaining power. Perhaps even more important is the level of organisation compared to the level of employment in an industry ('density'). Three industries are very highly organised in this sense. They are mining, the railways and Post Office employees, all of which probably have over 75 per cent of eligible employees in membership. Windolf and Haas (1989: 148) cite coal mining (and motor vehicles) as industries with a density of 90 per cent. But employees in the motor-vehicle industry are organised in the amorphous 'metal' industry which embraces occupations as diverse as steel making and light engineering. Industries with roughly 40 to 50 per cent density are metal, the public services, chemicals, printing and leather. Something like a third of the employees in textiles, timber, education and the arts are organised, whereas low densities are to be found in construction, catering, commerce and agriculture (Jühe et al. 1977: 62–78). Regionally, the highest trade union density is found in the Saar and the north (Grochla and Gaugler 1990: 2395).

The notion of trade union density can be analysed further with the aid of Table 6.2. By using the same table, it is also possible to explore the areas of interunion competition, although by comparison to pre-Second World War period this has not been all that significant. Finally, it is possible to analyse the concept of total trade-union membership mentioned earlier. A broad breakdown of the structural features of employees prior to unification is shown at the top of the table. Since the same structural features will emerge in the east, it is a good starting point for an overview of trade union density by broad occupational groups. Four introductory points must be made. First, the source of the data is a sample survey. Second, since the 1987 population census, this major data source no longer distinguishes between white-collar employees and manual workers – a reflection of the fact that there has been a convergence in their conditions of employment. Third, recall that the activity rate of females in the east was shown above to be double that of females in the west. Finally, it is not possible to fully understand the structure of the German labour force and trade unions without considering the

10 per cent of employees known as *Beamte*. Such a consideration will follow very shortly.

Initially, however, consider the total trade-union membership figures shown in Table 6.2. It can be seen that, in 1989, 7.86 million members were affiliated to the DGB. This represented the bulk of the total membership of 9.46 million. Moreover, the decline in total membership in 1959 referred to above was wholly attributable to a decline in DGB membership (Schnabel 1989: 135). However, the DGB membership had recovered by 1970 from the 1967 recession: it was 1973 before the DBB recovered and 1976 in the case of the DAG (*ibid*.). DAG membership was higher in 1989 than its previous peak in 1982; DGB membership was lower in 1989 than its 1981 peak, as was the membership of the DBB. Schnabel (1989) finds that the determinants of trade union growth in West Germany during the period 1955–86 were similar to those in other industrial countries, notably wages, prices, employment and unemployment. The first three variables are positively related to trade union growth, while unemployment is negatively related. The negative trend working against unionisation is more or less compensated for by the positive effect of other determinants, which are mostly related to the business cycle and which may be even partly influenced by trade unions. However, Schnabel's best estimation still leaves a quarter of trade union growth 'unexplained' – implying that unquantifiable and unsystematic influences may be at work.

Beamte (or public servants) are a unique German institution. They represent a social stratum in their own right. They receive a contract on appointment which specifies lifetime tenure and they enjoy guaranteed salary levels, together with

Table 6.2 Proportion of *Beamte*, White Collar Employees and Manual Workers organised in Trade Unions in 1989

Employees and unions	Beamte		White-collar employees		Manual workers		Totals		Females	
	No.	(%)	No.	(%)	No.	(%)	No.	(%)	No.	(%)
Employees in employment[1] (000)	2,424	9.8	11,612	47.0	10,682	43.2	24,713	100	9,724	39.3
Trade Union Members (000) of which										
DGB[2]	807.4	50.4	1,833.3	73.5	5,220.4	97.3	7,861.1	83.1	1,882.6	78.4
DBB[3]	701.2	43.7	72.7	2.9	19.7	0.4	793.6	8.4	216.3	9.0
DAG[2]	–	–	503.5	20.2	–	–	503.5	5.3	227.3	9.5
CGB[2]	95.1	5.9	84.8	3.4	124.8	2.3	304.7	3.2	75.8	3.2
Total	1,603.8	100.0	2,494.4	100.0	5,364.9	100.0	9,463.0	100.0	2,401.9	100.0
Density (i.e proportion of the relevant employee-group organised)		66.2		21.5		50.2		38.3		24.7
of which										
DGB		33.3		15.8		48.9		31.8		9.4
DBB		28.9		0.6		0.2		3.2		2.2
DAG		–		4.3		–		2.0		2.3
CGB		3.9		0.7		1.2		1.2		0.8

Source: IW *Zahlen* 1991: 11 and 117 (author's translations and calculations)

Notes: [1] Based on sample survey data (rounded)
[2] At 31 December 1989
[3] At 30 September 1989

generous non-contributory pension rights. In addition, they are not required to contribute to the unemployment-insurance fund while the employer assists with their private health-insurance contributions. In return, they are in theory required to accept certain limitations on their private lives. They are also required to relinquish the right to take industrial action. The Constitutional Court decided in 1993, however, that *Beamte* could not be used as strike breakers (FAZ 7 April 1993). This judgement – which overruled earlier findings by the Federal Labour and Public Administration Courts – was made as a result of an appeal by the postal workers against *Beamte* being substituted for its members when they took strike action. Note, therefore, that the term *Beamte* is often carelessly translated as 'civil servant'. Yet occupations classified as *Beamte* are not confined to civil servants, even if the term is broadly defined in the German context to typically include an appreciable proportion of employees in Federal, Länder and local-authority government. The term *Beamte* applies in addition to some members of the armed forces, judges, the police and customs officials. Teachers and university professors, as well as Bundesbank, Post Office and railway officials are also *Beamte*. For example, 60 per cent of Post Office employees are *Beamte* (*Statistisches Jahrbuch* 1992: Table 13.27). (It will be clear from this example that there is an appreciable overlap in the salary scales of senior *Angestellten* and the relatively lowly paid *Beamte*.) The unions representing *Beamte* are sometimes thought of as being purely lobby-organisations. They are probably more successful in maintaining parliamentary representation than the trade unions which negotiate collective agreements (Jühe *et al.* 1977: 154; McPherson 1971: 122–7).

It can be seen from Table 6.2 that the total density of *Beamte* (66.2 per cent) is relatively high. This high degree of organisation has to be compared to one in two manual workers and about one in five white-collar workers. Table 6.2 also shows that the DGB has been as successful as the DBB (*Deutscher Beamtenbund*) in organising *Beamte*. There are two types of *Beamte* organisation. The first is the professional association – that is to say an organisation which prefers the term 'association' to that of 'trade union'. Some of these associations are independent, others are affiliated to a central organisation. By far the largest central organisation is the DBB (807,400 members) which was established in 1950. A very small minority of its affiliated membership (see Table 6.2) are not *Beamte* and the associations responsible for such membership take part in the appropriate negotiations between the relevant employers' associations and other trade unions.

The most important independent association is that of the armed forces (DBV – 235,000 members). This association is the first of its kind in German history. Both active and former personnel – irrespective of rank – are eligible for membership and there are specialised departments for each service. Other independent associations are those of judges and attorneys (12,000) and university professors (8,000).

The other type of *Beamte* organisation carries the title 'union' and is affiliated to the DGB. These unions organise employees in education, the police, the Post Office, the railways and the various sectors organised by the ÖTV. All of them, to varying degrees, also organise white-collar employees and, with the exception of the educational union, manual workers. This again results in multi-purpose organisations which are represented on a number of negotiating bodies. The ÖTV may also often find itself technically negotiating in both the private and public sectors, since a number of municipal enterprises are registered in the legal form of private corporations. These DGB unions (with the probable exception of the police union) have challenged the long-held legal opinion that *Beamte* do not have the right to strike. Work-to-rules have been staged in the Post Office, on the railways, in tax offices and, during peak holiday periods, by air traffic controllers. This, of course, constitutes a form of industrial action but confrontation has been generally avoided by Federal and Länder authorities. A strike ballot for a one-day warning strike was prepared by the education union in 1972 and this union supported the 35-hour week claim which is explored below.

Similarly, some of the DGB unions and the DAG have competed for white-collar membership. The main areas of competition for members are commerce, banking and insurance (i.e. HBV in the DGB). The only other area of any significance is the public services, although ÖTV has always had far more white-collar employees in membership. Relations between the

DAG, on the one hand, and HBV and ÖTV, on the other hand, deteriorated over the years. Of late, however, there is increasing evidence that the DAG and HBV have cooperated, especially during industrial disputes (*Die Zeit* 13/92). A similar distinction to the one just drawn between *Beamte* organisations can be made in the case of white-collar unionism: the DAG is perceived as less militant than the DGB affiliates. In addition, the wage policies of the DAG and the DGB affiliates differ (Owen Smith *et al*. 1989: 111–16). This has all probably had an adverse effect on union density. It is important to see why.

Unlike the *Beamte*, the density of the white-collar employee group is low – just over one in five are organised in trade unions (see Table 6.2). The success of the DAG in this respect has been somewhat limited: the proportion of white-collar employees in the labour force organised by the DAG secularly fell from 10 per cent in 1951 to 4.3 per cent in 1989 (IW *Zahlen* 1989: 122; Table 6.2). On the other hand, the DGB unions more than doubled their white-collar organisation during the period 1950–89 – from 10.5 per cent to 23.3 per cent of their membership (calculated from DGB *Geschäftsberichte* and Table 6.2). Even the DGB rate of growth, however, was not sufficient to achieve anything more than a constant proportion of white-collar employees organised in DGB unions. This was because the number of these employees increased over three and a half times between 1950 and 1989 (3.2 million to 11.6 million), whereas the number of manual workers increased by only 8 per cent (9.9 million to 10.7 million) (BMA *Statistisches Taschenbuch*: 2.6; Table 6.2). Yet manual workers are on average twice as likely to join a trade union. Moreover, the proportion of employees in higher education increased during the 1980s – and there is a negative relationship between educational attainment and union density (Windolf and Haas 1989: 158–9). As a result the aggregate union density of the DGB and the DAG fell from 51 per cent in 1950 to 34 per cent in 1989 (IW *Zahlen* 1988: 123; calculated from Table 6.2). More particularly, white-collar union density has fallen from 29 per cent to 22 per cent – indeed, white-collar density now stands at almost half the level of 1931 (Hirsch-Weber 1959: 150; Table 6.2). It is this decline which would have to be arrested if aggregate union density is to recover. But this is precisely the area where inter-union competition is at its most intense. On the other hand, it is probably job characteristics that account for the low organisational density of females, some of whom are classified as white-collar employees. They are concentrated in small firms, in a few industries and occupations; about a third of them work part time. Interestingly enough, the degree of positive feeling towards union membership shown by both females and males seems to be identical (Windolf and Haas 1989: 153–4).

If one concentrates on absolute changes instead of relative increases in both white-collar and female unionisation, one can see that changes in the structure of the labour force were reflected in the structure of trade unionism. Total white collar membership of the DGB and DAG grew from just under a million in 1950 to almost 2.4 million in 1989; meanwhile, the number of manual workers increased by barely 400,000 from a base of 5 million (Hirsch-Weber 1959: 148 and 150; Table 6.2).

There are three associations affiliated to the CGB – one for manual workers, one for white-collar employees and one for public service employees. These three associations have, in turn, 18 trade unions in membership: 9 manual; 6 white-collar and 3 public service unions. Total membership of these unions was 304,700 in 1989. They are accorded somewhat tenuous negotiating rights in a number of industries. Coverage in the manual workers' association is of an industrial nature, reflecting to a large extent the predominantly manual worker organisations in the DGB (construction, metal, chemicals, mining and so on). The German Association of Commercial and Industrial White-Collar Employees was founded in Hamburg in 1950 in order to restore the former association of German clerks and its emphatic opposition to socialisation, Marxism and all forms of collectivism. It acknowledged the 'national characteristics of Christendom', the nation being a fundamental fact (Hartfiel 1966: 154–5; Kerr 1954: 542; Schuster 1973: 118). Second, the Association of Female White-Collar Employees is the only German trade union exclusively for women. It was founded in 1951 according to an old tradition 'guided by the thought of national solidarity, carried by the spirit of Christian ethics' (Hartfiel 1966: 156).

This survey of trade union structure can be concluded as follows. Historically, inter-union competition played a role in the lack of success in organising the growing proportion of white-collar workers. An alleged radical influence in the HBV may have caused some relatively minor disaffection to the DAG, although these two unions began to cooperate more closely early in the 1990s. Moreover, the growth in GEW membership may also be constrained by its militant stance. Similarly, the GK lost members during the prolonged merger talks with the printers, again because of the latter's perceived militancy (*Die Zeit* 16/89). The unique German institution of *Beamte* also causes organisational problems. Although not a serious problem, the Christian wing of the movement is still an alternative form of unionisation for DGB members. Nonetheless, there is a strong minority presence of Christian democrats in DGB unions. Indeed, successive Christian democrat Federal governments have consulted the trade unions on legislative change. Finally, in the post-wall era the east proved to be a fertile recruiting ground for the western trade unions.

TRADE UNION POLICY

In order to trace policy evolution, it will be useful to catalogue the main bargaining issues:

- ensuring a growth in pay rates sufficient to compensate for inflation and secure rising living standards
- determining the length of holiday entitlement
- reducing the length of the nominal working week
- influencing the course of other non-wage items (or 'fringe benefits')

When this wide view of collective bargaining is taken, it can be inferred that total labour costs in Germany are among the highest in the industrialised world. But it must be emphasised that this problem did not suddenly emerge with unification. If measured by the reaction of the Bundesbank to double-digit pay claims, for example, the increase in interest rates in 1991–2 followed the precedent of 1973–4 (Figures 4.2 and 4.4). Taking a somewhat arbitrary view, it can be said that the 1950s and 1960s represented a period of regaining and then consolidating real living standards. In the 1970s, non-wage benefits received more attention, while a radical reduction in working hours was the main bargaining issue of the 1980s. This is not meant to imply, of course, that the nominal working week was not reduced prior to the 1980s. But the first phase of its decrease preceded the rise in unemployment which accompanied the first oil price shock of 1974; when it emerged as a controversial bargaining issue in the 1980s, it was seen by some unions as being a means of redistributing the total volume of work (Bosch 1990: 611; Franz 1984: 629; Seifert 1991: 495–7). As will be shown in the 'problems' section below, the employers and State wanted to see more 'flexibility' in the labour market.

But the generalisation about the course of bargaining issues can be partly illustrated by comparing the course of labour costs at the end of the 1970s and the 1980s. By the middle of 1979 DGB unions had secured nominal pay increases averaging 4.6 per cent – approximately the same as the rate of inflation. This compared with 5.2 per cent in 1978 and 6.7 per cent in 1977. Reference is being made here to the average gross increase in pay per employee, excluding employers' social-insurance contributions and other non-wage items. While the increase in this average represented some real gains, they were not the primary cause for concern by the authorities. An even bigger policy problem was that pay for hours worked was constituting a smaller and smaller proportion of total labour costs. For example, in engineering (if one assumed pay for work done = 100), the index for average non-wage labour costs in 1970 was 47.6. By 1978 it had reached 68.2. This latter index yielded the following when subdivided: holiday and sick pay 27.3; holiday and other bonuses 13.5; and social-insurance contributions 27.4. Pay for work done had increased by 86 per cent since 1970; other labour costs had risen by 166 per cent (Himmelmann 1979: 259; IDS *International Report* 78). The clear trend was one of introducing both extra holiday pay and annual bonuses.

Subsequently, both white-collar and manual employees (who by then usually had the same holiday entitlement) became entitled to six weeks' annual holiday. Virtually all employees became entitled to an annual bonus equivalent to one month's pay (the literal translation of which is 'the thirteenth month's pay'). The trade unions were also beginning to seek a further reduction in working time. It is in the context of all these reforms that the social-policy developments analysed in Chapter 5 may be seen. The mandatory six-week period for sick pay met by employers was another such improvement. It should thus be appreciated that German unions are both a party in the field of collective bargaining within a *given* type of society and a movement for social reform (Hirsch-Weber 1963: 279–81; Kerr 1954: 536 and 555; Limmer 1966: 143–8; Roll 1939: 92).

By the end of the 1980s, nominal pay rates were increasing more modestly than at any time since 1950. Indeed, real pay rates had fallen over the previous year for seven years out of the ten-year period 1980–89 (BMA *Statistisches Taschenbuch*: 1.15). The first problem – already seen in Chapter 3 – was that relatively large deductions were being made from pay. Towards the end of the decade, average gross pay per employee was increasing at an annual rate of 3 per cent. The rate of increase in tax on pay *and* social-insurance contributions was over 4 per cent. Second, in two out of the three years when real pay rates rose (1986 and 1987), there was virtual price stability (Figure 4.4). But both before and after GEMSU, price inflation increased (Figures 3.10 and 3.11). On these two grounds, therefore, the relatively high pay claims at the beginning of the 1990s were to be expected. In the west, it is important to note, these pay claims would probably have been made even if the GEMSU treaty had not been signed. The 1990 tax reform – planned well before GEMSU – admittedly had an impact on real pay: it increased on average by 4.9 per cent (BMA *ibid*.; Figure 3.3). However, the income-tax surcharges in 1991 – a direct consequence of GEMSU – resulted in real pay falling by an average of 0.8 per cent (*ibid*.).

On the other hand, German holiday entitlements were internationally the highest (*Economist* 15 February 1992: 45). Furthermore, general trade union policy was to secure a 35–hour week in all sectors. The metalworkers' and printing unions were in the vanguard and they signed agreements which were to achieve that goal by 1995 (Bosch 1990: 617; Seifert 1991: 495). In 1990, a quarter of collective agreements specified a nominal 35-hour week (by 1995); a further two-thirds set nominal weekly hours at between 36 and 39 hours (WSI 1991: 93). Consequently, hours worked in manufacturing were the lowest in the world. Indeed, the general reductions in working time left Germany in 1990 with the shortest standard annual working time (1,648 hours) of all western industrialised countries: the equivalent statistic for the UK was 1,769 hours, the USA 1,904 and Japan (1989) 2,143 (Neifer-Dichmann 1991: 512). The cost implications of all these items is dramatically conveyed by Table 6.3. For example, in 1991, the average statutory non-wage labour costs analysed in Chapter 5 added 36.9 per cent to the wage bill for work done in industry and construction. A further 46.9 per cent was added by agreements reached either at the regional level between trade unions and employers' associations, or at the enterprise level between the works council and employer. Hence, total non-wage labour costs added on average 83.8 per cent to the wage bill for work done. In the banking sector –

where the unions were particularly militant in 1992 – employers paid on average DM 102.50 in 'fringe benefits' for every DM 100 paid for work done. Note the predictable uniformity in statutory non-wage items, but the major differences in collective and enterprise agreements.

But, as shown immediately above, these problems were already palpable at the end of the 1970s. For example, the Dresdner Bank had run a fairly regular series of international comparisons on labour costs in its *Economic Quarterly*; two such analyses appeared in August 1978 and November 1981. In 1981, it was shown, among other things, that British total hourly labour costs in manufacturing were 57 per cent of those in West Germany. However, at current DM exchange rates labour productivity was only 50 per cent of German levels. Hence, unit labour costs were 14 per cent higher in Britain ($57/50 \times 100 = 114$ per cent). The critical difference between the two countries is therefore the gap in manufacturing productivity. One of the underlying causes was the higher ratio of capital to labour in Germany. O'Mahony (1992: 52–3) estimated this ratio in 1987 to be 38 per cent higher, although her estimate of the overall productivity gap was 22 per cent per worker hour – considerably lower than the 40 per cent estimates made by other researchers (*ibid*.: 46). As well as greater capital intensity in Germany, lower skill levels *below* degree level in the British labour force in manufacturing may be another contributory factor to the inferior British performance (*ibid*.: 53–4). The greater number of hours worked in British manufacturing, which is due to higher overtime working, was most pronounced in engineering, vehicles and metals. On the other hand, British performance improved in the food, drink and tobacco industries when output per worker hour

Table 6.3 Non-wage Labour Costs in the Industrial, Construction and Service sectors
(enterprises with 50 or more employees)

Costs, contributions payments	*Percentage of remuneration for work done: 1991*				
	Industry and construction	*Wholesale sector*	*Retail sector*	*Banking sector*	*Insurance sector*
Employer's social-insurance contributions[1]	23.7	22.7	23.8	24.7	23.8
Paid national holidays and similar[2]	5.4	5.0	4.6	5.3	5.6
Sick pay	5.4	4.2	4.5	4.2	5.0
Other statutory non-wage labour costs[3]	2.4	1.5	1.4	1.1	1.2
Statutory non-wage labour costs: Total	36.9	33.4	34.3	35.3	35.5
Holiday pay	20.6	17.7	18.3	15.5	19.3
Special payments (bonus and '13 months' salary' payments)	10.0	8.2	8.1	21.2	15.2
Company pension-scheme contributions	9.0	4.4	3.3	16.5	17.4
Long-term savings with tax concessions	1.4	1.3	0.9	2.2	1.4
Other non-wage labour costs	5.9	4.2	6.6	11.8	8.7
Collectively-agreed and enterprise-level non-wage labour costs: Total	46.9	35.8	37.3	67.2	62.0
Total non-wage labour costs	83.8	69.2	71.5	102.5	97.5

Source: *KND* 17/92 (author's translation)

Notes: [1] This percentage differs from actual enterprise contribution rates because the basis for calculation is remuneration for work done. Remuneration for work done corresponds to total labour costs minus aggregate non-wage labour costs (see also Table 5.1)
[2] For methodological reasons, this row is calculated assuming a constant number of national holidays
[3] Insurance against industrial accidents, occupational disease; statutory payments for nursing mothers (see Table 5.1.)

instead of per worker was used as a comparative yard stick, although Germany still had a slight advantage. Perhaps significantly, the median plant size in both countries is greater in those industries where there is a productivity advantage (*ibid*.: 49 and 51). During the period 1968–87, the productivity gap reached a peak of 50 per cent in 1979–81. There was a substantial narrowing of the gap in the 1980s. Whereas German manufacturing output increased by 40 per cent between 1968 and 1987, however, the increase in Britain was 10 per cent; similarly, during the same period manufacturing employment in Germany fell by only seven per cent, compared to a decrease of 37 per cent in Britain. Moreover, 2.1 million of the three million jobs lost in British manufacturing during the period 1968–87 were shed in the 1980s.

This raises the central dilemma as far as the effects of collective bargaining are concerned: do the monopolistic influences exercised in both the labour and product markets by German unions and large companies influence wage determination in favour of highly unionised groups, or do large companies employ better-qualified, and therefore more productive and better-paid employees?. Neumann M. *et al.* (1980) of Nuremberg University found evidence of both effects, plus other efficiency gains. Their conclusion was that the two effects appear to cancel each other out. Conversely, Neumann M.J.M. *et al.* (1990) of Bonn University found that contract wages negotiated at the industry level followed the economy-wide growth in labour productivity. In addition, they found evidence of union influence having an adverse effect on employment, even though this was contrary to the union stance of neutrality in this respect. Schnabel (1991) surveys work which indicates that the negative and positive effects of unions on productivity almost counterbalance each other – although if anything the negative effects predominate. The relative degree of balance in Germany probably results from a legal prohibition of union wage differentials, and the unions' post-war contribution to the harmonious functioning of the economy (*Ordnungsfaktor*). A similar degree of balance with respect to the effects of German trade unions on real wages and productivity (with the latter predominating) was found by Wanik (1984). Finally, in attempting to resolve the 'puzzle' of why the inter-industry wage structure is similar in Germany and the USA – in spite of fundamental differences in the degree of unionisation – Fels and Grundlach (1990)

suggest that firms may raise wages above market-clearing levels in order to increase employees' effort.

It is also appropriate at this stage to consider the extent to which the western trade union structure and policy was rapidly introduced into the new Länder. The Hans Böckler Kreis (1990) saw no alternative, but warned that radically different attitudes had emerged over the forty-year period so that two contrasting movements had developed in totally different economic systems. They also warned that trade-union preparations for EC 1993 should not be neglected because of adapting to the changes caused by unification. Moreover, as Hoene (1991: 18) pointed out, in the planned eastern economy a labour market had not existed – except for some fringe black-market categories. The labour force had been allocated by plan, with the right to work anchored in the constitution and a network of highly subsidised social facilities (such as nurseries) provided by the State. In such a system the unions became purely administrative organs. The western unions rapidly filled the employee-representation vacuum created once a market economy was introduced. The rapid adjustment of eastern wage levels towards those prevalent in the west was effected by the West German unions who quickly assumed responsibility for wage negotiations in the new territory (Neumann 1991: 17–18). It was in the unions' interest in the 1990 pay round to achieve high wage increases immediately because this promised to attract a numerically strong eastern membership. It would also protect the western membership from potential wage competition. As a result, the wage round leader (the metal workers) achieved a stepwise progress to reach western standards by 1994. Similarly, public service employees were to achieve equality by 1995. Hence, wage levels in the two parts of the economy began to converge after unification. At the end of 1991 eastern negotiated wage rates had reached approximately 60 per cent of the western standard (MRDB 2/92: 5). However, the chairman of the DGB estimated that when considered net of fringe benefits and working-time differences, real earnings in the east would remain 30 per cent below western levels in the mid-1990s (FT 10 April 1991).

Nonetheless, one of the most striking consequences of GEMSU was the enormous increase in eastern real wages that accompanied it; there were also reductions in the length of the nominal working week, with 40 hours common to many agreements (Akerlof *et al*. 1991: 56). Some combination of five factors is probably responsible for the wage increases in the east (*ibid*.: 57–64):

- as compensation for higher social-insurance contributions and the removal of price subsidies
- in the interests of equity between east and west
- as a reflection of trade union perceptions about their eastern members' economic welfare
- in order to enhance trade union solidarity between east and west, as well as reducing the possibility of wage cutting in the west
- as a result of management offering no effective resistance to union pay claims

A survey based on a total of 663 questionnaires (*ibid*.: 43), plus an estimation that wages exerted an important influence on costs and therefore employment (*ibid*.: 25), caused these researchers to qualify these views. Hence, a variation of the possible explanations for rapid pay rises is that this was a rational goal for the unions to pursue. Higher earnings would produce higher unemployment benefits in the ultimate contingency, although the government was committed to maintaining high employment levels. Recruitment of new members in the east could therefore be boosted without unduly undermining bargaining power in the west because of the presence of a pool of desperate unemployed eastern competitors in the labour market.

Rationality was only the first of two levels on which this aspect of trade-union wage policy could be viewed. Employers' associations, the Bundesbank, the Federal government and the economic research institutes all took a highly critical view of union policy. The union posture changed perceptibly following the first all-German election when the government pledged no one would be worse off as a result of unification. Prior to this, the DGB put forward the notion of forgoing part of any pay claim and paying the proceeds into a special fund earmarked for investment in the east – a notion that was subsequently revived and applied much more generally by the Federal government, even though the leader of IG Metall was sceptical about the proceeds of such a fund finding their way to the east (*Der Spiegel* 8/91; *Guardian* 3 April 1992). (Following the election, the DGB would probably have been content to allow growth and skill shortages in the west to dictate the pace of pay rises. Because of the severity of the 1992–3 recession, however, this plan would have attracted little support from its affiliates.) The Federal government continued to advocate a 'solidarity pact'. Their favoured model was to surcharge unemployment-insurance contributions. In order to also include *Beamte*, the Federal government proposed postponing their 1993 and 1994 salary increases for four months in each case. (Other public-sector employees in the west received a three per cent increase from the beginning of 1993.) This still meant that the self employed would not contribute to the 'pact'. As a result, some commentators favoured including *Beamte* and the self employed in the unemployment-insurance surcharge or 'solidarity contribution'. As things transpired, the 1993 pay increase for senior *Beamte* was frozen for four months; Federal government ministers decided to forgo a pay rise for two years.

A few policy implications of GEMSU should be emphasised at this stage. The trade unions seemed to attract more adverse criticism for their stance on pay equalisation than the Federal politicians who promised costless unification and the Bundesbank's policymakers who overreacted and savagely deflated the economy. Yet Chapter 3 demonstrated that the belated indirect tax rises designed to contribute to the costs of unification were inflationary, while Chapter 4 showed that the Bundesbank's Council were already obsessed with domestically generated inflation prior to GEMSU. Monetary targeting, moreover, was carried out using an aggregate behaving in an unpredictable manner and in any case set inappropriately low. True, by 1993 the threat of international speculation against the DM was partly brought about by Germany's inflation rate being untypically higher than in other G7 countries. But the recessionary trends in the German and other EC economies were exacerbated by German monetary policy. (Chapter 8 concludes with an assessment of whether these trends represented structural decline rather than a cyclical blip.) It was also seen in Chapters 3 and 4 that both the Federal government and the Bundesbank's Council subscribed to supply-side doctrine. Taken to its logical conclusion this should have produced, among other things, a perfectly functioning labour market. Pay rates would fall until employment levels recovered – see the concluding section below. A more realistic alternative was put forward by Akerlof *et al.* (1991). This alternative, which will also be discussed in the concluding section of this chapter, envisaged subsidisation by means of a 'self-eliminating flexible employment bonus'. It is only necessary here to point out that this subsidy was more realistic in two senses. First, it recognised the disastrous effect of GEMSU exchange rates which had hopelessly overvalued assets in the east and destroyed East Germany's export markets. Second, Chapters 7 and 8 will demonstrate that German capital and product markets function in a largely irretrievably imperfect manner. (Some economic strengths may nonetheless have resulted from the nature of these markets.) As a result of resolute opposition to the equalisation process, however, the first official strike held in eastern Germany for sixty years took place in 1993. This dispute is analysed at the end of this section. Before that stage of the argument is reached, however, there are a number of evolutionary features of West German union policy which require analysis.

It is not, of course, meant to imply that disputes were unknown in West Germany prior to unification. However, trade union bargaining power was constrained in important respects. True, there is free collective bargaining in the sense that the decision to conclude an agreement is essentially left to the bargainers (see *Tarifautonomie* above). But the Collective Agreements Act 1949 (as amended in 1952, 1969 and 1974) lays down the possible contents of a collective agreement. It also regulates the applicability of the agreement, defining the parties (trade unions and employers' associations) who may conclude such agreements and finally provides that all agreements must be registered at the Federal Ministry of Labour. These agreements are detailed, diverse and numerous. Something like 300,000 are registered in the specially created section of the Ministry. Some may be in respect of only a particular region's wage agreement, applying to a particular industry during the current annual wage round (*regionale Lohnabkommen*). More rarely there will be similar agreements with federal-wide application (*bundesweite Tarifverträge*). Finally, there will be a whole series of more comprehensive and general agreements (for three to five years) which cover holiday pay, holiday entitlements, lengths of the working week and so on (*Mantel-* or *Rahmentarifverträge*). Once registered, agreements are legally binding on both parties and both the Federal and Länder governments have powers to enforce the conditions therein as statutory minima (*Rahmentarife*). Militant action during the currency of an agreement breaches the 'peace obligation' which derives from the legally binding nature of agreements: such a breach could result in litigation (Aaron and Wedderburn 1972: 132; Hofmeier 1976: 5; Kendall 1975: 124; Kerr 1954: 539; Owen Smith *et al.* 1989: 82; Reichel 1971: 469.) The employer, but not the union, may register plant agreements (Reichel 1971: 473).

In addition, the Federal Labour Court laid down a rigorous case law on the conduct of industrial disputes and the DGB and BDA both built up their own strict codes of practice. The emergence of case law coincided with a hardening of attitudes on the part of employers (Cullingford 1976: 26–7). The trend in unofficial action showed a marked upward trend in the 1960s, even though unofficial strikes are strictly speaking illegal (Clark 1979: 243; Hofmeier 1976: 6; Kendall 1975: 130n). But in 1974 the DGB revised its

voluntary code of conduct in three important respects. First, strikes could be used to achieve legislative aims and strike action could be used if negotiations seemed to be serving no useful purpose – as opposed to strikes being a measure of last resort; second, the DGB maintained that there was no law to support the Federal Labour Court's 1958 ruling that strike ballots can be defined as industrial action – affiliates should therefore feel free to prepare for industrial action in this or any other way; third, in the event of employers retaliating with a lockout, affiliates should lay down rules on whether and how selective emergency work should be carried out by their members (Incomes Data Services *Report* 192). In the 1970s and 1980s relatively bitter official strikes took place in the public sector and the 'metal' industry (Owen Smith *et al.* 1989: chs 7 and 9).

It has just been seen, however, that the collective bargaining system was delivering the goods. Possibly as a result of this factor, the Federal Republic loses comparatively few days per worker through strike action. Where strikes have occurred, however, important breakthroughs have been made – the phased introduction of the 35-hour week being a particular case in point. Moreover, all unions have strict rules about the procedure to be followed before a strike is called, including in most cases at least 75 per cent of those voting in a strike ballot being in favour of strike action. The DAG also requires only a 25 per cent vote in favour of ending a strike (Dittmar 1978: 152–4).

Finally, the silence of the constitution on the question of the lockout has not prevented the Federal Labour Court from ruling in 1955 (and 1971) that employers also have the right to take retaliatory action. In effect this has inhibited unions from staging selected strike action at strategically important plants, which would have enabled them to reduce the costs of strike action. In such circumstances the employers' association may legally encourage a lockout of any or all union members in as many plants as it chooses. The Labour Court's ruling has consistently been challenged on three counts. First, that a lockout is not analogous to strike action. Second, the employer's bargaining power lies in his ability to withdraw or reduce employment opportunities and his pricing decisions affect real wages. Third, the balance of power is already unequal, with the employer having the advantage (*Die Zeit*, 13/78). Further, all the costs of strike action fall on the union, because there can be no call on public funds (supplementary benefits, etc.) or tax refunds in the event of strike action. However, another factor which more conceivably reduced trade union bargaining power was a decision of the Federal Labour Court in 1967 that closed shops are contrary to the constitution (Cullingford 1976: 14–15). Where union density is high, however, the law may on occasions be disregarded (Miller 1978: 340). Indeed, Windolf and Haas (1989: 149, 155–6) show that in large firms in particular there is a positive effect on union membership which arises from the existence of a highly organised works council: unions have relied on this system as a means of enforcing 'quasi-obligatory membership'. Theoretically – as will be seen in the next section – there is an important legal distinction between collective bargaining at the company and regional level. There should accordingly be a strict separation of powers.

In the first significant post-war dispute over pay and conditions of service, the issue was one of equality between manual workers and white-collar employees, particularly in the terms of sick pay. The strike – although it had *very* important national implications – took place in Schleswig-Holstein. It began on 24 October 1956 and ended on 14 February 1957. It involved 34,000 engineering workers and affected 38 plants. The strikers, who were members of IG Metall, received the equivalent of half pay from the union during the strike. The employers formed a 'solidarity fund'. The strike committee, besides publishing a four-page daily newspaper, ran a huge entertainment programme for strikers and their families. A majority of 88 per cent had voted in favour of strike action; the first proposals by the mediator were rejected by 97.4 per cent. On 30 January 1957 IG Metall signed a compromise agreement only to have it rejected by a 76.2 per cent majority. The union's advice was again rejected in early February, but the majority fell to 57.7 per cent and this meant a return to work (the necessary majority for continuing the strike was 75 per cent). There were two important consequences. First, a major step towards equality with white-collar workers (which was subsequently realised when an Act governing sick pay was introduced by the Federal government in 1957). Second, in 1958 the Federal Labour Court declared that the first strike ballot had been held five days before the peace obligation had expired, although the union had denied this. The court found for the employers and awarded them DM 18 million damages against the union. However, the employers did not press for payment but settled for the reintroduction of a conciliation agreement. (This paragraph was drawn from: Aaron and Wedderburn 1972: 41n, 133 and 153; Cullingford 1976: 25; Grosser 1974: 312; Kendall 1975: 125; Owen Smith *et al.* 1989: 39 and 86; Rajewsky 1970: 69–74; Schuster 1973: 54).

The next serious confrontation occurred

in 1963, this time in the Nordwürttem-berg-Nordbaden region where both IG Metall and the employers (led at this juncture by Hans Schleyer) took equally militant lines. Indeed, when this annual phase of collective bargaining is completed, a broadly acceptable pattern for the rest of the economy will normally have emerged. (Note again, therefore, the *national* implications of *regional* collective bargaining.) The employers planned a wide offensive for 1963 and instead of a few key firms being strike bound (as the union had intended when it received an 85 per cent backing for the strike) 900 firms employing 450,000 in two regions staged a lockout for the first time since 1928. IG Metall then held a strike ballot in the Ruhr, and other DGB unions pledged support, but the Economics Minister acted as conciliator and persuaded both sides to accept a compromise 5 per cent increase.

In 1957–8 and 1963 the decisions of the labour courts and the tactics of employers reduced the official strike propensity. However, in 1968 the dramatic recovery of the economy from the 1967 recession brought about increases in profits which outstripped the increase in wages. Hence by September 1969 there was a rank and file revolt. The number of working days lost in 1969 was a negligible factor (249,000); it was the unofficial nature of this short period of strike action which was the significant feature. Income distribution had suddenly been skewed in favour of the employers and West German employees were being required to work for 1969 profits at 1968 wages (Riemer 1983: 177–8). IG Metall and the coal miners' union were therefore both obliged to renegotiate agreements (*ibid.*: 73; Cullingford 1976: 30–2). Greater rank and file pressure was exerted on trade union leaders after 1969. In 1971, 4.5 million working days were lost through lockouts

(1.9 million) and strike action (2.6 million) – at that stage the highest total in the post-war history of the Federal Republic; 21.8 working days per 100 employees were lost as a result of strike action (BMA *Statistisches Taschenbuch*: 3.4). Only the 35–hour week confrontations in 1978 and 1984 resulted in a comparable ratio: 21.4 and 28.6 respectively. Another notable exception was the ratio of 11.7 in 1951 – but the issue in that year was codetermination, as will be shown in the next section. The ratio was otherwise often less than one in the period 1952–89.

Confrontations during the 1970s and 1980s involved at least four important bargaining considerations. First, in the case of the somewhat abortive chemical workers strike in 1971 there was inflexible opposition from the employers to a pay claim. The opposition was on the grounds that financial losses were being incurred. Large dividends were nevertheless declared (Cullingford 1976: 46 and 52; Dzielak 1978: 63ff; Ebsworth 1980: 66–7). A similar situation obtained during the north German dock strike of 1978. Second, the public-sector strikes in 1974 were in effect caused by government pay policy; a similar attempt at imposing an incomes policy was made in 1981, 1982 and 1992 (Clark 1979: 254; Owen Smith *et al.* 1989: 106 and 116). Third, a threat of technological unemployment in the printing industry was the primary cause of the fairly frequent confrontations in this industry (Himmelmann 1977). A similar fear provoked the IG Metall strikes in North Baden in 1978 (*Die Zeit*, 15/78). Lockouts were again used during the printing and engineering strikes in 1978. It induced both unions to file 35,000 law suits to have lockouts declared illegal. (In June 1980 the Federal Labour Court confirmed its 1955 and 1971 rulings that retaliatory lockouts are legal.) Fourth, the steel industry strike in late 1978 was called to press a claim for a 35-hour week in order to offset the mounting redundancies. The claim as such failed and the employers again responded with a lockout; rank and file anger also turned on IG Metall after a settlement was reached (Owen Smith et al. 1989: 196 and 249). This gave a fillip to union attempts to renegotiate its procedure agreement so that warning (token) strikes could be held during negotiations. At the end of 1979 an agreement was reached which limited the duration of the peace obligation to six weeks – two weeks before the expiry of an agreement and four weeks afterwards. In retrospect, the 1978–9 strike marked a breakthrough. But the major 'metal' industry strike of 1984, followed by large-scale token strikes in 1987–8, secured the virtual transition to the 35-hour week in that industry (ibid.: 212–13).

The final settlement in the 1991 pay round – which again affected steel workers – was reached in February 1992 only after a vote overwhelmingly in favour of strike action. It was for a 6.4 per cent increase in pay which was below the 6.7 per cent average for that pay round. But it removed any hope of a rapid reduction in the record rates of interest and contributed to the formulation of union pay claims in the 1992 pay round. In banking, a settlement of 5.4 per cent was reached after token strike action. The BDA emphasised that the banks were in an incomparably more prosperous economic position than all other sectors, including the public service. They joined the Federal government and Bundesbank's policymakers in warning that other settlements should not exceed the 4 per cent inflation rate. Indeed, the Federal government rejected a conciliated public-sector settlement of 5.4 per cent, stating that 4.8 per cent plus a lump sum payment was its final offer. In principle,

this dispute resembled the course of its 1974 predecessor: the Federal government was attempting to implement a pay guideline via the public sector. As in 1974, this produced a rank and file demand for strike action. There were, however, two differences from 1974. First, the high costs of unification were increasingly acknowledged by the Federal government and there had been a consequent appeal for a solidarity pact. Second, there had been no public-sector conciliation machinery in 1974. Before 1992 and 1993 are analysed in a little more depth, therefore, both the evolution of conciliation and government involvement in pay determination must be examined.

Third-party involvement, in the form of conciliation, has in fact been an important strike substitute, particularly in the more prominent controversies; the 35-hour week disputes would undoubtedly have been more prolonged if conciliators had not been involved (ibid.: 126 and 212). In 1968 – according to one of the few other pieces of empirical research in the area – there were 293 conciliation agreements between trade unions and employers' associations. They covered about 10.3 million employees (Königbauer 1971: 15). Perhaps 5 per cent of all wage settlements are reached by means of conciliation. There had been well over 1,000 conciliations by 1972 (Külp et al. 1972: 15). The Federal Labour Court 'demands that a strike is preceded by an arbitration procedure' (Bendix 1978: 44). It is only after this stage that both parties are released from their peace obligation. The DGB and BDA concluded a basic conciliation agreement in 1954 and this model was adopted in agreements among their affiliates (Owen Smith et al. 1989: 37–9). This gave rise to a voluntary system which contrasted to the compulsory Weimar system, although the Federal Ministry of Labour had threatened an Arbitration Act when a voluntary system did not initially materialise after a 1950 agreement between the DGB and BDA (Aaron and Wedderburn 1972: 297).

Politicians will generally offer their services as mediators after a strike has commenced and the normal arbitration procedure has been exhausted. At the time of the first post-war threatened lockouts in 1962, the prime minister of Baden-Württemberg (Dr Kiesinger – a future chancellor) persuaded the parties to return to the negotiating table. During the more bitter, and escalating, 1963 strikes and lockouts, the federal Minister of Economics (Professor Erhard) intervened and chaired meetings between the two parties. The Minister of Labour in North Rhine-Westphalia (NRW) involved himself in the 1976 printing and the 1978–9 steel strikes and lockouts, and the mayor of Hamburg intervened during the 1978 dock strike. Following an 87 per cent majority vote in favour of strike action in the Ruhr steel industry, the prime minister of NRW (Johannes Rau) assisted the bargainers in reaching an eleventh-hour settlement in 1992. This latter dispute possessed many typical characteristics of post-war German collective bargaining: a claim based on profits in the previous time period; union complaints that increased taxes had undermined members' living standards; the Bundesbank implying that interest rates would be raised above their already record levels if it regarded the settlement as inflationary; the settlement being regarded as a benchmark by other unions; public sector employers determined to set an example in terms of pay restraint; and the economic research institutes isolating wage inflation (as well as government spending) as being an obstacle to a revival of economic activity.

In the meantime a much more forma-lised system had emerged in the public sector. Until 1974 there was no machinery for arbitration of interest-disputes in the public sector (McPherson 1971: 190–1). Major disputes had not previously occurred in this sector. The 1974 strikes and a number of work-to-rules, however, followed the general pattern of a relative increase in militancy. As a result of the 1974 strikes, a conciliation agreement was reached by the parties in the public sector (Owen Smith *et al.* 1989: ch. 7). It was used for the first time in 1976 (Keller 1983; Owen Smith *ibid.*). Its credibility was undermined in 1992 when the Federal government declined to accept the majority recommendation of the conciliation committee. This was because the employers' side had a preconceived 'guide-line'. Yet the cause of the 1974 strikes and the resort to conciliation in 1982 and 1983 were the result of analogous negotiating stances by government (Owen Smith *ibid.*). Following large majorities in the public-sector unions favouring strike action in the west, widespread strike action took place in 1992. Although the costs of unification had become a contentious policy issue, the credibility of the conciliation agreement was undermined by the employers' attempt to keep any settlement below 5 per cent, compared to the unions' claim for 9.5 per cent. Since an offer of 4.8 per cent had been made prior to the conciliation, and the conciliation committee had recommended a 5.4 per cent increase in pay, the bargaining issue was whether a confrontation should take place over such a small difference (FAZ 27 April 1992). Even the signal given to other bargainers by the acceptance of the conciliators' recommendation would have been salutary under the circumstances: both the engineering and construction industries faced a similar claim/offer configuration.

Consider also the more general role of government in collective bargaining, as opposed to its more direct influence in the public sector. Although the principle of free collective bargaining (*Tarifautonomie*) constrains overt government intervention, it is necessary to recall the phase of Concerted Action. In 1967 there was, by German post-war standards, quite a serious recession. The Economics Minister of the time therefore introduced the Promotion of Economic Stability and Growth Act. This Keynesian-based Act sought among other things to establish the voluntary co-operation of the trade unions in a type of incomes policy (Lembruch and Lang 1977: 202; Hudson 1980). Employers and government would also be represented. Hence a formal attempt at wage moderation was channelled through an institution known as 'Concerted Action'. This attempt to introduce an incomes policy and distributive equity was an integral part of the new approach to stabilisation and exchange-rate policies discussed in the budgetary policy section of Chapter 3. This policy framework was dubbed the 'new economics'.

Informal efforts in this direction had been attempted as early as 1960 and 1963, but they were without any real measure of success (Cullingford 1976: 34). However, the first two years of Concerted Action were successful in terms of wage restraint: there was a remarkable correlation between government guide-lines and actual basic wage and salary movements (Clark 1979: 248). Not surprisingly, as economic growth began to exceed the growth in real wages, there was some rank and file disenchantment; as profits increased with rapid economic recovery in 1968 and 1969, rank and file discontent could ultimately be no longer suppressed. The result was the unofficial 1969 strikes. 'Social symmetry' had become an 'empty formula' (Riemer

1983: 177). The two foremost proponents of the new economics – Schiller and the SVR – had been unable to make good their distributive promise to labour (*ibid.*: 178). As a result, the wage restraint effects of Concerted Action were less successful after 1969. There was a change in the DGB approach: every effort was made to include variables other than money wages. Long-term policy issues, as well as prices and profits, received attention from the union side. In effect, Concerted Action became a forum for an exchange of general information. The SVR, on the other hand, became obsessed with profit margins; the latent threat of joblessness was its main labour-market penalty as early as 1971 (*ibid.*: 189–90). Moreover, when companies raised prices in 1973, rather than matching union wage restraint, IG Metall faced another rank-and-file rebellion (*ibid.*: 193–4). It was little wonder that this union relinquished its traditional initiative in wage rounds. In 1974 the mantle passed to the ÖTV and the bitter public-sector conflict ensued.

In 1977, the trade unions boycotted the 40th session of Concerted Action. This was as a protest against an employers' challenge in the courts of the statute which extended co-determination rights (see below). Following the failure of the challenge, preliminary contact between the employers and trade unions to discuss economic problems began again, although a full, formal resumption of Concerted Action was ruled out. The fall of the social-liberal coalition in 1982 marked the end of efforts to stimulate formal contact between the trade unions and the Federal government. In 1985, after much preliminary work, tripartite talks with the BDA were scheduled to recommence (IDS *International Report* 247). Pension reform was to be one of the topics but another social-insurance issue – the events leading up to the Act to Safeguard the Neutrality of the Federal Labour Office (Chapter 5) – caused the DGB to withdraw in protest.

Sufficient background material has now been provided for a further consideration of the eventful years of 1992 and 1993. It will be recalled that the public-sector dispute in 1992 resulted in strike action. The conciliators' award of 5.4 per cent had not been accepted by the Federal government. Ultimately, the government settled for 5.5 per cent. But the ÖTV leadership had raised expectations of a slightly higher settlement and the deal was rejected in the subsequent ballot. This unique situation was resolved by the imposition of the settlement and the voting out of office of a union executive. Subsequently, IG Metall, the construction workers and, following conciliation, IG Medien all settled for 5.8 per cent. IGM, in spite of its experiences in 1969 and 1973, also made a settlement of 3 per cent for the following year. Given the forecasts at that time of a 4 per cent inflation rate, along with the increase in VAT in 1993, a decrease in real pay was inevitable. In other words, the settlement was a prelude to the moderation in pay claims considered to be the unions' contribution to the solidarity pact. Recall also that earnings historically increased more rapidly than in competitor economies. West Germany's superior productivity growth record meant, however, a slower comparative rise in unit labour costs. This situation still obtained within the EC at the beginning of the 1992 pay round (FT 8 May 1992). In addition, the fall in labour's share in the national income, which had commenced in 1982, had also continued (BMA *Statistisches Taschenbuch*: 1.9). (It was seen above that the goal of reducing working hours had been substituted for high pay claims.) *The Times* (17 January 1992) had argued that 'German

unions have unfairly been made the scapegoat for the cost of unification.'

The 1993 pay round in the west was just as intriguing. It clearly illustrated the critical policy linkages. ÖTVs claim was for 5 per cent, compared to 9.5 per cent at the beginning of the previous pay round. This claim immediately raised hopes that the eventual level of settlements would be around the 3 per cent mark – a level that the Bundesbank's policymakers considered necessary to stem inflation in the west. Reductions in short-term interest rates could then be made. On 2 February 1993, the ÖTVs leader (Monika Wulf-Mathies) held a confidential discussion with the Federal interior minister, before which she had insisted that the 2.8 per cent offer was unacceptable. She had added that there would have to be a '3' before the decimal point, having possibly recalled the previous year's ballot defeat. The settlement announced later was for 3 per cent and the Bundesbank's Council – which was meeting on the same day – reduced the discount rate from 8.25 per cent to 8.0 per cent and the Lombard rate from 9.5 to 9.0 per cent (see Figure 4.4d). (Turbulence within the ERM had persisted since September 1992. The Irish punt had been devalued by 10 per cent the weekend prior to the Council's meeting on 2 February 1993 and the Danish krone was under severe pressure. High interest rates in the EC were causing steep rises in unemployment.) Subsequent private-sector settlements confirmed the trend to moderation, with increases below inflation.

It was, however, the vexed question of pay equalisation between east and west which was the major policy issue. There were two essentially extraneous factors. First, within the EC the British government was stressing the country's relatively low wages and social charges. Advertisements had appeared in the German press extolling this comparative advantage. (Fears of 'social dumping' were raised: companies would be attracted to low-cost member states, thereby depressing earnings and other conditions of employment in EC economies where social charges were higher – see Table 6.3 above and the discussion of the social charter at the end of the industrial democracy section below.) Second, eastern European economies offered prospects of labour costs which were 10 per cent of German levels. Domestically, employers in the 'metal' industry unilaterally withdrew in February 1993 from a prevailing agreement which would have meant a phased pay increase of 26 per cent. Such a withdrawal was a unique event in the post-war period. IG Metall suspected, probably correctly, that the dispute would endanger the west's national bargaining system. Attempts at conciliation failed, although a significant modification to the chemicals agreement was achieved by this means. There were 85–95 per cent majorities in favour of strike action in the 'metal' industry. In consequence, there was a campaign of gradually spreading strike action during the first fortnight of May. Ultimately, the compromise settlement retained the principle of equalisation, but postponed its achievement until 1996 – two years later than originally envisaged. Moreover, individual companies could invoke a further postponement if this would improve the probability of their remaining economically viable.

The previous paragraph is therefore full of implications for the possible future course of collective bargaining in both east and west Germany. In particular, Germany's national bargaining system may not survive intact. This system may promote stability and avoid leapfrogging at plant level, although it is seen as producing inflexibility by some observers. In addition, the termination of a collective agreement did not augur well for the conduct of industrial relations in the united Germany. In a limited sense, the situation resembled the deterioration in bargaining relationships at the end of the Weimar Republic (Owen Smith et al. 1989: 33–4). A further indication of change was the emergence during the 1980s of a new generation of union leaders who were not active during the post-war reconstruction. There was also evidence of a gradual increase in rank and file militancy after 1969, but the Federal Republic's strike record remains low by international standards. A number of constraints operate which would in any case tend to reduce strikes: case-law developments, lockouts, third party involvement, strike ballots and the peace obligation. Moreover, there was an extension of codetermination rights during the 1970s and, along with the existence of works councils with bargaining rights at establishment level, this perversely somewhat undermined the trade unions – at least during the period 1952–72. Attempts by trade unions to introduce criteria other than profitability and efficiency into company decision making were met by the successful resistance of the internal board members (Streeck 1984a: 397). These were the opposite effects to those intended by the unions: they had perceived the extension of industrial democracy as a means of furthering wider policy aims. In addition, even though the Bonn constitution does not contain sections on labour and social matters, such reforms were seen as part of the social framework – as already shown in Figure 5.1. Within the social framework itself, however, the questions of unemployment and the reform of the social-insurance systems had become more urgent policy issues (Nutzinger and Backhaus 1989: 169; Chapter 5 above). Nonetheless, the notion of an economically *and* socially efficient enterprise is an aim of the SME (Grochla and Gaugler 1990: 412). Hence, because of the fundamental importance of developments in industrial democracy to an account of the German labour market, such developments are now examined.

DEVELOPMENTS IN INDUSTRIAL DEMOCRACY

When the British created the German Steel Trusteeship Administration, in order to decartelise and deconcentrate this industry, they invited the trade unionists to participate in the process. In 1947, eight large concerns were broken down into 24 smaller companies, each with the two traditional boards of directors. (The supervisory board (*Aufsichtsrat*) meets about four times annually and concerns itself with long-term strategy. A collegiate executive board (*Vorstand*) elects a 'spokesman' who, in effect, acts as chief executive. The executive board is responsible for day-to-day management.) In accordance with the British edict, the supervisory board of each new steel company was composed of five employee representatives, five shareholders' representatives and an eleventh member from the Trustee Board (Berghahn 1986: 213–14 and 219; Spiro 1954: 1115). The executive board was expanded to include a union-nominated labour director who was to co-operate closely with the works council. Members of the works council were elected representatives of both manual and white-collar workers. This council provided two members of the supervisory board; a further member was provided by the industry's union and the DGB supplied one member directly and nominated the fifth (Spiro *ibid.*).

In 1950 it became clear to the unions that legislation which did not envisage employee representation on supervisory boards was a distinct probability. Strike ballots were therefore conducted in both the iron and steel industry and coalmining (the *Montan* industries). Majorities of over 90 per cent in both industries were in favour of strike action if the CDU government did not agree to place the extant system of industrial democracy on a statutory footing. The unions also pressed for the legislation to extend the iron and steel model to coal – an industry in which the unscrambling process had been even more difficult. Adenauer, the Federal Chancellor at that time, expressed the view that such a strike threat was political in character. Ultimately, however, he was forced to make an eleventh-hour concession and in 1951 the Co-determination Act confirmed the parity and labour director provisions described in the previous paragraph. An 'impartial' eleventh man on the supervisory board, however, was now elected by a majority of at least three on each side; otherwise a complex mediation procedure is required. Moreover, two representatives on the supervisory board are proposed by the works council, two by the union and a further 'outsider' by the DGB. These provisions were extended to the coal industry by the same Act with the result that the strike threat was lifted in both industries. For many, this Montan model of industrial democracy was to become the symbol of social justice in post-war West Germany. (On this paragraph, see: Berghahn 1986: 223–9; Hirsch-Weber 1959: 92–3 and 151ff; McPherson 1951: 24–5; Schuster 1973: 37–8; Sturmthal 1964: 61; Taft 1952: 310; Wächter 1992: 260).

This still left the rest of German industry without legislation on 'codetermination' as defined by the 1951 Act. Hostility between the employers and unions increased as a national two-day newspaper strike, protest strikes and demonstrations were mounted to secure the same codetermination rights as those secured in the Montan industries. Cooperation was also withdrawn from government committees. A vitriolic criticism of the post-war co-operation between the unions and the British occupational forces was launched in the BDAs journal (Hirsch-Weber 1959: 113). The trade unions were to emerge from the conflict discredited, in spite of their insistence that their claim did not represent an abuse of power in view of their contribution to Germany's economic recovery (Anthes *et al.* 1972: 92). Ultimately, the statute enacted (the Company Constitution Act (1952)) was a diluted form of its 1951 predecessor (Berghahn 1986: 230). Employee representation on the supervisory board of joint stock companies outside of the Montan industries was one-third of the total membership; there was no labour director; works councils were given slightly more authority than under the 1920 Act because social, economic and personnel functions were added to their statutory powers; employee candidates for the supervisory board were suggested by the works councils. Even more dimensions have thus been added to the somewhat vague term 'codetermination'. For this reason, the more general term 'industrial democracy' is used in this section. As Spiro (1954: 1114) points out, a completely new arrangement of policy making at this level was implied by these developments.

Nonetheless, the effect of the 1952 Act was to render the unions largely ineffective at plant level. Industrial democracy, which started life after two world wars as a compromise between conflicting political and social pressures, neither secured the envisaged transformation of society, nor the increase in union influence at plant

and national level which was originally intended by its advocates (Kerr 1954: 554–5). During Weimar, the main union organisation was 'squeezed into a narrow corridor between the works councils caring for the daily plant interests of the workers and the SPD catering for visions of social reform' (*ibid.*: 545). Although the works councils were theoretically the 'long arm of the union' reaching into the plant, they were an arm without a hand (*ibid.*: 538). After the Second World War, works councils had sprung up spontaneously in many plants. (The councils had been abolished by the Nazis in 1933, but their members had continued to act as unofficial advisers to their fellow workers.) Legal recognition of the reconstituted councils was granted by the Allies in 1946 (Sturmthal 1964: 54; Taft 1952: 308). Following the 1952 Act, however, the unions had to wait a further 20 years before legislation somewhat more in accordance with their aspirations was to be passed – a development which will be further explored immediately below. In effect, therefore, bargaining has been carried out at *two* levels. The *first* level is the regional agreement negotiated by the relevant trade union and employers' association in the conditions of free collective bargaining described above, while the *second* level involved grievance handling and supplementary bargaining on a statutory basis between the works council and the individual employer. This caused wage drift: effective earnings at company level tend to exceed the minima agreed at regional level. Moreover, the unions have been kept, to pursue the earlier metaphor, at arm's length. Contact with the rank and file member tended to be minimal and the unions became centralised (Kerr 1954: 537 and 540–1; McPherson 1951: 23; Miller 1978: 339 and 343).

Unions nevertheless attempted to

develop a distinct system of work place representatives. Such attempts gathered real momentum after the 1967 recession (Miller 1978). Until this recession the trade unions had never really given up hope of exercising a higher degree of control over the councils. In any case a very high proportion of works councillors are also active trade unionists. Moreover, many councillors also hold positions on the trade unions' works committees. But these councillors tend to identify with their company. This is particularly true of the chairmen: the considerable developments that have been made in extending the recognition of lay union representatives at plant level have tended to be vitiated by works council chairmen who take the view that their full-time role within their company or plant is of more value in enhancing the welfare and financial gains of their constituents. (*Die Zeit* series 'Between Two Stools' 42/78 to 49/78 inclusive; Hartmann 1979: 78–81; Miller 1978: 340 and 346–7.) It should be added that the chairmen of works councils tend to become entrenched. Many company council chairmen are also involved at the level of their own plant as works council chairmen. In addition, it is not unusual to find that they are also members of their company's supervisory board. This type of contact with management is to most chairmen the only positive method of ensuring their company's and constituents' continued prosperity, a point which was made in the Biedenkopf Report (Streeck 1984a: 397). Because chairmen are generally the repositories of such vast amounts of information, they become career specialists in this function. There is overwhelming evidence that tenure and these qualifications go together in large-size firms (Hartmann 1979: 74–8).

There were other factors that tended to undermine trade union influence.

Although a threatened general strike during the controversy preceding the 1952 Act did not materialise, the BDA nevertheless suggested that action be taken against the printing union because of the two-day stoppage it had called. Following a number of adverse lower court decisions and various expert professors' opinions – including one written by the future president of the Federal Labour Court – the printing union voluntarily paid damages in an out-of-court settlement (Aaron and Wedderburn 1972: 327–8; Bunn 1960: 664–5; Rajewsky 1970: 36–8). Moreover, the former chairman of the printing union, who, following Böckler's death a few weeks after the agreement on the 1951 Act, had been elected chairman of the DGB, was ousted from his post in favour of the IG Metall chairman who had taken part in the more successful 1951 campaign (Hirsch-Weber 1959: 110–11; Schuster 1973: 42). A separate statute (Employee Representation in the Public Sector, 1955) was enacted to cover the public services. The rights embodied in the 1951 and 1952 Acts were not granted, although similar bodies to works councils were to be established. The only exception was the railways where one-quarter of the supervisory board are employee representatives and a labour director is one of four executive board members. A spate of mergers in the Montan industries led to the Codetermination (Supplementation) Act, 1956 (Berghahn 1986: 245). This Act specified that parity of representation in the supervisory board was to be maintained in the event of over 50 per cent of the operations of a company remaining in the Montan sector.

However, the setting up of the Biedenkopf Commission in 1968, together with an SPD/FDP coalition after the 1969 federal election, eventually led to the 1972 Company Constitution Act and the

1976 Codetermination Act. Recall above all the elements of a Pyrrhic victory in the 1952 Act. The main trade union criticisms of the practice of industrial democracy were that the minority of employees on supervisory boards felt that they lacked real influence; interests could be better represented on the works councils; shareholders retained their option to veto new investment; even in the Montan industries, the labour director was concerned only with the *consequences* of commercial and technical decisions – the latter being taken by his fellow directors; works councillors and trade unions lacked information because of the restrictions in terms of secrecy placed on their representatives on supervisory boards (Däubler 1975). For all these reasons, the DGB was quite adamant that parity representation should be extended to all supervisory boards.

The position of the labour director would still present particularly difficult problems. In effect, the Montan trade unions had regarded him as their representative on the executive board. However, while nominated by labour he is responsible to, and can be removed by, the entire board. His well paid and influential position tend to make him a member of the managerial class (Kerr 1954: 558). Moreover, when the Montan Act of 1951 was placed on the statute book there were 71 mining and 34 steel-producing companies. Many mergers between 1952 and 1968 reduced the number of companies subject to this Act to 31 in mining and 28 in steel (Adams and Rummel 1977: 6). Labour directors often therefore became directors of personnel affairs in the individual plants of the merged companies. Indeed, by the middle of 1969, the German coal industry was in a critical state; many mines were fused into one consolidated company which accounted for 94 per cent of the productive capacity

in mining (Hartmann 1970: 139–40). Again this resulted in the functional demotion of 28 labour directors.

The Biedenkopf Report (1970) gave a clear endorsement to what it saw as the success of the Montan Act. A key recommendation for industries outside the Montan sector was that employee representation on supervisory boards should be increased; shareholders' representatives should, however, retain a clear majority (Berghahn and Karsten 1987: 204; Cullingford 1976: 68). This was because employee representation in the Montan industries had fostered cooperation (Streeck 1984a: 397). Perhaps the Commission was more impressed by the pacifying effects which employee participation had on organised labour than by the sense of participation which it imparted to individual employees. On the other hand, the Commission indicated how collusion between the executive board and the works council tended to pre-empt the somewhat limited powers of the supervisory board. Finally the joint management-labour 'Economic Committee' was considered to be superfluous because information was exchanged at other levels (Hartmann 1975: 56–7).

Attempts were made in the 1972 Company Constitution Act to extend the roles and rights of trade unions at plant level. A trade union could now initiate proceedings in the labour courts, a majority of a sizeable work group (as opposed to one quarter of the whole works council under the 1952 Act) can vote for attendance of the union at council meetings; timely invitations to *each* individual council meetings must, however, be sent and 'the employer retains considerable control over the entry of the union official to the plant' (Roberts 1973: 349–50). The Economic Committee became an obligatory, employee-only body under the Act. Where a works council is larger than nine members strong, a Works Committee deals with the day-to-day business of the council. A company with several plants is obliged to recognise and facilitate the election of a company-wide council. Councils are also legally entitled to be informed of management's *intended* actions. Finally, there was recognition for the rights of minority workers (foreign workers, young persons and the disabled).

When the 1976 Act reached the statute book, it provided for a 6:6 supervisory board ratio for firms employing between 2,000 and 10,000 employees. Over 10,000 but under 20,000 employees meant that the ratio would be 8:8 and 10:10 for firms with over 20,000 employees. This Act thus created a third system of employee representation on supervisory boards: the Montan system remained intact, while firms employing between 500 and 2,000 employees retained the 1952 Act's one-third representation. If there are 10 employees' representatives under the 1976 Act, three are from the unions and seven are chosen from the employees – one of whom must be a senior executive. The shareholders' representatives are elected at the company's annual general meeting. A chairman and his deputy are then elected by a two-thirds majority of the supervisory board. In the event of deadlock the shareholders provide the chairman, the employees his deputy. A two-thirds majority on the supervisory board is also required for the appointment of the executive board. If necessary, the chairman has a casting vote. Finally, the labour director is appointed on the same terms as other members of the executive board.

The biggest stumbling block was the representation of senior executives. In effect, this organised group became yet *another* social and industrial entity (Bendix 1978: 136; Hartmann 1975: 63;

Roberts 1973: 359). Election procedures and the role of the labour director are further contentious issues. In the eyes of the DGB the new Act had resulted in only a diluted form of parity representation on the supervisory board. For some employers, the Act represented a fundamental attack on private-property rights and they took the matter to the Federal Constitutional Court (BMA 1979: 263–7). The Court ruled in 1979 that the Act was a vehicle for peaceful social order. It was felt that in view of the size of firms falling within the scope of the Act, the help of employees was required if the constitutional right of freedom of choice in trade and occupation was to be safeguarded (Berghahn and Karsten 1987: 253). Once again it can be seen that both the employers and the unions were concerned with a power relationship (Thimm 1981: 15).

There then followed a major controversy in 1980 when Mannesmann argued that the Montan model no longer applied in its case. This was because steel had come to represent a fairly small proportion of total turnover. The SPD's liberal partners supported the Mannesmann case (Thimm 1981: 17). Thus an Act of 1981 duly gave the opportunity to companies in this position to opt out of the Montan model provided they gave six years' notice. Mannesmann immediately announced that it would abandon the system in 1987; two years later Thyssen gave notice that it would withdraw in 1989. Salzgitter and Klöckner were also involved. These moves embittered the trade unions. Partly as a conciliatory gesture, the 1981 amendment was repealed in 1988. As a result, a parent company which does not itself undertake activities in the Montan industries nonetheless remains subject to the 1951 Act as long as any Montan subsidiary accounts for at least 20 per cent of its total turnover or employs at least 2,000 persons (IDS *European Report* 324).

What, then, does 'industrial democracy' imply and what are its economic effects? Some of the implications of employee representation on supervisory boards have already been discussed in this section. In addition, it will be shown in the next chapter that the chairmen of the supervisory boards tend to be bankers. Together with chief executives, they can dominate decision making. In any case, the executive board by its very nature can reach decisions that are difficult for the somewhat more desultory supervisory boards to overturn. This difference is more clearly brought out by a literal translation of the German: *Vorstand* is to stand in front and *Aufsichtsrat* is an advisory council. As the Biedenkopf Commission pointed out (Streeck 1984a: 398), parity codetermination led to a greater degree of professionalism on the part of management and a consequent independence from shareholders; management also held preparatory meetings with employee representatives prior to supervisory board meetings. Perhaps a more surprising feature of industrial democracy in practice is the fact that only 20 per cent of all enterprises with more than five employees have a works council, although virtually all large enterprises observe this legal requirement (Owen Smith *et al.* 1989: 78). Note also that works councils can bring a varying degree of influence to bear on an employer. In descending order in terms of influence are codetermination, consultation, and a general right to information. Above all, the careful distinction which must be drawn between these three areas demonstrates the need to exercise caution when using the term 'codetermination'. Admittedly, as will now be shown, the codetermination of personnel policy by a

works council probably represents the most advanced form of industrial democracy currently being practised in the industrialised world. (The nominated labour director and his contacts with the works council in the Montan model is possibly a somewhat poor second, especially if the Biedenkopf finding that this office had been absorbed into higher management is taken into account – Nutzinger and Backhaus 1989: 179.) All that need be borne in mind is that codetermination is only one aspect of industrial democracy.

Nonetheless, it is necessary to be clear about what constitutes 'codetermination'. If the term is to have any meaning, this aspect of industrial democracy must be confined to those areas where the employer is required by the 1972 Act to obtain the works council's approval before implementing or changing the employment contract. 'Joint decision making' may be a clearer expression. The range of items affected in this manner is impressive from an industrial democracy point of view. The list includes working hours, including overtime and short-time working, holiday arrangements, payment systems, recruitment and training procedures, reorganisation of working practices, redundancy compensation and alternative employment arrangements, and social amenities (Adams and Rummel 1977: 9). Because works councils are not permitted to take strike action, elaborate arbitration arrangements must be invoked in the event of a dispute – the costs of which are the responsibility of the employer (Owen Smith *et al.* 1989: 66–7). However, these complex arrangements, along with fears of employer retaliation and victimisation, may contribute to the relative rarity of arbitration cases (*ibid.*: 77–8). (It must be borne in mind that works councillors enjoy statutory protection against unfair dismissal; for that matter, the employer is required to afford them reasonable and fully-remunerated time off for training and council business.) Moreover, the parties are required at their monthly meetings to exhibit a spirit of cooperation in the interests of both employees and the company. On the other hand, given the potential for a fundamental reorganisation of personnel management, it is little wonder that many smaller companies in Germany have turned a blind eye to these statutory requirements.

A works council must be consulted in advance about a proposed redundancy programme; its scale and selection procedure then shade into a codetermination matter. This is because the works council can enforce the formulation of a redundancy payment plan (Grochla and Gaugler 1990: 1750). There must also be consultation about individual dismissals; where a complaint against unfair dismissal is lodged with a labour court, an applicant's employment contract cannot be terminated. Other general changes in both the size and composition of the labour force are also consultation matters. Informational rights boil down to being acquainted with general trading conditions, proposed technological changes, merger proposals and managerial reorganisations. These latter rights therefore largely coincide with matters at least in theory determined by the supervisory board. But the nature of matters discussed by the supervisory board cannot legitimately be communicated to the works council by employee members of that board. This in turn raises another problem. To what extent is there a conflict of interest between the obligations of a supervisory-board director elected by employees and the responsibilities of that director as a trade-union official or works council member? Two examples arose during the 1992 and 1993 wage rounds described at

the end of the previous section. First, the ÖTV leader (Monika Wulf-Mathies) was also deputy-chair of Lufthansa's supervisory board. The serious financial difficulties of the airline led to a return to the 40-hour week, even though this could conceivably have been cited as a precedent for other 'special cases'. Second, the highly regarded leader of IG Metall (Franz Steinkühler) was forced to resign just after the east-west pay equalisation dispute. He had been a supervisory-board member at Daimler-Benz, VW and Thyssen, but had used confidential information from Daimler for insider trading. (The prevalence of insider trading is discussed in the corporate finance section of Chapter 7.) On the other hand, the presence of the deputy-leader of IG Metall on BMW's supervisory board meant that he was able to use his offices to object to a report that the company did not intend recognising a union when it opened a new plant in the USA (FT 29 July 1992). (This move is summarised in the corporate ownership and control section of Chapter 8, although it can be noted here that BMW's chief executive claimed that costs would be one third lower at the (highly subsidised) new plant.)

The economic implications of industrial democracy were subjected to a gradually increasing series of studies from about 1975. The Biedenkopf Commission (1970) had argued in favour of increased employee representation on supervisory boards, although it opposed parity. This opposition to parity was not based on any clear evidence of reduced profitability in the Montan industries; it was assumed that profitability was better secured by capital owners and management (Nutzinger and Backhaus 1989: 168). Because the 1976 Act fell short of parity, its provisions are not very far from the ideas embodied in the Biedenkopf Report (*ibid.*). Note that profitability and the composition of the supervisory board – along with the role of the labour director – were the principal concerns of the Biedenkopf Commission; this represented a breakthrough, although there was still a lack of a clear theoretical framework and a shortage of systematic factual evidence (*ibid.*: 179). As Jones indicates (*ibid.*: 194) by drawing a parallel with British experience, the subsequent debate was dominated by the ideological hostility to the undermining of private-property rights. The West German employers' resort to litigation over the 1976 Act is the *cause célèbre* in this respect. Such a reaction at once suppresses and avoids the issue of how property rights embodied in jobs can be protected – a subject which will be shortly addressed. Suffice it for now to echo Rothschild's view (*ibid.*: 159–60) that two different sets of goals are implied when one considers the employers' and the trade unions' stances. They need not conflict – but they might.

It is therefore necessary to outline the various goals of industrial democracy. Two points will emerge. First, surprisingly little is known about its value to its intended beneficiaries, namely employees (Scholl 1986: 153). Second, extremely difficult methodological and data problems are encountered when carrying out empirical research work. Reliance on superficial case studies, the typically low response rates to questionnaires, the relatively short time periods covered and the creative accountancy contained in company reports are major examples of these difficulties. However, there was an obvious need to investigate the German models in a dispassionate manner.

Furubotn (1985) assumes parity representation of employees and shareholders on a supervisory board which, by law, is empowered to make strategic policy decisions for the firm. The internal structure and behaviour of the enterprise are also controlled by this board, and a system of third party involvement resolves any deadlock arising from a tied vote. Under such a regime, both parties have the incentive to reach agreement on the distribution of potential productivity gains. These gains stem from the reduction of conflict derived from the restructuring of the firm. But such gains could also be derived from improving informational rights, rather than this form of codetermination. Indeed, it is necessary for its advocates to show that codetermination yields greater net advantages than other participatory systems. More importantly, whereas Furubotn's limited theoretical model shows immediate gains, the effects in the longer period are much more uncertain. It is notable that where the Montan model has been chosen, emphasis has been placed on the ideal role of the supervisory board and productivity is the key economic variable.

Svejnar (1981) estimated the relative effect of the Montan model on earnings. If unconstrained, the effect in mining was zero but in iron and steel it was 6.5 per cent; by constraining the effect of codetermination to be identical in both industries the effect was estimated to be 6.2 per cent. This latter overall estimate indicated that trade unions in West Germany had a far lower impact on earnings than codetermination. This is attributed to their primary functions being of a social and political character, although from a broader perspective it is impossible to separate the unions from the participatory institutions on which they are represented. Moreover, the high level of non-wage costs referred to in the previous section were not included in Svejnar's estimations. However, the estimation was based on the few firms and relatively small proportion of the labour force in the Montan industry.

Benelli *et al.* (1987) tested data drawn from companies affected by the 1976 Act; they had found it difficult to obtain an extensive database for the Montan industries. They point out that the 1976 Act was originally expected to cover 7 million employees and 650 companies; three years later, roughly 50 companies had changed their charters and 120 had reduced their labour force below the 2,000 threshold – thus leaving 480 companies included under the Act. Codetermination defined in this sense was found to have little effect on corporate operations and performance. It was suggested that one potential reason for such results was that corporate decision making may have already adjusted to the historical influence of the 1952 Act, to which the companies had previously been subjected. Gurdon and Rai (1990) also estimated the effect of the 1976 Act. Their evidence was mixed in that productivity seemed to have declined but profitability increased. A slightly more favourable, though not conclusive, argument in favour of participation was adduced. But yet again 'codetermination' is defined as consisting of the presence of employee representatives on supervisory boards.

Yet the Biedenkopf Commission had acknowledged that manpower policy and planning had received more attention in the Montan industries; moreover, where the workforce is 'strong', dismissals tend to be infrequent, and wages and fringe benefits are high (Streeck 1984a: 397 and 415n). This type of 'productivity coalition' is a new form of manpower policy (*ibid.*). Such a manpower policy assumes the need for continuous retraining and redeployment in accordance with the needs of technological change. Moreover, the statutory requirement that redun-

dancy compensation plans be negotiated is not seen as being irreconcilable with a market economy: an employee should be adequately compensated for the loss of his or her job, especially at a time of high unemployment (Grochla and Gaugler 1990: 1751). Other studies of advances in industrial democracy have revealed the importance of work conditions for employee involvement: unqualified workers tend to be excluded from direct interest articulation ('voice') and they therefore rely on the traditional labour market option of handing in their notice ('exit') (Nutzinger and Backhaus 1989: 181). Incidentally, these two options were dramatically illustrated by the deterioration in the position of East German women on unification. Their previous superior child-benefit, child-rearing and maternity leave regulations were abolished in favour of the western system on unification. Amid some evidence in the east that the number of abortions increased and pregnancies fell from the beginning of 1990, Rudolph *et al.* (1990: 39) asked why women reacted so moderately when the future of their professional careers and economic independence was at stake; why had they chosen 'exit' rather than 'voice'?

The exit option is a manifestation of an individual employee's frustration at not being able to voice dissatisfaction with certain work conditions (Kraft 1986: 670). Hence, the type of manpower policy mentioned in the Biedenkopf Report is more significant for employee involvement than representation on a supervisory board. In any case, as already demonstrated, the works council is the most powerful component of employee representation ('collective voice') in Germany (*ibid.*: 703). Using this type of approach, it can be shown that decision rights have a significant negative effect on quits (*ibid.*). Such rights have an equally powerful effect on recruitment practices and absenteeism. Stability, as measured by turnover rates, as well as job security, are therefore major effects of a strong works council (Scholl 1986: 165–6). Perhaps these effects have to be distinguished from the fall in quits in response to increased job insecurity after 1973–4; but at the same time dismissals rose while recruitment diminished in conditions of decreased profitability (OECD *Economic Survey* 1985: 41). Nonetheless, a reasonable, though necessarily tentative, inference is that unit labour costs may be lowered as a result of the presence of a strong works council. Such an inference stems not just from the 'stability' aspects of industrial democracy just explored, but also from its contribution to flexibility *within* an enterprise – an absolutely critical test of efficiency in labour markets (see below). As Wächter (1992: 260) argues:

In economic terms, a legally imposed system of worker participation would be unharmful and possibly productivity enhancing if the employment system develops strategies which intensively utilise and involve human resources . . . Instead of 'external flexibility' the participatory firm will strive for 'internal flexibility'.

Moreover, Frick (1990) has shown that the average percentage of disabled employees is significantly higher in firms with a works council compared to firms without such an interest representation. It should be added that, curiously enough, German firms may be breaking the law in two respects in this latter context. First, since they have more than five employees, their employees should have a works council. Second, under the Handicapped Persons Act 1974, six per cent of the total number of employees (where this total exceeds 15) should be disabled persons; otherwise a monthly penalty of DM 150 for each

unfilled place is payable. The average ratio in 1987 was five per cent. In a later analysis (1992), Frick demonstrated that in spite of the legal obligation to employ a given proportion of disabled persons, the risk of dismissal among this group of employees was not very much less than non-disabled persons.

The somewhat surprising conclusion here must be that the most critical levels of industrial democracy (the works council and individual employees) have been neglected, for differing reasons, by German employers, trade unions and academic observers. It has nonetheless been these very areas on which the EC policy makers were able to make some progress. One refers here to the relevant proposals in the Social Charter, or 'chapter' as it became known following the Maastricht EC summit. The fairly significant progress made in respect of EC-wide works councils contrasted with the more tortuous evolution of proposals for employee participation at board level. An appropriate concluding note to this section will therefore be a comparative summary of the EC proposals for an extension of industrial democracy.

Perhaps the principal reason for the relative lack of progress in policy proposals for worker participation at board level was its inclusion in more general proposals for the introduction of an EC-wide 'Euro PLC'. The initial proposal by the Commission was made in 1972 (EC *OJ* C131 12/72). It was 1983 before the first amended version could be issued, although the employee-participation proposals remained largely unchanged (COM *Document* (83) 185 and (91) 372). Four alternative models of employee participation were put forward: first, employee representation on supervisory boards; second, participation in appointing members of the supervisory board by means of a process of cooption; third, separate employees' representative bodies at company level; finally, participation through collectively-agreed procedures analogous to the three preceding models. This Euro plc *à la carte* was derived mainly from the British insistence that national cultural differences should be reflected in the model chosen by each member state (*Die Zeit* 25/91). The influence of the German tradition can therefore be seen in one model; the French/Belgian models influenced another EC model; the Italian (and Swedish) versions were very roughly reflected in yet another model, while the British, the Spanish and the Greeks had no history of codetermination.

On the other hand, as EC 1993 approached, various institutions of the EC fairly expeditiously put forward proposals for the establishment of European works councils as part of the Social Charter. To this end, a proposed directive issued by the Commission affected companies and groups with at least 1000 employees, and which owned establishments with a minimum of 100 employees in two or more member states (EC *OJ* C39/10 2/91).

The introduction of the single market in 1993 was seen by the EC as generating opportunities for cross-border mergers, takeovers and joint ventures. Given this process of concentration, all the relevant advisory and policy-making institutions within the EC felt that 'fundamental Community social rights' would be at risk. Hence, a Social Charter which defined these rights was prepared. The Charter applied to both employees and the self-employed. It laid down the major principles relating to the pay and other conditions of employment of EC citizens. These principles were embodied in a series of rights, ranging from the freedom of movement to the employment rights of adolescents, the elderly and the disabled. Particularly relevant here are:

- the right to freedom of association and collective bargaining
- the right of an employee to information, consultation and participation

The member countries with high cost, high benefit social security systems such as France and Germany were less anxious about the concentration trends predicted by the EC than by the locational disadvantages which would arise if the low cost members were not required to implement the Social Charter. Moreover, as shown above, high total labour costs have led German employers in particular to seek rapid productivity gains; Germany also had a relatively developed system of industrial democracy. Significantly, VW's employees in member countries anticipated the EC legislation by establishing a European works council. By contrast, Britain is traditionally a low money wage and low social insurance contribution country with no recognisable form of industrial democracy.

Not surprisingly, the high cost countries insisted on the full implementation of the Charter. Bonn's Employment Minister (Norbert Blüm) welcomed the EC's works councils proposals, whereas then the British Employment Secretary (Michael Howard) thought that the benefits of the single market would be dissipated if the 'unnecessary and damaging proposals for EC social legislation' were permitted to 'impose cost burdens on industry and harm competitiveness' (*Wirtschaftswoche* 29 March 1991; *Employment Gazette* 5/91: 253). Under the ECs proposal the councils' costs would be met by employers. Perhaps the 'opt out' clause negotiated by the British government at Maastricht represented among other things its strength of feeling against this and other aspects of the Social Chapter. If the other eleven member states proceed on the basis of a majority vote, however, this approach could leave UK companies with European-wide interests without influence on matters of fundamental importance to their future. Moreover, the admission of Austria, Sweden, Finland and, possibly, Norway as early as 1995–6 could well enhance the chances of the German model's acceptance and increase the UK's isolation.

The EC estimated that the costs of its European works council proposal would be functionally related (COM *Document* (90) 581: 33–4) to:

- the number of participants (maximum 30)
- the number of member states involved (between 2 and 12)
- travel expenses
- translation requirements (oral and written)
- accommodation
- leave of absence to attend meetings
- documentation

The EC envisaged that the council would meet management representatives at least once a year for information purposes, twice if consultation is necessary. Note that the proposal did not envisage the introduction of the codetermination powers of the German works councils. Moreover, the competence of the council would be limited to those matters which concern the enterprise as a whole, or at least two establishments situated in different member countries. Taking a scenario which assumed 30 members from several member countries, and therefore with fairly sophisticated translation requirements, the cost was placed at 'some tens of thousands of ECUs'. But this community-wide company would have 'at least some thousands of workers'; the maximum cost per employee in such a case would be 10 ECUs per year (*ibid.*). Normally the cost

would be much less and unit labour costs would probably fall as increased employee involvement caused a rise in productivity. Again, the most significant reaction came from Germany where employers already meet such costs. The cost was considered by German employers to be less relevant than the remoteness of the proposed council from the employees it represents.

CONCLUSION: LABOUR MARKET PROBLEMS

Each of the above sections makes a contribution to general efficiency considerations. 'Efficiency' in this context is concerned with the extent to which the labour market adjusts to changing conditions. This adjustment process can take some combination of three basic forms:

- by a variation in the level and structure of employment
- by a variation in wage rates
- by a variation in the quality of labour as a result of active intervention by training agencies

Labour market flexibility along these lines can be seen as a necessary condition for higher employment levels, but not one that is sufficient in itself (Franke 1988: 15). If labour turnover, and if flows on to and off unemployment registers, as well as the effects of fixed-term employment contracts are all quantified, a relatively high degree of flexibility is seen to be inherent in labour markets (*ibid.*: 16–17).

It will also be noticed that the above three criteria combine market and institutional forces. In other words, the notion that the decentralisation and deregulation of labour markets would alone resolve the problem of adjustment is expressly rejected. As Soskice (1990: 36 and 61) has shown, institutional goals are now back on the agenda. Consider the market mechanisms which, 'if left to themselves', would contribute to a convergence of the (per capita) income-generating capacity of east and west Germany (OECD *Economic Survey* 1992: 71–2):

The initially low level of wages in eastern Germany would remain low, as many non-viable enterprises closed down and unemployment rose. Unemployment and low wages would give rise to two movements: workers would move from eastern to western Germany in search of jobs, at higher wages; while existing enterprises in eastern Germany would be mostly not very profitable, new investment would be highly profitable at low eastern wages (though profitability might be reduced by infrastructure deficiencies) and hence capital would flow east. Some changes in wage differentials could be expected: to induce managers to work in the new Länder, their earnings might have to be higher than in west Germany, whereas those of their employees would probably be lower since the majority of easterners would be unwilling or unable to migrate in search of higher wages. As these opposite flows of capital and labour took place, prices would adjust – real wages would rise in eastern Germany and returns to investment decline, while in the west wage growth would be dampened and returns to new investment would tend to rise.

As the OECD adds, ideas of fairness and the need to retain support among the eastern population for the shift to a market economy were the first reasons for state intervention. Second, additional financial incentives to invest in the new Länder were necessary. These incentives were to compensate for uncertainty and to prevent the new Länder becoming dependent on low-technology, low-wage employment. Third, although return migration was

likely once income and employment opportunities improved, there would in the meantime be pressure on the social infrastructure in the west; there would also be the danger of a vicious circle developing, whereby the most productive eastern labour would migrate thus undermining further the incentive to invest and inducing further outward migration. It will also be seen below that the eastern wage *structure* did indeed adjust quite rapidly, but the stylised response predicted by the pure theory quoted above did not occur. Moreover, the 1992–3 recession undermined the incentive to invest even in the west. If anything, foreign investment by German companies increased – see the trade sections of Chapter 8. Admittedly, all this poses the dilemma which arises if a prosperous economy with a highly advanced social-policy system attempts to integrate a totally different economy. It must be added, however, that previous recessions in the west had left a controversial legacy of intervention in the labour market.

In 1969, the AFG thus committed the Federal government to a framework of social and economic policy which would maintain a high level of employment and continuously improve the structure of employment (Grochla and Gaugler 1990: 1292). This Act was seen as a means of promoting economic growth. It assigned a highly interventionist role to the Federal Labour Office (Chapter 5). But the Office's active labour market policies were soon to become dwarfed by its expenditure on unemployment benefits. Moreover, the comparatively efficient technique of vocational training, together with a relatively advanced industrial relations system, did not prevent a steep rise in unemployment after the first crude oil price shock in 1973–4 (Kühl 1987; Figure 6.3). For Soltwedel (1988) the most outstanding feature of the West German labour market after 1973 was its poor employment creation record; between 1973 and 1986, employment increased in the USA by 24 million, whereas it declined by one million in West Germany. This scarcity of jobs coincided with a rising demand for jobs as demographic influences began to operate.

The rise in unemployment was attributed by some commentators to the insufficient adjustment of real wage rates and the wage structure following the oil crises (*ibid.*: 156; Gross 1988; Hellwig and Neumann 1987: 127). After the first two oil price shocks – in 1973–4 and 1979–81 – a positive real labour cost gap opened up because real labour costs were rising faster than productivity (OECD *Economic Survey* 1985: 36–7). The insufficiency of such adjustment was attributed to institutional rigidities and legislation which made it difficult and costly to dismiss employees (Gross 1988: 519; Hellwig and Neumann 1987: 116 and 121). In short, the collective bargaining and industrial democracy legislation analysed above was being called into question. By using real wage flexibility and employment adaptability, the OECD (*Economic Survey* 1988: 59) contrasted the German situation with Japan and the USA. In Japan real wage rates were found to be highly flexible, with a correspondingly small need for employment adjustment; in the USA employment was highly responsive to output growth and real wages were moderately flexible. Stafford (1988: 229) adduced similar evidence. On the other hand, Allen (in Owen Smith 1981: 89) referred to the cost advantages which Japanese employers accrue from their buffer stocks of 'temporary' workers. Moreover, in order to have maintained the long-term equilibrium rate of West German unemployment at 1.9 per cent

following the two oil price shocks, Gross (1988: 517) estimated that the wage–productivity ratio – a proxy for real wage rates – should have declined by 26.5 per cent between 1973 and 1982. Quite apart from the policy implications of such wage cutting, the time period of Gross' model (1973–83) is far shorter than the period of 1963–86 studied in a rival model (Flaig and Steiner 1989: 398). This rival model estimated that output dominated employment behaviour in West German manufacturing, relative prices playing only a minor role. Nonetheless, Sengenberger (1984: 323 and 327) saw a clear-cut shift in the competing models of economic and social development of West Germany; the collapse of the Federal liberal-social coalition in 1982 was traced back to the FDPs insistence that the social state be dismantled, thus stimulating more competition in the labour market.

The reader will identify the influence of 'supply side' economics in the previous paragraph. To achieve a lower unemployment rate, the received theory of the SME would have had to have been abandoned. A fundamental restructuring of the AFG and collective bargaining would also have been required. Most policy makers clearly viewed the complete adoption of these radical prescriptions as unacceptable, although the Federal conservative-liberal coalition introduced a series of measures designed to increase flexibility (see below). In any case, Franz (1983: 69 and 74–5) estimated that with unemployment at 10 per cent in the Spring of 1983, inflationary pressure would not have been increased by demand management policies aimed at reducing unemployment. He also suggested training programmes for the long-term unemployed. Such findings do not necessarily contradict the 'natural rate' of unemployment tested by Gross and reported in the last paragraph. As the

OECD points out (*Economic Survey* 1987: 64), such a 'rate' may well differ from the 'non-increasing inflationary rate' estimated by Franz. In addition, although the OECD (*ibid*. 1988: 60–1) confirmed the existence of regional wage rigidity, there was no evidence of any overall *rise* in labour market rigidities. Again, the bargainers' established practice of using a key pay settlement as a datum for federal-wide settlements in any pay round explains the comparatively small dispersion of wage increases but strongly dispersed regional unemployment rates (*ibid*.). This practice was also applied to the newly-unified Germany. It was shown above that it possesses rational elements. It must also be borne in mind that effective pay rates at company level show a wider regional variation. Underlying all the arguments in this paragraph is the European preference for income and job security with social-insurance provisions for the unemployed (Vogler-Ludwig 1989: 76).

Indeed, a number of positive arguments were advanced in favour of the active labour market policy stance contained in the AFG. Kühl (1987: 44–5) estimated that unemployment in 1975 was 25 per cent lower than it would have been without active labour market policies. However, this employment effect tended to diminish. By 1985 it was under 14 per cent. This may well have been a lagged response to the varying proportions of total expenditure accounted for by active labour market policies and unemployment benefits: in 1974 the respective proportions were 46 and 34 per cent; in 1983 they were 35 and 52 per cent (*ibid*.: 45). Moreover, the total costs of unemployment should be compared with the costs of active labour policies. In 1985, the annual average cost per unemployed person was DM 24,684. This was the sum of DM 13,819 in lost tax revenues and social-insurance contributions, along with DM 10,865 in average unemployment benefit (*ibid*.: 45–7). Hence, total unemployment in 1985 (2.3 million) caused a financial loss of DM 57 billion. The value of output forgone, assuming an average productivity of DM 55,000 per year, was over DM 125 billion – about eight per cent of GDP. Moreover, if the additional social-insurance contributions payable by the Federal Labour Office on behalf of the unemployed are added to the average costs per unemployed person, the sum increased to DM 25,500. Active labour market policies, on the other hand, cost on average about DM 36,000 per year (*ibid*.). Hence, 70 per cent of the costs of active intervention in the labour market were 'met' by the alternative policy of allowing unemployment to rise. This was before the employment effects of job creation were taken into account; it was also net of the improvements in productivity and competitiveness accruing from the enhanced human capital embodied in the 3.7 million persons who attended vocational and retraining courses between 1973 and 1986.

There was another policy response to the re-emergence of large-scale unemployment, as well as the general slowdown in employment growth. The purpose of the Job Promotion Act 1985 (*Beschäftigungs-förderungsgesetz*) was the creation of greater flexibility. Fixed-term contracts, part-time work, job sharing, employee leasing by agencies, a narrower definition of unfair dismissal, lowering the cost of redundancy programmes and restricting the use of overtime were all elements of this piece of legislation. This type of policy development was aimed at creating 'non-standard' employment because the forms of employment envisaged deviated from the 'standard model' of European employment practice (Büchtemann and Quack 1990). It was not clear, however, that the previous more restrictive policy stance in West Germany had led to significantly less temporary working than in the UK (Casey *et al.* 1989: 463). The major difference between the two countries lay in the composition of the temporary labour force: in West Germany, this segment of the labour force was mainly male and full time, whereas in the UK it was mainly female and part time (*ibid.*: 464–5). Any spread in temporary employment in West Germany varied in degree in various sectors and firms, and for different reasons; more than 90 per cent of such employment was on a fixed-term contract (Büchtemann and Quack 1990: 317; Dombois 1989: 368). In 1987, about two million employees were on fixed-term contracts in West Germany, 16 per cent of them working part time (Franke 1988: 16). There was also little change to the part-time ratio as a result of the Act, most of the change occurring prior to its enactment (Büchtemann and Quack 1990: 316 and 319; Franz 1984: 630). Hence, the German employers quoted an OECD survey which demonstrated that, by 1989, 13 per cent of all West German employees were working on a part-time basis, compared to 6 per cent in Italy but 22 per cent in the UK (KND 65/91). Seifert of the WSI (1991: 508) estimated a relatively small increase (from 13.1 to 14.2 per cent of the gainfully employed) for the period 1984–90. Even more significantly, in both 1980 and 1989 over 90 per cent of the part timers in the insured population were female (IW *Zahlen* 1991: 19). (In 1992, the 50-year-old regulation which prevented manual females – but not their white-collar analogues – from working night shifts was found to be discriminatory and therefore unconstitutional by the Constitutional Court). Finally, as Büchtemann and Quack (1990: 328) make clear, it is wrong to equate non-standard

and precarious employment. Serious disadvantages and lack of protection tend to cumulate in certain categories of non-standard work such as marginal part-time employment or short-term temporary job arrangements which offer no opportunities for eventual permanent employment.

During the 1980s, the employers too were consistent advocates of the need to increase flexibility. This was seen as a more viable means of reducing unemployment than the trade union policy of redistributing the total volume of work by reducing the working hours. Ultimately, the trade union aim was increasingly focused on reducing the length of the working week, or the supply of hours per employee. Initially, however, the metalworkers and printers pursued this aim, while in construction and chemicals emphasis was placed on reducing the supply of persons by early retirement (Seifert 1991: 497). Following each settlement in the metalworkers' disputes, both parties achieved their aims. The unions conceded greater flexibility in the structure of working time and the employers conceded a shorter nominal working week – although it should be added that the union also began to see advantages for its members in increasing flexibility, sabbatical leave being one example (Bosch 1990: 616 and 619). Quite significantly, it was left to individual employers and works councils to implement more flexibility in working hours – another example of the 'internalisation' of flexibility. 'Stability' was also enhanced by the long-term nature of the agreements (*ibid.*: 617; Wächter and Stengelhofen 1992: 28).

Several difficulties are encountered when assessing the economic aspects of reducing working time. A central issue in the debate is the extent to which wages will be affected if working hours are reduced. The polar positions are, on the one hand, leaving hourly nominal pay unchanged or, on the other hand, increasing hourly pay to such an extent that weekly, monthly or annual pay remains unchanged (Franz 1984: 626). During the 1980s, the unions secured a reduction in hours with weekly pay unchanged. There was thus a cost-side impact. But there may well be another impact: output per worker (productivity) probably rises as working hours fall (*ibid*.: 644). Greater flexibility in the structure of working hours was implemented concurrently and this changed labour utilisation and raised labour productivity. Induced capital investment also raised productivity but made industry less employment intensive (Neifer-Dichmann 1991: 514–16). Hence, the decrease in unemployment, or the employment effect of decreasing working hours, would be smaller, the higher the increase in productivity. An alternative employment effect would be derived from any increase in the demand for the product. Note also that the employment effect is constrained by the extent to which unemployed persons do not possess the requisite skills; even assuming a potential recruit possesses the necessary skills, jobs may also not lend themselves to being divided between an increased number of persons (*ibid*.: 517–18). In spite of unemployment, therefore, firms – particularly small firms – began to complain about a shortage of labour (*ibid*.: 518–19).

It is therefore hardly surprising that attempts to estimate the employment effects of reducing working time are controversial. Moreover, the methodologies used are extremely varied, which partly explains the disparate results; and all estimates come up against the difficulty of isolating the influence of cyclical fluctuations on employment levels (Seifert 1991: 497 and 500–1). In spite of methodological disparities, however, the estimated em-

ployment effects of reducing working time seem to be positive. Seifert (*ibid*.: 505) suggested that between 385,000 and 514,000 jobs were maintained or created during the period 1985–90. Thus 20 per cent of the increase in employment during this period can be attributed to reductions in working time. Bosch (1990: 619) added that the 35-hour dispute in 1984 stimulated a comprehensive evaluation of traditional working-time practices.

However, separating the employment effects of working-time reductions from those of economic growth and technical and organisational change is difficult (*ibid*.: 624). Indeed, Neifer-Dichmann (1991: 511–14) attributed employment trends exclusively to economic growth, not working hours. She added (*ibid*.: 520) that whereas the 1984 and 1987 working-time agreements allowed greater freedom in the distribution of working hours, the 1990 agreement introduced the possibility of individually differentiating working hours. As a result general reductions in working time may be a thing of the past. If the unions responded by attempting to fix maximum working hours, they may contravene the Collective Agreements Act which stipulates that only minimum conditions can be specified unless a departure can be shown to be in the employees' favour (*ibid*.: 520–1). Finally, the attitude of works councils will determine the extent to which enterprises could take advantage of flexible working hours (*ibid*.). In capital-intensive enterprises, for example, it was thought that equipment would be used more intensively if a system of rota days off was introduced (Bosch 1990: 621).

A general concluding note can be extracted from Seifert (1991: 508). By 1990, the average size of the economically active population in the west was 28.4 million – the highest employment level since the war and an increase of 7.9 per cent over the low point of 1983. The number of registered unemployed in the west, on the other hand, declined by a comparatively small amount – from a peak of 2.304 million in 1984 to 1.882 million in 1990. This apparent rigidity in unemployment could be attributed (*ibid.*) to:

the growing labour force participation of women, the increase in both national and immigrant workers as a result of demographic trends, and the rapid rise in the influx of ethnic Germans from eastern and south-eastern Europe, as well as from the former GDR (all of which) raised the potential labour force by rather more than 2 million since 1983.

Consider particularly how these problems have very little relationship to the implications of unification. It was conceded at the outset that without explicit government involvement, market forces would not produce a politically acceptable level of employment in the east. Norbert Blüm, the Federal employment minister, contended that active labour market policies in the east had reduced unemployment there by two million, as well as providing new skills (BA *Presse Informationen* 14/92). The most dramatic adjustment, however, affected females. Official scenarios calculated that the female participation rate in the former GDR would 'adjust' to the much lower West German level (Rudolph *et al.* 1990: 39). Such an assumption implied that one million females in the east would have to permanently withdraw from the labour market. It was also seen when discussing Figure 6.4 above that various subsidies were used to facilitate the transition of the eastern labour market to western standards. On the other hand the east German wage *structure* changed quite rapidly; by 1991 it closely resembled the pattern in the west

(Krueger and Pischke 1992: 34–5). A major feature of this wage structure was the tendency for government and union policies to maintain the wages of low-skill employees above the equilibrium level (*ibid.*: 37). But it was probably the absence of a vigorous economic recovery which remained the main impediment to adjustment (MRDB 12/92: 4).

A persuasive adjustment mechanism for, in effect, the eastern labour market was advocated by Akerlof *et al.* (1991). As already seen in Chapter 1, they had shown that the short-run viability of east German industry would be substantially improved by a reduction in labour costs. In the case of a 75 per cent reduction in labour costs, 88 Kombinate employing 77 per cent of the industrial labour force would have become viable (*ibid.*: 28). But in the absence of massive productivity improvements – hardly feasible without *long-run* technological change – substantial subsidisation would be necessary. A self-eliminating flexible employment bonus (SEFEB) was therefore proposed (*ibid.*: 80). The bonus was flexible because it was governed by a formula which linked eastern and western wage rates; it was self eliminating because its value fell to zero as wages in the east approached western levels. Moreover, the SEFEB had five major properties in terms of its costs to government. First, existing jobs would be preserved and new ones would be created. Second, as already shown in this section, unemployment insurance payments would decline, but income tax and social-insurance contributions would rise, as a result of higher employment levels. Third, politically undesirable migration from east to west would be reduced and the level of social unrest thereby lowered. Fourth, previously unviable firms would become more attractive to private buyers, thus speeding up the process of privatisation.

Finally, unlike the case of the usual form of (a constant) wage subsidy, trade unions would have to consider the employment effects of pay increases.

Many special job-creation schemes were in fact introduced. All of them involved an element of subsidy. But they all lacked the flexibility of the SEFEBs. Consider the special scheme based on the Employment Promotion Act (AFG). The subsidy offered was identical to average monthly rate of unemployment benefit. It was therefore neutral in costs as far as the Federal Labour Office's expenditure was concerned, but left prospective employers with initial high labour costs. Half way through 1993 the take-up rate had been only 15,000, whereas funds to support 70,000 had been earmarked for the year as a whole (BA *Presse Informationen* 52/93). Significantly, as early as October 1992 the Treuhandanstalt had been involved in the scheme (this institution is discussed in Chapter 8). This was with a view to eliminating some of the high initial labour costs. Taken together, the general concluding note above and the notion of SEFEBs just discussed give valuable insights into the likely areas where flexibility will become necessary in German labour market affairs. Cutting unemployment benefit is not a viable alternative. Many of those affected are not entitled to this benefit. In any case, the number of job searchers would fall at a time when the former indigenous sources of west German labour are on the wane.

Lower wage settlements and greater flexibility in working conditions thus became increasingly seen as policy imperatives. Government, employers and unions recognised that Germany was in deep crisis. At the end of 1993, VW and IG Metall reached a pioneering agreement to bring in a four-day week at the company's domestic plants in order to save 30,000 jobs. Basic monthly wages remained unchanged but IG Metall agreed to cuts in some fringe benefits. Similarly, Mercedes secured a cost-cutting deal as the price for locating its new mini car in Germany. Early retirements were one feature of this agreement. At the same time, employers' associations were being pressured by the small business sector to introduce more flexibility into pay deals. In view of the outcome of the dispute over the equalisation of pay rates between east and west, the engineering employers predictably served notice to terminate the existing wage and holiday contracts – an unprecedented move designed to secure cost-cutting agreements. Moreover, proposals for deregulating the labour market were unveiled by the Federal government at the beginning of 1994. Private employment agencies were to be legalised, thus ending the BA's monopoly on job placements. Special inducements for the long-term unemployed to take seasonal or low-paid community work were envisaged, as were moves to encourage more part-time work in both the public and private sectors. Somewhat surprisingly, the FT (19 January 1994) took the view that Anglo-American experience in the 1980s suggested that liberalising employment regulations encourages companies to hire more women, young people and immigrants to work part time for relatively low wages in the service sector. This chapter, therefore, must be concluded on a pessimistic note. In order to compete with the Pacific basin and eastern Europe, the superior working conditions which had evolved as a part of the SME were undermined. Social and, for that matter, environmental protection had been subordinated by GATT to 'free trade', or the unfettered right of multi-national corporations to seek the least-cost location from their point of view.

7

BANKING AND FINANCE

INTRODUCTION

The German banking system possesses three distinctive features. First, the casual observer may conclude that the German banking scene is dominated by the Big Three commercial banks – the Deutsche Bank AG, the Dresdner Bank AG and the Commerzbank AG. However, although these private-sector banks do indeed wield a great deal of market power, the ownership of the bulk of Germany's banks in fact lies in the hands of the public authorities and the cooperative banking movement. It would be equally wrong to view the private sector as consisting solely of the Big Three: there is a rich variety of banks within this sector. In short, three forms of ownership are represented among the economy's top banks, namely private, public and cooperative. Linked to the question of ownership, of course, is the more complex issue of control – an issue which is also considered in this and the subsequent chapter.

Second, the institutions belonging to three banking groups – irrespective of ownership – provide a full range of *both* commercial and investment banking services. This is the well-known *universal banking* principle. On the liabilities side, the banks accept short-term sight, time and savings deposits, along with long-term funds in the form of fixed-term de-

posits and issues of savings bonds and bank bonds. On the assets side, they grant not only short-term advances but also medium and long-term credits and loans. They also provide brokers' services, generally deal in securities and accept seats on the supervisory boards of non-banking companies. These off-balance-sheet activities generate a good deal of revenue for the commercial banks – particularly the Big Three. The exceptions to the general universal banking rule are the *specialised* banks which confine themselves to narrow fields such as the financing of mortgages, instalment sales and the performance of other specialised functions. The postal giro and savings banks are also classified under this heading. But in many cases these specialised banks are either subsidiaries of the universal banks or are state-owned. Nevertheless, it would be impossible to fully understand the methods of funding the national debt, or the post-war recovery, without examining the roles of the financial institutions which make up the specialist sector.

Third, until the 1960s, public and cooperative sectors felt inhibited by their charters from entering the more risky investment fields. Further, only the central institutions of the public and cooperative banking sectors are allowed to own equity capital in non-banking institutions, whereas the commercial banks, particularly the Big Three, have not been constrained in either of these ways. As a result, their industrial influence is quite extensive and policy prescriptions have ranged from calls for nationalisation to the advocacy of minor corrections. The private-sector banks, on the other hand, have become increasingly involved in retail banking. There has thus been a growing degree of competition between the three sectors in all areas of banking.

German banks, particularly the Big Three, are consequently involved in all the markets for financial services. These markets, both in terms of the manner in which they function, and in terms of their regulation, possess a number of peculiarities. The securities markets consist of equity and bond markets. When considering the equity market, it is necessary to extend the analysis to include the general relationship between the banks and the non-financial corporate sector. When considering the bond market, it is necessary to include not only public bonds but also the mortgage and other bank bonds which will be referred to in the housing finance section below. Finally, banking and insurance products became more markedly integrated in the 1980s (*Allfinanz*). This process continued, at a somewhat less hectic pace, into the 1990s. The central issue will be whether the efficiency of financial intermediation has been improved or impaired by the German banking system. In short, is Germany likely to become an international financial centre (*Finanzplatz Deutschland*) during the 1990s?

An examination of the basic structure and legal forms of banking, therefore, is followed by more detailed analyses of the private-sector, cooperative, public-sector and special-purpose banks. The rise of *Allfinanz* can be included in such an analytical framework. This leads to a consideration of prudential regulation and its

revision. The various financial markets are then discussed, including some observations on *Finanzplatz Deutschland*. Finally, an examination of some general aspects of banking – developments in profitability, competition and the international field – demonstrates the dramatic growth of, and change in, post-war banking. (It will be recalled that central banking was examined in Chapter 4.)

A general working hypothesis is that there has been a general process of concentration in German banking. The process of horizontal concentration recommenced in the private banking sector during the 1950s; it was followed by a phase of vertical integration when private mortgage banks were absorbed by the re-emerged private universal banks. These processes of horizontal concentration and vertical integration were later emulated within both the public and cooperative sectors (Pohl 1986: 11–12). The ownership, control and the external influence of these increasingly concentrated units have all become central issues of economic policy. Unification simply further exacerbated these critical factors: there was simply no western-style banking system operating in the east and all three sectors rapidly established themselves in the new Länder.

BASIC STRUCTURAL FEATURES

The banks differ considerably in business structure, size, legal form, administrative organisation and in their main fields of business activities. The structure of the German banking system is illustrated in Figure 7.1. This figure confirms the basic divisions between universal and specialist banking. It also illustrates the varying forms of ownership – private, cooperative and public. These three groups of banking institutions are each affiliated to separate central associations which serve as interest and public relations organisations (not shown in Figure 7.1). The private-sector banks are affiliated, through their Länder associations, or their specialist private mortgage or shipping bank associations if appropriate, to the Association of German Banks (*Bundesverband deutscher Banken eV; eV = eingetragener Verein* or registered charity); branches of foreign banks are also represented by this organisation. Some of the public sector banks – the savings banks and their central giro institutions (*Landesbanken*) – are affiliated to the German Savings' and Giro Association (*Deutscher Sparkassen- und Giroverband eV* – DSGV), while the *Landesbanken* again, plus the public-owned mortgage and special purpose banks, are all affiliated to the Association of Public Sector Banks (*Verband Öffentlicher Banken eV*). Finally, the Association of German Urban and Agricultural Cooperative Banks (*Bundesverband der Deutschen Volksbanken und Raiffeisenbanken eV*) represents the collective interests of the cooperative banks.

Although the number of affiliates to the Bundesverband deutscher Banken (BdB) does not exactly coincide with the Bundesbank data in Figure 7.1, it will be useful to apply the types of ownership in Figure 7.2 to private-sector banking.

In 1991, the total number of banks affiliated through their Länder or specialist associations to the BdB was 252. (In addition, the BdB looked after the interests of 58 branches of foreign banks represented in the Federal Republic). Among its affiliates, there were 130 AGs. There were also 48 GmbHs, as well as six banks of the remaining type of corporate entity defined in Figure 7.2, namely KGaA. With the exception of the Big Three, virtually all private-sector banks registered as compa-

nies are in either the 'regional and other commercial banks' or 'private mortgage and shipping banks' categories of Figure 7.1. Finally, the BdB had affiliates from the 'private bankers' category in Figure 7.1. In fact, there were 67 limited partnerships (KG), general partnerships (OHG) and relatively small banks which belong to a sole proprietor (*Einzelfirma*). As their legal form indicates, management and ownership in the case of the smaller private banks tended to coincide (Peltzer and Nebendorf 1973: 19).

THE PRIVATE-SECTOR COMMERCIAL BANKS

The relatively sudden transformation of Germany into a first-rank industrial nation owed much to the equally dramatic rise of her universal banking system. Since the underdeveloped capital market could not meet the enormous demands of emerging industry, the banks were encouraged to act as sources of industrial finance.

Such was the unique origin of German banking. It was the beginning of its crucial relationship with German industry. The Deutsche and the Dresdner Banks, along with the Commerz- and Discontobank, were therefore the products of the sudden upsurge in banking activity that followed the founding of the Second Reich. They were obliged to forge the type of organised credit system which in Britain was apportioned among numerous financial intermediaries (Marshall 1932: 341).

In 1870 the Deutsche Bank was founded as an AG under Royal charter in Berlin (Deutsche Bank 1970: 6). Later in the same year a new Companies Act meant that a Government licence was no longer required and 30 other newly-founded banks were founded in 1870 alone. During the 1873–5 financial crisis, however,

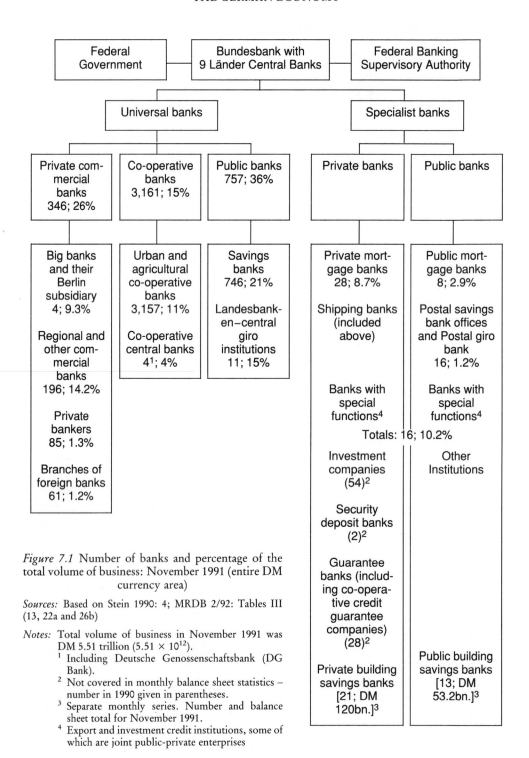

Figure 7.1 Number of banks and percentage of the total volume of business: November 1991 (entire DM currency area)

Sources: Based on Stein 1990: 4; MRDB 2/92: Tables III (13, 22a and 26b)

Notes: Total volume of business in November 1991 was DM 5.51 trillion (5.51×10^{12}).
[1] Including Deutsche Genossenschaftsbank (DG Bank).
[2] Not covered in monthly balance sheet statistics – number in 1990 given in parentheses.
[3] Separate monthly series. Number and balance sheet total for November 1991.
[4] Export and investment credit institutions, some of which are joint public-private enterprises

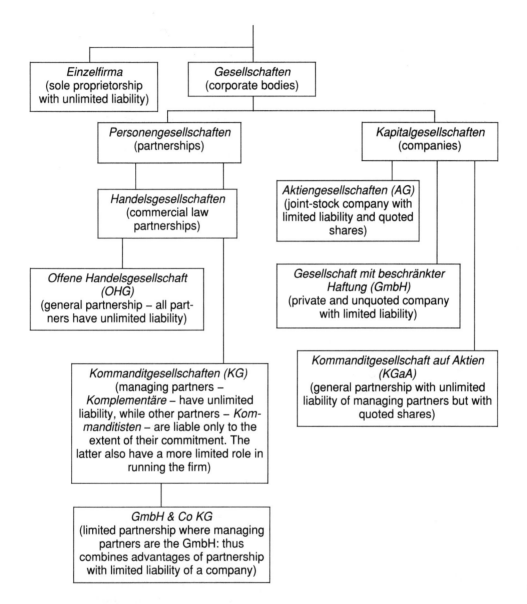

In addition, there are publicly-owned undertakings, co-operatives and both mutual insurance and building loan associations. Many public-sector undertakings register their subsidiaries in the AG, GmbH or Co form. Subsidiaries of the co-operative banks are registered as *eigentragene Genossenschaften (eG)* – i.e. registered co-operatives with or without limited liability. Finally, there is a silent partnership *(stille Gesellschaft)* whose capital contribution qualifies as debt rather than equity. This form of participation enables foreign investors to gain substantial tax advantages.

Figure 7.2 Various forms of ownership in Germany

Sources: Based on Beinert 1991: 2–14; Lawrence 1980: 30–1; MK various; Mueller *et al.* 1978: 49

nearly 50 banks had to be dissolved. Because the Deutsche Bank initially operated mainly abroad, it had avoided the company promotion fever (*ibid*.: 10). It began thereafter to take over other banks and rapidly acquired the status of a big bank. From then onwards it became closely involved in electrification with Siemens and AEG (Eglau 1990: 20). On the eve of the First World War the bank's world-wide activities included interests in electricity, railroads and oil. Its capital, which had already multiplied six times by 1895, stood at RM 200 million. By the time it had merged with the Disconto-Gesellschaft in the late 1920s, the bank was handling roughly 50 per cent of the business done by all the big Berlin banks.

The post-Second World War history of banking is probably the best example of the failure in attempts by the western Allies to deconcentrate dominant enterprises. The Deutsche Bank was divided into ten separate institutions (Pohl 1986: 103). As a result of a change in the law in 1952, these ten regional banks were merged into three area banks which covered the northern, central and southern areas of the country (*ibid*.: 104). In 1957 another legal change led to these three institutions in turn being merged to form the Deutsche Bank AG – thus becoming once again Germany's largest bank. This process, as Shonfield (1965: 242) suggests, consisted of legal changes which were often adjustments to suit the facts. An inexorable process of reconcentration began almost immediately after the Big Three had been broken up by the Allies. On its formal re-constitution in 1957, the Deutsche Bank had 16,597 employees and a balance sheet total of DM 7.6 billion. By 1990 these figures had reached 68,600 and DM 404.7 billion respectively (IW *Zahlen* 1992: 65). Its directors – particularly its chief executives

– have been highly influential in the formulation of both financial and industrial policy (Eglau 1990). As will be seen shortly, this applies particularly to Hermann Josef Abs. The Deutsche also went through another period of rapid expansion under Alfred Herrhausen who was a close confidant of Federal Chancellor Kohl during the 1980s. Herrhausen was assassinated in 1989. In 1990, the Deutsche was Europe's fifth largest bank (Table 7.1).

The history of the Dresdner Bank followed a similar pattern, except that this bank's administrative headquarters moved to Berlin in 1884 (Dresdner Bank, *Wirtschaftsberichte*, November 1972). The Bank retains the name of the city in which it was founded, along with house colours (white and green) which are the same as the flag of the former Kingdom of Saxony. Again, the small regional groupings into which the bank was divided following the Second World War, were succeeded in 1952 by three larger geographical groups – covering the south, west and north respectively. These three banks were merged to re-form the Dresdner Bank AG in 1957, since when it has remained Germany's second largest bank (see Table 7.1). One of the Dresdner's post-war chief executives (Jürgen Ponto) was also assassinated – in 1977. In January 1990, the Bank's executive board held its regular meeting in a specially-chartered train en-route to Dresden where a symbolic reception was held to mark the re-establishment of the bank's representation in that city (FT 31 January 1990).

After its foundation, the Commerzbank took rather longer to gravitate to Berlin. This is because its predecessor, the Commerz- und Discontobank, was founded in Hamburg in 1870, in order to avail itself of the commercial potential of the northern Länder's main port (Commerzbank 1970: 39). Some movement

Table 7.1 Germany's Top Twenty Banks in 1990

Rank in Germany	Rank in Europe		Capital		Assets		Pre-tax profit
			$m	Percentage change	$m	Rank	$m
1	5	Deutsche Bank	10,413	8.3	267,702	1	1,631
2	13	Dresdner Bank	6,424	4.6	189,500	2	1,022
3	18	Commerzbank	5,055	17.0	144,501	3	695
4	28	DG Bank	3,708	23.2	136,450	6	363
5	29	WestLB	3,680	5.9	137,279	5	72
6	32	Bayerische Hypo	3,549	14.8	116,772	7	475
7	33	Bayerische Vereinsbank	3,536	26.3	137,723	4	485
8	42	KfW	2,850	4.7	90,112	9	115
9	47	BayerischeLB	2,414	9.1	103,720	8	148
10	60	NorddeutscheLB	1,798	5.1	82,143	10	131
11	63	BfG Bank	1,739	22.2	40,326	16	79
12	69	Landeskreditbank Baden-Württemberg	1,523	7.7	40,704	15	10
13	80	SüdwestLB	1,261	28.7	58,979	12	73
14	85	Wohnungsbau- Kredit Berlin	1,209	8.5	18,156	31	99
15	89	Helaba	1,188	1.3	58,101	13	68
16	90	BHF Bank	1,168	2.2	25,748	21	161
17	96	Wüstenrot Holding	1,072	5.3	23,228	24	153
18	102	Hamburger Sparkasse	980	5.5	19,463	30	143
19	106	Deutsche Girozentrale	922	75.6	63,508	11	70
20	112	SGZ Bank	856	5.8	19,484	29	122

Source: Extracted from *The Banker*, September 1991: 60

towards Berlin began in 1891, but it was not until 1920 that Berlin finally became its base. Again the deconcentration process resulted in the bank being divided into nine separate regional institutions in 1947–8. This was followed in 1952 by a merger forming three larger organisations to serve the north, west and south of the Federal Republic. As in the other cases, the original parent body re-emerged in 1957. It is particularly important to compare the Commerz with both the BV and WestLB (a description of the BV follows immediately below, while the WestLB is analysed in the section on public-sector banks). The Commerz's balance sheet total was less than that of the WestLB in the 1970s, but it will be seen from Table 7.1 that, when measured by capital, the Commerz was Germany's third largest bank in 1990. Although special factors had resulted in the DG Bank (discussed in the cooperative banks' section) being in fourth position on this measure, it had a smaller balance sheet total than the BV and the WestLB. On the other hand, the Commerz's balance sheet total – not shown in Table 7.1 – also placed it in third position in 1990 (*Die Bank* December 1992). In 1991, however, its balance sheet total was again less than WestLB and only marginally greater than the BV (*ibid.*). By

1992 the BV – with a balance sheet total exceeding DM 250 billion – had moved up to fourth position at the expense of the Commerz (*Banker* March 1993). But by virtue of its extensive nation-wide presence, and for traditional reasons, the Commerz is still included in the phrase 'Big Three'. In any case, it will be concluded below that the private-sector banks, including the Commerz, returned excellent profit figures in the early 1990s. Moreover, it will also become apparent that balance-sheet expansion reflected concentration and the rush for growth. Capital-adequacy requirements were accordingly changed – see the prudential arrangements section.

Although a study of the evolution of the Big Three reveals many similarities, there seem to be traditional differences in management style. The suggestion here is that managerial responsibilities are perhaps more widely shared in the Deutsche Bank than at the Commerzbank, where a more rigidly enforced decision-making hierarchy exists. The Dresdner Bank perhaps lies between the two extremes. During the Commerzbank's adverse experience in 1980, Herr Lichtenberg was called back from the chairmanship of the supervisory board to again become, temporarily, chief executive. This was because the previous incumbent had resigned on grounds of ill-health. Lichtenberg took three actions. First, the supervisory and executive boards received no performance-related payments. Second, he announced that he expected the staff to work harder and ordered all bank managers to a meeting at Head Office. Third, he vigorously embarked on the task of finding a new chief executive – a post to which Dr Walter Seipp of the WestLB was appointed, holding the post until his retirement in 1991. Seipp confirmed that the Commerzbank was overcentralised

and bureaucratic, but unlike other large companies with such a centralised structure it did not possess a strong system of financial controls (FT 30 July 1982). He reconstructed the bank in such a way that its profitability reached unprecedented levels (*Euromoney* July 1991).

As already noted above, it is really the legal form of a private-sector bank which determines whether it is statistically grouped in either the 'regional and other commercial banks' or the 'private bankers' group. All banks registered as companies belong to the former. Moreover, the term 'regional' cannot be taken too literally: while most banks in the group operate only in a certain part of Germany, some are not confined to one region and consequently maintain branches in most parts of the country (Schneider *et al.* 1978: 13). The BfG Bank, which was established by the trade unions, is also statistically classed in this group. Because of both its origins and developments during the 1980s, however, it is discussed in a separate section.

It will be seen from Table 7.1 that the two largest banks in the 'regional' group are the Bayerische Vereinsbank (BV) and the Bayerische Hypotheken- und Wechselbank (Hypo-Bank). These two Bavarian (*Bayerische*) private-sector banks have a long history: the Vereinsbank was established in 1780 and the Hypo-Bank in 1835. In addition to conducting a full range of universal banking business, these two banks, together with the relatively much smaller (DM 3 billion balance sheet total) Norddeutsche Hypotheken und Wechselbank (Nordhypo Bank), traditionally operate as mortgage banks on a large scale. These institutions are therefore legally permitted to issue mortgage and communal bonds to finance their long-term loans. In other words, their loans are refinanced by long-term bond issues

(Stein 1977: 13 and 1979: 19 and 42). This differs from the practice in other commercial banks which have to carry out mortgage business through subsidiaries. The closely interwoven nature of housing finance, bond issues and the unique institutions engaged in these activities will be analysed in a separate section below. Among other things, it will be shown that this business accounts for a 25 per cent share of the banking market.

The BV's mortgage business has always been conducted throughout Germany, although it was only in recent years that its commercial banking business was extended beyond the frontiers of Bavaria. Hence its immediate post-war growth was tied closely to industrialisation in Bavaria, later followed by a series of take-overs or part-acquisitions of a number of small private banks. It also took substantial shareholdings in cities such as Hamburg, Düsseldorf, Frankfurt and Saarbrücken. In many ways, however, the most important merger involving the BV was when it merged with the formerly Bavarian government-owned Bayerische Staatsbank in 1971. As a result, the newly constituted private-sector bank entered *Fortune Magazine*'s top fifty international banks outside the USA (*Fortune Magazine* August 1972: 160; Peltzer and Nebendorf 1973: 18). When ranked by assets in 1990, it was larger than the Hypo; but it was slightly smaller in terms of its capital (see Table 7.1).

In the 1970s, the Hypo-Bank emerged strongly as a result of its active shareholding policy, particularly in breweries. These latter holdings sparked off some controversy, for the Hypo-Bank acquired about 20 per cent of the Federal Republic's beer market (Rutherford 1974: 32). Moreover, links between the Hypo and Dresdner Banks resulted in the formation of a company with a 15 per cent share

of the beer market (Peltzer and Nebendorf 1973: 18; Vogl 1973: 47). After a three-year absence, the Hypo returned to the top fifty banks outside the USA in 1975 (*Fortune Magazine* August 1976 : 244). As shown in Table 7.1, it was Germany's sixth, and Europe's 32nd, largest bank in 1990.

Merger activity within the 'regional and other banks' statistical grouping has also resulted in the emergence of the Berliner Handels- und Frankfurter Bank (BHF Bank), as well as the Vereins- und Westbank, Hamburg (Stein 1977: 18). At the time, these two banks occupied ranks in the top twenties and thirties respectively with balance sheet totals of about DM 17 billion and DM 9 billion (Stein 1977: 40) – far behind the Bavarian pair and the BfG Bank.

PRIVATE BANKERS

Private banking in Germany has a long and important history (Pohl 1986: 18). Approximately twenty of the private banks operating in the Federal Republic were founded before 1800 (Stein 1990: 30). But the total number of such banks has decreased rapidly since the 1920s, mainly as a result of competition from the other banks. In 1928 there were more than 2,000 private banks; by 1933 the number had fallen to 750 – another causal factor being a banking crisis. After the Second World War there were 300 private banks in the land area which became the Federal Republic and by 1970 there were 163 (Peltzer and Nebendorf 1973: 19; Stein 1990: 21). On the revised 1986 statistical basis, the number of private banks had fallen to 84 in 1991 (Figure 7.1).

One should not conclude, however, that this group has completely lost its significance, even though the group's share in the total business volume was halved between 1970 and 1991. (Prior to 1970, those institutions which remained had experienced higher than average growth – Peltzer and Nebendorf 1973: 20). They are distinguishable from the large and regional banks by the fact that they do not carry out mass business, and by the additional fact that they maintain no, or only a few, branches. Given the recent rise in staff and equipment costs (see below), this absence of branches is a cost advantage. On the other hand, a considerable cost disadvantage historically arose from the relatively low intake of funds from non-bank sources, with the consequent higher-cost need to borrow from within the banking system (*ibid.*: 20). Nonetheless, the most important target customers have always been multi-millionaires who expect sound financial advice on an absolutely confidential basis.

On their lending side, there are considerable differences within the group. Some private bankers operate on an international or supra-regional basis, while others are purely local in character (Stein 1990: 31–2). While some private bankers deal mainly with export financing, others favour domestic business. Domestic specialisations for the major private banks are in industrial and investment activities, while the smaller institutions manage instalment sales finance. Hence the larger private bankers tend to resemble the English merchant bankers. Sal. Oppenheim jr & Cie., Cologne-Frankfurt, which was founded in 1789, was the largest private bank in 1988 with a balance sheet total of DM 13.7 million (*ibid.*). Its decision to sell its controlling stake in Colonia Versicherung AG to Groupe Victoire meant that Germany's second largest insurer passed into French hands in 1989. On the other hand, the purely local private banker typically has a relatively small balance sheet total (Peltzer and Nebendorf 1973: 19).

During the 1980s, the private banks became highly sought after acquisitions by large German and foreign banks. Hence, most of the large German banks enjoyed a presence in this sector. More significantly, however, other European banks regarded this type of purchase as being the only means of transforming their fringe representation in German banking in the run up to EC 1993. For example, in 1990 Barclays purchased Merck, Finck – a highly prestigious private bank based in Munich. (A member of the von Finck family helped in the nineteenth century to found what became the two largest German insurance companies: Allianz AG and Münchener Rückversicherungsgesellschaft AG – see Figure 7.3 below). The Federal Cartel Office was not opposed to the takeover of Finck by Barclays (BT 1991: 115). Similarly, Lloyds held the majority stake in Schröder, Münchmeyer, Hengst (SMH) which it acquired after this private bank had over-extended itself by heavy lending to a client who went bankrupt (Ogger 1992: 85–6; also see the section on prudential arrangements below). Midland held the controlling stake in Trinkaus und Burkhardt, although this bank became a KGaA. Corporate status does not necessarily exclude banks from acting *inter alia* as private bankers, but to retain the exclusive status of a private bank such companies must remain in private family ownership with untraded shares (Stein 1990: 30).

The private bankers have trained some of the economy's most influential figures: for example, Hermann Abs, and Robert Pferdmenges, as well as – his father was also caretaker in the Dreyfus household – the long-serving head of trade union banking and business, Walter Hesselbach (Eglau 1980: 125; Engelmann 1978: 191).

The latter pioneered the formation, in 1974, of West Germany's largest business group under one roof. The holding company was the Beteiligungsgesellshaft für Gemeinwirtschaft (Hartrich 1980: 236; IW *Zahlen* 1981: 87). This mammoth organisation – which collapsed during the 1980s – included the BfG Bank which is analysed below. Another influential figure formerly associated with the private bankers is Otto Lambsdorff – the former Federal Economics Minister and leading member of the FDP. He was general manager at the Trinkaus Bank.

Abs became banking's most important figure in the post-Second World War era. He had begun his career, before the war, as an apprentice in a small private bank in Bonn (Eglau 1980: 121; Englemann 1987: 57; FT8 February 1994). His knowledge of international finance, however, resulted in his being appointed head of the Deutsche Bank's foreign operations while still in his thirties. After the Second World War, it was he who assumed the unofficial managerial responsibilities which were to lead to the Bank's eventual reconstitution (Hartrich 1980: 233). Although interned by the British after the war, and officially banned from the Deutsche Bank, Abs became the first general manager of the special institution set up to channel Marshall Aid counterpart funds into industrial and housing re-development – the state-owned Reconstruction and Development Loan Corporation (*Kreditanstalt für Wiederaufbau* – KfW) (Eglau 1990: 37–9; Englemann 1987: 60; Shonfield 1965: 276–8). This institution has become the nation's largest special-purpose bank, specialising in low-interest loans for regional development (Figure 7.1 and Table 7.1). Moreover, Abs' knowledge of international finance enabled him to reduce West Germany's reparation payments from DM 20 billion to DM 14 billion (Eglau 1980: 124).

Even when he had moved back to head the reconstituted Deutsche Bank, Abs remained on the KfW's supervisory board, initially as its deputy chairman, then as its chairman. At the Deutsche Bank he remained chief executive for many years, before moving over to the chairmanship of its supervisory board and, finally, becoming honorary president. During the early 1960s he occupied so many seats on the supervisory boards of other companies that the 1966 Act to limit the number of such seats any banker could hold was dubbed 'Lex Abs'. One of his successors at the Deutsche Bank – Erhard's nephew, Dr Wilfried Guth, the bank's joint chief executive – had also served as an executive board member of the KfW.

Abs shared with Pferdmenges the role of advising Adenauer on economic policy and relations with the Allies, while Erhard, Schäffer and Vocke were perhaps left to manage the national economy (Chapter 3; Hartrich 1980: 159). Vocke also belonged to Adenauer's small group of advisers, but Pferdmenges, a wealthy partner of the Sal. Oppenheim private bank, also became a close personal friend of Adenauer's (Eglau 1980: 123–4; Engelmann 1978: 66). Among other things, he assisted with the financial arrangements responsible for the resurgence of the August-Thyssenhütte, the Ruhr steel-making complex. With Pferdmenges' help the chief executive who re-built this huge concern for the Thyssen family (Hans Günther Sohl) was able to raise finance from the major banks, the Federal Government and the Marshall Aid funds (Hartrich 1980: 216).

Hence one should infer that the private bankers had a proud tradition and an influential economic role. The collapse of the Herstatt Bank (see below) shocked their fraternity. For the then head of Merck, Finck & Co., for example, it was a catastrophe which, had it happened to him, would have resulted in his 'never again showing his face in public' (*Die Zeit* 19/80). The SMH crisis (also see below) caused confidence to be shaken, too. However, its reputation remained more or less intact (Pohl 1986: 113).

THE COOPERATIVE BANKS

Cooperative societies, organised along the lines pioneered by Robert Owen, were founded in Germany during the nineteenth century by Frank Hermann Schulze-Delitzsch (1808–83) and Friedrich Wilhelm Raiffeisen (1818–88). They followed the principle of self-help amongst artisans and peasants respectively in an attempt to defend them against the new claims of industry (Hesselbach 1976: 12–13). The Raiffeisen cooperatives, the first of which opened in Neuwied in 1865, consisted of a network of agricultural credit institutions which enabled farmers to borrow money to meet bills which were presented before the revenue from annual harvests was derived (Henderson 1975: 129). Much the same principle – that is providing credit in anticipation of future revenue – applied to the Schulze-Delitzsch cooperative banks, which became known as Volksbanken, and which were established in *urban* areas in parallel to the Raiffeisen cooperative banks in *agricultural* areas. The bulk of the members' assets were held outside of the cooperatives in the form of their human capital and, to a certain extent in rural areas, their resources and property (Bonus and Schmidt 1990: 187).

The typical cooperative operated in a small geographical area. Members possessed adequate information about each others' loan status, thereby removing the informational asymmetries, uncertainty and monopoly power which would have led to an outside lender charging exorbitant loan rates; but they lacked the expertise to make investment judgements for their transient surplus funds (*ibid.*: 187 and 193). Following the deaths of the movement's two founders, and a change of the law which enabled members to take limited liability, Wilhelm Haas (1839–1913) established a three-tier structure of local primary cooperatives, regional central banks and a national coordinating body. The regional banks thus not only began to act as the local banks' liquidity managers and refinancing centres, but also supplemented their services where they could not afford the necessary staff or facilities (DG Bank 1981: 11). This model was used in West Germany: the local banks held a majority of shares in the regional banks which in turn held most of the share capital of the national bank. By the end of 1988, there were five regional banks; four were AGs, while only the largest was an eG (see Figure 7.2; Stein 1990: 40). In addition, the country's largest home-loan association (Schwäbisch Hall) and the eighth largest insurance company (R+V Versicherungen) are part of the group.

The rural and urban cooperative banks have flourished. One indication of this success is the size of their national institution (the DG Bank – Deutsche Genossenschaftsbank, see Table 7.1). The very nature of the cooperative banks means that their most important business lies in the savings and short- or medium-term lending business, even though they increasingly conduct their business as universal banks. Their business has expanded rapidly partly because the Act of 1889 allowed them to add a further 50 per cent to their equity capital when determining their lending ceiling. (Under the Banking Act a bank's lending for many years was not permitted to exceed eighteen times its equity capital – see the prudential arrangements' section below). This additional 50 per cent arose from the legal form which nearly all urban and most rural cooperative banks adopt – i.e. *beschränkte Nachschußpflicht* or the limited liability of their members to make additional contributions should their bank become insolvent. (Two of the ten largest cooperative banks were AGs in 1988, the remainder being eGs.) Because this legal concession enabled the cooperative banks to expand their business, the savings banks' association, which contended that the local authority owners have full liability anyway, lobbied for their enabling Act to be amended so as to grant them a similar concession. This would have given them an opportunity to further expand their own business, although they were in any case far larger than the cooperative group. In the 1985 amendment to the Banking Act (see 'prudential arrangements' below) this call by the savings banks for an addition to the guarantors' uncalled liability to the liable capital was in effect rejected: in what was termed a 'compromise' solution, the uncalled members' liability in the cooperative sector was to be successively reduced to not more than 25 per cent over a period of ten years (MRDB 3/85: 38).

If one considers the three universal groups cited in Figure 7.1, however, deposits held by the cooperative banks increased more rapidly than those held by the savings banks during the period 1950–87; the same is true of balance sheet totals and, to a lesser extent, lending (Bonus and Schmidt 1990: 184). Moreover, if measured by deposits, lending and balance sheet totals, the commercial banks' market shares decreased during the same period.

Within the cooperative movement itself, the number of primary banks has decreased, while membership has expanded. As a result, the average number of members per cooperative association increased from 118 in 1907 to 3,147 in 1987 (*ibid.*: 195). Nonetheless, this growth of cooperative banking has brought about some fundamental changes in the movement. Shares have become very low risk assets because the probability of insolvency is low. Yet relatively high dividends have been paid, irrespective of results – thus leading to the shares acquiring the characteristics of fixed-interest securities (Bonus and Schmidt 1990: 197). This absence of risk has left shareholders with no permanent reminder of their direct ownership of the local primary bank and their indirect ownership of the upper two tiers. In any case, share capital accounts for only 32 per cent of equity capital and the property rights of the banks' owners have been sharply curtailed (*ibid.*: 198). One consequential problem with the cooperative banks resembles that of the dilemma posed by the proxy-voting system dominated by the Big Three (see below): relative small groups of members, who are the owners, find it difficult to exercise control over management. Each member has only one vote, just as one share in an AG gives one vote to its owner (*ibid.*: 209 and 212–13). In effect, the cooperative member seems to have surrendered control to management in return for a virtually riskless investment. Interestingly enough, the regional association of the cooperative banks reacted adversely to an FDP proposal in Hesse that the savings banks be partly privatised by pointing out that the taxpayer rather than the proposed private owners would bear any risk (*Wirtschaftswoche* 24/89: 50).

This leads to a consideration of the role of the central institutions of the cooperative banks. As shown in Figure 7.1, by 1991 they had fallen to three in number, plus the DG Bank. The gradual fall in their number – there had been 19 in 1957 – was initially the result of a series of mergers among the regional central banks themselves. During the 1980s, however, the DG bank initiated a process of taking over the role of the regional central banks, initially in Bavaria (Stein 1990: 40). The traditional role of the regionals had been similar to the central institutions of the savings banks (*Landesbanken*), namely acting as cheque clearing houses and central banks, although the overall coordinating power of the DG Bank has always been much more powerful than its immediate equivalent in the savings bank sector (*Deutsche Girozentrale*) which is half owned by the *Landesbanken*. (The other half belongs to the DSGV.) For example, whereas each *Landesbank* went international in its own right (see below), the international aspirations of the cooperative banks were channelled into the DG Bank. The DG Bank also manages the liquidity of the cooperative banking sector. In short, the DG Bank became a fully-fledged universal bank (Pohl 1986: 141). All this is remarkable since the DG Bank was established in its present form in only 1975 (DG 1981: 7–8).

But this process of centralisation, along with the rapid growth in the average size of the local cooperative, have undermined the original notion of local cooperation among relatively small numbers of farmers or small and medium-sized businessmen in urban areas. Such a small unit would, it is true, be unable to compete with the other two banking sectors. In any case, in 1985 the DG Bank was obliged to absorb the Bavarian regional bank when the latter ran into liquidity problems caused by property speculation (Pohl 1986: 145). However, proposals for further centralisa-tion in 1989 – which would have completely removed the second tier and made the DG Bank Germany's second largest bank – were bitterly opposed by two of the remaining five regional central banks. Ultimately, the two smallest regional central banks agreed to merge their interests with those of the DG Bank – the reason for its succeeding the WestLB as Germany's fourth largest bank in 1990 (see Table 7.1). Prior to this merger, the smallest regional had been poised to merge with the second largest of the remaining three regionals. Meanwhile, the largest of the regionals made a DM Eurobond issue under its own name (FT 28 April 1989; DM Eurobonds are discussed in the *Finanzplatz Deutschland* section). (The three remaining regionals jointly have about half the balance sheet total of the DG Bank.) The Federal Cartel Office (BT 1991: 115) found the mergers between the DG Bank and two of the regionals to be consistent with German anti-trust law but pointed out that the traditional three-tier structure of cooperative banking had been further undermined. This development was somewhat sceptically debated by juxtaposing its extravagance and its inevitability (Bonus et al. 1988).

Shortly after the merger, Helmut Guthardt (the chief executive of the DG Bank, who had masterminded the reorganisation) was forced to resign over a bond repurchasing agreement made by a senior trader without the bank's knowledge. The agreement resulted in losses of DM 600 million. The irony was that the repurchase agreement had been made with a French bank and the intention behind the reorganisation had been to prepare for the EC-wide competition in financial services which would result from EC 1993. It was thought that the larger cooperative banks in the EC could provide linked services, not least by moving away from their traditional wholesale services and into investment banking. The DG Bank also found itself holding the bulk of the shares in the embattled, former trade union, Co op enterprise, having failed to reach agreement to purchase the trade union's insurance company (Volksfür- sorge). At the beginning of 1991 Asko Deutsche Kaufhaus AG acquired a 70 per cent share in the Co op and began a radical process of rationalisation. (It will be shown in Chapter 8 that this led Asko into financial difficulties.) Well after EC 1993, however, the issue facing Herr Guthardt's replacement (Bernd Thie- mann, formerly chief executive of the Norddeutsche LB) will be whether some form of organisation involving the membership is possible, rather than emulating the other large universal banks, a role assumed by the DG Bank. Unwinding what Thiemann called the 'mismatched position of grandiose pro- portions' between assets and liabilities would have to precede such efforts (FT 25 September 1992). Capital injections were necessary to cover problems created in the recent past, and to meet the strict new capital adequacy requirements (see the section on prudential requirements). In addition, provisions of DM 690 million in 1992 meant the bank broke even (FAZ 20 February 1993).

As Bonus (1986) has demonstrated, the cooperative association is characterised by a precarious equilibrium between 'centrip- etal' forces (benefits of collective associ- ation), and 'centrifugal' forces (benefits of independent operation). But the *Landesbanken* and the central institutions of the cooperatives share the problem of relying on their respective banking sys- tems for their funds, as well as holding their member banks liquidity. In the case of the cooperatives' central institutions such deposits account for three-quarters

of their volume of business. Variations in the cost of such funds affect the profita- bility of the central institutions (MRDB 8/81: 18–19).

THE BfG BANK, *ALLFINANZ* AND INSURANCE

Around the turn of the century, parallel to the development of consumers' societies, the trade unions began to form insurance companies, hotels, building societies and housing associations (Hesselbach 1976: 26). Although the desire to manage their own funds dates back to the formation of German trade unions, however, the first trade union banks postdate the coopera- tive agricultural and urban savings banks. Trade union banks of the Weimar Republic showed some tendency to universal banking activities, but their primary function was to act as *Haus- banken* to the trade unions (*ibid.*: 89). A wider set of objectives was established after the Second World War. As was the case with the Big Three, however, regional banks – six in number in this instance – were established in 1949 and 1950. In 1953, these banks were joined by the Berlin-based Bank für Wirtschaft und Arbeit. Following the Federal Act permit- ting amalgamation of banking institutions in 1957, one common establishment, the Bank für Gemeinwirtschaft (BfG), was formed. Its headquarters are in Frankfurt and it became one of the economy's top banks (see Table 7.1).

Another feature which the BfG had in common with the other big banks was its shareholdings in other banks and specialised credit institutions such as hire purchase companies and building socie- ties. In places like Hamburg, Frankfurt and Düsseldorf, it went into partnership with well-established private banks which – as seen above – tend to have expertise in investment matters and function rather like the British merchant bank. In addition, the BfG had links with the public-sector savings bank movement (*ibid*.: 94–5). Finally, the bank also established representation in London, New York, Luxembourg, Hong Kong and Moscow (Stein 1990: 28).

During the 1980s, the BfG became something of a pawn in two developments. The first development was the collapse of important parts of the trade unions' business empire, while the second development was the dramatic change in the relationship between banking and insurance. Since the BfG was itself an important part of the trade unions' holding company (Beteiligungsgesellschaft für Gemeinwirtschaft AG – BGAG), it was bound to be even more affected by the Co op's financial difficulties than the DG Bank. In addition, the failure of Neue Heimat – the property and construction subsidiary of the BGAG – also caused losses for the BfG. To make matters even worse, both Neue Heimat and the Co op became involved in major corporate scandals (Ogger 1992: 78–84). Finally, the only remaining part of the BGAG – the insurance giant Volksfürsorge (Vofü) – could not be readily sold because of the enhanced salaries and other conditions of employment enjoyed by its employees. This factor finally deterred the DG Bank from adding Vofü to its R + V holding, although there had also been internal disagreement about the proposed purchase as early as 1987. The BfG itself also had a rather poor image in terms of relatively high pay, overstaffing and therefore low productivity.

Late in 1986 the Aachener and Münchener Beteiligungs AG (AMB), the holding company of West Germany's fifth largest insurance group and at the time 20 per cent owned by Royal Insurance of the UK, made a successful DM 1.9 billion bid for a 50 per cent plus one share stake in the BfG. This was the harbinger of what in the second half of the 1980s became one of the most important developments in financial services in the post-war period, namely the intensive cross selling of insurance and banking products all under one roof. The German term for this change in marketing strategy – *Allfinanz* (multi-purpose financial services) – suitably summarises this development. As part of this trend, in 1989, AMB took a 25 per cent holding in, and managerial control of, Vofü. This latter bid was made in conjunction with the purchase of another 25 per cent stake in Vofü by the Italian insurer La Fondiaria, although early in 1992 AMB bought this latter holding too.

Apparently little was done by the BfG chief executive at the time of the takeover (Thomas Wegscheider) to rationalise the BfGs activities. His continued support for the Co op led to the bank, as that organisation's chief domestic creditor, having to write off bad debt; loans to Poland, the SMH bank and Korf Steel also led to losses (*Der Spiegel* 2/90; also see the section on prudential arrangements below). Profits were only DM 50 million in both 1987 and 1988, in the latter case only made possible by the sale of the bank's new prestige 37-storey building in Frankfurt am Main (*Wirtschaftswoche* 3/90). (The Deutsche thereby acquired a third tower to add to its famous 'debit and credit' towers. The BfG may eventually repurchase its present office block from a bankrupt Scandinavian property developer.) The BfG's record in this respect was compared to the Commerzbank prior to Seipp's appointment (see above). With the support of the BGAG members of the supervisory board, the chief executive of AMB (Helmut Gies), asked for

Wegscheider's resignation. In March 1990 the former head of the *Landesbank* in Rhineland Palatinate (Paul Wieandt) was appointed, not least because of his experience in rationalising his previous institution. Although Wieandt wanted the bank to remain universal in character, he set about closing smaller branches in large cities and discussing redundancy compensation with the BfG's works council. New consumer groups were also targeted. In addition, AMB injected DM 250 million into BfG and wrote down its investment in the bank by DM 633 million at the end of 1990 (FT 21 March 1991).

During 1990, as a prelude to EC 1993, AMB approached the 72 per cent state-owned French insurer Assurances Générales de France (AGF) with a view to a cooperative venture (FAZ 10 July 1992). AGF rejected AMB's terms and independently built up a 25 per cent holding in AMB which the German company refused to enter in its share register. Following complex and vituperative litigation, AGF succeeded in registering its voting rights at AMB's AGM in late 1992. Meanwhile, the state-owned French Crédit Lyonnais had been conducting exploratory but somewhat protracted negotiations with the Commerz, again with a view to reaching a cooperative agreement prior to EC 1993 (FT 17 July 1991). As early as July 1992, however, AGF pledged a controlling interest in BfG to Crédit Lyonnais. The acquisition of a majority holding of 50 per cent plus one share in the BfG by the French bank was duly approved at AMB's AGM – and therefore in time for the beginning of EC 1993 (FT 31 December 1992). AMB retained a 25 per cent stake in the BfG, as did the BGAG (*Economist* 9 January 1993). Consequently, the Crédit Lyonnais became Europe's largest bank, leaving the Deutsche in third position behind Crédit Agricole on balance sheet

totals (*Der Spiegel* 29/92; FAZ 10 July 1992). Concurrently, the restructuring of the BfG had continued. Including own-account trading results, the group reported profits of DM 221.1 million in 1991, compared with a loss of DM 389.9 million at the end of 1990 (FT 24 June 1992). However, at the parent bank there were losses at the partial operating level, reflecting extraordinary costs associated with restructuring. Provisions against doubtful sovereign debt also rose by DM 3.2 billion. Productivity at the BfG had been boosted, however, and profitability was expected to improve further when its portfolio of low-yield bonds matured in 1994. Moreover, Crédit Lyonnais injected badly-needed capital. (Like the DG Bank, the BfG required capital to cover its past losses and the new capital adequacy requirements.)

There are two lessons for the present analysis. The first is a case study of the relative power of supervisory board chairmen and chief executives already discussed in Chapter 6; the second is concerned with the pre-EC 1993 integration of finance markets. With respect to the first point, Gies – who had become chairman of the supervisory board – subsequently announced that the AMB's chief executive was to be replaced by his opposite number from Vofü (SZ 15 July 1992). This did not prevent shareholders from censuring Gies at the 1992 AGM for the acquisition of the BfG. The second point is much more significant from an economic point of view. While France is Germany's most important trading partner and vice versa, mutual penetration of each country's financial service industries had remained a pipe dream. (Private banker Oppenheim's decision in 1989 to sell its shares in Colonia to Victoire was an exception.) The relatively rapid developments discussed in the previous paragraph thus represented a dramatic breakthrough. Even though the German banks and insurance companies – particularly the Dresdner/Allianz and Münchener Rück – had expressed concern about AMB's lack of success in rationalising the BfG, they had taken no relatively dramatic steps to resolve the serious problems in two of the economy's large banks and insurance companies. This leads nicely to the sequel to AMB's 'chaotic' AGM in 1992 (TVF 31 December 1992). La Fondiaria – the Italian insurer – had a 20 per cent stake in AMB. At the AGM Fondiaria opposed the registration of AGF's stake in AMB, but it was ruled that the Italian company had itself failed to register its own shares in time. This threw the development of a European cooperation deal between AMB, Fondiaria and Royal Insurance into doubt. Moreover, in May 1993 a group of German financial institutions purchased Fondiaria's stake in AMB. As a result, Allianz achieved a total holding of about 28 per cent in AMB; the Münchener Rück, which is linked to Allianz through a large cross shareholding, acquired a total holding of 8.6 per cent in AMB; the Dresdner Bank, which is partly owned by Allianz, raised its shareholding in AMB to 14 per cent; the Deutsche Bank purchased the remaining 10 per cent of Fondiaria's stake (*Economist* 15 May 1993).

The link between the Dresdner and Allianz was noted immediately above. These two companies also formed an *Allfinanz* pact in 1988. In July 1991, Allianz AG – by far Europe's largest insurer – took a 22 per cent stake in the Dresdner, the latter having undertaken to retail the former's life insurance policies through its branches. (About the same time, various other major industrial and financial companies formed two holding companies which each accounted for a further 10 per cent shareholding in the

Dresdner, thereby dissolving the tradition that no shareholder owned more than 5 per cent of the bank's share capital – *Die Zeit* 34/91). The Federal Cartel Office ordered the Allianz to reduce this holding, and the Monopolies Commission had earlier recommended a thorough overall of the regulatory framework in insurance (MK VII). In a dramatic U-turn, however, the Office later withdrew its objection (FT 5 October 1992; the Office's work is explored in the anti-trust sections of Chapter 8). Allianz became so influential in the Dresdner's affairs that the latter's chief executive decided to move to the chair of the bank's supervisory board lest the then recently retired chief executive of Allianz took the post (FT 1 July 1992). Moreover, when the close business cooperation between Allianz and the Deutsche was severed – also in 1988 – the Deutsche decided to establish its own life insurance company. On the other hand, the Deutsche continued to hold equities worth over DM 4 billion in Allianz, plus a further DM 1 billion in Münchener Rück (Eglau 1990: 79; *Euromoney* January 1990). Other business reasons caused the Deutsche's diversification: West Germans were already placing one-third of their savings in tax-effective life insurance, and there was a distinct probability that the traditional low-interest savings deposits of German banks would become less popular as savers looked for new products (*Economist* 1 September 1990). These developments took further shape in 1992 when the Deutsche bought 30 per cent of the share capital of the family-owned Gerling insurance company. Gerling was estimated in IW *Zahlen* (1992: 65) to be Germany's fourth largest insurance concern and the company was one of Europe's leading industrial insurers (*Handelsblatt* 13 July 1992); in addition, the Deutsche purchased a 51 per cent holding in Deutscher Herold (FT 26 October 1992). Hence, two powerful new forces emerged in Germany as a result of the *Allfinanz* phase. They were the Allianz/Dresdner axis and the Deutsche. It is possible to view this near duopoly as a reaction to the French entry into the market.

It is surprising that there has not been more controversy about 'the economic power of the insurers'. A whole section below will have to be devoted to this phenomenon as far as the banks are concerned, such is the degree of policy concern in this field. Yet the Monopolies Commission has criticised the effects on policy premia of the regulatory framework supervised by the BAV (Bundesaufsichtsamt für das Versicherungswesen) (MK VII: 339):

. . . Policyholders in France, Britain and the USA have much further-reaching possibilities . . . [to tailor] their individual insurance needs. The standard extent of insurance cover approved by the BAV tends to be more comprehensive . . . There is also a much more pronounced differentiation of premium rate characteristics [in these other countries].

This situation may well have changed with the introduction of the EC life and non-life insurance directives in 1994, and if EC 1993 had thereby resulted in British and French companies introducing their pricing policies into Germany. Similarly, the directives would presumably have affected the higher premia and costs of German insurance relative to other EC member states (Deregulierungskommission 1991: 22–3). Given the above developments, however, it is unlikely that there will be a great deal of change.

Moreover, in contrast to the competition between the three sectors in banking, the economy's two largest insurers –

Allianz and Münchener Rück – hold 25 per cent of each other's equity. Their chief executives sit on each other's supervisory boards. Their head offices are on the same street in Munich. In 1989 Allianz had an investment portfolio which was equivalent to 5 per cent of (West) Germany's GNP; in 1991 it was probably larger than Sweden's GDP (*Economist* 15 April 1989 and 2 November 1991). Shares in many top German companies and banks were in this portfolio. When these shareholdings are added to the system of reciprocal representation on the supervisory boards of other major companies, as illustrated in Figure 7.3, the significance of Allianz in the German financial sector becomes unmistakable. In addition, Allianz's holdings abroad include Britain's Cornhill Insurance company, although it had earlier failed to take over Eagle Star. In 1990, it succeeded in fighting off a rival bid and took over 51 per cent of the East German Deutsche Versicherung, acquiring the remaining 49 per cent in 1991. The rival bid had been led by Colonia and the consortium had also included Nordstern – in which Colonia has a stake – and R+V. This near monopoly holding in the east again raised objections from the Cartel Office.

THE PUBLIC SECTOR: *SPARKASSEN* AND *LANDESBANKEN*

The savings banks (*Sparkassen*) movement in Germany has a longer history than both the cooperative and trade union banks: encouraging the small saver became the responsibility of the public authorities at the beginning of the nineteenth century. Since this task was to be undertaken on a local basis, it was the local authorities who either voluntarily took the initiative of establishing savings banks or, after 1838,

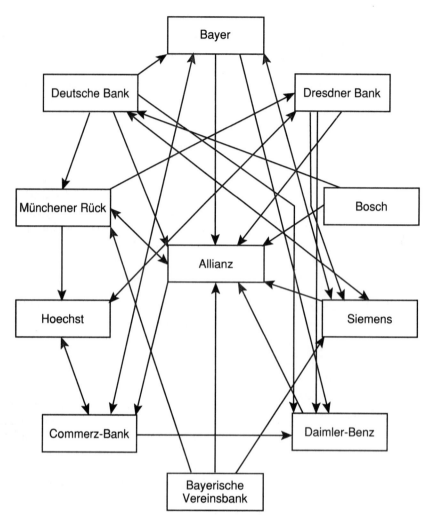

Figure 7.3 Germany plc: Allianz at the centre
Source: Wirtschaftswoche 51/91

were required by statute to perform this function.

Nowadays savings banks generate a large excess of liquidity. The larger institutions among them are also some of the world's larger banks. The Hamburger Sparkasse, for example, stands at number 18 in Table 7.1. This latter institution belongs, however, to a small group of seven savings banks whose charters are drawn up on the basis of private – as opposed to public – law. Strictly speaking, therefore, they could conduct business outside of their own areas but have voluntarily refrained from doing so. They belong to their own association of 'free' savings banks (*Verband der Freien Sparkassen*). Although the group is small in number, it accounts for 8 per cent of the total savings banks' business volume.

In addition to Hamburg, the savings banks of Bremen, Stuttgart and Frankfurt/ M were all in the 'top ten'. In 1989, the Frankfurt free savings bank took over the city's savings bank.

In 1909 a giro or cheque clearing system was introduced into the savings banks' sector. Today this system is operated by the *Landesbanken* which also act as regional central banks in the various Länder of the Federal Republic. Although the ownership of this upper tier is complex (see below), the savings banks and Länder governments have historically been the owners of the *Landesbanken*. The *Landesbanken* therefore manage the immense liquidity of the savings banks and act as house banks to their Land government. In other words, the savings banks provide retail banking services but pass to the *Landesbanken* requests for specialised tasks and wholesale banking services such as foreign exchange and securities trading – directly analogous functions to the upper tiers of the cooperative banks. Whereas the history of some *Landesbanken* can be traced back to the mainly specialist 'public' banks established during the eighteenth century, it was the roles assumed at the beginning of this century which set the *Landesbanken-Girozentralen* (to give them their full title) on the road to their present-day significance in the West German banking system (VÖB 1981: 6 and 12). Because the *Landesbanken* provide finance for public sector projects and offer a complete range of commercial and investment banking services, they perform the universal banking functions emphasised at the beginning of this chapter (*ibid.*: 16). Both the savings banks and the *Landesbanken* are subject to statutory control at the regional level, but the nationwide and international banking activities of the *Landesbanken* have excited considerable controversy, as will

be shortly shown. It will be appreciated that as the *Landesbanken* became more concentrated, the central problem for the owners of these banks was influencing policy decisions.

In the post-war period, the savings banks widened their range of services to compete with the commercial banks (BSA 1978: 22). Historically, they had largely concentrated on savings deposit business and the corresponding long-term lending, whereas they began making increasing inroads into the short-term deposit and credit business. Although specialising primarily in lending to medium and small-sized industry and the self-employed, the larger among the savings banks, and more particularly the *Landesbanken*, also engage heavily in large-scale lending business, providing finance to industry and taking part in issuing syndicates (BBk 1971: 9). Indeed, the customers of the Big Three, *Landesbanken* and central cooperative banks primarily consist of large-scale borrowers. They have permanent access to the Euromarkets, which operate on small margins (MRDB 8/81: 17). These banking groups are therefore exposed to keener competition than the smaller savings banks and credit cooperatives, which supply credit predominantly to medium and small-sized firms and to individuals who can draw less readily on the Euromarkets.

The *Landesbanken* and their central institution are large by both domestic and international standards. An indication of their size is the fact that five of the 12 institutions appear in the top 20 banks of the Federal Republic – see Table 7.1. A series of mergers between 1969 and 1972 created the giant Westdeutsche (WestLB), the Bayerische LB and the Norddeutsche (NordLB). These three banks were destined to become the pace makers in two decades of public-sector acquisitions. As early as 1969 the WestLB was already at rank number six in *Fortune*'s list of top fifty banks outside the USA (*Fortune* August 1971: 156). The NordLB first appeared in the list as number 49 in 1970 (*ibid.*). This was followed by the first Bayerische LB appearance at number 44 in 1972 (*ibid.*: September 1973: 211). By 1973 the Bayerische moved up to rank number 36 because its loans made on a trust basis were included among its assets (*ibid.*: August 1974: 182 – it is common in Germany for banks to serve as trustees for loans not provided by the bank themselves but by other corporations).

In 1977 the then head of the WestLB (Dr Ludwig Poullain) was thinking in terms of merging with another Landesbank which at the time was in the top ten, namely the Hessische (Helaba) – a proposal which was considered again during the 1980s. This would have created the largest bank in Europe whose operations may have dominated banking in central Germany. The reasons for the eventual breakdown in the negotiations are therefore instructive. The WestLB was owned by the Land government of NRW and four associations of savings banks. The Helaba was owned by the Land and one savings bank association. Hesse wanted equal representation in any merged bank and eventually the Land government sold its share to the savings bank association. This meant that the latter could provide more capital free of public budget constraints. But equality of representation in any merged bank still proved a stumbling block. Meanwhile, mergers in the north between the NordLB and the LBs in Bremen, Hamburg and Schleswig-Holstein, and in the south between the LBs in Bavaria, Baden-Württemberg, Saarland and the Rhineland Palatinate were being considered. Had all these proposed mergers materialised, there would

have been prior to unification only three LBs in southern, central and northern Germany. But the weighting of representation was the ostensible reason for the absence of agreement, a topic taken up again below. Moreover, one of the reasons Wieandt left the LB in the Palatinate for the BfG was that he would have become number two if a proposed merger with the Bayerische LB had been agreed (*Wirtschaftswoche* 3/90).

As things transpired, in 1992 the WestLB and SüdwestLB (see below) defeated a rival bid from Helaba to win approval for a 50 per cent controlling stake in the Palatinate's LB (FT 26 October 1992). A little later, the WestLB joined with the NordLB in taking a 49.5 per cent holding in the LB Schleswig-Holstein (FAZ 11 December 1992). The executive board of the Schleswig LB had preferred an alliance with the NordLB. On the other hand, the president of the regional savings bank association had favoured the WestLB, which ultimately obtained by far the largest holding in the Schleswig LB. Significantly, he believed that within a few years there would be three blocks of LBs; they would be concentrated on the WestLB, the NordLB and the Bayerische LB (SZ 10 December 1992). In terms of balance sheet totals, these three LBs had indeed become the 'big three'. To this end, it is important to add that the Bayerische LB had succeeded in gaining a 25.1 per cent blocking minority in the LB Saar at precisely the same point in time (FAZ *ibid*). Nonetheless, the WestLB was by now the most prominent public-sector bank.

Prior to considering the remaining small LBs, therefore, the ascent of the WestLB and the other prominent LBs should be charted. Serious consideration could not be given to the first WestLB-Helaba merger proposal because Dr Poullain had been forced to resign in 1977 after a controversial and expansionist career at the bank. Soon after his trial for accepting consultation fees from a financier had commenced, his successor as chief executive of the WestLB (Dr Johannes Völling) was also forced to resign in 1981 as a result of the losses arising from the need to refinance long-term lending through high-cost short-term borrowing; a similar situation had also led to a re-shuffle at the Commerz, although health reasons were also a factor in this case. (Poullain was later cleared by the courts and the question of his claim for compensation for unfair dismissal further embarrassed the WestLB. He became financial adviser to Max Grundig in 1982.) The WestLB had earlier – in 1973 – lost DM 270 million in foreign exchange deals, while the Helaba had lost at least DM 2 billion as a result of ill-judged banking decisions and property speculation. These latter financial disasters led to the resignation of the then Helaba chief executive, Dr Wilhelm Hankel, who had previously been chief economist at the KfW. This episode probably arrested the Helaba's ascendancy and it slipped gradually in terms of relative balance-sheet growth. Other notable losses were those incurred by the NordLB (DM 270 million on an investment in cameras which suffered badly from Japanese competition), the Württembergische (DM 400 million in high-risk construction company losses) and the Badische (DM 80 million when the private Herstatt Bank collapsed). Hence, only the Bayerische among the big four avoided a direct financial scandal – although a former Bavarian finance minister who became its chief executive was alleged to have undertaken privately remunerated duties (*Der Spiegel* 53/87).

In 1975, Dr Heinz Sippel became the first banker to be appointed chief executive of the Helaba, and the first senior commercial banker to defect to the WestLB (Dr Walter Seipp) significantly became head of its international division in 1974. (Seipp left a post at the Deutsche Bank which would almost certainly have given him a seat on the board; following Poullain's resignation he was made a vice-chairman in charge of international business – FT *Banking Survey* 1980: 18.) But one of Sippel's conditions in accepting the appointment was that the bank's expansion would not be curbed in order to merely re-assume its role as manager of the savings banks liquidity. The new chief executive at the WestLB, Friedel Neuber, possessed 10 years' experience on the bank's board, along with experience in both local political circles and in the savings banks. Since the assets of the *Landesbanken* had expanded at such a rapid rate during the 1970s, and since the larger ones were owned on an equal basis by the appropriate Land government and savings bank association, banking expertise coupled with an ability to deal successfully with the Land politicians and savings banks representatives on the board, are prerequisites for any *Landesbank* chief executive. After all, the Land acts as guarantor, and politicians have been forced to resign when their LB has had financial difficulties. All things considered, therefore, Neuber provided the element of management continuity the WestLB needed after the turbulence of the 1970s (*Euromoney* October 1991: 66). He became Germany's most widely-quoted banker following the assassination of Alfred Herrhausen of the Deutsche (*Wirtschaftswoche* 38/90: 52). If Reuter (Daimler-Benz), Kopper (Deutsche Bank) and Schieren (Allianz) were regarded as the three most powerful businessmen in Germany, Neuber was a strong candidate for the fourth most powerful position (FT 26 October 1992).

In 1989, the WestLB acquired the European operations of Britain's Standard Chartered Bank. However, the WestLB wished in return to gain an influence in merchant banking and was given a 50 per cent stake in Standard Chartered's merchant bank. This latter institution became Chartered WestLB Ltd (CWB). In effect, therefore, the two banks 'merged' their merchant banking and corporate finance activities – another example of cross border alliances in anticipation of EC 1993 (FT 10 October 1989). At one fell swoop the WestLB therefore gained access to the merchant bank expertise in London and overcame the obstacle of not having the access to Frankfurt which the Helaba merger would have endowed. It also gained access to Standard Chartered's international network. The Federal Cartel Office did not oppose this merger because it represented a rise of only 0.02 per cent in the WestLB's domestic market share (BT 1991: 116). At the end of 1992, WestLB Europa Group, a joint subsidiary of WestLB and SüdwestLB, acquired the remaining 50 per cent in CWB (WestLB Annual Report 1992). (Recall that the emergence of SüdwestLB still has to be analysed.) SüdwestLB had previously taken the same size of stake when it merged its Swiss subsidiary with WestLB's Swiss operations in January 1992; it also has a holding of 25 per cent plus one share in WestLB International SA (Luxembourg) (*ibid.*). Further, the Belgian BEAL group was acquired by the WestLB in order to 'strengthen' its presence in Latin America (*ibid.*). The WestLB also expanded its non-bank shareholdings. A significant development in the bank's portfolio during the 1992–3 financial year was the increase from 10 per cent to 86 per cent of its shareholding in the Thomas Cook travel and financial company. Finally, Schneider-Lenné (1993: 68)

points out that there is only one case where a German bank's holding in a domestic non-bank is around the 50 per cent mark: WestLB owned 49.7 per cent of the Horten department store.

For historical reasons, there were two *Landesbanken* in Baden-Württemberg: the Badische Kommunale LB and the Württembergische Kommunale LB which was also known as the Landesbank Stuttgart. These banks were founded in 1917 and 1916 respectively. After the Second World War they remained separate entities in spite of the formation of the new Land of Baden-Württemberg from territory which had formerly been three independent Länder. Both banks were entirely owned by the savings banks through their respective associations. The local authorities therefore stood as guarantors. Remaining separate entities had probably cost these two banks a more prominent place in the process of concentration among the LBs. There is a separate house bank for the Land of Baden-Württemberg: the Baden-Württembergische Bank AG with a Land holding of 90 per cent. Another bank – the Landeskreditbank Baden-Württemberg (LKB) – carried out the remaining duties normally transacted by the Landesbank; these entail granting credit for second mortgages and infra-structure development programmes. One of the biggest savings banks in the Federal Republic (*Landesgirokasse*) also operated on an untypically large scale in the Stuttgart/Württemberg area. During the 1980s a merger between the two LBs owned by the two associations of savings banks resulted in the emergence of the SüdwestLB. It can be seen from Table 7.1 that this new Landesbank was in the top twenty German banks in 1990 – but the LKB still had a larger capital base. The share capital of SüdwestLB is 35 per cent owned by the Baden Association, the remaining 65 per cent belonging to the Württemberg Association. At the beginning of 1989 the LKB became an independent agent; a similar institute which assisted in economic development programmes in Bavaria – the Bayerische Landesanstalt für Aufbaufinanzierung – remained wholly owned by the Bavarian Land government and was classified as a special-purpose bank (Stein 1990: 51–2).

In Saarland, prior to the BayerischeLB's acquisition of a 25.1 per cent stake, the *Landesbank* was 76.5 per cent owned by the regional association of savings banks, the Land government owning the remaining 23.5 per cent. As a result of the Bayerische's purchase, the association's share fell to 57.3 per cent and the Land's stake to 17.6 per cent (FAZ 11 December 1992). In Hamburg the Land has a 100 per cent stake in the *Landesbank*, although as shown above it is dominated by its 'free' savings bank. The Bremer Landesbank is 75 per cent owned by the NordLB. This therefore leaves only 25 per cent of the share capital in the hands of the Bremen Land government, a situation cited by the larger LBs as an example of regional interests not being submerged as a result of minority representation. The NordLB itself is 60 per cent owned by the Land of Lower Saxony and 40 per cent by the savings bank association, whereas the Bayerische LB is equally owned by the equivalent institutions in Bavaria. The Rhineland-Palatinate and Schleswig-Holstein LBs were also equally owned by the Land and savings bank association. As seen above, however, in 1992 the WestLB and SüdwestLB purchased stakes in the Rhineland LB and the WestLB and NordLB bought holdings in the Schleswig LB. The savings bank in Berlin carried out the LB's functions until becoming officially known in 1990 as Landesbank Berlin. It then began merger talks with three other Berlin banks, including the Berliner Bank whose majority shareholder was the city-state's government. The other two banks were a mortgage bank and a building association and together the four banks would become the sixth largest bank in Germany (cf. *Economist*, 23 October 1993).

Summarising, it can be said that the balance-sheet growth of the big three LBs was quite spectacular. By 1992, the WestLB had group total assets of DM 275 billion; the equivalent figure for the Bayerische LB was over DM 200 billion, while the NordLB's total was approaching DM 150 billion. It was not until the late 1960s that the *Landesbanken* became controversial institutions, that is when they looked abroad for new investment opportunities. Until this time there had been ample investment opportunities in the domestic economy, both within private industry and with post-war infrastructure reconstruction. Meanwhile, the larger savings banks had become serious domestic competitors in both investment sectors. They also began to deposit funds with the private-sector commercial banks. By entering fields of low profits and high risks, the *Landesbanken* inevitably created problems for themselves. With the exception of the Hamburg and Bremen, all the *Landesbanken* now have the almost mandatory representation in Luxembourg – something sought by all West German banks going international. Only the strength of their public guarantee has saved them from financial disasters which may have bankrupted a smaller private commercial bank. On the other hand, the Association of Public Sector Banks emphasises that its affiliates are not primarily profit-orientated institutions but rather represent one wing of the traditional dual – private and public – system of banking in the Federal Republic (VÖB 1981: 18).

SPECIAL-PURPOSE BANKS

The role of Hermann Abs in the post-Second World War formation of the Reconstruction and Development Loan Corporation (Kreditanstalt für Wiederaufbau – KfW) has already been discussed in the section on the Private Banks. Moreover, its origin was considered in Chapter 1, while its role in the new Länder was discussed at the end of Chapter 2. In view of the conclusion to the previous section, a perspective of the KfW's relative importance can be gleaned from the fact that its balance-sheet total in 1991 was behind the WestLB and Bayerische LB, but ahead of the NordLB (*Die Bank* December 1992). The evolution of the bank since its establishment in 1948 is even more significant here, however. This is because all banks in the heterogeneous group about to be studied were established for a specific purpose. Originally, the KfW was used to administer funds arising from foreign (mainly US) aid to West Germany under GARIOA (Government and Relief in Occupied Areas) and the European Recovery Programme (ERP or, more popularly, 'Marshall Aid'). This 'ERP special-fund' (*ERP-Sondervermögen*) is still the official term for the public funds allocated by the KfW. (Another principal public fund established about this time – the Equalisation of Burdens or *Sondervermögen Ausgleichsfonds* – also still exists to further social programmes and support the *Mittelstand* described in Chapter 8. The banks responsible for the administration of this fund will be analysed below.)

When the physical goods supplied in the form of aid were sold to German consumers, a DM counterpart fund was generated (Wallich 1955: 365). It was this fund which was used for vital capital investment in the process of reconstruction. The credit created on the basis of the counterpart funds was administered by the KfW, initially under the supervision of the American authorities. Later, the Federal Government assumed responsibility. Credit creation for capital investment purposes was not inflationary because food imports and consumption were supplied under foreign aid (*ibid.*). Counterpart funds played a strategic role in German investment; counterpart investment was probably the most carefully planned of all capital expenditures (*ibid.*: 175).

As Shonfield indicated (1965: 276–7) the KfW became a banker's bank – a valuable source of additional long-term credit which had two effects. First, the government could legitimately create credit out of the counterpart fund in a regime where its power to do so was otherwise constrained by the independence of the Bundesbank. Second, the credit so created supplemented the exiguous resources of the commercial banks since it was their task to recommend and guarantee their customer's applications for investment loans. Hence all the technical competence of Germany's universal banking system, already demonstrated above, was brought to bear on the removal of bottlenecks where small amounts of capital investment would produce a disproportionately large return.

The KfW thus received interest on its loans and eventual repayment. Its assets expanded until they totalled, in 1980, DM 53.7 billion (*Annual Report*); a decade later, as shown in Table 7.1, it was Germany's ninth largest bank on an asset count and eighth largest on capital. As a result of miscalculated interest-rate risks (in common with many other banks) its net income had slumped in 1980 to DM 11.7 million from DM 69.8 million on assets of DM 50.2 billion in 1979. Its balance sheet total (1990) was DM 164 billion and its capital of DM 1 billion was held on the following basis: 71 per cent by the Federal Government; 20 per cent by the Länder; 9 per cent by the federal ERP-Sondervermögen (BMF *Beteiligungen* . . . 1990: 46).

More recently, the KfW has had three major roles. First, it acts as a development-aid bank by acting for the Federal government. It scrutinises applications for aid, issues contracts for approved projects, administers the loans and progresses projects in underdeveloped countries (Stein 1990: 48). Such projects are assessed by the bank's own expert advisers. Second, the KfW plays an important role in financing direct exports. Third, the bank has become an extremely active agent of official regional policies (Shonfield 1965: 279). Allied to this domestic regional development function is the emphasis placed on aid to small businesses. Hence a longer and wider view of investment prospects are taken by the KfW than would be the case with an ordinary commercial lender. This was exemplified in the preparations for the 1982 federal budget when it was decided that DM 400 million would be paid into the KfW for low-interest loans. Further, as indicated in Chapter 2 and immediately below, the KfW provided investment funds to the new Länder. Its net income (1990) was DM 161 million and its loans totalled DM 30.9 billion. Of this amount, DM 20.3 billion was earmarked for domestic investment grants, DM 7.2 billion for export guarantees and DM 3.7 billion for overseas aid (BMF *Beteiligungen* . . . 1990: 47).

In short, the KfW was launched to balance the ERP books. But over the years it has become an important source of investment credit. The liberal policies of the KfW in this respect probably gave the Bundesbank greater flexibility to pursue its more conservative monetary policies. Note, however, that the owner/controller (principal/agent) problem was resolved by the Federal government delegating full policy responsibility to the KfW's executives.

The KfW had a 20 per cent holding in the DM 65 million share capital of the Berliner Industriebank AG, Berlin; 68 per cent belonged to the ERP-Sondervermögen; 4.8 per cent to the Land Berlin and the remaining 7.2 per cent to 'other shareholders' (*ibid.*: 201). This bank was founded in 1949 to foster the growth of the economy of West Berlin by granting medium and long-term loans at favourable interest rates. Again its early capital was almost entirely supplied out of the ERP special fund, although later tax concessions under the Berlin Aid Act attracted some private deposits (Stein 1977: 29). In 1990 its balance sheet total amounted to DM 7.7 billion and its net income to DM 21.9 million (BMF *Beteiligungen* . . . 1990: 170). The economic problems created prior to unification by the isolated location of West Berlin implied a need for this special-purpose bank (Chapter 2). On its privatisation in 1992, its promotional activities were transferred to the KfW and a special-purpose bank whose history is about to be traced (Ausgleichsbank). The Berliner Industriebank's post-unification role is then mentioned.

There are two major banks which owe their origins to the post-war attempts to integrate the expellees and refugees. In both cases a second specially created fund (*Sondervermögen Ausgleichsfonds*) was initially used for capitalisation purposes. The two banks concerned are the Deutsche Siedlungs- und Landesrentenbank (DSL-Bank – Housing and Agricultural Mortgage Bank), and the Lastenausgleichsbank (Bank für Vetriebene and Geschädigte), Bonn – where the sub-title literally translated means 'Bank for Expellees and (War) Disabled (BfVG)'. The former bank (DSL-Bank) resulted from an amalgamation of two separate banks which carried out each of its two main functions until 1966. Its basic activity consisted of financing rural restructuring programmes, particularly in areas which attracted a large number of expellees and refugees in the immediate post-war years (BMF *Beteiligungen* . . . 1979: 245; Stein 1977: 30). As well as raising capital from the Equalisation of Burdens fund, this bank attracted capital from the Federal Government, which was its main 'shareholder'. The remainder of its capital was owned by various Länder governments, although the Federal share increased to 98.99 per cent in 1981 (BMF *Beteiligungen* . . . 1980: 263). A further source of funds was the capital market. The BfVG was established in 1950 to assist, by means of low-interest loans, in the process of integrating expellees, refugees and war victims into the economic life of the newly emergent Federal Republic (BMF *Beteiligungen* . . . 1979: 291; Stein 1977: 29). Although the bulk of its nominal capital value was held by the federal Equalisation of Burdens fund (88 per cent), the remaining 12 per cent lay in the hands of the federal ERP special fund.

Important changes took place during the 1980s in both of these banks, partly in recognition of the fact that their original functions were largely obsolete. The DSL-Bank had long since become involved in the general rationalisation of agriculture. In 1989, 48 per cent of this bank was privatised. The majority shareholder in the specially-created holding company remained the Federal government, as well as a half of one per cent token holding by Bavaria and Berlin (BMF *Beteiligung* . . . 1990: 55). The BfVG became the Deutsche Ausgleichsbank in 1986. Its functions are the support of small businesses and professional services (*Mittelstand* – see Chapter 8), as well as being active in various social policy areas (Stein 1990: 50). Its share capital is owned by the Federal government, either directly or through the off-budget ERP and Ausgleichsfonds (BMF *Beteiligungen* . . . 1990: 53). The DSL-Bank, with a balance sheet total of DM 49.3 billion in 1990, is over double the size of the Deutsche Ausgleichsbank, whose balance sheet total in that year was DM 23 billion (*ibid.*: 54 and 56).

Including the ERP funds in their charge, three of these special-purpose banks (the KfW, Berliner and Ausgleichsbank) became the principal intermediaries for the Federal government's investment programmes in the east (MRDB 8/92: 25). Total loans approved by these three banks reached DM 51.6 billion in 1991, three-quarters of which (DM 38.5 billion) represented funds earmarked for the east. Between 1989 and 1991, their loan commitments amounted to DM 106.3 billion, whereas in the three previous years they totalled DM 41.7 billion (*ibid.*: 26). Refinancing was partly via public budgets, and partly through loans raised by the institutions themselves. As a result their recourse to the capital market significantly increased (Figures 7.4c and 7.8b below). As already mentioned, the Berliner's promotional activities were absorbed by the other two banks when the Berliner was privatised in 1992 (MRDB 5/93: 56). (Its loan commitments in 1992 were estimated at only DM 4.7 billion, compared to the KfW's DM 29 billion and the Ausgleichsbank's DM 13.3 billion; from these total commitments of DM 47 billion, DM 35.4 billion represented commitments in the new Länder – *ibid.*).

Also classified in the special purpose category are the Deutsche Bau- und Bodenbank AG (housing finance); the Landwirtschafliche Rentenbank (food production finance) and the Deutsche Verkehrs-Kredit-Bank AG (transport finance). All three of these public-sector banks contributed to the elimination of the various post-war shortages. The housing finance institution became an almost fully-owned subsidiary of the much larger Deutsche Pfandbriefanstalt (Depfa-Bank) which, prior to its partial privatisation in 1991, became the Deutsche Pfandbrief- und Hypothekenbank AG (Knauss 1990: 33). (A *Pfandbrief* is a special kind of mortgage bond issued by German mortgage banks. Mortgage bonds are discussed in the housing finance section below). In 1988 the Depfa-Bank had a balance sheet total of DM 63.5 billion (Annual Report). The Federal Government privatised its 65.06 per cent stake in 1991, leaving several federal agencies with minor stakes (BMF *Beteiligungen . . .* 1990: 48; Tofaute 1993: 13). It is instructive to note that a falling stock market had prevented the Depfa-Bank's partial privatisation in Autumn 1990 (Figure 7.6b; *Wirtschaftswoche* 51/90). Finally, the sole holder of the nominal capital of the transport industry's bank – the Federal Railways – sold 24.9 per cent of the equity in 1988 (Tofaute *ibid.*; Table 8.5 below). This bank supervises rail-freight users' credit payments and also acts as a central bank for the railway's cooperative banks.

As in the case of the KfW, therefore, the major conclusion must be that the reconstruction of the post-Second World War economy owes much to the credit created by the various specially formed, publicly-owned banks.

There are also special purpose banks which are owned by various financial consortia. In 1952 a group of the most significant German export banks founded the AKA Ausfuhrkredit GmbH (export credit company, the legal form of GmbH being adopted in 1960) (Stein 1990: 47). In 1974, the Industriekreditbank AG, Düsseldorf (established in 1949) and the Deutsche Industriebank, Berlin (established in 1924) finally merged, having been closely associated for a number of years. The resultant institution has as its title a compound of the names of the two banks which formed the new company. It makes medium and long-term loans to firms which fall into the median size category. Institutional investors and the issue of bonds supply the bank's funds and ownership is mainly vested in the large banks and insurance companies. Its balance sheet total in 1988 amounted to DM 22.6 billion (*ibid.*: 33). Hence, once again the industry-orientated nature of German banking may clearly be seen.

A final special purpose bank is of particular interest in the context of the next section. It is a consortium established in 1974 to handle domestic and foreign payment transactions and to bridge possible liquidity shortages in the banking sector (*ibid.*: 52–3). Its title is the Liquiditäts-Konsortialbank GmbH and its capital was raised from all groups in the banking sector: the Bundesbank holds 30 per cent of the share capital; the private banks also hold 30 per cent; the savings banks 26.5 per cent; the cooperative banks 11.0 per cent; the BfG 1.5 per cent and the instalment sales financing institutions hold the remaining 1 per cent. Non-banking business is not handled and the partners can be obliged to make supplementary payments.

PRUDENTIAL ARRANGEMENTS AND THEIR REVISION

As shown in Figure 7.1, banking institutions (*Kreditinstitute*) are subject to the official supervision of the Federal Banking Supervisory Authority (*Bundesaufsichtsamt für das Kreditwesen* – BAK). Prior to the introduction of this arrangement under the Banking Act (KWG) in 1961, bank supervision of banks and the fixing of their interest rates had been carried out by the Länder (BBk 1991: 6). This element of centralisation not only led to a new era in prudential regulation, it was also the prelude to the complete abolition of controls on bank interest rates in 1967, with a consequent rise in competition in the banking sector (Denton *et al.* 1968 174–5). Hence, German banking is characterised by a strict and closely administered regulatory environment and a highly competitive and densely banked market (Steinherr 1991: 347). Within each of the three sectors, however, there has been a process of concentration (Pohl 1986).

Section 1 of the KWG defines the term 'banking institution' as meaning any enterprise engaged in banking business where this business requires a commercially organised operation (Obst/Hintner 1991: 227). Such a broad definition is then more specifically delineated (Schneider *et al.* 1978: 60–1; BBk 1991: 23):

1   The acceptance of monies from others as deposits, irrespective of whether interest is paid (deposit business or *Einlagengeschäft*);

2   the granting of loans and acceptance credits (credit business or *Kreditgeschäft*);

3   the purchase of bills of exchange, promissory notes and cheques (discount business or *Diskontgeschäft*);

4   the purchase and sale of securities for the account of others (securities business or *Effektengeschäft*);

5   the custody and administration of securities for the account of others (custody business or *Depotgeschäft*);

6   the transactions designated in the Act on Investment Companies or *Gesetz über Kapitalanlagegesellschaften* (investment fund business or *Investmentgeschäft*);

7   the incurring of the obligation to acquire claims in respect of loans prior to their maturity;

8   the assumption for others of guarantees and other sureties (guarantee business or *Garantiegeschäft*); and

9   the effecting of transfers and clearings (giro business or *Girogeschäft*).

It will be immediately apparent that Section 1 of the KWG has a wide-ranging application. Any of the types of business listed above, even if only a small part of total business, constitute a 'banking institution', providing the business requires a commercially organised operation. There are, however, a number of institutions specifically exempted from supervision under the KWG (Section 2). These include the Bundesbank and the KfW which is subject to the direct supervision of the Federal Government. Insurance companies which do not typically carry out banking, the social security departments of the Federal Labour Office and the Post Office savings bank/giro operations are also among the exempt institutions (Obst/Hintner 1991: 227; Schneider *et al.* 1978: 33 and 63). (The insurance industry is subject to separate, but equally stringent, regulation by the BAV – see above. In view of its extended range of operations, the Postbank will be included in the provisions of the KWG from 1996 – MRDB 1/93: 41; also see the deregulation section of Chapter 8.)

Any banking institution operating in the Federal Republic, including branches of foreign-owned banks, must obtain a banking licence from the BAK. Further, the BAK operates in close cooperation with the Bundesbank, the latter passing on the various financial reports made by the banks and being actively involved in supervision (BBk 1991: 5–6). Under Section 44 of the KWG the BAK is also entitled to launch its own investigations into the affairs of a particular banking institution (Schneider *et al.* 1978: 134–7). The BAK has exercised its powers under the KWG to issue the Principles I and Ia which respectively control the domestic loan/equity capital and the foreign currency/equity capital ratios of the banking sector. Finally, the keystone of the Second Amendment to the KWG was the new powers accorded to the BAK enabling it to virtually step in and conduct the affairs of a bank in financial difficulties. It is therefore necessary to examine many of the points made in this paragraph in a little more depth.

Between 1962 and 1974 18 banks were forced into liquidation (*Die Zeit* 18/74). By far the largest of these banks was the Bankhaus I.D. Herstatt KG, Köln which failed in 1974. Its total assets were DM 2.075 billion, but its losses through currency speculation and fraud totalled DM 1.2 billion. This disaster roughly coincided with the WestLB and Helaba losses. The major difference, of course, is that the *Landesbanken* are in the public sector and they have the unlimited guarantee of the Länder behind them. In effect this prevented insolvencies in these latter cases, although the guarantee system meant that Land politicians were directly involved. In the case of the Herstatt collapse, the private banks formed a 'fire-fighting' fund. All small Herstatt depositors were recompensed in full, while half of the largest

institutional investor's assets were purchased. The idea of a comprehensive joint liability was repugnant to those organisations which could point to their well-tested deposit guarantee systems, namely the savings and cooperative banks (MRDB 7/76: 20). However, the major central associations of the banks agreed to substantially improve their deposit guarantee facilities. Naturally enough, the bigger private-sector banks also rail against the scheme because it has so far been the smaller banks which have run into liquidity crises.

Banking without any risk at all would, of course, be hard to imagine – even under a system of massive control. But the debate over the degree of control in West Germany became particularly intense following the Herstatt collapse. There were two issues. The first issue effectively consisted of agonising about the degree of control in a social market economy. The second issue was concerned with preventing a recurrence of the Herstatt fraud. Basically, it had been the move from fixed to free exchange rates in 1973 which shifted the costs of foreign currency speculation from the central bank to the rest of the banking system. Herstatt made use of its Luxembourg subsidiary and also made fictitious claims to Swiss balances, in order to speculate on the forward exchange market. Even after the fraud had been discovered, it took three years to investigate the matter and bring charges against the owner and seven of his bank's officials. Although the main hearing began in 1979, it took place initially in the absence through ill-health of Herstatt himself and his foreign currency dealer. By 1981 the case had cost DM 2.8 million and *Die Zeit* (9/81) was speculating that proceedings would have to be eventually dropped under the ten-year rule.

A second amendment to the KWG

which came into force on 1 May 1976 marked the conclusion for the time being of the Federal government's efforts to remedy the weaknesses in German banking which had come to light through bank failures – especially the Herstatt closure – and other difficulties in the banking system. It was made clear that the Amendment had to be considered in conjunction with (MRDB 7/76 17):

i) The introduction of Principle Ia (*Grundsatz* Ia) to limit the risks arising from foreign exchange deals.
ii) The improvement of deposit guarantee facilities by the banking associations.
iii) The appointment of a commission to study 'basic banking questions' [the Gessler Commission].

Principle Ia required that at the close of business on each business day a bank's open position in foreign currencies and, from 1980, in precious metals shall be strictly controlled so as not to exceed a given proportion of the bank's equity capital (Obst/Hintner 1991: 235; Schneider *et al* 1978: 42 and 174–7). (Principle Ia had to be substantially amended as a result of EC 1993 – see below.) Principle I, on the other hand, had laid down the basic rule that loans and shares included in the balance sheet must not exceed 18 times the equity capital (Obst/Hintner *ibid.*: 234). At the time, Principle I was not always observed by the Luxembourg subsidiaries of West German banks. It will be seen shortly that this potential loophole was tightened in 1985, while the '18 times' regulation was modified in line with the EC Solvency Ratio Directive.

The amendment itself sought to tighten-up the reporting requirements and restrict large loans. Those provisions concerned with reporting requirements were related to the Herstatt collapse; they were designed to enable officials at the Bundesbank and the BAK to gain more prompt information about the actions of bank officials. Under the clauses dealing with large loans, no individual large loan – including undrawn commitments – could exceed 75 per cent of a bank's equity capital; the five largest loans – including again loans promised – were not to exceed three times the equity capital; all large loans combined – this time only those actually taken up – were not permitted to exceed eight times the bank's equity capital (*ibid.*: 77–81). Every other month borrowers whose indebtedness exceeded DM 1 million were reported to the Bundesbank (KWG: Section 14); the Bundesbank would then inform – in general terms – all affected banking institutions if any one borrower had several such loans (MRDB *ibid.*: 81–2). (With the passage of time, the number of such reports understandably increased. The reporting threshold was therefore raised to DM 3 million as from mid-1993 – MRDB 1/93: 41). Lending to the Federal Government and West German public authorities, however, did not require equity backing.

Surely the keystone of the amendments lay, however, in the powers given to the BAK. This is because only the Authority may now file a petition for bankruptcy – and then only after efforts at re-organisation have failed and when means of compensating depositors have been found (MRDB 7/76: 21–2; Schneider *et al.* 1978: 141–9). Such measures for a time prevented another Herstatt-type failure, with the consequent serious loss of confidence at home and abroad. After all, one of the immediate side-effects of the Herstatt episode was to induce something akin to near-panic, with a subsequent decline in bank deposits.

The third amendment to the KWG came into force on 1 January 1985. It was partly prompted by the Gessler Commission's Report (see below), but equally by the failure in 1983 of another important and hitherto prestigious private bank (Schröder-Münchmeyer-Hengst & Co – SMH). As mentioned above, SMH came close to collapse after excessive lending – partly channelled through Luxembourg and Switzerland – to the IBH building machinery group which later failed. The German banking community stepped in again, this time with a DM 800 million rescue package. Lloyds Bank took over the healthy parts of SMH. An EC directive on the consolidation of bank supervision was also an important element of the amending legislation of 1985 (MRDB 3/85:40).

Within a five year transitional period, the banks were required to consolidate the results of most of their foreign operations and apply stricter lending rules. Under these revised regulations, the banks were thus required to publish consolidated accounts for all subsidiaries in which they had at least a 50 per cent stake (Obst/Hintner 1991: 243). Principle I was amended accordingly. The maximum lending regulation of 18 times a bank's own funds (paid-up capital plus reserves) was then applied to the new total amount lending as per the consolidated balance sheet (MRDB *ibid*). Moreover, a bank had to limit its lending to any single customer to 50 per cent of its capital, as opposed to the previous limit of 75 per cent – a limit which SMH had probably exceeded by routing some of its lending via foreign markets. (The EC Large Exposures Directive later caused a further modification of this regulation – see below.) It was fortunate for the banks that a few years of high profits had enabled them to strengthen their capital base and build-up their reserves. Principles I and Ia were again revised with effect from October 1990. This revision was necessary to limit risks arising from off-balance sheet transactions (BBk 1991: 7).

It should be added that a bank's liquidity is assessed by means of Principles II and III (BBk 1991: 9 and 118–19). Some 4,300 banks have submitted reports on their compliance with all Principles and it can be said that the vast majority observe the various regulations (BBk *Report* 1991: 78–9). For example, the '18 times' ceiling embodied in Principle I, expressed as an annual average for all institutions, was about '13 times' for the period 1981–91 (*ibid.*). The small minority of cases where overshooting occurred were due to special circumstances acceptable to the BAK.

The exposure to the various risks which the authorities sought to limit, therefore, tended to arise from the re-establishment of international banking links by the German banks. It will be evident that tighter regulation has been introduced as rapidly as necessary – but deregulation to prepare for EC 1993 was a more gradual process as will be seen when *Finanzplatz Deutschland* is discussed below. Moreover, further amendments to the KWG in the 1990s translated EC regulations into national law. These legislative developments will be discussed in a moment, but one significant stumbling block affected the unique mortgage bond – the characteristics of which are discussed in the housing finance section below. Suffice it for now to say that this is a traditional and significant part of Germany's fixed-interest securities market – so much so that bond issues as a whole are analysed as part of the housing-finance section. Of particular note here is the fact that in Germany this bond is perceived to be a safe investment instrument by virtue of strict legal provisions (MRDB 4/92: 27). These legal requirements arise not only from the KWG, but also from the Mortgage Bank

Act, as amended in 1974, 1988 and 1990. The bonds issued by these banks – which also include the partial refinancing of public-sector debt – are controlled by statute. There is a prudential requirement that such paper must not exceed sixty times liable capital and public-sector lending to other EC states must not exceed 15 per cent of total mortgage loans (*ibid.*: 23). From 1990, there was no restriction on the proportion of wholesale deposits from institutional investors. This provision marked the culmination of a process stretching back to 1974, prior to which only retail deposits were permitted. As a result, since 1984 mortgage banks have been subjected to the Bundesbank's minimum reserve requirements (MRRs – see the *Finanzplatz Deutschland* section below). Amendments were also made to the Building Savings Banks Act in order to permit these institutions to operate outside Germany. As a result, they were authorised to acquire interests in an extended range of foreign enterprises, and also to grant loans secured against real estate located outside Germany (MRDB 11/90: 34). This legislation was particularly formulated with EC 1993 in mind. At the same time the permitted range of their domestic activities was widened, as well as their refinancing arrangements (*ibid.*). Special transitional provisions were made for Mortgage Banks and Building Savings Banks when bringing Principle I into line with the risk weightings of the EC Solvency Ratio Directive (MRDB 3/93: 52–3).

The fourth amendment to the KWG paved the way for the implementation of the European banking market from 1 January 1993. A free movement in banking services, or a 'European passport', enabled all EC banks to establish a physical presence in, or provide cross-border services to, other member states. Such a far-reaching liberalisation of markets presumed the harmonisation and mutual recognition of financial systems. Harmonisation by means of implementing various EC Directives had been under way for several years. The fourth amendment to the KWG implemented two further directives, namely the Second Banking Coordination and the Own Funds Directives (MRDB 1/93). Moreover, Principle I was amended to take account of the Solvency Ratio Directive. Although the Basle Capital Accord formed the basis for the Own Funds and the Solvency Ratio Directives, the Basle Accord primarily applied to banks operating on an international level, whereas the EC Directives applied to all banks (MRDB 3/93: 48). The EC Capital Adequacy Directive, which harmonises capital adequacy standards for the security business of banks and other security dealers throughout the EC, would necessitate further revisions to Principle I and a complete revision of Principle Ia (*ibid.*: 55). Finally, the Large Exposures, Investment Services and Second Consolidation Directives all provide for further harmonisation in EC bank supervision and would therefore entail further changes to the KWG (MRDB 1/93: 41).

As a result of the Second Banking Coordination Directive, a central feature of the new piece of legislation amending the KWG provided for the mutual freedom of establishment of branches in other EC member states. It also permitted the provision of cross-border financial services by EC banks. In both cases, EC banks are subject to supervision by the home country authorities. A potential host country is accordingly notified by the BAK that an aspirant institution possesses adequate capital. A comprehensive mutual exchange of information normally permits the home-country's regulator to take remedial action, although in emergencies the host country's regulator may intervene. The new section 53(c) of the KWG extended this European passport to any non-EC state provided that either the EC has concluded an agreement with, or, in the case of bilateral agreements, certain prudential criteria are satisfied by, such a third country (*ibid*.).

Also under the amended KWG, reliability checks were expanded so as to include shareholders as well as managers. Hence, any shareholder owning 10 per cent or more of the capital of a banking institution, or controlling voting rights over the same threshold, is obliged to satisfy the BAK that the requirements for sound and prudent management are met. The same test is applied to anyone acquiring such a holding, or increasing any holding above the levels of 20 per cent, 33 per cent and 50 per cent of voting rights or capital. Moreover, the failure of the BCCI banking group led the legislators to provide for an inspection by the BAK of the effectiveness of supervision in integrated groups of companies (*ibid*.). In the event of the BAK finding the results of any of its investigations unacceptable, a licence can be withheld. A trustee may be appointed to exercise voting rights. New regulations on shareholdings in the non-financial sector were also introduced for the transitional period expiring in 2002. Individual holdings were limited to 15 per cent of the bank's equity capital, while total holdings could not exceed 60 per cent of that capital. Provided that the remaining portion of equity capital is not used for another purpose, it may be employed to exceed the 15 per cent and 60 per cent limits.

To meet the requirements of the Own Funds Directive, the definition of a bank's own funds was amended so as to distinguish between core capital and additional capital. Core capital must be avail-

able to a bank for unrestricted and immediate use to cover risks or losses as soon as these occur; additional capital is of a lower quality because it is either not shown in the balance sheet, or is not liable and repayable (*ibid*.: 39). Banks must have a core capital which amounts to at least 4 per cent of their risk assets and the additional capital must not exceed the core capital. A further 4 per cent of risk assets may be covered from additional capital. Both individual banks and banking groups must therefore have a minimum capital of 8 per cent of the weighted risk assets (details of the weighting arrangements appear in the next paragraph). Note that only core capital equalled the equity capital specified in the '18 times' regulation. In other words, gross core capital consists entirely of own funds (paid-up capital, less own and cumulative preference shares, plus published and approved reserves). Net core capital is arrived at by deducting losses and intangible assets, and it is this concept which is the required minimum coverage for weighted risk assets. A number of items hitherto not regarded as capital were included in the additional capital concept, including, much to the chagrin of Bundesbank officials, undisclosed reserves (*ibid*.: 39–40). The narrower capital concept was thus applied to large exposures until the EC Large Exposures Directive was translated into German law later in 1993.

As already indicated, the new Principle I embodied the Solvency Ratio Directive. The '18 times' ratio described above was replaced by the conventional minimum ratio of 8 per cent of capital as defined above. Hitherto, the ratio had been 5.56 per cent, the reciprocal value of 18 times the equity capital. In effect, therefore, the 5.56 per cent was reduced to 4 per cent of equity capital, and a further 4 per cent based on additional capital was added.

This had the effect of raising minimum capital requirements by 44 per cent – from 5.56 per cent to 8 per cent of the new 'own funds'. However, the list of risk assets requiring the support of a minimum 8 per cent of capital was significantly extended compared with the former Principle I. This list basically comprised all asset items, as well as most of uncompleted transactions (MRDB 3/93: 48). The counterpart risk weightings of 0 per cent, 20 per cent, 50 per cent and 100 per cent provided for in the old Principle I continued to apply, although some structural modifications were made (*ibid.*: 50). Because of the significant extension of capital adequacy embodied in the fourth amendment to the KWG, the limits of the risks in Principle Ia were adjusted. They were reduced by 30 per cent – to an amount equivalent to the original level of capital adequacy (5.56 per cent). Principles II and III remained basically unchanged. Although Principle Ia would not apply to banks holding a 'European passport', it would continue to apply to banks from non-EC states. By way of contrast, and despite the principle of home-country control, all banks would still be required to observe Principles II and III.

This latter process of European unification therefore took place on the basis of the EC 1993 treaty. Since this treaty preceded GEMSU, it was yet another important process which had no direct relationship with German unification. Such a conclusion also applies to the *Allfinanz* process seen above, and to the establishment of *Finanzplatz Deutschland* described below. All these developments thus indicate the extent to which GEMSU simply incorporated East Germany into a series of ongoing processes.

CORPORATE FINANCE

Germany's highly integrated and industry-orientated banking system stems from what became *per force* a traditionally close relationship between mutually dependent sectors of the economy. The banks trade in their corporate customers' shares and advise them on financial matters. Nearly half the sight and time deposits of the corporate sector are held by the private commercial banks (Stein 1977: 14). Big commercial banks dominated the business of lending to the giant corporations – in fact, bank loans far outranked stock issues as a source of capital for West German industry (Dyas and Thanheiser 1976: 56). This small equity base was a distinguishing feature of German enterprises when compared to the Anglo-Saxon capital market (OECD *Economic Survey* 1986: 48–9). Further, the commercial banks are collectively important in terms of their loans to small and medium sized firms. However, they face more competition from the savings and cooperative banks in the latter field. Nonetheless, as the improved profitability (and therefore self-financing ability) of West German blue-chip companies increased in the 1980s, all the banks focused their attention on *Mittelstand* companies. In consequence, when valued at market prices (as opposed to book values) the largest firms in both Germany and Britain had similar ratios of debt to equity. Smaller firms in both countries relied more heavily on bank borrowing. The big difference lay in the medium-sized firm sector (not in the top 100 companies but employing more than 200 employees): medium-sized German firms also relied more heavily on bank financing, but the British firms in this category had more equity capital (McWilliams 1991). As the large West German companies came to rely on self financing, however, the ratio of liquid assets to bank debt reached the highest level in 1987 since the 1960s and the gearing ratio had fallen steeply (OECD *Economic Survey* 1989: 21).

From the point of view of corporate finance, this retention of profits and the substantial increase in reserves as part of internal funding endowed the executive directors (and non-executive directors from the banks in some important cases) with a greater degree of policy discretion. From a macroeconomic point of view, however, the consistently greater significance of ploughed-back profits, relative to equity financing, poses some problems (MRDB 10/91: 21). Ultimately, it means that capital is tied up in the company and is thus withheld from the allocative function of the capital market. For that matter, company pension funds are also generally retained as a source of internal funding – with an identical macroeconomic effect. Moreover, given the relatively high risk of insolvency among small and new enterprises, a sound equity position is essential for this source of innovative investment, long-term growth and employment creation (*ibid*.: 25). For these and other reasons, the role of equity finance assumed a greater theoretical and practical significance in the 1980s. Indeed, such considerations went right to the heart of Germany's future importance as a financial centre – as will be shown in the next section. Before this discussion can be attempted, however, it is necessary to isolate the links between the banks and the non-financial sector.

The influence of the big banks from a competition policy point of view boils down to their direct shareholdings, their proxy voting and representation on their corporate customers' supervisory boards (Eckstein 1980: 465–6). Any analysis of

these three factors is, however, complicated by methodological difficulties and the contentious nature of the debate on 'the power of the banks' (*Der Spiegel* 4/ 71; Ponto 1971). There had been a parliamentary enquiry in the early 1960s (BT IV 2320). But as the BdB (1989) points out, the debate reached its first high point at the beginning of the 1970s. Demands for nationalisation of the (private) banks, and the abolition of the universal banking system played a role in the establishment of the Gessler Commission in 1974. Already at that stage, the Monopolies Commission was conducting its own survey into banking. It was to base important parts of its first two biennial reports on its findings (MKI and MKII). It will be also recalled that during this period there was a crescendo in the debate on industrial democracy analysed in Chapter 6. In the present context, codetermination was posited as one means of controlling the economic power of West German enterprises (*Der Bürger im Staat* 1973). The public debate was rekindled by the takeover of MBB by Daimler-Benz in the 1980s (Steinherr 1991: 360). As a result, the BdB (1989) pointed out that the Monopolies Commission's thesis that the banks were responsible for forging the merger overlooked the role of the Federal government in initiating the merger talks.

The methodological difficulties mentioned in the previous paragraph arise from differing sample sizes and the nature of these samples, although an examination of the samples themselves enables one to glean much about the structure of German enterprises (see Figure 7.2). It must be said at the outset that the number of AGs was declining while the above research surveys were taking place. Quite apart from being subjected to more stringent reporting requirements, an AG must have a separate supervisory (non-executive) board. A

GmbH, on the other hand, is not subject to the latter requirement until its labour force exceeds 500. In effect this means that all AGs – irrespective of size – must observe the codetermination legislation analysed in Chapter 6. Significantly, the OECD (*Economic Survey* 1986: 59) reported that while the decline in AGs was taking place, the number of GmbHs increased fivefold. Moreover, there are far fewer AGs in West Germany than PLCs in the UK, and it should be added that under 500 German companies were listed on the stock exchange with only 30 shares being regularly traded (*ibid.*: 46). Nonetheless, it will be seen in Chapter 8 that the 50 largest industrial enterprises in Germany – most of which are AGs – account for half the total turnover of German industry. With these factors borne in mind, it is possible to briefly summarise the differing data bases of the empirical research into 'the power of the banks'.

The 1964 survey relied on data collected in 1960 from 425 quoted AGs, including 34 banks (Shonfield 1965: 251n). The Gessler Commission (1979: 123) collected some of its data in 1974 from 2,036 non-bank AGs, although its analysis concentrated on 74 quoted AGs, including 66 non-banks. A survey was also made of 336 banks (*ibid.*: 122). The Monopolies Commission also carried out its survey in 1974. It assembled its sample (MKII: 286 and 560–4) from the 98 largest non-bank AGs and the two largest (non-bank) KGaAs. It was therefore necessary to 'compensate' for 33 companies which appeared in its top 100 list, but which did not fall into the appropriate corporate form (*ibid.*: 135). For example, there were 19 GmbHs among its top 100 companies, but these were excluded from its sample. The Gessler Commission (1979: 125–6n) expressly referred to the differences

between its own and the Monopolies Commission's results and samples. Moreover, these surveys preceded, of course, the increase in employee representation on supervisory boards as a consequence of the 1976 Act (see Chapter 6). Two subsequent surveys were Gerum *et al.* (1988 – quoted by Edwards and Fischer) and the BdB (1989). The former investigated 281 AGs which had more than 2,000 employees in 1979, while the BdB confined its analysis to the holdings of the 10 largest private-sector banks in 1986 and 1988–9 (BdB 1989: 19). It is notable that the Gessler Commission included 6 of these 10 banks to demonstrate their significance to its enquiry (1979: 443–5, for example). In addition, the BdB used the top 100 enterprises from *Die Welt's* 500 listing, eliminating 13 of the 100 because their legal form (KG, OHG and Einzelfirma) did not require them to have a supervisory board (BdB 1989: 20). Whereas the BdB criticised the Monopolies Commission for relying on obsolete data, Steinherr (1991: 360n) found the BdB data difficult to interpret.

All the surveys are at least consistent in one respect. Taken as a whole, the direct shareholdings of all the domestic banks in non-banking companies are relatively small. In Table 7.2, for example, the Gessler Commission's estimate of direct shareholding is about 9 per cent of total share capital. Rutherford (1974: 32) quoted a Bundesbank survey which put the figure at 8 per cent. Using more recent data from the same source, but including investment funds which are owned by the general public but usually managed by the banks, Edwards and Fischer (1991: 24) estimated the total direct bank equity holding to be 10.3 per cent in 1984 and 11.6 per cent in 1988; this direct holding by the banks and investment funds was reported as being 11.4 per cent of total

Table 7.2 Bank Holdings in 74 large West German quoted companies: 1974–5

Banks	Percentage share of equity capital	Percentage share of voting right at AGMs	Percentage share of supervisory board membership	Percentage share of supervisory board chairmanship
Deutsche Bank	3.5	18.6	5.3	24.3
Dresdner Bank	1.6	11.8	2.7	8.1
Commerzbank	1.0	4.5	1.9	1.4
All three above	6.1	34.9	9.9	33.8
Other banks and investment companies	3.0	27.8	8.0	16.2
Total all banks	9.1	62.7	17.9	50.0

Source: Gessler Commission 1979: 467 (author's translation)

share capital in 1989 (*Wirtschaftswoche* 21/92). The Bundesbank itself (MRDB 10/91: 27) put this form of share holding at 10 per cent in 1990, as did the *Economist* (3 February 1990: 91). Moreover, a comparison of the structure of share ownership in the UK and Germany produced respective holdings by the banks of 3 and 9 per cent (BEQB 1984: 370). But German companies regularly make large provisions to add to their reserves, while their share capital is valued at issue rather than market price. Profits are therefore underplayed – in complete contrast to Anglo-Saxon practice. Nonetheless, an unadjusted estimate for 1989 in the BdB sample (1989: 7 and 14) compared a total share capital holding by the banks of DM 1.68 billion to the DM 2.85 billion share capital of the chemical company BASF. The BdB concluded that the banks' total direct share holdings were overestimated and were in any case being reduced.

How do these holdings by the banks relate to other institutional and private shareholdings? The *Economist* (*ibid.*) concluded that the 10 per cent holding by the banks, plus a further 35–40 per cent accounted for by cross-company hold-

ings, gave 'little incentive to German companies to worry about the price of their shares'. Insurance companies and pension funds owned only 5 per cent of shares – as opposed to 60–70 per cent in Britain and the USA. There seems to be little disagreement that German non-financial companies hold about 40 per cent of all shares (MRDB and BEQB *ibid.*; *Wirtschaftswoche* 21/92). Pension funds also remained unimportant in Germany, although insurance companies doubled their shareholdings in the 1980s. At the end of 1990, however, equities made up only 10 per cent of their total portfolios of securities (MRDB *ibid.*). (An important caveat is that Allianz AG – Europe's largest insurance company – was also a very significant shareholder, as already seen in the BfG section above.) Perhaps 'close to half' of the remaining shares in quoted companies were held by foreigners at the end of the 1980s (*Economist ibid.*). When the holdings of non-financial companies were netted out the Bank of England reached a figure for 1982 of 35 per cent for non-residents, compared to 5 per cent in the UK (BEQB *ibid.*). The Bundesbank unnetted estimate for 1990 was 14 per cent, almost double the comparable statistic for 1970; as a result of the Federal government's privatisation programmes, however, public-sector share holdings were halved during the 1980s to reach 5 per cent of total share ownership in 1990 (MRDB *ibid.*). Particularly notable, therefore, is the corresponding decline in share ownership by German households: from 27 per cent of total holdings in 1960 to 17 per cent in 1990 (*ibid.*). This trend decline occurred in spite of the numerous efforts made to increase the wealth holding of households in the form of equities as part of the SME (Gurdon 1991). In fact there were only 4.2 million shareholders in Germany in 1990 – just under 4 per cent of the total population (FT 23/24 May 1992). At the same time, it must be borne in mind that the rapid increase in the number of shareholders in the UK – to 12 million, or 21 per cent of the population, in 1990 – can be easily misconstrued: the vast majority owned only one or two shares.

Summarising the evidence, it can be said that cross-holdings in the non-financial sector are a critical feature of the German scene. In 1989, they amounted to 40 per cent of total share capital, compared to 17 per cent in France and only 4 per cent in the UK (*Wirtschaftswoche* 21/92). Foreign holdings, on the other hand, are relatively large: 20 per cent in Germany, 15.3 per cent in France, 8 per cent in the UK and 6.7 per cent in the USA (*ibid.*). Some implications of these foreign-owned shares and cross-holdings will be examined in the section on mergers and acquisitions in Chapter 8. For now, it need only be indicated that there are limitations placed on voting rights at AGMs. Also note that the influence of German pension funds and insurance companies is limited: they own 2.7 per cent of all shares, compared to an equivalent holding of 4.5 per cent in

France and 54 per cent in the UK (*ibid.*). Finally, banks and investment funds have a direct shareholding of 11.4 per cent of total share capital in Germany, compared to 35.1 per cent in France and 9 per cent in the UK (*ibid.*).

So why have the banks been subjected to a high degree of critical attention? As Table 7.2 also indicates the direct share holdings of the domestic banks are heavily concentrated, the Big Three alone owning about two-thirds of the total. (The 1964 survey produced the same proportion – Denton *et al.* 1968: 68). Moreover, the value of the Deutsche Bank's shareholdings in quoted companies alone was estimated at DM 11 billion in 1989, equivalent to 52 per cent of its own share value at that time; these shareholdings amounted to 10 per cent of the share capital of non-banks (Eglau 1990: 61). A principal example of the controversy surrounding these holdings – as will be shown in the next chapter – is the quarter of Daimler-Benz owned by the Deutsche; the same bank also has a joint holding, of over 25 per cent each, with the Commerzbank in Karstadt, the country's leading chain store. Furthermore, the Big Three are strongly involved in construction and metals. Hence the holdings of the Big Three are heavily concentrated in certain sectors (Eckstein 1980: 467). These holdings often overlap and it may well be the case that all three major banks are collectively the most frequent shareholders in the country's top concerns. For example, the Monopolies Commission has consistently published data to support such a view, although it must again be emphasised that the insurance giant Allianz AG held the largest single number of shareholdings (MKI: 140 and 155; MKVIII: 202). Perhaps not surprisingly, in view of what has been said about its growth, the WestLB more than doubled its shareholdings between 1985 and 1991 – from DM 1.75 billion to DM 4.36 billion (*Die Zeit* 31/92). A policy response to this degree of concentration was perhaps inevitable. In 1990 the anti-trust Act (GWB) was extended to cover abuses of their dominant position by banks and insurance companies.

Yet these shareholdings are seen as a duty in the sense that, rather like some trade union leaders during the period of post-war reconstruction, many executives in the banking world believe that each social group has a duty to contribute to the harmonious functioning of the econ-omy – a so-called *Ordnungsfaktor*. A manifestation of this view occurred in 1975 when the Deutsche Bank bought up the Flick family holding in Daimler-Benz, thus increasing its total shareholding to 56 per cent. This was to prevent the Shah of Iran extending his country's industrial ownership in the Federal Republic, having already purchased a holding in the Krupp company. In any case, the Quandt family holding in Daimler-Benz had been sold to Kuwait (Eglau 1980: 176). (It will be necessary to return to the subject of family holdings in Chapter 8.) In 1979 the Deutsche divested itself of 25 per cent of its shareholding in Daimler-Benz by creating a new holding company. This holding company was misleadingly known as Mercedes Holding, even though it had no direct connection to the world-famous Daimler subsidiary of the same name. When Mercedes Holding shares were launched on the stock market, two major vehicle holding companies bought up 50 per cent of the equity. The Big Three and Allianz had substantial hold-ings in both of them. Hence, any take-over bid could be repelled. It is little wonder that the banks' equity stakes in general are the subject of fairly frequent comment (for example: *Der Spiegel* 11/89 and 36/89; *Euromoney* January 1990;

Economist 22 June 1991). On the other hand, one of the most significant capital market developments in the first half of the 1990s was the decision to disband Mercedes Holding and launch Daimler-Benz on the New York stock exchange – see the section on mergers and acqui-sitions in Chapter 8.

There are other ways in which the banks influence decision-making in the non-banking companies. Above all, the share of the private-sector banks in the security business far exceeds their share in the balance sheet total for all banks (Stein 1977: 13). It is in this sense that the 26 per cent of the banks' total business volume accounted for by the private banks in Figure 7.1 represents only the tip of the iceberg – and this is even more true of the Big Three's 9.3 per cent. In *absolute* terms, 4.6 million out of 11.8 million of all secur-ities deposited outside the Bundesbank in 1990 were in the custody of the private banks (*Beilage zu 'Statistische Beihefte zu den Monatsberichten der Deutschen Bundesbank' Reihe 1 7/91*). But by *value* the securities held at the private-sector banks represented over two-thirds of all domestic bonds, more than three-quarters of domestic shares, 65 per cent of all dom-estic investment trusts' certificates and 78 per cent of foreign bonds (*ibid.*).

Further, of the 4.6 million security deposits held by the private-sector banks in 1990, nearly 3 million were held by the Big Three (*ibid.*). Half the shares left for safekeeping with the private banks were also held by the Big Three. This endows the banks, and particularly the Big Three, with considerable influence, for the fol-lowing reason. Provided a bank has the written permission of its customer, it may, for renewable 15-month periods – revocable at any time during that period – exercise a proxy voting right at share-holders' meetings (*Depotstimmrecht*). A shareholder's voting instructions must be followed; alternatively, the bank notifies the shareholder of how it proposes to vote at the AGM if the shareholder does not give any instructions (Schneider-Lenné 1992: 20). (Note that banks are the traditional custodians of securities. To reduce costs, by obviating the need to physically transfer securities between bank vaults, most securities are lodged with the securities' clearing system (*Kassenverein*). Computer transfer can thus be rapidly effected when securities are traded. (ndc 1973: 188–9; Stonham 1982: 110–11).) The 1964 enquiry – one of the few relatively early pieces of empirical evidence on concentration in general – found that this proxy voting system gave the banks voting control over 60 per cent of the total capital of quoted companies (BT IV 2320; Denton *et al*. 1968: 69). This proportion was confirmed in the 1970s by the Gessler Commission – see Table 7.2. It was probably implied by the BdB which also posed the legitimate question: 'who would replace the banks at AGMs?' (1989: 11 and 21). Or, as Schneider-Lenné (1992: 20–1; 1993: 69) puts it, what practicable alternative would prevent unstable and random majorities, particularly at the time of a take over bid? On the other hand, the system is the subject of increasing criticism, not least for its inefficiency and the manner in which it undermines shareholders' rights (Steinherr 1991: 362 and 377; Ogger 1992: 31–2; Wenger 1990 and 1992). According to the 1964 enquiry, approximately 70 per cent of proxy votes were cast by representatives of the Big Three (Hartrich 1980: 223; Kaufmann 1973: 264). From the Gessler sample (Table 7.2), the proportion was estimated at 56 per cent, which is still, of course, quite high. Banks also loan their votes to each

other – a system known as *Stimmenleihe* (Shonfield 1965: 250 and 252).

There is a positive correlation between the extent of a bank's direct and proxy shareholding and the number of supervisory board seats it controls (Eckstein 1980: 470). Hence, by virtue of both of their own holdings and their proxy voting rights, according to the 1964 enquiry, the banks held about one in three of the *non-employee* supervisory board seats in 318 of West Germany's biggest enterprises (Denton *et al*. 1968: 70; Kaufmann 1973: 264). When account is taken of the fact that the Gessler enquiry (1979: 445) did not deduct employees' representatives on supervisory boards when calculating the 17.9 per cent shown in Table 7.2, the magnitude of bank *non-employee* representation was 28 per cent; indeed, in its bigger survey, the Commission (1979: 123 and 598) also found the proportion of non-employee seats to be about one-third, although in 65 per cent of these supervisory boards the banks held only one seat. The Monopolies Commission (MKII: 300) found that the banks held 15 per cent of the total supervisory board seats, and 22 per cent of non-employee seats. Once the number of seats had been increased to accommodate the requirements of the 1976 Codetermination Act, the proportion of non-employee seats on supervisory boards held by the banks may have fallen somewhat. Domestic banks held 16 per cent of these seats in the 1979 sample; by 1989 officials of DGB unions held 32 per of the employee seats compared to the bankers' 20 per cent holding of the non-employee seats (Edwards and Fischer 1991: 33; BdB 1989: 9 and 20).

In the first three samples, however, the proportion of 'bankers' seats' on supervisory boards held by the Big Three was around 55 per cent (MKII: 301; Shonfield 1965: 251–2; Table 7.2). Similarly, in 1972 an analysis of the top nine companies by sales indicated that out of a total of 168 supervisory board seats, 37 were held by bankers, 23 of whom came from the Big Three (Rutherford 1974: 35). For private-sector banks as a whole, the proportion in the 1989 sample was 65 per cent (BdB 1989: 20). The Deutsche alone held 400 seats in 1989, an increase of about 160 since 1976 (Eglau 1990: 127). There was also another element of concentration if representation on *companies'* supervisory boards as opposed to the number of *seats* on those boards is considered: in all the samples, at least one bank was represented on the supervisory boards of between 71 and 90 per cent of the non-bank AGs (Denton *et al.* 1968: 69; Gessler 1979: 123; MKII: 301; BdB 1989: 20). As already seen in the section on private banks, in 1966 'Lex Abs' limited the number of these directorships which could be held by an individual banker to ten. However, in two samples there was a fairly high probability that a bank representative would be chairman of a supervisory board; in a third sample a similarly high probability was arrived at if the vice-chairman was included (MKII: 303–5; Shonfield 1965: 251; Table 7.2). This probability falls substantially in the 1989 sample, where only chairmen are considered (BdB 1989: 20). Holders of these two posts are endowed with special responsibilities which distinguish them from ordinary members of the supervisory board. For example, their status entitles them to be consulted, with a virtual right of veto, about capital expenditure plans.

It was, then, the industrial influence of the Big Three, along with the growing problems raised by the international expansion of German banking, which led to the two enquiries during the 1970s. As already indicated, the first enquiry was conducted by the standing Monopolies

Commission (MK) – a government advisory body which was established in 1973. A second edition of its 1973–5 biennial report was published in 1977 (MKI). Chapter III was concerned with 'Banking and Concentration'. The Commission returned to the same theme in its 1976–7 report which was published in 1978 (MKII – ch. IV). The titles of the Commission's reports are a good indication as to the zeal with which it has pursued its task. Again as already indicated, the second enquiry was conducted by the specially-constituted Gessler Commission, a body which included authorities from the main banking sectors, the Bundesbank, the supervisory authorities, the universities, Finance Ministry and trade unions. Its composition was no doubt responsible for its somewhat schizophrenic approach to policy recommendations: the report is replete with pros and cons, as well as majority and minority views.

Of these reports, those of the Monopolies Commission adopted a more hawkish assessment of the relationship between banks and industry. Competition was being eroded not just because the bigger banks tended to gain a competitive advantage over the smaller ones, but also because the big banks had access to information on such things as the creditworthiness of both their existing and newly-formed corporate customers. There was, therefore, a long-term tendency for the banks to acquire bargain-price stakes in enterprises of above-average worth. The Gessler Commission was asked to express a view on whether an upper limit should be placed on direct holdings, as well as looking into the growing problem of banks using foreign subsidiaries as a means of granting credit well above the legal limit for their parent banks. In its report, the Gessler Commission took a more moderate policy stance compared to the one taken by the Monopolies Commission. Bank holdings in industry, which were part of the German traditional universal banking system, were not seen as necessarily a bad thing.

However, the Gessler Commission could not agree on a maximum holding: the majority recommended the 25 per cent plus one share of a company's capital which is the legal minimum required to block a change in the statutes of a West German company (para 99). But a 'substantial minority' proposed that holdings should not exceed 10 per cent, including any transient holding of up to 5 per cent for share-trading purposes (para 104). The majority recommendation excluded this 5 per cent holding (para 100). On the other hand, the MK (I para 568) had recommended that a bank's equity holding in a non-banking company should not normally exceed 5 per cent. Where this limit was exceeded, voting rights should in any case be limited to an equivalent of 5 per cent. One member of the MK entered a note of reservation in which he recommended a maximum holding of 20 per cent (para 569).

The Federal Government seemed at one stage to have settled for a 15 per cent ratio with a large number of exceptions. But quite apart from the Finance and Economics ministries being under politicians of differing persuasions, the shaky Bonn coalition was more preoccupied with its budgetary position in the early 1980s (Chapter 3 above). In any case, the banks may have reduced some of their holdings to 25 per cent in anticipation of legislation. Indeed, in the early 1980s some holdings may have been drastically reduced to provide reserves normally provided by profits (see below). Ultimately, the supply-side orientated Kohl administration decided not to proceed with the majority Gessler recommendation in its 1985 amendment to KWG (MRDB 3/85: 36).

The crucial relationship between banking and industry is further illustrated by the fact that not only are the banks represented on the boards of large companies, but that the large companies are, in turn, represented on the boards of the Big Three (Annual Reports). An example of this is the traditional relationship between Siemens and the Deutsche Bank. Long-standing links of this description are common. Continuity is also maintained by the practice of normally appointing a retiring chief executive of a bank to its supervisory board, usually as chairman (Denton et al. 1968: 70). This was seen to be the case when the careers of Abs and Lichtenberg were discussed above.

The ownership of the Big Three themselves was not dominated by any single large shareholder, at least until Allianz became influential at the Dresdner. They have also demonstrated, in the main, a record of being remarkably sympathetic shareholders in other companies. The banks generally have been very restrained in their dividend demands and have almost always tended to place a company's long-term interests above the need for short-term profits. Above all, the economic recovery of West Germany would have been impossible without the Big Three and without their long and close relationship to the big industrial and commercial corporations. The German banks were especially well equipped to know where the worst investment gaps were, and where the addition of a relatively small amount of capital – public or private in origin – would remove bottlenecks and produce a disproportionately large return (Shonfield 1965: 277).

The banks also took risks with their own capital, often lending ten and even twenty times their own capital funds to one borrower (Hartrich 1980: 230). A striking example of this risk financing was the re-organisation of the Carl Zeiss Optical Works. (At the end of the war, the plant in East Germany was taken over by the Soviet military government.) Another example of lending money 'on a plan and a promise and little else' involved the post-war rebirth of the Pittler Company of Leipzig, for fifty years an important East German machine tool producer (*ibid*.: 231). The textiles and glass industries were re-established in the same way (Mellor 1978: 149; Wallich 1955: 283).

Another industrial role played by the banks – again led by the Big Three – is that of mounting rescue operations when companies run into financial difficulties, a role in Britain readily left to the state. The Dresdner Bank had its own executive for retrieving corporate failures – Dr Manfred Meier-Preschany. In the late 1950s he organised the rescue of an ailing bicycle and motor cycle concern – Victoria-Werke in Nuremberg. In the early 1970s he led the search for a buyer when the plant engineering company of Zimmer was failing. It became one of the most profitable parts of Britain's Davy Corporation. His most challenging task, however, was in forming a consortium of 25 banks in order to inject new capital of DM 1 billion into the troubled electrical giant AEG-Telefunken and the government untypically and reluctantly gave guarantees worth DM 1.6 billion (*Economist* 26 March 1983 and 7 December 1991). This was one of those companies which had a large number of small shareholders (MKIII: para 342). When the banks met to consider further financial aid in 1981, however, they took umbrage because Meier-Preschany and not the Dresdner's chief executive and AEG supervisory board chairman (Hans

Friderichs) chaired the meeting (*Die Zeit* 46/81: 24). (Friderichs was later involved in reorganising the bankrupt Co op group – see the section on the BfG above.) More will be said about AEG in Chapter 8. But by 1982 sharply falling sales and cheap imports in household appliances and electric motors had also endangered the family-owned Bauknecht company. In this case 22 banks were involved.

Similarly, in the recession of 1966–7, another world-famous firm – Krupp of Essen – ran into one of its recurrent financial crises, the previous ones having been in the 1870s, 1920s and early 1950s (Manchester 1969: 907–8 and 923–4). No one could imagine that Bonn would permit the troubled company to go bankrupt, but Abs, Krupp's friend in the banking world, took a hard line with Schiller's full backing. At a climactic semi-secret meeting in March 1967 in Düsseldorf's Dresdner Bank, Schiller, Blessing and twenty-eight top figures from the world of finance (quite apart from the confidential nature of the meeting, there was not room for the 235 savings banks' and insurance companies' executives entitled to attend), it was decided that the company would go public (*ibid*.: 928 and 930). Schiller made it clear that the government was leaving the rescue operation to 'a few banks'. Krupp himself had nominated Abs and Werner Krueger of the Dresdner; they were to be joined by Otto Brenner of the metal-workers' trade union, Professor Bernard Timm of the rapidly expanding BASF chemical company, together with an academic and a research and development expert (*ibid*.: 934).

When the steel industry as a whole faced the third post-war recession at the end of the 1970s, bank lending to this sector increased. In effect this reduced both the state subsidies being paid to the sector and the concomitant need to fund such subsidies from either public borrowing or tax revenue. More specifically, Klöckner, Germany's third largest steel group, was making heavy losses. Its capital re-organisation was partly the brainchild of the deputy chairman of its supervisory board, whose full-time employment was membership of the management board of the Deutsche Bank (Dr Alfred Herrhausen). A consortium of twelve banks was formed to raise half of the capital required. In 1988, the Deutsche Bank averted the closure of Klöckner & Co, one of Germany's major trading companies (Schneider-Lenné 1993: 68). This company was then sold to the newly privatised VIAG conglomerate (FAZ 12 December 1992). However, the near-collapse of Klöckner-Werke steel concern in 1992 still affected the Deutsche because it held shares in the engineering wing of the former Klöckner family empire (KHD AG, Cologne). During the 1992–3 recession, Klöckner-Werke had run into even worse financial difficulties than those experienced by other steel makers. Although its creditors agreed a rescue plan that largely kept the Bremen plant in operation, the pertinent question was whether writing off a large amount of debt was an unambiguous gain for the wider European steel industry. After all, the cancellation of 60 per cent of Klöckner's debt effectively amounted to a substantial subsidy from the German banks (FT 8 June 1993). (The settlement proceedings of 'equalising' assets and liabilities (*das Vergleichsverfahren*) under German law permits debt to be written off and the enterprise thus remains open; it is clearly a less drastic process than liquidating assets on closure.) The technicalities and source of the subsidies would be deemed irrelevant in the EC. Instead, subsidised steel producers in Spain and Italy would become more determined to hold their ground. A

final illustration of bank involvement is the fate of Sachsenmilch AG, which was established in the east following unification. Although it was a subsidiary of the west's Südmilch AG, and supported by the Deutsche Bank, it was forced to file for bankruptcy in mid-1993. It was the only eastern company to be listed on the stock exchange. This threw Südmilch's balance sheet into disarray and the company applied for settlement proceedings.

Jürgen Ponto (1971) contended that the power of the banks was far less than was often thought. For example, the banks had virtually no direct or indirect representation in Parliamentary government, yet because of budgetary deficits and state spending in the modern economy, the banks had become the objects rather than the subjects of politics. For that matter, there was no equivalent of the direct intervention of the Bundesbank in any other economic sector. Further, the massive demand for capital, which was a feature of the modern economy, was usually supplied from a multiplicity of sources. In any case, 95 per cent of a bank's assets represented, in one form or another, customers' deposits, the contractual repayment of which had to be honoured. In terms of ownership, much of the banking industry was in the public and cooperative sectors and trade unions were also represented on supervisory boards. Finally, if 'power' means bringing the knowledge and experience of many banks and many bank employees to bear on economic problems, then this 'power' should be extended, not curtailed. As Cable (1985: 121) points out, this latter hypothesis embodies the assumption that the equivalent expertise cannot be purchased elsewhere. Nonetheless, one of Ponto's successors as chief executive of the Dresdner also expressed the view that the banks offered expertise, adding that for this reason bankers were seen as welcome advisers (*Der Spiegel* 36/89). The BdB (1989: 12–13) rehearsed similar arguments. In addition, it posed questions which are at the centre of any debate about 'the power of the banks'. What alternative organisations could prevent unwelcome takeovers, assist companies in financial difficulties and provide finance for *Mittelstand* businesses? Which other organisations could represent the interests of shareholders and prevent minorities from dominating AGMs? It will be necessary to address these vital questions in the section on mergers and acquisitions in Chapter 8.

In short, it is little wonder that the Big Three banks are often known as the 'prefects' of German industry (Hardach 1980: 152), although their depositors and borrowers are as a rule more interest-minded than those of other banking groups (MRDB 8/81: 19). Cable (1985: 130) found a significant, positive relationship between the degree of bank involvement in leading industrial companies and their financial performance. His main hypothesis (*ibid.*: 121) was that bank participation conferred the advantages of an internal capital market. Thus bank representation on supervisory boards *could* remove informational asymmetries that would otherwise lead to credit rationing and onerous lending terms in the provision of debt finance. There was, therefore, a close similarity between Cable's reasoning and those arguments adduced above when the origins of the local cooperative banks were discussed, namely the elimination of outsiders, a consequential reduction in lending charges and a probable lowering of agency costs. But there is more difficulty in the Cable case in deciding the precise methods by which banks contribute to the increased profitability of non-banks. Representation on super-

visory boards is, in itself, only one plausible method (*ibid.*). In Germany, the market for corporate control is much less competitive than in the Anglo-Saxon world because of the barriers to entry, cemented by the role of banks and interlocking directorships (Steinherr 1991: 367). This collusive behaviour, or at least restricted competition, has been a consistent target of the Monopolies Commission (*ibid.*: 362–3).

Viewed from another angle, it could be argued that in a proxy-voting system the shareholder (or principal) has little monitoring capacity over the bank (or agent) which may have wider objectives than value maximisation (*ibid.*). Steinherr (*ibid.*) thus concluded that the proxy-voting system is a fundamental departure from the 'one-share-one-vote' principle. This is attributable to the fact that the banks have more votes than the shares they own. On the other hand, where there is a large number of shareholders, proxy voting gives the banks the ability to have a decisive effect at AGMs and also gives them the incentive to acquire sufficient information to monitor and judge managements effectively (Edwards and Fischer 1991: 43). In this sense, proxy voting makes it far less difficult for single shareholders to exercise control over their managers. This represents another method of resolving the dilemma first raised with respect to the cooperative banks. The fact remains, however, that bank representation on supervisory boards, though significant, is not dominant – and there is some evidence that these boards do not collectively possess enough information to evaluate the executive board (*ibid.*; also see the section on industrial democracy in Chapter 6). Such a view is not inconsistent with the presumption that bankers who are chairmen, or even deputy chairmen, of supervisory boards are in a more advantageous position to regularly obtain vital information. Numerous examples of these chairmen exercising influence, irrespective of whether they are bankers, are given in this book. Finally, bank lending in Germany, as already seen, is a much more important source of finance for small companies without supervisory boards. Given the absence of such bank representation, therefore, it cannot be argued that information asymmetries have been removed resulting in lower loan costs (*ibid.*: 42).

There are thus two polarised arguments. On the one hand, as the *Economist* (7 December 1991) points out, the Edwards and Fischer (1991) study suggests that the partnership between Germany's banks and the non-financial corporate sector is more loosely defined than is commonly supposed. If Frankfurt bankers are more frequently seen on factory floors than their London counterparts, it is, it seems, as much for cultural and historical as for institutional reasons. On the other hand, and in complete contrast, Steinherr (1991: 371–2) argues that a bank-based financial system is rather costly for the non-bank sector. He tentatively concludes on the basis of his data that in such a system the securities market is underdeveloped because corporate control is less efficient; further, managers of banks and non-banks have large free cash flows and are not subjected to strict board controls; finally, outside financial resources are expensive in Germany. It can be said with much more certainty that the process of deregulation in the second half of the 1980s had the fundamental aim of making Germany more prominent as a centre for financial services, or *Finanzplatz Deutschland*. This process is therefore considered in the general context of this paragraph in the next section.

DEREGULATION AND *FINANZPLATZ DEUTSCHLAND*

An internationally attractive financial centre is regarded as a prerequisite for the cost-effective performance of a wide variety of assignments involving the provision of finance; such a centre also makes a direct contribution to GNP and employment (MRDB 3/92: 23). In addition, European financial markets were obliged to prepare for the increased competition which would emanate from the high degree of free capital movements embodied in EC 1993. Even more generally, a greater degree of global interdependence in these markets dictated the speed with which sophisticated computerisation had to be introduced. Such a costly process implied the need to attract sufficient business so as to ensure the intensive operation of this equipment. In short, the key issues here are the extent to which non-residents have access to the financial markets, and the degree to which international financial developments are reflected on the domestic scene. At the centre of the debate about Germany's adjustment to these emergent demands lay the two features analysed at some length in this book. They are the tight control exercised on monetary policy by policymakers at the Bundesbank (see Chapter 4) and the universal banking principle (see above).

Consider first the monetary-policy argument. There are two schools of thought which use equally pertinent time horizons. Protagonists of the Bundesbank's policy stance refer to the fact that the main steps towards the liberalisation of financial markets were taken much earlier in Germany than in most other OECD countries. Full convertibility and largely free capital movements were introduced in the late 1950s; interest rate regulations were abolished in 1967 (Gallant

1988: 10; MRDB *ibid*.; OECD *Economic Survey* 1986: 49). Further, 'the residual trifling exchange controls (were) abolished in 1981' (BBk 1989: 39). But restrictions on some capital inflows were maintained, most notably a 25 per cent coupon tax on non-residents' income from bonds. This measure was introduced in 1965 because under a fixed-exchange regime domestic liquidity could not be easily controlled. It was abolished in December 1984, retroactively effective from August of that year. Antagonists of the Bundesbank's stance see this latter date as marking the real beginning of the deregulation of German financial markets (*Euromoney* April 1992: 55; Steinherr 1991: 350). The *Economist* (28 January 1989) attributed the liberalisation to the innovative spirit of Karl-Otto Pöhl.

Irrespective of the merits of each case, purchases of DM domestic bonds by non-residents became more significant following the measures introduced in 1984, although they fluctuated wildly. The main stimulus to purchases by non-residents was an appreciation of the DM against the US$. A major deterrent was the abortive attempt to introduce a withholding tax in 1989. In what follows, it will be necessary to distinguish between gross and net domestic bond sales. 'Gross sales' refer only to initial sales of newly issued securities, not, however, resales of repurchased bonds; 'net sales' are gross sales less redemptions at market values plus/less changes in issuers' portfolios of their own bonds (MRDB tables VII[1 and 2]n). As one would expect, purchases of DM domestic bonds by non-residents are normally lower than purchases by domestic non-banks. (Net purchases or net sales of foreign bonds by residents – at transaction values – are also included in these data – *ibid*.). Low interest rates and low-cost government borrowing combined, how-

ever, to cause a reversal in 1986: non-residents' net purchases of domestic bonds were DM 59 billion, while purchases by domestic non-banks were only DM 12 billion (MRDB table VII[1]). Moreover, net purchases by non-residents reached a record of DM 133 billion in 1992, domestic non-banks having purchased only DM 29 billion. This compared to DM 60 billion and DM 128 billion respectively in 1991. Indeed, foreign investors and domestic banks became the only purchasers of DM domestic bonds in 1992. In that year, when net sales of bonds increased at record rates and the German bond market became one of the world's leading markets, domestic non-banks were net sellers of bonds (*ibid*.; Bayerische Landesbank *Money and Capital Markets* April/May 1993). Apart from price gains due to falling yields, non-residents were benefiting from the relative stability of the DM. The domestic bond market's capacity for absorbing public issues increased markedly compared to 1990: never before had it been possible to place such enormous amounts of fixed-interest securities (Bayerische *ibid*.). Domestic non-banks had clearly substituted other forms of savings (see the discussion around Figures 7.9a and 7.9b below). However, the yield curve was returning to normal, and fixed-interest securities were likely to become more attractive to residents as short-term interest rates fell (see Figures 3.10 and 4.4d).

It is when one turns from the domestic bond market to the international financial markets that one finds virtually all the elements that Bundesbank officials would view with trepidation. Writing as early as 1974, Park (page v) noted how the international, or 'Euro', market had diversified within a decade into a bewildering array of sub-markets. It was no longer possible to understand the Eurobond market without also studying other Euromarkets (*ibid.*). In the foreword to Gallant (1988: ix), Yassukovich referred to the 'mythology' which the Eurobond market had developed during 25 years. The Eurobond market, he continued, 'represented a theatre for innovation and experimentation'. Gallant himself (*ibid.*: 1) correctly adds that Eurobonds were invented when there were great restrictions on the movement of money as well as high taxation on the issuing of securities and on investment income. Whole industries 'grow up around the basic urge to circumvent authority'. Hence, the first Eurobond was issued in 1963, and since then the Eurobond market had grown to become the largest source of international borrowings, with an explosive growth in the bull markets of the mid-1980s. Yet Gowland (1991) could still afford to largely ignore the German international bond market. This was because by the late 1980s nearly all transactions in German government bonds took place in London or Luxembourg, although the German bond market had become part of the Eurobond market and was not a separate entity (*ibid.*: 7 and 107). In other words, the Bundesbank's policymakers were in danger of losing control of the German bond market. The dilemma that they faced resembled the one which caused all the machinations surrounding policy determination on the EMS and EMU (see Chapter 4). It was Hobson's choice: if the emergence of a DM Eurobond system could not be prevented, exert the maximum amount of control! It was a difficult choice, given the barriers against the inflows of foreign capital which had been historically erected, even though there had been a significant relaxation in 1980 whereby the regulations on capital imports had been relaxed in the face of a falling DM (Stonham 1982: 124–5; Chapter 4 above also

refers). Heartened by a substantial current account surplus, however, Bundesbank officials introduced the 1984–5 measures – not least by following the example of the USA in abolishing the withholding tax on non-residents which was deducted at source (Gallant 1988: 85; Gowland 1991: 34). These were indeed the first real steps in liberalising West German financial markets. It made it less difficult for foreign borrowers to access one of the world's least volatile bond markets. Ironically, this lack of volatility was because of the Bundesbank's concentration on long-term stability (Gallant *ibid.*: 87).

Prior to 1985, then, there were other controls on the bond market. Non-residents wishing to issue DM denominated bonds were required to designate a German bank as the lead manager. Representatives from six German banks, with an observer from the Bundesbank, consequently determined the calendar of DM Eurobond issues. (It has already been seen that DM-denominated bonds issued by foreign borrowers are usually known as 'DM Eurobonds'; in the Bundesbank's statistics they are known as 'bonds issued by non-residents' and for inclusion at least one German bank must be involved as a member of the issuing syndicate or the selling group – MRDB *Beiheft* 2. Moreover, unlike bonds issued in other currencies, *all* DM bonds must be issued in Germany. Hence, in the present analysis, 'DM domestic' bonds are issued by residents, whereas non-residents issue 'DM Eurobonds'. 'International DM' or 'foreign DM' bonds could also be used in the latter context – Benzie 1992: 15–17). But for many years the West German bond market was not very significant for foreign borrowers, not least because of a queueing system which depended on the Bundesbank's foreign exchange policy.

As a result of a package of measures in

May 1985, however, the regulation of DM Eurobonds was modified. Subsidiaries of foreign banks in Germany were allowed to be lead managers in underwriting DM Eurobond issues, although branches of foreign banks were still excluded from the market. Net sales of DM Eurobonds increased from DM 9 billion in 1984 to DM 21 billion in 1985, but such issues did not expand much further, even ignoring the exceptionally low sales in 1987. In 1991, for example, these sales amounted to DM 19 billion, compared to net domestic issues which totalled DM 228 billion (MRDB table VII[2]). Issues also remained generally within the purview of syndicated German banks, although issues lead managed by foreign-owned German banks rose to 30 per cent of gross sales in 1990 and 1991 (MRDB 3/92: 25). Not surprisingly, a flurry of activity preceded the ill-fated withholding tax on domestic interest income for a six-month period in 1989. Some German issuers used a foreign vehicle. Hence, 31 per cent of the record DM 41 billion issued by non-residents in 1988 was on behalf of domestic borrowers (*ibid.*: 24). Moreover, the banks' purchases in the domestic bond market increased after 1987 to compensate for the decline in some loan business (*ibid.* 4/89: 15). On the other hand, the Federal Bond Consortium, lead managed by the Bundesbank, was also extended in 1986 so as to include foreign-owned German banks. In 1992, there were 55 such banks out of the total of 113 banks in the consortium (MRDB 3/92: 27).

Until 1985, the Bundesbank also restricted the types of bonds which could be issued. For instance, floating rate bonds were not permitted. This had the effect of driving West German banks to establish subsidiaries and increase their presence in more deregulated markets, notably Luxembourg. It also made it more diffi-

cult for the Bundesbank to enforce its minimum reserve requirements. Following the May 1985 measures, the Bundesbank waived its restrictions on bonds with special features; more specifically, floating rates and zero-rated bonds were permitted. These types of bonds, particularly the zero rated, were generally not all that attractive. Fixed-rate bonds continued to predominate. Moreover, all DM Eurobond issues must have a minimum maturity of two years. This prevents domestic banks issuing minimum-reserve-free paper through their foreign subsidiaries which would be subject to the minimum reserve requirement if issued by the German bank direct (*ibid.*: 25). Notice also that reference has continually been made to the role of banks as key issuers. Although industrial bonds exist in Germany, they are a negligible factor: only DM 3 billion were in circulation at the end of 1992, compared to a total DM bond circulation of over DM 2.25 trillion (they are omitted from Figure 7.4a and Table 7.3 illustrates their insignificance). This was mainly because West German companies preferred to tap other Euromarkets, where the issue procedure had been historically far less regulated. Last, but by no means not least, the Bundesbank continued to insist on the market for DM issues being based in Germany (*ibid.*).

For chronological reasons, it is necessary at this stage to consider the developing position of minimum reserve requirements (MRRs). As implied in the previous paragraph, they have constrained the development of *Finanzplatz Deutschland*. For that matter, minimum-reserve policy was influenced in 1992 by a further critical development in the issues of DM securities (see below). Nonetheless, MRRs were criticised on several grounds (OECD *Economic Survey* 1986: 53):

It has been argued that MRRs are an extra tax on banking business, thus discriminating against this sector. Moreover, as the Bundesbank now relies more on open market operations, the MRRs would seem less important for the conduct of monetary policy, evidenced also by the fact that MRRs ratios have not been changed since 1982. However, the Bundesbank continues to consider MRRs as an important instrument because they act as an 'automatic brake' to money creation. Furthermore, the banks are the only deposit takers benefiting from the stock of deposits with no, or very low, interest rates. Banks also enjoy access to the lending facilities at the Bundesbank. In view of these privileges granted to the banks, some tax on them would not seem unreasonable although it remains debatable as to how much that tax should be.

Perhaps the Bundesbank's policymakers bowed to the inevitable by making a number of changes to MRRs. Consider the points arising from the above quotation:

- the Bundesbank's policymakers did indeed come to rely increasingly on open market operations – notably with the banks (see the first three sections of Chapter 4)
- MRRs applied rigourously would undoubtedly curb the banks' monetary creation powers but the Bundesbank's interest-rate policies have been geared to controlling the demand for money (see the discussion around Figure 4.4d)
- since the appearance of the above quotation, MRRs have in fact been reduced three times, increased only once and their pattern has been significantly changed: MRRs are sizeable only sight deposits; they amount to only 2 per cent on time and savings deposits (MRDB table V[1])

- the latter (interest-bearing) types of deposits represent the areas where German banks were especially vulnerable to competition from abroad, particularly Luxembourg where many of them had established subsidiaries
- nonetheless, Bundesbank officials contend, increasingly unconvincingly, that MRRs are the best monetary tool in a decentralised system; demand can be forecast and frequent intervention by a central bank in the money market is thereby avoided
- it is, however, conceivable that MRRs will gradually be abolished; the Bundesbank might prefer to maintain its restrictions on direct access to the money market, but legislative change could enable the banks to launch money-market funds (see the remarks on certificates of deposit and commercial paper below)
- since the MRRs on savings accounts have been reduced to almost insignificant levels, German banks may be forced by competition, particularly from Luxembourg, to pay more realistic interest rates on their savings deposits; they paid a uniform 2.5–3 per cent over the four years to 1992 and the Cartel Office launched an investigation (FT 16 September 1992)
- although still hardly generous in view of the high Bundesbank short-term interest rates, 'special' savings deposits were introduced by the banks to encourage the recovery in savings in the early 1990s (see the discussion around Figure 7.9a below)
- in short, MRRs were not conducive to the development of *Finanzplatz Deutschland*

The argument thus reverts to what remained a closely controlled market even after the 1984 and 1985 measures (Gallant

1988: 86). There was still dissatisfaction with what in 1992 became more formally known as DM issues. In that year, an official statement by the Bundesbank confirmed that all DM-denominated issues must continue to be made solely through banks domiciled in Germany (MRDB 7/92: 37). It was emphasised that this regulation also applied to domestic issues (*ibid.*: 38). The main reason for the clarification of this 'anchor principle' was the emergence of a commercial-paper market, a market which will be discussed in more depth following an examination of the German stock market. Of critical importance here is the fact that by virtue of the Bundesbank statement foreign non-banks were given access to DM Eurobonds with a maturity of less than two years, as well as to the commercial-paper market. Foreign banks continued to be restricted to issuing DM-denominated bonds and notes with a minimum maturity of two years. In deciding whether a foreign institution was a non-bank or a bank, Bundesbank officials would use the criteria elaborated in section 1 of the KWG. (These wide-ranging criteria can be found at the beginning of the section on prudential arrangements above.)

There were a number of other changes (*ibid.*). Foreign banks with branches in Germany were also subsequently permitted to lead manage DM issues, provided they possess a full issues department; non-German banks could become the principal paying agent; the requirement that all issues be subject to German law was abolished; issues no longer had to be listed on the German stock exchange; and issues could be made without inclusion in the German securities clearing system, or *Kassenverein*, which was described when proxy-voting was considered in the corporate finance section above. Bundesbank regulations on DM issues were thus further relaxed to meet the requirements of EC 1993 and in response to developments in the international capital markets. These deregulatory measures coincided with the prelude to the exchange-rate upheavals within the ERM. As a result, speculators were bound in any event to be attracted to DM securities and, at the same time, the costs of issuing and investing in DM Eurobonds had been reduced by deregulation (*Economist* 16 January 1993). Ironically, the UK Treasury raised DM 5.5 billion in October 1992 in order to replenish its foreign-currency reserves following the unsuccessful intervention on the forex market. This was the largest-ever DM Eurobond issue and, because of its prestige and size, the Deutsche was chosen as the lead bank (*Euromoney* December 1992). For the same reason, that is the gyrations within the ERM, Italy made the second largest issue (DM 5 billion) in January 1993. Further sovereign and supranational issues were to be expected. Frankfurt am Main had become at least a fledgling Euromarket in its own right – in spite of the intervening strains of unification.

Because of the historical importance of mortgage bonds, a fuller analysis of bond sales appears in the next section. However, the reader will already have gathered that DM Eurobonds compete with a wide range of domestic instruments in Germany. An overview of the bond market can be culled at this stage from Figures 7.4a, 7.4b, 7.4c and 7.4d. Figure 7.4a shows the relative importance of the principal domestic and DM Eurobonds. Recall that industrial bonds were too insignificant to be included (they amounted to only DM 3 billion in December 1992). It is evident, however, that the total circulation of bonds, including industrial bonds, was DM 2.267 trillion at the end of 1992. Although public bonds have grown in importance, the various types of bank bonds remain, in aggregate, the most important bonds in circulation (see Figure 7.4b, where 'total' includes industrial bonds). The mortgage banks, special-purpose banks and *Landesbanken* ('other') are the main bank-bond issuers (Figure 7.4c). Briefly put, it is still generally true to say that the German bond markets serve primarily as a means through which banks intermediate in raising and investing longer-term funds (BEQB 1984: 370). The Federal government issues most of its bonds direct. For this reason it accounts for the biggest proportion of public bonds (Figure 7.4d). Moreover, the significance of efficient and cost-effective borrowing was accentuated by the marked surge in the Federal Government's borrowing requirements in the wake of unification (MRDB 3/92: 27).

Three further points should be noted with respect to public bonds. First, the local authorities are of negligible significance in this context. They had a constant DM 150 billion outstanding after 1987. On the other hand, the significant increase in Länder issues following GEMSU is particularly conspicuous in 1992 (Figure 7.4d). Second, many of shadow budget items analysed in the budgetary policy section of Chapter 3 are included in the 'direct unity costs' category shown in Figure 7.4d. More specifically, these items are: the German Unity Fund (from 1990), the GEMSU currency conversion equalisation component of the Debt Management Fund (from 1991), the (reactivated) ERP special assets (1992) and the Treuhand (also 1992). It is instructive to juxtapose these costs of unification with Germany's emergence as an international bond market. By the end of 1992, the 'direct unity' items together accounted for 15 per cent of outstanding public bonds (DM 125 billion from DM 832 billion).

On the other hand, their total circulation was under half of the other rapidly expanding category of bond, namely DM Eurobonds. Third, from 1987, the Federal Post Office collectively carried a larger bond debt than the railways (DM 56 billion compared to DM 37.5 billion in 1992). The preparation of these public enterprises for privatisation is considered in Chapter 8.

The dominance of the bond market and, conversely, the relative underdevelopment of equity finance, are two key features of German economic development. Historical experience with monetary instability has inevitably influenced attitudes in the securities' markets. It is little wonder, therefore, that the fixed-income bond is preferred to the risk implied in holding equities. There is admittedly some evidence that this element of risk aversion is on the wane: 40 per cent of German shareholders are under 35 (*Economist* 3 July 1993). Nonetheless, the relative size of the bond and equity markets, which can be demonstrated in a variety of ways, reflects the significant residual predilection for fixed-income securities. The most poignant demonstration of this preference is the vast difference between the dealing in bonds and equities on the German stock exchanges. (There are eight exchanges – see below.) Bearing in mind that securities can be listed and issued on more than one exchange, it is still possible to say that almost 90 per cent of business on all exchanges in 1991 was in bonds (ADB *Jahresbericht* 1991). Moreover the nominal value of bonds in circulation in the early 1980s was over seven times larger than the equivalent measure of activity in the share market; by 1991 this factor had increased to over eleven (BEQB 1984: 370; MRDB *Beiheft* 2: Tables 5a and 16). In view of the subsequent analysis, however, Figure 7.5 contains a comparison of the nominal value of bonds and the market value of ordinary shares quoted on the German stock exchange. During the period 1974–92, their respective average values were DM 863 billion and DM 293 billion. As early as 1978/79, and again in 1984/85, the Council of Economic Advisers advanced the view that this shortage of equity capital was leading to insufficient real investment and low growth rates (Hax 1990: 107). This was because firms with insufficient equity capital are risk averse in their investment decisions.

All this does not, of course, detract from the fact that the relative rate of return on equities compensates for the risk factor. Such a statement is illustrated by means of Figures 7.6a, 7.6b and 7.6c.

In Figure 7.6a, the annual average relative yields of bonds and equities are plotted for the period 1951–91. So as to be consistent with Figures 7.4 above, the bond yield in Figure 7.6a is on outstanding bonds. This is in contrast to Figure 3.11 where the yield on newly issued bonds was more relevant. The equity yield, on the other hand, is measured as the average annual dividend on the average market value of a DM 100 par value ordinary share (MRDB *Statistische Beihefte* Reihe 2). Given this definition, the average annual yield on bonds – and indeed the average yield for the period as a whole – is higher than the equity yield. This is because no account has been taken of the annual average change in equity capital values. The rate at which these values have changed over the period 1951–91 is proxied by means of the FAZ general share index in Figure 7.6b. A total rate of return on equities is then arrived at by summating their average annual yield and capital values in Figure 7.6c. Hence, over the period 1951–91 the long-run average annual total return on equities was 15.79

per cent (Figure 7.6c), compared to an average bond yield of 7.25 per cent over the same period (Figure 7.6a). The higher degree of risk on equities is illustrated by the standard deviation of the total return on equities during the time period in question (27.95 per cent), which compares during this period to a standard deviation of only 1.28 per cent on bond yields.

It can also be seen from Figure 7.6c that there was only one year during the 1970s with an above average rate of return on equities (1975). Even during the bullish markets of that year, however, UK companies tapped equity markets to a substantially greater extent than German ones (BEQB 1984: 371). On the other hand, it can also be seen from Figure 7.6c that in five out of the ten years 1980–9 there was a higher than average return. An upswing in share prices began in 1982. It was followed by four further years of growth, culminating in the FAZ index reaching 676.37 in 1986 – 2.7 times higher than its 1982 level. In 1987, the October crash on Wall Street clearly had serious repercussions on the German share market. The spectacular recovery in 1988 was given further momentum by the fall of the Berlin wall, new issues reaching a record market value of DM 28 billion in 1990 (MRDB *Stat Beihefte* 2: Table 14). The Gulf war and the hike in crude oil prices to $US 40 a barrel – to say nothing about a belated appreciation of the true costs of unification – caused the market to end 1990 with the FAZ index 18 per cent lower than in 1989.

During the 1980s, the strongest growth was achieved in 1985, a year in which the AEG share, on the strength of being taken over by Daimler-Benz, reached over DM 200 – compared to DM 23 in 1982. From the end of 1984 to 1990, the number of AGs and KGaAs rose by 554 to reach 2,682, although the number of these enter-

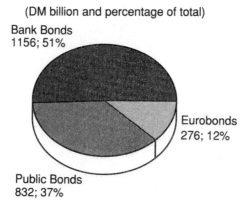

(DM billion and percentage of total)

Bank Bonds
1156; 51%

Eurobonds
276; 12%

Public Bonds
832; 37%

Figure 7.4a Bonds in circulation: December 1992
Source: MRDB *Stat. Beihefte* 2: Tables II (4a) and III (2)

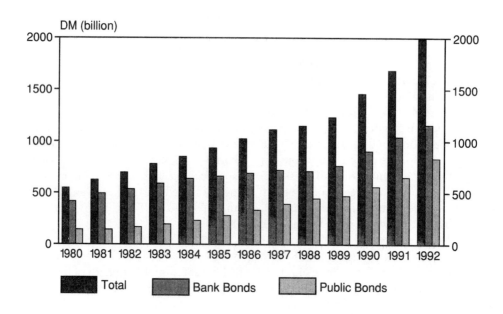

Figure 7.4b Domestic Bonds in circulation
Source: MRDB *Stat. Beihefte* 2 Table II (4a)

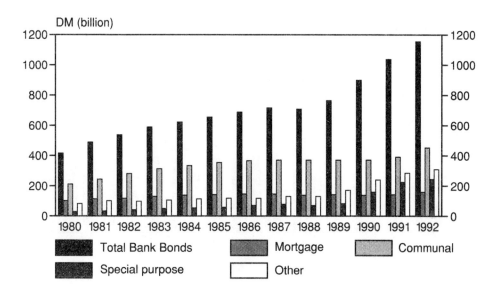

Figure 7.4c Bank Bonds in circulation

Source: MRDB *Stat. Beihefte* 2 Table II (4a)

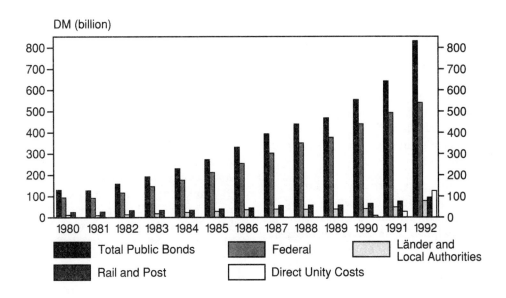

Figure 7.4d Public Bonds in circulation

Source: MRDB *Stat. Beihefte* 2 Table II (4f)

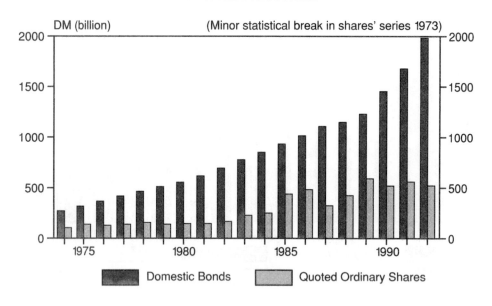

Figure 7.5 Securities in circulation
Sources: Dresdner Bank, *Stat. Reihen*; MRDB *Stat. Beihefte* 2

prises listed on the domestic stock exchange rose by only 52 to reach 501 (MRDB 10/91: 23). Nonetheless, the mostly bullish market had made it much easier for quoted companies to raise equity capital because they were able to realise relatively high subscription prices when selling new shares. Indeed, these propitious circumstances gave the appearance of a belated breakthrough for equity finance which also rekindled the Federal Government's interest in privatisation (*Economist* 12 April 1986):

Falling oil prices, virtually no inflation, forecasts of rising demand and a string of strong company results, together with the residual whiff of (the 1985) bull market, have induced German institutions and individuals to shed some of their customary reluctance to buy shares.

At the end of 1991 there were 519 listed companies, the highest number for twenty years; however, the number had risen to only 521 at the end of 1992 (MRDB *ibid* and *Beiheft* 2: Table IV[2]). The fact that soaring share prices were a prerequisite for the reemergence of shares may be taken as an indication of how unattractive this source of funding had appeared to companies. In 1990, however, share issues raised over 25 per cent of long-term funds – a proportion not known since the 1950s and 1960s; indeed, in 1983 securities as a whole constituted only 11 per cent of total liabilities for German non-financial companies, compared to 36 per cent for British companies (*ibid.*; BEQB 1984: 369). Ranked by market capitalisation as a percentage of GNP (that is 21 per cent in 1991), Germany still lay well behind Japan, Britain, Switzerland and the USA; on the same basis, her stock market was about the same size as France's.

A necessary condition for the consolidation and even continued advancement of equity finance was the removal of easily identifiable constraints. As well as the

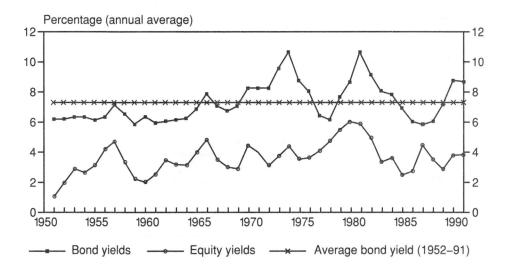

Figure 7.6a Annual yields on bonds and equities

Source: Plotted from Dresdner Bank *Stat. Reihen*

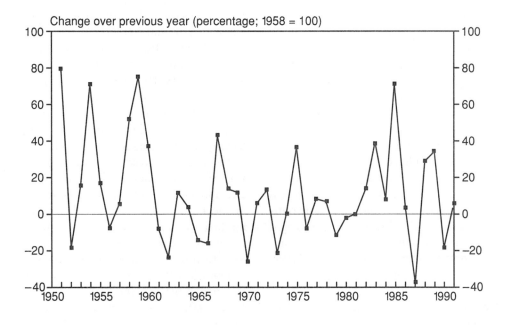

Figure 7.6b Annual change in FAZ General Share Index

Source: As Figure 7.6a

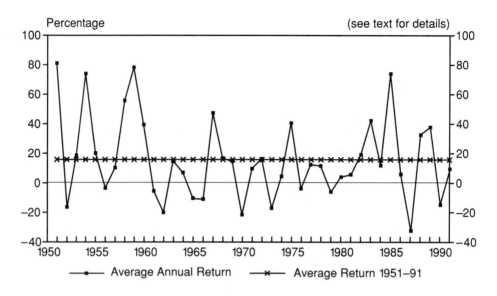

Figure 7.6c Total rate of return on equities
Source: Calculated from Figures 7.6a and 7.6b

general public attitude to buying shares, there were powerful institutional and tax reasons for what became known as the 'equity gap'. Yet the rivalry with Bonn and other European centres to attract the European Central Bank, along with the ambition to regain business lost to London and other financial markets, provided Frankfurt am Main with equally powerful reasons for reform. Rather more dubiously, Frankfurt's geographical location was considered appropriate for the assumption of a pivotal role in financing eastern and central Europe. Berlin and Munich, on this criterion, were more optimal locations. Frankfurt's relatively rapid post-war development as a financial centre was another matter. Consider, however, the emergence of all these problems:

Competition between exchanges Most of the old Länder possessed their own exchanges. Although these exchanges were governed by inter-Länder treaties,

there was a strong tradition of independence. Chronologically, the exchanges were established as follows (ndc 1973: 179–82): Hamburg (1558); Frankfurt am Main (1585); Berlin (1685); Hannover (1785); Munich (1830); Bremen (1850); Stuttgart (1861); Düsseldorf (1875). Following unification, there were thus eight independent stock exchanges, all situated in the old Länder – although Saxony was pressing for the establishment of exchanges in Dresden and Leipzig. This was therefore another issue on which attempted centralisation would be resisted in the Bundesrat. However, there was a marked concentration of business within the eight exchanges: 82 per cent of the total turnover of shares in 1991 occurred in Frankfurt (67 per cent) and Düsseldorf (15 per cent) (cf *ibid*.: 182; Stonham 1982: 103). On the number of dealings in securities – an obviously less significant measure, with considerable overlap – Frankfurt predominates, with Düsseldorf,

Munich and Hamburg of similar size (ADW 1991). Under the chief executive of the Frankfurt exchange – Rüdiger von Rosen, the 'dynamic former aide' to Herr Pöhl (*Economist* 28 January 1989) – efforts were made to improve computer links, reduce duplication and present a joint stand abroad. Von Rosen's innovations culminated in the Frankfurt exchange becoming an AG in 1990, with German banks holding 80 per cent of the capital. He also pressed the case for Frankfurt to become the base for Deutsche Börse AG, a new holding company which would provide central services for the eight exchanges. Von Rosen became its first chief executive and the other seven exchanges duly took a 10 per cent stake in the new company. By 1993 the *Kassenverein* securities clearing system (see proxy-voting above), the DTB (see computerisation below) and the Frankfurt exchange were all under one roof. They had all been merged into Deutsche Börse AG. This project was supported by the Finance Ministry as part of a package of measures aimed at promoting *Finanzplatz Deutschland*. But would this overcome the duplication in listings and, more especially, the quotation of different prices at each of the eight exchanges? Von Rosen was demoted as a prelude to efforts to introduce common technology and shared services in Frankfurt (*ibid.* 20 March 1993; also see passage on technology below). The political battles had been won in so far as Deutsche Börse existed as a legal entity; pure management skills were subsequently required to ensure that the new organisation functioned (FT 7 May 1993).

Insider trading The Frankfurt exchange is thus a dominant force, but this exchange had to deal with a number of insider-trading and tax-evasion cases, particularly, but not exclusively, in 1991. Moreover, insider trading was institutionalised: there

is no German phrase for the practice. The dominance of the banks does not help. As early as 1973, it was pointed out that this would prevent harmonisation within the EC (ndc 1973: 183). The banks act at one and the same time as both chief agents in corporate financing on the capital market, and as investment advisers and securities' dealers (*ibid.*). In other words, they possess sensitive information on both the demand and supply sides of the market. As well as dealing for clients, moreover, they reserve the right to deal on their own account (*Eigengeschäfte – ibid.*: 194). By building on the procedure of its Morgan Grenfell subsidiary, the Deutsche Bank hoped to introduce Chinese walls between different bank departments and place rigorous restrictions on own account trading in 1992 (FT 3 April 1992). Yet no potential conflict of interest, in terms of transparency, was perceived in the Deutsche providing its executive director for capital markets as the chairman of Deutsche Börse's supervisory board, notwithstanding the fact that similar links between financial and non-financial companies are common. In addition, the leader of Germany's largest trade union (Franz Steinkühler of the IG Metall) was forced to resign in 1993 because he had used information gained on the supervisory board of Daimler-Benz to profit from share transactions. This event was evidently more newsworthy than the entrenched role of the banks – for coverage in English see: the *Economist* 29 May 1993; FT 19, 24 and 26 May; *Guardian* 26 May; *Independent on Sunday* 30 May. IG Metall banned its officials from owning shares in companies where they sit on supervisory boards, although employee directors were permitted to retain employees' shares; the latter securities are subject to special conditions and cannot be openly traded (FT 30 June 1993). Notwithstanding the fact that this type of event further undermines public confidence in equity investment, it may have at least accelerated the frequently postponed legislation to outlaw insider trading. This legislation was the responsibility of the Federal Finance Ministry. (Such a framework was in any case required by the 1989 EC directive to make insider trading illegal by mid-1992; Germany's Act might reach the statute book in mid-1994.) Insider trading also reinforced the growing view that companies were not managed in the interests of their shareholders, thereby leaving the agency problem unresolved (Ogger 1992: 55; Steinherr 1991: 371; Wenger 1987: 219; also see the sections on the cooperative banks, *Allfinanz* and corporate finance above, as well as the section on mergers and acquisitions in Chapter 8). Earlier, (January 1991) a regulation was waived which had previously required the ministry's permission prior to the issue of new securities. Procrastination in introducing institutional and legal reform in the area of insider trading was, in fact, the major restraint on the development of *Finanzplatz Deutschland*. Compare, for example, the above Bundesbank measures enforced by international competition in the Eurobond markets with the complacency of the banks and Federal Government when it came to stock market reform.

The complex market structure For many years, there were two separate markets, albeit with a confusing and confused distinction (Stonham 1982: 105–8). First, official trading in all bonds and equities admitted to official listing by each exchange's listing committee was carried out on the exchanges between 1130 and 1330 daily – extended to three hours from 1030 in January 1990 (*amtlicher Verkehr* or *Handel*). Trading on the official exchanges is carried out by official market match makers, or brokers/jobbers

(*amtliche Kursmakler*). The market match maker compares buy and sell orders, and fixes the opening and closing prices for both single quotations (*Einheitskurse*) and continuous quotations (*variable Kurse*). As their title implies, *amtliche Kursmakler* are appointed by the Federal or Land Minister of Finance. When bunds are issued, they cooperate with Bundesbank officials. In 1991, there were 111 *Kursmakler*, 40 of whom were at the Frankfurt exchange (ADW 1991). Second, there is a two-tier unofficial exchange. The first tier consists of regulated unofficial dealing, a hybrid 'regulated free market' or 'semi-official market' (*geregelter Freiverkehr*). This market is basically regulated by civil law. Trading also takes place on the floor of the exchanges, the participants being almost identical to the official market, and trading in the same issues to a large extent. The second tier of the unofficial exchange is where trading takes place away from the floors either during official hours, or, more likely, by telephone and telefax outside of the restricted opening hours of the official exchange. The banks' dealers (*Händler*) and independent brokers (*freie Makler*) undertake the trading in both tiers of the unofficial market. There were 162 independent brokers in 1991, 79 of whom had been admitted to Frankfurt exchange; yet there were 377 bank dealers admitted to the Frankfurt exchange alone (*ibid.*). Numerous other employees may be admitted to the exchanges, with or without the right to deal. (Journalists are in the latter category, for example. But a measure of the relative insignificance of the stock exchanges is that all 30 of the closing prices of the blue-chip shares are announced within a few minutes at about 1345 on *Deutschland Funk* each trading day. There is almost continuous television coverage during trading in the USA. Nonetheless, the DAX 30 index commands more interest in Germany almost daily – see below.) This market system was made even more complex by liberalisation. A third tier (*geregelter Markt*) was added to the stock market by a Federal Act in 1987 (Frankfurter Wertpapierbörse 1992: 28). A related Act sanctioned the setting up of risk-capital investment companies in the form of AGs which could 'transmit' equity capital raised in the stock market to enterprises not qualified for stock-exchange listing. It was thus intended to reduce listing costs and relax disclosure rules for small and medium-sized businesses. In the event, the legislators' expectations were only partially fulfilled: fewer than twenty risk-capital investment companies had supported less than 200 firms by 1992. In 1991, the official market was responsible for 13,719 dealings, the regulated unofficial market made 990 deals and the *geregelter Markt* 4,108 (ADW *ibid.*). There are, for obvious reasons, no data on transactions made using the second tier of the unofficial market. Legal reform of trading was understandably still delayed in 1993.

Computerised price information, trading and hedging It is here where the greatest strides were made towards *Finanzplatz Deutschland*. A continuously updated German share price index (DAX) was introduced in 1988. DAX covers the top 30 listed companies representing 80 per cent of equity-market turnover and its introduction was mainly a prelude to the opening of the equity-options section of a financial futures market in January 1990 (DTB, *Deutsche Terminbörse*; a bund trading section was added in September 1990). These innovations were in response to international competition, not least from London where 30 per cent of the trading in German blue-chip shares also took place on the International Stock Exchange SEAQI system. In response to this latter off-exchange trading system, seven German banks (including the Big Three) launched a screen-based trading system in December 1989 (IBIS, *Integriertes Börsenhandels- und Informationssystem*). By October 1991, following fairly serious teething troubles, IBIS was being used to trade DAX shares and as the third method of issuing Federal bonds – the other two methods being the banks' and Federal consortia outlined above. Both the *amtliche* and *freie Makler* were disenchanted with the banks for setting up IBIS. Instead, they set up their own screen-based systems (MATIS and MIDAS respectively). Since this would have added three off-exchange trading systems to the eight stock exchanges, the banks sold IBIS to the Frankfurt exchange, thus enabling both groups of *Makler* to access its data base. Because the new system endangered both floor trading and the regional structure of exchanges, brokers continued *pro tem* to operate alongside the new system and regional stock and bond operations also continued. There is, however, a firm intention to implement a more extensive electronic dealing system for shares and fixed-interest securities later in the 1990s.

Sources of equity finance and equity prices The organisation of social-insurance funding, as well as the internal retention of company-pension contributions as a cheap and tax-exempt source of investment finance, meant that pension funds were a negligible institutional investor. (The company pension schemes alone totalled DM 200 billion in 1990, but they would not have received corporation-tax credit if invested on the open capital markets.) As already shown, tax-exempt contributions to life insurance funds had induced the banks to establish *Allfinanz*. A further disincentive was the par value of at least DM 50 for German shares – the initial offer price of which was 400 per cent higher in 1989. (Allianz – the top share in 1990 – had a market value of DM 2,000.)

Tax disincentives Although capital gains tax is not payable on equities held for longer than six months, corporation tax (36 per cent in 1991) and investment income tax (25 per cent) were both deducted at source from distributed profits. A tax-credit is then issued for inclusion in tax returns. Interest on bank savings accounts and on fixed-interest investment vehicles, on the other hand, was paid in full. Tax evasion was much easier than was the case for dividend payments. The effects of the 10 per cent withholding tax on fixed-interest vehicles were seen in Chapter 4 but recall that the tax had to be withdrawn after only six months in 1989. The Federal Constitutional Court enjoined the legislature in 1991 to introduce a more consistent system. As a result, most interest from bank accounts became no longer eligible for tax (see below). In general, it could also be said that the total tax burden fell as debt was substituted for equity capital. Additional taxes impeded the sales of shares. Hence, with effect from 1 January 1991 the stock exchange turnover tax or securities transfer tax (*Börsenumsatzsteuer*) was abolished. Similarly, from 1 January 1992 capital or stamp duty payable on the first acquisition of shares in companies (*Gesellschaftsteuer*), along with the tax on bills of exchange (*Wechselsteuer*), were also terminated. Undertakings to remove these tax constraints had been consistently made since 1982.

There were several implications for *Finanzplatz Deutschland*. The turnover tax had effectively curbed the growth of money-market instruments such as commercial paper (CP), certificates of deposits (CDs) and floating-rate notes. Given the extremely slender margins on these short-term investment instruments, even a small tax would have rendered such trading unprofitable. As early as 1986, Bundesbank policymakers had decreed that for the purpose of enforcing its MRRs, the issuing of DM-denominated CDs should be confined to Germany (OECD *Economic Survey* 1986: 52). At the same juncture, MRRs were imposed on bearer securities issued by the banks for maturity periods under two years. This had the effect of restraining the growth of these highly liquid securities which had circulated freely in the USA and UK since the 1960s. (Also recall that the German banks paid relatively low rates of interest for their retail deposits – see the above discussion on MRRs. This made CDs an unattractive alternative means of retaining an adequate level of bank deposits to finance advances.)

Similarly, Bundesbank officials had indicated that it had no objections to CP being issued in Germany, although they expressed anxiety about any developments which might undermine its minimum reserve policies (MRDB 3/92: 26). On the other hand, with the termination of the need to seek finance ministry approval to issue new securities, which coincided with the abolition of the turnover tax, the DM CP market overtook its sterling counterpart by 1992. The total value of programmes amounted to DM 25 billion by February of that year, with the Deutsche as chief dealer – initially for Daimler-Benz, but with Treuhand becoming the biggest domestic issuer. The Federal Post Office also issued CP. In August 1992, foreign non-banks were permitted by the Bundesbank to have direct access to the CP market rather than through the intermediary of a German subsidiary (MRDB 5/93: 62). In effect, MRRs prevent both foreign and domestic banks from tapping the CP market for their own purposes. In any case, issues of CP compete with wholesale bank lending to top-quality borrowers. Competition, especially from the Euro CP market, keeps interest rates fairly close to money market rates (*ibid.*: 64).

Consider these changes. Banks do not underwrite the CP which they are involved in placing, and thus do not pledge to purchase unsold paper or give credits to the issuers. CP is therefore excluded from measures of capital adequacy under the Federal Banking Supervisory Office's Principle 1 (MRDB 3/92: 26). CP is usually issued by large corporations, especially during periods of restrictive monetary policy when credit is tight. Potentially, universal banks could lose high-quality borrowers to the CP market, thus lowering the quality of their loan portfolios. They would therefore have to rely on CP issues generating higher commission receipts from these off-balance sheet transactions. Similarly, CDs were close substitutes to the low-interest deposits held by the banks and which constituted a traditional source of cheap funding. But CDs, having originated in the USA in the early 1960s, spread to the UK in 1968. EC 1993 therefore meant more competition from this vehicle. Moreover, they are a potential alternative to other short-term funds such as treasury bills. They therefore constitute a parallel money market – hence the reason for the Bundesbank insisting that they remain subject to its MRRs. On the other hand, CP was held by domestic or Luxembourg-based unit trusts (30–40 per cent of the market), along with an estimated further 25–30 per cent with domestic insurance companies (FT 3 September 1992). Central banks were the only foreign investors, with companies holding 25–30 per cent. This left relatively little for the

banks to use as money market funds and the growth of the market was said to be constrained by this factor (*ibid.*).

Consider next insider trading. For most German banks, traders took no risk but rather acted as 'order fillers' in an uncompetitive market; the average German bank trader was therefore underpaid and undermotivated (*Economist* 27 July 1991: 4; 31 August 1991: 15). They were, however, allowed to trade on their own personal accounts. Such a system was open to abuse if traders exploited inside information or put their own and their bank's interests before that of their clients. Where a shareholder paid a higher price for a share as a result of its value being artificially inflated by insider trading, it did not augur well for the future manner in which interests would be represented. The agency problem arises yet again: will corporate control of non-financial companies be exercised in the shareholders' interests? (By juxtaposing the underdevelopment of the German stock market and bank equity stakes, it will be recalled that Steinherr (1991: 371) concluded that the agency problem was not well resolved.)

But were the German banks becoming more interested in acting as the dominant European financial intermediaries, rather than retaining their traditional links with industry? Given the strength of the DM and Germany's normally high current account surpluses, there is at least an attractive *a priori* case for agreeing with Steinherr's contention (1991: 374), that Germany should have been a major exporter of financial services. Yet as Steinherr goes on to show, Germany was the ECs largest importer of such services. On the other hand, a plausible alternative argument would be that Germany's visible trade balance derived from her comparative advantage in manufacturing. Even after EC 1993, therefore, she could have continued to import financial services if other EC states held a comparative advantage in this field. But the priority accorded to achieving the goal of *Finanzplatz Deutschland* gathered its own momentum. As a result of insider-trading allegations, the Deutsche announced that it would impose rigorous limitations on own-account trading (FT 3 April 1992). It was seen in the notes on insider trading that the system of control was to be modelled particularly on practice at Morgan Grenfell, its UK merchant banking subsidiary (acquired in 1989). It will also be seen in Chapter 8 that the changing scene in mergers and acquisitions was another reason for the Deutsche's purchase of Morgan Grenfell. (Interestingly enough, it was the 'confident handling of foreign-exchange dealings and high investment in computer technology' that attracted LTU and the WestLB to Thomas Cook – *Sunday Times* 7 June 1992.)

Similarly, the tax evasion allegations had particular relevance to foreign investors. It was contended that *Freie Makler* had been involved in widespread and illegal dividend stripping for a number of years. This practice consisted of foreigners selling shares to German nationals prior to dividend payments. German investors then obtain a dividend and the tax credit on same, whereas the foreign investor would not have received the tax credit. A final phase would be for foreign investors to repurchase the shares at a lower price. Historically, foreign investors were an important impetus to the stock market. Indeed, in 1986 and 1989 foreign purchases of equities were significantly greater than domestic non-bank purchases (MRDB *Stat Beihefte* 1). In 1990 and 1991, however, domestic non-bank purchases reached the record heights of DM 41 billion and DM 33 billion, compared to foreign net sales (DM – 3 billion) in 1990

and negligible purchases of DM 1.5 billion in 1991.

It was a curious economic coincidence that many of the changes noted above reached their crescendo as unification occurred. EC 1993 was the proximate cause. To a certain extent, this applies to housing finance. For this reason, the analysis now turns to this uniquely German form of financial intermediation.

HOUSING FINANCE AND BOND ISSUES

It is appropriate to initially consider some salient features of the German housing market and policies. Writing in the early 1970s, Hallett (1973: 120–1) enthusiastically reported:

The Federal Republic's most distinctive achievement is probably in the field of housing and town and country planning . . . Housing policy is, perhaps, the clearest example of the 'social market economy'.

As in other sectors, however, it would be fallacious to consider that there has been a uniform approach to housing policy during the post-war period, or that the market has functioned in a frictionless manner. Tomann (1990: 919–21) incisively distinguishes four phases of housing policy covering each of the four decades between 1950 and 1989. Since his paper was completed, unification has produced – in housing as elsewhere – a fifth policy challenge which will at the very least dominate the 1990s. Such a scenario is broadly consistent with the various phases of more general economic development analysed in Chapter 1. In any case, a serious housing shortage had already started to develop in the west prior to GEMSU (see Figure 7.7b below). As a result, a number of policies were introduced, or even reintroduced. By 1992, some of these measures were seen as an illustration of 'the great extent to which the housing sector has been protected from interest rate movements in the capital market in the past few years . . .' (MRDB 8/92: 23).

Before the evolution of housing policy can be examined, therefore, it is necessary to specify the policy instruments. It will be seen that they have all affected the banking sector and bond market. As Börsch-Supan (1986: 380) indicates, government intervention takes place both on the demand and the supply side of the market, taking the form of housing allowances (*Wohngeld*), tax subsidies, and rent and eviction control. The instruments themselves – putting tenants' protection aside for a moment – fall under the two broad headings of either government subsidies or tax allowances. The following may be categorised as subsidies:

- social housing grants traditionally made to landlords as an inducement to provide rented property at low controlled rents
- housing allowances (first introduced in 1965) paid to tenants on low incomes and revised upwards over time
- premia which gained increasing importance in the post-war era even though their value was progressively reduced after 1975; they are available to prospective owner occupiers who comply with the deposit requirements of a savings contract with a building savings bank

The instruments which can be categorised as tax allowances are:

- capital gains tax exemption (since 1987) provided the property is not sold within two years of purchase

- depreciation allowances for both landlords and owner occupiers
- deductibility of contractual deposits at a building savings bank
- special tax credits (*Baukindergeld*) for all children in owner-occupiers' households
- from October 1991 owner occupiers may deduct interest payments up to DM 12,000 per annum for the first three years following the purchase of a newly-built house

It will be recalled that there was an acute housing shortage for several years following the Second World War, a shortage which had been brought about by both war damage on the housing stock side, and by the influx of ethnic German expellees and refugees on the demand side (Chapters 1 and 6 above). The severity of the housing shortage would have led to increases in rents had the system of rent control not been retained, initially at 1930 prices. Tenants in these pre-1948 rent-controlled dwellings also enjoyed security of tenure. The rebuilding programme designed to ameliorate the shortages was embodied in the 1950 and 1956 Housing Construction Acts, both of which provided tax and interest concessions, as well as earmarking considerable public funds (Hardach 1980: 151). Moreover, the programme was given impetus by two peculiarly German institutions, both of which had their origins in the 1920s. First, housing advisory services were channelled through home-construction guidance centres (*Heimstätten*). These were non-profit making bodies which provided architectural, legal and financial services to organisations, companies and individuals with building proposals (Hallett 1973: 123). In view of the emphasis placed on Länder autonomy in Chapter 2, it is interesting to note that each Land government became the largest shareholder in the Heimstätten, along with local authorities, banks, insurance companies and – the second institution responsible for the impetus to housing provision – housing associations. These latter institutions were completely exempt from taxation and were required to plough back all but 4 per cent of their annual profits into the association. Their ownership was vested in co-operatives, trade unions and churches. About one half of the publicly-assisted social housing programmes (*sozialer Wohnungsbau*) were channelled through the housing associations. It is important to note that the aim of the social housing programmes, which were introduced in the 1950 Act, was to provide rented accommodation for low-income families at subsidised and controlled rents. Such dwellings are a traditionally important part of the German housing stock. More generally, private individuals and, to a lesser extent, building firms also provided rented property for which general grants and tax allowances were available. Whereas rents for this latter type of property were set at more economic levels, they were also subject to control. The 1956 Act sought to encourage owner occupation by savings premia and various tax allowances. In this respect, the 1956 Act supplemented the Home Building Bonus Act of 1952 (Gurdon 1991: 596). But there was a disincentive to buy a home because of the growing supply of relatively cheap rented housing.

An Act in 1960 began a process of rent decontrol in the private-rented sector. (This excluded social housing, of course.) Initially, the pre-1948 stock was targeted at a local level. From 1965, rent control on other forms of property were abolished, although controls remained in force in Berlin, Hamburg and Munich. Rent decontrol was generally contingent upon

shortages having been eradicated and additions to the housing stock during the 1960s were not significantly different from the 1950s (Hills *et al.* 1989: 2; Figure 7.7a below). By the end of the decade additions to the housing stock slowed down and there were high rent increases (*ibid.*). Some protection for tenants against rent increases imposed by some private landlords was therefore considered necessary (Hardach 1980: 151). This culminated in the Rent Regulation Act (1971) which regulated rent increases for existing tenants, complemented by security of tenure (*Erstes Wohnraum-Kündigungs gesetz*) (Tomann 1990: 921). Further legislation in 1975 extended the provisions on security of tenure (Börsch-Supan 1986: 381). Each new tenancy accorded an opportunity for an unregulated increase in rent. The rent of existing tenants is determined by a complex process of indexation which establishes a standard rent for comparable accommodation. In effect, this system yields a rent level for sitting tenants which is a lagged average of the rent for comparable units; eviction is permitted only if (*ibid.*):

- the tenant is in breach of contract (failing to pay his/her rent, for example)
- the landlord or a close relative requires possession
- the appropriate economic usage is being frustrated (where the zoning laws permit business usage, for example)

In the latter case, the landlord was required to satisfactorily demonstrate that his firm's economic viability is being endangered. Something of a loophole was probably provided by the Constitutional Court in 1992. If a landlord notified the tenant that the property was required for conversion, further security against conviction was limited to a five-year period. It was alleged that this would particularly affect older tenants living in city-centre locations where conversion to luxury flats would provide landlords with lucrative sales (*Die Zeit* 32/92). In the longer run it would exacerbate the shortage of low-cost rented properties. Legislation planned for 1993 was designed to tightly curb conversions which would constitute permissible grounds for eviction.

Prior to its downfall in 1982, the Schmidt government further amended the details of the regulatory framework for rent adjustment, as well as reducing assistance for social housing programmes. These two measures largely assisted the Kohl government's intention to deregulate the housing market after 1982. Low-income groups were protected by increased reliance on the housing allowance scheme introduced in 1965; indeed, there was a policy shift from subsidised social housing – the joint responsibility of Federal and Länder governments – to housing allowances which are part of the Federal budget. The Act (*Wohngeldgesetz*) provides a right to a rent subsidy to enable a family to secure a basic minimum standard of accommodation (Hallett 1973: 126). On this basis, an acceptable level of rent payable by the family should not account for more than 15–25 per cent of a household's disposable income (see the incidence of taxation section in Chapter 3). An imputed rent is calculated for owner occupiers. The difference between this notional rent and the actual rent payable for the calculated minimum standard of housing is met by a housing allowance, or rent subsidy. The nominal value of the maximum allowance varies with family income, size and region. Since the main Act (1970), the allowance has been adjusted every 3–5 years. Rent inflation between 1981 and 1985 meant that the proportion of claimants whose rent rose

above the maximum limit increased from 31 to 53 per cent. An upwards adjustment of the allowance in 1985 caused this proportion to fall back to 31 per cent (Tomann 1990: 928). The Act was extended to the new Länder in 1991 and its provisions were again updated in 1992. As indicated in the social security section of Chapter 5, in practice 95 per cent of beneficiaries are tenants. In the event, the Kohl government made no attempt to amend the rent regulation provisions inherited from the Schmidt government. In spite of an emerging housing shortage, these provisions were no longer regarded as a major impediment to the supply of rented housing (Hills *et al.* 1989: 3; Figure 7.7b below). There was also an additional demand for housing as a result of the inflow of the *Aussiedler* and *Übersiedler* considered as the third wave of migrants in Chapter 6.

A major legislative revision in the housing market during the 1980s was brought about by the failure of the trade-union owned housing association Neue Heimat. At its peak in the late 1970s, Neue Heimat had owned 330,000 homes and controlled a further 240,000. It was western Europe's biggest property company. But in the early 1980s, its management were found to have circumvented the 4 per cent rule by establishing satellite property companies for speculative purposes at home and abroad. There was a somewhat bizarre episode in the rescue attempts when, in 1986, a Berlin baker purchased what remained of the company for DM 1. Much more illuminating from the point of view of this chapter, however, is the fact the creditor banks vetoed the sale. Ultimately, Heinz Sippel – who had earlier saved Helaba – was called out of retirement in order to supervise the disposal of the company's assets. At the end of the decade the Neue Heimat AG retained only a handful of employees to supervise the affairs of its pension fund (*Der Spiegel* 22/89). Housing associations in general had also lost their tax privileges, although the 1990s marked the advent of new depreciation allowances. Their precarious financial situation will probably induce them to write down their assets, thereby reducing any anticipated tax revenue (Hills *et al.* 1989: 27). The absence of profits, moreover, means that tax concessions for depreciation cannot be used to increase profitability; in such circumstances there is no incentive to invest in new rented housing. Nonetheless, from 1990 the tax position of the housing associations became identical to that of private landlords. Both parties also remain eligible to receive subsidies towards the provision of social housing.

For a number of reasons, then, the 1990s began with a housing shortage in the west. In addition to the factors already mentioned, a further reason was possibly the conservative-liberal coalition's erratic approach to social-housing programmes. Falling investment in social housing may also have been partially demand induced. The evidence is mixed. Total Federal and Länder support for these programmes was DM 9 billion in 1983; it had fallen to under DM 4 billion by 1987 and 1988 but then recovered to reach over DM 8 billion in 1990 (*Der Spiegel* 1/91). Moreover, there had been a pronounced secular decline in the provision of social housing. Between 1950 and 1956 the completions target for this type of property had been 1.8 million and the target was exceeded (Hallett 1973: 129). In 1952 and 1953, social housing respectively represented 69 per cent and 57 per cent of all additions to the housing stock (*ibid.*: 122). Since 1978, the official statistics of the Federal Economics Ministry have included an estimate of both publicly assisted and 'other'

social housing projects; even on this basis, however, the proportion of social housing in total completions had fallen to 17 per cent by 1989 (BMWi *Leistung* . . . 1989: 48). (The category 'other' refers mainly to 'second round' advances by the special-purpose banks.) Moreover, social housing was only 12.6 per cent of the total housing stock in 1987, of which 9.1 per cent was provided by housing associations (Hills *et al.* 1989: 2). Private landlords provided a further 41.7 per cent of the housing stock outside the social-housing rented sector, and 42 per cent of the stock was owner occupied (*ibid.*). This could indicate a demand-driven decline in social housing, not least as a result of the gradual rise in owner occupation induced by the 1956 Act (Hallett 1973: 131). Some caution is necessary here: 1989 marked the trough in the Economics Ministry's definition of social housing. The number of completions (40,000) was under half of the completions in 1985 and 1991 (BMWi *Wirtschaft* . . . 1992: 62). This could be interpreted as a reflection of changing supply-side conditions. Irrespective of the merits of each case, however, perhaps the effect of the social-housing measures on total housing starts can be gauged from Figure 7.7a below. More generally, as the supply of rented accommodation failed to keep pace with demand, the rents paid by new tenants from 1988 began to rise strongly in both nominal and real terms (*Die Zeit* 16/90; Tomann 1992b: 8). Börsch-Supan (1986) had estimated that the tenancy regulations would have such a nominal effect. Average real rents for all tenants, on the other hand, showed only a relatively small increase (Tomann *ibid.*). In other words, established tenants enjoyed low-cost accommodation relative to new entrants into the rented sector. Moreover, about half of the tax concessions for housing were by the nature of things received by the top five per cent of taxpayers (*Der Spiegel: ibid.*). This was probably one reason for the rise in the proportion of one-family housing starts to be mentioned below. Certainly the re-emergence of a readiness to acquire residential property triggered fiercer competition among the suppliers of housing finance (MRDB 11/90: 33).

Rents also rose strongly in the east following unification. In the large cities there was a three–four year waiting list. By western standards, every fifth home was in an uninhabitable state of repair (SZ 2 March 1991). Half the housing stock had been built before 1919 (*Der Spiegel* 1/91). As in other cases, GEMSU resulted in the value of these physical assets being converted at the arbitrary exchange rate of OM 2: DM 1. An enormous housing-sector debt of DM 51.3 billion had also been converted using this rate (Tomann 1992: 7). Local housing associations and cooperatives bore a proportionately higher debt on their predominantly post-war housing. Debt in these sectors, with a debt moratorium on interest payments until the end of 1993, would rise from DM 36 billion to approximately DM 50 billion (*ibid.*: 11). There was no private market to speak of and rent income barely met the administrative costs. Inevitably, the previously highly subsidised rents were incrementally phased out. A mark-up of DM 1 per month per square metre in the general rent level, plus a limited contribution to operating costs where appropriate, were introduced in October 1991 (*ibid.*: 10). Supplemented western housing allowances were introduced at the same time. A second round of rent increases in January 1993 was intended to provide strong incentives for maintenance and upgrading. The full increase was applied only to properties in good condition. By continuing this adjustment process, it is hoped

to achieve comparable rents (*Vergleichs-miete*) by 1995. Although the average rent burden in the east was well below that in the west, however, the unification treaty committed the authorities to take income growth into account when determining rent increases. The slump in eastern output thus constrained the policy makers somewhat. Nonetheless, the substantial financial requirements in the field of housing construction in the east opened up new growth opportunities for the western housing-finance institutions.

A brief comparison of the British and German housing markets will serve to emphasise the nature of the (West) German owner-occupier market. In relation to incomes, house prices in the UK at the end of the 1970s lay between 3 and $3^{1}/_{2}$ times average gross annual earnings, whereas in West Germany the factor was more in the order of between 5 and 8 (Bradley 1979: 941). In other words a new flat in Germany in the late 1970s cost DM 150,000, and the figure for a new house was well over DM 200,000 (BSA 1978: 12). By the beginning of the 1990s the average price of a house in Germany was more than twice that in Britain (*Economist* 20 June 1992). During most of the 1980s the ratio of house prices to income rose in the UK but fell in West Germany, although by 1989 the trends in the ratio for each country were reversed (Muellbauer 1992: 540). Above all, the relative rate of return from investing in housing has several times exceeded 60 per cent per annum in Britain – until the bubble burst in 1989; in Germany for most of the 1980s the relative rate of return on housing was negative, and even prior to this period it never reached spectacular levels (*ibid.*: 543). In short, 'Germans buy houses as places to live, while for the British portfolio investment is an important consideration' (*ibid.*: 545). There were wide regional disparities in Germany – as one would expect from the factors discussed in Chapter 2. In the southern Länder of former West Germany the average house price at the beginning of the 1990s was DM 530,000; in the old northern Länder the average was DM 300,000 (FAZ 10 July 1992). Somewhat paradoxically, average prices in Dresden and Leipzig began to approach those of Hannover. House prices in Frankfurt am Main increased by 20 per cent in 1991 but decreased by 5 per cent in London (*Economist* 20 June 1992). In view of all these factors, therefore, there is a relatively lower level of owner occupation in (West) Germany than in the UK – only about 43 per cent compared with about 65 per cent (Holmes 1992: 150). Britain's tax system was skewed in favour of home ownership, whereas it has been shown above that more emphasis was placed on the supply of rented accommodation in Germany. Notwithstanding the shortages which developed in Germany during the second half of the 1980s, by the mid-1970s there was hardly anywhere in the country where the would-be tenant could not find a passable choice of flats or houses at reasonable rents (BSA 1978: 8).

An enormous output of housing induced by subsidies and various tax concessions, then, gradually resolved the quantitative aspect of the problem until the late 1980s. By 1990, the western housing stock had reached nearly 27 million, 20 million of which had been completed since the founding of the Bonn Republic (BMWi *Leistung* . . . 1989: table 4.42; IW *Zahlen* 1992: 111). Figure 7.7a illustrates this dramatic growth pattern of housing. The annual output of housing fell below the half million mark only at the beginning and at the end of the period 1950–75. Indeed, a peak of 714,200 was reached in 1973 when many builders were bank-

rupted by the speculative over-building of accommodation intended for renting (Bradley 1979: 941). Initially, the credit squeezes following the two oil price shocks, then the deregulation of rents for new tenants, followed by a drop in the provision of social housing and the modification of some tax allowances have all conspired to constrain the demand for, and supply of, rented accommodation. Projections of housing availability around the mid-1990s, such as that made in Figure 7.7b, indicate that demand will significantly outstrip supply. One of the major issues to be addressed during the 1990s – in both west and east Germany – will be the future course of social-housing provision. As in other housing sectors, risk sharing and incentives for efficiency will dominate the discussion (Hubert and Tomann 1990).

Further, although there is a marked cyclical variation in the type of completion, about 45 per cent of the housing built in 1980 consisted of one-family dwellings; in 1960 the figure had been only 20 per cent (BMWi 1982: Table 4.42; Dresdner Bank *Wirtschaftsberichte* June 1982). During the same time period the multi-family type housing unit had fallen from 55 per cent to 30 per cent of all completions. For most of the 1980s the multi-family dwelling was again dominant, but by the end of the decade nearly half of the completions were one-family dwellings again. It was thought at one stage that this important qualitative change in the housing market may be accompanied by a trend towards a greater degree of owner-occupation (BSA 1978: 14). Such a change took place in spite of the advantages under income and land tax laws of including a self-contained flat in newly built accommodation, a provision abolished during the 1980s. For much of the post-war period, income tax relief was not given on mortgage interest

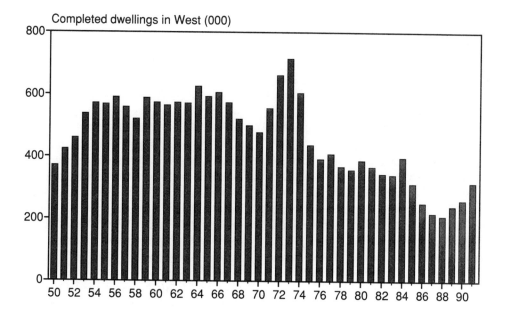

Figure 7.7a Annual additions to the housing stock

Source: As Figure 7.6a

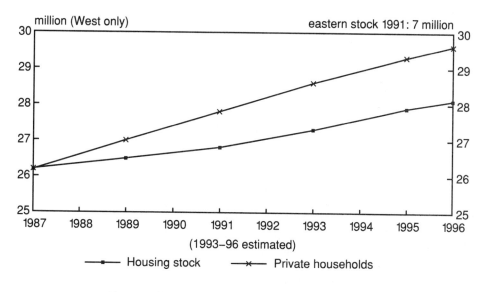

Figure 7.7b Housing stock and number of households

Source: *SZ* 19 February 1993

payments in West Germany. Such a scheme was implemented in 1983 but abandoned in 1987 on grounds of cost and the tax reforms illustrated in Figure 3.3 (Tomann 1990: 921). In 1991, however, the mortgage-relief instrument described at the beginning of this section was introduced (MRDB 8/92: 24). In addition to these more recent tax relief measures, there were numerous other tax advantages of which mortgagors may avail themselves. Not the least of these attractions is the Building Savings Premium to which long-term contract savers with building savings banks were entitled – see below. Real personal disposable income is also relatively high, helped by the maximum 53 per cent income tax rate and relatively low inflation (see Chapter 3). For all the reasons given in this paragraph, therefore, it seemed reasonable at the end of both the 1970s and 1980s to predict that the housing finance institutions would attract a growing clientele. During the 1980s, however, they experienced some difficulties, accompanied by change. Since these institutions are unique to Germany and account for 25 per cent of banking business, they must now be examined.

A first mortgage, up to a legal maximum of 60 per cent of the mortgageable value of a property (*der Beleihungswert*), is normally lent directly by a commercial or savings bank, or through a mortgage bank. Mortgage banks specialise in mortgage lending to finance both owner-occupation *and* the building of accommodation for renting. The commercial banks generally sell first mortgages provided by their mortgage bank subsidiaries, although they are prepared to offer long-term building finance up to 80 per cent of the total cost or buying price based on the borrower's creditworthiness and secured only by a second mortgage. Total mortgage packages are increasingly offered by the com-

mercial banks and mortgage finance altogether accounts for 25 per cent of the commercial banks' business. This proportion compares to the 50 per cent of lending by the savings banks in the form of long-term loans for housing finance and for capital expenditure by local authorities.

Building savings banks, on the other hand, cater mainly for owner occupiers. Some 23 per cent of the flow of funds into owner-occupied residential capital is administered by these institutions (Börsch-Supan and Stahl 1991: 266). They are therefore best seen as specialist institutions which extend loans to depositors after completion of a contractual savings plan, the loans being secured by second mortgages exclusively used for the acquisition, renovation or improvement of private homes. This system has been succinctly described as indiscriminate, guaranteed and insulated (BSA 1978: 18). It is indiscriminate in the sense that anyone may take out a savings contract. It is guaranteed because anyone fulfilling contractual obligations has a right to a loan, and it is insulated because the closed nature of the business separates it from the interest rates prevailing in other sectors of the money market. Hence, the fixed interest rates paid to contract savers will sometimes be highly competitive, while at other times they will be substantially below other nominal rates (Boléat 1978: 10). But the real value of the return on savings contracts was greatly enhanced by the various bonuses paid under the Savings Premium and other Acts (BSA 1978: 18 and 23). These bonuses attract funds from savers who have no intention of purchasing a property with the result that as much as 25 per cent of total contract savings emanate from this source, making this the only really developed contractual scheme in the Federal Republic. Notwithstanding these bonuses, however, the disadvantage of the closed system in which the building savings banks operate is that they are unable to offer loans sufficient in themselves to finance house purchase. Thus the analysis can now focus on the nature of the mortgage package as such. This package will be sold to the borrower at the first point of contact, be it a commercial, savings or building savings bank. Indeed, arranging such packages, and savings contracts, are the main functions of a building savings bank office and the many foreign visitors may be struck by the almost complete absence of cash transactions at these offices.

Hence, assuming that a savings contract with a building savings bank has been observed for an agreed period (between 18 and 36 months), and also assuming that 20 per cent of the purchase price is provided from the buyer's own funds, the Dresdner Bank, for example, would arrange a package of a further 50 per cent from its mortgage bank and 30 per cent direct from its own resources. The mortgage bank would issue a matching bond and the borrower would pay a fixed rate of interest on that part of the loan. Similarly, the borrower would also pay a fixed rate of interest, over an agreed period, of the 30 per cent loan. A capital sum equal to half of the total loan would have to be repaid by means of a second mortgage at the end of about an eight-year period. Since the total loan was equal to 80 per cent of the purchase price, therefore, the savings contract with a building savings bank would enable the borrower to repay 40 per cent of the purchase price at the end of eight years. This contract would, in turn, become the basis for a loan equal to the amount payable to the mortgage bank when 50 per cent of the contracted amount had been saved – subject normally to a waiting period. (For many years the savings-to-

loan ratio was 40:60 but lengthening queues caused most building savings banks to change the ratio to 50:50.) Both these contractual savings and the loans they produce carry low fixed rates of interest, usually 3 and 5 per cent respectively. A similarly strong vertical integration is to be found throughout the (West) German system of housing finance (Bradley 1979: 940).

The generic term for the institutions providing building finance in the Federal Republic is *Realkreditinstitute*, a term which is clearly linked to the concept of real estate. As already shown, there are a number of institutions in the field. The reason for this is that it would be impossible for most people to borrow nearly all the price of a house because the burden of mortgage repayments, even at relatively low rates of interest, would represent an intolerably high proportion of net income (Bradley 1979: 938 and 942). This is why the mortgagor usually purchases a property by means of a mortgage package consisting of a sizeable deposit from his or her own funds, a first mortgage supplied by a commercial, mortgage or savings bank and a second mortgage, usually provided on the basis of a savings contract by a building savings bank. Additionally, loans from the Federal and Länder Governments may have financed approximately 9 per cent of all mortgage lending (BSA 1978: 17).

Figure 7.1 indicates that in 1991 there were 28 private-sector mortgage banks (*Hypothekenbanken*). In the public-sector there were a further eight mortgage banks (*Öffentliche Hypothekenbanken* or *Grundkreditanstalten*). Similarly, there were 21 private building savings banks (*Bausparkassen*), together with their 13 public-sector counterparts (*Landesbausparkassen*). (This writer prefers the translation 'building savings banks' because the public-sector *Sparkassen* were known as 'savings banks' above; as already indicated, however, building savings banks are just as much concerned with loans.) In 1988, four out of the five largest private mortgage banks, and several smaller ones, were owned by the Big Three – the Deutsche actually owning two of the top five (Stein 1990: 42). The DG Bank is classified in the official statistics as being the owner of the remaining private mortgage bank in the top five. As would probably be expected, the BV had controlling holdings in three of the top ten, with the Hypo owning 75 per cent of another member of the 'top ten'. (The Bayerische LB had a 25 per cent stake in one of the BV's mortgage banks.) These rankings were changed slightly in 1990 and 1991 when the partially privatised DePfa-Bank appeared at number one (see the section on special-purpose banks above). Its balance sheet in 1991 totalled DM 67 billion, appreciably in front of the DM 48 billion total recorded by the Dresdner-owned number two (*Kreditwesen* 22/92). Nevertheless, the general concentration in the pattern of ownership of the largest mortgage banks persisted (*ibid.*; *Börsenzeitung* 24 October 1992).

The public-sector mortgage banks represent the earliest development in the *Landesbanken* system. They stem from the eighteenth century *Landschaften*, *Ritterschaften* and nineteenth century *Stadtschaften* (agricultural and urban societies – VÖB 1981: 6). Interestingly enough, two of the three remaining *Landschaftsverbände* – which were of Prussian origin – hold shares in the WestLB. They actively promote their local economies. In the mid-1980s, the largest public mortgage bank (Wohnungsbauförderungsanstalt des Landes Nordrhein-Westfalen – Wfa) had a larger balance-sheet total than the largest private mortgage banks, although it was only about half of the DePfa-Bank (Pohl 1986:

170). Much to the chagrin of the private-sector banks, ownership of the Wfa was transferred to the WestLB in 1992, thereby enabling the WestLB to increase its equity capital by DM 5.9 billion (WestLB Annual Report 1992: 11). Capital adequacy – as seen at the end of the section on prudential arrangements – was an issue at this juncture.

Mortgage banks traditionally raise their funds either by issuing mortgage bonds (*Hypothekenpfandbriefe*) or – in order to finance the increasing amount of lending to the public sector – by the issue of communal bonds (*Kommunalobligationen*). 'Public sector' is used in a wide sense in this context. Loans are made to the Federal and Länder governments, as well as to local authorities and other domestic authorities and EC member states. The term 'mortgage bank' is therefore a little misleading. Nonetheless, bonds issued by these institutions constitute a very important sector of the fixed-interest securities market – even though long-term deposits became an increasingly important part of their funding in the 1980s. Such deposits rose from DM 87 billion in 1980 to DM 226 billion in 1991, and those of private mortgage banks, which are included in these data, from DM 32 billion to DM 140 billion (MRDB 4/92: 26). Moreover, most of these deposits were raised on the wholesale money market. During the same time period, the total increase in mortgage bonds was less pronounced – from DM 156 billion to DM 306 billion. All the increase in such bond issues was attributable to the private mortgage banks, thus leaving the few remaining public mortgage banks relying mainly on long-term deposits.

Predictably, the sales of mortgage bonds have roughly reflected the fluctuations in house building and the level and movements of interest rates. For example, redemptions exceeded new sales in 1987, 1988 and 1990 – with the result that net sales were negative in these years (MRDB *Statistische Beihefte* Reihe 2). The sales of communal bonds, on the other hand, displayed a rapid growth in the second half of the 1970s. This growth rate was so dramatic that communal bonds became much more significant than mortgage bonds in fixed-interest business. Between 1975 and 1992 gross sales of communal bonds quadrupled, so that by 1992 they totalled over DM 134 billion; indeed, they became an important constituent of total gross bond sales as from the 1967 recession – see Figure 7.8a.

This sudden upsurge in the gross sales of communal bonds contributed to the high positive skewness of total gross bond sales, as can be gauged from the relative sizes of the medians and means in both total and communal gross bond sales during the period 1950–91 – see Table 7.3.

Similarly, as Table 7.3 also indicates, other bank bonds and, to a lesser extent, public authority bonds contributed to the rapid expansion of gross bond sales from 1970 onwards. (Although industrial bonds have been included in the 'total' category of Figure 7.8a, it is again emphasised that they are of negligible significance. Indeed, they registered zero gross sales in 1990 and 1992.) The proceeds of 'other' bank bonds, which are principally issued by the *Landesbanken*, tend to be extended as credit to industry and trade (MRDB table VI[2n]). As shown in Figure 7.8b, their growth coincided with the growing concentration and expansion of the *Landesbanken* after 1970. Indeed, these bonds did not exist in the 1950s. Gross sales of public-authority bonds also displayed a significant increase during the 1967 recession, but the most dramatic change occurred from the early 1980s onwards

(Figure 7.8a). Since these latter bonds are issued by the authorities themselves, they compete with communal bonds in this sense. Redemptions of communal bonds in 1990 exceeded newly sold bonds; net sales were therefore negative (MRDB *Statistische Beihefte* Reihe 2). Nonetheless, the banks clearly remain the dominant issuers. Finally, it should be added that some of the privately-owned mortgage banks are engaged in the finance of shipbuilding, an activity which clearly involves the provision of medium and long-term loans.

Not surprisingly – in view of what has been said in this section thus far – the business environment for private and public mortgage banks changed considerably during the 1980s. The growth of mortgage lending slackened; at the same time, the demand for communal loans flattened out as the public authorities adopted a consistent budgetary consolidation policy and increasingly switched to direct capital market borrowing (MRDB 4/92: 21). (This latter remark applies notably to the Federal government.) Even the upsurge in public debt on unification was refinanced without any particular resort to communal bonds (Figures 7.8a and 7.8b). As will be shown in Figure 7.10 below, however, the mortgage banks more or less maintained their proportionate share in the total business volume. This was, however, due to the performance of the private mortgage banks which in 1991 accounted for 75 per cent of the business transacted by the mortgage banks (see Figure 7.1 – which also shows that these banks collectively held larger market shares than the Big Three and local cooperatives). Privatisation and changes to the legal form of some public sector mortgage banks have also brought about some changes in the official statistics which give a somewhat misleading impression of the relative

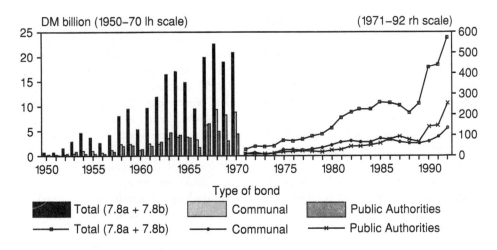

Figure 7.8a Gross Domestic Bond sales (total sales and Public Debt funding)
Sources: Dresdner Bank *Stat. Reihen*; MRDB *Stat. Beihefte 2*

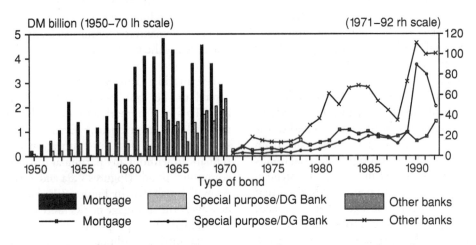

Figure 7.8b Gross Bond sales (mortgage and non-mortgage Bank Bonds)
Source: As Figure 7.8a

importance of private and public mortgage banks.

Competition in mortgage lending also intensified towards the end of the 1980s. This decade began with high rates of mortgage lending by the private mortgage banks – not least against the existing housing stock (MRDB 4/92: 24). Even between 1983 and 1987 these banks achieved a higher rate of expansion in mortgage lending than other banks. However, the resumption of the growth in demand for housing loans did not benefit them. Interest rates were rising and mortgagors preferred variable-rate loans. (Since mortgage banks mainly deal in fixed interest

Table 7.3 Gross Bond sales: 1950–1991 inclusive (DM billion)

Type	Median	Mean	Pearson coefficient of skewness
Total	27	93	1.683
Mortgage	5	9	1.429
Communal	9	27	1.744
Special purpose and DG Bank	2	9	1.170
Other bank	3	22	1.840
Public Authorities	7	26	1.476
Industrial[1]	0.4	0.5	0.831

Source: Calculated from Dresdner Bank *Statistische Reihen*

Note: [1] Because of their relative insignificance these (non-bank) bonds are omitted from the text and from Figures 7.8a and 7.8b

business, most lending is funded at matching rates of interest and maturities.) Universal and cooperative banks particularly increased their shares of the mortgage market, although the nearest rivals to the mortgage banks remained the savings banks (*ibid.*: 25). Moreover, the rekindled interest of the government in promoting low-cost rented housing resulted in 'second round' loans channelled through the special-purpose banks.

But whereas mortgage banks traditionally relied on (fixed interest) bonds for their source of re-finance, the savings banks attract the largest proportion of savings deposits and savings bonds (*Sparbriefe*) – the latter being a fixed-interest, non-marketable security (see Figure 7.9a). Whereas the savings banks traditionally dominated the market for savings bonds, however, they have faced growing competition from the cooperative banks. In 1975, 77 per cent of these bonds were issued by the savings banks, with only 1.4 per cent being sold by the cooperatives; by 1990, the savings banks' share had fallen to 60 per cent but the cooperatives accounted for 27 per cent (MRDB *Statistische Beihefte* Reihe 1). On the

other hand, these two forms of savings have grown spectacularly – as can be seen from Figure 7.9b. Although bond sales broke all records during the first quarter of 1993, moreover, domestic non-banks clearly preferred savings deposits and savings bonds. These two vehicles were expected to comfortably attain the respective levels of DM 800 billion and DM 250 billion in the first few months of 1993 (Bayerische Landesbank *Money and Capital Markets* April/May 1993). Compared to a decade earlier the growth in these two vehicles outpaced the rival five-year special federal bonds and federal savings bonds, even though these latter products provided about 30 per cent of total federal borrowing in early 1993 (*ibid.*). Taken together, savings deposits, savings bonds and five year special federal bonds amounted to DM 1.2 trillion in February 1993. Above all, however, savings deposits – made more attractive by the relatively new 'special' savings accounts – were clearly recovering from the downturn at the end of the 1980s. It must also be recalled that savings deposits in Germany are an entirely separate entity from time and sight deposits. Hence, for many years, mortgage lending patterns tended to reflect the nature of re-financing: the savings banks issued vari-able rate loans, repayable over 25 or 30 years, whereas the mortgage banks issued relatively short-term loans at over 5 to 7 years at fixed rates of interest, the matur-ity of these loans matching the maturity of their bonds (Boléat 1978: 11). However, increases in applications from prospective owner occupiers tended to have the effect of lengthening the average mortgage-bank loan and increasing the number of fixed rate mortgages offered by the savings banks (BSA 1978: 15).

Because they are classified separately, savings deposits held at building savings banks are not included in Figure 7.9a (also see Figure 7.1). In 1975, 1980, 1985 and 1990, total savings deposits at these insti-tutions (in DM billion) were respectively 76, 111, 123 and 125; only a negligible proportion of these deposits were of an inter-bank nature – DM 1 billion in 1990, for instance (MRDB 11/90: 42 and 7/92: Table III(22a). Large private building savings banks operate throughout West Germany. Interests in some of them were acquired by the commercial banks in the 1970s (Bradley 1979: 940). But the biggest changes took place during the second half of the 1980s, partly to prepare for the competitive threats posed by EC 1993 (Tomann 1990: 924). More specifically, these changes resulted from the trend to *Allfinanz* first noted in the BfG section above. Many building savings banks forged links with universal banks and insurance enterprises, and most of the others began to supplement their product ranges by means of appropriate coop-eration agreements (MRDB 11/90: 33). Conversely, universal banks and insurance enterprises identified additional opportu-nities in the building savings market. As a result, in order to further increase the

number of financial services offered under one roof, the Deutsche (1987) and the Dresdner (1988) established their own building savings banks (Stein 1990: 45). The Commerz agreed to cooperate more closely with the Leonberger Bausparkasse and obtained a 40 per cent holding in this institution (*ibid.*). The two largest build-ing savings banks remain the Schwäbisch Hall and Wustenrot, with the DG Bank controlling the former. Public-sector building savings banks, on the other hand, operate regionally because they are an integral part of the *Landesbanken* system (BSA 1978: 16).

Although they are almost as big as the British building society movement, German building savings banks do not dominate the market in the same way: they provide only 40 per cent of total housing finance, much of which is concen-trated on the financing of new dwellings. Building savings banks also differ from British building societies in that both the rate of interest they pay on savings con-tracts, and the interest rate which they receive on loans are fixed. Hence in respect of variable interest rates, the sav-ings banks tend more to resemble the British building societies (Boléat 1978: 11). Moreover, repayments to building savings banks are kept as short as possible. Consequently, annuities are high and loans are usually paid off in eight to twelve years. Finally, unlike the British building societies, the building savings banks do not operate as major savings institutions. This is because of the strength of the savings bank movement which attracts a savings volume over four times larger than the private-sector building savings banks (MRDB *Statistische Beihefte* Reihe 1).

Börsch-Supan and Stahl (1991: 265) therefore correctly refer to the completely closed and self-financing system rep-

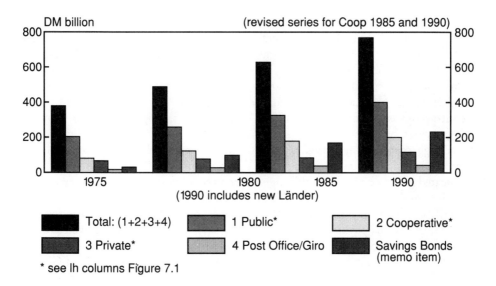

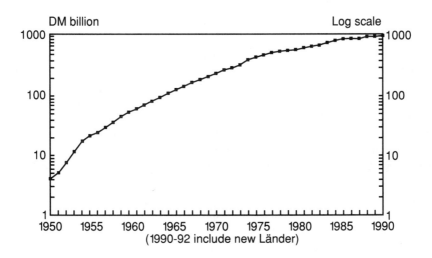

Figure 7.9a Non-bank Savings Deposits/Savings Bonds

Sources: Stat. Jahrbücher 1980 and 1991

Figure 7.9b Growth of total Savings Deposits and Savings Bonds

Sources: Dresdner Bank *Stat. Reihen*; MRDB Table IV (3)

resented by the German building savings banks as 'unique'. Only contracted savers are eligible for loans. Given the high degree of government involvement in pension-fund business already discussed in Chapter 5, the 'dedicated savings and loan contract system' administered by the building savings banks contributes effectively to aggregate savings (*ibid.*). The government subsidy strongly influenced this dedicated savings behaviour, although it must be emphasised that this subsidy has steadily declined since the mid-1970s. Until 1975, the bonus payable was 25 per cent, but it was reduced to 23 per cent in 1975 and to 18 per cent a year later; by 1989 it had fallen to 10 per cent and additional bonuses for each eligible child were abolished (*ibid.*: 269; MRDB 11/90: 38). Moreover, the income ceiling above which no housing bonuses were payable was not changed between 1975 and 1990; the adjustment in 1990 was significantly below the rate of inflation since 1975. The degree of total subsidy also varies across occupational groups. This is because all taxpayers are permitted to write the building savings deposits off their taxable income as part of their deductible expenses. But an upper limit is placed on the total tax allowance which may be written off (see the section on the incidence of taxation in Chapter 3). All the social-insurance contributions referred to in Chapter 5 are included among the deductible expenses. This means that the special category of public-sector employee analysed in Chapter 6 (*Beamte*) – mainly because of their non-contributory pension scheme – gained most from the subsidy because their tax allowance was not exhausted (Börsch-Supan and Stahl 1991: 271). The extent of the write off is affected in the taxpayer's favour by the basic allowance which is deductible from insurance contributions *prior* to the deduction of the

amount deposited in a building savings contract during the tax year. This basic allowance was raised to DM 8000 for a married person in 1990, although the eligible amount for deduction was reduced to one half of the savings deposit, still subject to the upper limit on allowances (MRDB 11/90: 38). This policy development favoured low-income families (Tomann 1990: 924). The relative rate of return, however, includes a very attractive second-mortgage package. Even without a government subsidy, therefore, the building savings contract is perceived as a desirable product. In short, these contracts were very popular among West Germans; they were held by every second household in 1983 and accounted for 20 per cent of total wealth (Börsch-Supan and Stahl 1991: 295).

But the system was put under severe strain during the 1980s. In fact, the balance sheet total and profitability of the building savings banks declined during the second half of the decade (MRDB 11/90: 42–3). The reasons are not hard to find. Building savings banks are handicapped by their normal method of refinancing. The system depends critically on a fairly healthy inflow of new savings. Given the low-interest nature of the business, refinancing from outside the system at market rates in order to reduce the waiting period for loans is clearly only possible to a limited extent. This vulnerability becomes particularly acute during periods of high interest rates outside the system. Not only did this factor affect the inflow of new funds at the beginning of the 1980s, but property prices were declining and alternative investment in financial assets was more attractive. In 1981 and 1982 the respective dramatic proportionate *falls* in newly opened contracts were −19.8 and −17.4 per cent (*ibid.*: 34). Even when new business started to recover in 1983 – contracted sums rose to DM 74.5 billion – terminations due to the cancellation and maturing of contracts continued to rise (*ibid.*). The trough was reached in 1987 when the net increase in contracts outstanding reached only DM 0.8 billion – the inflow having been DM 85.7 billion but cancellations and completions of contracts reached DM 84.9 billion. In other words, the decline continued into a period of low-interest rates when bank loans were being offered on comparatively favourable terms. (The trends in interest rates were analysed in Chapter 4.) The progressive dismantling of the subsidy and tax relief referred to above further undermined the competitive position of the building savings banks. The situation improved somewhat after 1987 and profits were ploughed back. As a result they were set to assume a major financing role again but will probably never regain their former importance due to the reduction in government support.

SOME GENERAL ASPECTS OF BANKING

Between 1950 and 1960, longer-term banking business became more prominent, with a consequent decrease in the relative importance of short-term business (MRDB 3/61: 27). As a result, those institutions which engaged more in long-term business – private and public mortgage banks, savings banks and *Landesbanken* – raised their proportionate share of total banking business. Expressed as a proportion of the total volume of business (see below), the mortgage banks more than doubled their share (5.9 to 12.8 per cent); the savings banks and their central institutions' share increased from 30.8 to 36.0 per cent. On the other hand, the commercial banks' share went down from 36.4 to 26.5 per cent (for the Big Three the

fall was from 19.1 to 12 per cent). The cooperatives' share also fell marginally – from 12.4 to 10.7 per cent (*ibid.*: 28–9).

From 1960 to 1970 the banks more than trebled their volume of business, a rate of increase in excess of that of GNP which, at current prices, doubled (MRDB 4/71: 29). There was also a fairly large number of mergers in West German banking. The pace of bank growth was, however, no longer so rapid as in the 1950s when, starting from the very low base after the currency reform, the business volume of the banks increased six-fold. For that matter, the business expansion in the banking sector during the 1960s was not as rapid as building savings banks and insurance companies, notably the former which benefited from government measures to stimulate savings (*ibid.*: 29–30). (Building savings banks, unlike the insurance companies, are part of the banking system. As seen at the end of the section on housing finance, they perform a specific banking function. They are thus subject to the provisions of the KWG which were outlined in the section on prudential arrangements. As seen in Figure 7.1, however, they are included in a separate data series. This prevents their inclusion, for example, in Figure 7.10 below.) Allowing for the break in the continuity of banking statistics caused by the 1968 revision, developments during the 1960s within the banking sector were a good deal more uniform than in the 1950s. Of all three branches of the universal banks, however, the commercial banks, and therefore the Big Three, recorded the smallest growth rate; the savings banks and *Landesbanken* enlarged their lead even further so that by 1970 they reached the two-fifths share of the total business volume from which they slipped fairly slightly thereafter (Figure 7.1 above; Figure 7.10 below). The cooperatives made the biggest advance during the decade from 1960 to 1970: the reporting ones grew from 8.6 to 11.5 per cent of the total business volume; including the non-reporting ones the growth was from 10 to 13 per cent. This generally more uniform rate was due to the fact that longer-term lending no longer grew more quickly than other types of business (MRDB 4/71: 30 and 32).

Although the volume of business again trebled during the 1970s, business conditions became less stable (MRDB 8/81: 14). In general terms, the 1970s ushered in a decade of wide fluctuations in the earnings position of the banks, as well as a tendency for the proportionate rise in staff and other operating costs to outstrip the increase in net interest and commissions (MRDB 1/78: 13–14 and 16). Aside from mounting staff costs, there were also higher rents for office space and data processing equipment, all of which were directly related to the continued strong expansion in business volume (MRDB, 8/80: 22–3). In this latter sense – the expansion of business volume – the German banks faced the dual problem of still making profits by keeping the growth of costs in check and at the same time keeping their shareholders content after a decade of shareholder-financed capital/asset ratio growth which created the banks' expansion of their lending limits. This profitability problem probably caught up with the German banks a full decade after it had hit German industry. Moreover, from 1 April 1967, there was a total abolition of the interest rate controls imposed during the 1932 banking crisis which, together with a further rapid extension of the branch network, paved the way for more general competition (MRDB 4/71: 31).

In the 1980s the banking sector again experienced a sustained period of rapid expansion. As a result, its total volume of business doubled (MRDB 4/89: 13). There were, however, some marked structural shifts among the main categories of banks and in the focal points of banking business. Some of these changes were a response to the global interdependence of finance markets. Foreign-owned banks operating within Germany increased in number, and German banks sharply expanded their activities abroad. Worldwide deregulation and EC 1993 provided additional boosts to this trend. The banks' contribution to total value added, which was increasingly derived from off-balance sheet transactions, continued to follow the upward trend which can be traced back to 1950 (*ibid.*: 14). By 1988, the proportion of gross value added by the banks in real terms reached 4 per cent and, somewhat untypically for the economy as a whole, the number of employees in this sector continued to grow. In 1988, 615,000 persons were employed in banking. It was again the cooperative banks which registered the highest average growth rate (*ibid.*: 17). By contrast, the public-sector and commercial banks, which in the 1970s had managed to hold their own, grew at rates below the overall average growth rate for the banking sector. The commercial banks, however, compensated by expanding their international business. After 1985, however, about half the growth in the market share of the cooperatives was due to a change in the statistics (*ibid.*: 18). Figure 7.10 shows the general picture in this respect.

GEMSU provided the banks with a further boost to growth. It will be recalled (Chapter 4) that the savings and cooperative banks in the East passed their funds on to the centrally-controlled Staatsbank. This latter institution's assets were its loans to the largely-uncompetitive state enterprises. East Germany therefore required a banking system geared to func-

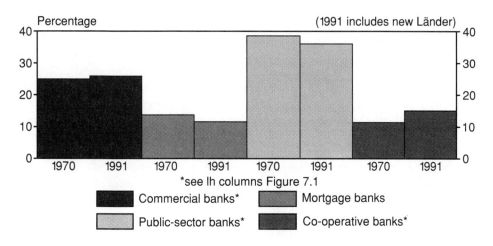

Figure 7.10 Shares in the total business volume of all banks
Sources: MRDB 4/89: 20; Figure 7.1

tioning in a market economy. Over 40 western German banks, including 35 from the private sector, enthusiastically provided such a system (Stein 1990: 70). The FT (1 July 1992) conservatively predicted that the number of their branches in the east would reach 1,000 by the end of 1993. Meanwhile, the large number of eastern savings and cooperative banks was set to continue to fall drastically as mergers continued to bring their average unit business volume nearer to that obtaining in the west (BBk *Report* 1991: 112). The DG Bank provided the eastern cooperative banks with central-banking services traditionally provided by the second tier in the west, although it has already been shown that this tier had rapidly contracted. In the savings banks' sector, a close association between east and west was facilitated by new legislation and the provision of central-banking services by the Deutsche Girozentrale. Before long this latter institution was being pushed back into its clearing-bank role by the *Landesbanken* – again resembling the situation in the west. Saxony established its

own Landesbank, although by 1992 the SüdwestLB had purchased a 25 per cent share in the Saxony LB. WestLB was active in Brandenburg, whereas Helaba assumed these functions in Thuringia. WestLB also took control of one of eastern Germany's most important special purpose banks – Deutsche Industrie und Handelsbank. Its initial partner – Deutsche Außenhandelsbank – had formerly belonged to the DDR Staatsbank and had handled East Germany's foreign-exchange business (BT 1991: 116). By taking over this franchise, WestLB established a presence in all of the new Länder (*Euromoney* October 1991: 68; WestLB Annual Report 1992). Perhaps most important of all, however, and as already seen in Chapter 4, the Deutsche and the Dresdner built up an extensive branch network with the Kreditbank – the latter being the most important successor to the DDR Staatsbank. The Commerzbank, by contrast, established its own network. All this early activity was risk free in so far as the Treuhand guaranteed to repay the debts of any defaulters (FT 1 July 1992).

Later, there were 'simmering tensions', followed by a 'public row', between the Federal Government and the private-sector banks over the relatively small flow of credit to east Germany (*Independent on Sunday* 20 June 1993). The big western banks criticised the economic-policy background; significantly, the big banks did not enjoy the degree of policy influence which they enjoyed during the early development of the SME.

Thus the re-emergence of banking in the Federal Republic during the 1950s and the 1960s resembles very much the general expansionary and merger trends of the economy at large. Similarly, the more cyclical-prone experience of the 1970s is also reflected in the banking sector, when profitability fluctuated widely under the influence of the general trends in interest rates and economic activity (MRDB 8/80: 19). The tightening of the Bundesbank's restrictive course in 1973 confronted the banks with a new situation (MRDB 5/74: 24). Hence at the end of the 1970s West Germany's powerful banking industry was experiencing its most difficult period since its reconstitution after the Second World War. Two further years of restrictive credit policy had resulted from the Bundesbank's protracted tight monetary policy. Long-term lending agreed in 1977 and 1978, when the banking system had a high level of liquidity, became difficult to refinance when the unanticipated balance of payments deficit led to a restrictive monetary policy. This helps to explain the descent in international terms of the seven members of the German top ten banks which were also among the international top fifty. Moreover, while most of the German banks registered declines in dollar-denominated assets – the fall for the group was 5 per cent – the Commerzbank's assets dropped even in domestic currency terms. This was exceptional: it

had only happened to other banks on three previous occasions while *Fortune Magazine* had been recording data over a seven-year period (*Fortune Magazine*, 10 August 1981: 220). Yet it has been shown that the Commerz staged a substantial recovery in the 1980s, a decade of record average profits for the banking sector as a whole. The 1990s began with the boost given by unification.

There are thus three features of banking which require further analysis:

- first, the fluctuations in domestic profitability during the period 1968–91
- second, high administrative costs, particularly in terms of personnel costs
- third, the international expansion of German banking

In order to examine the profitability record of the banks in a little more depth it is necessary to define 'the volume of business', 'operating result (or net operating income)' and 'pre-tax profits'. This is because annual data on these variables has been collected by the Bundesbank since 1968. However, some caution is necessary when examining these published data because the banks have large reserves – both hidden and disclosed – on which they may draw or which they may replenish.

The (nominal) volume of business represents an enlarged balance sheet total since it includes endorsement liabilities and bills drawn by the banks in circulation (MRDB 3/61: 26 and 10/79: 15n). As from 1976 the volume of business also included the foreign branches of commercial banks; in 1979 the statistic was further extended to cover similar branches operated by the *Landesbanken* and since 1988 the foreign branches of special purpose banks have also been included (MRDB 8/91: 24n). The (partial) operating result – that is excluding own account trading – is defined as (MRDB 11/76: 16, 18 and 20):

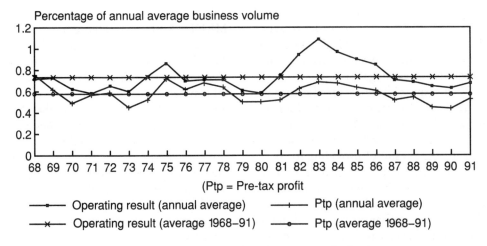

Percentage of annual average business volume

(Ptp = Pre-tax profit

```
——■—— Operating result (annual average)        ——+—— Ptp (annual average)
——×—— Operating result (average 1968–91)       ——●—— Ptp (average 1968–91)
```

Figure 7.11 Operating result and pre-tax profit (banks)
Sources: MRDB 8/81: 14 and 8/92: 40

Interest received − interest paid + commissions received − commissions paid − administrative costs

or

net interest received + net commission received − administrative costs

(where net interest received is by far the most important source of income for the banks and is functionally related to the volume of business and levels of interest rates during a specific period of time; also where staff costs are by far the larger proportion of administrative costs; if fees, own account trading and so on were taken into account, net interest would be of declining importance).

Pre-tax profits (taxes on income, earnings and net assets) are defined as:

Operating results + excess of other receipts over other expenses (where the latter is typically a negative item)

Figure 7.11 illustrates the troughs in overall profitability of the West German banks in 1970, 1973 and 1980, as well as the peaks in profitability in 1975 and 1983, the latter marking a period of sustained high

profits. It is also possible to see that the decline of profitability in 1979 was followed in 1980 by an overall stabilisation. However, there were marked differences in individual cases. Within the top ten group of banks, for example, only four banks produced an increase in profits (the Deutsche, Bayerische VB, Bayerische LB and DG Bank). Three of the four increases were relatively small, especially when viewed in conjunction with the relatively high falls. Only the DG Bank significantly improved on its patchy profit performance of the 1970s, although it too had problems and was showing a loss by 1981. Among the top four private-sector banks, only the Deutsche raised its dividend in 1980: from 9 to 10 per cent, a level retained in 1981. The Bayerische Vereinsbank held its dividend at 9 per cent in both 1980 and 1981, while the Dresdner cut its rate from 9 to 6 per cent in 1980, followed by a cut to 4 per cent in 1981. In both 1979 and 1981, the Commerzbank did not pay a dividend at all and offered some of its holding in a mortgage bank for sale. It thus became the first major West German bank in the post-war period to miss its dividend payment and to sell assets to draw on hidden reserves in order to avoid declaring a loss. The BfG also began to dispose of some of its subsidiaries in order to counter its earnings crisis.

What seems to have occurred is that the write-downs for definitive loan losses and for actual and latent risks in national and international banking business all rose sharply. As a result of providing for these risks, the banks' pre-tax profits in 1981 rose less steeply than the operating result. A fillip to profitability was, however, given by the expiration of fixed interest loans made during a period of low interest rates. Hence, as measured by the operating result, all banking groups except the *Landesbanken* and the private mortgage banks were able to improve their profitability in 1981, though to varying degrees. Overall profitability in 1981, as measured by the operating result as a percentage of business volume, was well above the 10-year average for 1971–80 (0.68 per cent) at 0.75 per cent. Pre-tax profits measured in the same way, however, were still below the average for 1971–80 (0.58 per cent) at 0.52 per cent (MRDB 10/82: 15–16).

The 1975 results were the best in banking history up to that time. One measure of profitability in 1975 is that net income in some cases was higher in absolute terms than in 1980. Even where 1980 profits were higher in absolute terms, the growth on 1975 was less than the 22 per cent growth in the retail price index. Moreover, since GNRP registered a negative change in 1975 (Figure 1.1), the record profits in banking require some explanation. They were attributable in the first instance to interest margins, or the differences between lending and borrowing rates. Although interest received (DM 94.3 billion) actually fell by −3.9 per cent on the previous year, interest paid (DM 65.0

billion) decreased by −10.8 per cent (MRDB, 8/91: 24). Hence net interest received increased both absolutely (DM 29.3 billion) and as a percentage of business volume, which at 2.24 per cent was only marginally below the peak of 2.27 per cent in 1983. Taken together these two ratios represented the highest values in the period for which comparable statistics exist (1968–91). A negative change in interest receipts and payments such as the one which occurred in 1975 is untypical. Significantly, however, this unusual configuration was repeated in 1983 when the respective absolute values of interest received and paid were DM 215.2 billion and DM 151.0 billion. Of equal significance is the fact that net interest received as a percentage of the average volume of business displayed a downward trend between 1976 and 1980 and again between 1984 and 1990. The extent of the fall in interest rates and the rapid rise in liquidity were presumably responsible for both these unusual negative changes in interest receipts and payments (Figures 4.4a and 4.4c). Not surprisingly, the proportionate rises in interest paid during the periods of low profitability were greater than those of interest received (MRDB 8/92: 40).

A second factor which accounts for the profitability peak in 1975 was the booming stock market. To this must be added, third, the steep rise in the sales of bonds, particularly communal bonds in 1975. Public authority and 'other' bank bonds sales had also generally increased rapidly during the 1970s, reflecting the growth in public indebtedness (Figure 7.8a and Table 7.3 above). Not only did this source of funds become more costly in 1980, however, but lending to enterprises and private individuals by the *Landesbanken* increased by only 6 per cent in 1980, compared to a 16 per cent increase in public-sector lending in the same year and 17 per cent in 1979. These increases in public-sector lending stem from the role of the *Landesbanken* as principal bankers to the public authorities. While hardly any risks attach to such assets, they are less lucrative profitability-wise than loans to private customers (MRDB 8/81: 19). Nevertheless, bond yields generally reached correspondingly high levels during the 1970s. The average annual yields of 10.6 per cent in 1974 and 1981 were post-war highs, along with above average yields for most of the period (see Figure 7.6a).

An equally propitious constellation of events boosted bank profits between 1982 and 1986. It enabled West German banks to recover from the doldrums of 1979–81 and ride out the SMH fiasco. This successful period was due partly to an export boom inspired by the strong dollar, partly to a resurgence of retail business, car sales and housing starts (*Euromoney* February 1985: 90). Interest margins recovered and many banks experienced a boom in their own-account trading in securities and foreign exchange. The banks also concentrated on prudence and efficiency following their tightening of lending ratios and the consolidation of group balance sheets (see the section on prudential arrangements). As *Euromoney* (*ibid.*) reported, only a rise in running costs in 1984 prevented the banks from beating their 1983 results. But the banks continued to operate in a very favourable economic climate in both 1985 and 1986. Record profits were reported by most banks and some, notably the Deutsche and Dresdner banks, increased their dividends or gave special bonuses to shareholders in order to reflect their success (FT 6 July 1987). By 1987, however, the slow pace of domestic economic growth, and the effects of the strong DM abroad, meant corporate demand for funds fell.

Although economic performance had fully recovered by 1989, net interest received did not grow vigorously again until 1990 (MRDB 8/91: 24). Moreover, the banks' volume of business expanded at an average rate of 8.9 per cent, the most rapid rise in bank assets since 1981. This rise was mainly attributable to the surge in retail and wholesale banking business which was one of the consequences of unification. As already shown, the banks spent most of 1990 building up their east German networks; this trend was expected to continue for a few years. Only the Dresdner posted a real increase in pre-tax profits, whereas the Deutsche's profits in 1990 were lower than its impressive performance in 1989 (*The Banker* September 1991: 50). Expansionist policies at the WestLB also caused pre-tax profits to fall back substantially. In addition, the banks as a whole transferred a much larger share of their annual profits to their published reserves (MRDB 8/91: 15). Finally, the large block of longer-term fixed-rate loans not funded at matching maturities and granted during the long period of low interest rates in the 1980s continued to reduce the banks' profit margins. On the other hand, short-term lending to domestic enterprises and individuals went up at an annual average rate of 11.5 per cent in 1990, compared with 7.7 per cent in 1989 and a decline of 0.2 per cent in 1988. There was a further surge in the demand for credit during 1991 and the banks' cost of funds declined – 30 per cent of the total liabilities of Germany's large banks were financed by deposits which yielded 3 per cent or less per year (FT 11 February 1992). The banks could loan these funds at up to four or five times that amount and at no risk where the Treuhand guaranteed the loans. As a result of cutting their costs and expanding their lending in eastern Germany, the increase in the respective operating profits of the Deutsche, Dresdner and Commerz were 17, 23 and 45 per cent (*Die Bank* December 1992; *Economist* 9 May 1992). Little wonder, then, that the FT (*ibid.*) could summarise the banks' experience in 1991 as follows:

At a time when German industrial companies are struggling to maintain profits and shareholder dividends in the face of a deteriorating economy, the banking sector is enjoying a boom . . . [the] Deutsche Bank signalled its confidence . . . when it recently increased its 1991 dividend by DM 1 to DM 15 a share.

For 1992 the Deutsche was expected to post profits of DM 5.66 billion, larger than the combined profits of the three next largest banks but not sufficient to stimulate an increase in dividends (FAZ 9 December 1992; FT 19 March 1993). The Dresdner reported double-digit profit growth but also no increase in dividends; both the BV and Hypo announced large leaps in profits; the chemicals group Hoechst, on the other hand, complained about the 'miserable' start to 1993 (FAZ 8 December 1992; FT 24 April 1993). The ten-month interim results of the top five private-sector banks in 1992 had certainly demonstrated the banking sector's resilience to the worst post-war recession (*Banker* March 1993). Moreover, group earnings at the Commerz grew by 15 per cent in the first five months of 1993; at the same juncture, it was announced that the engineering group KHD expected to only break even for the second year in succession (FT 7 July 1993). Management at the five large private banks were, however, warning about their sharply increased risk provisioning. Steinherr (1991: 377–8), on the other hand, concludes that competitive pressure in German banking has not generated competitive pricing. He attri-

butes high profitability to this non-competitive pricing.

Notwithstanding these latter – albeit important – points, the recovery of profitability in 1990 followed a number of rather less profitable years (MRDB 8/92: 29). During the following year (1991), the operating result and pre-tax profit rose strongly and reached record absolute levels; interim reports for 1992 suggested that this trend was continuing (*ibid.*). Moreover, the eight-year downward trend in net interest received was halted: expressed as a proportion of the annual average volume of business – the interest margin – there was a rise from 1.72 per cent in 1990 to 1.79 per cent in 1991.

On such a note, it is appropriate to move on to the second item for discussion in this section, namely administrative costs. In Germany, a dense network of sophisticated savings institutions services an economy in which there is traditionally a high propensity to save. Both the emergence of the dense banking network and savings opportunities owe a lot to the public and cooperative sectors. Originally the savings banks were opened to everyone, whereas the cooperatives served only their own members, of which there were 11 million prior to unification (Bonus and Schmidt 1990: 195). Over time, the agricultural and urban cooperatives have moved much closer together and the services they offer are similar to those offered by the savings banks. Hence all three do not differ radically in the structure of their business or their customers (MRDB 8/81: 18). However, the cooperatives remain the property of their members, while the savings banks are still normally owned by the local authorities. That is why the cooperative sector afforded such a good example of the shareholder agency problem when it was discussed above.

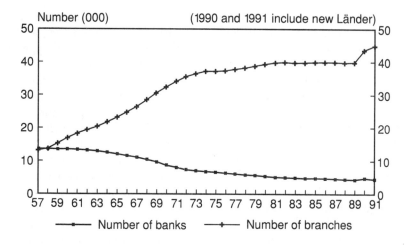

Figure 7.12 Number of banks and branches
Sources: MRDB 8/81: Table 25a, and 5/92: 26a

In 1991, with over 3,000 local cooperative banks and over 700 savings banks, together having 37,546 branches in east and west, these parts of the banking sectors provided the most extensive banking network in Europe (MRDB 5/92: Table III[26b]). After the currency reform, both sectors expanded more rapidly than the private sector, culminating in the cooperative and public-sector banks accounting for over half of the total volume of banking business (Figure 7.1). Over three-quarters of all savings deposits and savings bonds, as well as over 80 per cent of the country's bank branches, are accounted for by the cooperative and public sectors. However, these sectors do not exert the overwhelming influence that their massive aggregate business volume suggests. Both sectors are fragmented, as is borne out by both the number of banks involved and the size of the branch networks.

Figure 7.12 suggests, however, that when one refers to 'a dense network of savings institutions', one is really nowadays emphasising the number of branches even more than the number of banks.

Notwithstanding the increase in the number of banks as a result of unification, the number of local cooperatives fell from 11,795 in 1957 to 3,147 in 1991, whereas in the same period their branches increased from 2,305 to 18,059 (MRDB 5/92 Table III [26b] – the statistics differ slightly from the November data used in Figure 7.1). The fall in the number of savings banks over the same period – from 871 to 734 – was not so dramatic, although here the impact of unification was more pronounced. (There were 546 savings banks in west Germany at the end of 1991.) Allowing for unification, the total number of savings banks' branches increased from 8,192 to 19,487. As already shown, the number of private bankers has also displayed a long-term downward trend, but the commercial banks generally, and the Big Three in particular, made a greater effort to build up their personal sector business. In consequence, the Big Three increased their branches in the above time period from 787 to 3,423, again allowing for the effects of unification. Hence, despite the decline in the number of banks, the number of bank branches has risen at a time of rapidly rising labour costs and rapid changes in banking technology. In the early 1980s, West Germany had one bank branch for every 1,400 members of the population compared to a ratio of one to 4,000 in Britain and one to 6,000 in the USA (*Die Zeit* 24/81: 25). As illustrated in this paragraph, one of the effects of unification has been to increase this density. Dividing the total population of 78 million (Figure 2.1) by the 44,000 branches shown for 1990 in Figure 7.12 yields an average 1,773 persons to each branch.

In this sense, then, West Germany is 'overbanked'. Even here, however, Steinherr (1991: 381–2) recommends some caution: the universal banking system implies that value added per bank branch 'can be bigger'. After all, the trend to *Allfinanz* has increased even further the number of services supplied at each branch. Moreover, taking interest-rate spreads into account – that is the lending less the borrowing rate – 'the density of the German retail network is not abnormal' (*ibid.*). Nonetheless, the pressures of rising staff costs and changing technology have inevitably induced some rationalisation. The problem of rising labour costs is an almost universal one in the German economy, not least in the banking sector (Table 6.3). Such costs typically represent two-thirds of total administrative costs in banking and they increased by 8.6 per cent in 1990, marginally less than the increase in the volume of business (MRDB 8/91: 24). As already indicated, the number of staff has increased secularly. The staffing problem is exacerbated by customer conservatism and inertia, although in view of the periodic banking crises and inflation this disposition is probably understandable. In other words, the German retail banking customer in particular may have to be cajoled into accepting new forms of bank-

ing service. Credit cards and other forms of cashless transactions, as well as automatic cash dispensers, all appeared more slowly than in most other industrialised economies. Another astonishing anachronism in an age of computerisation is the existence of an independent clearing system in each banking sector. However, towards the end of the 1970s there were increasing signs of German savers shopping around. This trend was accompanied by a growing interest-rate consciousness among savers (BMWi *Leistung* . . . 1980: 30). Customers tended to move away from low interest savings accounts into short-term instruments offering higher rates. This new practice began at a time when interest rates were on an upward trend but was not maintained. It has already been seen that a sizeable proportion of bank customers accept a fairly meagre return on their savings. Unlike the practice in British banks, though, these low retail rates are not used to cross-subsidise cheap sight-deposit banking. On the contrary, German banking fees are imposed quite arbitrarily and can be at the same time incredibly extortionate.

The third and final topic in this section concerns the international aspects of German banking. The expansion of West German banks abroad was one of the major developments in world banking during the 1970s, though it is apparent that the relatively slower growth in assets and profits brought about some decline at the end of that decade. The domestic reasons for the fall in profitability have already been analysed. Internationally, it is clear in retrospect that world banking as a whole was creating problems for the 1980s. This was because of the kudos placed on balance sheet growth and international expansion. When combined with the liquidity created by Arab surpluses, this led to fierce competition among banks to lend. The profitability and even soundness of such lending played a relatively minor role in credit creation.

Including foreign branches of the private commercial banks in the Bundesbank's statistics from 1976 resulted in, for that year alone, an average business volume increase of DM 20.8 billion (MRDB 1/78: 21n). Of this sum, DM 14.1 billion was attributed to the Big Three, while the remaining DM 6.7 billion was attributed to the 'regional and other commercial banks group'. Similarly, including the foreign branches of the *Landesbanken* from 1979 resulted in a statistical increase of DM 8.9 billion (MRDB 8/80: 27n). During the two years up to mid-1979 the total external liabilities of the banks increased by no less than DM 40 billion to reach roughly DM 122 billion (MRDB 10/79: 28). By far the greater part of this increase (DM 27 billion) was in the form of longer-term capital inflows. Mortgage and *Landesbanken* in particular placed an increasing amount of DM borrowers' notes running for more than four years (and therefore not subject to reserve requirements) in other countries. In this way they financed a large part of their substantial lending to domestic private and public borrowers, so that the aggregate long-term external liabilities of the banks almost doubled (to reach DM 60 billion) between 1977 and 1979. Since the total external assets of the banks displayed a smaller expansion than liabilities, the overall balance was DM 16 billion in 1977 but DM −0.7 billion in 1979.

Every sector of the German banking industry went international during the 1970s. In effect, this means that all the major West German banks had either direct or syndicated representation in the principal financial centres. West German banks therefore lend and borrow abroad, either as individual institutions or as part of a syndicate. Overseas business, for example, accounted for 25 per cent of the Deutsche's total business in 1992 (FT 20 May 1992). A further corollary is that foreign banks sought direct or syndicated representation in West Germany. Three consequences will therefore be briefly examined: first, the implications of the Luxembourg subsidiaries of the German banks; second, loans made to East Europe and the Middle East 'petro dollars'; and, finally, the alleged difficulties experienced by foreign banks in gaining entry into the German banking system.

Subsidiaries of West German banks were established during the late 1960s and 1970s in Luxembourg – 'a place known for its liberal banking regulations' (Commerzbank 1980: 5). In other words, the strong presence of West German banks in Luxembourg resulted from the fact that they were not required to observe the minimum reserve requirements imposed by the Bundesbank at home. Domestic regulations also stipulated that a bank's lending may not exceed its equity capital by more than eighteen times – the so-called Principle 1 of the Supervisory Authority (issued under the KWG). In some Luxembourg subsidiaries, much to the consternation of both the Bundesbank and Supervisory Authority, the capital to loans ratio reached around 1:28 instead of the German minimum 1:18. It was in this way that the German banks used these subsidiaries as vehicles for their dramatic international growth. What especially concerned the authorities was the private sector's inability to build up adequate reserves to cover loan losses. After a lengthy campaign by the authorities, and when the banks were facing a profit crisis at the end of the 1970s, a voluntary agreement was reached with the private and cooperative banks. Under this agreement the banks agreed to provide the supervisory authorities, on a regular basis, with consolidated accounts including data on wholly-owned foreign subsidiaries. As seen in the section on prudential arrangements, the authorities were not satisfied with the operation of these voluntary arrangements and this resulted in the KWG being amended in 1985. Profitability of the Luxembourg subsidiaries was in any case relatively low. In 1990, the published pre-tax profit of these subsidiaries was almost halved compared to 1989; it also fell below the average for 1980–89 (MRDB 8/91: 21). Yet in 1992 the banks advertised the higher returns on deposits which were held at their Luxembourg branches (*Guardian* 9 September 1992). Such deposits were not subject to the new tax regime which was introduced from 1 January 1993. It was not perfectly clear why the banks, or the general public, were so disenchanted with the new tax, given that the Constitutional Court had required its introduction on grounds of equity. It was a vast improvement on the hapless withholding tax imposed for a few months in 1989 (Figure 4.6b). Foreign investors were excluded from the new tax, and most domestic taxpayers were unaffected because of the high amounts of interest income not subject to tax. The tax-free allowance was DM 6,100 for all single persons and DM 12,000 for a married couple (TVF 29 January 1993). This meant that the following rates of interest could be applied tax free to the following balances held by a single person, double for a married couple (*Handelsblatt* 21 January 1993): 5 per cent: DM 122,000; 6 per cent: DM 101,666; 7 per cent: DM 87,142; and 8 per cent: DM 76,250.

Perhaps the large capital outflows implied that interest earned abroad, particularly in Luxembourg, would not be declared for tax, and past tax evasion on domestic accounts would be detected if

these accounts were left in Germany (FT 14 December 1992). On the other hand, Steinherr (1991: 384–5) demonstrates that, in spite of persistent current account surpluses and tight local regulations, German banks hold the lowest proportion of their assets abroad.

In turning to the Polish payments crisis as an example of the difficulties caused by the rapid international expansion of German banking, one must bear several points in mind. Above all, the German banks played a vital national role in financing the rapid recovery of Germany's foreign trade: during the 1950s and 1960s the Deutsche Bank alone financed about a third of all the country's foreign trade (Deutsche Bank 1970: 43). Further, the strong DM made it relatively easy for the West German banks to raise funds. Enormous oil-dollar funds flowed on to the Euromarket – in 1981 alone the total was expected to reach DM 80 billion (*Die Zeit* 22/81: 25). Two of these factors – a strong DM and financing a booming export trade – increasingly encouraged the pursuit of asset growth rather than profitability. The risks involved in extending credit well in excess of equity capital seemed to be acceptable.

But those risks suddenly became greater at the end of the 1970s. Interest rates rose to unprecedented heights internationally and the banks found themselves saddled with long-term loans made when rates had been much lower but re-financed with short-term funds at higher rates. A mounting balance of payments deficit added to the problems: such current and capital account problems were new to the West German authorities during the period under review. Events in Iran and, more particularly, in Poland were bound to exacerbate the difficulties in which the West German banks already found themselves. This was because West German banks are heavily committed in financing their economy's traditional trade with East Europe as a whole. Hence in international banking terms Poland's financial crisis hit Germany's banks hardest. A decade later their exposure in the former USSR was creating similar difficulties. Germany was owed around DM 50 billion, including both commercial and government loans (*Economist* 12 December 1992). Russia was paying very little and 600 commercial banks, led by the Deutsche, reluctantly agreed to the postponement of repayments. This rescheduling cost DM 8 billion (FT 6 April 1993). Trade debts were a particularly serious problem: many of the debts were owed to small German firms. Substantial amounts of other aid such as further credit facilities, export credit guarantees, the costs of the repatriation of military personnel to the former Soviet Union and economic reforms were also agreed for 1993–4 (*ibid.*). Yet post-communist Russia represented a potentially important market for east Germany in particular – see the trade section of Chapter 8.

It was seen in Figure 7.1 that 61 foreign banks have branches in West Germany. It was also seen that they account for only 1.2 per cent of the total volume of business. There are two reasons for this. First, although the large US banks have had branches in Germany since shortly after the Second World War, West Germany became something of a Mecca for foreign banks only from the late 1960s. Second – and this is a more important, if highly controversial, point – the small proportion of the business volume accounted for by the foreign banks was attributed to unfair and anti-competitive practices of the native German banks. Discrimination in this sense was frequently alleged; some Japanese bankers went as far as saying that the west German financial community

was a closed society (BSA 1978: 26). However, some evidence of a gradual opening up has been seen in the sections on private banks and deregulation above. Indeed, what the Bundesbank (MRDB 3/ 92: 27) saw as 'the conspicuous attractiveness of the financial centre Germany' resulted in a large increase in the number of foreign banks with subsidiaries operating in Germany. Between 1984 and 1991 this number doubled, reaching 132 at the end of this period.

Not surprisingly, Germany's unique universal banking system is central to the foreign banks' difficulties. As already emphasised, this system has resulted in extraordinarily close links between the big domestic banks and industry. In addition, the ties within the financial sector itself were stressed when *Allfinanz* and the stock exchanges were discussed. Historically, the basic allegation was that this system was used by major West German banks to exclude foreign banks (FT *Banking Supplement* 1979: V). It was even alleged that foreign banks were asked to temporarily take a loan to a West German company back at the end of a financial year so that problems with the West German bankers on the company's supervisory board could be avoided (FT *ibid.* 1980: III). However, business done with some of the larger West German companies may well have been booked outside of Germany, even though it was arranged by West German staff (FT *ibid.* 1981: IV). Profits too may be taken elsewhere. Another method of gaining access to West German corporate companies was, of course, to take over one of the smaller West German banks. Examples of such moves were given in the section on the private bankers. Such moves may also improve low profitability, for this is another feature which tended to characterise foreign banking in West Germany

(MRDB 10/79: 19 and 10/82: 28). One major factor in this respect is that the business of both foreign banks and private bankers involves a significant proportion – between a half and two-thirds – of short-term business. They were therefore better able than other banks to adjust their lending terms very flexibly to the higher cost of funds (MRDB 8/81: 18). But the advent of *Finanzplatz Deutschland* had a palpable effect on the general attitude to foreign banks and practices – as can be readily seen from the section on this topic.

CONCLUSION

West German financial institutions were forced to reconsider their role during the 1980s. Their response to international competition, not least the pressure of EC 1993, was evident during the *Allfinanz* saga, and in their changing role vis-à-vis *Finanzplatz Deutschland*. The Gessler Commission's recommendations, particularly on the banks' industrial holdings, and the Bundesbank's concern with the lending loophole created by the presence of the Luxembourg subsidiaries were both legislative nettles. The latter was grasped – perhaps imperfectly – but the former remains a controversial policy issue. Schneider-Lenné (1993: 68) insists that the German banks will have no difficulty in observing the ECs directive on holdings in non-banks. Shareholder activists, however, are more perturbed by proxy voting and the presence of the banks on supervisory boards.

Almost in time for the arrival of EC 1993, the Allianz/Dresdner axis and the Deutsche Bank had taken effective control of the insurance industry and Frankfurt am Main's DM Eurobond market was showing great potential. (The introduction of the EC's insurance directives was postponed until 1994.) Such developments

were more viable than those in the City of London, where institutions seemed more geared to relying on windfall gains from privatisation and speculation during the occasional Black Wednesday to bolster profits! Progress was thus made in improving Frankfurt's competitiveness as an international financial centre. This was yet another issue which was almost unrelated to the repercussions of unification. Stock market practices still required some modification, but during the 1980s the Bundesbank's approach to bond issues and the role of foreign banks changed dramatically. Federal tax and legal impediments to financial growth were also removed, otherwise the incongruity of one the world's most powerful industrial economies remaining a financial backwater would have become even more obvious as the full effects of EC 1993 made themselves felt. Given its trading activities on behalf of the Federal government, the Bundesbank had a major interest in efficient, transparent and cost-effective financial markets (MRDB 3/92: 28). The Bank itself gave a clear undertaking that it would 'continue to focus its efforts on safeguarding the stability of the DM', thereby 'preserving a major comparative advantage' of *Finanzplatz Deutschland* (*ibid.*: 31).

This does not gainsay the gratuitous fillip to domestic growth which the banks, and indeed insurance companies, enjoyed as a result of unification. They were arguably the single largest beneficiaries, particularly when compared to the more desultory penetration of west German industry into east Germany – a topic to be considered in the next chapter. German private-sector banks were in a particularly strong position even during the 1992–3 recession. They had not, as in much of Europe, had to contend with a catastrophic asset deterioration on residential or commercial property portfolios, and they follow a more conservative provisioning policy against foreign exposure than most (*Banker* March 1993). Their reserves are enormous and any unforeseen, embarrassing lending or trading errors can be quickly camouflaged. EC 1993 had lowered the costs of entry into other EC states. Moreover, the BV and Hypo banks saw southern and central Europe as their obvious backyards (*ibid.*). Finally, as German banks expand into the rest of Europe and beyond, market share considerations, along with non-quantifiable strategic advantages, are likely to be more important than immediate profit prospects.

This writer (1983: 269) concluded a previous study of German banking as follows:

What is beyond doubt is that there will be further attempts at legislative reform, although budgetary and more general economic policy issues preoccupy the minds of Bonn politicians at the time of writing. Nevertheless, as the *Financial Times* (3 September 1981) suggested, the commercial banks may hope that further reform can be postponed until profitability is restored, and perhaps even until a 'more amenable' Government is ruling in Bonn. On the other hand, the sudden willingness on the part of the banks to part with their 'long-treasured' share-holdings in the non-banking sector has been seen by *The Times* (10 September 1981) as not just a result of the squeeze on profits, but also to some extent the SPD/FDP Government's undertaking to legislate on banking.

It is patently obvious that Bonn's budgetary and general economic problems were even more of a preoccupation in the early 1990s. Generally, the profitability of the banks was adequately restored in the 1980s, and there was a 'more amenable' government in Bonn (CDU/CSU/FDP). Precise evidence on the banks' degree of influence in non-banks is by the nature of things extremely difficult to obtain – as was shown in the section on corporate finance. By the same token, it is almost impossible to accurately judge the significance of the Luxembourg subsidiaries. There is traditionally a high degree of confidentiality in all the banks' dealings – as the legislators found when they were enjoined by the Federal Constitutional Court to introduce a more equitable system of taxation on interest income. By and large, it seems that the historical relationship with the non-banks, and the degree of circumvention of monetary policy via the Luxembourg subsidiaries, will both remain policy problems. This in no way underestimates the domestic changes wrought by *Allfinanz* and *Finanzplatz Deutschland*.

INDUSTRY, TRADE AND ECONOMIC POLICY

*(Written with Stephan Burger [Privatisation]
and Lothar Funk [Trade])*

INTRODUCTION

Differences in a number of policy perceptions between German and Anglo-Saxon economists make a consideration of the title of this chapter appropriate. It will be noticed that the general term 'economic policy' has been preferred. This is because it combines the notions of 'industrial' and 'competition' policies as they have evolved in Germany. 'Economic policy' likewise avoids the controversy which has been generated by the respective roles of industrial and competition policy (Neumann in Cowling and Tomann 1990: 222; Sturm 1989b: 155–60). More specifically, within the theoretical framework of the SME the term 'industrial policy' has negative connotations: 'advocates of industrial policy deviate from the regulatory policy path of competition' (Sauter in Cowling and Tomann 1990: 234). Yet the regulatory policy path of competition – as seen in Chapter 1 – really means in Anglo-Saxon, particularly US, parlance the presence of strong anti-trust legislation. As Berghahn has demonstrated (1986: 32, 100 and 140), the major objective of such legislation in the USA was to preserve the principle of competition and to protect it against misuse. This approach permitted the US authorities to draw a sharp distinction between the decartelisation and deconcentration of German industry after the war. It will be shown below that German legislation designed to 'regulate' competition policy consists of precisely identical strands, namely controlling cartels and attempting to prevent the abuse of market-dominant positions. It will also be shown below that the effect of such legislation is regularly reviewed by the Monopolies Commission (MK).

Significantly, the MK distinguished carefully between competition and industrial policy in its ninth biennial report (MK IX). Specific attention was paid to governments influencing trade flows by means of subsidies, an issue considered in the section on strategic trade, competition and industrial policies below. Hence, Klodt (in Cowling and Tomann 1990: 285) illustrates the semantic problem by classifying competition policy as the EC Commission 'centrally slowing down inefficient subsidy races among member countries in high-tech industries'. In fact, the EC's competition *and* industrial policies were reflected in the 'Commission's determination to eliminate unauthorised government subsidies to industry and to clamp down on illegal restrictive and monopolistic practices, rather than wait for protected and inefficient industries to fail in the face of foreign competition' (Owen and Dynes 1992: 154). But EC competition policy itself was confined to the implications of cross-border mergers and acquisitions (*ibid*.; Woolcock *et al*. 1991: 11). True, the French, Italians and many large European companies favoured using competition policy as surrogate for industrial policy, but the Germans and British successfully argued that their own highly developed merger-control policies should form the basis of EC competition law (Woolcock *et al*. 1991: 19).

Although a strong case against industrial policy is presented by German economists and policy makers, Germany has, and has always had, its own brand of industrial policy (Sturm 1989b: 161). A number of loopholes were found to justify the amount of state support given to industry (*ibid*.). For example, German industrial policy was influenced by an overt shift in emphasis after 1967 (Cowling and Tomann 1990: 37). The active structural policy which was introduced at that stage formally sought to promote macroeconomic objectives by microeconomic policies (Peacock *et al*. 1980: i). The example given by Peacock *et al*. (*ibid*.) is the case where economic growth is believed to be 'export led'. In such a case, structural policies should concentrate on diverting resources by tax and subsidy measures, for example, towards exporters. As this policy framework advocated direct government intervention in the economic system, it was in direct conflict with the received theory of the SME. Yet the trend in government subsidies alone had been almost continuously upwards during the post-war period (*ibid*.: para 4.9). On the other hand, any discussion of industrial policy must also include an account of privatisation and deregulation programmes. In this chapter, therefore, it will be necessary to consider the various aspects of anti-trust policy, together with other policies which have affected the competitive and structural characteristics of German industry.

Suffice it to say at this stage that the term 'industrial policy' has *dirigiste* tones for many Germans. For example, the chief executive of Daimler-Benz has expressed this view, although he significantly added that the EC required a common framework within which the market economy could operate (FT 8 March 1993).

Also by way of introduction, a further feature of the German industrial landscape must be mentioned. It was shown in the previous Chapter (Figure 7.2) that the legal forms of ownership are quite manifold. Moreover, the domestic holders of shares in the largest companies fall into four equally varied categories (Rutherford 1974: 29; Vogl 1973: 43). First, the financial institutions, mainly the large banks, own strategically placed blocks of shares. Second, there are powerful and rich families with holdings in important companies. Taken together, the banks and families thus highlight *two enduring features* of the German corporate scene. The Flick family was the most important family to reemerge in post-war Germany. During the 1980s, however, the company was subjected to the first hostile takeover in German corporate history (see the section on mergers and acquisitions below). Other famous families include the Quandts (see the corporate control section below), the Fincks (see the section on private bankers in Chapter 7) and the Haniels (founders of GHH). Such a list is far from exhaustive. One could add, for example, the families or individuals such as Siemens (founded in the mid-nineteenth century) and Grundig (founded after the Second World War) whose companies also played a vital role in technical innovation and exports. Nor does it take account of the foundations (*Stiftungen*) to which families like Bosch and Thyssen hived off respectively 85 and 11 per cent of their shares (Rutherford 1974: 44–5). The Siemens family holdings held in this form may have diminished (*ibid*.: 42). Note also that the demise of the corporate influence of the Krupp family – and the rescue mounted by the banks – were both briefly traced in the previous chapter. The Krupps, like several generations of the Haniels, now leave the running of the business to professional managers. On the other hand, the Henkel family – owners of the economy's fourth largest chemical concern – still play a significant corporate role. All these examples set the scene for the subsequent discussion of industrial concentration and, more particularly, export-led growth; they are thus deliberately confined to Germany's past and present industrial prowess in these senses. Sectors such as the mass media, exemplified by the presence of Bertelsmann and Axel Springer in the 'top 100 industrials', would have been added to a more widely defined list. Third, there are assorted types of Federal, Länder and local authority organisations, although it will be shown that the process of privatisation has had something of an impact here. Fourth, there is the traditional owner of a small shareholding. It was emphasised in the previous chapter, however, that the large banks often exercise corporate influence on behalf of this latter group.

Figure 7.2 also demonstrated that the first important distinction which must be made is between the usually small one-man (or family) businesses – the backbone of the *Mittelstand* – and the various corporate bodies. Moreover, it was shown in Chapter 1 that the *Mittelstand* is a central element of SME theory. For this reason, shedding light on the role of the *Mittelstand* in post-war growth will be an early task in this chapter. Note for now, however, that the corporate bodies themselves may, in turn, be divided into partnerships and companies. Some of

the larger family-owned companies are registered in the form of partnerships. However, most of the very large companies in West Germany are AGs, that is full public companies with limited liability and quoted shares. The private and unquoted limited liability companies (GmbH) are usually much smaller than AGs, although some holding companies and firms in trust-ownership such as Robert Bosch have taken the GmbH form. There are also some large share-quoted partnerships (KGaA). For example, the former Flick family holding company – for much of the post-war period one of Germany's largest companies – became a KGaA towards the end of its existence, although for most of the time it was a KG. Henkel is also a KGaA with the majority of the shares being owned by the family (MK IX: 212 and 214). Cross-company holdings result in cooperation between the different forms of companies. Daimler-Benz, for instance, was closely associated with the Flick group, which owned 38 per cent of the company (Dyas and Thanheiser 1976: 81). Quandt – also responsible for the spectacular revival of BMW – held another 14 per cent and the Deutsche Bank 31 per cent. This ownership structure changed during the 1970s (see below). Nonetheless, the company was significant among motor vehicle manufacturers in that it remained highly profitable at the end of the 1970s (*Business Week*, 20 July 1981: 100). Whether its subsequent diversification was a wise policy became one of the most frequently aired topics in West German industrial affairs.

Hence, any reference to 'industrial structure' in Germany, immediately raises complex issues. Yet again, unification simply added an extra dimension to these complexities. For example, it will be seen in the trade sections below that the debate about *Standort Deutschland* (West

Germany's potential as a competitive industrial location) embraced the cost implications of taxation, interest rates and wage bargaining for a number of years prior to unification (also see Chapters 3, 4 and 6 above). As already indicated, however, perhaps the most important issue requiring initial clarification in this chapter is the need to resolve the apparent paradox between Germany's reputation for being the home of a thriving small and medium-sized business sector (known as the *Mittelstand*) yet at the same time possessing some of the most dominant multinational corporations. This will therefore be the starting point of this chapter. As a general principle, however, the central finding throughout the chapter will be that German industrial enterprises are large and critically important when accounting for Germany's economic power.

INDUSTRIAL STRUCTURE

What, more precisely, is the *Mittelstand*? It consists of an extremely heterogeneous group of small and medium-sized businesses located throughout the German economy. In its normal usage, it refers to companies and partnerships represented in industry, commerce, the residual parts of the service sector, the professions (*freie Berufe*), and *Handwerker*, a term which was roughly translated in Chapter 6 as 'handicraft trades'. A more detailed account of *Handwerker* follows shortly. It should be noted, however, that the term *neuer Mittelstand* is occasionally, but fallaciously, used to describe mid-ranking *Beamte* and *Angestellten* who were more appropriately defined in Chapter 6. Moreover, in its widest – and equally careless – usage the term is used also to include agriculture.

A working definition of those small and medium-sized enterprises correctly included in the term *Mittelstand* is based on the quantitative criteria of turnover or employment (Commerzbank *VWL Bericht* 11/85):

- industry: small = annual turnover of up to DM 2 million or up to 50 employees; medium = DM 2 million to DM 25 million or 50 to 499 employees
- wholesale: small = up to DM 1 million or up to 9 employees; medium = DM 1 million to DM 50 million or 10 to 199 employees
- retail: small = up to DM 500,000 or up to 2 employees; medium = DM 500,000 to DM 10 million or 3 to 99 employees
- transport, news media, *Handwerker* and other services provided by both companies and the professions: small = up to DM 100,000 or up to 2 employees; medium = DM 100,000 to DM 2 million or 3 to 49 employees

Thus if one excludes distribution, transport, hotels and catering, along with those small and medium-sized businesses which use mass-production techniques, there remains a group of *Mittelstand* enterprises known as *Handwerker*. This amorphous business sector includes, for example, the baker who produces his own bread and confectionery for sale in his own corner shop, or the cabinet maker who supplies his neighbourhood with wooden products from tables to coffins. Plumbers, tailors, glass craftpersons and coppersmiths are further examples. Although the number of *Handwerker* enterprises fell from roughly 750,000 to 500,000 between 1960 and 1980, thereafter this statistic remained fairly static in the west (*Die Zeit* 25/80; BMWi *Wirtschaft* . . . 1992: 68). Total turnover of these enterprises increased during the same period (1960–91) from

DM 80 billion to almost DM 580 billion; on the other hand, employment in this sector remained fairly constant at about 4 million persons (*ibid*.). It has already been seen (Chapter 6) that one third of all apprenticeships are served in *Handwerker* enterprises. For this reason, *Handwerker* are often referred to as the economy's 'mentors'.

When distinguishing between small, medium and large enterprises, the Federal Ministry of Economics uses more general categories of turnover and employment than those referred to above (Jeske in Stern 1992: 141). Small businesses are defined as having an annual turnover of up to DM 1 million, or employing up to 49 persons. Medium businesses have an annual turnover of between DM 1 million and DM 100 million or between 50 and 499 employees. Large companies thus have an annual turnover of over DM 100 million or over 500 employees. Köster (1991: 53) thus demonstrates that the *Mittelstand* small and medium-sized enterprises – that is with under 500 employees – account for 1.9 million companies in the west, compared to only 3,600 large companies. *Mittelstand* companies on this definition employ 12 million persons – two thirds of all private-sector employees. They are responsible for training 80 per cent of all apprentices. Half the private-sector GDP is generated by these companies and they undertake 40 per cent of total investment. Using the turnover definition of under DM 100 million, Jeske (*ibid.*: 142) more or less confirms the size distribution of companies in terms of numbers (two million small/medium, compared to 4000 large). Significantly, however, the relative magnitude of sales is found to be divided equally between, on the one hand, the small/medium businesses and, on the other hand, the large companies (*ibid.*: 143). Not that there are

no links at all between these two groups of enterprises. Heinz Dürr, for example, came from his family's business to rescue the giant electrical concern AEG. After unification, he took over the job of merging the two railway systems.

Support for *Mittelstand* companies was a constant element in West German economic policy dating back to the use of Marshall Aid counterpart funds being channelled through the KfW (see Chapters 1 and 7). Such *quasi*-government backing lowers the barriers to entry and expansion. As in all economies, of course, it has become increasingly difficult to start a small business which tends to be at its most vulnerable in its early years. However, there are numerous examples of policy developments designed to ameliorate this feature of the market economy. Is history set to repeat itself? Predictably, the *Mittelstand* was all but destroyed in the east. One of the biggest challenges of the 1990s will therefore be reintroducing this vital characteristic of German economic life. There was already some indication of such a revival in the new Länder as reliable statistical evidence began to emerge in 1991 (BMWi *Wirtschaft* . . . 1992: 68–9). During 1992, however, one of the effects of the post-unification recession engineered by the Bundesbank in response to inflationary pressures was a notable increase in the bankruptcy rates among newly-founded firms in the east (TVF 24 February 1993). Lack of sufficient expertise was another cause of failure.

There is a final significant feature of *Mittelstand* companies. Simon (1992) found that they frequently dominate the world market for their product. This export success, moreover, tends to date from the 1950s and 1960s. Although usually highly specialised, the *Mittelstand* companies in his sample made every effort to cater for their foreign customers' requirements. Because of this attention to detail and quality, their overseas' customers tended to ignore the tendency for high West German labour costs to be passed on in the form of relatively high prices. However, their flawless engineering and lavish customer service has increasingly met with Japanese price competition (*Economist* 6 March 1993). The analysis will return to export shares and competition below. Significantly, though, Simon uses BMW as an example of a company that set out to increase its exports to Japan. But when BMW entered this market in 1981 it was already West Germany's twenty-seventh largest industrial enterprise in terms of its turnover (*Die Zeit* 36/81). By 1991, it was eleventh by turnover and thirteenth by employment – see Table 8.1 below. These data place BMW well beyond the DM 100 million/500 employees maxima referred to above. By way of a curious coincidence, however, BMW's chief executive voiced concern for the future of the *Mittelstand* during the deep recession of 1993. Many of the motor industry's suppliers were small companies who were feeling the brunt of the big price reductions for their components (*Independent* 26 March 1993).

The dominance of such large industrial enterprises will be a recurring theme throughout this chapter. Some perspective in this respect is therefore essential. On unification, industry accounted for only about one third of total employment, although it also generated one third of GDP (OECD *Economic Survey* 1992: 120). Within the industrial sector of the western economy in 1990, 52 per cent of all employees worked for enterprises with over 500 employees (IW *Zahlen* 1992: 67). These enterprises also accounted for 58 per cent of total industrial turnover (*ibid.*). Moreover, it will be shown below that

West Germany's remarkable export-led growth is attributable to the industrial sector. It is in this sense that one needs to distinguish between the received theory of the SME – a thriving small business sector being an indicator of economic and social welfare – and the proximate cause of Germany's economic prowess. This distinction can be initially drawn in the following manner. Bannock (1976: 56) reported that Germany had many more small businesses than the UK and their share of output and employment was much higher. Concentration in both countries was increasing, but the decline of the small firm sector appeared to be somewhat faster and certainly more widespread among the different branches of the economy in Britain. However, small and medium-sized businesses accounted for a smaller share of *industrial* employment and *industrial* production in West Germany than in any other OECD country (Peacock *et al.* 1980: para 4.25 – emphases added). Nonetheless, the number of programmes assisting small and medium-sized business enterprises in general had increased considerably in the FRG, as had the amount of government expenditure for such purposes (*ibid.*: para 4.26).

Having established the relative size of West German industrial enterprises, it is possible to proceed to a review of Germany's most important companies in turnover and employment terms. This is principally achieved by means of Figure 8.1 and Table 8.1, both of which contain such data.

It must be first noted that the data used in calculating the ratios in Figure 8.1 are subject to relatively minor errors. The reasons are instructive. Above all, employment levels at the individual company level by 1991 included in some cases turnover and employment in the new

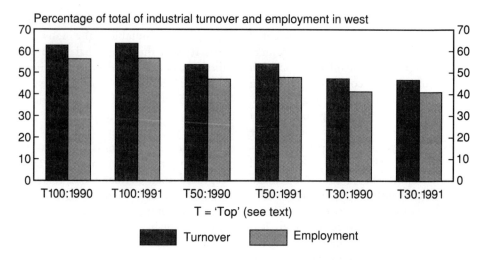

Figure 8.1 Turnover and employment in large industrial companies

Sources: *Die Zeit*; *Stat. Jahrbuch*; IW *Zahlen* (author's translation and calculations)

Länder. Indeed, total international turnover and employment for some of the large international groups may be included in some numerators. But as made clear in the figure, these numerators have been expressed as a percentage of total (international) turnover and west German industrial employment – where 'industrial' is defined to include manufacturing and mining but not construction (*Statistisches Jahrbuch* 1992: 205). Total domestic industrial turnover was about 70 per cent of total industrial turnover in 1990 and 1991 (*ibid.*). In 1991, however, industrial turnover in the east represented only 5 per cent of total industrial turnover (IW *Zahlen* 1992: 69). Domestic employment by the top ten industrial companies accounted for about two thirds of their total employment in 1989 (*Die Zeit* 34/90). For the economy as a whole the proportion would probably be significantly larger. Nonetheless, subject to these qualifications, an overall picture of dominance emerges from Figure 8.1. Two comparative dimensions of this picture are pre-

sented. First, 1990 is compared to 1991. Very little change in the degree of dominance is discernible in this fairly static sense. (In Table 8.4 below, it will be shown that the degree of dominance over a longer time period has significantly increased in turnover terms). Second, the dominance of the top 30 companies, relative to both the top 50 and top 100, is also apparent from Figure 8.1.)

Turnover and employment within the top 30 industrials themselves are compared in Table 8.1. Again the comparison is for the years 1990 and 1991. Notice first the prominent position of Daimler-Benz. The emergence of this conglomerate – whose turnover exceeded the Irish Republic's GNP in 1991 – will be analysed below. For now, it is instructive to note that a decade earlier there had been serious losses at AEG, but Daimler-Benz was highly profitable. During the 1980s AEG was acquired by Daimler-Benz. This is a good example of how some large companies accrued large financial reserves which in turn enabled them to finance takeovers.

Table 8.1 The 30 largest industrial enterprises

Rank 1991	Rank 1990	Company	Sector	Turnover 1991 DM million	Turnover 1991 Percentage change over 1990	Profits (−losses) DM million 1991	Profits (−losses) DM million 1990	Employees End 1991	Employees Percentage change over 1990
1	1	Daimler-Benz	Motor vehicles/Aerospace/Electrical	95,010	11.1	1,942	1,795	379,252	0.7
2	2	VW	Motor vehicles	76,315	12.1	1,114	1,086	260,137	−0.3
3	3	Siemens	Electronic/Electrical	73,008	15.5	1,792	1,668	406,000	8.8
4	4	VEBA	Energy/Chemicals	57,201	8.5	1,223	1,209	114,537	7.2
5	6	Hoechst	Chemicals	47,186	5.2	1,357	1,696	179,332	3.7
6	5	BASF	Chemicals	44,799	−1.0	1,056	1,111	129,434	−3.9
7	8	RWE	Energy	44,100	9.7	1,200[1]	1,186	105,840	8.4
8	7	Bayer	Chemicals	42,401	1.8	1,835	1,903	164,200	−4.0
9	9	Thyssen	Steel/Machinery/Commerce	36,562	1.0	520	690	148,557	−0.7
10	10	Bosch	Electricals	33,600	5.6	540	560	177,200	−1.4
11	11	BMW	Motor vehicles	29,830	10.0	783	696	74,238	4.6
12	13	Opel	Motor vehicles	27,149	14.5	1,075	1,327	56,782	−1.2
13	18	Preussag	Steel/Energy/Commerce	25,455	33.7	425	350	71,654	−0.8
14	14	Ruhrkohle	Coal mining	24,700	7.8	83	171	122,469	2.5
15	12	Mannesmann	Machinery/Steel	24,315	1.6	263	464	125,188	1.0
16	17	VIAG	Holding	23,587	21.4	405	336	74,122	32.7
17	15	Ford	Motor vehicles	22,360	7.7	142	270	48,171	−3.9
18	16	Metallgesellschaft	Metals/Equipment	21,180	6.8	179	262	38,173	18.5
19	19	M.A.N.	Machinery/Commercial vehicles	19,031	0.5	406	328	64,170	−2.7
20	26	Ruhrgas	Energy	15,275	25.3	789	664	10,105	9.4
21	20	Krupp	Steel/Machinery	15,134	−2.8	305	217	53,115	−10.0
22	22	IBM Deutschland	Electronics	14,802	11.1	473	692	31,536	−0.7
23	23	Bertelsmann	Mass media	14,483	8.8	540	510	45,110	3.7
24	24	Deutsche Shell	Mineral oil/chemicals	13,687	7.0	547	358	3,294	1.2
25	21	Degussa	Chemicals/Precious metals	13,305	−4.5	99	147	34,482	−1.5
26	27	Henkel	Chemicals	12,950	7.7	443	429	42,040	8.3
27	28	Esso	Mineral oils	12,610	9.9	507	441	2,366	−1.9
28	31	Phillipp Holzmann	Building	11,003	18.5	51	17	40,410	9.7
29	25	Hoesch	Steel	10,108	−19.6	127	103	44,200	−15.3
30	32	Deutsche Unilever	Food products	9,799	6.5	348	339	29,046	6.1

Sources: *Die Zeit* 34/92 and 31/91; *Fortune* 27 July 1992   Note: [1] Estimated

This huge degree of liquidity generally persisted in 1991 among domestically owned enterprises, total liquidity probably being DM 1670 billion (*Die Zeit* 34/92). Figure 8.2 shows how profits and self-financed investment grew during the 1980s. Between 1981 and 1989 general industrial profits doubled (*Die Zeit* 34/90). Further, *Die Zeit*'s 'top 100' listing showed that two thirds of the industrial companies in the list had increased their profits during the accounting year of 1989 (*ibid.*). Only seven companies in the list had incurred losses. In 1989, Daimler-Benz's management were able to draw DM 6.5 billion from reserves in order to impress international investors and Mitsubishi – with whom they were seeking cooperation deals (*ibid.*). As a result, their published profit was larger than the total profits of the next four largest companies in the 'top ten' (VW, Siemens, VEBA and BASF). Moreover, at the end of the 1980s, the reserves of Daimler-Benz alone (by then Germany's largest industrial company) were placed at FFr 75 bil-

lion, closely followed by those of Siemens at FFr 70 billion but leaving the comparatively liquid British GEC with FFr 15 billion well behind (*Best of Business* Winter 1989–90). But the commitment of large industrials to investment in the east was not over impressive (see Table 8.2).

The profits of Daimler-Benz as early as 1980 contrasted with the losses within West Germany of Ford and Opel, the latter being a subsidiary of General Motors. Indeed, at an international level Daimler-Benz exceptionally boosted profits, even outclassing the Japanese motor companies which shared this distinction (*Business Week* 20 July 1981). This was at a time when 'the history of international business (was being) written in red ink' (*ibid.*). Also in the motor industry, the deteriorating financial situation of VW was noticeable. Although history was repeating itself to a certain extent later in 1991, there were at least no losses recorded in the motor vehicle industry within Germany (Table 8.1). Internationally, however, General Motors reported the largest loss ever by a

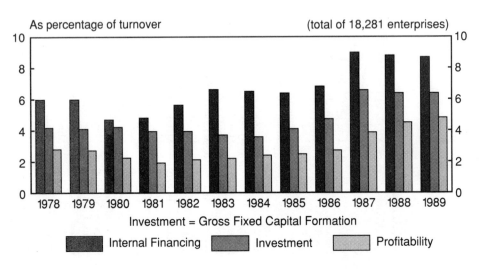

Figure 8.2 Finance, investment and profitability (18,281 enterprises)

Source: MRDB 10/92: 36

Table 8.2 The largest investors

Rank	Company	Capital investment (1991)		of which domestic		of which in eastern Germany		Planned in east
		DM million	% change on 1990	DM million	% change on 1990	1991 DM million	1992 DM million	DM million
1	VW	8,529	64	5,000	66	300	1,400	5,000[1]
2	Daimler-Benz	7,231	11	6,115	8	n.a.	n.a.	2,500[2]
3	Siemens	5,003	14	3,400	24	250	450	
4	VEBA	4,912	14	4,800	25	1,025	1,407	7,000[4]
5	BASF	4,800	8	2,081	−10	40	720	
6	RWE	4,429	55	3,700[5]	36	530	n.a.	
7	Hoechst	3,586	6	1,878	6	n.a.	n.a.	580[1]
8	Bayer	3,074	−17	1,600	−16	n.a.	n.a.	650[3]
9	Thyssen	2,713	−3	2,100	−4	214	436	
10	Bosch	2,273	−19	1,464	16	80	120	
11	BMW	2,123	3	1,856	−2	61	n.a.	
12	IBM	1,745	4	1,745	4	n.a.	n.a.	
13	VIAG	1,701	55	1,242	36	500	n.a.	
14	Mannesmann	1,500	15	1,231	28	90	150	
15	Ruhrkole	1,395	1	1,395	1	0	0	

Source: *Die Zeit* 34/92 (author's translation)

Notes: [1] To the end of 1995
[2] 'In the next few years'
[3] To the end of 1993
[4] To the end of 1996
[5] Accounting year 1990/91 (1991/92 : DM 4.7 billion)

company not owned by its government, while Ford suffered the biggest loss in its history (*Fortune* 27 July 1992). 'Profits took a sickening dive' at this level, while 'German results benefited from the glow of unification' (*ibid.*). The situation in the German motor industry changed dramatically in 1992–3. VW, for example, accounted for 3 per cent of GDP; although its turnover increased by 12 per cent in 1992, its pre-tax profit fell by 66 per cent (*Independent on Sunday* 4 July 1993). In the first quarter of 1993, VW lost DM 1.25 billion on a 12 per cent decline in sales (*Guardian* 15 June 1993). Cyclical and structural factors were responsible, both at VW and other manufacturers. The response was dramatic – see the sections

on corporate control and *Standort Deutschland* below.

To the predictable importance of the motor vehicle industry must be added electrical and electronic engineering as indicated by the presence of Siemens (Germany's largest employer in the private sector) and Bosch in the 'top 10' by turnover (Table 8.1). Similarly, the chemical giants – Hoechst, BASF and Bayer – also appear in this top ranking. Two of the mechanical engineering giants – Thyssen and Mannesmann – appear in the 'top 10' by employment. Another important mechanical engineering/ commercial vehicle manufacturer – MAN – was sixteenth by employment. There are thus four industries which dominate

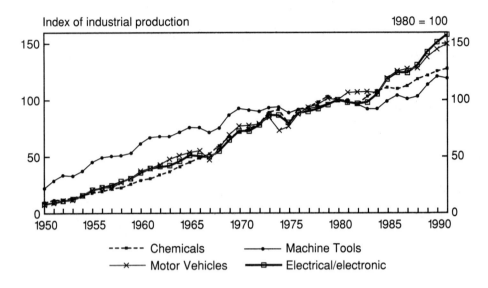

Figure 8.3 Some growth industries
Source: Plotted from Dresdner Bank, *Stat. Reihen*

the German economy. They are motor vehicles, other forms of mechanical engineering, electrical and electronic engineering and chemicals. An indication of their recovery and growth during the post-war period may be gleaned from Figure 8.3.

However, in the steel industry, in which Thyssen and Mannesmann also have interests, there were several analogies with the serious situation a decade earlier – culminating in the closure crises of 1987 and 1993, as well as the Klöckner 'equalisation' in 1992. (Equalisation is not to be confused with liquidation. The former is a process of writing down debt until an enterprise is commercially viable – see the references to Klöckner and Südmilch in the corporate finance section of Chapter 7). In 1980, Klöckner and the then state-owned Salzgitter were unable to pay dividends. The coal giant Ruhrkohle, the economy's tenth largest employer among the companies listed in Table 8.1, suffered

a set back in profits in 1991. In the same industry, the smaller Saarbergwerke – fifty-fourth on turnover in the top 100 of 1991– incurred a DM 59 million loss. (Subsidised output by the German coal industry had been developing into a controversial issue for some time.) Other energy concerns – RWE, Preussag, VIAG and Ruhrgas – gained either from acquisitions in, or supplying energy to, the east. The fluctuations in energy and steel output are illustrated in Figure 8.4, from which it can be seen that steel and coal experienced a number of negative decreases in demand. The spur of unification also favourably affected the only construction company in the top 30 (Philipp Holzmann). It should be added that the three subsidiaries of the Federal Post Office and, on unification, the Railways, occupied the two top positions as employers. (Neither of these public-sector organisations is shown in Table 8.1, but they both employed over 500,000 persons

– *Statistisches Jahrbuch* 1992: 13.3 and 13.27).

Finally, the rapid economic expansion in the 1950s and, to a lesser extent, the 1960s was conducive to both industrial growth and concentration. The growth path of the economy was traced as early as Figures 1.1 and 1.3, but Figure 8.3 shows how rapidly industrial production rose in the vitally important export industries. Again the growth trend slowed down in the 1960s, and there were cyclical fluctuations in the 1970s and, albeit to a lesser extent, in the 1980s. The trends in concentration will be further analysed in the anti-trust sections below. First, however, a brief survey of corporate ownership and control is necessary.

CORPORATE OWNERSHIP AND CONTROL

As the Monopolies Commission (MK) data in Table 8.3 make clear, 68 per cent of the top 100 enterprises in 1990 were of the AG form. (The reader is reminded that Figure 7.2 contains a schematic expression of the different corporate forms in Germany.) When the other two types of companies (GmbH and KGaA) are added to the AG, the proportion in both 1980 and 1990 reached 87 per cent. Further, of the partnerships and sole proprietorships which accounted for the remaining 13 per cent only the Oetker family's food manufacturing business was for many years classifiable as an industrial concern (MK III para 325). Oetker appeared in the MK's top 100 until 1990; following a restructuring it stood at 56th in *Die Zeit*'s industrial listing of 1991 (*Die Zeit* 34/92; MK VIII: 184–5). The reader will thus have gathered that the MK's listing contains non-industrial concerns, including, therefore, companies in the financial sector. Indeed, this approach created comparative difficulties when the influence of the banks in corporate finance was

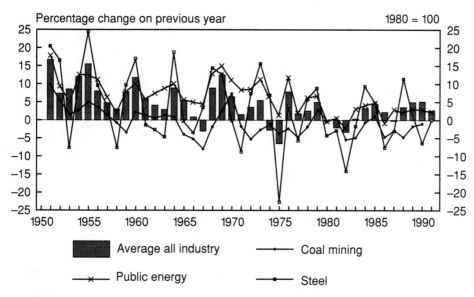

Figure 8.4 Industrial fluctuations

Source: As Figure 8.3

Table 8.3 Legal forms of the Top 100 Enterprises

Legal form	Number of companies			
	1976	*1980*	*1986*	*1990*
Sole proprietors	2	–	–	–
AG	68	66	67	68
KGaA	2	3	3	2
GmbH	17	18	18	17
OHG	2	1	2	2
KG	3	7	7	4
GmbH & Co KG	3	2	–	3
Others	3	3	3	4
Total	100	100	100	100

Sources: MK III: para. 324; IV: para. 421; VIII: para. 451; and IX: para. 453

Note: The Monopolies Commission has observed on the relative stability over time in the legal position of ownership (II, para. 265 and III, para. 325). Even under the slightly different criteria employed after 1980 (IV, para. 422), this generalisation remains valid

considered in Chapter 7. Nevertheless, utilising the MK's data set for a brief investigation into the ownership of West Germany's 100 largest companies will give valuable insights.

The MK regularly undertakes an analysis of what it defines as the top 100 companies. Its 1978 analysis relied on capital ownership, whereas from 1980 shares in value added were used. (It can be seen from Tables 8.1 and 8.4 that *Die Zeit*'s ranking is by turnover.) In 1990, the MK's ownership structure of the top 100 – defined as holdings of over 50 per cent – indicated (MK IX: 219):

- the majority of capital ownership of 30 of the top 100 companies was extensively distributed
- individuals and families (including *Stiftungen*) had majority interests in 23 of the top 100 enterprises
- over 50 per cent of the capital of 17 of the top 100 companies was foreign owned
- the various parts of the public sector owned over 50 per cent of the capital in eight companies
- only two companies were majority-owned by other top 100 companies, and one of these companies was the restructured co op enterprise which in 1990 was jointly owned by the DG and BfG banks but sold to Asko in 1991 (see the previous chapter and *ibid.*: para 458)
- there was no majority holding in 16 companies of the top 100, although 14 of these companies were holding companies belonging to members of the top 100 – five of the 14 being majority owned by members of the top 100 when their capital holdings were aggregated (*ibid.*: para 462)
- the remaining four companies were subject to some other form of majority holding

The introductory remarks on ownership made at the beginning of this chapter are thus substantiated by this breakdown. Moreover, when considering the diverse ownership of the 30 companies cited immediately above, it should be recalled that the banks often act on behalf of the small shareholder. For instance, in the case of BASF, which for most of the 1970s was the largest of the three chemical combines, the Deutsche Bank was entrusted with more than 25 per cent of these proxy votes (MK II: para 552). There may have been a similar situation at Bayer (*Die Zeit* 23/82). When compared to the early 1980s, however, the major difference in the majority ownership structure is the absence of trade union enterprises (see the BfG section in Chapter 7).

As well as analysing the structure of ownership in terms of majority holdings, the MK examines cross holdings within the top 100. It will be recalled that the controversy over the perceived 'power of the banks' stems partly from this exercise (see the corporate finance section in Chapter 7). Hence, together with the mammoth Allianz insurance company, the Big Three banks were in aggregate the largest shareholders in their fellow top 100 enterprises (MK IX: 209–10). In 1990, both the Allianz and the Deutsche Bank held shares in 15 of the top 100; the Dresdner Bank had stakes in eight enterprises and the Commerz in seven. Moreover, the banks and insurance companies were in some way associated with the 17 mergers and acquisitions within the top 100. On the other hand, enterprises from outside the top 100 held when aggregated majority stakes in seven of the top 100 companies. Finally, the MK estimates an 'interdependence ratio' for the top 100. Theoretically, though totally unrealistically, this ratio could reach 100 per cent if every company in the top 100 belonged to other companies within this statistical population. It is nevertheless instructive to note that the ratio was 12.6 per cent in 1990 – a rise of 1.7 percentage points over 1988.

As Schneider-Lenné (1992: 11) points out there is no German expression for 'corporate control'. As she also indicates, however, this does not mean that the basic problem of corporate control does not exist. This problem – first raised in the context of both cooperative banks and corporate finance in Chapter 7 – boils down to ownership and management typically being in separate hands. Such a problem in turn raises the question of the extent to which management pursues its own goals at the expense of shareholders' interests. For example, should dividend maximisation and the threat of takeover, both of which are induced by the Anglo-Saxon system, be important company goals? Moreover, it was seen in Chapters 6 and 7 that there are three locations of decision making at company level: the executive and supervisory boards, and the AGM. Two central features of corporate control were shown to be the presence of employee and bank representatives on the supervisory board. (Recall that the works council also has to be informed of changes in corporate control. Its chairman's support is particularly important.) Powers arising from the banks' direct holdings and proxy-voting rights, along with the impact of cross holdings held by the non-financial corporate sector, were also seen to exercise influence at the AGM. In this sense it would be wrong to think of the three institutions of control – the two boards and the AGM – as being a hierarchy. The elements of conflict and cooperation between these three institutions is best exemplified by the following case study of the motor vehicle industry. (The extraordinary emergence of *Allfinanz* is an equally interesting, if not to say extraordinary, case study of this aspect of corporate control in the financial sector – see the section on the BfG in Chapter 7.) Finally, there are two further aspects of corporate control (or lack of it!) which are well illustrated by a case study of the motor industry. The first aspect is diversification, while the second aspect is direct foreign investment.

In spite of their undoubted economic success, all three of the major German-owned vehicle companies – Volkswagen AG, Daimler-Benz AG and BMW AG – have been to varying degrees the scenes of power struggles, and their policies have been influenced by minority shareholders (Dyas and Thanheiser 1976: 81). For example, by the late 1950s BMW had liquidity difficulties and the Deutsche Bank executives who were respectively chairmen of the BMW and Daimler-Benz supervisory boards proposed that the two companies should merge (Rutherford 1974: 39). But the small shareholders of BMW joined Herbert Quandt in resisting the proposal at an unusually bitter and protracted AGM. (AGMs are normally fairly lengthy, well-attended social occasions – Vogl 1973: 57). Equally significantly, the chairman of the BMW works council (Kurt Golda) also supported Quandt. After the 1959 BMW AGM, however, the merger plans were allowed to lapse and the Quandts became key shareholders. Under the guidance of the new chief executive (Paul Hahnemann) sales rocketed – they nearly doubled between 1960 and 1963 (when the company paid its first post-war dividend), and then grew at an average annual rate of 23 per cent between 1963 and 1972. Hahnemann's marketing techniques had clearly succeeded. He had capitalised on the excellent engineering skills already at BMW. But a new chief executive was appointed by Quandt in 1969, and sales executive Hahnemann was obliged to tender his resignation to Quandt in 1971. This event

remains shrouded in mystery. His successor as chief executive (Eberhard von Kuenheim) was an engineer. He remained in office until 1993 and he enjoyed the continued support of the works council chairman until the latter retired in the late 1980s. Von Kuenheim basically concentrated on the product successfully marketed by his predecessor. In other words, BMW did not for a long period emulate the diversification of its product and plant locations introduced by VW and Daimler-Benz (see below). Indeed, in 1991 the increasing output of BMW cars began to converge very closely on the declining volume produced by Mercedes, although both manufacturers were producing well over 500,000 units per year (*Die Zeit* 14/92). In fact in 1992 BMW exceeded Mercedes' 530,000 units for the first time. A measure of the severity of the recession which hit both companies, however, is that both manufacturers had eventual annual targets of over 600,000 units. Von Kuehnheim's retirement in 1993 coincided with this serious recession which, he predicted, would cost his industry as many as 300,000 jobs (*Independent* 26 March 1993).

In the early 1990s, however, BMW broke with tradition when it also announced that it would be building an assembly plant in the USA and cooperating with Rolls-Royce in aeroengine design and production. But BMW was able to draw on VW's disastrous experience in the USA. Although VW's decision making is examined below, it can be noted here that the company purchased an unfinished Chrysler plant in Pennsylvania, inheriting a disgruntled, unionised labour force (Beaver 1992: 20). VW also installed an American management and produced body panels in West Virginia, from where they were transported by road. Product quality, normally a valuable sales promotion for VW, was also initially inferior. BMW obtained a green-field site in South Carolina which included an airport large enough to accept jumbo jets carrying parts from Bavaria (*Independent on Sunday* 9 May 1993). Like VW, BMW received generous subsidies from the Americans, including a 20-year freeze on tax payments (*Guardian* 24 June 1992). Production costs would also be lower, Japanese competition was intense, and the dollar was far stronger than it had been during the first half of the 1980s (FT 1 July 1992; also see the trade section below). In addition, start-up costs were rather less important than several qualitative factors. It also represented BMW's sole investment outside of Bavaria.

Other chief executives were appointed at an inopportune time from the point of view of their future careers. Kurt Lotz of Volkswagen was a good example. In 1968, he succeeded the legendary Professor Heinrich Nordhoff who had been appointed by the British in 1948 (Hartrich 1980: 219). Following the currency reform, VW had rapidly extended its operations in Lower Saxony (BMF *Das Industrielle* . . . 1962: 163). By 1960, when motor-vehicle production in West Germany passed the two million mark, every second vehicle exported had been produced by VW (BMF *Der Bund* . . . 1961: 163). In spite of a noticeable decline in US motor-vehicle imports, VW succeeded in raising its sales there by 25 per cent (*ibid.*). Not surprisingly, the company was seen by the Federal government, but not by its joint owner Lower Saxony, as a prime candidate for privatisation (see below). But in spite of the phenomenal success of the Beetle, Nordhoff left a narrow product range, heavily dependent on exports (Beaver 1992: 20). True, Audi was acquired in 1965, in order to move up-market. Nevertheless, the VW supervi-

sory and executive boards were at odds about future strategy. (VW is an interesting, if extreme, case. Government and union representatives occupy seats on the supervisory board. Achieving a consensus is difficult and time consuming – *ibid.*) Further, the attempt in 1969 to purchase NSU and merge it with Audi ran into opposition from minority shareholders at NSU (Vogl 1973: 58–9). Again, there were protracted AGMs, this time with legal representation and threats of law suits. All this unfavourable publicity, especially bearing in mind that VW was still 40 per cent public owned, was an important reason for Lotz's dismissal in 1971. His successor, Rudolf Leiding, had been in charge of Audi and the remaining NSU shareholders almost immediately accepted a substantially revised VW offer for their shares.

Between 1971 and 1974 Leiding introduced new models and on two occasions forced the supervisory board to dismiss colleagues on the executive board who disagreed with him. Leiding himself left in the middle of a slump in sales when VW ran up nearly DM 1 billion in losses over the two year period 1974 and 1975. He had made himself unpopular with the majority of the supervisory board, particularly when he appealed over the heads of the unions for wage restraint (*Fortune* 13 August 1979). Perhaps like Lotz before him, he had also underestimated the influence of the Federal and Lower Saxony SPD governments who were at the time both part-owners of VW (Vogl 1973: 52). (The Federal government sold its remaining holding in the 1980s – see the section on privatisation below.) Nonetheless, as Beaver puts it (1992: 21) 'Leiding forced a stagnant company to innovate.' In a relatively short period, his radical product restructuring was consummated by the marketing of the highly-successful Golf.

The abrasive Leiding was replaced by the diplomatic Toni Schmücker in 1975. Schmücker was a former Ford executive. He was forced by heart trouble to resign in 1981, although by then he had achieved Leiding's ambition to open a manufacturing base in the USA. The aim was to reduce costs in order to offset the effects of Japanese competition. Operationally, product-wise and financially the plant in the USA was not a success. Schmücker's replacement (Carl Horst Hahn) was ultimately forced to close the plant in the USA and concentrate instead on manufacturing and sales in Europe, Asia and Latin America (*ibid.*: 24). It was also necessary to resolve the problems created by the disastrous (1979) foray into office machinery by selling Triumph-Adler at a knockdown price to Olivetti (Ogger 1992: 160). There were, however, two noteworthy aspects about Hahn's appointment by the VW supervisory board. First, he was one of the members of the VW management board dismissed in 1972 by the then supervisory board on the insistence of Leiding, even though he had been at VW under Nordhoff since 1959. Second, he had subsequently been chief executive of Conti-Gummi – a tyre group which he pulled back from near bankruptcy and which was also situated mainly in Lower Saxony (see the section on mergers and acquisitions below). Shareholders there received their first dividend for eight years just prior to Hahn's re-appointment to VW, although after his departure profits fell again. This experience was correctly expected to stand him in good stead for the 1980s for, after five profitable years, VW was again almost in the red by 1981. In this sense Hahn's appointment resembled that of Schmücker, since the latter re-organised the troubled Rheinstahl company before joining VW at the time of the 1975 financial crisis. Hahn was persuaded to take the VW job by the newly-elected chairman of the VW supervisory board (Hans Birnbaum). Birnbaum was also chief executive of the then state-owned Salzgitter steel plant which was not only situated near to the main VW plant at Wolfsburg, but also gave Birnbaum links within the rationalising steel industry. Hahn attempted to lead the group through a potentially more successful phase of international expansion. The plants in Mexico, China and the former Skoda company in the Czech Republic were fairly well placed to benefit from the expected expansion of sales in those areas; even the Seat affiliate in Spain was thought to be capable of withstanding the more intense competition within the EC. But his European plans were to be drastically curtailed by his successors. Whether this was attributable to Hahn's ineptitude or the Bundesbank's credit squeeze will become clearer towards the end of the 1990s.

In January 1993, Hahn was succeeded as chief executive by Ferdinand Piëch. Again, there were similarities with previous appointments to the office of chief executive. Piëch had built up a reputation for resolute management – but this time exclusively within the VW group at Audi. He is the grandson of Ferdinand Porsche, who had invented the Beetle. His appointment was approved, of course, by the supervisory board which contained the head of IG Metall and the prime minister of Lower Saxony. The critical question was the extent to which the supervisory board would support Piëch's enforced rationalisation policies. Sales had slumped as a result of the recession in both domestic and export markets. As well as this cyclical factor, however, there were indications of structural problems in Germany. Piëch estimated that VW's production costs exceeded Japanese manufacturers' by 30 per cent (FT 28 January

1993). In March 1993, Piëch announced the appointment of a ruthless cost cutter whom he had controversially headhunted from General Motors (José Ignacio López de Arriortúa). Klaus Liesen of Ruhrgas, as chairman of the Supervisory Board, was also involved in the appointment. The move was also dramatic because VW has been shown to have a corporate culture prone to growing its management in-house. This appointment was thus as much a response to the erosion of VW's competitive base as another change in the style of corporate control. In this sense, the analysis anticipates the section on *Standort Deutschland* below. By June 1993, López had revealed his plans to build a revolutionary factory in his Basque birthplace. Suppliers would be required to provide complete modules rather than parts for assembly on a production line. New methods of producing a small car in 12 hours would be tested. Although a redundancy programme was confirmed, productivity and quality improvements in VW's existing plants were already evident. There had perhaps been one significant difference at GM over the location of López's proposed new plant. Hungary might have been preferred to Spain because labour costs were even lower. By July, however, plans for the Spanish plant had been abandoned and VW's supervisory board held an emergency meeting in August to discuss recent business developments. There were court proceedings alleging that López and senior colleagues were still in possession of confidential GM documents when they arrived at VW. The chairmen of the works councils at both VW and Opel (GM's German subsidiary) issued a plea for their managements to consider the effects of their dispute on sales and jobs. Piëch's position was undermined when he was called to account by the prime minister of Lower Saxony.

Finally, Liesen began to distance himself from both Piëch and López. (The material in English for this paragraph was extracted mainly from the *Economist* 29 May and 28 August 1993; FT 10 and 26 June; *Guardian* 15 June, 21/31 July and 5/7 August; *Independent on Sunday* 4 July; *The Times* 30 March. Readers who have German would derive further benefit from consulting the contemporaneous accounts in the German press.)

Family and foreign-owned holdings in Daimler-Benz have already been mentioned in Chapter 7. It was shown that the Deutsche Bank increased its stake in the company by purchasing the Flick holding in 1975. The intention was to prevent the Shah of Iran purchasing the Flick block of shares in Daimler. (The holding company which was later formed was dissolved in 1993 – see the mergers and acquisitions section below.) Although the Quandt family sold its shares to Kuwait, the Deutsche remained the largest shareholder. It was therefore the Deutsche's chief executive (Alfred Herrhausen) who chaired the supervisory board. He cooperated with Edzard Reuter who ultimately became Daimler's chief executive during the final phases of the company's diversification in the 1980s (see Figure 8.5). Reuter had been the preferred candidate of both the trade union and the Deutsche as early as 1983 (FT 4 May 1988). Initially, however, the chief executive's post was held by Reuter's rival (Werner Breitschwerdt) who was a trained engineer and committed to keeping Daimler, like BMW, as a manufacturer of high-quality cars – a saga reported in some depth by the *Economist* (27 April 1991; 3 June and 16 September 1989; 7 May and 12 November 1988; 12 December 1987). Breitschwerdt was forced into early retirement in 1987. Daimler continued its policy of diversification, not least in the type of car it intended producing. In early 1993, the chief executive designate of Daimler's car subsidiary Mercedes-Benz (Helmut Werner) announced that the subsidiary would be broadening its product range, pruning management, transferring assembly to Spain, South Korea and Mexico and searching for international partners, especially in components (FT 27 and 28 January 1993). A little later, in April 1993, Reuter indicated that the expected annual output of cars would fall to 486,000 – a far cry from the earlier target of 600,000. He also announced the company's intention to build a car plant in the USA. But a comparative case study of this and other decisions by Daimler appears in the section on *Standort Deutschland* below.

Having assembled the paramount features of ownership and control, the analysis can now draw some conclusions.

When it comes to the structure of companies, there is some confusion about where decision-making powers reside. Chief executives perhaps tend to be somewhat harassed, but they are certainly very busy persons. For example, Leiding is reputed to have worked ten hours a day, seven days a week in his first eighteen months at VW, while Abs of the Deutsche Bank claimed in the early 1970s that he had not taken a holiday since 1956 (Vogl 1973: 97). Rutherford (1974: 28) concludes that these types of working practice are average for West German chief executives. Perhaps understandably, they may tend to be somewhat insular, but more controversially Rutherford insists that they are not all that well informed about world affairs in general (*ibid.*). Abs' resolution of Germany's external debt problem (Chapter 1) would belie this view. Even more controversially, doubts have been cast on their efficiency (Ogger 1992; Vogl 1973: 96). On the other hand, some studies cite their educational qualifications, or even their achievements

as 'self-made men', as being highly respectable (Copeman 1971: 18–22; Engelmann 1978: 209). However, the need to import foreign executives, epitomised by the appointment of López at VW, lends some credence to Ogger's suggestions that senior German managers are in their 50s, physically fit and mentally alert, but the products of an ineffectual and conformist career path (*ibid.*: chs 3 and 6). Nevertheless, sufficient has been said in this section to indicate that lack of success tends to threaten their positions. The basic question is whether German managers became increasingly complacent as a result of undoubted past success. In short, while successful they remain highly-paid and receive extremely generous fringe benefits; in return – although shielded as far as possible – they have no claim to uninterrupted leisure time (Engelmann 1978: 102–3 and 113). It has also been shown that there is a great deal of overlap in company control. Chief executives from one company may chair the supervisory board of another company. However, cross mandates (executives from company A becoming non-executives at company B and *vice-versa*) are not permitted (Schneider-Lenné 1992: 14).

Perhaps sufficient evidence of a system favouring industrial concentration has now been assembled. How this system has operated in an anti-trust sense can therefore now be examined.

ANTI-TRUST POLICY: THE LEGAL FRAMEWORK

German law on competitive restraints has evolved separately and independently of the law on unfair competition (Heidenhain and Schneider 1991: 17). Two major statutes reflect this distinction. They are the Act against Unfair Competition (*Gesetz gegen den unlauteren Wettbewerb*

– UWG) and the Act against Restraints on Competition (*Gesetz gegen Wettbewerbsbeschränkungen* – GWB).

The UWG is generally aimed at preventing unethical business practices, whereas the GWB is intended to preserve competitive market structures (OECD 1981a: Section 2.1). There is a more rudimentary difference between the two acts, however. Originally designed to protect trader against trader, the UWG is deeply rooted in Germany's industrial history. It dates from 1909, having replaced a similar Bismarckian act of 1896. In 1980, amendments to the UWG extended its provisions to consumer protection. More generally, amendments have followed historical precedents and in this sense the UWG is similar to statutes in some other countries. For instance, misleading advertising is forbidden. Indeed, German law in principle prohibits, and is hostile to, comparative advertising (Mittelstaedt 1991: 76). In contrast, the GWB derived from US pressure after the Second World War (see below). Its provisions were intended to be revolutionary as opposed to the evolutionary nature of the UWG. In short, the GWB provides a legal framework which purports to protect competition, whereas the UWG defines the rules of competition. It will be shown that the GWB is principally enforced by the Federal Cartel Office (Bundeskartellamt – BKA), whereas the UWG is enforced directly through the courts. For example, in 1992, when Metro and Asko proposed to forge a link which would have produced one of the world's largest retail chains and rival Daimler-Benz and Siemens in turnover terms, the BKA was concerned only with the sectors in which anti-competitive market dominance would probably emerge. The proposed merger was fairly expeditiously approved when Metro-Asko gave certain undertakings, even though it left only three retail groups with about a 50 per cent market share. On the other hand, the retail trade association had been conducting a seven-and-a-half year court case against alleged unfair commercial tactics by Metro (FT 8 December 1992).

It may have already been gathered that the history of the GWB is more complex yet more relevant for policy formulation during the post-war period. More specifically, cartels of various kinds were historically legitimate in German law (Gordon 1928: 14, 23 and 139). Indeed, both the Courts and the State displayed a distrust of competition, and cartels were in some cases compulsory (Marburg 1964: 81–3). Under the 1923 Act the Minister for Economic Affairs, a supervisory agency and a Cartel Court were all given powers to intervene in the public interest and prohibit certain abusive practices of cartels and market-dominating enterprises. Such powers were never forcefully exercised and effective control of monopolistic and restrictive business practices was not achieved (Voigt 1962: 177–81; Mueller *et al*. 1981: 14; OECD 1981a: Section 0). Indeed, the 1923 Act preceded a period of strong and comprehensive concentration (Stolper *et al*. 1967: 123; Braun 1990: 49 and 50). By 1930 there were over 3,000 cartel arrangements, or, as they are classified immediately below, 'horizontal market agreements' (Berghahn 1986: 21).

When Erhard's Economic Council was asked to make legislative proposals, the decartelisation and deconcentration statutes enacted by the Western Allies were still in force (Mestmäcker 1980: 391). The aspiration of the Council and, later, the Federal Government was to legislate against the two fundamental anti-trust problems: restrictive business practices and concentration. Restrictive business practices are cartel arrangements which either involve *horizontal* collusion aimed at enforcing an agreed pricing policy within an industry and excluding new entrants, or involve *vertical* attempts to fix the prices at which an industry's goods are re-sold. Horizontal restraints are characterised by the common purpose of the parties (Hoffmann and Schaub 1983: 135). They are dealt with in the first part of the GWB. Vertical restraints are reciprocal or individual agreements. They are less homogeneous than cartel arrangements and are defined in the second part of the Act (*ibid.*). The concentration problem, on the other hand, is concerned (rarely) with pure monopoly, more frequently with market dominance and, most frequently, with oligopoly. Indeed, market dominance and oligopoly are defined fairly rigorously in Section 22 of the GWB, a section which stands at the beginning of the third part of the Act (Heidenhain and Schneider 1991: 189 and 191):

- an enterprise is market dominating . . . if it has a market share of at least one-third for a specific type of good or service
- [oligopoly conditions obtain] where either three or fewer enterprises have a combined market share of 50 per cent or more, or where five or fewer enterprises have a market share of two-thirds or more

Thus once mergers were controlled after 1973 (see below), the substantive criterion for prohibition was the expectation that the merger would result in, or strengthen, a market-dominating position (Möschel 1987: 526–7). Moreover, firms in a dominant market position may not abuse this position, an example being cutthroat pricing to drive a competitor out of the market (*ibid.*: 535 and 537). (Similarly, a restraint of competition must be

shown to be a likely influence on market conditions, rather than adopting a strict *per se* prohibition – *ibid.*: 528). Absolute market size is also a criterion under the GWB. Thus, market domination is deemed not to exist where an enterprise has a turnover of under DM 250 million. Similarly, the oligopoly assumptions do not apply where an enterprise has a turnover of under DM 100 million. Two important inferences about the nature of German pragmatism in the field of antitrust policy may be drawn from what has been said about the GWB. First, any enterprise may acquire and maintain a market dominating position from which it may derive competitive advantages in a non-abusive manner; such a position would be illegal in the USA (Heidenhain and Schneider 1991: 57). The MK proposed in 1980 that the BKA should be empowered to dissolve market-dominating enterprises, but no legislative action was taken (*ibid.*). In effect, then, the BKA must demonstrate that an enterprise is exploiting, or as a result of a merger or acquisition would be exploiting, its position in an *abusive* manner. Second, as early as the 1960s – in other words at an early stage in the Act's evolution – a notion of 'workable competition' emerged (Hoffmann and Schaub 1983: 105). The debate on the meaning of this term revolved around whether market developments could be predicted, or, alternatively, whether the current stage of a given market in terms of expansion and contraction should influence rule making.

First the Allies, and later sections of the CDU and industry, insisted that the legislators should concentrate on cartels. In effect, therefore, the GWB which, after seven years of deliberations, reached the statute book in July 1957 was a cartel-prohibition law (Marburg 1964: 92; Voigt 1962: 190). When it came into effect on 1

January 1958, however, there were a number of exemptions to horizontal agreements which considerably weakened the Act (Denton *et al.* 1968: 59; Dyas and Thanheiser 1976: 54; Voigt *ibid.*). Horizontal restrictive business practices are prohibited but renewable exemptions may be permitted by the BKA in the event of contingencies such as economic crises, rationalisation and foreign trade regulation. Basically, Section 1 of the GWB spells out the prohibition, Sections 2–7 the exemptions, while Section 8 enables the Economics Minister to override Section 1 in the public interest (Audretsch 1989: 583–8). The GWB therefore reflected its drafters' conviction that competition was not an end in itself but rather the normal means of improving efficiency and securing technological change (*ibid.*: 581–2). As the BKA confirmed, in some markets rationalisation through cooperation – that is by means of cartelisation – is preferable to free competition (*ibid.*). In both 1973 and 1983, there were over 200 legal cartels in West Germany (*ibid.*: 591). Hence, only horizontal agreements are known as 'cartels' (*Kartelle*) in German terminology (OECD 1981a: Section 2.0). Unlike the Sherman Act in the USA, the GWB does not contain a general prohibition of such arrangements (Heidenhain and Schneider 1991: 22). Further, an indication of vertical weakness of the 1957 Act was that resale price maintenance was legally protected. Finally, although the newly established BKA could control the abuse of economic power by dominant enterprises in certain specified ways, it had no powers to act against a merger which it adjudged to have an adverse effect on the structure of a market (*ibid.*: 81).

Following considerable controversy about the operation of the GWB, the Act was amended in 1965. Above all, the crude cartel-prohibition nature of the GWB

became even more evident. The incomparably more important movement in concentration was slipping completely by the BKA – as its president made abundantly clear (Voigt 1962: 199 and 200). Once again resistance within the Government's own party resulted in the continuation of resale price maintenance. However, the amended GWB contained a much more precise definition of mergers which were to be registered with the BKA, although the exemptions of certain types of cartels were extended. Taken together, the amendments modified but did not fundamentally alter the 1957 Act (Denton *et al.* 1968: 61).

But the amendments carried through by the SPD/FDP coalition in 1973 did radically change the GWB (Heidenhain and Schneider 1991: 19). Retail price maintenance was abolished, and the control by the authorities of both illegal cartels and market-dominating companies was made easier. Merger control in its present form was introduced in these amendments, the term 'merger' encompassing mergers, acquisitions of assets or holdings and other forms of affiliations between enterprises (Mueller *et al.* 1981: 69). The Monopolies Commission (Monopolkommission – MK) was also established. About this time fines were imposed by the BKA on seven breweries – DM 7 million – and seven leading enterprises in the special steels industry – DM 2.3 million – for price agreements in their respective associations (OECD 1981a: Section 3). A further amendment to the GWB in 1976 brought newspaper mergers within the scope of the Act – an issue which was to exercise the minds of the MK in a number of reports (MK III ch 3; VIII and IX ch 5).

There were further significant amendments in 1980 (Heidenhain and Schneider 1991: 19). These amendments again intensified the control of mergers and extended the scope of the pre-merger notification procedure. Finally, a fifth set of amendments which came into force in 1990 empowered the BKA to control mergers and acquisitions even where a stake of less than 25 per cent of the voting capital is procured. The only test in this latter case is whether considerable restrictive influence is exercised over the acquired enterprise (OECD *Economic Survey* 1990: 42). (Lowering this shareholding-acquisition threshold, particularly where a bank simultaneously obtained shares in the same company, was a subject of controversy within the MK – MK VI: 448–9.) Previously exempted sectors – banking, insurance, transportation and public utilities – were also brought into the scope of the Act by the 1990 amendments.

It can thus be said that the GWB gradually evolved between 1957 and 1990. During this fairly lengthy process, its provisions became by international standards both comprehensive and complex (Heidenhain and Schneider 1991: 20). The GWB's main targets are, first, cartels which set out to influence prices, levels of production and other market conditions through restraint of competition. There are a number of exceptions and a number of areas have not yet been settled by case law (*ibid.*: 27). However, recent cases suggest the willingness of the courts to extend the scope of their powers over cartels (*ibid.*). Its second and third targets are the abuse of market dominant positions and, since 1973, mergers. In 1973 resale price maintenance was also prohibited (with minor exceptions), although recommended prices are still allowed (Cable 1979: 21). In short, the large West German enterprises had lived with the doctrine of competition for barely a generation (Dyas and Thanheiser 1976: 62). It should be added, however, that Article 66 of the ECSC (Paris) treaty, as well as Articles 85

and 86 of the EEC (Rome) treaty, also deal respectively with mergers involving firms in the coal, iron and steel industries and restrictive inter-firm agreements and abuses by market-dominating firms in relation to all other products and services (Markert 1981: 294–8).

Summarising, then, anti-trust law is implemented in the first instance through the BKA whose work is based on the GWB. This work boils down to (OECD Economic Survey 1987: 58):

- prohibiting cartels and other constraints on competition (subject to certain exceptions)
- acting against the abuse of market power
- preventing mergers which create or strengthen market dominance

While the second provision has not been very effective in practice, the first and last have worked reasonably well. Indeed, a strict system of merger control is the central plank of competition regulation and the BKA's main activity. There is some empirical evidence that actions by the BKA have tended to reduce corporate profit margins in the short run, while the deterrence effect may be more limited in the longer run (*ibid.*: 65). On the other hand, it must be emphasised that mergers in Germany usually take the form of one enterprise purchasing a majority stake in another enterprise – full acquisitions are accordingly relatively rare (Franks and Mayer 1990: 196–7). Given this background, a more detailed account of the GWB can now be attempted.

ANTI-TRUST POLICY: THE OPERATION OF THE GWB

In order to gain some insights into the operation of the GWB, it is necessary to have a knowledge of the five institutions which are allocated with powers of enforcement.

First, the BKA has wide powers to investigate, search and seize documents, and question witnesses. It is mandatory to notify mergers meeting certain criteria to the BKA. Specifically:

- (i) mergers are subject to control and pre-merger notification where either one of the parties has a turnover of at least DM 2 billion, or two or more of the parties have a turnover of at least DM 1 billion each
- (ii) mergers are subject to control and post-merger notification where the parties have a combined turnover of at least DM 500 million
- (iii) mergers are subject to post-merger notification only, where the turnover thresholds in (i) or (ii) are reached and where an independently-controlled enterprise with a turnover of less than DM 50 million merges with another party, although to avoid the unimpeded acquisition of relatively small companies by large concerns from falling outside the scope of merger control, any two merging companies with respective turnovers of at least DM 4 million and DM 1 billion are subject to control
- (iv) mergers are subject to post-merger notification only, where the affected market for goods or services has been supplied for at least five years and the turnover is less than DM 10 million – such markets having been considered by the policy makers to be too small for dominant-firm influence

As would probably be expected, there is very little quantitative relationship between the reporting of mergers subject to control, and mergers where notification only was required. For example, in 1981, a total of 618 mergers were reported to the

BKA, 214 of which were in the 'notification only' category; the respective statistics for 1989 were 1,414 and 269 (BT *Drucksache* 12/847: 10). (Later data were affected by the Treuhand's privatisation activities.) Nonetheless, in carrying out its duties, the BKA exercises a *quasi*-judicial function, imposing prohibitions and fines where it deems such action necessary. Its biennial reports appear during each year ending with an odd number, whereas the MK's appear every even year. The MK regularly consults with the BKA as, for example, the *Vorwort* to the MK's ninth biennial report made clear.

Second, as already seen in Chapter 7, the MK publishes opinions on the development of concentration and competitive structures. It consists of five independent advisers and the titles of its biennial reports are indicative of its findings:

- More Competition is Possible (MK I)
- Continuing Concentration among Large Enterprises (MK II)
- Merger Control remains a Top Priority (MK III)
- Progress in the Measurement of Concentration (MK IV)
- Economic Criteria in the Application of Anti-Trust Legislation (MK V)
- General Economic Opportunities and Risks Associated with the Increasing Enterprise Size (MK VI)
- Extending the Framework of Competition (MK VII)
- Competition Policy Facing New Challenges (MK VIII)
- Competition Policy versus Industrial Policy (MK IX)

The Commission's clearest concern is the erosion of competition – an essential feature of the SME. Nonetheless, in view of the postulated advantages of concentration – economies of scale and international competitiveness – perhaps the basic dilemma facing anti-trust enforcement agencies, especially the Ministry of Economics, was best brought out by the title of the ninth report. A great deal of emphasis is therefore placed on these factors below. Moreover, it will be shown in this chapter that privatisation, regulation and subsidies form an equally important part of industrial policy. Their effects on competition policy have been subject to a series of wide-ranging debate.

Third, the first court of appeal against the decisions of the BKA is the Berlin court of appeal (*Kammergericht*). This court reconsiders both the legal and the factual basis of the Office's decisions. Fourth, the next stage of appeal (the Federal Supreme Court – *Bundesgerichtshof* – BGH) is also the highest instance of legal appeal in West Germany. At this fourth level, however, appeals are considered on points of law only. In both cases, the courts contribute to the clarification and evolution of German anti-trust law – a feature which delineates Germany from the rest of the EC.

Finally, in the case of an appeal against a merger prohibition, the Federal Minister of Economics may also become involved. As the merger will already have been prohibited by the BKA, he is required to first request a special report from the MK. Thus the Minister has over the years investigated several cases and approved appeals on the following grounds (Baur 1980: 460): the safeguarding of the petroleum supplies – Gelsenberg/VEBA; safeguarding energy provision – VEBA/ BP; the maintenance of employment – textile machinery manufacturer Artos/ Deutsche Babcock; the preservation of technical potential – Hüller/Thyssen; international competitiveness in, and the domestic supply of, aluminium products – VAW/Kaiser. In the case of VEBA and VAW companies were involved which

were at the time partly state-owned. The classic case, however, was Daimler-Benz/ MBB merger in 1989. Daimler had already (in 1985) taken at least controlling interests in AEG, MTU and Dornier. (In the case of MTU, Daimler raised its holding to 100 per cent by buying out MAN's 50 per cent joint-venture share. In 1990, AEG made a negative 8.8 per cent return on its equity capital, although members of the executive board each received DM 1.2 million – Ogger 1992: 97). During the 1980s this takeover activity thus transformed Daimler into a conglomerate covering motor vehicles, electrical products and aerospace (see Figure 8.5). In the early 1990s, Daimler added the Dutch Fokker company to its aerospace group, thus making it Europe's largest concern in this field (*Die Zeit* 31 July 1992).

The BKA vetoed the takeover of MBB on competition grounds, but the Bonn government supported the move on the grounds that it would no longer be necessary to provide public support for the Airbus. Another justification for the approval given by the Economics Ministry was that Germany's technological independence would be increased. In both its special and biennial reports, the MK supported the BKA's opposition to many of the mergers cited immediately above. However, the decision by the BKA not to prohibit the Daimler-Benz/AEG merger, caused the MK to doubt whether the GWB 'in its present form' provided sufficient control over large mergers (MK VI: 450). The MK added that large conglomerate mergers were questionable in terms of both competition and social policy (*ibid.*). Moreover, a majority decision by the MK to support in principle the Daimler/MBB merger brought about the resignation of its then chairman. As well as dissenting on the grounds that competition would be fundamentally distorted, he contended (FT 4 August 1989) that:

. . . the MK appeared to reflect developments within Germany and at the EC under which state interference with the economy was becoming increasingly accepted

There was thus the type of combined reference to competition and industrial policies described in the Introduction to this Chapter. Nonetheless, the Minister has generally made his approval of mergers subject to certain restrictions and conditions (Mueller *et al.* 1981: 99). As

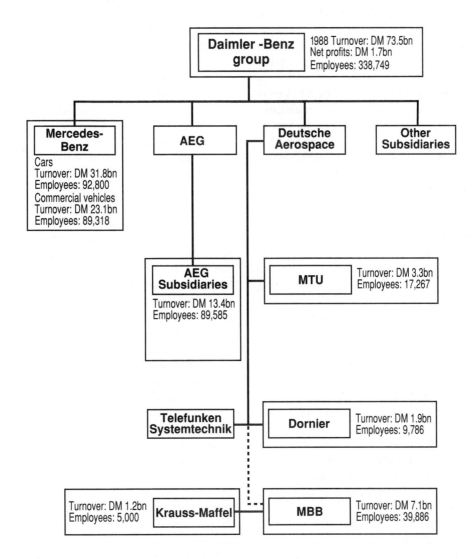

Figure 8.5 Growth of Daimler-Benz in the 1980s

Source: FT 13 September 1989 (1988 figures)

Baur (1980: 461) points out, this gives the Minister the opportunity to mould the areas of activity of large enterprises according to his own ideas.

But the salient point here, as Tillotson (1980: 65–6) lucidly argues, is that the finer points of national merger law give way to the economic facts of life. He cites the Karstadt and Neckermann merger. Karstadt was the largest departmental store in West Germany, indeed in Europe, while Neckermann before the merger was the third largest mail order retail company and the second largest operator of package tours (Markert 1981: 309). The BKA took the view that Karstadt, together with three other major department stores, had to be regarded as a market-dominating oligopoly that was likely to be strengthened by the acquisition of a major mail order retail firm. However, it accepted that Neckermann was in such a critical financial state that only the merger with Karstadt would avoid bankruptcy and save the jobs of Neckermann's 19,000 employees. The BKA saw that for it to go through the process of first prohibiting the merger only for the Minister to later approve it on the grounds of overriding national interest would in practice have meant that the rescue of Neckermann would have come too late.

In comparing the Karstadt/Neckermann case with the abortive attempt by GKN to take over Sachs (see below), Tillotson (ibid.) concludes that although Karstadt was the largest department store in Europe, it was German-owned; GKN, on the other hand, was not German-owned and Sachs did not require rescuing. But Karstadt did not bring Neckermann's losses to an immediate halt. By 1982, losses had reached DM 400 million (Die Zeit, 47/82). Moreover, the Metro-Asko case which was cited above bore certain similarities to the Karstadt/Neckermann issue. Asko had acquired the loss-making Co-op group in 1989 and was predicted to be running into severe financial problems by 1992 (FT 8 December 1992). In effect, the BKA must have realised that the Minister would allow Metro to save jobs by approving the takeover. Hence, the BKA required the two companies to sell stores with a total turnover of DM 1.2 billion in return for its approval. (The combined group's turnover was DM 60 billion – ibid.)

Nonetheless, it is necessary to keep a sense of perspective. Between 1973 and 1989 a total of 10,849 mergers were notified to the BKA (Heidenhain and Schneider 1991: 82). Only 90 of these mergers were prohibited by the BKA, but almost all these decisions were appealed (ibid.). Less than half became ultimately effective. Moreover, a private communication in the possession of the author indicates that there were almost 3,000 mergers examined by the BKA in 1989 and 1990, about 500 of which were not subject to control. From the balance of 2,500 mergers over which it had jurisdiction, the BKA prohibited only eighteen. The parties involved appealed against thirteen of the prohibitions. The Kammergericht upheld the majority of the BKA's prohibitions, although where cases were further appealed to the BGH, the BKA successfully defended only about half of its decisions. Ministerial intervention is a relatively rare occurrence. For example, Woolcock et al. (1991: 12) point out that the Minister had invoked these reserve powers on only seven occasions 'since 1973'. In any case, the BKA examines a constant flow of merger casework. About 95 per cent of its case load is cleared within one month. The remainder is subjected to fuller scrutiny which may last up to one year. During these detailed investigations, the parties frequently give undertakings which enable the merger to be cleared. Alternatively, parties often informally submit and discuss merger proposals which they feel may not receive BKA approval; such consultations are not included in the official notification statistics (Heidenhain and Schneider 1991: 82).

At the end of the 1970s, the Federal Government, the MK and the BKA all shared the view that it had proved impossible to stop the growth of concentration, particularly as a result of mergers involving large and very large enterprises. Two types of cases were involved (Baur 1980: 445). First, mergers as such between large and very large enterprises. The two classic mergers of the early 1970s were the purchase of considerable holdings in Rheinstahl by August-Thyssen and, similarly, Mannesmann's purchase of a 51 per cent stake in Demag (Vogl 1973: 232 and 241). In both cases, this represented a merging of steel and engineering interests in the Ruhr (Rutherford 1974: 44). The other type of merger involved financially powerful and large enterprises purchasing small and medium sized firms in order to penetrate new markets. The forward integration of chemical firms into the lacquer and dye industry was one example (Baur ibid.).

An example of the trend in merger control is the case involving the British-owned multinational Guest, Keene & Nettlefolds Ltd (GKN) and the German family-owned Sachs AG. There were many side-issues involved, not least the implications of further foreign intervention and the behaviour of the Sachs family. Of relevance here, however, are the processes by which decisions were made and the implications of the case for merger control, although matters were confused by the fact that the proposed merger was supranational in character.

Hence, Tillotson (1980: 47–53) demonstrates that by late 1975 GKN had applied for the necessary consents to the merger from all the appropriate authorities: the UK Office of Fair Trading, the BKA and the European Commission. As the merger involved products falling within the sphere of the ECSC, the European Commission was charged with dual control jurisdiction under both the ECSC and EEC treaties. In view of the absence of Sachs from British markets, the UK authorities did not consider the case relevant; the EEC thought that competition would not be appreciably affected, while the ECSC authorised the proposed merger under Article 66. It was the BKA which opposed the merger. The GKN/Sachs case therefore merits a little more discussion.

In 1975, GKN declared its intention of eventually obtaining a 75 per cent holding in Sachs. GKN's product range included motor vehicle components and it already held a stake in the West German transmission manufacturer Uni-Cardan. Sachs was part-owner of Fichtel & Sachs which supplied 80 per cent of the West German clutch market. GKN's steel-making division would have been in a position to supply the processing undertakings of the Sachs group with the finished and semi-finished steel products which Sachs previously bought on the open market (ibid.: 43). In addition, GKN's reliance on a vulnerable UK car market (with less than half the output of the West German industry) would have been reduced and Sachs' turnover would have more than doubled GKN's existing Uni-Cardan business in West Germany. Finally, the executive board at Sachs were re-assured by the excellent relationship between GKN and Uni-Cardan.

But in May 1976 (two months before the ECSC and EEC announced their decisions) the BKA issued a prohibition order. The grounds were that the proposed merger was contrary to the GWB since it would lead to a strengthening of a dominant position through an accretion of financial power. GKN appealed to the Berlin high court and, as an indication of its determination, purchased a 24.98 per cent stake in Sachs. Sachs' profits were high at the time and the chairman of GKN moved on to their supervisory board. After the Berlin court had upheld GKN's appeal, the BKA appealed to the BGH. This time the (1978) ruling went in favour of the Office, so GKN appealed to the Economics Minister. However, before the Minister reached a decision, GKN withdrew its application. After selling its shares in Sachs to the Commerzbank, GKN increased its Uni-Cardan holding to over 80 per cent. Notice how GKN observed the German practice, disposing of its 25 per cent stake to a bank rather than offering them to the public via the stock exchange. Deals like this, that is transactions outside the stock exchange system, lower the public image of the exchanges (Stonham 1982: 114). In 1980 the then state-owned Salzgitter steel works was seriously interested in Sachs – although by now the profits picture had deteriorated badly. Sachs was ultimately acquired by Mannesmann in 1987 (MK VIII: 185–6). Ogger (1992: 159) rightly questions the wisdom of this acquisition, especially as it marked part of the five-year process which saw Mannesmann's turnover increase by a half, but its profits plummet. The *Economist* (9 July 1988) thought that the opposition to the GKN bid mounted by the BKA was based 'on narrow, technical grounds', whereas the BKA maintained that the 'Europeanisation' of the market subsequent to the GKN offer meant that Mannesmann did not acquire a dominant market position (FAZ 30 April 1987). Significantly, the

Economist (*ibid*.) added that 'the spirit of 1992 would almost certainly tip the balance the other way today'.

Yet the 1980s opened with the successful completion of a merger between two other British and West German companies – that is between Pilkington Brothers and Flachglas AG, West Germany's largest glass maker. Pilkington's motivation had been similar to that of GKN's: West Germany's economic growth rate was still expected to be much faster than Britain's and expansion within the European glass market had been a formally stated tenet of Pilkington's policy since the early 1970s (FT 12 March 1982). Following a hearing in Berlin and other investigations, the BKA approved the purchase by Pilkington of a 62 per cent stake in Flachglas. The only condition – which proved fortuitous for Pilkington's – was that the British company should abandon its plans to purchase an ailing pair of Belgium-Dutch glass companies. There were two differences from the abortive merger efforts of GKN and Sachs, however. First, the highly profitable Flachglas was already foreign owned – by the French BSN group. Second, at the end of the 1970s GKN turnover (£1.8 billion) was about six times that of Sachs, while Pilkington's (£629 million) amounted to only around three times that of Flachglas. A somewhat more tenuous link between the two cases is that the controversial chief executive of Fichtel & Sachs – Dr Walter Trux – became head of Flachglas in 1981. Why, then, did the GKN/Sachs proposed merger fail?

Undoubtedly, the GKN/Sachs case arose at a time when mergers and the consequent process of concentration seemed to be getting out of hand. It is important to emphasise the reasoning behind the authorities' decisions. The decisive point to the Office was that the merger

would have given Fichtel & Sachs sufficient financial strength to prevent newcomers from entering the market or to
deter competitors (Baur 1980: 447). Put
another way, the BKA was seeking to distinguish between actual and potential
competition (Tillotson 1980: 59). Further,
GKN's strong market positions in other
fields of motor component manufacture
would bolster Sachs' dominant market
position still further. The Berlin appeal
court, in attempting to emphasise the crucial test of trade restraint, criticised the
Office for its distrust of size alone. For its
part, the MK pointed out that the appeal
court was making the assumption that
enterprises may be so big that their market
position could not be further strengthened. In effect, this meant that the largest enterprises would escape any control
of mergers (Baur 1980: 448).

When the BGH published its written
judgement it stressed that potential competitive forces were already rather weak
because of the significant advantage possessed by Sachs. If the merger were
allowed, these forces would disappear
completely as a result of the increase in
financial power and the consolidation of
related markets (*ibid.*: 449). However, as
Baur correctly argues (p.450), this meant
that restraint of trade was no longer the
major test but rather the structure and size
of the acquiring enterprise – characteristics independent of the particular market
situation. In fact in affirming the BKA and
reversing the Appeal Court, the BGH
went as far as to assert (Markert 1981: 307;
Tillotson 1980: 57 – emphases added) that:

. . . the *highly conglomerate* and financially very powerful first party, . . . is
active in the *vicinity* of the market to the
overall extent of 40 per cent.

As Tillotson (*ibid.*) argued, however, it
was doubtful whether GKN could be de-

fined as 'highly conglomerate'. Indeed,
conglomerates as such were hardly known
at that juncture in West Germany (Dyas
and Thanheiser 1976: 90). The transmu-
tation of Daimler-Benz in the 1980s was
another matter. Moreover, in its WMF/
Rheinmetall judgement a few years later,
the BGH departed from its GKN/Sachs
decision, a development welcomed by the
MK for the following reason (MK VI: 449
– emphasis added):

. . . the *market proximity* of the merger
partner gives no indication of the probability of the use of financial power in the
markets in which the acquired company
operates.

In spite of the fact that the West
German economy has been dominated by
large firms and cartels for a century, the
significance of the GKN/Sachs case was
that it was found to influence legislators
when debating the 1980 amendments.
Three factors consequently now lead to a
presumption that a merger has created or
strengthened a dominant market position.
First, a proposed merger of the GKN/
Sachs type where an enterprise with a DM
2 billion turnover in its previous financial
year, attempts to take over an enterprise
which has a market dominating position in
one or several markets in which its aggregate turnover exceeded DM 150 million
(Mueller *et al.* 1981: 87 and 159). Second,
where an enterprise with a DM 2 billion
turnover attempts to take over an enterprise operating in a market in which small
and medium-sized businesses together
hold a two-thirds share of the market, and
the merging enterprises would subsequently control a 5 per cent share of that
market. Third, where large enterprises
with a collective turnover of DM 12 billion, at least two of which each have a
turnover of DM 1 billion, propose to
merge.

These size criteria were added to the market-share criteria of the 1973 amendment. These latter criteria had defined market domination as, first, a single enterprise having a market share of one-third (Mueller *et al.* 1981: 145). Second, in the case of three or fewer enterprises, the share is 50 per cent, while for five or fewer the share is two-thirds. The cartel authorities thus do not have the power to dissolve market-dominating enterprises; they simply use the criteria to prohibit abuses and, in some cases, mergers (*ibid.*: 47). Moreover, a legal presumption in no way proves that a position of market dominance in fact exists (Baur 1980: 453).

Although merger control dates only from the 1973 amendments of the GWB, it soon became evident that the minimum size threshold for exemption from merger control (DM 50 million turnover) was pitched on the high side. In consequence, large enterprises found that it was possible to avoid reporting certain mergers by acquiring small firms in markets formerly dominated by small and medium-sized enterprises (Mueller *et al.* 1981: 85). This led to a severe deterioration in the competitive structure of these markets, since between 1973 and 1979, 1,390 out of a total of 3,388 notified mergers were covered by this exemption. Hence the 1980 amendments included a rider to the DM 50 million exemption. This was to the effect that control could be exercised if an enterprise with a turnover of more than DM 4 million is taken over by an enterprise having a turnover greater than DM 1 billion.

Other provisions aimed at preventing circumvention were also included in the 1980 amendments to the GWB. For example, the acquisition of shares in another enterprise is now held to constitute a merger if the acquired shares, together with the shares already held,

equal either 25 per cent or 50 per cent of the voting capital. In other words, there are now two separate share thresholds which could conceivably apply to a company acquiring first 25 per cent and then later up to 50 per cent of another company. Further, even if the acquired shares do not reach 25 per cent of voting rights, but the acquiring enterprise is granted an agreement effectively giving it such control, then a merger is considered to have taken place. Similar provisions apply to interlocking directorates. However, the acquisition of shares by a bank does not constitute a merger if the bank acquires the shares with the intention of selling the shares in the market, does not exercise any voting rights with respect to the shares, and sells them within one year of the acquisition (Mueller *et al.* 1981: 76). In fact, because of explicit exemptions in the GWB, its provisions applied mainly to manufacturing industry and mining (Cable 1979: 23). As shown in the last section, however, the 1990 amendments widened the scope of the Act.

A lot of what has been said tends to imply that intervention by the authorities, particularly in the merger field, came too late to prevent a re-emergence of concentration. A central hypothesis of the previous chapter was that a similar degree of concentration in banking also re-emerged. During the debate in the run up to EC 1993, however, it was a mergers-control model activated by a turnover threshold and enforced by a separate and politically independent authority which was strongly advocated by the Germans (Woolcock *et al.* 1991: 17 and 19). Hence, in September 1990 a new EC regulation gave the Commission authority to monitor mergers between companies where combined global turnover exceeds ECU 5 billion; prior notification of an intention to merge is required, copious information must be given and fines may be imposed for non-observance (Owen and Dynes 1992: 168). But it is now time to look at trends in business concentration throughout the period 1950–90.

FACTORS CONDUCIVE TO GROWTH AND CONCENTRATION

In considering the process of diversification among the top 100 enterprises in West German industry, Dyas and Thanheiser (1976: ch 7) distinguish three groups of companies. Their methodology is followed here. Since their analysis is confined to the period 1950–70, however, it is supplemented with a commentary on the subsequent period. First, there was a somewhat surprisingly large group of low diversifiers. Second, there was a group of post-war diversifiers. Third, there was a group of companies which were traditionally diversified.

A great majority of the low diversifiers were in industries where the conditions for diversification were generally unfavourable. By far the largest number of enterprises (23 out of 39) in this group were in capital-intensive areas such as steel, oil and motor vehicles. Also included here was Ruhrkohle which was formed in 1968 from 20 coal mining companies because of the critical state of the coal industry. This problem of over-production in coal plagued most major steel companies since they had vertically integrated coal mining into their company structure. On the other hand, some of the industries in this group experienced very fast growth – motor vehicles, electrical engineering and household appliances, for example. In the case of the latter two industries there were also apparently good opportunities for diversification. In size, the enterprises in this group ranged from

some of the very largest of the top 100 industrial concerns (VW, Daimler-Benz and Thyssen) to the smallest.

The post-war diversifiers represented the smallest of the three groups at 29 companies of the top 100. Although differing somewhat from the previous group, there was some overlap: half of them were in either the heavy industries, or those with limited possibilities for technological transfers. The other half were in electrical, mechanical and chemical engineering. A dozen West German-owned companies diversified into technologically-related fields. Among them were three major steel producers – Mannesmann, Rheinstahl and Hoesch. Mannesmann's post-war history is typical of many West German companies: the imposition of Allied deconcentration; the reconstruction of former links and scopes, followed by horizontal expansion by merger or joint ventures with (or acquisitions of) competitors. One such joint venture by the Mannesmann group was with Thyssen, its major competitor in steel tubes. Another enterprise of particular interest in this group of post-war diversifiers is the family-owned Oetker concern. This enterprise diversified into both industry and brewing during the post-war era. Bosch also diversified.

A number of features of these post-war diversifiers should be emphasised. Above all, the post-war diversification strategies of West German companies in this group, while obviously broadening the scope of the enterprise concerned, rarely fundamentally changed their characteristic features. Technological relatedness was the predominant factor. Diversification, it is important to add, was accompanied by horizontal and vertical integration. The most prominent examples of this were the big steel companies, which had been forcibly deconcentrated after the Second World War. Diversification did not become an important strategic priority to most of them until well after a decade of efforts to re-establish vertical links and horizontal scope.

An outstanding feature of the third group (traditionally diversified enterprises) is that it includes many of the world-famous names of West German industry. Companies such as Krupp, Siemens, Bayer and Zeiss all enter the analysis.

Bayer is, of course, one of the big three chemical groups – the other two being BASF and Hoechst. Although deconcentrated by the Allies, all three companies have displayed a process of forward integration. By the end of the 1970s, however, these three international giants were plagued by over-capacity, falling demand and oil price rises – something they had in common with the rest of the world's chemical industry. Their joint market shares are quite sizeable.

Similarly, in electrical engineering Siemens shared a market leadership with AEG for most of the period under review. Both companies originally had the major part of their capacity in Berlin. During the 1950s AEG concentrated on re-building its capacity within West Germany, whereas Siemens was already expanding its international and technological strength. AEG, as already shown in Chapter 7, was rather heavily orientated towards the production of consumer goods – a factor which was to contribute to the deterioration in its financial position during the 1970s. This was because of intensifying Japanese competition. Siemens grew almost entirely from internal expansion, while AEG considered both acquisition (latterly abroad as well as at home), and collaborative ventures of equal strategic value (also see Vogl 1973: 239). Ironically enough, AEG's venture into nuclear power with Siemens was also

a loss-making operation. In 1978 Siemens bought out AEG's stake (and losses) in Kraftwerk-Union, the nuclear company in question. Hence, at the end of the 1970s, Siemens was a multinational, relatively profitable giant, while AEG was a loss-making albatross with holdings all over the world. However, even Siemens announced redundancies and slightly smaller profits in 1981.

Both of these electrical giants were involved in diversification strategies during the 1980s. As seen in Figure 8.5, AEG became part of the Daimler-Benz conglomerate. It thus became part of what at the time was one of Europe's financially strongest groupings. Siemens possessed even larger liquid reserves. In 1990, it acquired Nixdorf computers which consolidated its position as Germany's largest private-sector employer. A year earlier, it had joined GEC in acquiring Plessey. Both AEG and Siemens were also involved in mergers in the household-appliance industry. An overview of this process can be gleaned from Figure 8.6. It should be added that Electrolux acquired a 10 per cent stake in AEG in 1992.

A slight digression on AEG's economic problems is in order at this stage. This is because of the insights it provides into the adjustment strategies of West German industry. Another company facing adjustment difficulties – significantly in the entertainment electronics business – was that of Grundig. Although this latter company fits into the Dyas and Thanheiser 'low diversifier' category, it will be well worth considering its problems with those of AEG at this juncture. The reason is that Max Grundig also felt beleaguered by Japanese competition. Indeed, as Dyas and Thanheiser point out (1976: 70–80), declining margins in entertainment electronics may have contributed to

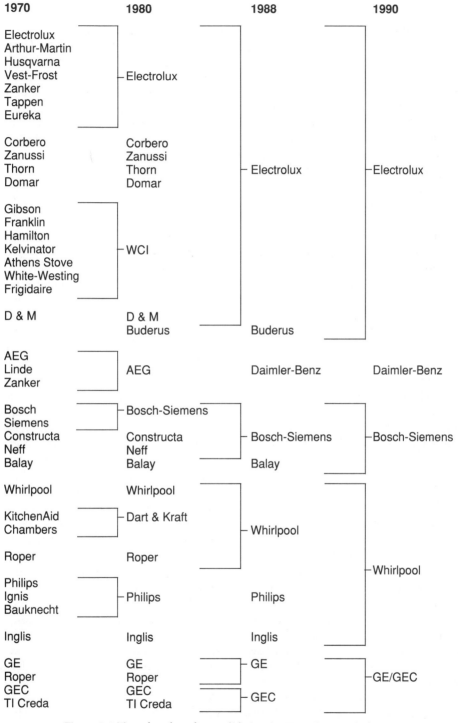

1970	1980	1988	1990

Electrolux
Arthur-Martin
Husqvarna
Vest-Frost
Zanker
Tappen
Eureka

Electrolux

Corbero
Zanussi
Thorn
Domar

Corbero
Zanussi
Thorn
Domar

Electrolux

Electrolux

Gibson
Franklin
Hamilton
Kelvinator
Athens Stove
White-Westing
Frigidaire

WCI

D & M

D & M
Buderus

Buderus

AEG
Linde
Zanker

AEG

Daimler-Benz

Daimler-Benz

Bosch
Siemens
Constructa
Neff
Balay

Bosch-Siemens

Constructa
Neff
Balay

Bosch-Siemens

Bosch-Siemens

Whirlpool

Whirlpool

KitchenAid
Chambers

Dart & Kraft

Whirlpool

Roper

Roper

Whirlpool

Philips
Ignis
Bauknecht

Philips

Philips

Inglis

Inglis

Inglis

GE
Roper
GEC
TI Creda

GE
Roper
GEC
TI Creda

GE

GEC

GE/GEC

Figure 8.6 Two decades of consolidation in West German industry
Source: FT 24 June 1992

Grundig's decision to abandon his diversification programme as early as the 1960s.

One of the major economic preoccupations in the 1980s was bound to be a search for a solution to AEG's problems. In Chapter 7 it was seen that the banks became large creditors. The Dresdner faced the largest losses, but the Deutsche Bank, Commerzbank, together with the Westdeutsche and Hessische Landesbanken, had all made large loans to AEG. In the 1970s, a succession of three chief executives were appointed and the Dresdner Bank's chief executive was the chairman of AEG's supervisory board. The government granted emergency financial aid in 1982 and further help was requested. At this juncture, other companies were considering take-overs of wholly-owned AEG subsidiaries, or existing partners were invited to extend their holdings. For example, Grundig, along with a bank consortium, were considering the purchase of AEG's television and radio company; similarly, the British company GEC, and later United Technologies of the USA, were at one time seen as possible partners in the electronics components division; Electrolux of Sweden was already considering the possibility of acquiring AEG's household appliances company (see Figure 8.2 and the surrounding discussion); the AEG Communications systems division was expected to become part of new telecommunications grouping owned by Robert Bosch and Mannesmann. In other words, the strategy was to hive off loss-making consumer goods divisions, and then become a smaller and more specialised undertaking based on the apparently more viable capital goods business. New capital would have to be attracted and this would in turn require the confidence of new investors. But in the early 1980s the holding company (AEG-Telefunken AG) – which was the main financing vehicle for the group – had debts to West German banks of DM 3 billion, unfunded pension liabilities of DM 2.6 billion and trade creditors of DM 1.7 billion. Application had been made to the courts to write down unsecured claims by 60 per cent. Following some rationalisation, Daimler-Benz ultimately assumed control in 1985 (Figure 8.5).

It was also intensifying Japanese competition in the consumer goods field which ultimately forced Max Grundig to offer a 75.5 per cent share in his company to the state-owned French electrical goods manufacturer Thomson Brandt (*Der Spiegel*, 48/82). Thomson Brandt was the second largest European company in this field, although it was ahead of Daimler-Benz and British Aerospace in defence electronics. It had originally been formed – along with its counterparts in the UK (GEC) and Germany (AEG) – to exploit the Thomson-Houston electricity patents. The largest company – Philips Eindhoven – already held an 18.7 per cent stake in Grundig (MK IV: para. 438). Significantly, Thomson Brandt lay not only behind Phillips but, at an international level, behind the world's two largest electrical concerns: Japan's Matsushita and Hitachi. Of equal significance is the fact that Max Grundig was reported as saying that his company, with a turnover of DM 3.5 billion, was far too small to withstand Japanese competition (*Die Zeit*, 48/82, 23). Further, both the French company and Grundig had been making losses, and only the fact that Thomson Brandt was state-owned enabled this French giant to find sufficient funds to make an offer for Grundig (*Der Spiegel*, 48/82; *Die Zeit*, 48/82). The proposed deal was, however, vetoed by the BKA. Grundig himself saw an increase in the Phillips' stake as a poor alternative, but he was permitted by the

BKA to allow the Dutch company to increase its stake in Grundig AG. More than 60 per cent of the capital was retained by the Grundig family, although the company's founder concentrated on his hotel interests until his death in 1989.

Having examined the nature of both AEG's and Grundig's problems, it is now possible to return to the Dyas and Thanheiser 'traditional diversifiers' category.

Also among the traditional diversifiers were family enterprises of the Ruhr. They can be divided into two groups. One pattern consisted of iron and steel manufacture as the point of departure, followed by backward vertical integration into coal mining and forward integration into mechanical engineering. Krupp, Thyssen and Haniel more or less followed this route. It was seen in the last section that this process also culminated with two massive mergers in the early 1970s, both of which involved the post-war diversifiers of Mannesmann and Rheinstahl. When steel output slumped at the end of the 1970s it was significantly the companies which had diversified most (Thyssen and Mannesmann) which avoided heavy losses. Krupp and Hoesch were obliged to merge their loss-making crude-steel capacity into a new company (Ruhrstahl AG), although the newly-founded company may have been undermined by proposals to merge the high-grade steel-making interests of Krupp and Thyssen. Ironically, at the end of the 1960s, Thyssen had made counter-proposals which prevented the merging of the steel interests of Hoesch and Mannesmann (*Die Zeit*, 36/82). As a result Hoesch spent a period of the 1970s in an unsuccessful venture with the Dutch steel firm Hoogovens. Hoesch was finally taken over by Krupp in 1991 (see below). The implications of this takeover are illuminating – see the section on mergers and acquisitions. Klöckner – the least diversified of West Germany's steel companies – did not pay a dividend after 1974, although at the beginning of the 1980s it was trying its utmost to diversify out of steel making. It eventually applied for an 'equalisation' hearing in 1992 (see the corporate finance section in Chapter 7). Moreover, Salzgitter was also involved in loss-making shipbuilding until its preparation for privatisation (see below). This state-owned enterprise had also to contend with the double disadvantage of its uneconomic home-ore based plant which until unification was located near the frontier-corridor. It was privatised in 1989, with Preussag taking a majority stake (MK IX: 195, 199 and 225; also see Table 8.5). Finally, the ailing steel company in the Saarland was financially restructured after being taken over by a French concern; it became Dillinger Hütte Saarstahl AG, falling from 36th to 45th place in *Die Zeit*'s listing between 1990 and 1991 (*Die Zeit* 34/92; MK IX: 196).

The other pattern of development began in the iron and steel trade. It involved Klöckner and Otto Wolff. Klöckner was broken up during the post-war deconcentration process, and was reformed by the family. As already seen, however, Klöckner remained heavily dependent on steel production. By 1970, however, it far exceeded its pre-war size in manufacturing as well as trading activities. Thereafter, the company ran into difficulties and was broken down by the banks into independent steel, engineering and trading divisions. (Reference was made to the financial deterioration of these companies in the corporate finance section of Chapter 7.) Wolff was not quite so important in absolute size. One family that did not fare so well was the Stimnes. Their mining and trading operations were taken over by VEBA, the rapidly expanding group which was completely privatised in 1989 (see Table 8.5).

MERGERS AND ACQUISITIONS

If investigations into the trend in mergers since the introduction of the GWB in 1958 are based on the statistics issued by the BKA, there will be a number of reasons for treating the findings with caution. First, reporting requirements were fairly precisely defined only after the 1965 amendment. This effectively meant that before 1967 the series is seriously incomplete. Second, legal and procedural changes in the 1973 and 1976 amendments make the preceding data not strictly comparable. After 1973 in particular the coverage was extended (Cable *et al*. 1980a: 101).

Nevertheless, it is clear even from these data that there has been a significant rise in merger activity since 1958. This statement is substantiated by Figure 8.7, in which the BKA data are reproduced. Even when allowance is made for an extension in reporting requirements, Figure 8.7 also indicates that there was an increase in merger activity in 1969–72. Such a surge was more or less contemporaneous with merger booms in the USA, Britain and elsewhere, which is suggestive of common underlying causal factors prompting mergers rather than the vagaries of statistical reporting (Bannock 1976: 56; Cable *et al*. 1980a: 101). Merger activity over the period 1968–91 also seems to be related to economic growth. This cyclical tendency is also supported by the insolvencies reported in Figure 8.7. Moreover, Figure 8.7 confirms the further increase in merger activity leading up to the 1980 amendments. It was shown in the last section that this latter increase was brought about mainly by large firms acquiring small

firms in markets previously dominated by the latter. Again, this level of merger activity was not disproportionate by international standards (Cable 1979: 10). Finally, preparation for EC 1993 and more general precautionary moves against international competition may have played a role in the dramatic increase in mergers during the period leading up to the 1990 amendments.

Cable (1979: 13–14) found that during the period 1958–77 there had been an increase in the proportion of mergers taking place outside the industrial sector. Within the industrial sector, however, mergers were heavily concentrated in a small number of industries. In descending order of merger incidence the top six industries for the period as a whole were chemical products, electrical engineering, machine tools, iron and steel, mineral oil products and food processing. These findings coincide with those of Dyas and Thanheiser (1976: ch 7) and Kaufer (1977: 81–2). Cable *et al*.. (1980a: 110–12) also confirm other aspects of earlier findings. In both the industrial and non-industrial sectors the majority of mergers were horizontal – that is between firms in the same industrial category. However, mineral oil showed an outstanding tendency towards forward vertical integration into commercial activities, while, to a lesser extent, the iron and steel industry was also involved in this activity. These industries were followed, at some distance, by motor vehicles, electrical goods and chemicals. But the results of statistical testings for alternative merger causes and effects in West Germany did not suggest significant community gains (Cable *et al*. 1980b: 245).

Moreover, it has been shown that the process of diversification and mergers which preceded the 1973 amendments to the GWB resulted in a high degree of concentration. In fact, before the GWB

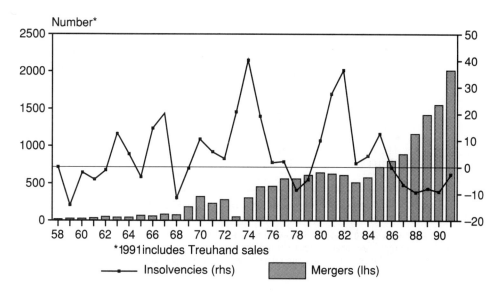

Figure 8.7 Mergers and insolvencies in West Germany

Sources: IW *Zahlen*; BK *Jahresberichte*

came into force in 1958, many of the pre-war enterprises were again as concentrated as they had ever been. These trends in concentration were accompanied by a phenomenal growth in output. Hence, overall industrial concentration undoubtedly rose during the post-war period as a whole. Between 1950 and 1970 the top 100 enterprises' share of total industrial turnover increased from about one-third to over one-half (Dyas and Thanheiser 1976: 101). In view of what has been said about the increase in mergers during the 1970s and 1980s, it will not be surprising to learn that concentration continued to increase. Hence, Table 8.4 demonstrates that by 1980 the top 50 enterprises' share of total industrial turnover was almost a half. By 1989 this proportion was over 54 per cent. Whether a simple merger count (Figure 8.7) or the share of turnover (Table 8.4) best captures the impact of mergers on competition depends not just on the absolute size of the merging firms, but also on size relative to the market. The growing share of turnover accounted for by a wide variety of industrial enterprises indicates, however, that much of West German industry is dominated by firms with large market shares.

The rich variety in types of ownership and influence in West Germany render simple generalisations invalid. In any case, reliable information about the extent of family ownership and family management is not normally available (Dyas and Thanheiser 1976: 78). Engelmann's book (1978) may have been something of an exception. Normally, however, even books explicitly concerned with the world's richest men tend to overlook the West Germans (Vogl 1973: 48). Some background knowledge on the Flick dynasty is, however, essential. This is because what had been a largely private company became the first target in Germany of a hostile takeover bid – in other words a bid opposed by the incumbent management

Table 8.4 The trend in industrial concentration, 1960–89

| Year | All industrial enterprises | | Top 50 enterprises | Col. (3) as percentage of col (2) |
	Number[1]	Turnover[2] (DM billion)	Turnover (DM billion)	
	(1)	(2)	(3)	(4)
1960	49,600	266.4	92.3	34.6
1972	44,246	657.2	281.5	42.8
1980	39,011	1,208.0	598.5	49.5
1989	37,920[3]	1,713.5[3]	915.6	54.4

Sources: Jordon 1976: 75; *Stat. Jahrbücher* 1981 and 1991: tables 9.1 and 9.3; *Die Zeit* 36/81 and 34/90 (author's translations and calculations)

Notes: [1] 1960 and 1972 with 10 or more employees; 1980 and 1989 with 20 or more employees
[2] 1960 including turnover tax; 1972, 1980 and 1989 excluding value-added tax
[3] 7.2 million employees; total wage and salary costs were DM 350.4 billion

It thus constitutes an almost perfect case study. It also probably had implications for the developments in German M&A policy during the 1990s. The bid itself involved what have been demonstrated to be typical elements of ownership in Germany: an important family (the Flicks in this case), a bank (the Deutsche), a recently fully privatised, acquisitive industrial concern (VEBA) and an eager prospective foreign purchaser waiting in the wings (Stora of Sweden). Disenchanted members of the family masterminded the takeover. Typically, however, family heirs to company fortunes in post-war Germany have tended to opt for an immediate and opulent retirement.

The company's founder, Friedrich Flick, remained a relatively unknown figure until the end of his life (Rutherford 1974: 36). In its obituary, the London *Times* (22 July 1972) referred to him as 'something of a recluse . . . famed for his exceptional modesty . . . but also a strong-willed, autocratic individual.' His eldest son (Otto-Ernst), who died in 1974, had a decade earlier resorted to litigation which resulted in a cash settlement in return for his relinquishing all claims on the family business. The case came about because of the father's continued domination of the company's affairs. The second son died in the war. The youngest son (Friedrich Karl) ultimately succeeded his father as the sole head of the Flick industrial empire. But the founder's will had decreed that Otto-Ernst's two sons (Gert-Rudolph and Friedrich Christian) should also participate in the company's management (*Der Spiegel* 22/89). Their uncle therefore made a settlement for the 30 per cent stake in the company that they held in conjunction with their sister (*ibid.*). Hence, relations within the dynasty remained acrimonious and it also became involved in one of the two major financial scandals during the first half of the 1980s, the other being the collapse of Neue Heimat – see the housing finance section in Chapter 7. (The decade's 'most spectacular corporate scandal' – the Co-op – occurred later – FT 6 March 1989.)

Flick's holding company (*Industrieverwaltung*) was acquired by the Deutsche Bank in 1985, prior to its being floated as Feldmühle Nobel AG in April 1986. The two nephews received a compensatory payment from the Deutsche Bank (*ibid.*).

This share issue was correctly seen as a watershed in German stock exchange history by the *Economist* (26 April 1986). The flotation was unique because (Franks and Mayer 1990: 228):

- it was a record new issue
- it was the first time that 100 per cent of a company's share capital had been offered via a new issue
- unlike many other issues, the shares were ordinary voting, as opposed to non-voting preference shares

In 1988, the two nephews of Friedrich Karl Flick (who had sold the original company to the Deutsche) made an unsuccessful bid for 51 per cent of the shares. They were dissatisfied with the management of the new company who reacted by achieving the required 50 per cent at the AGM for a five per cent limit to voting rights, irrespective of the number of shares held (*ibid.*: 229). Schneider-Lenné (1992: 15) estimates that twenty AGs have such voting restrictions. The resolution at the AGM received the proxy-voting support of the Deutsche, although its use of such a voting block in this custodian role was not limited by the voting restriction. In 1989, a shareholder group led by the two nephews secretly accumulated a 40 per cent stake in Feldmühle and sold the shares to VEBA AG (*ibid.*). Of particular interest is the fact that the 40 per cent stake was spread over the coalition of seven individual investors, thereby overcoming the 5 per cent voting restriction and avoiding the requirement at that time that individual interests over 25 per cent were to be disclosed. VEBA's acquisition was duly approved by the BKA. Subsequently, VEBA raised its stake to 50 per cent and then sold this holding to Stora of Sweden. Even though Stora later resold Feldmühle-Nobel's non-paper activities to Metallgesellschaft, it is ironic to note that the main reason for the introduction of voting restrictions at AGMs had been to curb the growth of foreign holdings (by OPEC countries) in the early 1970s (*Economist* 23 February 1991; FT 4 July 1991 and 22 December 1992). In view of the fact that the restriction was circumvented in this case, it is superfluous to enquire whether a coalition of employees' and banks' representatives exercised on the supervisory board provided what Franks and Mayer (1990: 206) usually term 'formidable' impediments. There was, however, bank involvement in the Stora sale to Metallgesellschaft. The Deutsche was involved in this successful bid, with the WestLB not succeeding in a counter bid (*Der Spiegel* 27/91). The tables were to be turned in the Krupp takeover of Hoesch (see below).

There were thus two departures from standard German practice. First, the voting restrictions were removed by some of the actors. Second, this was done against the express wishes of the Deutsche Bank, the Deutsche itself having sided with the incumbent management. This type of share dealing was more reminiscent of Anglo-Saxon practice with all its possible implications for the inferior economic performance that this system seems to engender. On the other hand, shareholders in Germany are disadvantaged by the absence of a takeover code. In other words, takeover rules and related disclosure requirements are far less strict – and a lot less developed – than in the UK (Schneider-Lenné 1992: 22). In Germany, a predator company does not have to disclose a shareholding in its intended acquisition until it reaches 25 per cent, compared to 3 per cent in the UK. For good or ill, however, challenging voting restrictions and a company's house bank were features of four further cases. They involved the tyre makers Continental and

Pirelli, the insurance case (AMB and AGF) to which detailed reference was made in the BfG section of Chapter 7, the acquisition of the Sabo lawnmower company by John Deere of the USA and the Krupp takeover of Hoesch. In a fifth case, the Mercedes holding company was dissolved. In effect, this had been formed in 1975 in order to prevent the Shah of Iran from buying the Flicks' large stake in Daimler-Benz. Despite its name, the holding company had no connection with Daimler's motor car subsidiary: it was a highly effective anti-takeover device.

Ostensibly, Pirelli's bid for Conti was motivated by the perceived need to withstand Japanese and US competition by building up a 15 per cent share in the international tyre market. The bid became public in early 1991 during the run up to EC 1993. Pirelli claimed to have assembled an alliance controlling just over 50 per cent of shareholders' votes, although Conti's supervisory board could block any offer provided it retained one more vote than 25 per cent of those voting at the AGM (*Economist* 23 February 1991). (Company law requires that the approval of 75 per cent of the shareholders is necessary for certain actions. Hence, any institution holding 25 per cent plus one share of a company's share capital is in a position to veto major company decisions. But it is a double-edged sword, as the AMB-AGF case demonstrates. In other words, this power of veto is what institutions may seek and they often content themselves with a holding of this magnitude. Clearly, this level of influence may only normally be gained in the share-quoted AG. Indeed, as Vogl suggests (1973: 65–6), probably the reason for many companies remaining GmbHs is to avoid such influence.)

The Deutsche, which was a major shareholder in Conti and which occupied the chairmanship of its supervisory board, initially supported Pirelli's bid. Support also came from Allianz (another major shareholder) and the prime minister of Lower Saxony, the Land in which Conti is located. But the major shareholders, along with Daimler-Benz, VW and BMW who had been persuaded to buy shares, later switched their support to Conti's chief executive who was an ardent opponent of the takeover. Although an EGM threw out the 5 per cent voting restriction, an uneasy truce was declared when the Deutsche dismissed the chief executive (*Economist* 30 November 1991). The voting restrictions were also opposed by the following two AGMs without any palpable influence on the company's management (*Die Welt* 7 April 1993). Pirelli renewed its takeover attempt during 1992, again without success (FT 1 July 1992 and 22 December 1992). In April 1993, Pirelli and its allies announced that they had sold the bulk of a 38 per cent stake in Conti. The Deutsche placed 28 per cent of these shares with institutional investors, having retained a further 5 per cent for itself (*Guardian* 6 April 1993). The remaining 5 per cent was kept by Italy's Mediobanca. Lower Saxony's government also remained financially committed (*Die Welt ibid.*). Conti had therefore been advised by the Deutsche which in turn relied on its fairly new UK acquisition Morgan Grenfell. It is intriguing, if futile, to speculate how the staff of this British subsidiary viewed the German M&A system relative to Anglo-Saxon practice. One refers here not only to the voting restrictions which provide a formidable barrier against hostile takeovers, but also to the tendency for German companies to pay lower dividends than British companies (see the discussion of taxation structure in Chapter 3).

Ultimately, the French insurer AGF

succeeded in having its voting rights recognised at AMB's AGM. But AMB's management had initially refused to recognise these rights – even though AGF had acquired just over 25 per cent of the German company's shares. AMB's justification was that AGF was trying to win control with the minimum necessary outlay. However, AGF found a buyer (Crédit Lyonnais) for AMB's troubled BfG bank and AMB's chief executive was forced to resign, even though his predecessor, who had acquired the BfG, remained as chairman of the supervisory board. As shown in the *Allfinanz* section of Chapter 7, the Allianz/Dresdner bank axis, along with the Deutsche, then all gained more shares in AMB. Presumably, this left a situation of stalemate should attempts be made to restructure AMB's operations. The Sabo case, on the other hand, which began in March 1991, was characterised by the removal of voting restrictions by a group of institutional shareholders led by Colonia Versicherung AG.

The Krupp takeover of Hoesch, also in 1991, signified new departures from established practice, too. At the outset, it can be noted that both companies had earlier made overtures to purchase Salzgitter (see the privatisation section). Hoesch was ruled out because further rationalisation in steel was deemed to be desirable, whereas Krupp's foreign shareholders were reported to have deterred the Federal government (FT 3 October 1989). Krupp and Hoesch had for a number of years seriously considered merging because of the mounting problems in the steel industry. It was considered that Germany – with six companies – was not well placed to fend off competitive pressures from abroad. For example, most EC partners had only one major steel producer. The WestLB significantly became involved in this case. It pulled off a coup by engineering the

successful takeover of Hoesch by Krupp (*Economist* 16 May 1992). The Deutsche Bank, Hoesch's house bank at the time, was taken by surprise when Krupp announced that it had secretly acquired a stake in its target. Such deals are usually conducted by one of the Big Three, mostly the Deutsche itself. Krupp, with the assistance of WestLB, had moved so rapidly and decisively that by German standards the takeover was hostile.

More change was implied by the dissolution of Mercedes Holding in 1993. First, it was regarded as a victory for shareholders' rights. Although individual and smaller institutional shareholders in Mercedes Holding received Daimler-Benz dividends, they had no direct vote in the comglomerate's affairs. In any case, half the shares in Mercedes Holding had been held by two holding companies which were in turn owned largely by the big banks and the Allianz insurance company. On the dissolution of Mercedes Holding, all its shareholders received a one-for-one issue in the main company, and the price of their shares increased. Second, the insider trading of Franz Steinkühler (the then leader of IG Metall) was disclosed at this stage – see the stock market section of *Finanzplatz Deutschland* in Chapter 7. Third, the existence of Mercedes Holding was one of the obstacles preventing Daimler's listing on the New York stock exchange. Its removal meant that Daimler was nearer making a large rights issue there. In other words, equal voting rights were accorded to each share and the anti-takeover device had been removed. However, Daimler also had to accept Anglo-Saxon disclosure and accountancy rules. Moreover, there was still dissatisfaction with the Deutsche's remaining 25 per cent stake in Daimler.

Is the writing on the wall for the corporate practices which characterised the German M&A scene until the above events? Certainly, changes are underway, and some of these changes can be linked to both *Finanzplatz Deutschland* (see Chapter 7) and *Standort Deutschland* (see the trade sections below). Note that a move towards the Anglo-Saxon system implies a move away from the features that characterise the Japanese corporate system. In Japan the typical industrial firm is also untrammelled by the threat of a market for corporate control and is supported by the long-term commitment of Japanese financial capital (Cowling and Tomann 1990: 204). These long-term perspectives have assisted the MITI approach (to be reviewed in the *Standort Deutschland* section). But the next task is to unravel the intricacies of the German public sector. Not only will some further valuable lessons on ownership emerge, but there will also be an opportunity to see how privatised conglomerates emulated the restrictive corporate practices to which reference has been made in this section. Indeed, they were endowed with some of these powers on privatisation.

PRIVATISATION, DEREGULATION AND SUBSIDIES

All three of these economic policies have played a role in the post-war period. This is the reason for considering each of them in separate sections. As an economic issue, privatisation has the longest post-war history. It was made even more complex by unification. For these reasons, its consideration covers a number of subsections. Chronologically, the privatisation debate began in the 1950s. Selling off the reconstructed public combines established during the Weimar republic, and then by the Nazis, transpired to be the major policy objective (BMF *Der Bund . . .* 1959: 66;

BMF *Das Industrielle . . .* 1962: 163 and 1966: 68; Hardach 1980: 34 and 189–90; Reuss 1963: 234–5). (Immediately following the Second World War, the reconstruction of these public-sector enterprises had received top policy priority – Tofaute 1993: 16). It will also be seen below that, at this juncture, another aim was to introduce a wider ownership of equity capital.

Subsidies were a major feature of the attempts to achieve economic and social structural change after 1967, although they had been used in an *ad hoc* but significant manner prior to this date (Peacock *et al.* 1980: 45–6). Deregulation came to be seriously considered in the second half of the 1980s – it was therefore a later product of the supply-side debate. An IfW study for the MK had estimated that only about half of total value added in West Germany was produced under a regime where market forces operated; the other half was either subject to government regulations or produced by the state itself (iwd2 22/90). Somewhat surprisingly, it was added that the latter estimate was probably on the low side as intersectoral regulations, subsidisation and import barriers had not been taken into account (OECD *Economic Survey* 1986: 25). On the other hand, some caution was necessary in interpreting the results because most of the highly regulated sectors in West Germany were also subject to regulation in most other countries (*ibid.*). Nonetheless, it is German practice to view anti-trust policy as a form of regulation. If its somewhat tardy enforcement is also included in any assessment of the SME, therefore, it follows that this post-war system operated in an entirely different manner from its text book conceptualisation. Moreover, Giersch *et al.* (1992: 218) point out that until the early 1970s West Germany could rely on the expansion of exports to sustain a high level of domestic regulation. (In other respects, the line of argument in the Giersch *et al.* book differs from the view of the SME taken by this writer. But perhaps their 'export machine' notion could be applied to impressive export surpluses achieved during most of the 1980s.)

Privatisation and deregulation are policy strategies for increasing the scope of the market in the production and allocation of goods and services by removing perceived harmful government controls, promoting competition, and reassigning property rights from the state to private persons or corporations. Both privatisation and deregulation are tributaries of the same main stream. They are concerned with the reduction of government intervention in economic affairs. Subsidisation, on the other hand, increases the state's role in resource allocation. Hence, subsidies can be seen as a means of maintaining existing structures or fostering structural change. The extensive discussion in West Germany of such a potentially wideranging *Strukturpolitik* has ideological overtones (Peacock *et al.* 1980: ch. 1).

Privatisation is, generally speaking, a transfer of rights in a particular form for which the recipient usually, but not always, pays a price. Following a privatisation, the regulatory environment determines the new owner's rights (Walters 1989: 189–90). Where there are conditions of natural monopoly, regulation is necessary to prevent higher prices. Privatisation in this type of case therefore implies replacing government intervention with new forms of control whose superiority has still to be demonstrated (Bös 1989: 238). Among the countries with the most obvious economic changes along these lines, the United States and the United Kingdom occupy a prominent position. Indeed, the expressions 'Reaganomics' and 'Thatcherism' characterise these economic policies, the aims of which were to

increase the flexibility of the economy, to improve resource allocation and, ultimately, to enhance the potential for economic growth. In the economic policy debate in Germany, the options for, and limits of, privatisation and deregulation also generated considerable interest. It was unification, however, which marked the watershed in this policy debate. The prelude to EC 1993 also caused more importance to be accorded to these topics (Giersch 1985).

Consider privatisation specifically. The transfer of state-owned assets to the private sector featured prominently on the policy agenda of many European economies, but in different dimensions. During the 1980s, the pioneers of the privatisation wave were Great Britain and France. In Britain critically important industries like telecommunications or gas were sold to the public, while in France large industrial conglomerates were privatised. In many other economies, especially West Germany, policy aspirations were more modest. In a sense this is surprising, because the economic and political factors favouring privatisation were strong throughout much of the 1980s. Hence, one might have expected West Germany to adopt a privatisation programme similar to that of Britain, especially given that the centre-right coalition government of Helmut Kohl was in power almost as long as the Thatcher government. Why did the privatisation programme in West Germany prove to be much more moderate than in other European countries? Was it because of a smaller privatisation potential or because of the lack of political will? It will be shown that, in west Germany, constitutional provisions, along with political constraints at the level of the Länder and local authorities, prevented wide-spread privatisation. The new Länder were eager to emulate these arrangements, although the privatisation potential was obviously far greater than in the west.

Since the public sector in the developed West European countries represents on average only 8.4 per cent of total production, the potential for privatisation is relatively low (Lipton and Sachs 1990: 300). This stands in contrast to the East European countries where the system employed in the former socialist economies necessitated the privatisation of whole economies (the share of public-sector production in the former GDR, for example, was 96.5 per cent in 1982). Given this dramatic difference between west and east Germany, there was scope for equally different privatisation goals and methods. It is therefore helpful to distinguish between privatisation in west Germany, which could be seen as one instrument of deregulation in general, and privatisation in east Germany where it was the main plank in the transition process. Moreover, there is a rich variety of privatisation methods (Cassel and Schipke 1992: 185; Schöler 1992: 267–72). Because of its complexity, however, it is first necessary to briefly survey the public sector in Germany.

THE PUBLIC SECTOR

In the SME there is a private sector of households and enterprises and a public sector which consists of numerous units. The public institutions belong to the Federal, Länder and local authorities. It is often not easy to discern the existence of a public enterprise and public involvement is more complex than in most other countries. This is principally because terminology varies between public authority, public agency, public company, public economic unit, public service and so on (Eichhorn 1991: 63). While there is no universally agreed definition of a public enterprise, the term is generally used to mean any government-owned or controlled unit that produces and sells industrial, commercial, or financial goods and services. This definition does not distinguish between wholly state-owned enterprises and those in which the state shares majority or minority equity with private sector owners. State-owned enterprises took on a wide variety of forms over the years, depending on the state of development of the economy as well as the government's commitment to state ownership and control of the means of production (Cowan 1990).

The diversity of the German public sector can be illustrated by considering its rationale, goals, responsibilities and legal forms (Brede and Hoppe 1986: 205–7). Its *rationale* ranges from industrial profit-making firms, founded in the public interest but entirely dedicated to national and international competition, to firms whose public purposes consist of the direct provision of utilities for the population, which are not always public goods in an economic sense. In fact, they include transport and communication services, electricity, gas, water, district heating, housing, banking and insurance services. Public enterprises are also 'instruments' of the state's administrative machinery in a broader sense. In addition to the familiar infrastructure function, public enterprises create the framework for market-orientated economic activity, in that they are seen as the classical instrument for controlling 'natural' monopolies, which are technically characterised by declining long run average costs (Pera 1989: 166). This means that the output of a single firm can be produced at lower total cost than by another greater number of firms because of economies of scale (lower long-term unit costs) or economies of scope (advantages through the joint production of several products). Furthermore, public enterprises are regarded as an instrument of regional and structural policy which embraces stabilisation and social policy. More recently, there have also been frequent references to their significance in the context of policies for promoting R&D (Fielder 1989: 457).

The public sector can also be characterised by the *goals* of public authorities and enterprises. Public enterprises with public-interest goals can be found within the public utility sectors of energy, gas and water, while public enterprises resembling private ones are represented by companies owned in the main by the Federal and the Länder governments. Among the commercially orientated enterprises, one finds public enterprises that compete with private business and have similar profit goals. Their revenue is assigned to the budgets of their owners to fulfil public goals (see, for example, the section on public-sector banks in Chapter 7). Those enterprises with public-interest objectives are prone to greater intervention than those which operate along commercial lines. In general, the greater the number of public goals allocated to an enterprise, the greater the degree of influence exercised. The following kinds of aim cause intervention by the different levels of government in their enterprises (Eichhorn 1991: 67):

- the maintenance or creation of jobs
- the stabilisation of the regional or local economy
- the creation of a balanced economic structure in the region
- the development of sectors with high growth potential
- the consolidation of the public budgets

As indicated above, *responsibility* for

German public enterprises rests with the Federal, Länder and local authorities. Following the privatisation programmes to be investigated below, the focal points of Federal ownership at the beginning of the 1990s were mainly in communications (Deutsche Bundespost), the railways, financial institutions (KfW – see Chapter 7), in housing and housing estates and in the field of R&D. Länder and local authority enterprises are mainly involved in the supply of electricity, gas and water, as well as banking (Fahning 1987: 186). The Länder pursue regional, the local authorities local aims (Brede and Hoppe 1986: 206).

Public enterprises are conducted in the *legal forms* of both private and public law. Some state monopolies subject to public law have been granted administrative independence without being accorded legal independence – the Deutsche Bundesbahn and the Deutsche Bundespost, for example. Other firms subject to public law have been granted their own corporate status – public-sector banks, for example. In the sector subject to private law, the legal forms with the greatest significance are those of AG and GmbH – with the relevant public authority (or authorities) being the owner(s) of the equity capital.

Two criteria have been used to differentiate the primarily administrative and the primarily entrepreneurial units in public ownership, namely a material and a formal attribute (Eichhorn 1991). From a material point of view public institutions can be characterized as public enterprises if they possess a substantial equity and a reasonable degree of autonomy in decision making. In most cases this economic independence is combined with legal independence, often including limited liability. When applying the formal criterion, the term public enterprise is used if there is any government economic activity embodied in independent forms of public and private-law enterprises. Defining the economic (and non-economic) activities themselves is simply a matter of referring to the articles of association.

PRIVATISATION: THE MAJOR ISSUES

One of the earliest references to *Privatisierung* was in *Die Zeit* at the time of the first privatisation wave in the 1950s (Hawkins 1991: 22n). The privatisation debate in West Germany therefore dates back more than forty years. The term 'denationalisation' was used contemporaneously in Britain. It was applied specifically to road haulage and steel (Rose 1989: 257n). The German debate therefore predates Thatcherism. Not surprisingly, the aims of privatisation in Germany have differed over time. For this reason, the arguments used over this relatively long period should be considered prior to an analysis of the actual extent of privatisation in the German economy.

The reader is first reminded of the particular significance of private property in post-war Germany; Eucken, one of the founding fathers of the economic system introduced into West Germany, postulated that private property is a constitutional element of market systems in general and the SME in particular (see Chapter 1). Above all, private ownership of the means of production performs four functions (Eucken 1952: 271; Gutmann 1991: 67):

- Without private property rights, genuine competition would not exist. One reason for such a stipulation arises from the freedom it endows to use or transfer the rights over a resource in a manner consistent with the owner's property rights and individual utility. Since a misallocation of re-

sources is thereby obviated, private property rights also perform a social function

- Private ownership of productive equipment is also a precondition for an efficient managerial control. The determination of the present value of expected profits (losses) of firms is made possible through private shareholders. An incentive is therefore given for the private share owners to obtain information about the main features of business and to control the managers. Managerial control ceases to be a public good

- A further advantage of private property rights is the opportunities generated for risk-sharing and the consequent diminution of risk. The creation of risk-taking institutions becomes viable

- Another characteristic function of private property is the minimisation of mistakes and errors through decentralised decision making. The preconditions are working capital markets which lead to an efficient allocation of capital. The allocation of capital between competing uses needs reliable information about alternatively accessible rates of return. This is a problem for state-owned enterprises since low profitability is often valued as a particular virtue by advocates of public ownership. High losses, irrespective of their cause, are regarded as acceptable (Hamm 1992: 143). The liability of the owner is the basic foundation for the minimisation of errors because the socialisation of losses is not compatible with an efficient allocation of resources

On strictly theoretical grounds, therefore, there is an incorrect belief in Germany that the policy decision to privatise requires justification. However, with the more fundamental decision to introduce a social *market economy*, the argument runs in the opposite direction: only in the case of market failure is the state permitted to intervene and then only if performance is likely to be more efficient when the possibility of political failure is taken into account. But a principal thesis of this book is that the theory and practice of the SME differed. For example, the pervasive nature of public enterprise has already been indicated. Specific illustrations will be given shortly. It will also be demonstrated that the inability of policy makers and advisers to distinguish between the theoretical model of the SME and its pragmatic operation created even more problems for east Germany.

Going arguably much farther than the SME theorisers, Adam Smith allocated three groups of tasks to the state (Lenel 1989: 33):

1 The state should provide external security.
2 It should also provide an appropriate legal system for the enforcement of laws.
3 Finally, it should erect and maintain 'those public institutions and those public works which, though they may be in highest degree advantageous to great society, are, however, of such a nature that the profit could never repay the expense to any individual or small number of individuals, and which it therefore cannot be expected that any individual or small number of individuals should erect or maintain'.

The scope of government involvement in Germany goes far beyond that. There are thus two basic sets of arguments used when justifying privatisation. First, there are political or ideological reasons and, second, economic reasons.

An initial insight into the *political or ideological reasoning* has in effect already been provided. Privatisation is an instrument to change the distribution of power within a society since decisions on prices, investment, and technology are taken out of the domain of public bureaucrats and policy makers and shifted to managers who (in theory at least) are responsible to private shareholders (Bös 1989: 219). Thus large-scale privatisation leads to a redistribution of private and public economic power. Moreover, the influence of the trade unions will typically be reduced by privatisation. It is therefore not surprising that the trade unions are among the main opponents of privatisation. In the DGB's set of basic aims announced in 1981, support was expressed for public enterprises; the extension of public ownership in economic enterprises was also advocated (Loesch 1983: 25). The German trade unions' opposition to privatisation stems mainly from the fear that privatisation would result in some members losing their *Beamte* status, some privileges, or perhaps even becoming unemployed (*Beamte* were discussed in Chapter 6). Since the BVG decided in 1993 that *Beamte* could not be used for strike-breaking purposes, presumably the employers' side saw even less reason for maintaining this employee classification.

Freedom and democracy are further arguments for privatisation: the extent of the public sector constrains private activities. Combining economic and political decision-making powers threatens the decentralised system of competition regulation; it also endangers the horizontal separation of power between the state, on the one hand, and the society on the other hand (MK VIII: 25; Brabant 1991: 35). Widening the ownership of economic assets could be another motive for privatisation. This could be achieved by giving preferential treatment to small investors, employees and tenants, thus structuring the sales of public assets so as to promote the wider ownership of economic assets. (This was an important, but unrealised, objective of Thatcherism. Small investors allocated with low-priced shares generally preferred the short-term capital gain which could be realised by selling to institutional investors. Short termism of this description dominates Anglo-Saxon practice. It will be shown that the West German first privatisation phase also introduced this uncharacteristic capital-market feature into normally more long-term German practice.)

Yet another argument in favour of privatisation was also seen in Chapter 1. It is the principle of subsidiarity (*Subsidiaritätsprinzip*: Nell-Breuning 1962). With the encyclical *Quadragesimo anno* of pope Pius XI in 1931 this became an important component of Catholic social teaching and over and above this a constitutional element of the SME in Germany (Vanberg 1988: 20). More recently, the principle of subsidiarity is also often used in the discussions about the EC. From a social philosophy point of view it offends against justice if higher units (for example, the state) take over tasks that small and subordinated units are also able to fulfil.

But in Germany many public enterprises are also owned by the Länder and by local authorities. Indeed, prior to the first world war the Länder derived almost 30 per cent of their revenue from their commercial activities (Konrad 1968: 45). Because of the growth in their financial needs, however, the Länder nowadays derive only a relatively small proportion of their revenue from business enterprises (*ibid.*). As would be expected, SPD governments of the Länder or social democratic mayors are opposed to privatisation. However, the CDU/CSU Länder have also retained their shares in public firms. The classic examples were Volkswagen in Lower Saxony and, even more superficially surprising, the opposition to privatisation in Bavaria led by Franz-Josef Strauß. On closer examination, however, the reasons for Strauß' opposition were extremely instructive. As chairman of the supervisory board of the Federal airline he was in a position to ensure that Lufthansa did not purchase Boeing aircraft rather than the subsidised European Airbus, part of which was manufactured in Bavaria. Privatisation might have undermined his position. Hence, in addition to yet another example of the potential influence of a supervisory board chairman, the more relevant factor here was the protection of the Land's business interests (Tofaute 1993: 12). Moreover, a group of free-market Economics professors added a further dimension to the argument (Kronberger Kreis 1993: 12). The growing influence of the North-Rhine Westphalian government, exercised indirectly through the WestLB, was seen to be as significant as the industrial holdings in VW (Lower Saxony) and the aero-space and surface-transport enterprises in Hamburg and Bavaria. They estimated that, provided these political constraints were removed, a privatisation programme in the west could realise at least DM 2 billion (*ibid.*: 9). They added, by way of illustration, that if all State holdings were sold, there would be sufficient to redeem the whole of the national debt, leaving a three-digit billion dowry which, if invested, would earn a two-digit billion stream of revenue. Relieving the growth in public debt as a consequence of unification was therefore proposed as a powerful reason for a thorough programme of privatisation (*ibid.*: 8). In spite of Federal privatisation programmes, public-sector ownership was expanding annually (*ibid.*: 44). Municipal and regional savings banks (*Sparkassen*), the Länder's house banks (*Landesbanken*), insurance holdings, local transport and electricity supply were some examples. Moreover, holdings in other utilities and airports could be added to the list. A start could at least be made by including the industrial holdings in VW, aerospace and surface transport held by the Länder with the relatively more successful privatisation programme carried out at Federal level (*ibid.*: 34). It will nonetheless be seen that there were significant constraints to a privatisation policy that do not exist in a unitary state like the UK. Unification made these differences more pronounced, as will shortly be shown.

The overlapping ownership in the energy utilities is particularly intriguing. As was seen in Table 8.1, Germany's largest energy concern in 1991 was RWE AG. The majority of its voting rights were still in public sector hands (MK IX: 217). Following GEMSU and its complete takeover of the construction company Hochtief, it became officially known simply by its initials (*ibid.*: 195 and 217). Prior to 1990, it had been registered Rheinisch-Westfälisches Elektrizitätswerk AG – a title which did not indicate its energy acquisitions in the east and construction. (As early as 1977, it had shared ownership of Hochtief with the Commerz and Merck Fink banks – MK II: 164 and 168. In 1990 it also had an 11 per cent holding in the construction company Philipp Holzmann AG; the Deutsche Bank held a further 30 per cent stake – MK IX: 207.) Similarly, the Bayernwerk AG was 60 per cent owned by Bavaria in 1990; the other 40 per cent belonged to the then recently privatised VIAG, in which Bayernwerk had a cross holding of one third (MK IX: 206–7, 211 and 215; Table 8.5 below). A total of eleven western energy utilities – most of which jointly

belonged to the Länder, local authorities and privatised concerns such as VEBA and VIAG – were listed in *Die Zeit's* top 100 industrials in 1991. Unscrambling these overlapping holdings for the purpose of privatisation would clearly be difficult. In addition, the direct-labour services of local authorities, along with the work which they offer for subcontract, is far reaching (Kronberger Kreis 1993: 14–16). These services enjoy tax exemption when carried out directly, but private subcontractors pay the full range of taxation discussed in Chapter 3 (*ibid.*: 31). The Federal railways and postal services also enjoy tax exemption.

Unification exacerbated the two problems of unscrambling western energy holdings and local-authority enterprises. Many local authorities in east Germany objected to the BVG about the electricity-supply contract awarded to the three large western utilities – RWE, PreussenElektra (a subsidiary of VEBA) and Bayernwerk – which had specifically formed Vereinte Energiewerke AG (VEAG) for that purpose (Boehmer-Christiansen *et al.* 1993: 367; DIW/IfW 1992: 16–17 and 57). These western utilities had moved into the east with haste trying to buy, divide and rule even before unification (Boehmer-Christiansen *ibid.*: 361). It is also interesting to note that the now fully privatised VEBA, along with its former subsidiary Preussag, were exerting monopoly power (*ibid.*: 365). Eastern local authorities viewed with enthusiasm the prospect of using 'monopoly' profits to finance their other activities; indeed, about 100 authorities entered into such projects (DIW/IfW *ibid.*; Deregulierskommission 1991: 79). A compromise suggested by the BVG was not accepted by some eastern local authorities and this had a deleterious effect on energy investment (BfG *Standpunkt* 3–4/93). Such infrastructure investment was of vital significance to the rationalisation and future use of brown coal for electricity generation, especially as the unsafe nuclear power stations in the east were all closed during 1990: the western utilities did not want to operate suspect and unpopular eastern reactors, or become engaged in a further round of public enquiries and protests (Boehmer-Christiansen *et al.* 1993: 366). Considerable progress had been made by the Treuhand privatisation agency in reducing by one half the output of brown coal and concentrating its production into two regional companies (DIW/IfW 1992: 15–17). Brandenburg, Saxony and Saxony-Anhalt insisted that both fields should remain active, though it transpired that an optimal output would require further rationalisation. Only seven of 38 sites would remain open but it was presumed that these three Länder should retain a major interest in any electricity consortium (*ibid.*). RWE, which already held similar interests in the less sulphurous and more economically mined field in the west, was also prepared to participate in a consortium. Similarly, Ruhrgas and VEBA purchased significant stakes in natural gas pipelines and mineral oil respectively (*ibid.*: 17–19). Supply of gas at the regional level was subcontracted to regional companies from west Germany, with British Gas also participating in two consortia (*ibid.*: 67 and 71). When the Treuhand's privatisation programme is quantified below, however, it will be seen that an appreciable proportion of total investment and employment guarantees were given by energy concerns.

The principal objective of privatisation, then, is improving economic efficiency and productivity. The *economic reasoning* for privatisation is therefore dominated by allocational arguments. They refer to efficiency, to market structure, and to the quality of public supply. State-owned enterprises are stereotyped as creating many problems of bureaucratic failure. Inadequate planning leads to substantial, yet ill-conceived investments. Political interference in routine operations guarantees inefficiencies, managers frequently find themselves contending with unclear, multiple or even conflicting objectives (Gayle and Goodrich 1990b: 9) In contrast, a private firm is conceived of as an institution in which prices and output are guided by the product market, while responsibility to the capital market constrains costs. Such a firm can trade, transfer partial ownership rights by the sale of shares, and also be acquired by investors who perceive unexploited profit opportunities. (It has been shown in both this chapter, and in Chapter 7, that the German capital market does not function in this manner.)

Moreover, the expected economic benefits from privatisation include increased production quantity and output quality, reduced unit costs, expanded employment, as well as growth opportunities in the long run, and the generation of new technologies. So the gains from privatisation could not only be derived from a static but also from a dynamic point of view. In the absence of competition and private ownership, managers of firms are not driven by self-interest to make profits in an economically meaningful sense; they merely strive to fulfil (or to successfully pretend to fulfil) the prescribed targets. As the firms could not go bankrupt, they have little endogenous incentive to improve their efficiency (Siebert and Schmieding 1990: 2). When accompanied by liberalisation, privatisation encourages the emergence of managers who are willing to champion an entrepreneurial, risk-taking culture (Gayle and Goodrich 1990b: 7). The change in management behaviour is caused by the reduction in government intervention and a stock market threat which requires a careful observation of share values (Kay and Thompson 1986: 19). Empirical studies comparing private and public firms seem to confirm that private enterprises are more efficient than public enterprises that produce the same goods or close substitutes (Picot and Kaulmann 1989, Borcherding 1982).

Finally, government budgets are influenced by the deficits and profits of those firms that are publicly owned in whole or in part. An important motive for privatisation is therefore the improvement of public finances. Privatisation can assist, at least in the short run, in balancing the national budget, reducing government expenditure, and financing capital investment programmes for the enterprises which remain in public ownership. Nonetheless, it has been argued on political and economic grounds that it would be better if all private goods were supplied without interference from government. Government could then concentrate upon the provision of pure collective goods, such as military defence and law and order (Rose 1989: 271; Hamm 1983:180). Alternatively, it could be argued that in order to secure a short-term increase in revenue for budgetary purposes, a privatising government forgoes the long run control its successors would otherwise have had over the levels of employment and human-capital formation within government enterprises (Bös 1989: 238).

PRIVATISATION IN WEST GERMANY

As mentioned above, the extent of privatisation in West Germany was not comparable to the magnitude achieved in other European countries. One reason for this is that in the post-war period there was neither a spate of nationalisation, nor were private-sector enterprises which experienced financial difficulties taken over by the Federal Government. As a result, government holdings in the Federal Republic were not as large as in many other European countries (Brede and Hoppe 1986: 209). It is also necessary to emphasise that the privatisation process in West Germany can be divided into two discrete periods. Within these periods contrasting arguments were used to underline the importance of privatisation.

In 1951, the CDU initiated a privatisation debate in the West German parliament because of the exposure of eastern European governments to central planning, especially in the soviet-occupied zone of east Germany. It was at this time that the former holdings of the Third Reich and Prussia were legally assigned to the Federal government (Konrad 1968: 41). A minor programme thus began in 1952 and it was officially confirmed in 1954 that privatisation should occur where this was in the public interest (*ibid.*). However, the first really significant privatisation programme in the west took place between 1959 and 1965. By this time, there was some public disquiet about the apparent contradiction between the SME theory and the actual extent of government intervention in the economy (Reuss 1963: 235). This first sizeable privatisation programme was to be realised by means of the sale of people's shares (*Volksaktien*), an idea adopted from Austrian practice. It was thought that only specific public firms could be privatised in this way. Two conditions had to be fulfilled in order to become a sought after company on the stock exchange. First, earning power as a basis for durable dividends and, second, a potential privatisation value of more than DM 1 billion was necessary to gain the required impact (Loesch 1988: 69–70). Consequently, there were only three possible government-owned firms likely to achieve a broad demand: Preussag, Volkswagen and VEBA. In the event, their respective privatised nominal value and initial number of subscribers were (Knauss 1989: 8 and 1990: 24; Konrad 1968: 42):

- Preussag (1959): DM 81.5 million; 216,000
- Volkswagen (1961): DM 360 million; 1,547,000
- VEBA (1965): DM 528 million; 2,600,000

This first major privatisation programme was launched at the CDU's pre-election conference in May 1957. The economics minister, Ludwig Erhard, promised to begin the programme by privatising Volkswagen, one of the state enterprises created by the Nazis in 1938. But the privatisation of Volkswagen required complex legislation and the Land government of Lower Saxony resolved to contest the ownership of Volkswagen. (In 1949, the British military government had surrendered control of VW, stipulating that Lower Saxony should exercise trusteeship on behalf of, and in consultation with, the Federal government – BMF *Das Industrielle* . . . 1962: 163). These problems forced the government to start its privatisation programme in 1959 with a trial sale of DM 30 million of new people's shares in Preussische Bergwerks- und Huetten AG (Preussag, as is became officially known in 1964), a subsidiary of the federal government's mining, chemical and electricity holding, Vereinigte Elektrizitäts- und Bergwerke AG (VEBA). Describing the problems in initiating a phased privatisation programme, the Federal government pointed out that its assets could not be disposed of in a random manner (BMF *Der Bund* . . . 1959: 5–6). They consisted of thriving and viable enterprises whose privatisation

must not only realise a social-policy aim, but must also pay due regard to the preservation of jobs, the economic significance of the enterprises and, last but not least, the more general economic effects (*ibid.*). Whereas widening share ownership was an aim which should not be confined to privatisation programmes, shares in Preussag represented a low-risk asset (*ibid.*).

A 'social discount' on Preussag shares was thus offered to persons whose taxable income was less than DM 16,000 a year, each purchaser being limited to five shares (Denton *et al.* 1968: 66). Preferential terms were offered to Preussag's employees (Hawkins 1991: 16). Demand for shares outstripped supply by a very large margin, although some shares were quickly resold (Denton *et al.*: *ibid*). However, in order to qualify for the concessionary rate most purchasers seemed prepared to retain the shares for at least five years (BMF *Der Bund* . . . 1959: 10). As the Federal government considered its experiment a great success, it decided to offer a second issue of DM 51.5 million, thus reducing the VEBA's holding to DM 23.5 million, or 22.39 per cent of the total share capital (*ibid.*: 9). In fact, one must distinguish carefully between the two issues. Preussag required an increase in its share capital (from DM 75 million to DM 105 million – Konrad 1968: 42). VEBA could not finance this out of its own resources and the Federal government would not do so. Hence, the capital increase of DM 30 million was achieved by a public flotation. It was the further DM 51.5 million which exclusively represented a people's shares exercise (*ibid.*: 45). No capital increase resulted from this second exercise and its objective was therefore purely concerned with social policy. There were two further sales of people's shares in 1961 and 1964 which combined both elements since they respectively raised Preussag's share capital to DM 157.5 million and DM 200 million (*ibid.*: 42). When there was a further increase in Preussag's share capital to DM 225 billion in 1965, the by then partially privatised VEBA was the sole purchaser (*ibid.*; BMF *Das Industrielle . . .* 1968: 73). At the end of 1969 VEBA sold this 26.5 per cent stake to the WestLB (BMF *Finanzbericht* 1971: 57). By 1975 this bank's holding had risen to about 40 per cent of Preussag's total share value (MK I: 153 and 163). Although this holding was later reduced, the original aim of the Federal government had been to secure a wider ownership of shares, with even proxy voting by financial institutions minimised by the personal attendance of the new shareholders at AGMs (BMF *Der Bund . . .* 1959: 10–11). Finally, it can be seen from Figure 7.6b that the sales in 1959 took place during bullish stock-market conditions. Moreover, Preussag shares successfully weathered the 1962–3 slump and rose considerably thereafter (Denton *et al*: *ibid*).

The problems preventing a partial privatisation of VW were ultimately resolved by an agreement drawn up by the Federal and Lower Saxony governments (BMF *Der Bund . . .* 1960: 5–6). In 1961, therefore, the Federal government was able to offer people's shares in VW. The company's share capital had been doubled to DM 600 million for this purpose and 60 per cent of this new amount was floated. In accordance with the settlement between the two governments, a further 20 per cent of the share capital was allocated to the Lower Saxony government in lieu of its claim on the company, while the Federal government retained the remaining 20 per cent (*ibid.*; Hawkins 1991: 16). Once again there was a restriction on the number of shares which could be purchased by any one applicant. However, share buyers

were allowed to pay a deposit of DM 100 for each DM 350 share and then pay the balance in three or six instalments over a period of one year. Discounts were again offered to small shareholders, but on this occasion the discounts were subject to the provision that shares would have to be retained for at least five years (Denton *et al.* 1968: 66). There was a large excess demand for the shares and their value rose from DM 350 to DM 700 following flotation (*ibid.*). They later peaked at DM 1,000 and even after falling back remained comfortably above their issue price. The Federal government's privatisation proceeds of about DM 1 billion were used to endow the Volkswagen Foundation which was established in 1960 to promote academic and technological research and teaching (Konrad 1968: 47). This sum was to be made available as a twenty-year loan to the Federal government at an appropriate rate of interest (*Der Bund ibid.*). The Foundation was also guaranteed the dividend on the 40 per cent shares which remained in public hands. There was some public criticism of both the Preussag and VW partial privatisations (Reuss 1963: 207–8 and 235–6). First, the state retained powerful minority positions and VEBA still held over 20 per cent of the share capital of Preussag, a proportion consolidated by VEBAs subsequent acquisition in Preussag in 1965. Second, 'enormous' profits accrued to those who purchased shares.

In 1965 the first privatisation programme came to something of an abrupt end with the privatisation of part of the Federal government's holding in VEBA. Its capital was increased from DM 450 million to DM 825 million through the new issue of people's shares. Repeating the Preussag technique, the Federal government initially floated only the capital increase of DM 375 million, thereby reducing its holding to 54.54 per cent of the company (BMF *Das Industrielle . . .* 1966: 68; Hawkins 1991: 17). Once again preference was given to VEBA's employees. The practice of offering discounts on a limited number of shares to small investors on relatively low incomes was also repeated. Because of an unexpectedly large demand for shares, an EGM approved the Federal government's proposal to float a further DM 153 million of the share capital (*ibid.*). Although this decreased the Federal government's nominal shareholding to 36 per cent, the EGM also decided that the voting rights of any single private-sector shareholder should be restricted to a maximum of DM 82,500, or 1/10,000 of the new share capital (BMF *ibid.*). Such voting restrictions were to prevent 'the danger of foreign infiltration by interest groups' (BMF *Der Bund . . .* 1959: 9; also see the section on mergers and acquisitions above). This differed in two respects from the Preussag and VW voting restrictions. First, the absolute restrictions were DM 105,000 and DM 60,000 and, second, they also applied to VEBA and the Federal and Lower Saxony governments respectively (BMF *Der Bund . . .* 1959: 9 and 1960: 7–8). On the other hand, VEBA was given four seats on the Preussag's supervisory board, while the Federal and Lower Saxony governments were each allocated two seats on VW's supervisory board (*ibid.*). To compensate for voting restrictions at VEBA, private shareholders were entitled to a mark-up of 1.5 per cent on any dividend payment. However, the shares fell back from their opening price soon after they were issued (Denton *et al.* 1968: 66). Indeed, this was the reason for the programme's demise (Hawkins 1991: 18):

During the first few weeks of trading, VEBA's share price rose to DM 241.

However, its price then fell back to around DM 215 as problems came to light in the company. The collapse in the price undermined the Western German people's confidence in people's capitalism. In view of the forthcoming September general election, the government was forced to undertake a massive support operation to stop the share price falling below DM 215, and hence prevent a fiasco. These people's shares turned out to be not quite the election gift the government had planned. The VEBA flotation marked the end of *Aktion Volkskapitalismus . . .* despite some speculation that Lufthansa would be privatised next.

The first privatisation programme has to be seen in the light of the conflict between the capital-market and allocation aims. On the one hand, the government's concept was that of 'universal welfare', or 'popular capitalism' (*Aktion Volkskapitalismus*). More specifically, lower-income groups should become shareholders. On the other hand, the potential of the stock exchange was to be strengthened. People's capitalism succeeded in achieving a broader dispersion of shares. West Germany could therefore be regarded as the mother country of large privatisations and broad dispersion (Knauss 1989: 23). But the collapse in share prices in 1965 (demonstrated above and in Figure 7.6b) undermined West German confidence in people's capitalism (Loesch 1983: 20). Hardach (1980: 155) concluded that the exercise was essentially a means of influencing the electorate. Moreover, the value of the Federal government's holdings rose inexorably after the inception of its privatisation policy. Hence, between 1953 and 1965 the value of these holdings rose from DM 1,461.8 million to DM 3,486.9 million (Konrad 1968: 44). Only the sales of VW and VEBA caused something of an abatement in the rise, and only VEBA's privatisation made a palpable impact on the Federal government's revenue from the sales of its assets (*ibid*.: 46). VEBA's share capital was subsequently raised to DM 1,031.25 million in 1971 and to DM 1,404 million four years later (BMF *Finanzbericht* 1973: 128 and *Beteiligungen* . . . 1975: 7). No shares were offered to the private sector on either occasion. By 1975, the Federal government's holding had thus increased to 43.75 per cent, while within ten years the number of private shareholders had fallen to 1.2 million from 2.6 million (*Beteiligungen* . . . *ibid*.; Knauss 1989: 8; also see the discussion around Table 8.5 below). Of the 106 cases of privatisation during the first privatisation period (1953–65) only 23 represented a disposal of direct holdings, with the proceeds from the remaining indirect holdings financially benefiting the main holding company (*ibid*.: 47). Undoubtedly, the principal example of this approach is that the Federal government received absolutely nothing from the Preussag sales. Finally, although the Federal government normally permitted its enterprises to reinvest their fairly substantial profits, it forfeited a potential annual revenue from Preussag and VEBA estimated at DM 70 million, in order to avoid investment of DM 30 million and DM 375 million respectively (Konrad 1968: 45–6).

THE SECOND PRIVATISATION DECADE

In view of what has been said about the opposition of the SPD to privatisation, it is not surprising that there was not a major privatisation programme after the general election of 1969, when the SPD was able to form a coalition with the FDP. Nonetheless, during the 1970s some thought was given to reducing the extent of the Federal government's holdings (Knauss 1988: 22–3). However, after Chancellor Kohl's victory in the general election in 1982 the privatisation programme was set in motion again. In his policy statement of May 1983, the Chancellor stated that the government would be 'restricted to the performance of essential functions'. In its 1984 Economic Survey, the Federal government gave express notice that it would 'privatise public property where this could be done without prejudicing the interests of the state'. In the 1989 issue of the same publication, the Federal government saw privatisation as belonging to a policy mix designed to stimulate more competition (*Die Zeit* 43/89).

In contrast to people's capitalism policy in the first decade of post-war privatisation, the arguments during this second phase derived from the German *Ordnungspolitik*. In other words, the aims were the revitalisation of markets, along with the promotion of personal freedom and performance, especially that of the German *Mittelstand*. Wealth formation by employees was no longer the rationale for privatisation. In any case, wealth formation was set on a far broader basis as early as the first wealth formation law in 1961 (Gurdon 1991: 596).

In 1983, the government reduced its holding in VEBA to 30 per cent as a signal for the resumption of the privatisation policy. About 4.5 million shares having a total value of DM 232 million were sold. This second partial privatisation of VEBA, which took place in January 1984, was carried out on the financial market through the medium of banks; they were required to give a preferential treatment to German subscribers. Though there was a discount for private investors, the quotation was too high to be attractive for small investors. In 1985 the government reduced its involvement in VEBA even further, this time from 30 to 25.7 per cent (see Table 8.5). Note that the state holding in VEBA was still sufficient to guarantee the power of veto to the government. In this sense privatisation in West Germany up to this time was only partial in nature (Oudenhoven 1989: 173). As also shown in Table 8.5, however, the full privatisation of VEBA took place in 1987. By 1990, the number of this company's shareholders (543,029) stood at half the 1975 level noted above. Although the vast majority of these shares were still held by private individuals, foreign institutional investors were becoming increasingly important (FT 27 November 1992).

In the Autumn of 1987, privatisation programmes in all European countries were interrupted by the crises on the stock-markets. But in March 1988 the West German government continued its privatisation plans – the first European government to do so. Within a two-month period, the remaining Federal stake in Volkswagen was sold, VIAG was completely privatised and the Deutsche Verkehrskreditbank was partially privatised. Privatisation consequently proceeded during this second phase mainly at the Federal government level. As in the first phase, it was in its indirect activities where the number of holdings fell most: from 827 in 1981 to 215 in 1989 (BMF *Beteiligungen.* . . . 1981 and 1989). The direct holdings of the Federal government – that is excluding the special assets of the ERP, LAG, Federal post office and railways – fell from 85 to 77 during the same period, although unification and deregulation had brought the number back up to 83 in 1990 (*ibid.*, including 1990). As can be seen from Table 8.5, between 1984 and 1989 revenue from sales of the major Federal assets amounted to DM 9.7 billion – a rather modest amount in relation to

both GDP and other economies (Stevens 1992: 6). There is a further similarity to the first phase in that the vast majority of these sales realised a relatively small amount of revenue. The sale of Federal holdings in VW, VEBA, VIAG and Salzgitter AG alone accounted for almost 90 per cent of total receipts from privatisation over the period in question (*ibid.*: 4).

The case of Salzgitter's privatisation is particularly interesting. Above all, it demonstrates that the Erhard popular capitalism era was definitely a thing of the past. Salzgitter was purchased for DM 2.5 billion by Preussag whose own privatisation process was shown above to be part of the said Erhard era. Preussag itself employed 26,000 persons at the time of the privatisation, compared to Salzgitter's 38,000. By 1991, however, Preussag had become the 15th largest industrial employer, and had also jumped from 18th to 13th on turnover terms (Table 8.1). In this sense, this privatisation contributed to the process of concentration explored in the anti-trust sections above.

One third of Preussag was in turn owned by the WestLB in 1990 (MK IX: 207). Moreover, Preussag was also only just recovering from a period of losses, having paid its first dividend since 1985. Prior to its privatisation, on the other hand, Salzgitter had gone through a process of rationalisation which had cost the Federal government DM 2 billion over a decade (FT 3 October 1989). Five of its six shipyards had been closed and had its management been permitted to purchase Fichtel and Sachs (see the anti-trust section above), its non-steel sales would have been higher than the 15 per cent of total sales accounted for by its electronic and machinery divisions (*ibid.*). Salzgitter had therefore become relatively profitable – it recorded a surplus of DM 90 million in the accounting year prior to its privatisa-

Table 8.5 Privatisation: calendar of events

Period/Company	Comments	Receipts (DM billion)
1984		
VEBA AG	Federal holding reduced from 43.7 per cent to 25.5 per cent	0.8
1986		
VIAG AG	Federal holding reduced from 87.4 per cent to 47.4 per cent, after capital injection	0.7
VW AG	Federal holding reduced from 20 per cent to 16 per cent	0.1
Industrieverwaltungsgesellschaft AG	Federal holding reduced from 100 per cent to 55 per cent	0.2
1987		
VEBA AG	Full privatisation	2.4
Deutsche Lufthansa AG	Federal holding reduced from 74.3 per cent to 65.4 per cent, after capital injection	0.1
1988		
VW AG	Full privatisation at Federal level[1]	1.1
VIAG AG	Full privatisation	1.2
Deutsche Verkehrskreditbank AG	Federal German Railways' holding reduced from 100 per cent to 75.1 per cent	0.1
1989[2]		
Schenker & Co. GmbH	Federal German Railways' holding reduced from 100 per cent to 77.5 per cent	0.1
Deutsche Lufthansa AG	Federal holding reduced from 65.4 per cent to 51.6 per cent, after capital injection	0.1
Deutsche Siedlungs-und Landesrentenbank	Federal holding reduced from 99 per cent to 51 per cent	0.2
Salzgitter AG	Full privatisation	2.5
Deutsche Industrieanlagen GmbH	Full privatisation	0.1
Total receipts		9.7

Source: OECD *Economic Survey* (Germany) 1990: 41

Notes: Table refers only to privatisation of federal holdings
    [1] Lower Saxony still owns 20 per cent of the share capital and is represented on VW's supervisory board (authors)
    [2] The Deutsche Pfandbriefanstalt was partially privatised in 1991 (authors). (See the section on Special-purpose banks in Chapter 7.)

tion (*Die Zeit* 43/89). By selling direct to Preussag, the Federal government avoided the two-year preparation required for a flotation. The revenue from the sale was therefore generated prior to the 1990 election, thereby assisting – on the eve of unification – in the then successful process of budgetary consolidation. One rationale put forward for the selection of Preussag was that both companies were located in Lower Saxony (*ibid.*). IG Metall, church representatives and even the Land's CDU politicians did not accept that the case had any merits (*ibid.*).

Finally, the potential for privatisation – and deregulation – was seen by the Federal government in the early 1990s as not being exhausted. The Federal Railways and parts of the Federal Postal Services were put forward as good examples (Leipold 1991: 141). A further reduction in the Federal holding in the state airline (Lufthansa) was also viewed as a possibility, as was the privatisation of the KfW (*Economist* 24 November 1990). But these were all longer-term propositions. Although the Federal post office had been divided into three sections (postal, telecommunications and banking – see below), Article 87(1) of the GG prohibited its sale to private investors. The necessary two-thirds majority for a constitutional amendment would have been difficult to obtain. Yet Deutsche Telekom was even put forward by the Federal government as a candidate for 'the people's share of the 1990s' (FT 11 August 1992). If this materialised, it would mark a return to the Erhard approach analysed above.

Lufthansa's complete privatisation was viewed as attainable by the end of the 1990s (*Guardian* 22 July 1992). Its problems at the beginning of the decade derived from the harsh economic and airline-industry environments, as well as ambitious expansion plans which backfired (FT

1 September 1992; Ogger 1992: 185). In three years, the number of Lufthansa employees had increased by 13,000 to 62,000 and its fleet from 120 to 275. In addition, unification meant increasing the number of loss-making routes. As a result, it began making losses in 1991 when its -732 per cent decline on the previous year's profits made it Europe's second worst performer (*Die Welt* 11 February 1993). The 1991 loss was the first in eighteen years (Ogger *ibid.*). A return to profitability was forecast by 1994–5 (FAZ 24 February 1993). Both the trade unions involved (the DAG and the ÖTV – see Chapter 6) accepted pay cuts and increased working hours, while the new chief executive made the point that British Airways had received strong government support when implementing its pre-privatisation recovery programme (FT *ibid.*).

The loss-making railways were expected to make accumulated losses of DM 420 billion by the end of the century. It was announced by the Federal government in 1993 that both networks – west and east – would be merged into the Deutsche Eisenbahn AG from 1994. (Like the postal services, the railways had been included as a matter for Federal administration in Article 87[1] of the GG. For that matter the foreign and fiscal services are assigned to the Federal government by this clause, but transforming the postal services into a joint stock company was an obvious next step.) Three component groups, dealing with track, freight and passenger traffic, would then permit partial privatisation. Non-essential property and subsidiaries such as the bus services could also be sold off. However, requiring the rail-track authorities to earn a commercial rate of return on their assets, or at least to break even, was seen by at least one German economist as a flaw in both the German and British proposals (FT 3

February 1993). Higher fares and line closures were the predicted results. To finance the Federal Railways it was also decided in February 1993 to privatise the state-owned motorway service areas in Germany. Motorway tolls and higher hydrocarbon duties were seen as other sources of financing the redemption of the railways debt.

PRIVATISATION IN EAST GERMANY

As emphasised in Chapters 1 and 4, post-wall Germany posed the challenge of integrating a former centrally planned economy into a larger, established market system. Moving from a centrally planned economy with government ownership of the means of production to a market economy should in the longer run improve incentives and increase economic efficiency. At a very early stage, it became clear that two processes would determine the size of the post-wall integration dividend. First, the process of privatisation in the east German economy, together with the success in assigning private rights to existing east German assets. Second, the integration process involving economic adjustments by existing firms and the creation of a broad base of new small and midsize businesses (Collier and Siebert 1991: 196). In short, it is the primary goal of any privatisation strategy to increase overall efficiency and assure that scarce resources are allocated optimally (Franz *et al.* 1992: 60).

But the privatisation programme in the east was not comparable to previous programmes. In order to understand the nature of the problems encountered, it is necessary to recall the extent of expropriation and centralisation which determined the economic framework of the former GDR (see Chapter 1). Above all, recall

that a large segment of the industrial sector was converted into VEBs and *Kombinate*. Thus, in 1988 virtually all industrial employment was accounted for by the state sector. In agriculture, collectivisation had resulted in the nationalisation of 90 per cent of all arable land. Private ownership was essentially confined to small-scale businesses, restaurants, and craft shops and these were permitted to exist only if they were 'predominantly based on personal labour' (Lipschitz and McDonald 1990: 57).

As a consequence, industry in the GDR exhibited the following weaknesses. Firms tended to keep huge inventories of raw material and intermediate goods as buffers against unexpected and unplanned developments. Industrial efficiency was severely impaired by a tendency towards self-production of inputs. This under-specialization was also reflected in the pattern of foreign trade. As the behaviour of firms was neither controlled by private owners nor by a capital market, managers had no pronounced incentives to keep the physical capital stock intact. New technologies were introduced only slowly and reluctantly. As a consequence of these shortcomings, the existing capital stock was mostly outdated, to a considerable extent physically run down and largely economically and environmentally obsolete (Siebert and Schmieding 1990: 3–6). Furthermore, GDR employment was heavily concentrated in sectors and branches that had been declining rapidly in the West. Taken together, agriculture, forestry and fishery, energy and mining, and the clothing, leather goods and textiles industries accounted for about 18 per cent of the GDR labour force as opposed to 9 per cent in West Germany (see also Figures 2.3a and 2.3b).

With the introduction of GEMSU, producers lost their well-protected and clearly segmented outlets. They were exposed to the competition of western firms. There was an urgent need to clarify property rights and privatise and reorganise state-owned enterprises. In addition, the oversized public administration had to be reduced (Klodt 1990: 3). Reorganisation has two different meanings (Bös 1991: 185). First it can refer to the reorganisation of the economy. In east Germany this was achieved in part by splitting up the *Kombinate*. Second, reorganization refers to the technological restructuring (or rationalisation – *Sanierung*) of any single industrial firm.

However, precisely how the transformation from a socialist economic order to a market economy could be achieved was a completely open question. As already emphasised in Chapter 1, one must resist the temptation to seek common patterns between West Germany in 1948 and East Germany in 1990 (Loesch 1990, Ehret and Patzig 1991). GEMSU led to an economic collapse in the new Länder. Apart from the financial support, the situation was not analogous to post-war West Germany. An important difference between the two starting points is that East German enterprises entered GEMSU as inefficient producers for the reasons mentioned immediately above. The marginal capital output ratio was higher than in 1948 which meant an increase in capacity requiring considerably higher investment. The wage determination process was different from 1948 because the wage level in East Germany on integration was completely out of line with productivity and wages were likely to grow faster than productivity.

On the other hand, the east German experience is unique among transition economies because the country inherited not only a complete set of institutions appropriate to advanced industrial countries, but also access to experienced administrators to run those institutions. Among these imports are the legal system, a system of property rights, and a set of courts; a social system, including unemployment benefits; a hard currency; a system of public finance; and a banking system with branches that opened immediately after unification (Dornbusch and Wolf 1992: 236). But the social union that went into effect simultaneously with the monetary and economic union extended also a social welfare system that had evolved to fit a relatively rich, well-developed economy (see Chapter 5). Furthermore, there was an understandable though unrealistic expectation that West German levels of real consumption could be achieved without closing the productivity gap between East and West. East German impatience for West German prosperity was enhanced by an entitlement mentality which survived the Communist economic system that fostered it. Similarly, the post-war western disposition of treating east Germans as western citizens fuelled unrealistic expectations. There was also a risk of extreme corporatism, in that the state and pressure groups could become increasingly influential in decision making. The consequent bureaucracy could become even more complex than the one which evolved in West Germany (Dichmann 1991: 308; also see the section on the public sector above). These psychological and political factors had the potential to complicate both the privatisation and the real adjustment processes of German economic integration (Collier and Siebert 1991: 10). Apart from these factors, however, the conditions for privatisation were better than in other eastern European countries. Unlike them, east Germany had the same currency and the same institutional framework as west Germany, and it therefore has the potential to attract the vitally necessary massive capital flows.

The core of the adjustment process was the restructuring of east German industry. In restructuring existing firms three different facets need to be distinguished: the legal independence of the constituent enterprises within the *Kombinate*, the economic efficiency of these individual enterprises and, last but not least, their ownership (Collier and Siebert 1991: 4). In the face of formidable competitive pressures, east German enterprises had to increase their efficiency by restructuring their input and product mixes. Cutting back the work force was clearly the most sensitive issue facing managers. Yet these aspects of rationalisation were closely linked to the issue of privatisation. To supervise this difficult process, the property rights of publicly owned firms were transferred to a new government trustee agency, the Treuhandanstalt. This institution – abbreviated to the Treuhand – is analysed in the next section, but what can be said about its theoretical aims?

A rational privatisation scheme ought to meet a variety of economic and political criteria (Siebert 1991a: 52):

- decisions in firms are dominated by economic considerations
- a dynamic process of structural change is possible
- capital is allocated to its optimum use in the economy
- managers are controlled by the capital market

The analysis in both this and the previous chapters has been largely devoted to showing that West German firms and the economy's unique capital markets do not operate in strict accordance with this version of rationality. Indeed, some researchers suggest a totally different scenario (Wenger 1987, 1990 and 1992). An

appreciable amount of analysis has also been devoted to removing the misapprehension that the ideal market economy model of a medium-sized firm run by its owners is the norm in west Germany (Flassbeck 1993: 91). Reconciling the frequently divergent interests of owners and controllers in large companies is a central corporate problem in the industrial market economies. Moreover, an enduring weakness in the West German economy was new business formation and this problem was confounded by the capital market being risk averse (Porter 1990: 377). Finally, anti-trust policy evolved following and during a period of intense concentration and public-sector enterprise remained a key feature of the economy (see above). The above criteria were therefore in effect setting new standards for the already chaotic economy of East Germany. Technological backwardness, environmental and ecological disasters, as well as inferior physical and human capital formation were all impervious to pure market reform. Yet the Treuhand was expected to support market forces (Beyer and Nutzinger 1991: 252). The central purpose of the Treuhand was therefore accelerating the process of structural adjustment, but its brief lacked clarity (Flassbeck 1993: 81):

A policy, such as the one in west Germany, which cushions structural change over long periods, was avoided . . . The Federal government feared the risk of new long-term subsidy situations just as much as the preservation of old structures . . . [The preferred policy configuration], partly for financial reasons and partly for reasons of order, [consisted of] currency reform, institutional adjustment, immediate inclusion in the world economy, the opening of markets and the resulting transformation shock . . . [Such a policy framework] assumed that companies in east Germany could be made competitive with relatively little expense and then privatised without further ado. The assumption has been rendered largely invalid by the nature of the currency union, wage developments and the disintegration of traditional markets in Eastern Europe. The Treuhand had to make decisions about structural policy without being able to fall back on clearly defined concepts of structural policy and follow them actively. In fact, matters of structural policy have so far not played a decisive role in the work of the Treuhand.

The bottom line was that the Treuhand itself became responsible for the rationalisation and other adjustments that the 'new' owners would have implemented under a perfectly operating system of privatisation (Beyer and Nutzinger 1991: 254).

THE *TREUHANDANSTALT*

The Treuhand was established on 1 March 1990 and began its work on 15 March. The formation of the institution therefore preceded GEMSU. Its initial aim was to administer collectively-owned property, the sale of which was not anticipated. Such property was considered to be indivisible, but transformable in its legal structure. An effective role for the Treuhand in the transformation process was therefore not conceivable. It was regarded as an institution for the trustee administration of collective property and therefore as an institution for securing public ownership (Kroll 1991: 12). The statutory duties of denationalisation and privatisation were contained in the Treuhand Act which became effective on 1 July as part of GEMSU. Under this Act state-owned enterprises were transformed into AGs or GmbHs, and a public trust fund for the administration of state property (the Treuhandanstalt) assumed temporary ownership, the term 'temporary' emphasising what was optimistically seen as the transient nature of the Treuhand's role (Beyer and Nutzinger 1991: 251–3).

The Treuhand was given a structure similar to a German public company: it was headed by an executive board (*Vorstand*) consisting of a president and four directors, who were to be appointed by the supervisory council (*Verwaltungsrat*). The supervisory council consisted of a chairman and 16 members. It was to monitor and support the operations of the executive board. The chairman and seven council members were to be appointed by the GDR government and the remaining members by the GDR parliament. West Germans entered the Treuhand in mid-July 1990. With the dissolution of the GDR in October 1990, the Treuhand in its current form started with less than 100 people, almost no initial knowledge of their vast inventory of companies, property and other assets, and no historical precedent to guide them in their functions. Following unification, the Treuhand was formally linked to the Federal Ministry of Finance in Bonn, but enjoyed wide-ranging autonomy in its decision making powers.

The privatisation of firms was recognised to be indispensable for the transition into a market economy, and the purpose of the Treuhand was consequently redefined. The new assignment was to rationalise firms, to make them fit for the demands of a market environment, and to transfer them into private hands. It took some time before some organisational and, more especially, personnel modifications enabled the Treuhand to meet its new terms of reference. It was late 1990 before the process of privatisation began.

Considerable progress was subsequently made.

The Treuhand became the owner of about 8,000 east German industrial enterprises, most of which had to be privatised. They possessed no fewer than 40,000 separate factories and the Treuhand thus became the world's largest holding company (Schuppert 1992: 188). In addition, it had to dispose of 45,000 establishments, 20,000 commercial businesses, 7,500 hotels and restaurants, 1,000 pharmacies, and numerous bookshops and cinemas (Dornbusch and Wolf 1992: 243). As a result, the agency was responsible for about 3.7 million jobs. The goal of privatisation implied the need to divide firms into smaller units. Organisational subunits of state monopolies had the option of declaring themselves legally independent units. The actual process of privatisation commenced in two steps. First, the VEBs were transformed into either AGs or GmbHs. This necessitated the production of articles of association and starting balance sheets. The deadline for submitting these documents to the Treuhand was 31 October 1990, but half the firms were granted extensions. Second, the Treuhand started to sell the companies. There were no restrictions on potential buyers, other than those imposed by the BKA. In particular, there were no constraints on the nationality of the buyers.

The Treuhand was subdivided into four departments reflecting the main tasks of the agency: Reconstruction, Privatisation, Labour Market/Social Policy, and Finance. In accordance with the Treuhand Act, the agency was thus not only charged with privatisation. One fundamental impediment to privatisation was that many east German enterprises had a negative value, since their costs exceeded their revenue. Such firms could be sold for their property, land or scrap value, but not to individuals or firms who were prepared to operate them. Hence, the Treuhand was faced with a choice of either subsidising or liquidating such loss making firms. Reconstruction and liquidation of state enterprises were, therefore, further options (Akerlof et al. 1991: 3). In anticipation of future privatisation revenues, the Treuhand was prepared to make financial injections and grant bridging loans which helped companies overcome liquidity problems during reconstruction. In the Unification Treaty the credit limit of the Treuhand was extended to DM 25 billion (Schnabel 1992: 247). As a result of the solidarity agreement designed to partially fund unification costs – reached with difficulty in 1993 – the Treuhand's borrowing limit was increased by a further DM 30 billion (FT 15 March 1993). Significantly, these additional funds were required both for the 'restructuring of core industries' which could not be sold, and for eradicating their environmental and ecological damage. Such restructured industries would, however, then become serious competitors for their recession-hit counterparts in the west. For example, the chemical industry queried if there were markets enough to absorb the east's output (FT 16 March 1993).

STAGES IN THE PRIVATISATION PROCESS

Five stages can be distinguished in the privatisation process since 1990. The first stage was the transformation of the Kombinate into legally independent enterprises and companies. This involved the Treuhand in providing assistance which enabled enterprises to carry out analyses of their competitiveness, ascertain their liquidity, acquire suitable legal forms of business organization and prepare 'opening balance sheets' in Deutsche Marks. A team of 80 top West German managers spent four months analysing balance sheets and restructuring plans in order to determine the future viability of an enterprise. These enterprises were then divided into six categories (Carlin and Mayer 1992: 329):

1 Profitable, therefore no further requirement for restructuring and can be privatised quickly.
2 Expected to be profitable, require little restructuring, can be privatised quickly.
3 Can probably be successfully privatised, disaggregated into
   (i) those that must produce a binding cooperation agreement (with purchaser) or be transferred to categories 5 or 6 and
   (ii) those that cannot be privatised immediately.
4 Appear capable of being profitable but have inadequate plans. Alternative plans were required.
5 Unlikely to become profitable, detailed investigations required.
6 Cannot be made profitable, bankruptcy or liquidation required.

Evaluations were based on whether an enterprise was 'potentially viable' (categories 1–4) with restructuring and 70 per cent of the firms were classified as potentially viable in this sense. The remaining 30 per cent were being re-examined. The Treuhand itself initially stated that 10 per cent of enterprises would have to be closed. Revised estimates put the closure proportion at 20 per cent to 30 per cent.

In the second stage the role of the Treuhand had to be clarified. Privatisation became its central goal in order to secure the transformation of centrally planned enterprises within the terms of the Treuhand Act. Following the principles of the SME, therefore, the Treuhand was required to privatise and utilise the public funds to promote the structural adjustment of the economy. It was also to support the reconstruction of firms by supplying loans for that purpose. But by the end of 1990 only 403 firms had been privatised.

The main task in the third stage of privatisation was to secure the liquidity of enterprises as a precondition for their resale and reconstruction. However, necessary liquidation strategies were to be devised. First and foremost, the Treuhand functioned as a 'lender of last resort' (Schmid-Schönbein and Hansel 1991: 463). Complete bankruptcy had to be prevented. The Treuhand consequently decided to take over 41 per cent of total financial requirements. There were no alternatives to this 'watering can principle'. At the end of 1991 only 730 firms needed an extension of credits. The relatively small privatisation programme in the service sector was nearly completed. Larger retail stores and smaller hotels were all privatised, as were 76 per cent of small stores and restaurants, along with 62 per cent of pharmacies. About 80 per cent of these firms were taken over by east German citizens (Deutscher Sparkassen-. . . 1992: 119). A *Mittelstand* therefore began to fairly rapidly emerge in the east. But only 20 per cent of industrial firms had been privatised. (It should be added that within the Treuhand the head office was in charge of firms with more than 1,500 employees, while the smaller firms were delegated to regional branches.) In the industrial sector, the speed of privatisation increased from 90 units in October 1990 to 321 in February 1991. By July 1991, 833 firms had been privatised by the head office and 2,153 by regional branches. At this stage, 435 firms evaluated as non-viable had been closed, affecting 76,360 employees (Siebert 1991b: 300).

⦿ The sales strategy of the Treuhand was significantly extended at the fourth stage. As already indicated, it was empowered to sell most of its enterprises for scrap or for redevelopment. But the Treuhand was reluctant to do so. Instead, it preferred purchasers to continue employing workers and to create new jobs. This clearly illustrates its concern about employment. The sales of firms by the Treuhand were thus contingent upon job guarantees, investment undertakings, sales prices and entrepreneurial potential (Berg 1992: 149–52). In fact, the decision to sell mainly depended on investment and employment commitments. The Treuhand therefore appreciably discounted its sale prices and assumed responsibility for large parts of the former liabilities of the enterprises it succeeded in selling. Where the buyer did not observe undertakings, compensatory payments to the Treuhand may have been required. Attaching such conditions reduced Treuhand's sales revenue.

An analysis of the various factors summarised in this section provides a useful profile of the Treuhand's activities. As the identification of enterprises proceeded, along with their transformation into legally independent organisations, so the total portfolio of companies on the Treuhand balance sheet increased. At the end of 1990, there were thus 10,952 enterprises, while in July 1992 there were 12,883 (iwd2 3/92: 93). However, the SVR (BT 12/3774: para 113) discounted over 650 enterprises either because they had been written off following mergers and segmentation, or were classified as forestry and mining entities. Similarly, nearly 2,000 further companies were excluded on the grounds that (*ibid.*):

- there had been 1,039 restitutions plus the provisional allocation of ownership in 69 further cases
- majority holdings had been sold in 541 companies
- 244 companies had been transferred to local-authority ownership – the antithesis of privatisation, thereby further exacerbating the public-sector ownership complexities described above
- 28 enterprises had been liquidated

In other words, by Autumn 1992, almost 4,500 enterprises had been fully privatised and about 5,200 remained officially on the books of the Treuhand (*ibid.*). Management buyouts may have accounted for 1,781 of the 4,500 full privatised enterprises. Of the 5,200 enterprises remaining, the Treuhand had begun to liquidate 1,788 and the balance of these companies were still to be fully privatised (Dresdner Bank *Trends* 2/93). Further progress was subsequently made. Hence, by the end of January 1993, Treuhand informed the authors that 4,998 enterprises had been fully privatised.

Working on a slightly different basis, Gemählich (1992: 56) estimated that at the end of 1991 about 5,000 firms had been completely or *partially* privatised, two thirds of them by the regional offices, one third by the Treuhand's central office. Investment promises of about DM 100 billion and job guarantees for nearly one million employees were obtained, about 40 per cent of the existing jobs in the privatised firms. In March 1992, more than two-thirds of agricultural and forestry enterprises, along with half the enterprises in mining, energy, steel, engineering and textiles, all still had to be privatised (Flassbeck 1993: 83). The Dresdner Bank (*ibid.*) reported that, by Autumn 1992, the Treuhand had received

1.32 million job guarantees and investment commitments amounting to DM 155.3 billion. There was a fair degree of concentration in these commitments. Over DM 30 billion of the investment undertakings, and 77,000 of the job guarantees, were made by west German energy concerns in conjunction with east German local authorities. Finally, there remained a hardcore of at least 2,400 enterprises, employing 400,000 persons, for which it had become increasingly difficult to find a purchaser (BfG: *Standpunkt* 3–4/93). Policy interest in the mid-1990s will therefore focus on the fate of these enterprises – many of which have 'stagnated' while in the ownership of the Treuhand (Flassbeck 1993: 94–5). It is difficult to escape the conclusion that the ethos of the privatisation process was at least partially misconceived. The process probably owed much to those policy observers who extolled the virtues of market forces and the perceived success of privatisation in the industrialised market economies (Fels and von Furstenberg 1989). Yet there were a number of disadvantages to this policy scenario, not least the implications of western companies dominating the ownership of eastern enterprises (Beyer and Nutzinger 1991: 258–9). The new Länder governments predictably became the most vocal advocates of an eastern *Industriepolitik* – a term which meant preserving firms with a 'regional significance' (*Economist* 27 March 1993). The Treuhand thus agreed to place at least 40 companies in Saxony's Atlas programme, which the agency would modernise and subsidise for one year. Thereafter, a further judgement was to be taken about their market prospects. Other eastern Länder considered cloning the Atlas model. Such a finite limit should be placed on all subsidy programmes. The obvious comparison here is the Akerlof model discussed in the adjustment section of Chapter 6. This approach is preferable to the immediate and ruthless operation of a market creed which was in any case not emulated in the west.

For these reasons alone, including entrepreneurial potential as an independent privatisation criterion is comprehensible only in the context of the Treuhand's predisposition to secure jobs. It is not necessarily compatible with the aim of creating efficient and competitive structures. From a competitive point of view such a criterion would be superfluous and the most efficient concept would be preferred. In competitive structured markets, the Treuhand would achieve the highest quotation, allowing unprofitable jobs to be eliminated. In a market economy without distortions, the Treuhand would maximize social welfare by maximizing the proceeds from privatisation. Each enterprise would be sold to the highest bidder, with no additional conditions of sale. However, the Treuhand's emphasis on employment safeguards can be justified because there was a major distortion in the east German economy. Wages were significantly above market clearing rates. Thus, in the absence of a job creation policy, employment in east Germany would be well below the socially optimal level so that the Trust was acting in the country's best interest by promoting employment as a major objective (Akerlof *et al.* 1991: 68). The enforcement of job guarantees meant in effect the privatisation of employment policy. Probably such a strategy was less costly than unilateral efforts by the state to create new jobs using traditional instruments of labour market policy (MK IX: 19–20). In several instances, the Treuhand accepted a symbolic payment of a single DM when the buyers of the firm gave explicit job guarantees.

The fifth stage was characterised by a revaluation of the aim of reconstruction and was accompanied by a public discussion about the ranking of the Treuhand's goals. Because of the rising unemployment in east Germany the discussion became increasingly political. The process of privatisation became rather sluggish, although given the integration with the far more affluent west Germany, a very 'effective' demand should in theory have existed. A long, drawn-out process of privatisation would have consequences not only for the rate of capital investment, but also for the financial needs of the institution entrusted with privatisation, the Treuhand (Heilemann 1991b: 145).

METHODS OF PRIVATISATION

The decision to use the Treuhand approach to privatisation had underlying political reasons. First, there was broad agreement that immediate and rapid privatisation was necessary. A sustained divergence of production levels and employment between east and west would generate large additional transfers and could lead to an inefficient and extremely costly structural policy (see below). Second, the conditions for privatisation differ from other eastern European countries where the free distribution of assets was advocated. These erstwhile centrally planned economies lacked a market system and the institution of private property. For these economies, many schemes were suggested for the direct transfer of shares, as a way of enforcing the privatisation process. One proposal has been to issue to the general public, free of charge, a large number of vouchers which could then be used for bidding at auctions. Another proposal was to put the shares of state-owned enterprises in a few holding companies, with the shares of holding companies in turn distributed to the public (Watrin 1991: 168). In East Germany new capital was more likely to be attracted because there was no exchange rate risk, no risk of changes in the institutional conditions and also a reasonable degree of political stability. The chosen privatisation procedure was designed to fully exploit these potential advantages of private capital transfers. A voucher system would be much slower. Furthermore, new management had to be established quickly since the firms required new strategies to compete successfully in an open economy. The voucher system does not easily solve this issue of corporate control (Siebert 1991b: 301). For all these reasons, the voucher system was never seriously considered in Germany and the Treuhand approach seemed better suited to prevailing conditions.

In principle, three types of privatisation methods were isolated (Siebert 1991b: 301). One extreme lay in 'informal selling', whereby the Treuhand negotiated with only one or a few buyers. The advantage of such a privatisation strategy is that it does not require much time. On the other hand, there may have been a shortage of bidders, thus driving down the selling price. As a consequence, the sale and price policy becomes ambiguous and possibly leads to distrust on the part of other potential buyers. A classic case was the solution for the former Kombinat Carl Zeiss Jena. The Baden-Württemberg firm Carl Zeiss of Oberkochen was preferred and extremely favourable conditions were negotiated. These conditions, which were gradually improved after the deal had been agreed, involved a Treuhand expenditure of more than DM 3.5 billion. Many other firms may well have been interested had the privatisation policy been clear at the outset (Priewe 1992: 71).

The other extreme form of a privatisation strategy is to use the stock market, which provides a reliable evaluation of a firm's value, including a market judgement on its economic viability. The privatisation of Sachsenmilch AG is one example of this approach. But in the case of the stock market there exist many preconditions which are not fulfilled. As well as the legal regulations, economic considerations are also important. An issuer will require assurances about earning power and potential yields, the status of the firm and no objection to publicity. Furthermore, stock issued on the stock market leads to a privatisation of ownership, but not automatically to a new concept or strategy for the enterprise. Yet the latter is at least of equally critical importance to the privatised company's future.

In between the two extremes (informal selling and a stock market issue) lies a formal bidding process: in contrast to a diminished market, formal bidding reveals the willingness to pay and the intentions of potential buyers. It has also the advantage of providing new management and injecting new capital. The bidding process is a mechanism that provides a substitute for a stock exchange. Such an institution did not in any case exist in eastern Germany – a situation clearly far worse than the underdeveloped system in west Germany (see Chapter 7). Privatisation in the formal bidding model is the result of negotiations on each single object, if possible with competing bidders. The basic idea behind this procedure is that nobody is better qualified than private entrepreneurs to find out the economic potential of the assets for which the Treuhand was trustee.

The Treuhand permanently extended its information network to reach a large scale of bidders. Investment banks and management consultants were engaged in the privatisation process. To soften the one-sided predominance of West German buyers, potential foreign buyers were able to consult Treuhand representatives in important industrial countries. Offices were established in New York and Tokyo and international invitations to tender were also issued. Moreover, the Treuhand introduced additional methods of attracting qualified management, new sources of capital and the establishment of independent enterprises in east Germany:

- Different forms of staff participation, especially management and employee buy outs, as well as management buy ins (purchase of firms by external executives) (Flassbeck 1993: 84–5; Beyer and Nutzinger 1991: 256–65). Mixed forms of three methods were also possible. The difficulties involved in raising capital restricts the initiative of management buy outs, except where firms require only a small amount of equity capital. By June 1992 there had been 1,350 privatisations through management buy outs with an average number of employees of 44 involved

- Private fund models provide further opportunities. For example, the German Industrial Holding Company (Deutsche Industrie-Holding-DIH). The DIH took over and reconstructed Treuhand firms to prepare for a later public issue on the stock market or a direct sale

- Another model with the assistance of the public authorities was developed in Saxony. A 'Saxony Fund' was established as a joint-stock company. With the capital from the fund and the advice of experienced managers from the private sector, firms were selected from the Treuhand's portfolio to be reconstructed and thereby contribute to the formation of an independent industrial *Mittelstand*. After reconstruction the firms could be sold or transferred to the stock market. The planned equity capital of DM 500 million was not provided by the state, but completely by credit institutions, insurance companies and other enterprises

- Finally, the Treuhand considered approaches to 'privatise' the reconstruction order. Enterprises with considerable reconstruction requirements of about 500 employees and more were affected (Thanner 1991: 24). Management companies were founded to take over Treuhand firms and reconstruct them before they were offered for sale. The main incentive for the executives from the private sector would be a later interest in potential privatisation revenues (Siebert 1993: 14)

To encourage investment in Eastern Germany, the government also introduced a comprehensive programme of incentives and subsidies which could provide over 50 per cent of the cost of investment. This programme was available without restriction equally to German and foreign investors. Direct incentives also are provided in the form of investment allowances or grants (Breuel 1992: 39):

- investment grants of up to 23 per cent of the total cost incurred
- grants up to 20 per cent of total cost associated with expansion of an existing business
- grants up to 12 per cent of total costs for purchases of capital equipment vital to the operation of the business
- accelerated depreciation allowances for fixed assets at a rate of 50 per cent,

30 per cent and 20 per cent over the first three years of operation

DIFFICULTIES DURING THE PRIVATISATION PROCESS

Returning to the term privatisation as such, it should be noted that a distinction must be drawn between privatisation of an economy, that is the growth of the private sector relative to the state sector, and the privatisation of firms, that is the transfer of ownership titles in existing firms into private hands. Given the dismal state of many firms and the time their privatisation inevitably consumed, the top-down establishment of capitalism can be at least retrospectively seen as being of rather limited importance. Instead, the growth of the private sector and hence the economic re-emergence of the former GDR was to a greater extent dependent upon the establishment of new private firms and the growth of existing small units (the bottom-up emergence of capitalism). A lengthy process of privatisation would inevitably have consequences not only for the rate of investment, but also for the refinancing needs of the Treuhand (Heilemann 1991a: 145). One of the first corollaries of any privatisation policy should therefore consist of ensuring that all obstacles to the establishment and expansion of small and new private enterprises are removed (Schmieding 1992: 98).

However, uncertainty over property rights was estimated to be the most important bottleneck to a self-sustained growth process. Thus in spite of all the efforts on the part of both the government and the Treuhand to induce privatisation there were the uncertainties arising from property rights which prevented fast and extensive privatisation. Allocative efficiency does not depend on how property rights are initially distributed: from the economic point of view, it does not matter how firms are privatised – whether they are sold or given away. The initial distribution of wealth may affect current saving and the allocation of capital but not the efficiency of capital allocation. What matters is that property rights are extensive, clearly defined and effectively enforced (Vaubel 1992: 112). It follows that property rights must be established. Unclear property rights were a major obstacle to investment in east Germany. Existing owners were not willing to invest and the previous owners would not do so either. Nor would new investors buy the contested properties and begin new businesses (Sinn 1992a: 103). Ultimately, everything hinged on the clarification of ownership.

In June 1990, the governments of West and East Germany published an agreement on the principle of privatisation, and the Volkskammer of the GDR passed a statute on the privatisation and reorganization of state-owned property. The agreement stipulated that the following principles would guide the privatisation process (Lipschitz and McDonald 1990: 57):

- Expropriations undertaken by the Soviet Military Government in 1945–49 would not be reversed, but an all-German parliament would have the right to determine appropriate compensation

- Expropriated or state-administered land and real estate would in principle be returned to the previous owners or their heirs. If, however, land or real estate had been used for other than its original purpose and could not be returned, compensation would be paid. This applied also to cases where the property has been legally acquired in good faith by citizens of the GDR

- Companies or holdings expropriated after 1949 would, in principle, be returned to their previous owners. For companies expropriated between 1949 and 1972, compensation might be paid in lieu of restoration of ownership rights

- The GDR authorities would establish an extra budgetary fund to finance compensation payments. Applications for the return of property or compensation would have to be submitted within a time period to be specified; this deadline would be no later than six months after the effective date of GEMSU. The authorities would ensure that no land or real estate, the property rights to which were unclear, would be sold before the expiration of the application period

The restitution principle has been severely criticised as the major mistake of the transformation process, but it should not be forgotten that respect for private property is essential for the functioning of a market economy. The commitment to respect property rights in the future is not quite credible if they have been disregarded in the past.

There are three different kinds of property that could be formally distinguished (Siebert 1992b: 10). First, land, including buildings (but not firms), where the previous owners have a right to restitution. Second, those firms which will be given back to their previous owners. Third, state-owned firms where new ownership has to be established. A major problem is that ownership of land and ownership of firms are not necessarily distinct and the assignment of property titles, together with the mapping of objects and titles of owners, may be inconsistent.

There were 1.7 million applications for restitution of the ownership of land and buildings, each of them requiring an administrative decision. Title records were not up to date and inheritance claims involved confirming relationships. It is little wonder that the process was complex (iwd2 39/92). Moreover, each administrative decision could be challenged in the administrative court system. Only about 130,000 claims for land and buildings had been dealt with at the end of 1992. It is estimated by experts that it will take a further ten years to determine these ownership claims.

The restitution of firms and land to former owners related to 17,000 cases with roughly 4,000 having been returned by September 1991 (Nunnenkamp 1992: 61). At the beginning of 1991, the German government had decisively diminished the principle of restitution in kind. On 29 March, Parliament passed the Act on the Removal of Obstacles to Privatisation of Enterprises and on the Promotion of Investment (*Hemmungsbeseitigungsgesetz* – Tietz 1991: 196–201). The core part of this Act consisted of several amendments to the Restitution Act and to the Investment Act facilitating the sale of enterprises and of property pending restitution claims of the former owners. Under the new Act, the Treuhand had farreaching competence to overrule former owners who did not present an investment programme equivalent to that of any other competing investor.

The restrictions on the nominal owner's power of disposition were suspended and a former owner's claim for restitution no longer impeded a sale if the following prerequisites and criteria were met (Breuel 1992: 40):

- the investment purposes for which real estate had to be used by the investor are to create or preserve jobs, in particular, building a production plant

or setting up a service company or to construct residential buildings
- the investment purposes with respect to enterprises were that the investor must create or save jobs or allow investments improving the competitiveness of the enterprise or at least continue the business of the enterprise, while the claimant under the Restitution Act leaves doubt as to whether he would do so

The Restitution Act authorises the Treuhand itself to decide on whether special investment purposes exist and, if so, to overrule the former owner's claim for restitution. The claim is then converted into a monetary claim for compensation direct against the Treuhand corresponding to the market value of the enterprise or to the selling price, whichever is the higher (Horn 1991: 146).

While the *Hemmnisbeseitigungsgesetz* improved the prospects for a faster process of privatisation, other obstacles remained. The reorganisation of the authorities proved to be a protracted process. They therefore operated inefficiently, leading to time-consuming and costly preprivatisation procedures. The equipment of the firms awaiting privatisation was often obsolete, in both a technical and environmental sense. The unsatisfactory infrastructure resulted in the type of concessions in the sales price described above. Restrictive legal regulations also made privatisation more difficult. For example, some agreements obliged investors to take over the entire staff of state-owned enterprises even though they required only sections of the labour force for the planned activities.

Another privatisation problem was the sale of uneconomically large units. This especially deterred potential *Mittelstand* clients. These units were split up and regrouped, so that firms which were more suitable for privatisation resulted. The legal foundation has been the *Spaltungsgesetz* from April 1991 (Welter 1992: 168). This statute produced an increase in the number of privatised firms. (From 8,000 in 1990 to 13,000 in 1992). As the reports of the Treuhand indicate, the *Spaltungsgesetz* also furnishes an explanation for the number of remaining units increasing even though progress in privatisation had been made.

THE EXTENT OF PRIVATISATION

Three years after GEMSU, the privatisation process was not completed. Considering the 13,000 firms which had to be privatised, and the relatively short time period involved, this does not detract from the performance of the Treuhand. Note, however, that an accelerating rate of privatisation after 1991 still led to observable differences between different sectors of the economy. Several factors accounted for the disparities in the rates of transformation.

High transformation ratios were achieved in sectors where sales were regionally concentrated and which were not exposed to intense external competition. In other words, these sectors are domestic market orientated and therefore in some cases produced non-traded goods. High transformation ratios can be observed in banking, construction and services. Construction derived particular benefits from the capital transfers from the west since they favoured building activities in general and, more especially, infrastructure construction (Hillebrandt 1992: 146). Related quarrying and brick works were also privatised fairly quickly, as were establishments in the food, drink and tobacco trades (BT 12/3774: para 113).

Less successful transformation ratios reflected difficult circumstances. Notable causes of these difficulties were uncertain property rights in agriculture, accumulated debt, antiquated and environmentally dangerous capital equipment in energy and mining and Comecon export dependency in parts of the industrial sector. Accumulated debt was DM 104 billion, of which the Treuhand inherited DM 70 billion (German Embassy (London) *Report* April 1993). Particular problems arose where industry's internationally competitive position was weak – and competitive disadvantages were considerable (high wages, low quality). In addition, former markets in the eastern European economies collapsed. The deficits incurred in privatising the machinery, motor vehicle, chemical, metal fabrication and textile industries were correspondingly high (Gruhler 1992: 104). In addition, the SVR (12/3774: para 215) emphasised privatisation difficulties in mining and the leather and shoe industries.

Firms classified by the Treuhand as already having been sold, or viable with reorganisation, do not constitute a reliable guide to the residual privatisation problems. In the remaining firms, half the employees were located in sectors which were confronted with acute problems of adaptation, again stemming from the collapse in trade with the East and a simultaneous slowing down of economic activity in the West (DIW 1992: 16).

It is now predictable that, as the end of the privatisation phase is reached, privatisation will not have been the financial success expected in mid-1990. At that time, productive property in the former GDR was estimated by the Treuhand to be worth about DM 600 billion, inclusive of land and property. Subsequent estimates indicated a probable final deficit in the region of DM 250 billion. Some of these liabilities arose from the special concessions made to facilitate the process of privatisation. But as already indicated revenue maximisation was not the major aim of the Treuhand. More importance was attached to the maintenance of employment and investment guarantees. In spite of this considered approach, however, political pressure on the Treuhand increased.

PRIVATISATION AND REORGANISATION

The statutory duties of the Treuhand were not confined to privatisation. In addition, the Treuhand Act required that the reorganisation of firms should be actively supported, provided that there was a viable product market which would permit long term survival. This legal provision has been a contentious subject. The Treuhand was criticised for placing too much emphasis on privatisation and neglecting reorganisation. It is important to define reorganisation in this context. In its narrowest sense, reorganisation means in principle that firms should be privatised since privatisation is considered the best method of reorganisation (SVR *Jahresgutachten* 1990: para 516). A broader interpretation of reorganisation indicates that firms should be supported in order to mitigate the adverse consequences of restructuring the enterprises, especially for employment levels. There is a finite limit to such financial support. The broadest interpretation of reorganisation implies that subsidies should be made available to firms that cannot be privatised. This no longer represents by definition an economic reorganisation (Maurer *et al.* 1991: 48).

Consequently, there are two discrete strategies for privatisation: reorganisation or immediate sale. When priority is accorded to reorganisation, firms are initially revitalised as far as possible. This includes the appointment of new management, changes to the organisational structure, the introduction of accurate accounting methods and staff reductions. The affected firms were offered for sale only after successful restoration. By adopting such an approach it was hoped that a higher sale price could be realised – an outcome in the interest of the public sector (Wild 1991: 10). When priority is accorded to an immediate sale, however, it can be justified on the grounds of the Treuhand's limited and insufficient information; obtaining more adequate information would have overloaded the Treuhand's resources (iwd2 41/91).

An assessment of the two approaches can be made by referring to the clause in the Treuhand Act which clearly states that firms should be reconstructed so as to prepare them for a competitive environment. This was not possible unless three fundamental conditions were fulfilled: the clarification of a viable unit, the formulation of an entrepreneurial concept, and the acquisition of the necessary financial funds. If this notion of reorganisation was accepted, the conflict between privatisation and reorganisation had less significance (Hax 1992: 146). But a further question had to be posed: should privatisation be brought about by selling potential firms to investors who have their own entrepreneurial concept or should reorganisation by the Treuhand precede privatisation?

If the issue is viewed in this way, it could be contended that the Treuhand was not in a position to reorganise a large pool of enterprises. The hypothesis that firms should first be reorganised and then sold is based on the implicit assumption that the Treuhand is better qualified to develop promising entrepreneurial concepts for a large number of firms than individual investors who single out the object which they regard as being suited for their own activities. But because of its legal construction, its size and multiple activities, the Treuhand was not equipped to actively organise the reconstruction of the firms. There was a lack of qualified entrepreneurs who could develop, assess and implement reconstruction plans. In contrast to the UK, where state-owned enterprises have been reorganized before privatisation, the scale is quite different (Deutscher Sparkassen- . . . 1992: 121). (It could be added that British privatisation was often preceded by the writing off of debt. In this sense Thatcherism had something in common with the Treuhand's policies.)

Moreover, when comparing reorganisation by the Treuhand to reorganisation by a private investor, the question of incentives arises. Since reorganisation requires funds for capital investment, acquirers of firms would either use their own funds or they will have to convince financial institutions that the acquisition promises an acceptable future rate of return. This was probably the best achievable guarantee that investment plans will be subjected to rigorous scrutiny. Less strict criteria may be applied in a reorganisation programme conducted by the Treuhand. The capital expenditure involved would be financed by the Treuhand or by credits guaranteed by the Treuhand – with the unsatisfactory possibility of the costs of any failure being borne by the taxpayers.

There was another aspect of using a Treuhand-type approach to privatisation. The Treuhand, although legally independent, remained a government agency and therefore could not be completely shielded from political pressure. In these circumstances there was always an understandable risk that criteria other than profitability would play a decisive role. Preserving jobs is the major example which has been consistently cited above. From time to time, moreover, in order to obtain loan guarantees the reconstructed firms were required to produce updated reconstruction plans. It was very likely that these firms would not follow the identical adjustment policies as they would do under market conditions (Hax 1992: 147). At the same time, privatisation afforded an opportunity to distinguish firms with a viable future from those which would not survive in an albeit imperfectly competitive environment. If all efforts to find a bidder fail, it could be concluded that a firm was not suited for reorganisation, and should therefore be closed.

Governments are tempted to mix privatisation with structural policy. Such an approach is probably doomed to failure because structural policy is more concerned with smoothing the transition for individual firms and protecting employment by subsidising declining industries. The solution to such a policy problem is arguably not to confuse the protection of persons with the conservation of inefficient firms. Persons who are threatened by unemployment should receive support – not the firm. Many academic economists are in a sufficiently detached position to argue that the preservation of obsolete industrial structures is a very costly form of supporting these persons. Provided market forces are assumed to be operating in a textbook manner, such a form of support could be viewed as detrimental to the economic recovery of a region (Siebert 1992b: 53; Hax 1992: 149).

DEREGULATION

Regulation in its widest sense constrains an economic agent's freedom of action or autonomy to determine the allocation of given resources. In other words, it prevents the undesirable consequences of unbridled competition. Property rights and contract law are two examples of regulation which are designed to provide a framework for ethical practices. If regulation blunts competition too severely by intervening directly into economic affairs, however, it may reduce the profit motive, raise prices, deter the introduction of technological change and confer considerable financial advantages on the regulated industries (iwd2 22/90). But regulated sectors are a product of particular economic circumstances. As with all economic principles, therefore, the case for outright deregulation may not be unambiguously plausible.

From mid-1983, attempts were made to abolish or simplify legal and administrative regulations. Some measures designed to reduce the costs of such bureaucracy seem to have been successful (OECD *Economic Survey* 1985: 31). But these measures did not influence the areas where government regulation strongly affected price formation, the entry of new firms and quantities supplied (*ibid.*). There were thus two significant developments in deregulation. First, the Federal government's decision in 1985 to appoint the independent Witte Commission on telecommunications. This commission reported in September 1987. Second, in December 1987, an independent commission of enquiry into 'anti-market' regulation was appointed. It will be apparent that this latter commission had a far-wider brief. Its inaugural meeting took place in March 1988 and it reported in 1991 (Deregulierungskommission 1991: v and vii). Note that it took a supply-side government five years to appoint the more general deregulation commission. There had been a good deal of prompting. For example, the OECD *Economic Survey* (1986: 26; 1987:

59) had twice published a summary table showing the extent of regulation in the West German economy. An extract from the table appears below as Table 8.6. (The original table also linked regulation and subsidisation, the latter being the subject matter of the next section.) Significantly, the table's source was a book coauthored by Professor Donges who became a member of the commission. The degree of regulation was therefore an issue which preceded unification.

The Deregulierungskommission (1991: 1) distinguished between constructive and special regulation. For example, anti-trust legislation is seen in Germany as constructive. It ideally creates the conditions where competition can operate. Special regulations, as the term implies, typically affect specific groups. The object of special regulation was to modify or even eradicate the perceived undesirable effects of competitive forces. An important section of these regulations applied to the 'service' sectors of the economy – transport, electricity supply, banking, insurance, the professions and *Handwerk* (*ibid.*: 13). Both state and privately owned enterprises were therefore involved. The legal framework affecting these sectors had the aim of ensuring 'acceptable results' in an economy where a division of labour operates within a market environment. But it was not easy to define 'acceptable results' (*ibid.*: 1). Moreover, a minority report by one member of the commission expressed scepticism about the labour-market recommendations made by other members (*ibid.*: 157–8). This scepticism was based on the premise that the labour market differed fundamentally from the other markets analysed by the commission. Nonetheless, the commission associated itself with the increasing criticism of the BA's monopoly of employee recruitment services. Finally,

Table 8.6 Government Regulation

Sectors	Market entry	Quantities	Prices
Agriculture, forestry and fishing	XXX	XXX	XXX
Electricity, gas and water	XXX	X	XXX
Coal mining	X	XXX	X
Other mining	X	X	0
Iron and steel	X	XXX	XXX
Oil processing	0	X	0
Shipbuilding	X	0	X
Aerospace	X	0	X
Food and beverages	X	X	0
Construction	0	0	X
Trade	0	0	X
Railways	XXX	XXX	XXX
Shipping	XX	X	XXX
Other transport	XX	XX	XX
Postal services	XXX	X	XXX
Banking	X	0	X
Insurance	X	0	XX
Housing	X	XX	XX
Educational services	XX	XX	X
Health and veterinary services	XX	XX	XXX
Other services	X	X	XX

Source: Donges, J.B. and Schatz, K.W. (1986) *Staatliche Interventionen in der BRD*, Institut für Weltwirtschaft, Kiel – extracted from OECD *Economic Survey* (Germany), 1987: 59

Note: [1] Regulation is through specific measures: 0 = minor, X = partial, XX = strong and XXX = very strong or complex

many of the highly subsidised sectors to be examined in the next section, along with the postal services, are also highly regulated. A general overview of regulation before the commission commenced its deliberations will be found in Table 8.6.

It can be seen from the table that the state-owned postal services – the partial concern of the Witte Commission – had strict entry and pricing regulations. Because the Federal Post Office retained its virtual monopoly over the postal, telecommunications and the postal giro system, cross subsidisation was possible. For example, when record profits of DM 3.3 billion on total sales of DM 46 billion were made in 1985, losses of DM 1.7 billion had been incurred on the postal services (FT 11 July 1985). Only relatively

minor changes in telecommunications had been introduced prior to the Witte Commission (von Weiszäcker and Wieland 1988: 30). On the grounds that there were no appreciable economies of scope, however, the commission recommended the separation of postal and telecommunication services (*ibid.*: 35). This proposal was in principle implemented by the Post Office and Telecommunications Act of 1989. With the aim of reducing cross subsidisation still further, the banking facility was also made a separate entity. (Each section was prefixed Deutsche Bundespost, followed by POSTDIENST, TELEKOM and POSTBANK; the Federal postal services minister retained overall control – BMF *Beteiligungen . . .* 1990: 173–96). In spite of the easing of some entry restrictions, however, about 80 per cent of the telecommunications market remained under the control of TELEKOM (OECD *Economic Survey* 1990: 42). This continuing lack of competition was reflected in the appreciably higher price of telephone calls relative to other countries (*ibid.*: 90n). In early 1990, for example, the cost of an international call was more than triple its counterpart in the United Kingdom. On the other hand, in 1991–2 TELEKOM invested DM 16 billion out of the total DM 66 billion spent on public infrastructure investment in the east (Dresdner Bank *Trends* February 1993).

It is also clear from Table 8.6 that the state-owned railways are highly regulated. This regulatory framework was established during the inter-war period (OECD *Economic Survey* 1988: 72). It was retained following the liberalisation of some markets in 1948. The fares on the West German federal railway system required the approval of the Federal transport minister who took into account social, structural and regional needs (*ibid.*: 73). Moreover, the railways had an obligation to meet community welfare needs such as the operation of unprofitable routes. Two thirds of the total rail subsidy of DM 13.7 billion in 1986 was accounted for by welfare and other regulatory obligations (*ibid.*). As already shown in the privatisation section, the amalgamation and debt redemption of the western and eastern railway systems are major policy challenges for the 1990s. It was also shown that some rail privatisation proposals were made in 1993. These proposals can also be found in the report of the Deregulierungs-kommission (1991: 43–4). For example, one proposal consisted of separating the rail network from other parts of railway business and allowing more general access to that network. The commission also

recommended that the role of the Federal transport minister should be drastically reduced. Uneconomic activities should be financed by minimised subsidies – for which external bodies such as Federal and Länder governments would be accountable. Finally, the use of anti-trust legislation should prevent collusion among providers of rail services. Virtually all the other transport media were also seen by the commission as requiring immediate and drastic deregulation (Deregulierungs-kommission 1991: 46–65). Their subsidies, particularly those of public road transport, added DM 6 billion to the DM 13 billion received by the railways in 1986 (EC 1990a: 32). In 1991–2, however, the eastern railways invested DM 22 billion of the total DM 66 billion of public infrastructure investment in the east (Dresdner Bank *Trends* February 1993).

Consider next electricity supply. Various provisions have created market-entry barriers in the generating sector of the industry (EC 1991a: 28–9). Generating plant may not be constructed, extended, modified or closed without permission. Such permission may be withheld in the public interest. Länder economics ministers are responsible for both this and price regulation. The generators, transmitters and distributors enjoy exemption from anti-trust legislation. This enables them to forge demarcation and licensing agreements. Predictably, the Deregulierungs-kommission (1991: 84) recommended that the exemption be abolished. In addition, the commission advised that the connected holdings of local authorities in all types of public utilities and local public transport services should be investigated (*ibid.*: 87). Where necessary, energy utilities should be privatised with a view to introducing more competition into energy supply. The commission also noted the incorporation of the eastern electricity-supply industry by the large western generators (*ibid.*: 78–9). Ironically, the legal and regulatory vacuum in the east during 1990–1 had induced particularly intense, even unscrupulous, competition among the western utilities (Boehmer-Christiansen *et al.* 1993: 356).

Both the banking and insurance sectors were analysed in Chapter 7. Prudential regulation of banking was, by implication, seen to be a necessary feature of economic control. Moreover, deregulation of the bond and stock markets was shown to be an essential element of the preparation for EC 1993 and *Finanzplatz Deutschland*. A particularly striking feature was the restrictions historically placed on the participation of foreign banks. The full effects of EC 1993 and the EC insurance directives will, however, not be immediately discernible. The commission recommended the abolition of the system of tied agents, the introduction of state-recognised insurance brokers and advisers, the ending of discrimination against foreign companies, a lifting of the monopoly enjoyed by public-sector insurers and a limitation on the cartel exemption of private health insurers (*ibid.*: 28–34). In short, insurance was a highly regulated and 'staunchly defended' market at the beginning of the 1990s (FT 19 June 1990). Domestic firms were set to fare better elsewhere in Europe than *vice versa* (*ibid.*). The *Economist* (21 November 1992) confidently predicted, however, that 'deregulation will force change upon German insurers faster than they imagine'. That prospect, the *Economist* incisively continued:

alarms some, especially those familiar with the savage competition in the deregulated markets of Britain and America . . . Germans are not cut-throat competitors. Foreign adventurers will be defeated by the formidable agent networks that sell most private insurance in Germany.

This quotation has to be juxtaposed with one from Giersch *et al.* (1992: 218):

. . . other countries – notably the United States, the United Kingdom and the Netherlands – have made quite courageous attempts at liberalisation . . . While there has been some deregulation in Germany as well – most of it in financial markets – the balance looks modest by international standards . . . liberalising the rigid West German shopping hours . . . took years of public debate . . . (before the shops were permitted) to extend their opening hours beyond the standard 6.00 or 6.30 to 8.30 on one single day of the week.

Notice first the sting in the tail with respect to shopping hours. It is a good example of the possible repercussions of deregulation. Prior to the (1989) agreement referred to in the quotation, the Shop Closing Times Act (*Ladenschlußgesetz*) had regulated these hours. Both the large department stores and the unions (the HBV and the DAG – see Chapter 6) had been opposed to extension of opening hours (FT 10 August 1989). The employers accepted the union proposal that the new hours be embodied in a revised framework agreement, thus overriding statute law and relying on companies with works councils to supervise the implementation of the agreement (see Chapter 6). In this sense the Federal government's efforts were sidestepped, although the government were not without empathy. Union membership, however, tends to be low in retailing. On average, about 20 per cent of shop employees are union members. The large developments on the outskirts of towns have a particularly low level of organisation. There was thus the problem which cannot be completely gainsaid. The problem was one of deciding whether relatively low-paid and unorganised employees should be exposed to US and, to a lesser extent, British opening hours. The bottom line was that shops be permitted to open until 2030 on Thursdays, but the 'long Saturday' closing time on the first Saturday of the month would be correspondingly reduced from 1800 to 1600 during the summer months.

Also consider the introduction of the single insurance market on 1 July 1994. The Länder building insurance monopolies will, for example, be abolished. In theory, a German will be able to shop around in eleven other member states. If the level of premia is of major concern, differing policy content may go unnoticed. Moreover, national regulatory standards and their enforcement may still differ, although EC-wide regulations will from 1995 admittedly require insurance companies to publish an accurate indication of their valuation. Where capital coverage is scant, customers will ostensibly be deterred. But obtaining information of this description is not costless and only fairly large corporate customers will surely be able to devote the time and financial resources to searching the market.

Finally, consider the use of the railways as instruments of redistribution and regional policies in the sense that they are required to retain unprofitable lines. This would be rejected by liberal economists who opposed distributionally modified pricing. Direct cash grants to those regarded as 'poor' are considered a more appropriate instrument (Walters quoted by Bös 1989: 231). An alternative liberal argument would be to issue vouchers so that the 'poor' can choose between competing transport media. The implied assumption is, of course, that the service (or services) will be supplied subject to an expectation of profit. Might this leave the 'poor' with, at best, scanty public transport or, at worst, with the provision of no service at all? Similarly, is there a finite long-run limit to the number of competing firms which can offer telecommunications services? Or, in a completely deregulated system, is the ultimate sanction of bankruptcy the best safeguard for consumer choice? Accurate answers to these and other questions would only be found by trial and error. It was seen in the privatisation section that the effects of implementing particular policy prescriptions are often different from those predicted by their advocates. Perhaps some caution is therefore necessary when it comes to deregulation.

SUBSIDIES

In this context, subsidy instruments have the potential to reallocate resources and have a budgetary cost (Ford and Suyker 1990: 39). Tax concessions – which play a major role in Germany – can be included in such a definition (ibid.: 51). It will become apparent that some industries noted as highly regulated in Table 8.6 are also highly subsidised. Moreover, since subsidies are a form of protection, it will be necessary to return to the topic in the trade sections.

Prior to unification, the most important recipients of subsidies – accounting for 80 per cent of total subsidisation – were located outside industry (OECD Economic Survey 1987: 56). Agriculture, housing and transport were the major recipients. Within industry, structurally weak sectors such as coal mining and shipyards received increasing shares and, as already seen in Chapter 2, firms situated in West Berlin and along the inner German border also received assistance. In addition, both the 'sunrise' aerospace industry and the steel industry – which was characterised by chronic over capacity – received assistance. The subsidies given to aerospace are considered in the section on strategic trade, competition and industrial policies below. The general principles involved in distinguishing between assistance to high-tech and declining industries are also discussed in that section, whereas the case study on NRW in Chapter 2 was concerned with problems in a declining region.

There are good reasons for including a brief analysis of the assistance given to agriculture. It has been contended that without the elaborate arrangements for government intervention, structural adjustment in this sector would have been more rapid (EC 1990a: 25). Industries such as textiles and clothing, leather and leather goods and construction had to contend with similarly exacting adjustment exigencies, although they did not receive the same intensity and diversity of government assistance as agriculture. Nonetheless, between 1970 and 1987 employment in the cited industries fell by 45 per cent compared to 42 per cent in agriculture (*ibid.*: 27; Wilmes 1992). It was concluded that the adjustment process in these industries had been 'successfully completed', whereas 'agriculture is more than ever dependent on the drip feed of subsidies' (*ibid.*). Moreover, producer prices would have aligned themselves to world market levels, and consumer prices for agricultural products would have been correspondingly lower.

Measures to protect agriculture date back to the 1870s. Then, and subsequently, agriculture became a decisive political force. In the meantime, Britain was going through a 'painful' but successful agricultural adjustment, Denmark and the Netherlands developed comparative advantages in some agricultural products, but countries like Germany postponed adjustment which led to a vicious circle of maladjustment and protection (Tangermann 1979: 246). As a result, in 1989 agricultural productivity in Britain was double the German level (iwd2 25/91). There was also an important paradox: in the 1870s Germany was already on its way to becoming one of the world's leading economies – see Chapter 1. Similarly, protective measures were reintroduced in the 1950s (EC 1990a: 25). Hence, agriculture was again protected during a period of record industrial expansion. Alongside national protection, Germany negotiated special conditions when the EC introduced its notorious CAP and MCA measures – with consequent higher prices and costs for German consumers and taxpayers (Tangermann 1979: 242, 249–50). Another paradox is that small farmers, who have borne the brunt of what adjustment took place, saw their incomes and alternative employment opportunities fall during the 1980s (Pfeffer 1989a and 1989b). Hence, total agricultural subsidies in 1985 totalled DM 21 billion (well over one per cent of GDP), or DM 1,300 per month for each person employed in agriculture (EC 1990a: 27). But only one third of this amount went to the farmers themselves. The other two thirds went to associated industries such as food, drink, tobacco and the wholesale trade, or was accounted for by storage and denaturing costs. One year later (1986), total agricultural support was estimated at 2.1 per cent of GDP (Ford and Suyker 1990: 49). Three years before unification, the extent of agricultural support resulted in at least two incisive denunciations (Donges *et al.* 1987; *Der Spiegel* 45/87–50/87 inclusive).

Agriculture was thus yet another area

where unification exacerbated an existing problem. As in other cases, moreover, the amount of time and resources required to effect the transformation process in eastern agriculture was initially underestimated (iwd2 44/92). By 1992, the Federal government had provided assistance totalling DM 12 billion, while EC's special provisions for east Germany had generated a further DM 2.4 billion (*ibid.*). Agricultural productivity in the east was even worse than in the west. Each 100 hectares required fourteen employees in the east compared to only two in the west (iwd2 25/91). Within eastern Germany, however, the productivity on holdings sold to individual farmers was over double that attained on farms privatised as cooperatives (iwd2 44/92).

There are two similarities between coal mining and agriculture – quite apart from their both being in receipt of subsidies and other forms of protection. (Reference is made here to hard (or bituminous) coal mining which, although largely concentrated in the Ruhr district, is also an important employer in the Saarland – see Chapter 2.) First, shortages in their output during the immediate post-war era gave way to over production. Second, there are consequent stockpiles which resulted from excess capacity. However, whereas agricultural output doubled between 1950 and 1986, the output of hard coal was roughly halved.

Over 80 per cent of total coal sales are made to the electricity supply and steel industries (EC 1990a: 27). Consequently, the two most important forms of protection for the coal industry are found in these areas. In electricity supply, a series of Acts since the 1960s (*Verstromungsgesetze*) induced the construction of coal-fired power stations and, from 1977, the industry committed itself to purchasing a fixed amount of German coal (*Jahrhun-dertvertrag*). Under the latter arrangement, power generators received subsidies financed from the *Kohlepfennig* – a levy in percentage terms added to electricity bills and related to the amount of electricity consumed. In 1990 the levy was 8.5 per cent, yielding more than DM 5 billion (*ibid.*). This agreement was due to expire in 1995 and it has received an unfavourable response from the EC. Its framers were not to know, of course, that this was the very year when, following unification, a new system of fiscal equalisation would have to be introduced (Chapter 2). By its very nature, the new system would essentially favour the eastern Länder and would therefore prove a competitor for financial resources. More specifically, the future employment needs implied by brown coal mining in the east would conflict with a possible increase in the output of subsidised hard coal mining in the west; moreover, mining in both parts of Germany faced stiff competition from Polish and Australian imports (Boehmer-Christiansen *et al.* 1993: 358, 364 and 366–7). Indeed, there are even wider ramifications (*ibid.*: 370–1):

Energy politics in the united Germany involve both a search for solutions to old problems (coal subsidies, nuclear power, competition) and for ways to reach new goals, such as energy efficiency, European integration, access to gas and oil supplies from Russia. In this search, environmental regulations continue to play a major role. The energy carbon tax is therefore much more than a purely environmental instrument . . . Nevertheless, there is as yet insufficient evidence for a paradigm shift toward an ecologically benign energy system.

The agreement between the coal mining and steel industries (*Hüttenvertrag*) dates from 1960. Under this agreement, the steel industry agreed to purchase fixed amounts of German coking coal. These sales were made at world prices which did not cover the costs of producing the coal. Subsidies were therefore paid to the coal producers by the Federal and Länder governments. The agreement was due to expire in the year 2000. Both the coal subsidies, and the direct protection of the steel industry which resulted in unprofitable capacity being kept in production, were approved under the ECSC treaty (*ibid*.: 27 and 28; Ohteki 1992: 88–94). During the 1980s domestic coal cost on average almost 70 per cent more than imported coal. At the end of the decade, Federal and Länder subsidies totalled DM 10 billion, or DM 4,400 a month per person employed in the industry (*ibid*.).

An account of the subsidies given to the shipyards is illuminating from many points of view. In spite of the dramatic increase in demand for subsidies to east Germany, along with the policy aim of reducing state spending in the west, subsidies to shipbuilding were increased in 1992 (FT 12 November 1992). However, whereas the Federal government had met the full cost of this subsidy until 1986, and contributed two thirds of the cost thereafter, from 1993 it shared half the cost with the affected northern Länder (SZ 8 December 1992). (More generally, half of all the subsidies are administered by the Länder, a system which gives rise to regional competition for subsidisation – OECD *Economic Survey* 1987: 57.) The northern economics ministers insisted that the low order book situation in 1992 was temporary (SZ *ibid*.). Capacity had to be preserved in order to maintain a competitive shipbuilding base for the upturn. Yet international competition and excess capacity had resulted in similarly successful pleas in 1977 (FT 24 October 1977). Moreover, as early as 1974, Langer

(188–9) had shown that of the twelve methods of government intervention used in the eleven most important shipbuilding nations, seven were used in West Germany. As a result, the industry exported 46 per cent of its output – albeit only a relatively negligible two per cent of total German exports (*ibid*.: 223–5). It also preserved its position as a dominant employer in the northern region (*ibid*.: 281). Indeed, Reuss (1963: 202) shows that the industry provided a liberal tax shelter up to 1958 and was probably overcapitalised as early as 1953. Given this entrenched position, the takeover of east German yards by western firms following unification raised the 'possibility' of continued support in this sector (OECD *Economic Survey* 1992: 51–2).

A direct consequence of the past protection accorded to the shipbuilding industry, then, was its continued reliance on such support in the early 1990s. On a *per capita* basis it received in 1990 DM 16,800 in subsidies – DM 2,000 more than agriculture but under a third of the support given to hard coal mining (FT 12 November 1992). Both the railways (DM 35,344) and aerospace (DM 22,283) also received more. (Hamburg is also dependent on the aerospace industry, it will be recalled – see Chapter 2.)

West German subsidisation as a percentage of GDP fell only very marginally during the 1980s. Between 1981 and 1986 the annual average was 2.5 per cent, relative to an average of 3 per cent of GDP for the EC10 as a whole (EC 1989a: 10). Although this annual average was 2.4 per cent in West Germany during the period 1988–90, it was above the EC12 average of 2.2 per cent of GDP (iwd2 44/92). It is therefore almost certain that the German average will remain significantly above the EC average during the period required to reconstruct the east German economy.

It should be emphasised that the cited proportions of GDP accounted for by subsidies had the advantage of EC-wide statistical consistency. Within West Germany somewhat higher estimates were made. The broadest measure, which included capital transfers and tax relief, reached a peak of 7 per cent of GNP in 1979, falling back to 6.5 per cent in 1984 (OECD *Economic Survey* 1984: 47). Using a measure similar to the one defined in the opening paragraph of this section, however, the OECD (*ibid*. 1992: 48) estimated that subsidies had fallen from 3.75 per cent of GNP in the mid-1980s to 3.25 per cent at the beginning of the 1990s. Critics of the solidarity agreement to fund transfers to the east (arrived at in 1993) expressed disappointment that no reduction in the extent of western subsidies had been agreed.

WEST GERMAN COMPANIES AND THE WORLD ECONOMY

Goods are exported by a company when the profit from a sale to a foreign country exceeds the profit on the home market, taking into account the costs of transport. Export markets are also sought in the event of low domestic demand, in which case they assist in sustaining a more balanced capacity utilisation where business cycles among nations differ. Moreover, a bigger market due to trade liberalisation can help to reap economies of scale (lower average costs).

From the point of view of the economy as a whole, exports foster income, employment and growth. As such, this does not differ markedly from domestic sales. But exports have the following additional advantages (Donges 1992: 3–4):

- the exporting country earns foreign currency which can finance imports of goods and services. These gains from trade consist of a higher quantity and variety of differentiated goods, internally non-available raw materials like crude oil and foreign technology which costs licence fees. Items like tourism, remittances by foreign workers, and payments to other countries and to institutions can also be financed
- They can foster competition which leads to more efficiency and a faster adjustment of supply to changes in demand
- Where trade barriers do not exist, therefore, exports and imports are important as each country will specialise in exports where it has a comparative advantage. The results, at least in theory, are a higher real income of all countries due to specialisation, less monopoly power and higher efficiency

In the post-war period the West German economy displayed many of the above features. It has been characterised by a continuous process of internationalisation. Rising levels of interdependence, both economically and politically, among the world's nations played a major role in this process. International trade and direct investment in other economies thus grew considerably. Foreign trade in goods rapidly became an important determinant of West Germany's national income. By the mid-1950s trade accounted for about 20 per cent of GNP. This ratio continued to rise. In 1990 over one third of Germany's GNP was derived from exports.

The spectacular rise in West Germany's share of world trade in goods is illustrated in Figure 8.8. It can be seen that between 1950 and 1990 West Germany's export share in world trade rose from 3.5 per cent to 12.1 per cent, with two peaks of 12.9 and 12.6 per cent in 1973 and 1987 respectively. Moreover, from 1986 to 1990, with the exception of 1989, West Germany headed the international export league table, ahead of the US and Japan (FT 1 December 1986; SZ 26 March 1991). In value terms during 1990 West Germany exported US$ 421 billion worth of goods, followed by the USA ($ 394 billion) and Japan ($ 286 billion) (KND 37/91). France ($ 216 billion) and the UK ($ 185 billion) were in fourth and fifth positions. It is important to also note that West Germany's share of world imports consistently grew less than exports during the period 1950–90 (see Figure 8.8). In 1950, her share of imports was 4.6 per cent; by 1990 it was almost 10 per cent. Further, east Germany is included in the 1991 data used in Figure 8.8. Hence, the dramatic effect of unification on the shares of visible exports and imports can likewise be seen in the figure. It was the only occasion on which the two ratios displayed convergence. On the other hand, the first two crude oil price shocks caused a deterioration in both ratios.

What were the long-run effects on the current account of this export achievement? Figure 8.9 contains a comparison of the trade, invisible and current account balances. The dominant role of the trade balance for much of the post-war period is immediately apparent. If the untypical years of 1949 and 1950 are excluded, the trade balance has always been positive. However, a relatively small trade balance has resulted in West Germany's current account slipping occasionally into the red. But this happened only in 1962, 1965 and 1979–81. Conversely, relatively large trade surpluses have produced correspondingly large current account surpluses. The second half of the 1980s are a particularly striking illustration of this factor. Indeed, the recovery in the trade balance after the 1980 record current account deficit soon led to steadily growing surpluses. The extent of the return to export-led growth during the 1980s should not be underestimated.

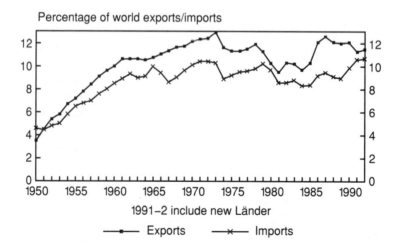

Figure 8.8 Share of world trade

Source: As Figure 8.3

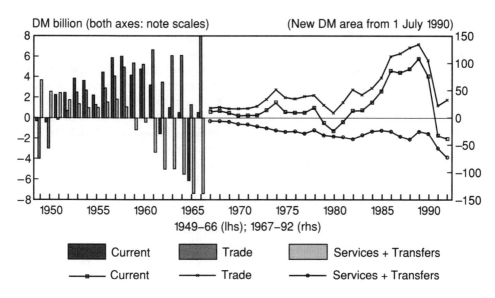

Figure 8.9 Current, Trade and Invisible Balances

Source: As Figure 8.3

At the beginning of the decade things looked very different (Riemer 1983: 4):

The world economy as a source of German vulnerability, as well as of strength, became apparent when the Federal Republic slipped within a matter of a few years from its usual position of export leader to that of export junkie and oil import addict.

Note, however, that the aggregation in Figure 8.9 of the two invisible items – services and transfers – shows a secularly worsening deficit after 1959–60. This aggregation was undertaken purely because it more conveniently illustrates the relationship between the trade and current account balances. Nonetheless, there has been an important difference in the behaviour of the services and transfer balances. Services are remunerated items such as travel, transport, insurance, government current transactions and income

from profits, interest and dividends (MRDB *Stat Beiheft* 3: Table 4a). The really notable deficit item has been travel, with insurance generally registering more minor deficits. There have been appreciable surpluses in the remaining three items. During the period 1980–90, therefore, the services balance was often positive. For example, the particularly rapid improvement in the current account in the years 1984–6 can partly be attributed to the positive service balance (Glismann *et al.* 1992: 160). Conversely, transfers – unremunerated invisible items in the current balance – have been an increasingly large deficit item. In the government sector, net contributions to the EC play a large role, whereas remittances by foreign employees are significant in the private sector (MRDB *ibid.*: Table 5a). In spite of the minor role played by occasional positive services balance, however, it can be concluded that the current account has been largely driven by the trade balance.

During the critical period of the first two oil price shocks (1973–82), for example, the balance of transfers and services had oscillated around −2.3 per cent of GNP. But the massive swings in the current account balance can in general be attributed to the variations in the DM value of the exports and imports.

In 1991 about 50 per cent of employees were directly involved in export production. Export dependence, however, differs markedly among industries. The motor-vehicle and machine-tool industries, which together account for more than one third of German exports, are especially dependent on world trade (Friedrich and Wiedemeyer 1992: 98). Furthermore, the foreign direct investment by West German enterprises grew considerably in the 1980s, whereas foreign direct investors were generally less and less attracted to West Germany (Mussel 1992: 101). In both 1990 and 1991 – when east Germany was attempting to attract foreign investment – net German foreign direct investment reached the record amount of over DM 25 billion (BMWi Wirtschaft . . . 1992: 98). Consequently, the stock of German overseas investment was DM 211 billion in 1990; this was DM 71 billion more than the stock of foreign investment in Germany (ibid.: 105). The USA was by far the largest host and donor country. Chemical, electrical and financial companies were the largest German direct investors overseas. These few numbers show that Germany, on the one hand, has considerable effects on the world economy, while, on the other hand, foreign economic policy and growth linkages affect Germany (Donges 1992: 2).

The economy of East Germany was far less integrated into the international division of labour. Her export ratio was about 22 per cent of GNP, while her world market share, including intra-German trade, was only 1.5 per cent. About half of her exports flowed to western countries, the remainder to the other socialist countries in the east. In 1989, trade accounted for about 2 million of East German jobs (Friedrich and Wiedemeyer 1992: 100). For a small industrialised country with only 16.4 million inhabitants this share was far smaller than in similar market economies like, say, the Netherlands which had an export ratio of 58 per cent of GNP. East Germany's inferior position was in the main due to her borders being closed against the west and underspecialisation. Giersch et al. (1992: 259), for example, point out that the East German 'metal manufacturing industry' produced 65 per cent of the range of goods in this category in the world, whereas the much more specialised and bigger West Germany produced only 17 per cent of the range. This bias against a rational division of labour was partly the consequence of a deliberate policy aimed at almost full self-sufficiency in most products.

Quite clearly, then, the eastern part of post-wall Germany had to emulate the more successful economy into which it had been incorporated. More specifically, what were the conditions which led to the west's superiority? An examination of the various phases in West Germany's international trade experience will afford a partial answer to this question. This is followed by an analysis of the structure of trade and Germany's role in international investment. Of particular importance here are three widely-debated issues. First, the future German competitiveness in the main export industries. Second, the related question of Germany's position in the global high-tech race. Third, the effects of German unification on international trade, although this is obviously a more recent strand in the debate. All three factors affect the German economy's potential to remain a leading exporter and international investor. They are well summarised by the German term for the debate (*Standort Deutschland*). Finally, attention is focused on the role of economic policy measures in fostering the quantity and the structure of a country's trade (Heidrich 1992: 8).

PHASES IN THE DEVELOPMENT OF TRADE

Following the war, the extent of the material damage done to the economy's productive potential was overestimated and there was still a substantially intact stock of human capital (Lang 1990). A rapid expansion of trade was the best way for a country with a large population, dependent upon large imports of food after the war, and almost no natural resources, to regain its position among the leading countries quickly (Walter 1992: 59). West Germany was soon in a position to take such a step. She therefore advocated a policy of trade liberalisation and took advantage (Bhagwati 1988: 3–9) of:

- the significant increase in world trade due to the Bretton Woods pegged exchange rate agreement of 1944
- the successive GATT rounds after 1947 which led to world-wide tariff cuts, particularly for industrial products
- lower transport costs and improved telecommunications
- the beginning of European economic integration which removed custom barriers within Europe

Economic development and integration into the world economy took place in West Germany with an unexpected dynamism. This self-reinforcing dynamism of real economic forces which led to the rapid recovery and reconstruction of West Germany was a result of a number of stimuli (Lang 1990). Among these stimuli was the special situation in which West Germany found herself as the loser of the Second World War. Cost conditions were exceptionally favourable because of the very modest real wage demands of a highly motivated and productive labour force. Unions had probably underestimated the rate of improvement in productivity. Among other factors, this caused relatively moderate wage demands. It also meant that the scope of supply-side growth and the rapid reduction of unemployment were not diminished by extraordinary high labour costs (Giersch *et al.* 1992: 73). In other words, low social-policy costs and a very elastic supply of labour improved the situation still further by their productivity-enhancing effects. The shortage of capital due to the very limited capital market was overcome by high business profits favoured by tax concessions. These conditions led to low consumption and incentives to private-sector investors from abroad. The rapid growth of productive capacity with its increasing rate of utilisation during the reconstruction period improved the availability of goods and increased exports in the new economic world order with again new demand enhancing multiplier effects and incentives for further private investment. As a result of all these extremely favourable conditions, price inflation was low.

The most important external factor for the West German export success during the 1950s was the protection provided by the fixed exchange rate regime of the new Bretton Woods international monetary system. A fixed parity of DM 4.20 to the US dollar stimulated German exports for a number of years and at the same time it constrained foreign competition in domestic markets. Indeed, the most important factors for Germany's success on the export markets was this undervalued exchange rate, along with the relatively low average rate of price inflation in the 1950s. Other contributory factors were the Korean war – which enabled the strengthening German economy to fill gaps in international markets – the considerable restrictions on international capital transactions and the low level of foreign tourism until 1957–8. It resulted in export-led expansion above all in the capital-good industries. As Giersch *et al.* (1992: 116) put it:

West Germany was transformed by a combination of good luck (high demand for capital goods) and policy (less inflation than abroad) into a country enjoying all the benefits of export-led growth.

In contrast, the other market economies had to face an accumulation of disadvantages in the post-war period. The victorious powers had to meet the cost of having financed the war mostly under existing market rules. They could not introduce a far-reaching currency reform, whereas West Germany largely eliminated the cost of financing the war in such a way. This laid a burden of considerable government debt on the other economies' shoulders. Another result of the war for the victorious European powers was a considerable debt to the USA which they had to settle under the fixed exchange rate system. Moreover, productive capacity which had been shifted largely to war production had to be reorganised for civil production. Where dismantling of obsolete plants in Germany took place, their reconstruction in the receiving countries as reparations did not enhance productivity as expected but only transferred obsolete technology. It also was the adverse effect that much labour was tied up with work which did not allow innovative activity (Lang 1990:

251). Last but not least, the victory over Germany had led the people of the other western market economies to have unjustified expectations for the future which could only be disappointed during the phase of reconstruction. Economic growth in these countries was adversely affected by demands for too high real wage increases in comparison to productivity. Trends in costs and demand brought about a situation in which these countries required goods imported from Germany for their own reconstruction (*ibid.*).

During the 1960s, there was a period of normalisation, when the German economy adjusted to international standards. A stable exchange rate – fixed at DM 4 from 1961 – in combination with stability-orientated economic policies meant a steady improvement in German industry's international price competitiveness. The real undervaluation of the DM again fostered exports whereas imports did not grow in the same amount (Weiss 1989a: 635). This had two contradictory effects within the domestic economy (Giersch *et al.* 1992: 126–39):

- Persistent overemployment and a strong influx of foreign labour which reduced the frictional costs of structural change and helped to maintain a fairly harmonious industrial climate; the labour force was reallocated to areas where the West German economy enjoyed long-term comparative advantages
- Early structural change away from industry to the modern service sector was prevented; the effects were manifest as soon as prices and the exchange rate were adjusted (on the collapse of the Bretton Woods agreement), and the dynamics of European integration came to a temporary halt

The increasing degree of undervaluation

of the DM against the US dollar promoted exports without stimulating imports to the same extent. Such a situation was possible as long as the share of savings was high by international standards (Francke 1983: 182). This enabled the Bundesbank, in spite of the imbalance in the foreign trade sector, to achieve price stability. Because of the fixed exchange rate, however, an increasingly restrictive monetary policy was required to prevent the money supply being boosted by a growth in bank liquidity. External factors thus dominated policy making. Restrictive monetary policies were increasingly pursued due to threat of high current account surpluses being converted into DM bank balances. Even when the Bundesbank's tight credit policy caused the 1967 recession, a combination of Schiller's new approach to fiscal policy and an export boom brought about an economic recovery (Riemer 1983: 118 and 147; also see the budgetary policy section of Chapter 3 above). Furthermore, the rapid integration into the world economy continued, although with a pronounced bias towards intra-European Community trade and heavy protectionism in agriculture and mining.

A number of internal and external factors thus led to the persistent trade balance surpluses in Germany during the 1950s and 1960s. The internal factors in the embryonic economy were, first, a highly motivated, well qualified and plentiful supply of young, geographically and occupationally mobile labour. Second, the pragmatic approach to the SME in which Erhard played an important role (see also Chapters 1 and 3). Erhard's policies stimulated corporate investment and labour productivity. External conditions also favoured German exports in the 1950s and 1960s. Stable exchange rates guaranteed by the Bretton Woods agreement favoured German international price competitiveness as much as the slower domestic cost increases due to the stability-orientated economic policies facilitated by a unique configuration of economic conditions. Tariff reductions, especially in industrial world trade, and the removal of customs barriers within Europe further enhanced the integration of world markets.

However, supply-side conditions deteriorated during the 1970s. With the collapse of the pegged exchange rate system, West German foreign trade was conducted in a more severe environment. Her ability to exploit an undervalued currency with revaluation potential was not as easy as during the 1960s and there was unrelenting upward pressure on the DM (Riemer 1983: 99). Several other factors also undermined the international competitiveness of the German industry, above all a sharp rise in labour costs and two oil price hikes. Moreover, the tough monetary policy of the Bundesbank after the introduction of the floating exchange rate system prevented the unfavourable supply-side shocks from developing into accelerating price inflation. For the West Germans the economic situation had deteriorated dramatically. The economy had stumbled into a severe recession and into a vicious circle of slow growth and high unemployment (Knappe and Funk 1992). In the short run, this scenario induced a lower level of aggregate demand and in the longer run a lack of investment. West Germany lost market shares to Japan, an economy which had become a new export power, particularly in the US market. In short, the competitive pressures from successful new exporters became more acute, especially as the high degree of DM's undervaluation was removed. Foreign observers were not quite so pessimistic. West Germany stood out in comparative terms as an enclave of relative prosperity and stability (Riemer 1983: 41). With the exception of 1974 and 1975, GNRP grew at a respectable rate (Figure 1.1). Indeed, Riemer (*ibid.*: 99) referred to 'the virtuous cycle of upward revaluation, enhanced stability and leeway for growth'.

The new successful exporters forced major traditional industries such as textiles, clothing, shipbuilding and iron and steel into further difficult adjustments due to an emerging new international division of labour. Newly industrialising countries, especially Hong Kong, Taiwan, Korea and Singapore possessed a comparative advantage in labour-intensive products as their labour unit costs are significantly lower. As a result, there was a partial rationalisation of the West German industrial structure in accordance with the principle of comparative advantage, but there was also a partial revival of protectionism. Although GATT left little manoeuvre for international trade restrictions, a worldwide resurgence in protectionism followed the first oil crisis. Many governments and agents proved adept at building up non-tariff barriers such as technical and legal obstacles and import quotas to national markets. Like many other countries, West Germany simultaneously protected domestic industries by means of extensive subsidies (Weiss 1989a and 1989b). The clamour for protectionism consequently produced an elaborate response (Funk 1990: 84–9).

There were other reasons for the rise in protectionism. In 1974–5 and 1979–81 the world economy had to bear two severe recessions with rapidly rising unemployment rates. As the cause was the externally induced crude-oil price shocks, import-competing firms also demanded more protection on these grounds. Furthermore, those economies which were able to register high growth rates during the 1950s and

1960s were unable to emulate their performance. It was decisively more difficult to overcome the steady structural changes of the economy without frictions. In other words, at growth rates of 1 or 2 per cent, employees displaced in the declining sectors had fewer alternative employment options than at a growth rate of 4 or 5 per cent. Accordingly, there was a higher demand for protection on these grounds, too. Finally, in addition to the support for traditional industries 'new industrial policy' and 'industrial targeting' came into vogue. Whether these latter policies promoted *Standort Deutschland* is a topic for later discussion. It can be concluded here that, in comparison to the 1950s and 1960s, protectionism during the 1970s damaged industry's flexibility. There was a consequent reduction in capital investment, employment and the pace of technological innovation. This catalogue of problems demonstrates the difficulties which faced Chancellor Schmidt when he was pressured to create the locomotive of international recovery (see Chapters 3 and 4).

Yet during the 1980s the West German trade surplus staged a dramatic recovery. In 1980 it had sunk to a level already attained in 1966. Thereafter it increased fifteenfold before it fell from a record high of DM 135 billion in 1989 to DM 92 billion in 1990. (Recall that Figure 8.9 includes east Germany after GEMSU. The plot of the trade balance therefore includes exports to the DDR before GEMSU, thereby increasing the 1990 balance to DM 105 billion.) Some straightforward reasons for this impressive performance will be given shortly. Initially, however, it has to be regrettably indicated that there seems to be no clear-cut explanation of the economic and policy causes of this phenomenal recovery. The economic controversy is best summarised as follows. Zinn

(1991: 264) describes the early 1980s as a 'supply-led export expansion', that is deflationary policies in the domestic economy obliging manufacturers to seek markets abroad. Yet supply-side policies are designed to improve expectations and thus stimulate investment, rather than exports. Hellwig and Neumann (1987: 138) thus contend that the initial stimulus untypically came from the domestic economy. Export-led growth as a result of high export surpluses may have begun as late as 1986 (Davidson 1992: 214).

What of the policy background to this recovery? The SVR had concluded in its 1981/82 report that it was essential to implement a policy of wage restraint and consolidation of the Federal budget, supported by a lower level of public spending. This would in turn stimulate a desirable rate of growth of private investment. It was thought that reducing the weight of state intervention in the economy would result in a process of 'crowding in' of private-sector expenditure which would in turn help increase the productive capacity of the economy. 'Such "crowding in" would be facilitated by the rational expectations of businessmen. In so far as the policy is credible businessmen will anticipate a relaxing of interest rates and a lowering of future tax levels, these being factors favourable to a recovery of economic activity' (Fitoussi and le Cacheux 1989: 136–7.). Some readers will recognise the salient economic doctrine of the time (rational expectations). Kohl's undertaking to introduce such a policy of fiscal consolidation was apparently sufficient to bring about a revision of the pessimistic expectations prevalent in 1982 (Hellwig and Neumann 1987: 138). However, inherited structures were preserved and fundamental reform was eschewed (*ibid.*: 140). On the eve of unification, therefore there had been no real supply-side adaptation. The extent to which economic fundamentals remained unchanged has been shown, for example, in the sections on privatisation, deregulation and subsidies. Meanwhile, the SVR contended that the competitive process is the driving force for the achievement of sustained growth and employment (Helmstädter 1988: 418). Only innovative competition enables businessmen to increase profit margins by creating new products which offer a more favourable ratio of value added to the costs of production (*ibid.*: 417). Provided the growth of real wages remains lower than the growth of productivity, unemployment will fall as firms invest at home rather than abroad (Neumann 1990).

What is the alternative view? Keynesians explained West Germany's role as the world's leading exporter as being at least partly due to domestic austerity. In these circumstances, West German firms could earn more from sales in foreign than in domestic markets. A stability-orientated, deflationary demand policy – as recommended by German supply-siders – did not lead to the expected private investment expansion but, in combination with other factors, to the persistently very high German current account surpluses and West Germany's ascent to the top of the export league in 1989 (Ambrosi 1990; Carlin and Jacob 1989; Issing 1989). In other words, weak domestic demand due to tight monetary and fiscal policies forced West German companies to shift their attention to export markets. Aggregate demand is still therefore able to support a higher level of employment than would otherwise be the case (Neumann 1990). This is opposed to the view of supply-side orientated economists. In their view, a trade surplus is evidence 'that a country saves more than it deems profitable to invest at home' (Giersch *et al.* 1992: 246).

More fundamental explanations of West Germany's high current account surpluses are fortunately possible. They boil down to:

- the qualitative features of West German goods
- economic growth in the USA due to Reaganomics in the early 1980s
- the fall in the price of imported crude oil (see Chapter 4)
- a renewed vigour in trade within the EC member states in the second half of the 1980s
- the real undervaluation of the DM in relation to other European currencies

It will be fruitful to consider each of these factors.

Qualitative factors can best be isolated as follows. A slightly technical but valuable method of clarifying the relationship between exports and imports is to consider the responsiveness of the quantity of any good demanded to changes in the level of income of those consumers or producers demanding that good. This income elasticity of demand is of great practical importance to businessmen and policy makers. In a growing economy, any product which has a low income elasticity (that is less than unity) will experience a declining share of total spending. Assuming world trade continues to expand, economies which export products with low income elasticities will incur balance of trade problems in the longer term. This is because the demand for exports rises more slowly than the propensity to import foreign products. British readers in particular will see that this is precisely the position in which their economy finds itself (Peacock et al. 1980: 18). All readers will already have anticipated that the West German position was diametrically opposite: the income elasticity of demand for her products was high from the time she re-entered

world markets (Giersch 1970: 14). In short, West German exports increased as world economic growth was reflected by rising incomes. A reasonable, if somewhat intuitive, inference is that her products embodied a number of comparative advantages which are difficult to quantify. It can be concluded that these features are qualitative in nature and that West German foreign trade to this extent relied on supply-side factors. These factors are determinants of export performance and the propensity to import. This can all be well summarised as follows (Thirlwall 1992: 8):

The growth of exports depends largely on the income elasticity of demand for exports in world markets which in turn depends on the supply characteristics of the goods produced and traded such as their design, technical sophistication, reliability, delivery and so on. If domestic goods are poor in this respect, the income elasticity of demand for exports will be low and the income elasticity of demand for imports will be commensurably high.

Moreover, it was seen when *Mittelstand* companies were considered above that until the onset of the 1990s quality was apparently more important than price in determining the demand for West German exports. Hence, price changes had a negligible effect on the quantities demanded, whereas the supply of exports rose quite significantly over time. In any case, Funke and Holly (1992: 508) found that a rise of 10 per cent in the world trade of manufactured goods raised West German exports by 7.8 per cent but the price of exports by only 1.3 per cent. But this happened on a level of already relatively high prices which in turn allowed high labour costs to be absorbed. In contrast, British and Irish managers do not seem to attempt to make and sell products similar to current west

German ones at the higher German price levels thereby gaining enhanced profits (Hitchens *et al.* 1992: 460). Part of the answer may be that British and Irish managers perceive that their investment and training costs would increase to achieve the better quality and no addition to profits would occur (*ibid.*: 461). Hence, the short termism which characterises Anglo-Saxon style capital markets has a direct counterpart in the manufacturing sector. However, British exporters may have served less sophisticated markets where price was a more critical factor, whereas West Germany's exports consisted of sophisticated high-technology products where price was not a major consideration (Peacock *et al.* 1980: 19 and 27n). Among other things, higher product sophistication implies greater technological sophistication. Anglo-German differences in this respect are reflected by the higher volume of German patents in the USA and the higher level of R&D expenditure in West Germany (Patel and Pavitt 1989). For example, in the 1980s the volume of firm-funded R&D in West Germany was more than double that in Britain (*ibid.*: 28). Moreover, not only was private-sector funding of R&D far higher in West Germany, but defence-related R&D accounted for a much higher proportion of the smaller R&D budget in the UK (*Economist* 11 November 1989; FT 18 June 1991).

During the 1980s, however, there were some ominous signs that Germany was losing her competitive advantage in a number of advanced industries (Porter 1990: 382). Indeed, although Germany regained her position as the largest applicant for patents at the German and European offices in 1992, the most glaring contrast with her Japanese and US rivals was her small number of high-tech applications (*Die Welt* 20 April 1993). There

was thus an ostensibly paradoxical spectacle during the 1980s: Germany's exports and patent applications were booming but many policy makers in one of the world's top exporting economies became increasingly concerned about her competitive future (*Standort Deutschland*). An entire section will therefore be devoted to this question below. Initially, however, the other factors responsible for the export boom of the 1980s will be considered.

Reaganomics was another important cause of the German export success in the early 1980s. A mix of over-stimulative fiscal policies and tight monetary action drove up the dollar from a low of DM 1.72 in January 1980 to a peak of DM 3.31 in March 1985. The US boom actually lasted from 1983 to 1989, but West Germany's share of exports to the USA increased only until the mid-eighties. In fact, exports to the USA decreased thereafter because of the steep recovery of the dollar from early 1985. At that juncture, US exchange-rate policy switched from a stance of benign neglect to one of an interventionist character and this is what led to a considerable fall in German exports to the US (Wohlers 1990: 273). Hence, although the USA remained Germany's most important non-European market as late as 1990 – accounting for one-tenth of all export markets – the share had fluctuated markedly. These fluctuations reflected both the volatility of the DM/US$ exchange rate and the business cycle in the USA (Walter 1992: 61). Nonetheless, in the early 1980s it was primarily the USA that induced the recovery of exports to the 'other industrial countries' plotted in Figure 8.10.

By way of a happy coincidence for West Germany, the fall in her exports to the USA was compensated for by Europe's emergence from the slow growth of the 1970s and early 1980s. The increase in her exports to the EC therefore immediately followed her success in the USA – as can be clearly seen in Figure 8.10. This figure also shows how the gradually enlarging EC took an increasing proportion of West Germany's exports. Of particular importance here is the fact that the level of 50 per cent of all exports was reached in 1986, thus illustrating the extent to which the EC provided an immediate alternative export market. Between 1986 and 1990 the EC's share in West German exports rose by more than four percentage points (*ibid*.: 65). This period coincides with the preparations for EC 1993 and West Germany's capital equipment manufacturers were notable beneficiaries of this boom (*ibid*.). It should be added that the share of the EC in Germany's total exports remained well above the 50 per cent mark following unification – as demonstrated in Figure 8.11. Indeed, the western European orientation of German trade can be fully recognised from the fact that 72

per cent of all exports went to the EC and 'other European industrial' market economies – an area which accounted for only one-third of world GNP (Figure 8.11). If the 'non-European industrial' market economies are added, the proportion rises to a dominant 85 per cent. (Industrial market economies supplied almost the same proportion of imports.)

West Germany's export boom was, on the one hand, attributed to the real undervaluation of the DM which was in turn partially engineered by the distinctive role of institutional power and the intervention in the foreign-exchange markets by the Bundesbank (Bulmer 1989: 27; Soskice 1990: 43–6). One possible result could be that the interests of the export sector were regarded as paramount by the Bundesbank and the DM exchange rate was kept deliberately low. Export-led growth would be the corollary (Davidson 1992; Riese 1987: 179). In addition, the real undervaluation of the DM was also due to

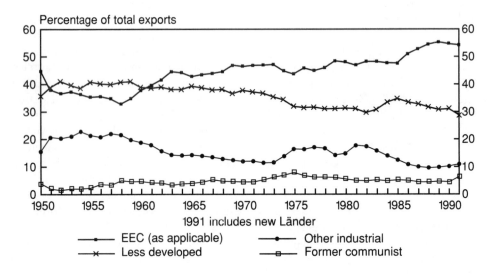

Figure 8.10 Major trading partners

Source: As Figure 8.3

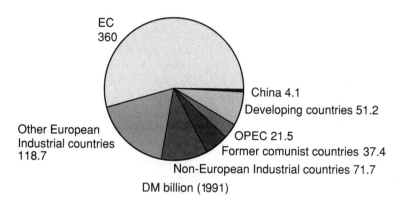

Figure 8.11 Exports by country groupings
Source: MRDB *Stat. Beihefte* 3: Table 2c

the refusal of other EMS countries to adjust the pegged exchange rates. As Michaelis (1991: 15) argues:

In the run-up to a realignment, there are usually coordinating discussions between Bonn and Frankfurt to determine the German position. In these exchanges the Bundesbank is guided by the necessities of monetary stability. In order to avoid [destabilising] speculative capital flows, the Bundesbank attaches great importance to 'timely and silent' adjustments. In principle, the Federal Government supports this basic concept of the Bundesbank. But since France in particular considers a devaluation of its currency as a sign of weakness, the Federal Government sometimes has to weigh the economic against the political aspects of a realignment (also see Issing 1992b).

On the other hand, others see the Bundesbank's currency policy as a balancing act between the longer-term requirements of low inflation and domestic monetary control and short-run pressing needs for coordinated exchange rate management and the promotion of internal demand growth (Dudler 1991: 309–10; Spahn 1989: 25–6).

But is there any evidence that the Bundesbank has been a party to boosting exports at the expense of domestic absorption? Such an employment policy came to be known as 'neomercantilist' (Riemer 1983: 50). In a wider context, the maximisation of national wealth on the basis of persistently large and favourable trade balances which benefited exporters at the expense of overseas customers was known as 'mercantilism'. (Presumably the Bundesbank's accumulation of foreign-exchange reserves are seen as the equivalent of the mercantalists' accumulation of gold – see Glismann *et al.* 1992: 164–5). In the later debate, the two terms were used interchangeably. It is true that there have been some periods when West Germany's monetary policy was guided by an exchange rate target rather than by domestic price stability. Current account deficits in 1979–81 may also have contributed to the Bundesbank's deflationary policy. But its autonomy was in the main used to keep the domestic inflation rate almost always below the average of the other industrial countries. This endowed exporters with a competitive real exchange rate. It would require sufficient cynicism and access to unobtainable information to test whether this was a contrived or co-incidental comparative advantage. Indeed, the orthodox view is that monetary policies favoured savers but were unfavourable to the immediate interests of West German industry (Riemer 1983: 48). For example, savers allied themselves with the SPD, the SVR and the Bundesbank in the revaluation controversy of 1969 – against the CDU and industry (*ibid.*). More specifically (*ibid.*: 51):

From the Bundesbank's point of view, the orientation of private banks and industrial clients toward exports is advantageous because it gives both sectors a stake in monetary stability. Low inflation rates keep German goods competitive.

There was also a broader base to the debate over the origins of West Germany's current account surpluses in the 1980s. It was argued that the balance of payments statistics do not conclusively show whether net capital exports are the result of surpluses on the trade and services accounts, or whether net capital exports are the cause of these surpluses (Neumann 1990). In this context, the term 'net capital exports' refers to both short and long-run capital movements. Neumann (*ibid.*) thus compares the small overall capital balance in 1982 with the large outflows in 1988 and 1989; since his article appeared, however, the deficit capital balance became smaller as the current account sank into deficit (Figures 4.6a and 4.6b). Nonetheless, there were two ways of viewing high export earnings (Sauernheimer 1990: 4). First, a current account surplus reflects the competitive nature of the goods and services exported. Conversely, capital outflows are stimulated by the deteriorating attractiveness of domestic production; this leads to a devaluation of the DM which stimulates exports. No evidence of such a devalua-

tion was found in Figure 4.5. Moreover, given the increasing variability of short-term capital movements – which were attributed to speculative movements in Chapter 4 – long-term capital movements, and even more specifically foreign direct investment, are arguably more relevant to the comparative propensity to invest at home and abroad.

When capital movements are viewed in this way, foreign direct investment is directly analogous to the internationalisation of capital markets (*Finanzplatz Deutschland* in Chapter 7) and the international migration of labour seen in Chapter 6 (also see Wagner 1991: 6–13). Economic growth can then be seen to have been related in the USA to employment growth, whereas the EC relied on productivity growth and Japan relied on both of these causal factors (Sauernheimer 1990). Two factors interpreted by some observers as demonstrating the erosion of Germany's competitive base (*Standort Deutschland*) can also be brought into sharp relief (*ibid.*). First, not only was growth in the EC, including West Germany, slower than in the USA and Japan during the 1980s, but West German companies started to undertake substantially more foreign direct investment. Second, it was undoubtedly true that West Germany was the world's major exporter, but her exports did not consist of high-technology products.

Moreover, the asymmetry between the recovery in export demand, profits and business saving on the one hand and the postulated slack in domestic investment on the other hand was considered by some observers to constitute an explanation for the simultaneous high export surpluses and deficiency in investment decisions until 1988. Although the use by West German manufacturers of export surpluses for investment may be viewed as 'mercantilist', it must be recalled that according to the supply-side paradigm such surpluses are evidence of a country earning more than it deems profitable to invest at home. Hence, before 1988, the cyclical upswing in the West German economy was not taken as evidence of a lasting improvement in supply-side conditions, even though its genesis can be traced back to the earlier sharp decline in imported raw material prices and the sustained, long-standing reduction in real unit labour costs (Giersch *et al.* 1992: 274). The country's attractiveness for mobile capital was also low, although other reasons played a role here (Fröhlich 1991, Mussel 1992). In 1992, conversely, the current account deficit of DM 39 billion – one per cent of GNP – was taken as evidence that domestic savings were not sufficient to finance investment activity and transfers to the new Länder (Dresdner Bank *Trends* April 1993). Long-term capital imports plugged this gap, representing Germany's deficit with the rest of the world (*ibid.* – but see Figures 4.6a and 4.6b).

Notice that the above arguments rely in the first instance on the postulated lack of investment decisions until 1988. More specifically, it was held that by this stage the rate of return on capital had resumed levels previously attained in the late 1960s (Giersch *et al.*: *ibid*). An argument which would tend to counter this view is that West German companies were awash with enormous liquidity in the 1980s (see Figure 8.2). It would seem that their profitability and self-financed investment recovered together from 1981 (*ibid.*). Moreover, the annual increase in gross real investment in plant and equipment was as high in 1985 (9 per cent) as it was in 1989, with 1990 understandably returning a record 13 per cent (BMWi *Wirtschaft* . . . 1992: 43). Between 1985 and 1990,

indeed, investment measured in this way increased by 44 per cent – from DM 153 billion to DM 220 billion (*ibid.*). Meanwhile, however, net direct foreign investment increased by 160 per cent, although the absolute numbers were far smaller: DM 10 billion to DM 26 billion (*ibid.*: 98). This latter outflow has been seen as evidence of a 'capital flight' due to inferior supply-side conditions in West Germany. But the liquid reserves of West German companies remained quite high during the same period, as the discussion around Figure 8.2 indicates. This implies that an appreciable part of these reserves was neither invested abroad (where rates of return were presumed by the 'capital flight' protagonists to be much higher), nor did the companies invest reserves in new (high-tech) products which would have increased their viability. The latter forgone competitive advantages are analysed below.

Consider for now the relative rates of return argument. As will also be shown below, foreign direct investment was directed towards those economies where West Germany also enjoyed substantial export markets. Providing ancillary services, as well as investing some of their export earnings, would thus be equally plausible reasons for foreign investment programmes undertaken by West German companies during the 1980s. In addition, it was seen in the section on corporate control above that the recovery, retention and expansion of market shares are all equally powerful reasons for investing in foreign markets. It was also shown that the rival US locations offered various investment inducements. Finally, Milner and Pentecost (1993) found that the reasons for inward investment into the UK were strongly related to market size. Drawing on their own and other research work, they found that access to a wider

EC market through relatively unrestricted exports was even more important than classic locational advantages such as lower labour costs.

There was, however, some policy concern about the system of concerted export promotion which dated from the 1950s, a system which was indeed dubbed 'neomercantilist' in the mid-1970s (Riemer 1983: 50–1; also see the section on the special-purpose banks in Chapter 7). As early as 1974, a robust free marketeer like Count Lambsdorff (FDP), at one stage the Federal Minister of Economics, expressed reservations about the export surpluses (*Die Zeit* 28/74). He compared them to the winnings of a consistently successful card gambler during his days as a prisoner of war. Ultimately, the card games could only continue when this persistent winner had been robbed! Deficit countries would not permanently be content with their lot and, even if they were, they would eventually lose their creditworthiness. Hence, when West Germany's persistent current account surpluses led to deflationary tendencies in the deficit countries, West Germany was accused by the US and some EC countries of pursuing a beggar-my-neighbour policy at the cost of its trading partners. West Germany and Japan were urged in both the late 1970s and 1980s to act as 'locomotives' by the deficit countries – see Chapter 3. This illustrates one reaction to persistent trade surpluses. Yet the USA and the UK continued to run up sizeable deficits. German unification disposed of the problem coincidentally in the sense that the current account surplus was dissipated and the demand for foreign goods increased. Relatively speaking, of course, current account deficits were still atypical and past export surpluses had made a fundamental contribution to West German affluence. It is equally instructive, moreover, to note

that the post-unification boom, and therefore the accompanying import boom, were in turn dissipated by the Bundesbank's credit squeeze.

So much for the causes of the high current account surpluses but what about their effects? Until the mid-1980s the dependence on US demand in a regime of flexible exchange rates created uncertainty because of exchange-rate fluctuations. This dampened medium-term sales and profit expectations, impeding a sustained investment upswing and higher growth rates among otherwise reflationary policies (Neuthinger 1989: 145). Thereafter, the policy-induced reduction of exchange rate risks, the build-up of excess liquidity in West Germany and the maintenance of low domestic interest rates in the face of monetary tightening abroad were likely to have strengthened business confidence and encouraged a recovery in corporate investment (Dudler 1991). Moreover, export surpluses, in combination with modest increases in wages and salaries and gains in the terms of trade, enhanced the profit share – especially after 1985 (Braun 1990: 219; Oberhauser 1991: 94–5). Such surpluses are coupled with rising profits if these surpluses do not lead to a decrease in private investment which was nearly always the case in West Germany (Scherf and Oberhauser 1990: 291).

At first sight, West Germany seemed to enter the 1990s in quite a sound economic position, although no fundamental supply-side reforms had taken place (Tietmeyer 1992: 4). Strong gains in employment interacted with virtual price stability and healthy growth. The consolidation of public finance had made good progress, and the high external surpluses of the 1980s provided a cushion for the expansion of imports and the throttling back of exports as a result of German unification. East Germany, however, was in a desolate state (Chapter 1 above; Döhrn 1991; Sinn and Sinn 1993: 45–51; Sherman 1990: 43–7). The necessary structural change and clarification of property rights would be a lengthy process (see, for example, the sections on the Treuhand above; Lang 1990: 252). Wants in the east, moreover, were directed towards greater consumption rather than towards improved performance and wage restraint. Of major relevance here, however, is east Germany's loss of its established markets in the former Soviet Union and the other eastern Europe countries. In addition, the east German economy had to adjust to a world of highly developed and established competitors (Lang 1990: 252):

All around the world these efficient competitors, including those from west Germany, are ready and easily able to meet east Germany's demand from their own excess capacities. The present productive capacity of east Germany is not suitable to wants in western markets and is superfluous to (its) own restructuring requirements.

Unification changed Germany's external position almost overnight. Given the existing high rate of capital utilisation in the west, it was only possible to meet the east's high demand for western products from foreign sources. As the current account sank into deficit, the capital account oscillated in the opposite direction: capital outflows of DM 135 billion in 1989 had become an inflow of the same magnitude by 1992 (Figure 4.6a). West German firms increasingly sold their goods in east Germany, temporarily accepting cuts in their shares of foreign markets. Moreover, in 1990 and 1991 German imports rose by 10 and 16 per cent, respectively. Hence, as well as west Germany, other economies benefited from unification, although to differing degrees. Issing (1992a: 4) estimated the benefit to European economies as equivalent to an average half percentage point increase in GNP in both 1990 and 1991. Germany thus performed the locomotive role in 1990 and 1991, a situation which had changed abruptly by 1992 when German high real interest rates caused general deflation and currency speculation (Bean 1992; Hankel 1993: 59; Pomfret 1991; Rybczynski 1993). Two possible foreign-trade scenarios for the rest of the decade were put forward. From the German point of view, one scenario was optimistic, the other pessimistic. The optimists believed that the decline in German exports was only temporary (Walter 1992). Krakowski (1993: 20–4), on the other hand, thought conflicts over income distribution were possible. Further problems like the slump in the world economy and the deterioration in the German age structure might lead to a further worsening of the current account – the latter due to dissaving by the elderly (Chapter 5 above; Meyer 1992, Müller 1992).

An assessment of these two scenarios involves attempting to gauge the probable future international competitiveness of the German economy (*Standort Deutschland*). This has been a hotly debated issue in west Germany for many years. The analysis therefore now turns to this topic.

STANDORT DEUTSCHLAND

This topic has been explicitly and implicitly discussed in virtually every chapter of this book. It has been a controversial subject since about 1985, with three of the five research institutes publishing reports on the topic during 1989 (Sauernheimer 1990: 3). Perhaps the Federal Minister of Economics (Günter Rexrodt) best summarised the wide-ranging nature of the debate (FT 4 May 1993):

- reduced enterprise taxation
- better promotion of R&D
- more flexible labour practices
- promotion of technical education, as opposed to academic disciplines
- a reliable energy policy, including nuclear energy
- accelerated privatisation of railways, roads and telecommunications

It will be noticed that many potentially controversial factors endow an economy with comparative advantage. (This advantage consists of best-selling products produced by technically advanced physical and human capital.) For example, the chief executive of a VEBA subsidiary argued that because two-thirds of his enterprise's electricity was generated using nuclear power, it had been possible to reduce prices over 10 years by 8 per cent (*Die Welt* 16 April 1993). Moreover, the IW compared Germany with thirteen other industrialised market economies and stressed the higher labour costs, corporate tax rates, environment protection costs and productivity in Germany (*Das Parlament* 5 March 1993). Lower working hours were also cited in these findings. Yet an opinion poll carried out in Germany demonstrated that nearly half of all respondents thought that Germany remained the optimum location for industrial investment (*ibid.*). Finally, the attractiveness of Germany to foreign as well as domestic investors was also included in the debate. Faltlhauser (1992: 40) demonstrated, for example, that Germany became a less popular location for US investment in the second half of the 1980s. It has also been shown above that there was an increased tendency for German companies to invest abroad during the 1970s and 1980s.

In the last analysis, there are thus two related aspects to this issue. First, to what extent have German manufacturers transferred the production of established products overseas for comparative-cost reasons? Second, to what extent have both domestic and foreign manufacturers introduced new products into the domestic economy because of comparative-cost advantages? To answer both of these questions, it is necessary to show how comparative competitive advantages are derived. It is also necessary to consider the process of post-war change in West Germany's comparative advantages.

The comparative competitive advantage of an economy in traded goods is obviously a function of the efficiency of its productive capacity. These factor endowments lead to capital-rich economies exporting capital-intensive goods; relatively labour-rich countries, on the other hand, have a cost-advantage in labour intensive goods (Funk 1990: 9–16). Similarly, countries with a high level of technical knowledge export highly technical products. Assuming the absence of tariff protection, a classic rule of international trade theory is that a country exports goods which utilise those factors with which it is relatively well endowed (German agriculture is a conspicuous exception – see the section on subsidies above.) A number of endowment conditions are given (climate, area and the natural environment). However, other endowment factors can be created (the infrastructure, the physical capital stock, the human capital embodied in the labour force at all levels, the technology of production, organisation and the attitude towards working and leisure time). But these latter endowment advantages are not constants; they change over time and there are considerable changes in the endowment advantages of some economies (Porter 1990: 80; Siebert 1985: 111). This means that some of the endowment factors influencing trade and growth are given; others can be influenced by policy and represent acquired comparative advantage. Improving the state of technology or increasing physical or human capital formation can therefore improve comparative competitive advantages in the long run. For example, West German optics firms were able to steadily improve product performance and quality because of the flow of highly-skilled employees from specialised university and apprenticeship programmes (Porter 1990: 79).

International trade also provides a larger market, and a larger market reduces costs through economies of scale (Bea and Beutel 1992). Hence, cost advantages derived by West German industrial enterprises were quite substantial. On average, these enterprises were 40 per cent larger than the median EC enterprise (*Die Zeit* 35/90). Cost advantages were particularly marked in motor vehicles, heavy engineering and chemicals. The general level of costs was 3 per cent under the EC average (*ibid.*). The equivalent statistic for France was 1 per cent under; Britain was 1 per cent over the EC average and Italy 4 per cent over. Moreover, the large German enterprises further increased in size as a result of EC 1993 and expansion in eastern Europe (*Der Spiegel* 27/91). Given the extent of German involvement in intra-EC trade, however, it became increasingly difficult to disentangle export shares in products falling under the same general classifications (*Die Zeit: ibid.*). Other EC trade problems were summarised by Flam (1992: 14–15.):

Intra-EC trade does not seem to be driven by comparative advantage based on factor endowment differences (as in the traditional Heckscher-Ohlin explanation of international trade) or industry-wide tech-

nological differences (as in the classical Ricardian theory), but rather by a combination of technological and other leads on the level of individual firms, as well as by imperfect competition, product differentiation, and economies of scale. [Only] a small share of trade is clearly based on factor endowments; [for example], the clothing and footwear exports of Greece and Portugal are based on an abundance of unskilled labour.

Nonetheless, the pattern of trade specialisation for many years consisted, very broadly speaking, of the less developed countries exporting primary products, the newly industrialising countries exporting 'low technology' manufactured goods (fuels, raw materials, fibres, fabrics and food stuffs) while the industrialised market economies exported manufactured goods like chemical products, machines and transportation equipment. Noteworthy changes then took place in the industrial sectors of the world economy. Standardised industrial products with a high labour intensity like textiles but also standardised industrial products with a high capital intensity like steel, radios, televisions, semiconductor chips and some chemical products have gradually become export goods of the newly industrialising countries and a number of less developed countries. These countries also began to manufacture products like motor vehicles whose production required the derivation of economies of scale as well as capital intensity. Only research and skill-intensive products like pharmaceuticals, electronics and data processing remained fairly exclusively in the advanced industrial market economies. This shift in comparative advantage particularly favoured the far east. In some respects, it was the reverse of the drift from 'north' Germany to the 'south' which was examined in

Chapter 2. In the international trade case each product also moved through its life cycle from being a new product to being an old one, but its geographical location *changed* during its life cycle (Vernon 1966). Innovation and new product development tend to occur in the major industrialised economies and reflect such factors as the highly educated and skilled work force and the relatively high level of expenditure on R&D. Once production no longer requires the R&D and the engineering skills of expensive labour forces it is economic to relocate production to other countries where the cost of standardised production is lower.

There are, however, more direct implications for the export composition of west and east German products. West Germany is well endowed with technological know-how, physical capital, a well-trained labour force and an efficient infrastructure (Braun 1990: 247). This implies that she will lose her international-trade advantage in later stages of the product cycle, especially if mass production is involved. It probably follows that the west can only be competitive in the early stages of the product cycle with 'intelligent products' (Siebert 1985: 113). Furthermore, economies like west Germany lose competitive advantages in established export industries due to internal factors, particularly where environment-policy measures raise the costs of industries which are unable to adapt their technology. In addition, there are the social-policy and labour-market institutional arrangements which have emerged with growing affluence (see Chapters 5 and 6 above). These internal factors have the effect of giving less and newly industrialised countries a comparative advantage in mass production work. The obvious

challenge for west Germany is the need to remain at the appropriate stage of her products' life cycles.

What degree of change is necessary in the structure of Germany's exports? West Germany had been particularly successful in mechanical, precision, optical and motor-vehicle engineering, as well as the chemical industry (Ohr 1992: 142). Furthermore, some smaller (*Mittelstand*) industries shared this success in world markets. In 1987, West Germany occupied the first position in fifteen out of the 35 two-digit product groups of the Standard International Trade Classification, ahead of the USA and Japan. But West Germany had an added advantage because of the wide variety of her exports. For example, only 10 per cent of her exports in 1985 came from industries which held a minimum share of 30 per cent of world exports (Porter 1990: 357–8). This breadth meant that relatively specialised industries, characterised by high levels of productivity, formed segments of export success (*ibid.*). Within those industries, however, both large and small companies were extremely export dependent. Large companies whose exports and foreign transactions accounted for over 40 per cent of their turnover in 1973 included VW, Ford, Opel, Siemens, Mannesmann, GHH and the three chemical giants (*Die Zeit* 2 August 1974). More specifically, the proportion of foreign turnover in the total turnover of some of the top industrial enterprises in 1990 was as follows (Perlitz 1993: 13):

- Bayer AG   78.3 per cent
- BASF AG   62.7 per cent
- BMW AG   61.5 per cent
- VW AG   60.4 per cent
- Mannesmann AG   59.8 per cent
- Siemens AG   55.1 per cent
- Thyssen AG   47.2 per cent

During the 1980s, however, West Germany lost parts of her world exports share in high-tech products. Many observers and actors regarded the relative decline of the German and other European computer and semiconductor industries as especially problematic. The only significant German-owned computer manufacturer is Siemens/Nixdorf, and the three major European chip producers – Philips, Siemens, SGS-Thomson – all experienced losses in 1990. Only one-third of European chip demand is met by European manufacturers. A loss of such markets may well become a problem in the 1990s because these products have displayed the strongest growth in international trade since 1980 (Hartwig 1990: 395). This in turn led to the fairly widespread fear that Germany in the 1990s was 'on the way to becoming a technological colony of global Japanese and American enterprises' (Seitz 1992a: 75). This point of view will be evaluated below.

There is also a fairly wide variation of export dependence among the Länder (Altmann 1992: 343). This is not surprising, of course, since industrial and regional dependency are both related. They are after all derived from the diversity of industrial products. As can be seen from Figure 8.12, Bremen has the highest export share with 38 per cent, and Brandenburg is lowest with only 9 per cent. Because of the collapse of their export markets, the new Länder generally have lower shares. (Hamburg also relies on the service sector – see Chapter 2). This variation in regional dependence is therefore another dimension of the changes required in product structure.

Hence, West Germany's specialisation lay in industries with high human and physical capital inputs, such as mechanical and electrical engineering, motor vehicles, chemicals, pharmaceuticals and medical equipment – all of which were heavily engaged in R&D (Müller-Merbach 1992).

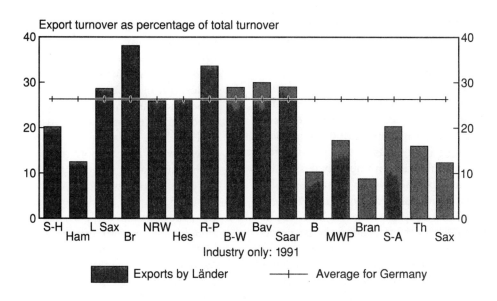

Figure 8.12 Export dependence of the Länder

Source: IW *Zahlen* 1992: 3

For the most important West German industries, the degree of dependence amounted to nearly 60 per cent. The export experience of these industries in the late 1980s, when they were engaged in restructuring for EC 1993, and in the early 1990s, was as follows (Frowen 1991: 109–12; de Smidt 1992; Aho 1991; Kudo 1992):

- In mechanical engineering, the impact of the single market was expected to be significant. Higher growth rates due to increased investment expenditure to raise efficiency throughout the EC made the expansion of productive capacity desirable. West Germany as the most important European producer of investment goods benefited in the late eighties from this development, and the mechanical engineering industry most strongly. In the late eighties Germany had to meet the upsurge in the demand for investment goods which led to high capacity use and investment until 1990. (Thereafter, international competitiveness declined due partly to higher labour costs and partly to the worldwide lower demand for investment goods – in other words both structural and cyclical factors (Link 1992). Germany, which had been the undisputed number one manufacturer of machine tools found itself thrust into a loss-making and vulnerable number two spot by the Japanese who were also hit by international recession (*Independent* 10 March 1993))

- In electrical engineering the prospects were already less promising in the second half of the 1980s. The same is even more true for the 1990s. As in other sectors, the small and medium-sized firms, which often specialise in supplying larger domestic industrial concerns, were subject to pressure to reduce prices as increased international competition forced large concerns to reduce costs. These larger companies often supply public-sector industries in Germany, such as the railways and telecommunications. Electricity supply is another large domestic customer. Until 1993 suppliers to these industries had little competition from abroad. With the liberalisation of government procurement more intense competition was expected. However, the rise in investment-goods demand from east Germany was probably set to compensate for any negative international effects on Siemens

- In the late 1980s motor vehicles was the third major West German export industry with an EC market share of about 40 per cent. Larger cars, for which the market in most EC countries increased, particularly benefited the German industry – and this was expected to continue into the 1990s (Frowen 1991: 110–11). West Germany enjoyed superiority over other EC manufacturers who specialised in the production of smaller vehicles. But in the 1990s the difficulties experienced by the main German car producers were also both structural and cyclical. Japanese car manufacturers were much more productive than European and German car producers – Europeans needed on average about 35 hours to build a car, Japanese car producers only 17. Their models find favour in both Europe and the USA. The established reputation of West German engineering and craftsmanship was no longer sufficient; costs required attention on the supply side (*Economist* 23 May 1992). Demand for German cars also fell in

1993 as a result of recession. Even BMW was hit and Mercedes aimed to broaden its product range (*Economist* 30 January 1993; FT 27 January 1993; *Guardian* 26 March 1993)

- Chemicals, pharmaceuticals and medical equipment were also affected by structural and cyclical factors. In Chapter 5 it was shown that the demand for drugs – normally a non-cyclical factor – was affected by the Federal government's health service reforms. In addition, chemical manufacturers in the UK, France and Italy were less subject to environmental legislation than their German counterparts, thus endowing them with a cost advantage. Production is mainly located in the Rhine valley, where strict environmental protection has been enforced. However, leaks which occurred at Hoechst in 1993, not least because they followed a series of previous Federal-wide accidents in 1992, further undermined public confidence (Focus 22 March 1993). Bayer, Hoechst and BASF all announced falling profits and dividends in 1993 (FT 10 and 18 March 1993). (In a wider context, Germany's huge exports of goods for recycling swamped capacity throughout the EC)

Even when unification is disregarded, therefore, the future prospects of Germany's international competitiveness were not unambiguously good. Yet in addition to the need for product innovation, the east's economy and foreign trade base required complete renovation. A strength on which east Germany could build, however, was the old ties to the countries of eastern Europe (Döhrn 1991). After all, many sectors of the east's economy specialised in meeting demand from the former Communist bloc. Linguistic and other links necessary for re-creating trade already existed. Given the parlous state of all these economies, export guarantees and subsidies would surely be warranted in this case. Joint ventures could also be a catalyst for strengthening long-term economic links (*ibid.*). Support for trade with eastern Europe could be seen as investment in a new market, albeit one whose economic and political future was likely to remain uncertain. On the basis of this reasoning west Germany should concentrate on its extant links with the industrial market economies, while east Germany should be encouraged to rekindle the links just described. But German enterprises reacted to this unprecedented situation by fostering the internationalisation of their production, especially by means of stepping up foreign direct investment (1990: DM 31.7 billion; 1991: DM 29.2 billion – BMWi *Wirtschaft* . . . 1992: 98). For that matter, prior to unification large West German firms had responded to the challenge of the growing interdependence in the world economy with foreign direct investment (FDI) in their traditional areas of strength (Fröhlich 1991; Oppenländer and Gerstenberger 1992).

Multinational enterprise thus came to be one of the most significant strategies of West German firms, as a consequence of which they joined the ranks of Japanese firms as international investors during the 1970s and 1980s. The increase in the stock of West German FDI was impressive (Heiduk and Hodges 1992: 163). From being barely DM 1 billion in 1961, it had risen to DM 211 billion by 1990 (BMWi *Wirtschaft* . . . 1992: 105; IW *Zahlen* 1979: 69). Since the stock was only DM 18 billion in 1970, it will be appreciated that most of the growth took place after that year. In spite of changes in this statistical series, it is possible to say that by 1980 at latest the stock of West German FDI was larger than the stock of direct investment by foreigners in West Germany (IW *ibid.* 1992: 45). This gap had reached DM 54 billion by 1991 (MRDB *Beilage zur Beiheft* 3: 6/93). The gap between the flows of FDI was dominated by increasing West German outflows after the mid-1970s (Braun 1990: 245). The outflow was unusually dynamic and scarcely influenced by the business cycle (Deutsche Bank *Bulletin* December 1985). When measured by the stock of FDI in the industrial market economies, West Germany moved up from sixth to third position between 1967 and 1976 (Hood and Young 1979: 67). The shares of both the USA and UK contracted, so that by 1976 the USA's share was 48 per cent, the UK's 11 per cent and West Germany's 7 per cent (*ibid.*). By the late 1980s, in terms of net long-term capital outflows – that is including both portfolio and direct investment – West Germany had replaced the UK and was second only to Japan (*Economist* 14 January 1989). Whether the capital outflows during the 1980s were attributable to 'capital flight' or the 'natural development' of West Germany into a mature economy was considered above. (As indicated in the discussion around Figure 4.6a, the persistently large current account surpluses in both the 1950s and the 1980s were inevitably complemented by strong capital outflows. An attempt was made to distinguish between short and long-term capital flows in Figure 4.6b. The 'capital flight' school would contend that during the 1980s capital outflows led to an exchange-rate depreciation and therefore export surpluses. The 'natural development' school would argue that the real exchange rate advantage demonstrated in Figure 4.5 led to export surpluses and, consequently, capital outflows.)

West Germany's FDI was, like her exports, predominantly orientated towards the industrialised market economies. In 1989, West German multinational firms were thus located in the USA (29.5 per cent of the total FDI stock), France (8.2 per cent), the Netherlands (7.7 per cent) and the UK (6.5 per cent) (IW *Zahlen* 1992: 45). Out of total West German FDI, the flow to the EC grew strongly after 1980: from 28 per cent in 1980 to 68 per cent in 1990 (BMWi *Wirtschaft . . .* 1992: 100–1). On the other hand, West German FDI flows to the USA decreased during the same period from 41 per cent to 13 per cent (*ibid.*). Industrially, the four largest exporters were also the four largest owners of productive capacity outside West Germany in 1988. Their rankings in these two respects differed, however. This can best be seen by comparing their percentage shares of total exports in 1989 with their percentage shares of the stock of FDI in manufacturing industry in 1988. The following data report these two shares, placing the stock of FDI in rank order (Heiduk and Hodges 1992: 174):

- chemicals: 10.1 per cent of exports; 33.0 per cent of FDI
- vehicles: 18.0 per cent of exports; 17.3 per cent of FDI
- electrical engineering: 8.6 per cent of exports; 15.3 per cent of FDI
- mechanical engineering: 19.0 per cent of exports; 8.9 per cent of FDI

But in the late 1980s the service sector (holding companies, banking and insurance) became the most important target sectors for German FDI, something that might become even more relevant in the 1990s (Faltlhauser 1992).

In order to illustrate these general patterns it is appropriate to examine typical globalisation strategies at company level. This is best accomplished by contrasting the strategies of two important German multinational firms – Daimler-Benz and BASF (Heiduk and Hodges 1992: 174–82). It will be shown that they followed very different globalisation paths. Yet these two firms give a fairly representative impression of the two general trends of the international pattern of FDI (*ibid.*: 183–5). Some implications for the declining Ruhr district will also be added to the detailed case study in Chapter 2 (*ibid.*).

Daimler-Benz and BASF domestically ranked first and sixth in terms of turnover in 1991 (Table 8.1 above). This was identical to their relative position at the end of the 1980s. An international perspective must also be highlighted here, however. In an international ranking of turnover these two companies were 10th and 37th in 1991, although BASF had slipped from 32nd in 1990 (*Fortune* 27 July 1992: 55). Daimler was below three petroleum multinationals – Shell, Exxon and BP. Three motor-vehicle manufacturers were also above Daimler – General Motors, Ford and Toyota. IBM was also above Daimler but, along with General Motors and Ford, IBM had registered losses in 1991. Although Daimler's sales plummeted from mid-1992, the international recession hit other companies too. Nonetheless, within Europe, Daimler in 1991 achieved the second highest turnover (US$ 93 billion), with Shell only DM 2 billion ahead (*Die Welt* 11 February 1993). Three other German companies – VW, Siemens and VEBA – were also in the 'top ten' European list for turnover, but no German company appeared in the list containing the ten most profitable companies in Europe (*ibid.*). But corporate growth has already been seen to be a more important German goal than profit maximisation. However, the very different globalisation strategies and different goals of Daimler and BASF can be summarised under the following headings:

- non-domestic turnover
- foreign investment
- numbers employed outside Germany
- joint ventures

As seen above, Daimler-Benz's strategy changed during the 1980s when the company increasingly became an integrated-technology firm by means of in-house technological developments, intensive R&D, but more especially by takeovers in the aerospace and electrical-engineering sectors. Daimler aspired to an internationally-competitive position as a result of its technological base combined with the resultant synergy, although problems emerged. Turnover outside West Germany as a proportion of total turnover increased from 55.4 per cent in 1980 to 66.1 per cent in 1984 (Heiduk and Hodges 1992: 176). At the end of the 1980s it dropped back to 61 per cent as a consequence of its domestic takeover policy. Although the proportion of total turnover accounted for by North American operations during the 1980s rose from 9.9 per cent to 17.1 per cent, it peaked at 26 per cent in 1984 (*ibid.*: 175). On the other hand, the European share of total turnover – including West Germany – increased as a consequence of preparations for EC 1993. As a result, European turnover rose from 63.8 to 66.7 per cent between 1980 and 1989, having initially fallen to 53.2 per cent in 1984. The recovery of European sales was the result of the intensive marketing of its cars, especially in Italy, France, Spain and the UK (*ibid.*: 176). But in 1992 domestic and European turnover fell marginally, whereas it rose in the USA by 8.2 per cent (*Die Welt* 7 April 1993). Significantly, Daimler also made an important shift in its locational and product strategy in 1993. As well as following its major rival BMW to the USA, it decided to extend its car product range into those segments showing good growth prospects (FT 6 April 1993):

We will not withdraw into an ivory tower of a 'mega-luxury class' but rather attack the Japanese competition in its own market niches by offering our own technologically superior product concepts.

Daimler already produced heavy trucks in the USA through its Freightliner subsidiary, but this was the first car manufacturing operation outside Germany on any scale. US state subsidies could be expected, as in the case of BMW and VW (see the corporate strategy section above). The BMW strategy of a green-field site in the south was also favoured. As a result, US production would be 'substantially cheaper' than in Germany (*ibid.*).

Because it did not pursue Daimler's policy of diversification and mergers, BASF reduced its domestic turnover from 42.2 per cent of total turnover to 31.9 per cent during the 1980s. Moreover, the proportion of total turnover attained within the EC – including Germany – decreased in the 1980s from 60.7 to 56.8 per cent (Heiduk and Hodges 1992: 180). This was due to BASF's policy of securing and expanding the important US market where the turnover share increased in the 1980s from 15.3 per cent to 22.1 per cent.

A powerful indicator of the degree to which both firms are internationally involved is their investment pattern. Daimler-Benz increased investment abroad in the 1980s except during the years of its major takeovers. Hence, in the mid-1980s the increase in investment abroad was particularly high (*ibid.*: 176). Following the completion of domestic takeovers, investment abroad increased at a rate slightly higher than that of domestic investment. BASF also invested increasingly abroad in the 1980s but not so much in the EC nations as Daimler-Benz.

During the 1980s the share of BASF's total investment abroad remained fairly high at between 46 and 33 per cent (*ibid.*: 182). The company invested particularly intensively in the USA – again with the aim of securing and expanding this important market (*ibid.*: 179). BASF thus concentrated on the demand for its existing products as opposed to the Daimler-Benz method of attempting to find strategic access to expected future markets. As such, the BASF strategy was not only more representative of many other large West German firms but was also similar to that of German medium-sized firms (*ibid.* and the remarks on *Mittelstand* firms above). BASF's product range has also not changed significantly, another thing the company has in common with *Mittelstand* companies. The share of turnover derived from each category of product remained stable. Technological progress was used to increase product differentiation. BASF did not attempt product diversification as was the case with Daimler-Benz. But both enterprises were more risk averse when investing abroad.

Unlike investment abroad, Daimler-Benz's domestic mergers did not affect employment policy at its foreign subsidiaries. At around 20 per cent of total employment, this proportion remained fairly stable even in the years of the takeovers (*ibid.*: 178). Relatively high domestic labour costs, combined with the fairly sudden and serious recession which began in 1992, caused the motor-vehicle subsidiary to announce a broadening of its product range, a pruning of management and the intention to transfer assembly to Spain, South Korea and Mexico (FT 28 January 1993). As already shown, an extremely important change in strategy later resulted in the US investment decision. Similarly, the aerospace division's product range – and employment abroad –

were both extended by the acquisition of the Dutch Fokker company. This gave Daimler access to established and possible future product and technological specialisation (*Die Zeit* 31 July 1992; FT 2 November 1992). A strategic alliance with Mitsubishi was a rather more nebulous factor to assess, especially in terms of its possible effects on employment and human-capital formation. This alliance involved joint research, information exchanges and possible joint products. Perhaps the alliance represented a new dimension in international technological cooperation between associate companies in the fields of electronics, services and aerospace. Examples of such cooperation already existed in the motor-vehicle industry (Renault-Volvo, General Motors-Saab, for example). Strategic action of this description could not only be a possible method of maintaining or achieving a leading position in the face of fierce international competition. It also clearly changes the qualitative structure of the labour force. Joint ventures and employment policies are therefore closely related. Corporate investment risks are also shared in these attempts to maintain a leading edge in know-how and technology. Daimler was hit by the 1993 recession: stocks of cars were high, thus preventing it from achieving Japanese-inspired lean production. Nonetheless, the company still hoped to maintain sales through exports (*Guardian* 7 April 1993).

BASF, on the other hand, increased non-domestic employment during the 1980s – from 25 per cent of total employment in 1980 to 34.9 per cent in 1989 (Heiduk and Hodges 1992: 183). In 1985, when involvement in the US market was intensified, there was a particularly marked increase. In 1993, when BASF experienced a recession, the company specifically indicated that it would maintain employment abroad but reduce the domestic share by about 4,000 jobs (FAZ 19 March 1993). This strategy was again a conventional response to both demand and cost factors, the latter being related to the high costs imposed by environmental regulations in Germany. On the demand side, many factors contrived to bring matters to a head (*Focus* 19 April 1993):

- 60 per cent of all chemical products were nearing the end of their cycle
- price competition was intensifying in the far east
- European motor-vehicle and electrical industries were breaking away
- the 1993 health-sector reform undermined the normally non-cyclical market for pharmaceuticals

All these factors stimulated the quest for overseas markets and joint ventures. Hence, in 1993 BASF announced three new joint ventures with the Chinese (FAZ 19 April 1993). This was in line with the perception of all three German chemical giants that the most rapidly growing markets were in the Far East (Focus *ibid.*). Moreover, all three chemical combines were conducting more of their R&D abroad: BASF and Bayer in the USA, Hoechst in Japan (*Die Welt* 16 April 1993).

Heiduk's (1989) study of the Ruhr district also indicated a high degree of international involvement. About 80 per cent of the firms in the region seemed to export abroad, and about 22 per cent were engaged in FDI. On the whole, therefore, it can be suggested from the fairly representative micro study of Daimler-Benz and BASF, along with apparent experience in the Ruhr district, that securing and opening up of foreign markets is the dominant reason for internationalisation of German firms. Furthermore, Heiduk (*ibid.*) significantly found that German small and medium-sized firms are relatively more active abroad than those of other industrialised countries. As would be expected, however, they almost always export to other industrialised countries, and, of course, there is an almost entire absence of FDI.

Thus far the analysis has been confined to West Germany's past external economic relations from the macro and a possibly representative micro point of view. However, the future competitiveness of both west and east Germany depends crucially on their ability to attract international investment (Berthold 1992; Krakowski *et al.* 1992). Such a definition of international competitiveness is not linked to the presence or absence of a current account surplus. As already indicated, the presence of such a surplus is partly the result of capital exports due to high regulation and labour costs – in other words, a lower return on capital employed. The main indicators of competitiveness in this sense will now be assessed.

It has been shown in earlier chapters that the West German economy is characterised by relatively high industrial costs. In spite of numerous reforms during the post-war period, there is a fairly high top rate for income tax and a relatively high corporation tax (Chapter 3; Kreklau 1992). The process of reform was brought to an abrupt halt by unification. A high standard of social-policy protection, particularly social insurance, has not only been an historical feature of the economy, it has also been an inherent component of the SME (Chapter 5). But employers' social-insurance contributions raise labour costs, as do the reductions in working hours and increases in pay. There were substantial gains in productivity, but unification brought the problem of having a substantial pocket of relatively low pay

in the east (Chapter 6). Cost enhancing consumer protection, the technical security of plant and equipment from the health and safety viewpoint and environmental legislation also all raise costs. These latter attributes are aimed at maximising the quality of life. But all these sources of high costs involve the need to raise productivity faster than competing countries, given that reducing costs would lower living standards. An alternative option is for German firms to relocate in lower-cost EC countries or the USA. Until unification a continued compensation for high costs through a correspondingly high level of productivity increases was seen as vital. It was achieved mainly by sufficient investment and further technological advances. (In a pessimistic scenario below, it will be argued that unification may have changed this adaptability in several respects.)

There are several indicators of competitiveness (Dunn 1992; Löbbe 1991; Ohr 1992). The exchange rate and international technology transfer have both been considered above. Research expenditure, research intensity and the number of external patent applications have also been mentioned. It is, however, salutary to note that whereas research expenditure in West Germany increased more than in the USA during the 1970s, their achieved increases of 27 and 21 per cent respectively were dwarfed by Japan's 81 per cent (Dunn 1992: 325). In the 1980s, West German R&D expenditure increased by 40 per cent, in the USA by 50 per cent and in Japan by 100 per cent (*ibid.*). Moreover, it has already been seen that the quantity of German patent applications conceals a qualitative weakness as far as new technologies are concerned.

Probably one of the most important indicators of competitiveness is FDI, although it is viewed in two distinct ways.

The first of the two views is that the relocation of West German industry had been proceeding for some time. The relevant indicator here is the increasing amount of west German direct foreign investment. Germany's position as a location for industry, it is further argued, is weakening because of lower expected rates of return and the consequent investment of domestic savings abroad. Most of this is forced saving in the following sense. As already seen, German companies can more easily waive a dividend payment without the threat of a takeover or substantial protest from small shareholders. On the other hand, this system probably induces more investment than the enforced distribution of profits under the Anglo-Saxon capital-market regime. If that investment is made overseas, however, employment prospects are probably undermined but the corporate sector enjoys a higher rate of return. Whether a greater degree of profit distribution would have resulted in a higher return for shareholders elsewhere is not relevant as far as this first view of FDI is concerned. The important point, as seen in the context of the 1980s above, is that a relative higher rate of return is derived from German corporate investment abroad.

The other view was also examined in the context of the 1980s. It is that FDI was simply the counterpart of the rapidly growing trade surpluses in West Germany. According to this hypothesis there was a close correlation between West German exports and her FDI – and the evidence is fairly convincing. This evidence consists of the correlation between exports and FDI already examined above. It should be added that 90 per cent of Germany's most important export markets were the most important host countries for West German FDI (Heiduk and Hodges 1992: 163; Faltlhauser 1992: 39). The second view therefore seems to be quite a powerful explanation. Furthermore, it must not be forgotten that West Germany possessed the potential to ensure that the requirements of *Standort Deutschland* were met. She was able to offer industrial investors a sound infrastructure, along with a propitious economic and social system which had produced a politically stable climate. A highly-skilled labour force and highly motivated management were additional advantages. All these qualitative advantages favoured the production of high quality goods (Soskice 1991). The following also bears reiteration. Provided the east is suitably developed the basis for trade with eastern Europe could be re-exploited. Apart from her central geographical position, east Germany has developed links in that direction.

What is to be learned from this discussion? It is certainly not enough to have only a contemporaneously successful and therefore attractive number of export goods. Arguably, devaluation, shorn of its political unpopularity and accepting the implied losses of real income, could always absorb increases in production costs and perhaps even make hitherto qualitatively unattractive goods internationally competitive. *Standort Deutschland* implies that the more long-term factors just outlined have to be taken into account. A loss of these factors means lower future competitiveness because of lower physical and human capital formation, along with a slower rate of technical progress. It is then that the necessary losses of real income due to devaluation will occur (Fels 1989: 2).

STRATEGIC TRADE, COMPETITION AND INDUSTRIAL POLICIES

The Monopolies Commission (MK IX: 516) devoted a significant part of its ninth biennial report to the conflict between industrial and competition policies in the field of foreign trade. This was because of the renewed interest during the 1980s in the extent to which governments can influence international trade by adopting a strategic trade policy. Relative resource endowments were no longer seen as being the main reason for international trade. More importance was accorded to economies of scale in production as a reason for international specialisation. Since government policy was assumed to exert an influence on trade flows, free trade and competition are constrained. The most obvious method for such government intervention is subsidisation. Notice that reference here is to real factors. Free international capital movements became a more important influence on exchange rates than trade during the 1980s – see the end of the section on monetary aspects of the balance of payments in Chapter 4. It is at the very least arguable that free trade and free international capital movements are incompatible. By adopting strategic trade policies, therefore, governments in the market economies sought to manage international trade rather than the international monetary system.

Apart from credit support, West Germany initially pursued a liberal foreign trade policy as far as industrial goods are concerned (Donges 1992: 20–2; Engelhard 1992). But since the fierce competition in mass-produced goods started in the 1970s, some old 'sunset' industries have been heavily subsidised. These were industries in which Germany had lost a comparative advantage. Furthermore, the emergence of new models of strategic industrial policies, along with the success of Japan in skill and technology-intensive goods, led to a policy of fostering 'sunrise' industries with potentially high worldwide monopoly profits. Although this strategic industrial policy was the subject of controversy among economists, regional interest groups utilised West Germany's federal system to secure its implementation.

Subsidies and government intervention as such were not new, of course – see Chapters 1, 2 and 3, and the sections on deregulation and subsidies above. It was the *Gestaltende Strukturpolitik* (active structural policy) which formalised their use. This economic policy was introduced by the grand coalition (1967–9) and was further developed by the social-liberal coalition (1969–82) (Tomann in Cowling and Tomann 1990; Peacock *et al.* 1980: 1–5; Riemer 1983). Further reform plans for a prospective and active industrial policy were in fact proposed during the 1970s but these far-reaching plans were not implemented (Tomann *ibid.*: 40). This was mainly because many politicians took the view that more entrepreneurial initiative was necessary to overcome the crisis after 1974. A structural policy was, however, subsequently pursued under the Christian-liberal coalition, although its philosophy and its instruments changed (Riemer 1985).

Active structural policy is a Keynesian concept. It is the converse of a neoliberal philosophy which treats the mainly self-correcting market economy as a natural or spontaneous order (Neumann 1990). The policy's aim was to stimulate economic growth by allocating productive factors to sectors with relatively high productivity levels and by developing the economic potential of new technologies and regions. Critics see it as a subsidising policy in the guise of a broader and more constructive policy. Two basic cases for sectoral economic policy were isolated by the social-liberal governments:

- government support for the socially unacceptable adjustment process in declining industries. This support took the form of investment aid to firms to avoid large-scale disinvestment in recessions and also the form of unemployment aid to reduce the social cost to employers of disinvestment decisions.
- Government support for the promotion of innovative industries which were regarded as embodying future technologies and whose expansion was perceived as requiring a stimulus. The major rationalisation was that the normally high risks could not be taken solely by the private sector (Stille in Cowling and Tomann 1990). In later policy debates, government assistance in this category became known as 'strategic industrial policy'.

Subsidisation in both cases was seen as transitional. In theory, there were built-in safeguards to prevent its becoming permanent. The main instruments of this protection were tariffs, quotas, voluntary export restraints on the part of foreign exporters and exceptions to anti-trust legislation which permitted cartel arrangements to ostensibly supervise capacity reduction in a socially responsible manner. In the 1970s this policy was principally used to, first, support shipbuilding and coal mining, the coal industry having already been concentrated into a single company (Ruhrkohle AG) in the late 1960s.(Abelshauser 1979; Dach 1992.) Second, a special ministry was built up to foster high-tech industries like aerospace, computers and nuclear power. There was a parallel development of programmes at Länder level. These pro-grammes took the form of regional aid to specially selected industries. Finally, local authorities vied with one another to attract industry by offers of cheap sites and infrastructure (Sturm 1989b: 165). Higher local tax revenue and lower unemployment were seen as the two main advantages.

In 1982 the government and the philosophy of structural policy changed. The new philosophy was inspired by the neo-classical one of minimal government intervention. There was to be no direct interference with sectoral or regional resource allocation (Stille in Cowling and Tomann 1990: 92; Molitor 1992). This meant that lame-duck industries would be permitted to decline more rapidly and support for new technologies would be withdrawn. But West German policies were more pragmatically implemented. As a result, there was no real difference from earlier practice. Indeed, subsidies increased substantially. Although there were some theoretical changes in political priorities, the structure of industry was largely conserved. Highly protected and ailing industries (agriculture, coal mining, shipbuilding, iron and steel) continued to receive support. But the international-trade sector was given something of a fillip. R&D intensive industries like electrical and mechanical engineering also received higher subsidies (Stille *ibid.*: 100).

Structural change was consequently seen as being hampered rather than enhanced by protection. West Germany's many actors attempted to follow diverse goals. Neither goals nor instruments were at all well coordinated – or even known – by the various actors (*ibid.*: 89). Declining industries were by definition protected from international competitive pressure from the newly industrialising countries. This normally slows down the pace of adjustment and results in higher profits –

or lower losses! There is an absence of an incentive to curtail production; further support is rather sought. Furthermore, protection of some declining industries harms other industries. It means an increased burden of taxation to fund subsidies and artificially inflated prices for raw materials. Their competitiveness is consequently undermined and this may induce requests for additional government intervention (Neumann in Cowling and Tomann 1990: 229).

An active strategic industrial policy in favour of 'sunrise industries' found special support from the German ambassador to Italy, Konrad Seitz (1992a). He argued that Germany and the rest of Europe were not keeping pace with the new industrial revolution in the future key technologies. A biotechnical industry had not even been established in Germany; the semiconductor, computer and consumer electronic industries were not very highly developed, and it was uncertain whether it would be possible to retain and develop the machine tool and telecommunications industries. Seitz believed that 'any economy which forfeits its competence in these areas will become dependent on the supply of key components from abroad, and will increasingly tend to lose the ability to develop new equipment and industrial establishments' (Seitz 1992b: 104). He therefore assumed a scenario of European economic dependency on Japan and, to a lesser extent, the USA. His conclusions and policy proposals have been widely debated in Germany:

- cooperation between the State and industry, in order to devise an overall strategy, is necessary
- it follows that a selective promotion of identified key industries is also necessary
- to foster strategic cooperation with

Japanese firms, it is essential to have freer access to the Japanese market
- an integrated framework for the global promotion of the German economy in the high-tech age should be formulated by an Advisory Committee for Strategic and Competitive Trade Policy

In theoretical terms, strategic and industrial policies are designed to increase national economic welfare by enabling exporters to charge prices higher than those necessary to keep them in business ('extracting monopoly profits or rents'). Monopolies tend, however, to be inefficient because there is no incentive to minimise costs. Moreover, most economists agree that the conditions for welfare-enhancing government intervention are very restrictive. Finally, several conditions must be fulfilled to shift monopoly profits ('rents') to the domestic economy:

- large economies of scale in the targeted industries
- no new entrants who would compete the rents away
- governmental ability to predict the competitive behaviour of oligopolistic enterprises
- the credibility of government commitments to support domestic industries
- no further reduction in the efficiency of firms due to government protection
- no retaliation by foreign governments
- no transfer of rents to national interest groups seeking government protection

But it must also be asked whether the alternative is technological dependence on other economies – in which case the arguments for and against industrial policy would have to be seen in a different light (Funk 1992; Keller 1992). For example, the heavy reliance on the import of semi-conductor products has been a particular cause of concern for some time in Germany and the rest of Europe. But the mere fact of being dependent on a particular technology does not necessarily justify the development of corresponding industries in one's own country (Starbatty and Vetterlein 1988: 114). It is true that Germany could cut off the supply of silicon; indeed, in the last analysis, the European market for a whole range of Japanese products could completely be closed against Japanese competition, which would have a significant effect on Japanese firms. But 'one can imagine how quickly Japanese car manufacturers would make representations to their prime minister' (ibid.: 115). Other observers feared only a delay in the supply of the latest generations of chips, which is again unlikely. As memory chip production entails very high R&D spending, extremely short product cycles and high static and dynamic economies of scale, only those enterprises that market their latest products worldwide as quickly as possible will earn the envisaged supernormal profits. One should also bear in mind that prices usually fall dramatically once products have been exposed to the market, and so do profits. In any case, no economy enjoys a technological monopoly with long-term prospects (ibid.: 113).

Yet another contention is that Japanese producers might restrict the volume by reaching cartel agreements to drive up prices. But the required degree of collusion is unlikely to exist as Japanese manufacturers are in fierce competition with one other. In any case, even cheaper suppliers in the Far East are flooding the world market with memory chips. Furthermore, the argument that the use of application-specific chips leads to divulgence of the system's technology is at best only partly correct. The assembly firms

have the option of programming the system's technology into the chips themselves. There is also the further option of running tests on the chips. On the other hand, if programming is done by the chip manufacturer (turn-key design), disclosure of the technology cannot be completely ruled out. Nevertheless, it must be borne in mind that these firms have a reputation to maintain, for they do want to sell their products (Keller 1992: 115).

Last but not least, the argument that technological 'neo-imperialism' can also come about as a result of Japanese direct investment in western Europe is equally unconvincing. Multinationals locate their plant on the basis of comparative advantages and the market potential of the host countries. Hence, where suitable conditions exist, R&D may well be carried out abroad. This also creates highly paid jobs in the host country. An example of such a direct investment by German and other European multinationals is that of biochemicals in the USA. This migration of R&D activities occurred due to the less restrictive legal requirements for biotechnology research in the USA. In short, government ministries face severe informational problems in attempting to formulate an optimal strategic trade policy. An ill-designed approach to 'rent-snatching' could quite well result in welfare losses for all participants (Funk 1990 and 1992; Greenaway and Milner 1986: 184; Siebert 1992c). All the same, there is a strong demand for protection. It stems from Europe's inferior position in international technological progress. Since the end of the 1960s, it has been accepted that a 'technological gap' existed between Europe and the USA; a similar gap later developed in favour of Japan (Legler 1992: 17). For the rest, it is likely that US firms which invested in the UK were more interested in access to the large EC market rather than 'protection jumping' *per se* (Milner and Pentecost 1993).

Three German industries in particular successfully lobbied for support from public budgets; they also sought joint ventures with their counterparts in other leading industrial countries (Seitz 1992a and 1992b). These industries are aerospace, microelectronics, and motor vehicles. In the aerospace industry economies of scale were pronounced. They result from learning-curve effects. Furthermore, barriers to entry were high and, without massive government support, newcomers would probably not have been able to compete with the dominant American producers. Bletschacher and Klodt (1992: 81 and 84) point out that European aerospace projects such as Concorde, the VFW-614 and Comet failed to capture a successful market. Yet the support given to the European consortium Airbus Industrie since the early 1970s may have enabled it to gain a significant position in the world market. But the degree of economic success is difficult to quantify. Such an exercise was attempted by means of a simulation using an IfW model (*ibid*.: 91–3). It was first assumed that Boeing had derived cost advantages by virtue of the learning-curve bedrock of previous production runs. Without subsidisation, therefore, the market entry of the Airbus would have been inhibited. Even given the estimated additional tax burden for European customers of US\$ 20 billion, however, the producers of the Airbus gained US\$ 17 billion and Boeing's prices were lower than they would otherwise have been. The impact of Airbus subsidies on European welfare in this case was positive, although Boeing and the rest of the world were 'losers'. When McDonnell-Douglas was included with Boeing, the market entry of the Airbus resulted in the

welfare change that was negative throughout the world.

The motor-vehicle industry is another graphic example of the possible ineffectiveness of a strategic industrial policy (Bletschacher 1992: 84). The basic idea, for instance, of the voluntary restraint agreement of Japanese car exports to the US market in the early 1980s was to enable American producers to catch up with Japanese lean-production techniques. But the technological gap did not shrink. After the agreement expired the gap was still as large. A similar development must presumably be expected from the similar agreement between the EC and Japan, an agreement which expires in 1999. Dicken (1992: 30) uses the term 'global car wars' to describe the trade situation which gave rise to these agreements. A better strategy of German car producers would probably be to increase productivity (Lange 1992: 30). In the meantime, Japanese manufacturers had successfully established themselves in the UK, thus deriving an entry into the post-EC 1993 market.

Manufacturing microelectronic integrated circuits also yields significant learning-curve effects. However, the barriers to entry here are low. This is because of the rather short product cycles. They imply that a learning-curve advantage in a specific chip generation does not imply an advantage in subsequent generations. The monopoly of dominant producers is therefore only transitory, as confirmed by history. The hierarchy of firms with respect to world market sales has significantly changed over time and across different segments of the chip markets. This leads to the conclusion that there are no rents that could be shifted by strategic industrial policy because competition among chip-producing firms is intense.

The example of the semi-conductor industry also implies that the dependency argument cannot really be used to justify assisting key industries. An example of the tardy nature of state policy when it comes to capitalising on market developments is afforded by the European Jessi and Eureka programmes, the results of which are lucidly described by Keller (1992: 115–16):

The example of the semi-conductor industry shows that the dependency argument cannot really be used to justify assisting key industries. Is a rather cumbersome state industrial policy a suitable way of handling such a dynamic area of high technology? It is more likely that it would always be lagging one step behind the helter-skelter developments in the market.

The point is exemplified by events surrounding the Jessi-project under the Eureka programme. The project was launched in 1989 at the urging of the three large European semi-conductor manufacturers Philips, Siemens and SGS Thomson. In order to ensure commercial success, an extremely tight timetable was drawn up; pilot production of the static 16 Mb chip was to begin by 1993 and that of the dynamic 64 Mb chip by 1996. The project costs were estimated at DM 8 billion, half of which would be met by national governments and the EC and the other half by industry. Philips' withdrawal from static memory chip technology and Siemens' decision to develop the dynamic 64 Mb chip in co-operation with IBM have already invalidated most of the original objectives of Jessi. It would seem that Siemens and Philips did not consider the development of memory chips within the Jessi framework to be worthwhile, despite state subsidies. It is also doubtful whether memory chips are strategically important in any case, as they are standardised mass-produced components. Memory chips account for only a relatively small part of semi-conductor production. The total world market for semi-conductors in 1991 is put at around $ 55 billion, of which just over $ 12 billion represents memory chips (MOS). The market in application-specific chips was even smaller, at $ 7.7 billion, and yet it is this kind of chip, rather than memory chips, that bears the hallmarks of key products.

The Jessi project is now focusing its sights more on these products. According to the German Research Minister Riesenhuber, the European microelectronics industry can survive only if there is also mass demand for application-specific chips in Europe. So-called 'flagship projects' should take care of this, in fields such as high resolution television, digital radio reception and mobile telephones. Chip producers and users and the suppliers of apparatus for chip production should co-operate across national borders in these projects. Since Jessi aims to establish independent European chip production, participation by non-European firms is accepted only reluctantly, if at all. The circle of potential participants is therefore biased towards European firms, despite the fact that non-European companies often have more to offer than their European counterparts as regards their complementary technological capabilities. This is demonstrated, for example, by the co-operation between Siemens and IBM on the 64 Mb chip.

Naturally, the analysis could now turn to the many examples of protectionism on the part of Japan and the USA. But this book is confined to the German economy and its possible future course. On the whole, the experience with industrial policy is generally discouraging, although it would be clearly wrong to say that West

Germany did not have such a policy (Sturm 1989b; Tomann in Cowling and Tomann 1990). Perhaps this is because the policy has been sector specific, although it will shortly be seen that the Japanese adopted a similar approach. Governments – at least European governments – do not normally seem able to pick a future winner *ex ante* because they do not possess sufficient information on the future state of the world market. Regrettably, from a European point of view, its large industrial concerns – which primarily mean the German ones – have also not generally retained the ability to pick future winners. Significantly, Klodt (in Cowling and Tomann 1990) concludes that EC 1993 will not endow the EC Commission with more influence over technology policy. This is because EC funds in this area are of minor importance. Klodt (*ibid.*: 285) concludes that the EC Commission would have to concentrate on '*competition* policy' which he defines as 'centrally slowing down inefficient subsidy races among member countries in high-tech industries'. Policy makers should, it seems, therefore refrain from strategic *industrial* and therefore trade policy.

Industrial policy in this sense is likely to become one of the most controversial issues in any future international consideration of economic policy. Summarising the situation, Paqué and Soltwedel (1993: 25–6) initially point out that the undoubted export success of Japanese companies in high-tech markets has even led some observers to predict that Germany and other European countries may become a technological colony of the Japanese industrial giants. Two opposing strategies are therefore postulated (*ibid.*). First, the opening up of markets and the strengthening of the principles of free trade in Europe would counter the inefficiencies of firms, dispersed national markets and protectionist policies. Alternatively, it is urged that Germany (or perhaps the EC) should develop a role equivalent to that performed by the Japanese Ministry of International Trade and Industry (MITI). In other words, the very existence of MITI implies a strategic trade policy which expressly acknowledges government involvement.

There are, however, several possible implications of the extreme free-trade approach, particularly if it is introduced unilaterally. These possible implications were well brought out in a scenario suggested by Roland Berger, the 'guru of German management consultancy' (*Independent on Sunday* 25 April 1993). East Germany should be viewed as a model for tomorrow's west Germany, with a greater emphasis on services and a shift away from labour-intensive manufacturing. This shift accepts the erosion of Germany's quality premium in so many traditional areas, such as machine tools, cars and chemicals. The only future investment that would make sense in Germany, in the east as in the west, would be high-tech and extremely capital intensive. Bypassing the UK as an alternative *Standort* – where labour costs, according to British official sources, are half of those in Germany – Berger suggests East Europe for future German labour-intensive investment. Labour costs there are only a tenth of those in Germany and these countries offer a meaningful home market when compared to Portugal or Malaysia. Germany should extend her service sector which excessive protection and regulation have made relatively small and inefficient. Berger therefore implicitly favoured a more dynamic *Finanzplatz Deutschland* approach rather than the one reviewed in the previous chapter. This would result in resistance from the Bundesbank policymakers, who would argue that the credibility accorded to German monetary policy derives from their firm direct and indirect control of the financial markets. That credibility, it would be argued, is the reason for favourable price-inflation expectations. And among other things, as seen above, West Germany's relatively low inflation rate endowed German exporters with a real exchange rate advantage.

It is important to be equally clear about the MITI approach (Cowling in Cowling and Tomann 1990: 203–7; Krugman and Obstfeld 1991: 273–4). The Japanese saw early on that static comparative advantage was not an adequate basis for national economic development. They would otherwise remain manufacturers of cheap toys and simple textiles. One key factor at the time of rapid Japanese development in the 1950s and 1960s was to protect domestic industry until it was fully competitive. Once foreign exchange and credit were no longer in short supply, and were thus no longer rationed, there were subtle changes in industrial policy from 1975 onwards. Planning is active rather than passive, selective rather than comprehensive. But the industries targeted since 1975 remain a small part of the Japanese economy. Moreover, the consumer goods which are so successful in foreign markets – motor vehicles and electronic products such as TVs and VCRs – were not the focus of the new industrial policy.

Other forms of government policies are nonetheless one of the main factors which determine the attractiveness of an economy for mobile multinational firms. To a lesser extent, such policies can also stimulate the inflow of highly-skilled personnel – a 'brain drain' to the sending country. As already indicated, immobile factors endow locational advantages and thus determine to what extent mobile factors can be attracted to an economy. Hence,

the more attractive the policy mix in this respect, the larger the inflow of FDI. Donor countries would eventually have to modify their own policies in order to adjust the outflow (Giersch *et al.* 1992: 245; Nicolaides 1992; Siebert and Koop 1993: 2–4). What policies are relevant here? Improving the general conditions for innovation and human capital formation can be achieved by allowing write-offs for R&D in a general way, thus stimulating basic research and building up an efficient educational system. The key dilemma is that intellectual property rights for invention must provide enough incentives to stimulate R&D as well as innovation on the one hand but, on the other hand, should markets be kept open so that newcomers can enter? A patent granting a short-run monopoly position and thereafter making the knowledge generally available is one possible method of resolving the dilemma.

Regional policy can also stimulate both national and international mobility. West German industry consistently pressured government at all levels for support. It normally received this assistance on its own terms, rather than in accordance with policy guidelines set by the state. Moreover, the theory and practice of industrial policy initiatives differ at the regional and local level. As emphasised in Chapter 2, the federal decision-making process is cumbersome. A coherent industrial strategy and the coordination of its implementation are both difficult, if not impossible, to achieve. As a result a suboptimal allocation of resources ensues. State support for industry was in Germany justified by a number of loopholes. First, the constitutional guarantee of the creation and maintenance of comparable living standards and career prospects throughout the country (see the sections on fiscal equalisation in Chapter

2). Second, the state's responsibility under the AFG to create and maintain high levels of employment has been used to justify subsidies to ailing industries, not least to combat subsidies received by competitors in other economies (see the case studies of NRW and Berlin in Chapter 2, and the description of the AFG in Chapter 5). Third, cases were made for securing international competitiveness – as seen earlier in this chapter. In practice, these and other loopholes led to a financing of regional developments by above all the federal government. In support, the Länder granted assistance to local authorities, mainly by means of funds for the development of an adequate infrastructure. The aim was to endow a domestic comparative advantage in the Land as a whole. Local authorities themselves attracted industry by offering cheap lands, attractive credit, improved infrastructure, and low fees for amenities.

An important local and regional industrial policy initiative, at the beginning of the computer age, was the opening of technology centres. They were charged with changing regional comparative advantage in the absence of classical infrastructure advantages. It was envisaged that these centres would combine R&D with management efforts to foster economic growth. They would also provide information services on technology and industrial innovations. The initiative for these centres came from both local authorities and Länder governments. They were pioneered in Baden-Württemberg, North Rhine-Westphalia and Hamburg. There were 55 such centres in the mid-1980s and they were located in the vicinity of universities and research institutes. The problem, however, is that the successful centres are in the more prosperous regions (Sturm 1989b: 165). For this reason, they may have exacerbated regional imbalances. Many of the more successful companies subsequently left the centres, while others remained loss makers after the envisaged period for official support (*Handelsblatt* 16/17 April 1993).

Industrial policy, then, is predominantly reactive and is not at all well integrated and coordinated among the different levels of government. Measures to support declining industries particularly follow no coherent strategy. They are mostly emergency programmes of an *ad hoc* character. Evidence shows that many policy goals are not achieved (Sturm 1989b and 1992). The political bargaining process results in a relatively thin spreading of subsidies instead of a discrimination in favour of economic growth. Furthermore, the tough competition at Länder and local authority levels may quite often result in inefficient subsidies: the value of financial inducements exceeds the proceeds from new industrial activities. Indeed, only an estimated 60 per cent of financial help has resulted in additional industrial activities (Sturm 1989b: 169). Finally, higher subsidies may well mean higher taxation.

CONCLUSION: RETROSPECT AND PROSPECT

Although the evolution of West German anti-trust law was fundamentally different from past German practice, its tardy development produced a somewhat muted impact. The post-war process of horizontal and vertical integration, which brought about a degree of concentration analogous to the inter-war period, was completed before mergers could be prohibited by the BKA. Even after the law was strengthened, further concentration was permitted. The growth of Daimler-Benz during the 1980s is almost certainly destined to become *the* classic illustration of this process. As the *Economist* pointed out (3 April 1993), Daimler also embodies other characteristics of German capitalism. Its majority shareholders are the Deutsche Bank and a holding company also owned by the banks. Only a third of its shares are traded. The prospect of Daimler seeking a flotation on the New York stock exchange is therefore intriguing, not least because the shield against takeover – the holding company – had to be dissolved. Foreign investors – and this usually means the biggest sources of equity finance such as US and British pension funds – demand higher corporate performance than the traditional German sources of corporate finance. The non-German approach would not permit restricted voting rights and hostile takeovers are fairly frequent. Accountancy regulations are also more rigorous. For all these reasons, other German companies may be reluctant to follow Daimler's example. Yet the enormous investment needs in east Germany and abroad, along with continued export growth, may well mean that corporate development will depend on tapping foreign equity finance. By their very nature, however, foreign equity sources will inhibit the traditional ability of large German companies to make longer term growth plans.

But the rapid recovery of West German industry during the 1950s was not only accompanied by a process of diversification: this period of unprecedented growth also resulted in a period of high profits. A high proportion of these profits was ploughed back and thus provided a further stimulus to corporate growth. Although the 1960s brought slower economic growth, German exporters continued to expand their share of world trade. Hence the spectacular recovery of the 1950s, combined with growing domestic prosperity during most of the 1960s,

were in the last analysis attributable to the resurgence of German industry. Such a resurgence was due to the widespread policy and public support which industry received. In a nutshell, most of this book has been either directly or indirectly concerned with the significance and revival of West German industry. By the end of the 1970s, however, steel, motor vehicles and chemicals were already running into difficulties. The notable exception in the motor vehicle industry was Daimler-Benz. In electrical engineering, AEG's position continued to deteriorate, and the banks were indicating that some support from the State may be necessary. By the end of the 1980s, as seen immediately above, structural problems had emerged. The post-unification boom concealed these problems, only for the recession subsequently engineered by the Bundesbank to bring them, along with a serious fall in domestic and foreign aggregate demand, very much to the fore again.

Evidence of the almost universal dominance of West Germany in electrical and mechanical engineering exports, when compared to Britain and France, was also given by Saunders (1978: 11 and 81–3). Some wider industrial evidence of the growth to this position of dominance may be gauged from the fact that in 1954 the export ratios of manufacturing industry in the UK and West Germany stood at 13.6 and 14.3 per cent respectively (Panic 1976: 118). By 1972, the respective ratios were 15.2 and 24.3 per cent. An obvious corollary is that the leading sectors of West German industry remained highly export orientated. This dependence is brought out if a particular aspect of the overall 26.3 per cent average industrial export ratio in Figure 8.12 is examined sectorally, bearing in mind that a decade earlier West Germany's average was very similar (25.3 per cent – Dresdner Bank

Wirtschaftsberichte 81/2). The top four industries in 1980 already had total sales of over DM 100 billion. Of these industries, mechanical engineering had an export ratio of 43.7 per cent, motor vehicles 41.0 per cent, chemicals 38.4 per cent and electrical engineering 29.8 per cent (Dresdner Bank *Economic Quarterly* July 1981).

It will also be noted from Figure 8.12 that on average over a quarter of industrial turnover is absorbed by exports. This leads to another measure of the size of industrial enterprises, namely the relative international size of West German companies. Between 1977 and 1980 seven West German enterprises were in the world's top 50 (*Fortune* 13 August 1979 and 10 August 1981). Not surprisingly, the industries in which a high degree of concentration has been found to exist – motor vehicles, chemicals, electrical and mechanical engineering (including iron and steel) – were all represented in the world's top 50. Another indication of relative international size was the high proportion of German companies in the top 100, and is brought out by a comparison with Britain, France and Japan (*ibid.* 1981: 218). Relative growth rates, even from such a sizeable base, had thus been respectable, even during the relatively depressed 1970s.

Panic (1976: chs 1 and 2) reports that between 1954 and 1972 West Germany's industrial performance outstripped that of Britain's in terms of the growth in net output, capital stock, employment, labour productivity and prices. Net output in manufacturing industry in this period increased at an annual average rate of 6.6 per cent in West Germany compared to 2.7 per cent in Britain. Moreover, this growth was more uniformly spread: the coefficient in variation across the various industries in West Germany was half that of Britain's. Similarly, the capital stock grew at an annual average rate of 7.4 per

cent in West Germany compared to 3.9 per cent in the UK. However, in both cases capital growth outstripped output growth. As a result, there was an annual average decline of capital productivity of −1.1 per cent in the UK and −0.8 per cent in the FRG. Since the inverse of this ratio is the capital/output ratio, therefore, this latter ratio was increasing (also see MRDB 1/80: 13).

Turning to the labour indicators, Panic first reports that the annual increase in employment in manufacturing industry was 1.9 per cent in the FRG. In the UK this statistic declined by −0.1 per cent. However, it will be recalled that absolute employment in manufacturing in the FRG has fallen since 1970 and the participation rates peaked in 1960. Nevertheless, labour productivity in the FRG increased at an annual average rate of 4.6 per cent compared to 2.9 per cent in the UK. This productivity differential was attributed by Pratten (1976: 61) to both economic and 'behavioural' causes. The latter group of causes includes 'manning and efficiency'. Finally, the rate of annual average price increases in the FRG was 1.6 per cent. In the UK it was 3.2 per cent.

Just as West German manufacturing industry, when compared to Britain's, surged ahead and captured valuable export markets in the period 1954–72, so she also made other significant gains. This period, however, preceded the tangible emergence of the various economic problems for West Germany. It will be recalled that these problems included relative high labour costs, stagnating and even falling capital investment, increasing crude-oil prices, an appreciating exchange rate, a secularly worsening invisible balance, direct capital outflows and increased protectionism. During the 1980s, more favourable trends in the DM/US$ exchange rate (until 1986), were followed by an increase in domestic investment. These two factors, together with falling crude-oil prices and a remarkable export boom, were sufficient to conceal the growing structural problems indicated by an inability to absorb the continued rise particularly in non-wage costs. Continued FDI and a lack of product innovation were fairly serious problems when the shock of unification occurred. Bemused by the probity of its monetary policy, the Bundesbank brought on the worst recession in the post-war period. Nevertheless, the economic gains made by West German industry in the majority of the years under review remain relevant. The overnight incorporation of the far less efficient East German economy inevitably caused problems. GEMSU's generous exchange rates made industry in the east even less competitive. Expectations of rapidly rising living standards in the east were fuelled by unjustifiable analogies with the genesis of the SME.

Only time will show whether an optimistic or pessimistic scenario for *Standort Deutschland* is accurate. The optimistic scenario predicts a recovery in the world economy and, as a result, German trade expansion particularly in both western and eastern Europe. In west Germany, EC 1993 will continue to boost growth. EMU – if it ever materialises in some form or other – could be an even greater boost to trade if a policy balance is struck between controlling inflation and stimulating growth. On these criteria, Chapter 4 demonstrated that doubt must be cast on the Bundesbank model. In east Germany, the outlook for a renewal of trade with eastern Europe offers substantial opportunities. Germany must not, however, underestimate the degree of competition from the fastest growing region of the 1980s: south east Asia and, more especially, Japan. In these regions there has

been almost no change in the fundamental strengths: labour force flexibility, openness to innovations, a high level of industrial technology and a gift of rapidly applying the results of research and successfully marketing the resulting products. These favourable features are combined with a market-economy policy stance and a forceful element of export promotion. Can Germany, notwithstanding the arguments at the end of Chapter 6, meet these challenges in view of its existing production set and its expected pattern of production in the future?

The pessimistic scenario contends competitive adjustment might be difficult, especially because the impact of integrating east Germany is frequently neglected (Krakowski 1993). The mere presence of east Germany might badly affect the ability of the whole country to attract international investment. Although Germany needs FDI, the east has not proved sufficiently attractive. The Treuhand sales to foreigners amounted to only 5 per cent of total privatisation proceeds (Faltlhauser 1992: 40). This might be due to the administrative problems and pessimistic expectations about *Standort Deutschland*. High interest rates and the perhaps somewhat overrated significance of budgetary deficits raised the cost of capital in Germany, although it was concluded in Chapter 3 that domestic bond yields and Germany's debt/GNP ratio, contrary to dire predictions, remained comparatively low. Higher taxes, especially as a result of the solidarity pact, may also be a deterrent. The decisive question in terms of international competitiveness is what returns investors expect in the future. Investment decisions therefore depend on expected future taxes, interest rates, labour costs and infrastructure developments (Krakowski *ibid*.: 23–4; Wohlers 1992: 140). Moreover, the supply of high quality management in west Germany might be reduced as virtually all the new management in the east had to be recruited in the west. This might in turn reduce the quality of production, distribution, and strategic planning which came to be associated with *Modell Deutschland* – an element that made West Germany so successful in comparison to the UK (Soskice 1991).

In spite of an innate propensity by Germans to occasionally agonise about the economic future, one should take seriously the dangers facing *Standort Deutschland*. Indeed, the German capacity to make a drama out of a crisis may well be the partial source of the recoveries staged in 1967, 1974 and 1981. Studies at the beginning of the 1990s still found evidence of the high quality and competitiveness of former years (Brenton and Winters 1992: 155; Hughes 1992: 442). But this situation could change dramatically, not least because of east Germany's inability to attract the required – and enormous – amount of domestic and foreign investment (Ohr 1992). Adjustment problems could ensue (Greenaway and Hine 1991). Perhaps the enormous inflow of long-term capital in 1992 (Figure 4.6b) may indicate that the corner is being turned. If the deflationary effects of the Bundesbank's interest-rate policy in the early 1990s is juxtaposed with the pessimistic and optimistic *Standort Deutschland* scenarios, an element of crystal-ball gazing is still required when considering the possible future course of the German economy. Figure 8.13 demonstrates how industrial production in the west initially continued to rise under the impetus of unification. What can be said about the proportionate influences of recession and loss of competitiveness on the subsequent dramatic decline? Will there simply be a repetition of the export-led recoveries which characterised the post-1967, 1973

and 1980 periods? It seems from Chapters 3 and 4 that these recoveries took place in spite of, rather than because of, the Bundesbank's monetary policy. By definition, export-led growth implies seeking markets where monetary-policy conditions are less restrictive. Moreover, it must be recalled that the downturn demonstrated by Figure 8.13 occurred at a time of international recession. In this sense, there are arguably resemblances to the second oil price shock. Others would retrospectively argue that the tough stance of the Bundesbank policymakers gave monetary policy credibility; this had an *ipso facto* positive supply-side effect.

If German competitiveness is adversely affected by the factors summarised in the pessimistic scenario, a future current account deficit would be seen as an expression of a decline in international competitiveness of the united Germany. There is a notable tendency to react by attacking institutions of the SME which have contributed to a high level of social cohesiveness and therefore economic prosperity. For example, dismantling the social-policy framework as a means of reducing non-wage costs and curbing industrial-democracy rights are often advocated (Frowen 1991: 113, Müller 1992). A reform of company taxation is under way, but will it see an end to the generous depreciation allowances and enormous corporate hidden reserves? Activating those reserves in a meaningful economic manner has been seen to be one of *Standort Deutschland*'s major problems. Similarly, before the Germans rush headlong into an elaborate process of privatisation and deregulation, they would do well to ponder US and UK experience. Creating and maintaining an adequate infrastructure – particularly in the east – may well be an area in which the public sector is superior to badly designed

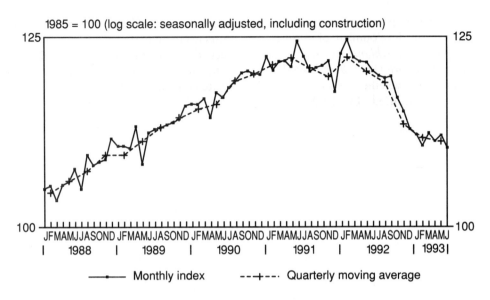

Figure 8.13 West German industrial production

Source: MRDB *Stat. Beihefte* 4: Table III (8)

privatisation and deregulation strategies. In any case, West Germany's persistent trade surpluses were historically determined by lower household savings and higher budget deficits on the part of many of her trading partners, most notably the USA. A permanent reversal of trade patterns would require a fundamental macroeconomic change from united Germany in these respects. The presence or absence of domestic economic and trade-policy reform will thus have little direct impact here. Moreover, Germany's FDI will tend to increase imports from subsidiaries overseas, while her invisibles will presumably remain fairly substantial deficit items.

It is the contrasts during the post-war decades which strike the observer. As was demonstrated in the early part of Chapter 1, such contrasts stretch right back into German economic history. However, to compare the shock of unification with the hyperinflation of the Weimar republic, or with the tragic collapse of the Great

Depression, completely underestimates the strengths on which the German economy can still draw. A stable financial system, large foreign currency reserves, a solid human and physical capital base and generally mature institutions all make analogies with the inter-war period quite spurious. That said, the history of targeting money-supply growth indicates that the over-reactions by the Bundesbank policymakers, prior to introduction of the wider ERM bands in 1993, would have pulled Germany and the rest of Europe into depression (see the discussion around Figure 4.4d). EMU, if it ever materialises, could therefore still become an organisation notorious for its high interest rates, price stability and rising unemployment. However, unification, it has continuously been shown, must be seen against the backcloth of the contrasting economic policies and prescriptions pursued in West Germany during the post-war decades. Although these changes did not have a fundamental impact on the nature of the SME, the development of *Allfinanz*, *Finanzplatz Deutschland* and the agonising over *Standort Deutschland* would all have occurred whether or not GEMSU had been introduced. EC 1993 played a major role here. Contrasting policy developments in numerous fields have, in short, been the main theme of this book. It is in this sense that they constitute an appropriate concluding note.

BIBLIOGRAPHY

Aaron, B. and Wedderburn, K.W. (1972), *Industrial Conflict: A Comparative Legal Survey*, Longman, London

Abelshauser, W. (1979), 'Von der Kohlenkrise zur Gründung der Ruhrkohle AG', in Mommsen, H. and Borsdorf, U. (eds), *Glück auf, Kameraden!*, Bund-Verlag, Köln

—— (1981), 'Wiederaufbau vor dem Marshall-Plan', *Vierteljahrshefte für Zeitgeschichte, 29*, pp.545–78

—— (1982), 'West German Economic Recovery 1945–1951: A Reassessment', *The Three Banks Review*, No.135, September

—— (1983), *Wirtschaftsgeschichte der Bundesrepublik Deutschland 1945–1980* (Edition 1241 – NF Band 241), Suhrkamp

—— (1984), *Der Ruhrkohlenbergbau seit 1945*, C.H. Beck, Munich

Abelshauser, W. and Petzina, D. (eds) (1981), *Deutsche Wirtschaftsgeschichte im Industriezeitalter: Konjunktur, Krise, Wachstum*, Athenäum/Droste Taschenbücher Geschichte, Königstein

Adams, R.J. and Rummel, C.H. (1977), 'Workers' Participation in Management in West Germany', *Industrial Relations Journal, 8* (1), pp.4–22

Adamy, W. (1990), 'Marktwirtschaft und Arbeitslosigkeit in der DDR – Zwei Seiten einer Medaille?', *WSI Mittelungen, 7*, pp.433–41

Adenauer, K. (1966), *Memoirs, 1945–53*, Weidenfeld and Nicolson, London

ADW (Arbeitsgemeinschaft der Deutschen Wertpapierbörsen), *Jahresberichte* (various), Frankfurt a.M.

AdwF (see Abbreviations listing) (1992), *Die Lage der Weltwirtschaft und der deutschen Wirtschaft im Herbst 1992*, München

Aho, M. (1991), 'New Perspectives on Germany (the EC), Japan and the United States', in Welfens, P.J. (ed.), *op. cit.*

Akerlof, G.A., Rose, A.K., Yellen, J.L. and Hessenius, H. (1991), 'East Germany in from the Cold: The Economic Aftermath of Currency Union', *Brookings Papers on Economic Activity, 1*, pp.1–105

Albeck, H. (1990), 'Lohnentwicklung entscheidet über die künftige Höhe der Beschäftigung', *Wirtschaftsdienst, 70* (9), pp.448–50

Alber, J. (1989), *Der Sozialstaat in der Bundesrepublik 1950–1983*, Campus Verlag, Frankfurt a.M./New York

Albrecht, D. and Thormälen, T. (1985), *Subventionen – Politik und Problematik*, Peter Lang, Frankfurt a.M., Bern, New York

Altmann, J. (1992), *Wirtschaftspolitik – Eine praxisorientierte Einführung*, Fifth Edition, UTB-Verlag, Stuttgart, Jena

Altmann, N., Köhler, C. and Meil, P. (1992), *Technology and Work in German Industry*, Routledge, London

Ambrosi, G.H. (1990), 'Angebotsorientierte Fiskalpolitiken der 1980er Jahre – Zukunftsmodelle für Europa?', in Spahn, H.-P., *op. cit.*

Ammermüller, M.G. (1990), 'Rentenversicherung: Stufen zum einheitlichen Recht im vereinigten Deutschland', *Bundesarbeitsblatt*, 11, pp.5–9

Anthes, J. et al. (1972), *Mitbestimmung: Ausweg oder Illusion?*, Ro Ro Ro Tele, Rowohlt Taschenbuch Verlag, Reinbek bei Hamburg

Ardagh, J. (1988), *Germany and the Germans*, Penguin Books, Harmondsworth (Hard cover: Hamish Hamilton, London, 1987)

Arnold, V. and Geske, O.E. (eds) (1988),

Öffentliche Finanzwirtschaft, Verlag Franz Vahlen, München

Audretsch, D.B. (1989), 'Legalized Cartels in West Germany', *The Antitrust Bulletin, XXXIV* (3), pp.579–600

BA (Bundesanstalt für Arbeit), *Presse Informationen* (various) (Federal Labour Office, Press Releases)

—— (1993), *Arbeitsmarkt 1992*

Bäcker, G. (1990), 'Wie sozial ist die soziale Marktwirtschaft? Zur Zukunft der Sozialpolitik' in Bundeszentrale für Politische Bildung, *Wirtschaftspolitik*, Bonn, pp. 330–49

Backer, J.H. (1971), *Priming the German Economy: American Occupational Policies 1945–1948*, Duke University Press, Durham, N.C.

Bade, F.-J. and Kunzmann, K. (1991), 'Deindustrialisation and Regional Development in the Federal Republic of Germany', in Rodwin, L. and Sazanami, H. (eds), *Industrial Change and Regional Economic Transformation: The Experience of Western Europe*, Harper Collins Academic, London

Bahnmüller, R. (1985), *Der Streik. Tarifkonflikt um Arbeitszeitverkürzung in der Metallindustrie 1984*, VSA-Verlag, Hamburg

Balz, M. (1990), 'Probleme einer Integration der DDR-Landwirtschaft in den EG-Agrarmarkt', *Ifo-Schnelldienst, 19*, pp. 9–18

Banker (various), London

Bank für Gemeinwirtschaft, *BfG: Wirtschaftsblätter* (various), Frankfurt a.M.

Banking World (various), London

Bannas, G. *et al.* (1990), *Der Vertrag zur deutschen Einheit: Ausgewählte Texte*, Insel Verlag, Frankfurt a.M. und Leipzig

Bannock, G. (1976), *The Smaller Business in Britain and Germany*, Wilton House, London

Barker, K. *et al.* (1985), 'Macroeconomic Policy in Germany and Britain', *National Institute Economic Review*, November, pp. 69–89

Baur, J.F. (1980), 'The Control of Mergers Between Large Financially Strong Firms in West Germany', *Journal of Institutional and Theoretical Economics (Zeitschrift für die gesamte Staatswissenschaft), 136* (3), pp. 444–64

BBk (1989/1982/1971), *The Deutsche Bundesbank: Its Monetary Policy Instruments and Functions*, Deutsche Bundesbank Special Series No.7, Third Edition, Frankfurt a.M. (as indicated, previous editions of this valuable pamphlet appeared in *1971* and *1982*)

—— (1991), *Banking Act of the Federal Republic of Germany*, Deutsche Bundesbank Special Series No.2, Third Edition, Frankfurt a.M.

BdB (Bundesverband deutscher Banken) (1989), 'Zur Diskussion um die "Macht der Banken"', *Informationen des Bundesverbandes deutscher Banken*, Köln

—— (1991), *Mitgliedsverbände und angeschlossene Institute des Bundesverbandes deutscher Banken e V*, Köln

Bea, F.X. and Beutel, R. (1992), 'Die Bedeutung des Exports für die Entwicklung der Kosten und die Gestaltung der Preise', in Dichtl, E. and Issing, O. (eds), *op. cit.*

Bean, C.R. (1992), 'Economic and Monetary Union in Europe', *Journal of Economic Perspectives, 6* (4), pp. 31–52

Beaver, W. (1992), 'Volkswagen's American Assembly Plant: *Fahrvergnugen* was not enough', *Business Horizons, 35* (6), pp. 19–26

Beinert, D. (1991), *Corporate Acquisitions and Mergers in Germany*, Graham and Trotman, London, Dordrecht, Boston

Bellermann, M. (1990), *Sozialpolitik: eine Einführung für soziale Berufe*, Lambertus-Verlag, Freiburg im Breisgau

Bellmann, L. and Lehmann, H. (1990), *Active Labour Market Policies in Britain and Germany and Long-Term Unemployment: An Evaluation*, paper presented at the EALE Conference, Lund, Sweden, 20–23 September, mimeo.

Bendix, D.W.F. (1978), *Limits to Co-determination?*, Institute of Labour Relations, University of South Africa, Pretoria

Benelli, G., Loderer, C., Lys, T. (1987), 'Labor Participation in Corporate Policy-Making Decisions: West Germany's Experience with Codetermination', *The Journal of Business, 60* (4), pp. 553–75

Bennecke, H. (1968), *Wirtschaftliche Depression und politischer Radikalismus: die Lehre von Weimar*, Günter Olzog Verlag, München/Wien

Bennett, R. (1991), 'Local Taxation and Local Economic Development Incentives in Britain and Germany', in Wild, T. and Jones, P. (eds), *De-industrialisation and New Industrialisation in Britain and Germany*,

Anglo-German Foundation Publications, London

Bennett, R.J. and Krebs, G. (1988a), *Local Business Taxes in Britain and Germany*, Nosmos Verlagsgesellschaft, Baden-Baden

—— (1988b), 'Regional Policy Incentives and the Relative Costs of Capital in Assisted Areas in Britain and Germany', *Regional Studies, 23* (3), pp. 200–18

Benzie, R. (1992), 'The Development of the International Bond Market', Bank for International Settlements *Economic Papers*, No.32, January

BEQB (Bank of England Quarterly Bulletin) (1984), 'Business Finance in the United Kingdom and Germany', 24 (3), pp. 368–75 (reprinted in *MRDB*, November 1984)

Berg, G. (1992), 'Privatisierung und Arbeitsplatzsicherung', in Ipsen, D. and Nickel, E. (eds), *op. cit.*

Berger, J. and Mohr, J. (1975), *A Seventh Man*, Pelican Original, Penguin Books, Harmondsworth

Berghahn, V.R. (1986), *The Americanisation of West German Industry 1945–1973*, Berg, Leamington Spa/New York

Berghahn, V.R. and Karsten, D. (1987), *Industrial Relations in West Germany*, Berg, Oxford/New York/Hamburg

Berthold, N. (1992), 'Wettbewerbsfähigkeit der deutschen Wirtschaft – Ein Standortproblem?', *Hamburger Jahrbuch für Wirtschafts- und Gesellschaftspolitik, 37*, pp. 159–71

Besters, H. (ed.) (1992), 'Vitalisierung der ostdeutschen Wirtschaft', *Gespräche der List Gesellschaft, 14*, Nomos Verlagsgesellschaft, Baden-Baden

Beyer, H. and Nutzinger H.G. (1991), 'Sanierung und/oder Privatisierung? Zur Umstrukturierung der ostdeutschen Unternehmen durch die Treuhandanstalt', in Westphal, A., Herr, H., Heine, M. and Busch, U. (eds), *Wirtschaftspolitische Konsequenzen der deutschen Vereinigung*, Campus Verlag, Frankfurt/New York

BfA (Bundesversicherungsanstalt für Angestellte) (1989), *Rentenreform '92*, Frankfurt a.M., Berlin

BfG:Bank AG, *Standpunkt* (various), Frankfurt a.M.

Bhagwati, J. (1988), *Protectionism*, Harvard UP, Cambridge, Mass.

Biedenkopf Report (1970), *Bericht der Sachverständigenkommission zur Auswertung der bisherigen Erfahrungen bei der Mitbestimmung*, Bundestag-Drucksache VI/334, Bochum

Billerbeck, U. and Deutschmann, C. (1982), 'Tarifpolitik mit politischen Skrupeln. Der öffentliche Dienst in den siebziger Jahren', in Billerbeck, U. *et al.*, *Neuorientierung der Tarifpolitik?*, Campus, Frankfurt a.M.

Bispinck, R. (1990), 'Tarifbewegungen im 1. Halbjahr 1990 – Durchbruch zur 35-Stunden-Woche und Beginn der Tarifpolitik in der DDR', *WSI Mitteilungen 43* (9), pp. 546–63

Blaschke, K. (1990), 'Alte Länder – Neue Länder: Zur territorialen Neugliederung der DDR', *Aus Politik und Zeitgeschichte*, B27/90, 29 June, pp. 39–54

Bletschacher, G. (1992), 'Strategische Handels- und Industriepolitik in der Automobilindustrie?', *Die Weltwirtschaft, 1*, pp. 68–84

Bletschacher, G. and Klodt, H. (1992), 'Strategische Handels- und Industriepolitik – Grundlagen, Branchenanalysen und wettbewerbspolitische Implikationen', *Kieler Studien*, 244, J.C.B. Mohr (Paul Siebeck), Tübingen

Blitz, R.C. (1977), 'A Benefit-Cost Analysis of Foreign Workers in West Germany, 1957–1973, *Kyklos, 30* (3), pp. 479–502

Blommenstein, H. and Marrese, M. (eds) (1991), *Transformation of Planned Economies: Property Rights Reform and Macroeconomic Stability*, OECD, Paris

Blüm, N. (1990), 'Sozialunion mit der DDR. Antwort in Historischer Stunde', *Bundesarbeitsblatt*, 7/8, pp. 5–7

BMA (Bundesminister für Arbeit und Sozialordnung) (1979 and 1990), *Mitbestimmung*, Bonn

—— (1985), *Maßarbeit*

—— (1989), *Die Gesundheitsreform '89*, Bonn

—— (1990), *Rentenreform '92*, Bonn

—— (1991), *Übersicht über die Soziale Sicherheit*

—— *Sozialberichte* (various), Bonn

—— *Sozialpolitische Informationen* (various), Bonn

—— *Sozialpolitische Nachrichten* (various), Bonn

—— *Statistisches Taschenbuch* (various), Bonn

BMF (Bundesministerium der Finanzen), *Beteiligungen des Bundes* (various), Bonn

—— *Das Industrielle Bundesvermögen* (various – 1960s predecessor of *Beteiligungen* above, published by the Bundesschatzministerium), Bonn

— *Der Bund Als Unternehmer* (various – 1950s predecessor of *Beteiligungen* above, published by the Bundesministerium für wirtschaftlichen Besitz des Bundes), Bad Godesberg

— *Finanzberichte* (various), Bonn

— Reihe: *Berichte und Dokumentationen* (various), Bonn

— Reihe: *Bürger-Informationen* (various), Bonn

— Reihe: *Politik-Informationen* (various), Bonn

— *Subventionsberichte* (various), Bonn

— (1983), 'Finanzbeziehungen zwischen Bund, Ländern und Gemeinden', in *Finanzbericht 1984*, Bonn, pp. 111–38

— (1988), 'Finanzbeziehungen zwischen Bund, Ländern und Gemeinden', in *Finanzbericht 1989*, Bonn, pp. 119–42

— (1990), *Haushaltsrecht des Bundes*

BMWi (Bundesministerium für Wirtschaft), *Leistung in Zahlen* (various), Bonn

— *Wirtschaft in Zahlen* (various), Bonn

Board of Inland Revenue (1980), *Income Taxes Outside of the United Kingdom (Federal Republic of Germany, 1976 to 1979)*, Second Edition, HMSO, London

Böckler-Kreis, H. (1990), 'Die geeinigten Deutschen Gewerkschaften in der Gemeinschaft der europäischen Staaten – Erklärung', *Gewerkschaftliche Monatshefte*, 41 (9), pp. 589–600

Boehmer-Christiansen, S.A., Merten D., Meissner, J. and Ufer, D. (1993), 'Ecological Restructuring or Environment Friendly Deindustrialization: the Fate of the East German Energy Sector and Society since 1990', *Energy Policy*, 21 (4), pp. 355–73

Bofinger, P. (1990), 'The German Monetary Unification: Converting Marks to D-Marks', *Review*, 72 (4), Federal Reserve Bank of St. Louis, pp. 17–36

Böhning, W.R. (1975), 'Some Thoughts on Emigration from the Mediterranean Basin', *International Labour Review*, 111 (3), pp. 251–77

Boléat, M.J. (1978), *An International Comparison of Housing Finance Systems*, The Building Societies Association, London, mimeo.

Bonus, H. (1986), 'The Cooperative Association as a Business Enterprise', *Journal of Institutional and Theoretical Economics*

(*Zeitschrift für die gesamte Staatswissenschaft*), 142 (2), pp. 310–39

Bonus, H. and Schmidt, G. (1990), 'The Cooperative Banking Group in the Federal Republic of Germany: Aspects of Institutional Change', *Journal of Institutional and Theoretical Economics (Zeitschrift für die gesamte Staatswissenschaft)*, 146 (1), pp. 180–207

Bonus, H., Steiner, J. and Wagner, H. (1988), *Dreistufigkeit im genossenschaftlichen Bankenverbund: Luxus oder Notwendigkeit?*, Fritz Knapp Verlag, Frankfurt a.M.

Borchardt, K-D. (1989), *European Unification: the origins and growth of the European Community*, Third Edition, European Documentation (Periodical 1/1990), European Communities, Luxembourg

Borcherding, T.E. (1982), 'Comparing the Efficiency of Private and Public Production: The Evidence from Five Countries', in Bös, D., Musgrave, R.A. and Wiseman, J. (eds), *Zeitschrift für Nationalökonomie*, Supplementum 2, pp. 127–56

Börsch-Supan, A. (1986), 'On the West German Tenants' Protection Legislation', *Journal of Institutional and Theoretical Economics (Zeitschrift für die gesamte Staatswissenschaft)*, 142 (2), pp. 380–404

Börsch-Supan, A. and Stahl, K. (1991), 'Do Savings Programs Dedicated to Home-ownership Increase Personal Savings?', *Journal of Public Economics*, 44, pp. 265–97

Bös, D. (1989), 'Arguments on Privatization', in Fels, G. and von Furstenberg, G.M. (eds), *op. cit.*

— (1991), 'Privatization and the Transmission from Planned to Market Economies. Some Thoughts about Germany 1991', *Annals of Public and Cooperative Economics*, 62 (2), pp. 183–94

— (1993), 'Privatization in Europe: A Comparison of Approaches', *Oxford Review of Economic Policy*, 9 (1), pp. 95–111

Bosch, G. (1986), 'The Dispute Over the Reduction of the Working Week in West Germany', *Cambridge Journal of Economics*, 3, pp. 271–90

— (1990), 'From 40 to 35 Hours. Reduction and Flexibilisation of the Working Week in the Federal Republic of Germany', *International Labour Review*, 129 (5), pp. 611–27

Boss, A. (1990), 'Sozialhilfe, Leistungsanreize und Sozialunion mit der DDR', *Die Weltwirtschaft*, 1, pp. 101–10

Boyer, H. *et al.* (1980), 'White Collar Unionisation in West Germany 1960–1976', *Industrial Relations Journal, 11* (5), pp. 63–73

Brabant, J.M. van (1991), 'Property Rights Reform, Macroeconomic Performance and Welfare', in Blommenstein, M. and Marrese, M. (eds), *op. cit.*

Bradley, J. (1979), 'Building Societies Would Find West Germany a Tough Market to Enter', *The Building Societies Gazette*, August

Brander, S. (1990), 'Die DDR als Investionsstandort aus der Sicht westdeutscher Unternehmen', *Ifo-Schnelldienst, 26/27*, pp. 9–13

Brandt, G. *et al.* (1982), *Anpassung an die Krise. Gewerkschaften in den siebziger Jahren*, Campus, Frankfurt a.M.

Braun, H. (1979), 'Soziale Sicherung in Deutschland', *Der Bürger im Staat, 29* (4), pp. 211–17

Braun, H.-J. (1990), *The German Economy in the Twentieth Century*, Routledge, London and New York

Brede, H. and Hoppe, U. (1986), 'Outline of the Present Status of the Privatization Debate in the Federal German Republic', *Annals of Public and Co-operative Economy, 57* (2), pp. 205–29

Breit, E. *et al.* (1984), 'Die neue Dimension in der tarif-politischen Auseinandersetzung. Der Arbeitskampf in der Metall- und Druckindustrie 1984', *Gewerkschaftliche Monatshefte, 35* (7), pp. 391–435

Brenton, P.A. and Winters, L.A. (1992), 'Estimating the International Trade Effects of "1992": West Germany', *Journal of Common Market Studies, XXX* (2), pp. 143–56

Bresciani-Turroni, C. (1968), *The Economics of Inflation*, Augustus M. Kelley, London, Third Impression

Breuel, B. (1991), 'A Social Market Economy cannot be introduced Overnight', *European Affairs, 5* (6), pp. 28–32

— (1992), 'Buy One, Get One Free: The Case for Germany's Treuhand', *The International Economy, 6* (1), pp. 37–40

Broadberry, S.N. and Fremdling, R. (1990), 'Comparative Productivity in British and German Industry, 1907–37', *Oxford Bulletin of Economics and Statistics, 52* (4), pp. 403–22

BSA (Building Societies Association) (1978), 'Building Societies and the European Community', *Report* of Working Group B: West Germany, London, mimeo.

BT IV/2320 (1964) – Deutscher Bundestag (1964), *Bericht* und *Anlageband* über das Ergebnis einer Untersuchung der Konzentration der Wirtschaft, *Drucksache*

— XII/847 (1991), *Bericht* des Bundeskartellamtes über seine Tätigkeit in den Jahren 1989/90, *Drucksache*

— 12/3774 (1992), '*Jahresgutachten* 1992/93 des Sachverständigenrates zur Begutachtung der gesamtwirtschaftlichen Entwicklung', Deutscher Bundestag, 12. Wahlperiode, *Drucksache* (SVR Reports are published by both the BT and privately by the Kohlhammer Verlag; see also SVR (1990))

Büchtemann, C.F. and Quack, S. (1990), 'How Precarious is "non-standard" employment? Evidence for West Germany', *Cambridge Journal of Economics, 14* (3), pp. 315–29

Buck, A.J. and FitzRoy, F. (1988), 'Inflation and Productivity Growth in the Federal Republic of Germany', *Journal of Post Keynesian Economics, X* (3), pp. 428–44

Budd, S.A. (1987), *The EEC. A Guide to the Maze*, Second Edition, Kogan Page, London

Buechtemann, C.F. and Schupp, J. (1992), 'Repercussions of Reunification: Transforming East Germany', *The Industrial Relations Journal, 23* (2), pp. 90–106

Bulletin of the European Communities (1990), 'Commission Statement on German Unification', Supplement 4/90, 3 October

Bulmer, S. (ed.) (1989), *The Changing Agenda of West German Public Policy*, Avebury Press (Gower), Aldershot

Bundesvereinigung der Deutschen Arbeitgeberverbände (1984), *Flexibilisierung der Arbeitszeit. Neue Tarifregelungen als Chance*, Köln

— (1985), *Zwanzig-Punkte-Programm: Für mehr Beschäftigung*, Köln

— (1990), *Wirtschaftsnachrichten*, Köln, March/April

Bundeszentrale für politische Bildung, *Informationen zur politischen Bildung* (various), Bonn

Bunn, R.F. (1960), 'The Federation of German Employers' Associations: A Political Interest Group', *Western Political Quarterly, 13* (3), pp. 652–69

— (1984), 'Federal Republic of Germany', in Windmuller, J.P. and Gladstone, A. (eds), *Employers Associations and Industrial*

Relations: A Comparative Study, Clarendon Press, Oxford

Burda, M. (1993), 'The Determinants of East-West German Migration: Some First Results', *European Economic Review, 37* (2/3), pp. 452–62

Burtenshaw, D. (1974), *Economic Geography of West Germany*, Macmillan, London

Buttler, F. *et al.* (1985), *Staat und Beschäftigung: Angebots- und Nachfragepolitik in Theorie und Praxis*, Institut für Arbeitsmarkt- und Berufsforschung, Nürnberg

Button, K. (1991), 'The Development of East-West European Transport in the 1990s', in CTRF, *Evolution in Transportation*, Quebec

Butzin, B. (1991), 'Regional Life Cycles and Problems of Revitalisation in the Ruhr', in Wild, T. and Jones, P. (eds), *op. cit.*

BVR (Bundesverband der Deutschen Volksbanken und Raiffeisenbanken) *Jahresberichte* (various), Köln

— *Zahlen* (various), Köln

Cable, J. (1979), 'Merger Development and Policy in West Germany since 1958', *Warwick Economic Research Papers*, No.150, Department of Economics, University of Warwick

— (1981), 'Merger Control Remains the Priority – the Third Report of the German Monopolies Commission', *Journal of Institutional and Theoretical Economics (Zeitschrift für die gesamte Staatswissenschaft), 137* (2), pp. 302–8

— (1985), 'Capital Market Information and Industrial Performance: the Role of West German Banks', *Economic Journal, 95* (1), pp. 118–32

Cable, J.R., Palfrey, J.P.R. and Runge, J.W. (1980a), 'Federal Republic of Germany 1962–1974', in Mueller, D.C. (ed.), *The Determinants and Effects of Mergers: An International Comparison*, Oelgeschlager, Gunn and Hain, London

— (1980b), 'Economic Determinants and Effects of Mergers West Germany 1964–74', *Journal of Institutional and Theoretical Economics (Zeitschrift für die gesamte Staatswissenschaft), 136* (2), pp. 226–48

Carlin, W. (1987), 'Economic Reconstruction in Western Germany, 1945–55: The Displacement of "Vegetative Control"', *Discussion Paper No.87–09*, Department of Economics, University College London

Carlin, W. and Mayer, C. (1992), 'Restructur-ing Enterprises in Eastern Europe', *Economic Policy, 15*, pp. 312–52

Carlin, W. and Jacob, R. (1989), 'Austerity Policy in West Germany: Origins and Consequences', *Economie Applique, XLII* (1), pp. 203–38

Carr, C. (1992), 'Productivity and Skills in Vehicle Component Manufactures in Britain, Germany, the USA and Japan', *National Institute Economic Review, 1*, pp. 79–88

Casey, B. (1986), 'The Dual Apprenticeship System and the Recruitment and Retention of Young Persons in West Germany', *British Journal of Industrial Relations, 24* (1), pp. 63–81

— (1991), 'Recent Developments in the German Apprenticeship System', *British Journal of Industrial Relations, 29* (2), pp. 205–22

Casey, B., Dragendorf, R., Heering, W. and John, G. (1989), 'Temporary Employment in Great Britain and the Federal Republic of Germany', *International Labour Review, 128* (4), pp. 449–66

Cassel, D. and Schipke, A. (1992), 'Privatisier-ung im Systemwandel Osteuropas', *List Forum, 18* (3), pp. 179–93

Cassel, D. *et al.* (eds) (1972), *25 Jahre Marktwirtschaft in der Bundesrepublik Deutschland*, Gustav Fischer Verlag, Stuttgart

Chauffour, J.-P., Harasty, H. and Dem, J. Le (1992), 'German Reunification and European Monetary Policy', in Barrell, R. and Whitley, J. (eds), *Macroeconomic Policy Coordination in Europe: The ERM and Monetary Union*, Sage Publications for the National Institute of Economic and Social Research, London

Cheshire, P. (1990), 'Explaining the Recent Performance of the European Community's Major Urban Regions', *Urban Studies, 27* (3), pp. 311–33

Chester, T.E. (1971), 'West Germany – A Social Market Economy', *Three Banks Review*, December

Chipman, J.S. (1981), 'Internal-External Price Relationships in the West German Economy, 1958–1979', *Journal of Institutional and Theoretical Economics (Zeitschrift für die gesamte Staatswissenschaft), 137* (3), pp. 612–37

Clarich, M. (undated), 'The German Banking

System: Legal Foundations and Recent Trends', mimeo.

Clark, J. (1979), 'Concerted Action in the Federal Republic of Germany' *British Journal of Industrial Relations, XVII* (2), pp. 242–58

Collier, I.L. (1991), 'On the First Year of German Monetary, Economic and Social Union', *Journal of Economic Perspectives, 5* (4), pp. 179–86

Collier, I.L. and Siebert, H. (1991), 'The Economic Integration of Post-Wall Germany', *American Economic Review, 81* (2), pp. 196–201

Commerzbank (1970), *100 Jahre Commerzbank*, Düsseldorf

—— (1980), *Worldwide Activities*, Frankfurt a.M.

—— *Economic Trends* (various), Frankfurt a.M.

Commission on Industrial Relations (1974), *Worker Participation and Collective Bargaining in Europe* (Study No.4), HMSO, London

Conjoncture (1990), 'German Reunification and its Consequences', March, pp. 43–50

Copeman, G. (1971), *The Chief Executive: and Business Growth*, Leviantan House, London and New York

Cornelsen, D. (1990), 'Die Wirtschaft der DDR in der Honecker-Ära', *Viertel Jahresheft*, DIW, 1/90

Coventry and District Engineering Employers Association (1972), *Labour Relations and Employment Conditions in the EEC*, Coventry

Cowan, G.L. (1990), *Privatization in the Developing World*, Praeger, New York/London

Cowling, K. and Tomann, H. (eds) (1990), *Industrial Policy after 1992*, Anglo-German Foundation for the Study of Industrial Society, London

Cullingford, E.C.M. (1976), *Trade Unions in West Germany*, Wilton House Publications, London

Curwen, P. (1992), 'The Economics of Social Responsibility in the European Community', *Economics, 28* (4), pp. 156–62

Dach, G. (1992), 'Der deutsche Steinkohlenbergbau im Binnenmarkt', *Wirtschaftsspiegel, 10*, pp. 2f.

Darrat, A.F. (1987), 'Money and Stock Prices in West Germany and the United Kingdom: Is the Stock Market Efficient?', *Quarterly Journal of Business and Economics, 26* (1), pp. 20–35

Däubler, W. (1975), 'Co-determination: the German Experience', *The Industrial Law Journal, 4* (4), pp. 218–28

Davidson, P. (1992), *International Money and the Real World*, Second Edition, Macmillan, London

Denton, G., Forsyth, M. and MacLennon, M. (1968), *Economic Planning and Policies: Britain, France and Germany*, Allen and Unwin, London

Der Bürger im Staat (various), Stuttgart

Der Gewerkschafter (1990), *Die DDR unter Druck*, Mai

Der Hans-Böckler-Kreis (1990), 'Die geeinten deutschen Gewerkschaften in der Gemeinschaft der europäischen Staaten', *Gewerkschaftliche Monatshefte, 41* (9), pp. 589–600

Der Personalrat (1990), 'Sozialunion zwischen der Bundesrepublik Deutschland und der Deutschen Demokratischen Republik', July/August, pp. 197–224

Deregulierungskommission (1991), *Marktöffnung und Wettbewerb*, C.E. Poeschel, Stuttgart

Der Spiegel (various), Hamburg

—— (1987), 'Landwirtschaft- der alltägliche Irrsinn', Nos 45/87–50/87 incl.

Detwiler, D.S. and Detwiler, I.E. (1988), *West Germany*, Oxford, Clio Press, World Bibliographical Series, Vol.72

Deutsche Bank (1970), *100 Years of the Deutsche Bank*, Frankfurt a.M.

—— *Annual Reports* (various), Frankfurt a.M.

—— *Bulletin* (various), Frankfurt a.M.

Deutsche Bundesbank (1991), *Die deutsche Wiedervereinigung (Wirtschafts-, Währungs- und Sozialunion): Auswahlbibliographie*, F2 Bibliothek und Archive, January

—— *Annual Reports* (various), Frankfurt a.M.

—— *Auszüge aus Presseartikeln* (various), Frankfurt a.M.

—— *Monthly Report* (various), Frankfurt a.M.

—— Statistical Supplements to the *Monthly Report of the Deutsche Bundesbank* (various), Frankfurt a.M.

Deutscher Bundestag, *Drucksache* (various), Bonn

Deutscher Sparkassen- und Giroverband e.V. (1992), *Ostdeutsche Wirtschaft im Wandel: Bestandsaufnahme und Perspektiven eines Aufholprozesses*, Stuttgart

Deutscher Sparkassen Verlag (1992), *A*

Versatile Partner in all Money Matters, Stuttgart

DG Bank (Deutsche Genossenschaftsbank) (1981), *DG Bank and its System: A Brief History*, Frankfurt a.M.

DGB, *Geschäftsberichte* (various), Bundesvorstand des Deutschen Gewerkschaftsbundes, Düsseldorf

Dichmann, W. (1991), 'Eigentums- und Arbeitsverhältnisse im Transformationsprozeß zur Marktwirtschaft – ordnungspolitische Aspekte am Beispiel der neuen Bundesländer', *List Forum, 17* (4), pp. 301–18

Dichtl, E. and Issing, O. (eds) (1992), *Exportnation Deutschland*, Second Edition, C.H. Beck, München

Dichtl, E., Raffée, H. and Wellenreuther, H. (1983), 'Public Policy towards Small and Medium-sized Retail Businesses in the Federal Republic of Germany', *Rivista Internazionale Di Scienze Economiche E Commerciali*, XXX (4–5), pp. 424–39

Dicke, H. (1988), 'The Economic Effects of Agricultural Policy in West Germany', *Weltwirtschaftliches Archiv*, 124 (2)

Dicken, P. (1992), 'Europe 1992 and Strategic Change in the International Automobile Industry', *Environment and Planning A, 24*, pp. 11–31

Diemer, G. (ed) (1990), *Kurze Chronik der Deutschen Frage*, Olzog Verlag (Geschichte u. Staat, Bd Nr. 288)

Die Sozialversicherung (various), Heidelberg

Dietzel, G.T.W. (1991), 'Die Neubildung der Bundesregierung', *Sozialer Fortschritt, 40* (3), pp. 53–6

Die Zeit (various), Hamburg

— *Die 100 grössten Industrie- Unternehmen in der Bundesrepublik* (annually), Hamburg

Dittmar, R. (1978), *Die Deutsche Angestellten-Gewerkschaft*, Droste Verlag, Düsseldorf

DIW (Deutsches Institut für Wirtschaftsforschung) (1990a), 'Szenarien der Bevölkerungsentwicklung in der DDR', *Wochenbericht, 57* (23–4), pp. 315–21

— (1990b), 'Liquiditätsengpässe der Sozialversicherung in der DDR', *Wochenbericht, 57* (39), pp. 559–61

— DIW *Wochenberichte* (various), Berlin

DIW/IfW (1992), 'Gesamtwirtschaftliche und unternehmerische Anpassungsprozesse in Ostdeutschand', *Kieler Diskussionsbeiträge*, 198/199, Institut für Weltwirtschaft, Kiel

Documentation (1977), 'The First Bi-Annual

(sic) Report of the Monopolies Commission', *The German Economic Review, 15* (2), pp. 155–74; reprinted in *The Anti-Trust Bulletin* (1978), *23* (4), pp. 667–87

Doetsch, W. (1990), 'Aktuelle Probleme der Rentenversicherung', *Deutsche Rentenversicherung, 7*, pp. 377–86

Dohnanyi, K. von (1990), *Das Deutsche Wagnis*, Droemer Knaur, München. (Extracts serialised in *Der Spiegel*, 39/90–42/90)

Döhrn, R. (1990), 'Konsequenzen einer deutschen Vereinigung für die Europäische Gemeinschaft', RWI-*Mitteilungen, 41*, s.195–204

— (1991), 'Exportnation Deutschland – Die außenwirtschaftlichen Verflechtungen Deutschlands', in Wehling, H.-G. (ed), *op. cit.*

Dombois, R. (1989), 'Flexibility by Law? The West German Employment Promotion Act and Temporary Employment', *Cambridge Journal of Economics, 13* (2), pp. 359–71

Donges, J.B. (1980), 'Industrial Policies in West Germany's not so Market-Oriented Economy', *World Economy, 3* (2), pp. 185–204

— (1992), 'Die Exportorientierung der deutschen Wirtschaft: Erfahrungen, Probleme, Perspektiven', in Dichtl, E. and Issing, O. (eds), *op. cit.*

Donges, J.B. *et al.* (1987), 'An Open Letter to the German Chancellor on Agricultural Policy', *The World Economy, 10* (3)

Donovan, M.H. (1977), *Official Grants and Financial Aids to Business in Western Europe: West Germany*, Graham A. Trotman, London (basic volume); 1978 and 1979 (supplements)

Dornbusch, R. and Wolf, H. (1992), 'Economic Transition in Eastern Germany', *Brookings Papers on Economic Activity, 1*, pp. 235–72

Dresdner Bank, *Economic Quarterly* (various) (translation of the principal *Wirtschaftsberichte* articles), Frankfurt a.M.

— *Statistische Reihen*, supplement to *Wirtschaftsberichte*, (also available in English) (various), Frankfurt a.M.

— *Trends* (various), Frankfurt a.M.

— *Wirtschaftsberichte* (various), Frankfurt a.M.

Dubrowsky, H-J. (1990), 'Schritte und Tempi der monetären Umstellung der DDR – Wirtschaft auf eine Marktwirtschaft', *List Forum, 16* (3), pp. 221–29

Dudler, H.-J. (1991), 'Monetary Control and Exchange Market Management: German Policy Experience from the 1985 Plaza Agreement for the 1989 Summit of the Arch', in Eckstein, Z. (ed.), *Aspects of Central Bank Policy Making*, Springer Verlag, Berlin a.o.

Dumke, R. (1990), 'Reassessing the Wirtschaftswunder: Reconstruction and Postwar Growth in West Germany in an International Context', *Oxford Bulletin of Economics and Statistics*, 52 (4), pp. 451–92

Dunn, M.H. (1992), 'Competitiveness and Technology Policy – The German Experience', *Jahrbücher für Nationalökonomie und Statistik*, 210 (3–4), pp. 315–31

Dütz, W. (1978), 'Die Beilegung von Arbeitsstreitigkeiten in der Bundesrepublik Deutschland', *Recht der Arbeit*, 5, pp. 291–303

Dyas, G.P. and Thanheiser, H.T. (1976), *The Emerging European Enterprise*, Macmillan, London

Dzielak, W. (1978), *Belegschaften und Gewerkschaft im Streik*, Campus Verlag, Frankfurt a.M.

Dzielak, W. et al. (1980), *Arbeitskampf um Arbeitsplätze. Der Tarifkonflikt 1978–79 in der Stahlindustrie*, Campus, Frankfurt a.M.

Ebsworth, D. (1980), 'Lay Officers in the German Chemical Workers' Union', *Industrial Relations Journal*, 11 (4), pp. 63–70

EC: Commission of the European Communities (1976), 'Action Programme in Favour of Migrant Workers and their Families', *Bulletin*, Supplement 3/76, Office for Official Publications, Luxembourg

— (1977), *Report of the Study Group on the Role of Public Finance in European Integration*, Vol.2: International Contributions and Working Papers

— (1987), *The Regions of the Enlarged Community – Third Periodic Report on the Social and Economic Situation and Development of the Regions of the Community – Summary and Conclusions*, Office for Official Publications of the European Communities, Luxembourg

— (1989a), *First Survey on State Aids in the EC*

— (1989b), *A Common Agricultural Policy for the 1990s*

— (1990a), Directorate-General for Economic and Financial Affairs, 'Country Studies: The Federal Republic of Germany', *Economic Papers*

— (1990b), *The Community and German Unification*, Vols.I and III, COM(90)400, Brussels

— (1990c), 'Background Report: The European Community and German Unification'

— (1990d), *Inventory of Taxes Levied in the Member States of the European Communities*, Thirteenth Edition

— (1990e), 'Taxation in the Single Market', *European Documentation: Periodical*, 6/90

— (1990f), Economic and Social Committee, 'German Democratic Republic', *Information Report* of the Section for External Relations, Trade and Development Policy on Central and Eastern European Countries (co-rapporteur: Mr. Jens Peter Petersen), FXT/74

— (1993), *Our Farming Future*

EC Mortgage Federation (1990), *Mortgage Credit in the European Community*, Brussels

Eckardstein, von Dudo et al. (eds) (1990), *Personalwirtschaftliche Probleme in DDR-Betrieben*, Rainer Hampp Verlag, Mering

Eckstein, W. (1980), 'The Role of the Banks in Corporate Concentration in West Germany', *Journal of Institutional and Theoretical Economics (Zeitschrift für die gesamte Staatswissenschaft*, 11 (3), pp. 465–82

Economist (various), London

Edding Commission (1974), *Sachverständigenkommission* 'Kosten und Finanzierung der beruflichen Bildung' Bundestag-Drucksache VII/1811, Bonn

Edwards, J.S.S. and Fischer, K. (1991), 'Banks, Finance and Investment in West Germany since 1970', *Discussion Paper* No. 497, Centre for Economic Policy Research, London

EEC (European Economic Community), *Reports on Competition Policy* (various), Brussels and Luxembourg

Eglau, H.O. (1980), *Erste Garnitur: Die Mächtigen der deutschen Wirtschaft*, Econ Verlag, Düsseldorf und Wien

— (1990), *Wie Gott in Frankfurt: Die Deutsche Bank und die deutsche Industrie*, Econ Verlag

Ehret, M. and Patzig, W. (1991), 'Ist eine Wiederholung des 'Wirtschaftswunders' möglich? Perspektiven für die Entwicklung in den neuen Bundesländern', *List Forum 17* (2), pp. 109–31

Eichhorn, P. (1991), 'Public Enterprises in Germany: Definition, Ownership, Objectives and Control', *Annals of Public and Cooperative Economy, 62* (1), pp. 63–79

Eltis, W. and Fraser, D. (1992), 'The Contribution of Japanese Industrial Success to Britain and Europe', National Westminster Bank *Quarterly Review*, November, pp. 2–19

Embassy of the Federal Republic of Germany, *Report* (various), London

Employment Gazette (1990), Department of Employment (various), HMSO, London

Employment Institute, 'How to End Pay Leapfrogging', *Economic Report, 5* (5)

Engelhard, J. (1992), *Exportförderung: Exportentscheidungen und Exporterfolg*, Gabler Verlag, Wiesbaden

Engelmann, B. (1978), *Meine Freunde – die Manager*, Deutscher Taschenbuch Verlag, Müchen, 6. Auflage. (One of several books by Engelmann (same publisher). There is one on millionaires with a very similar title.)

Engelsing, R. (1973), *Sozial- und Wirtschaftsgeschichte Deutschlands*, Vandenhoeck and Ruprecht, Göttingen

Erd, R. (1978), *Verrechtlichung industrieller Konflikte*, Campus, Frankfurt a.M.

— (1982), 'Zur rechtlichen Einbindung gewerkschaftlicher Betriebspolitik in der Bundesrepublik Deutschland', in Kühne, P. (ed.), *Gewerkschaftliche Betriebspolitik in Westeuropa*, Duncker and Humblot, Berlin

Erdmann, G. (1955), 'Die Schlichtungsvereinbarung vom 7. September 1954', *Recht der Arbeit, 1*, pp. 1–3

Ergun, T. (1975), *Some Economic Implications of Migration to Western Europe since 1945 with Special Reference to Turkey*, unpublished MSc Thesis, Loughborough University of Technology

Erhard, L. (1962), *Prosperity Through Competition*, Thames and Hudson, London, Third Edition

Eser, T.W. (1989), 'Der Einfluß der Europäischen Gemeinschaften auf die regionale Wirtschaftspolitik in der Bundesrepublik Deutschland', *Trierer Beiträge zur Stadt- und Regionalplanung, 17*, Universität Trier

— (1991a), *European Unification, Federalism and Regional Policies in Germany*, English abstract of Paper given at the German-speaking section of the Regional Science Association, Lisbon, mimeo.

— (1991b), *Europäische Einigung, Föderalismus und Regionalpolitik*, Zentrum für Europäische Studien, Universität Trier

Estrada, J. and Fugleberg, O. (1988), 'Interfuel Competition in France and West Germany', *Energy Policy, 16* (3), pp. 292–96

Eucken, W. (1952), *Grundsätze der Wirtschaftpolitik*, J.C.B. Mohr (Paul Siebeck), Bern/Tübingen

Euromoney (various), London

European Parliament, Directorate-General for Research (1990a), 'The Impact of German Unification on the European Community', *Research and Documentation Papers*, Working Document No.1, 6–1990

— (1990b), 'The Impact of German Unification on the European Community' (the consequences of German unification for the European Community's agricultural and fisheries policy), *Research and Documentation Papers*, Addendum to the Working Document No.1, 6–1990

Fahning, H. (1987), 'Finanzierungsformen der regionalen und örtlichen öffentlichen Unternehmen in der B.R.D.', *Annals of Public and Co-operative Economy, 58* (2), pp. 185–94

Falke, J. et al. (1991), *Kündigungspraxis und Kündigungsschutz in der Bundesrepublik Deutschland*, Bundesministerium für Arbeit und Sozialordnung, Bonn

Faltlhauser, K. (1992), 'Standort Deutschland – Defizite und notwendige politische Maßnahmen', *Politische Studien*, Sonderheft 4, pp. 35–51

Faust, K. (1992), 'Technologische Wettbewerbspositionen im Licht der ifo Patentstatistik', *Ifo-Schnelldienst, 32*, pp. 1–20

Federal Employment Institute of the FRG, several editions, undated, Nürnberg

Federal Labour Office (Bericht der Bundesanstalt für Arbeit) (1974), *Ausländische Arbeitnehmer 1972/73*, Bundesanstalt für Arbeit, Nürnberg

Feinberg, R.M. (1986a), 'The Effects of European Competition Policy on Pricing and Profit Margins', *Kyklos, 39*, pp. 267–87

— (1986b), 'The Interaction of Foreign Exchange and Market Power Effects on German Domestic Prices', *The Journal of Industrial Economics, XXXV* (1), pp. 61–70

Feix, N. (1973), *Integration oder Rotation?*,

Institut für Empirische Soziologie, Saarbrücken

Fels, G. (1988), 'Technical Change and Rationalisation – Is Technology Threatening Jobs?', *Studies on Economic and Monetary Problems and on Banking History*, No.22, v. Hase and Koehler Verlag, Mainz, pp. 19–33

—— (1989), 'Standort Bundesrepublik – Die Wettbewerbsfähigkeit der deutschen Wirtschaft', *Volkswirtschaftliche Korrespondenz der Adolf-Weber-Stiftung*, 28 (7), München

Fels, G. and Furstenberg von, G.M. (eds) (1989), *A Supply-side Agenda for Germany*, Springer-Verlag, Berlin

Fels, J. and Gundlach, E. (1990), 'More Evidence on the Puzzle of Interindustry Wage Differentials: The Case of West Germany', *Weltwirtschaftliches Archiv*, 126 (3), pp. 544–60

Fest, J.C. (1977), *Hitler*, Pelican Books, Harmondsworth, London

Fichter, M. (1993), 'A House Divided: A View of German Unification as it has Affected Organised Labour', *German Politics*, 2 (1), pp. 21–39

Fielder, M. (1988), 'Investment by Public Enterprise in the Federal Republic of Germany', *Annals of Public and Co-operative Economy*, 59 (4), pp. 455–73

—— (1989), 'Investment by Public Enterprise in the Federal Republic of Germany', *The American Journal of Economics and Sociology*, 59 (4), pp. 455–73

Filc, W. (1990), 'Wirtschaftliche Vereinigung Deutschlands im internationalen Zusammenhang. Devisenmarktanalyse für das zweite Vierteljahr', Institut für Empirische Wirtschaftsforschung, August

Filc, W. and Winkler, A. (1991), 'Monetäre Voraussetzungen marktwirtschaftlicher Reformschritte in den Staaten Osteuropas', *Kredit und Kapital*, 24 (2), pp. 175–97

Filip-Köhn, R. and Ludwig, U. (1990), 'Dimensionen des Ausgleichs des Wirtschaftsgefälles zur DDR', *DIW-Diskussionspapiere*, No.3, DIW

Financial Times (various), London and Frankfurt a.M.

—— Banking, 'Banking in West Germany', *Financial Times Survey* (various), annually, London and Frankfurt a.M.

—— West Germany, 'West Germany', *Financial Times Survey* (various), annually (usually October), London and Frankfurt a.M.

Finley, L.K. (1989), *Public Sector Privatization. Alternative Approaches to Service Delivery*, Quorum Books, New York

Fiorelli, F. (1991), 'Economic Dynamics in the "Powerful Areas" of Europe: the Case of the Ruhr', *Journal of Regional Policy*, 11, pp. 91–103

Fishbein, W.H. (1984), *Wage Restraint by Consensus*, Routledge and Kegan Paul, Boston and London

Fitoussi, J.-P. and Cacheux, J. le (1989), 'Growth and Macroeconomic Policies in OECD Countries', *International Social Science Journal*, 120 (2), pp. 127–48

Flaig, G. and Steiner, V. (1989), 'Stability and Dynamic Properties of Labour Demand in West-German Manufacturing', *Oxford Bulletin of Economics and Statistics*, 51 (4), pp. 395–412

Flam, H. (1992), 'Product Markets and 1992: Full Integration, Large Gains?', *Journal of Economic Perspectives*, 6 (4), pp. 7–30

Flassbeck, H. (1993), 'The Treuhandanstalt: Attempt at a Provisional Assessment', in Bae, J.-Y. (ed.), *Two Years Since German Unification: Economic Evaluations and Implications for Korea*, Korea Institute for International Economic Policy/Friedrich Ebert Stiftung, Seoul

Flemig, G., Langfeldt, E., Schatz, K.-W. and Trapp, P. (1990), 'Bundesrepublik Deutschland: Wirtschafts- und Währungsunion mit der DDR stützt die Konjunktur', *Die Weltwirtschaft*, 1, Institut für Weltwirtschaft (Halbjahresschrift des Instituts)

Flink, S. (1930), *The German Reichsbank and Economic Germany*, Greenwood Press, New York (reprinted in 1969)

Flockton, C.H. (1990), 'The German Economy and the Single European Market', *Politics and Society in Germany, Austria and Switzerland*, 2 (3), pp. 54–70

—— (1992), 'The Federal Republic of Germany', in Dyer, D. (ed.), *The National Economies of Europe*, Longman, Harlow, Essex

—— (1993), 'The Declining Performance of the East German Economy', in Kolinsky, E. (ed.), *Recasting Germany*, Berg, Oxford

Flockton, C.H. and Esser, J. (1992), 'The Labour Market Situation and Labour Market Policy in Germany after Unification', in Padgett, S., Paterson, W. and Smith G. (eds), *Developments in German Politics*,

Macmillan, Houndsmills, Basingstoke, Hants

Ford, R. and Suyker, W. (1990), 'Industrial Subsidies in the OECD Economies', *OECD Economic Studies*, No.15

Forschungsstelle zum Vergleich wirtschaftlicher Lenkungssysteme (1991), 'Zur Transformation von Wirtschaftssystem. Von der Planwirtschaft zur Sozialen Marktwirtschaft', *Arbeitsberichte zum Systemvergleich, 15* (2), Second Edition, Philipps-Universität, Marburg

Fortune Magazine (various), Time Inc., Los Angeles, USA

Francke, H.-H. (1983), 'Notenbankpolitik und internationaler Handel: National differierende Strategien. Eine Fallstudie: Japan – Bundesrepublik Deutschland', in Dams, T. and Kunihiro, J. (eds), *Internationale Wirtschaftsbeziehungen: Japan – Europäische Gemeinschaften – Bundesrepublik Deutschland*. Duncker and Humblot, Berlin

Franke, H. (1988), 'Economic Growth, Stability and the Labour Market', *Studies on Economic and Monetary Problems and on Banking History*, No. 23, v. Hase and Koehler, Mainz, pp. 7–23

Franke, H.H. and Hudson, M. (1984), *Banking and Finance in West Germany*, Croom Helm, Beckenham, Kent

Frankfurter Allgemeine Zeitung (various), Frankfurt a.M.

Frankfurter Institut (1990a), *Wirtschaftsreformen in der DDR – Das Soziale in der Marktwirtschaft, 29*, February

— (1990b), *Europäische Währungsunion-Wettbewerblichen Weg jetzt ebnen, 2*, March, pp. 1–6

— (1990c), *Wirtschaftsreformen in der DDR – Wettbewerbsfähige Arbeitsplätze schaffen, 32*, June, pp. 1–6

Frankfurter Wertpapierbörse AG (1992), *Grundzüge der Zulassung von Wertpapieren zum Börsenhandel* (published by the Börse, Frankfurt a.M.)

Franks, J. and Mayer, C. (1990), 'Capital Markets and Corporate Control: A Study of France, Germany and the UK', *Economic Policy, 10*, April, pp. 189–231

Franz, A., Schipke, A. and Groszek, A. (1992), 'Privatization in Poland: A Property Rights Approach', in Kremer, M. and Weber, M. (eds), *Transforming Economic Systems: The Case of Poland*, Physica-Verlag, Heidelberg

Franz, W. (1981), 'Employment Policy and Labor Supply of Foreign Workers in the Federal Republic of Germany: A Theoretical and Empirical Analysis', *Journal of Institutional and Theoretical Economics (Zeitschrift für die gesamte Staatswissenschaft, 137* (3), pp. 590–611

— (1983), 'The Past Decade's Natural Rate and the Dynamics of German Unemployment: A Case Against Demand Policy?', *European Economic Review, 21* (1–2), pp. 51–77

— (1984), 'Is Less More? The Current Discussion About Reduced Working Time in Western Germany: A Survey of the Debate', *Journal of Institutional and Theoretical Economics (Zeitschrift für die gesamte Staatswissenschaft), 140* (4), pp. 626–54

— (1990), 'Fiscal Policy in the Federal Republic of Germany', *Empirical Economics, 15* (1), pp. 17–54

Frerich, J. (1987), *Sozialpolitik*, R. Oldenbourg, Munich/Vienna

Frick, B. (1990), *Internal Labor Markets and the Employment of the Severely Disabled*, Second Joint Loughborough-Trier ERASMUS Seminar, mimeo.

— (1992a), 'The Influence of Works Councils on the Dismissal of Severely Disabled Employees', IAAEG, Trier, mimeo.

— (1992b), *Betriebliche Schwerbehindertenbeschäftigung und interne Arbeitsmärkte*, Campus, Frankfurt a.M.

Friedman, M. (1980), *Free to Choose*, Secker and Warburg, London

Friedrich, H. and Wiedemeyer, M. (1992), *Arbeitslosigkeit – ein Dauerproblem im vereinten Deutschland? Dimensionen, Ursachen, Strategien*, Leske + Budrich, Opladen

Frischmuth, B. and Wahl, J. (1990), 'Finanzausgleich zur Angleichung der Lebensverhältnisse in den Bundesländern', *Lehrstuhl für Volkswirtschaftslehre mit Schwerpunkt Finanzwissenschaft*, Universität Passau, November

Fritsch, M., Wagner, K. and Erkhardt, C.F. (1991), 'Regionalpolitik in Ostdeutschland. Maßnahmen, Implementationsprobleme und erste Ergebnisse', *Wirtschaftsdienst, 71* (12), pp. 626–31

Fritzsche, B., Gebhardt, H., Heilemann, U. and Loeffelholz, H.D. von (1991), 'Perspektiven und Optionen der deutschen Finanzpolitik 1991 bis 1994', *Wirtschaftsdienst, 71* (1), pp. 19–32

Fröhlich, H.-P. (1991), 'Der internationale Kapitalverkehr – Quantitative Bedeutung und ökonomische Funktion', in Wehling, H.-G. (ed), *op. cit.*

Frowen, S.F. (1991), 'A German Perspective of a European Single Market and EMU', in Davidson, P. and Kregel, J.A. (eds), *Economic Problems of the 1990s – Europe, the Developing Countries and the United States*, Edward Elgar Publishing Limited, Aldershot

Funk, L. (1990), *Inter- and Intra- Industry Trade, Commercial Policy, and the Political Economy of Protection*, unpublished Diploma Thesis, University of Trier

—— (1992), 'Strategische Industriepolitik auf dem Prüfstand', *Fortbildung, 37* (3), September, pp. 68–71

Funke, M. and Holly, S. (1992), 'The Determinants of West German Exports of Manufactures: An Integrated Demand and Supply Approach', *Weltwirtschaftliches Archiv, 128* (3), pp. 498–512

Fürstenberg, F. (1984), 'Recent Trends in Collective Bargaining in the Federal Republic of Germany', *International Labour Review, 123* (5), pp. 615–30

Furubotn, E.G. (1985), 'Codetermination, Productivity Gains, and the Economics of the Firm', *Oxford Economic Papers, 37* (1), pp. 22–39

Gäbe, W. (1991), 'De-industrialisation and Industrial Restructuring in the Rhine-Neckar Area', in Wild, T. and Jones, P. (eds), *De-industrialisation and New Industrialisation in Britain and Germany*, Anglo-German Foundation Publications, London

Gallant, P. (1988), *The Eurobond Market*, Woodhead-Faulkner, Cambridge

Garlich, D. (1977), *Steuerungsprobleme zentralstaatlicher Planung in der Bundesrepublik*, International Institute of Management, Discussion Paper 77-17, Berlin

Garlich, D. and Hull, C. (1977), *Central Control and Information Dependence in a Federal System*, International Institute of Management, Discussion Paper 77-102, Berlin

Gaugler, E. (1979), 'Mitarbeiter-Kapital im Arbeitgebenden Unternehmen', *Finnish Journal of Business Economics*, 4-1979, Special Edition

Gaugler, E. *et al.* (1978), *Ausländer in deutschen Industriebetrieben: Ergebnisse einer empirischen Untersuchung*, Peter Hanstein Verlag, Köningstein/Ts. (Part of a wide-ranging series of empirical studies, all of which are published by Hanstein – see both the Introduction to this Gaugler volume and Kremer and Spangenberg below.)

Gayle, D.J. and Goodrich, J.N. (1990a), *Privatization and Deregulation in Global Perspective*, Quorum Books, New York

—— (1990b), 'Exploring the Implications of Privatization and Deregulation', in Gayle, D.J. and Goodrich, J.N., *op. cit.*

Gebhardt, H., Heilemann, U. and Loeffelholz H.D. von (1989), 'Finanzhilfen der Bundesrepublik für die DDR: Umfang, Formen, Wirkungen', *RWI-Mitteilungen*, pp. 323–48

Geimer, R. and H. (1978), *Science in the FRG: Organisation and Promotion*, Fourth Edition, Deutscher Akademischer Austauschdienst, Bonn

Geiselberger, S. (1972), *Schwarzbuch: Ausländische Arbeiter*, Fischer Taschenbuch Verlag, Frankfurt a.M.

Gemählich, P. (1992), 'Erfahrungen und Politik der Treuhandanstalt', in Ipsen, D. and Nickel, E. (eds), *op. cit.*

Genosko, J. (1986), 'Der wechselnde Einfluß des Subsidiaritätsprinzips auf die wirtschafts- und sozialpolitische Praxis in der Bundesrepublik Deutschland', *Jahrbücher für Nationalökonomie und Statistik, 201* (4), pp. 404–16

Gerhaeusser, K. (1991), 'Firm Size and R&D Expenditure – A Decomposition for the West German Economy', *Economic Letters, 37*, pp. 459–63

German Politics (1992), Special issue on Federalism, Unification and European Integration, 3 (1)

Gerstenberger, W. (1990), 'Das zukünftige Produktionspotential der DDR – ein Versuch zur Reduzierung der Unsicherheiten', *Ifo-Schnelldienst, 7*, pp. 13–22

Geske, O.-E. (1991), 'Die Finanzierung der ostdeutschen Länder nach dem Einigungsvertrag', *Wirtschaftsdienst, 71* (1), pp. 33–9

Gessler Commission (Bericht der Studienkommission) (1979), 'Grundsatzfragen der Kreditwirtschaft', *Schriftenreihe des Bundesministerium der Finanzen, 28*, Fritz Knapp Verlag, Frankfurt a.M.

Giersch, H. (1970), *Growth, Cycles and*

Exchange Rates – the Experience of West Germany, Almqvist and Wiksell, Stockholm. Republished (in German) in: *Konverse Fragen der Wirtschaftspolitik* (B. Piper and Co. Verlag, München, 1971.) (Page references in this book are to the German edition.)

—— (ed.) (1983), *Wie es zu schaffen ist: Agenda für die deutsche Wirtschaftspolitik*, Deutsche Verlags-Anstalt, Stuttgart

—— (1985), *Eurosclerosis*, Kiel *Discussion Papers*, No.112

Giersch, H., Paque, K-H. and Schmieding, H. (1992), *The Fading Miracle: Four Decades of Market Economy in Germany*, Cambridge U.P., Cambridge

Glastetter, W., Paulert, R. and Spörel, U. (1983), *Die wirtschaftliche Entwicklung in der Bundesrepublik Deutschland 1950–1980*, Campus Verlag, Frankfurt a.M/New York

Glismann, H.H. *et al.* (1992), *Weltwirtschaftslehre II – Eine problemorientierte Einführung*, Fourth Edition, UTB-Verlag, Göttingen

Glos, M. (1992), 'Do We Need a Strategic Industrial Policy à la Miti?', *Intereconomics*, 27 (3), pp. 107–11

Gordon, A.P.L. (1928), *The Problem of Trust and Monopoly Control*, George Routledge and Sons, London

Gossweiler, K. (1975), *Grossbanken, Industriemonopole, Staat*, Verlag des Europäischen Buches, West Berlin

Gowland, D. (ed.) (1991), *International Bond Markets*, Routledge, London

Graham, F.D. (1967), *Exchange, Prices and Production in Hyperinflation: Germany 1920–1923*, Russell and Russell, New York (re-issued)

Grebing, H. (1969), *The History of the German Labour Movement*, Oswald Wolff, London

Greenaway, D. and Hine, R.C. (1991), 'Intra-Industry Specialization, Trade Expansion and Adjustment in the European Economic Space', Journal of Common Market Studies, XXIX (6) pp. 604–22

Greenaway, D. and Milner, C. (1986), *The Economics of Intra-Industry Trade*, Blackwell, Oxford

Greza, G. (1974), *Germany in Our Time*, Pelican Books, Harmondsworth

—— (1975), *Sozial – Report*, Inter Nationes, Bonn

Grochla, E. and Gaugler, E. (eds), (1990),

Handbook of German Business Management (2 volumes), Verlag C.E. Poeschel, Stuttgart/Springer-Verlag, Berlin

Gross, D.M. (1988), 'The Relative Importance of Some Causes of Unemployment: The Case of West Germany', *Weltwirtschaftliches Archiv, 124* (3), pp. 501–23

Grosser, A. (1974), *Germany in Our Time*, Penguin Books, Harmondsworth

Grottian, P. *et al.* (1988), *Die Wohlfahrtswende*, Verlag C.H. Beck, Munchen

Gruhler, W. (1978), 'Rationalisierungsinvestitionen und Beschäftigung', *Beiträge zur Wirtschafts- und Sozialpolitik*, 52, 1/1978, Deutscher Instituts-Verlag, Köln

—— (1992), 'Privatisierungsbilanz der Treuhandanstalt', *iw-trends*, No.3, pp. 97–104

Guardian (various), London/Frankfurt

Guillebaud, C.W. (1939), *The Economic Recovery of Germany (1933–1938)*, Macmillan, London

—— (1971), *The Social Policy of Nazi Germany*, republished by Howard Fertig, New York

Gurdon, M.A. (1991), 'The Politics of Property in the Federal Republic of Germany', *International Labour Review, 130* (5-6), pp. 595–611

Gurdon, M.A. and Rai, A. (1990), 'Codetermination and Enterprise Performance: Empirical Evidence from West Germany', *Journal of Economics and Business, 42* (4), pp. 289–302

Gutmann, G. (1991), 'Euckens konstituierende Prinzipien der Wirtschaftspolitik und der ordnungspolitische Wandel in den Ländern Osteuropas', in Forschungsstelle zum Vergleich wirtschaftlicher Lenkungssysteme, *op. cit.*

Hagedorn, K. (1991), 'Financing Social Security in Agriculture: The Case of the Farmers' Old Age Pension Scheme in the Federal Republic of Germany', *European Review of Agricultural Economics, 18* (2), pp. 209–29

Hallett, G. (1973), *The Social Economy of West Germany*, Macmillan, London

Hamm, W. (1983), 'Was tun mit den öffentlichen Unternehmen? Sanierung, Entmonopolisierung, Privatisierung', in Giersch, H. (ed.), *op. cit.*

—— (1988), 'Nationale Wirtschaftspolitik als internationaler Standortfaktor', in Dürr, E. and Siebert, H. (eds), *Weltwirtschaft im Wandel*, Verlag Paul Haukpt, Bern/Stuttgart

—— (1992), 'Privatisierung – ein Schlüssel-problem freiheitlicher Ordnungen', *ORDO Jahrbuch für die Ordnung von Wirtschaft und Gesellschaft, 43*, pp. 139–56

Hanby, V.J. and Jackson, M.P. (1979), 'An Evaluation of Job Creation in Germany', *International Journal of Social Economics, 6* (2), pp. 79–117

Hankel, W. (1993), *Die sieben Todsünden der Vereinigung. Wege aus dem Wirtschaftsdesaster*, Siedler Verlag, Königswinter

Hansen, U. (1990), 'Delinking of Energy Consumption and Economic Growth: The German Experience', *Energy Policy, 18* (7), pp. 631–40

Hansson, A.H. (1990), 'The 1948 West German Economic Reforms: a model for Eastern Europe?', *Discussion Paper*, No. 90-05, Department of Economics, The University of British Columbia, Vancouver, Canada

Hardach, K. (1980), *The Political Economy of Germany in the Twentieth Century*, California UP, Berkeley/Los Angeles/London

Harden, I. (1990), 'EuroFed or "Monster Bank"?', National Westminster Bank *Quarterly Review*, August, pp. 2–13

Hardes, H.-D. (1974), *Einkommenspolitik in der BRD*, Herder + Herder, Campus: Studien, Frankfurt a.M.

—— (1981), *Arbeitsmarktstrukturen und Beschäftigungsprobleme im internationalen Vergleich: Theoretische und empirische Analyse am Beispiel von USA, Großbritannien und der Bundesrepublik Deutschland*, J.C.B. Mohr (Paul Siebeck), Tübingen

Härtel, H.-H. (1991), 'Lohnpolitik im vereinten Deutschland: vorschnelle Vereinheitlichung der Tariflöhne birgt Gefahren', *Wirtschaftsdienst, 71* (1), pp. 7–10

Hartfiel, G. (1966), 'Germany', in Sturmthal, A. (ed.), *White-Collar Unionism*, Illinois UP

Hartmann, H. (1970), 'Co-determination in West Germany', *Industrial Relations, 9* (2), pp. 137–47

—— (1975), 'Co-determination Today and Tomorrow', *British Journal of Industrial Relations, XIII* (1), pp. 54–64

—— (1979), 'Works Councils and the Iron law of Oligarchy', *British Journal of Industrial Relations, XVII* (1), pp. 70–82

Hartrich, E. (1980), *The Fourth and Richest Reich*, Collier Macmillan, London

Hartwig, K.-H. (1990), 'Bundesrepublik Deutschland: Bleibende Dominanz in Europa?', in Cassel, D. (ed.), *Wirtschaftssysteme im Umbruch: Sowjetunion, China und industrialisierte Marktwirtschaften zwischen internationalem Anpassungszwang und nationalem Reformbedarf*, Verlag Franz Vahlen, München

Hautsch, G. (ed.) (1984), *Kampf und Streit um Arbeitszeit*, Verlag Marxistische Blätter, Frankfurt a.M.

Hautsch, G. et al. (1979), *Stahlstreik und Tarifrunde 1978/79*, IMSF, Frankfurt a.M.

—— (1984), *Der Arbeitskampf um die 35-Stunden-Woche. 'Flexi-Konzept' des Kapitals und die Zukunft der Gewerkschaften*, IMSF, Frankfurt a.M.

Hawkins, R.A. (1991), 'Privatisation in Western Germany, 1957–1990', National Westminster Bank *Quarterly Review*, November, pp. 14–22

Hax, H. (1990), 'Debt and Investment Policy in German Firms: the issue of capital shortage', *Journal of Institutional and Theoretical Economics (Zeitschrift für die gesamte Staatswissenschaft), 146* (1), pp. 106–23

—— (1992), 'Privatization Agencies: The Treuhand Approach', in Siebert, H. (ed.), *op. cit.*

Healey, D. (1989), *The Time of my Life*, Penguin Books, London

Heide, von der, H.-J. and Cholewa, W., 'Stellung und Aufgaben der kommunalen Gebietskörperschaften in der regionalen Wirtschaftsförderung', in Eberstein, H.-H., *Handbuch der regionalen Wirtschaftsförderung, Achtzehnter Rahmenplan*, Verlag Dr. Otto Schmidt KG, Köln

Heidenhain, M. and Schneider, H. (1991), *Das Recht gegen Wettbewerbsbeschränkungen/ German Antitrust Law*, Fourth Edition, Fritz Knapp Verlag, Frankfurt a.M. (Previous editions were with Mueller, R. – see below.)

Heidrich, W. (1992), 'Innovationsstandort Deutschland', *Wirtschaftspolitische Diskurse, 35*, Forschungsinstitut der Friedrich-Ebert-Stiftung Abteilung Wirtschaftspolitik, Bonn

Heiduk, G. (1989), *Internationalization Strategies of German Firms: The Case of Three Industries in the Ruhr Region*, paper presented at the Annual Meeting of the Euro-Asia Management Studies Association, 'International Business and the Management of Change', Nagoya, 6–8 December

Heiduk, G. and Hodges, U.W. (1992), 'German Multinationals in Europe: Patterns and

Perspectives', in Klein, M.W. and Welfens, P.J.J. (eds), *Multinationals in the New Europe and Global Trade*, Springer Verlag, Berlin

Heilemann, U. (1991a), 'The Economics of German Unification – A First Appraisal', *Konjunkturpolitik, 37* (3), pp. 127–55

— (1991b), 'The Economics of German Unification Reconsidered', *Intereconomics, 26* (6), pp. 296–304

Heine, M. and Walter, D. (1990), 'Sektorale und räumliche Auswirkungen der Stukturanpassung in der DDR', *Wirtschaftsdienst, 70* (8), pp. 402–5

Heise, A. (1991), 'Wirtschaftsförderung in den neuen Bundesländern', *Wirtschaftsdienst, 71* (11), pp. 578–81

Heller, W.W. (1950), 'The Role of Fiscal-Monetary Policy in German Economic Recovery', *American Economic Review* (Proceedings of Sixty-Second Meeting: Economic Policy in Occupied Germany), *40* (2), pp. 531–47

Hellwig, M. and Neumann, M. (1987), 'Economic Policy in Germany: was there a turnaround?', *Economic Policy*, No.5, pp. 105–45

Helmstädter, E. (1988), 'The Irrelevance of Keynes to German Economic Policy and to International Economic Cooperation in the 1980s', in Eltis, W. and Sinclair, P. (eds), *Keynes and Economic Policy*, Macmillan, London

Henderson, W.O. (1975), *The Rise of German Industrial Power 1834–1914*, Temple Smith, London

Henke, K-D. (1990), 'Das Gesundheitssystem im gesamtdeutschen Einigungsprozeß', *Wirtschaftsdienst, 70* (8), pp. 353–8

Henning, F.W. (1974), *Das industrialisierte Deutschland 1914–1972* (UTB 337), Ferdinand Schöningh, Paderborn

Hennings, K.H. (1982), 'West Germany', in Boltho, A. (ed.), *The European Economy: Growth and Crisis*, OUP, Oxford

Hentschel, V. (1983), *Geschichte der deutschen Sozialpolitik, 1880–1980*, Suhrkamp, Frankfurt a.M.

Henzler, H. (1992), 'Managing the Merger: A Strategy for the New Germany', *Harvard Business Review, 70* (1), pp. 24–9

Herb, K. (1979), 'Verlauf und Ergebnis des Arbeitskampfes in der Eisen- und Stahlindustrie', *Gewerkschaftliche Monatshefte, 30* (3), pp. 137–45

Hesselbach, W. (1976), *Public, Trade Union and Cooperative Enterprise in Germany*, Frank Cass, London

Hickel, R. (1991), 'Anleihe zur Finanzierung der Kosten der ökonomischen Sanierung des Wirtschaftsgebiets der ehemaligen DDR', *WSI Mitteilungen*, January, pp. 54–5

Hildesheim, M.G. (1990), 'Das Fremdrentengesetz – Eingliederung von Aussiedlern in die gesetzliche Rentenversicherung', *WiSt, 19* (1), p.33

Hillebrandt, V. (1992), 'Aufgaben der Treuhandanstalt im Erneuerungsprozeß', in Besters, H. (ed.), *op. cit.*

Hills, J., Hubert, F., Tomann, H. and Whitehead, C. (1989), 'Shifting Subsidy from Bricks and Mortar to People: Experiences in Britain and West Germany', *Welfare State Programme Discussion Paper*, WSP/41, March, LSE

Himmelmann, G. (1977), 'Der Arbeitskampf im Druckgewerbe 1976', *Der Bürger im Staat, 27* (3), pp. 176–82

— (1979), 'Sozialpolitik der Tarifpartner', *Der Bürger im Staat, 29* (4), pp. 258–62

Hirsch-Weber, W. (1959), *Gewerkschaften in der Politik*, Westdeutscher Verlag, Köln und Opladen

— (1963), 'Die Gewerkschaften: Interessengruppen oder soziale Bewegung?', *Gewerkschaft Wirtschaft Gesellschaft*, Bund-Verlag, Köln, pp. 275–82

Hitchens, D.M.W.N., Wagner, K. and Birnie, J.E. (1992) 'Measuring the Contribution of Product Quality to Competitiveness: A Note on Theory and Policy', *The Economic and Social Review, 23* (4), pp. 455–63

Hoene, B. (1991), 'Labor Market Realities in Eastern Germany', *Challenge, 34* (4), pp. 17–22

Hoffman, D. and Schaub, S. (1983), *The (sic) German Competition Law* (Legislation and Commentary), Kluwer Law and Taxation Publishers, Deventer, The Netherlands

Hoffman, W.G. (1965), *Das Wachstum der Deutschen Wirtschaft seit der Mitte des 19. Jahrhunderts*, Springer-Verlag, Berlin, Heidelberg, New York

Hofmeier, K. (1976), 'Partners or Adversaries', *Sozial-Report*, 4-76(e), Inter Nationes, Bonn-Bad Godesberg

Hölker, F-J. (1984), 'Die Ordnung der Energiewirtschaft der Bundesrepublik Deutschland', *Annals of Public and Co-operative Economy, 55* (4), pp. 413–31

—— (1986), 'Entmonopolisierung der Energieversorgung?', *Annals of Public and Cooperative Economy, 57* (4), pp. 513–21

Holmes, M.J. (1992), 'The European Market for Mortgage Finance and 1992', in Mullineux, A. (ed.), *European Banking*, Blackwell, Oxford

Hommelhoff, P. (ed.) (1991), *Treuhandunternehmen in Umbruch: Recht und Rechtswirklichkeit beim Übergang in die Marktwirtschaft*, RWS-Forum 7, Verlag Kommunikationsforum, Köln

Homze, E.L. (1967), *Foreign Labor in Nazi Germany*, Princeton UP, New Jersey

—— (1976), *Arming the Luftwaffe: the Reich Air Ministry and the German Aircraft Industry 1919–1939*, University of Nebraska Press

Hood, N. and Young, S. (1979), *The Economics of Multinational Enterprises*, Longman, London and New York

Hopkins, S.V. (1953), 'Industrial Stoppages and Their Economic Significance', *Oxford Economic Papers, 5* (3), pp. 209–20

Horn, E-J. (1982), 'Management of Industrial Change in Germany', *Sussex European Papers*, No.13, Sussex European Research Centre, University of Sussex

Horn, N. (1991), 'Privatisierung und Reprivatisierung von Unternehmen. Eigentumsschutz und Investitionsförderung im Lichte der neuesten Gesetzgebung', in Hommelhoff, P. (ed.), *op. cit.*

Hrbek, R. (1990), 'Die EG und die Veränderung in Mittel- und Osteuropa', *Wirtschaftsdienst, 70* (5), pp. 247–55

Huber, P. and Wiegert, R. (1978), 'Der künftige Arbeitsmarkt', *Der Bürger im Staat, 28* (3), pp. 183–8

Hubert, F. and Tomann, H. (1990), 'Leistungsanreize und Risikoteilung in der Wohnungsbauförderung', *Zeitschrift für Wirtschafts- u. Sozialwissenschaften, 110* (2), pp. 239–59

Hudson, M. (1980), '"Concerted Action": Wages Policy in West Germany, 1967–77', *Industrial Relations Journal, 11* (4), pp. 5–16

Hughes Hallett, A.J. and Ma, Y. (1993), 'East Germany, West Germany, and their Mezzogiorno Problem: A Parable for European Economic Integration', *The Economic Journal, 103* (2), pp. 416–28

Hughes, K.S. (1992), 'Trade Performance of the Main EC Economies Relative to the USA and Japan in 1992-Sensitive Sectors', *Journal of Common Market Studies, 30* (4), pp. 437–54

Hutchinson, T.W. (1979), 'Notes on the Effects of Economic Ideas on Policy: The example of the German Social Market Economy', *Journal of Institutional and Theoretical Economics (Zeitschrift für die gesamte Staatswissenschaft), 135* (3), pp. 426–41

Hutton, S. and Lawrence, P. (1981), *German Engineers: the Anatomy of a Profession*, OUP, Oxford

Hutton, S.D., Lawrence, P.A. and Smith, M.H. (1977), 'The Recruitment, Deployment and Status of the Mechanical Engineer in the German Federal Republic', *Report* to the Department of Industry, London, Parts I and II. (Part I, pp. 1–94, contains a general introduction; Part II, p. 95 onwards, contains the results of a survey.)

IDS (Incomes Data Services Limited) (1990), Country Profile (West Germany), 'Unification Recasts National Mould', *IDS European Report*, 343, July

—— *European Report* (formerly *International Reports*) (various), London

ifo-digest (various), München

Ifo-Schnelldienst, 7/90, 'Das zukünftige Produktionspotential der DDR ein Versuch zur Reduzierung der Unsicherheiten'

IG Chemie (1981), *Projekt Schichtarbeit – Gesamtergebnis der Problemanalyse*, (i) Langfassung, (ii) Kurzfassung, (iii) Tabellenband, Hauptvorstand, Hannover

ILO (International Labour Office) (1945), *The Exploitation of Foreign Labour by Germany*, ILO, Montreal

Informationen zur Politischen Bildung (various), Bonn

Institut für Empirische Wirtschaftsforschung (1990), 'Zins und Wechselkurswirkungen der deutschen Währunsunion – Devisenmarktanalyse für das erste Vierteljahr', May

Institute of Economic Affairs (1976), *Job 'Creation' – or Destruction?*, London

Ipsen, D. and Nickel, E. (eds) (1992), *Probleme der Einheit. Ökonomische und rechtliche Konsequenzen der deutschen Vereinigung*, Metropolis-Verlag, Marburg

Issing, O. (1988), 'Recent Trends and the Bundesbank's Monetary Policy', *Prospects*, Swiss Bank Corporation, 1/88

—— (1989), 'Balance of Payments Adjustment Problems – The Case of West Germany', in Fair, D.E. and Boissieu, C. de (eds), *The*

International Adjustment Process. New Perspectives, Recent Experience and Future Challenges for the Financial System, Kluwer Academic Publishers, Dordrecht

— (1992a), 'The Impact of German Unification on the Members of the European Community', Deutsche Bundesbank: *Auszüge aus Presseartikeln*, No. 2, pp. 3–6

— (1992b), 'Theoretical and Empirical Foundations of the Deutsche Bundesbank's Monetary Targeting', *Intereconomics, 27* (6), pp. 289–300

Issing, O. and Masuch, K. (1992), 'EWS, Währungsunion and Kapitalallokation – Neue Perspektiven durch die Wiedervereinigung', in Köhler, C. and Pohl, R. (eds), *Währungspolitische Probleme im integrierten Europa*, Duncker and Humblot, Berlin

iwd1 (Institut der deutschen Wirtschaft), *iwd-Nachrichten* (various), Köln

iwd2 (Informationsdienst des Instituts der deutschen Wirtschaft) (various), Köln

IW (Institut der Deutschen Wirtschaft), *Zahlen* (various), Köln

— (1991), *Das begrenzte Risiko*, Second Edition

Jäckel, P. (1990), 'Planungen der Industrieunternehmen: Tendenz weiter steigend', *Ifo-Schelldienst, 26–27*, pp. 3–8

Jacobi, O. *et al.* (1974), *Gewerkschaften und Klassenkampf: Kritisches Jahrbuch, 1974*, Fischer Taschenbuch Verlag, Frankfurt a.M.

Jacobi, O., Keller, B. and Müller-Jentsch, W. (1992), 'Germany: Codetermining the future?', in Ferner, A. and Hyman, R. (eds), *Industrial Relations in the New Europe*, Blackwell, Oxford

Jeffery, C. and Savigear, P. (1991), *German Federalism Today*, Leicester University Press, Leicester and London

Jeffries, I. and Meltzer, M. (eds) (1987), *The East German Economy*, Croom Helm, Beckenham, Kent

Jochimsen, R. (1989), 'Wirtschaftliche Entwicklung in der Bundesrepublik Deutschland – unter besonderer Berüksichtigung der Nord-Süd-Diskussion', Lecture Paper, 19 May, Goethe Institut, London

Jochmann-Döll, A. (1990), *Gleicher Lohn für gleichwertige Arbeit: Ausländische und deutsche Konzepte und Erfahrungen*, Rainer Hampp Verlag, München and Mering

Johnes, G. and Hyclak, T.J. (1988), 'Wage Inflation in Europe: the Regional Dimension', *Regional Studies, 23* (1), pp. 19–26

Johnson, N. (1973), *Government in the Federal Republic of Germany*, Pergamon Press, Oxford

Johnson, N. and Cochrane, A. (1981), *Economic Policy-making by Local Authorities in Britain and Western Germany*, George Allen and Unwin, London

Jones, P.N. (1990), 'West Germany's Declining Guestworker Population: Spatial Change and Economic Trends in the 1980s', *Regional Studies, 24* (3), pp. 223–31

Jordan, R. (1976), 'Entwicklung und Stand der wirtschaftlichen Konzentration in der Bundesrepublik Deutschland – Ein empirischer Überblick', *WSI Mitteilungen, 29*, August, pp. 71–7

Jühe, R. *et al.* (1977), *Gewerkschaften in der Bundesrepublik Deutschland: Daten Fakten Strukturern*, Deutscher Instituts-Verlag, Köln

Kahn, G.A. and Jacobson, K. (1989), 'Lessons from West German Monetary Policy', Federal Reserve Bank of Kansas City, *Economic Review, 74* (4), pp. 18–35

Kaufer, E. (1977), *Konzentration und Fusionskontrolle*, JCB Mohr (Paul Siebeck), Tübingen, 1977

Kaufmann, G. (1973), 'Banken in der BRD', *Der Bürger im Staat, 23* (4), pp. 256–64

Kaula, K. (1989), 'Bericht zur Lage', *Die Ersatzkasse, 69* (7), pp. 261–78

Kay, J.A. and Thompson, D.J. (1986), 'Privatisation: A Policy in Search of a Rationale', *Economic Journal, 96* (1), pp. 18–32

Keeney, R.L., Renn, O. and Winterfeldt, D. von (1987), 'Structuring West Germany's Energy Objectives', *Energy Policy, 15* (4), pp. 352–62

Kellas, J.G. (1991), 'European Integration and the Regions', *Parliamentary Affairs, 44* (2), pp. 226–39

Keller, B. (1983), *Arbeitsbeziehungen im öffentlichen Dienst. Tarifpolitik der Gewerkschaften und Interessenpolitik der Beamtenverbände*, Campus, Frankfurt a.M.

Keller, D. (1992), 'Should Europe Provide Selective Assistance for Key Industries?', *Intereconomics, 27* (4), pp. 111–17

Kendall, W. (1975), *The Labour Movement in Europe*, Penguin Books, Harmondsworth

Kennedy, E. (1991), *The Bundesbank: Germany's Central Bank in the International*

Monetary System, Pinter Publishers, London

Kerr, C. (1952), 'Collective Bargaining in Postwar Germany', *Industrial and Labor Relations Review*, 5 (3), pp. 323–42

—— (1954), 'The Trade Union Movement and the Redistribution of Power in Postwar Germany', *Quarterly Journal of Economics, 68* (4) pp. 535–64

Kindleberger, C.P. (1967), *Europe's Postwar Growth: the Role of Labor Supply*, Harvard UP, Cambridge, Mass.

Kissel, O.R. (1990), 'Arbeitsrecht und Staatsvertrag (zur Errichtung der Währungs-, Wirtschafts- und Sozialunion)', *Neue Zeitschrift für Arbeits- und Sozialrecht, 7* (13, 20), pp. 545–52

Klauder, W. and Kühlewind, G. (1990), 'Längerfristige Arbeitsmarktperspektiven in einem zusammenwachsenden Deutschland', *Arbeit und Sozialpolitik, 44* (8/9), pp. 264–70

Klemmer, P. (1990), 'Modernisierung der ostdeutschen Wirtschaft als regionalpolitisches Problem', *Wirtschaftsdienst, 70* (11), pp. 557–61

Klemmer, P. von and Schrumpf, H. (1990), 'Probleme einer ökonomischen Umstrukturierung der DDR aus regionalpolitischer Sicht', RWI-*Mitteilungen, 41*, pp. 117–30

Kliemann, H.G. and Taylor, S.B. (1964), *Who's Who in Germany*, Third Edition (2 vols A-N and M-Z), International Book and Publishing, Munich

Klodt, H. (1990a), 'Arbeitsmarktpolitik in der DDR: Vorschläge für ein Qualifizierungsprogramm', *Die Weltwirtschaft*, 1, pp. 78–91

—— (1990b), 'Wirtschaftshilfen für die neuen Bundesländer', *Wirtschaftsdienst, 70* (12), pp. 617–22

—— (1990c), 'Government Support for Restructuring the East German Economy', Kiel *Working Paper*, No. 450

Klopstock, F.H. (1949), 'Monetary Reform in Western Germany', *Journal of Political Economy, 57* (4), pp. 277–92

Kloss, G. (1985), 'The Academic Restructuring of British and German Universities and Greater Efficiency: A Comparative Perspective', *Oxford Review of Education, 11* (3), pp. 271–82

Klump, R. (1989), 'Einführung in die Wirtschaftspolitik', Vahlen, München

Knapp, M. (1981), 'Reconstruction and West-Integration: The Impact of the Marshall Plan on Germany', *Journal of Institutional and Theoretical Economics (Zeitschrift für die gesamte Staatswissenschaft), 137* (3), pp. 415–31

Knappe, E. (1974), *Möglichkeiten und Grenzen dezentraler Umweltschutzpolitik. Bekämpfung externer Nachteile durch Verhandlungen*, Duncker and Humblot, Berlin

—— (1983), 'Reform der Krankenversicherung', in Giersch, H. (ed.), *Wie es zu schaffen ist: Agenda für die deutsche Wirtschaftspolitik*, Deutsche Verlags-Anstalt, Stuttgart

Knappe, E. and Funk, L. (1992), 'Inflexibilität, Lohnstruktur und Arbeitslosigkeit', *Trierer Diskussionsbeiträge*, No. 28, Social Administration and Management, Universität Trier

Knauss, F. (1988), 'Privatisierungspolitik in der Bundesrepublik Deutschland', *Beiträge zur Wirtschafts- und Sozialpolitik Institut der deutschen Wirtschaft, 160*, Deutscher Instituts-Verlag, Köln

—— (1989), *Unternehmen und Sondervermögen der öffentlichen Hand – Zum 'wichtigen Bundesinteresse' und zur Privatisierung von Bundesbeteiligungen*, Fachbereich IV, Universität Trier

—— (1990), 'Privatisierung in der Bundesrepublik Deutschland 1983–1990. Bilanz und Perspektiven', *Beiträge zur Wirtschafts- und Sozialpolitik Institut der deutschen Wirtschaft, 183*, Deutscher Instituts-Verlag, Köln

KND (*Kurz-Nachrichten-Dienst*) (Bundesvereinigung der Deutschen Arbeitgeberverbände, Press Releases) (various), Köln

Knerr, B. (1991), 'The Impact of Transfers to Agriculture Through the German Tax System', *European Review of Agricultural Economics, 18* (2), pp. 193–208

Knieper, O. and Schmidt, H.-W. (1990), 'Bestandsaufnahme und Probleme der Neuorientierung der Energiewirtschaft in der DDR', RWI-*Mitteilungen*, pp. 29–40

Knieps, F. (1990a), 'Das Gesundheitswesen und die Krankenversicherung im beigetretenen Teil Deutschlands', *Arbeit und Sozialpolitik, 44* (11/12), pp. 392–7

—— (1990b), 'Auf dem Weg zur Sozialunion? Erste Anmerkungen zum *Staats*vertrag über die Schaffung einer Währungs-, Wirtschafts- und Sozialunion zwischen der Bundesrepublik Deutschland und der Deutschen

Demokratischen Republik', *Arbeit und Sozialpolitik, 44* (6), pp. 197–9

Knott, J.H. (1981), *Managing the German Economy: Budgetary Politics in a Federal State*, Gower, Lexington, Mass; Toronto

Koch, K. (1989), 'Industrial Relations', in Koch, K. (ed.), *West Germany Today*, Routledge, London

Koch, U.E. (1981), *Angriff auf ein Monopol*, Deutscher Instituts Verlag, Köln

Kohl, H. (1987), *Preserving Creation, Mastering the Tasks of the Future: Government Policy 1987–1990*, statement by Federal Chancellor Helmut Kohl to the German Bundestag on 18 March 1987, Press and Information Office of the Federal Government

Kommission der Europäischen Gemeinschaft (1990a), 'Die deutsche Frage europäisch lösen – Die Europäische Gemeinschaft und die DDR', *EC Informationen, 12*, March

—— (1990b), 'Europäische Landwirtschaft muß bezahlbar bleiben', *EC Informationen, 13*, April

Königbauer, G. (1971), *Freiwillige Schlichtung und tarifliche Schiedsgerichtsbarkeit*, Gustav Fischer Verlag, Stuttgart

Konrad, H.-M. (1968), 'Privatisierung öffentlicher Unternehmen – Bestandsaufnahme und finanzpolitische Würdigung', *Die Öffentliche Wirtschaft, XVII* (1), pp. 41–7

Kopstock, F.H. (1949), 'Monetary Reform in Western Germany', *The Journal of Political Economy, 57* (4), pp. 277–92

Korff, H.C. (1983), 'Germany's Planning and Budgeting', *Public Budgeting and Finance, 3* (4), pp. 57–70

—— (1990), 'Europäische Landwirtschaft muss bezahlbar bleiben', *EC Informationen*, No. 13, April

Körner, J. (1990), 'Letze Steuerschätzung für die Bundesrepublik', *Ifo-Schnelldienst, 24*, pp. 11–20

Köster, T. (1991), 'Der Mittelstand als Richtpunkt der Ordnungspolitik', *Orientierungen zur Wirtschafts- und Gesellschaftspolitik, 50* (4), pp. 52–6

Kowalski, J.S. and Rothengatter, W. (1991), 'Development Prospects for European Transport Between East and West' from ECMT (European Conference of Ministers of Transport), *Prospects for East-West European Transport*, ECMT Publications, Paris

Kraft, K. (1986), 'Exit and Voice in the Labor Market: An Empirical Study of Quits', *Journal of Institutional and Theoretical Economics (Zeitschrift für die gesamte Staatswissenschaft), 142* (3), pp. 697–715

Krakowski, M. (1993), 'Alternatives and Consequences for Integration of Two Economic Systems', in Bae, J.-Y. (ed.), *Two Years Since German Unification: Economic Evaluation and Implications for Korea*, Korean Institute for International Economic Policy/Friedrich Ebert Stiftung, Seoul

Krakowski, M., Lau, D. and Lux, A. (1992), 'Auswirkungen der Wiedervereinigung auf den Industriestandort Deutschland', *Wirtschaftspolitische Diskurse, 32*, Forschungsinstitut der Friedrich-Ebert-Stiftung, Abteilung Wirtschaftspolitik, Bonn

Krautkrämer, U. (1979), 'Arbeitslosenversicherung', *Der Bürger im Staat, 29* (4), pp. 239–42

Kreklau, C. (1992), 'Die deutsche Wirtschaft im Sog des japanischen Wirtschaftswunders?', *Politische Studien*, Sonderheft 4, pp. 22–34

Kremer, M. and Spangenberg, H. (1980), *Assimilation ausländischer Arbeitnehmer in der Bundesrepublik Deutschland*, Peter Hanstein Verlag, Königstein/Ts

Kremer, U. (1992), 'Industriepolitik im Vormarsch? – Eine Zusammenstellung zur aktuellen industriepolitischen Debatte', *WSI-Mitteilungen, 45* (5), pp. 274–83

Krieger-Boden, C. (1987), 'Zur Regionalpolitik der Europäischen Gemeinschaft', *Die Weltwirtschaft, 1*, pp. 82–96

Kroll, H. (1991), *Strategie und Verlauf der Privatisierung in den neuen Bundesländern*, Institut für Angewandte Wirtschaftsforschung e.V., Berlin

Kronberger Kreis (1993), *Privatisierung auch im Westen*, Frankfurter Institut für wirtschaftspolitische Forschung e.V., Bad Homburg

Krueger, A. and Pischke, J-S. (1992), 'A Comparative Analysis of East and West German Labor Markets: Before and After Unification', *Working Paper*, No. 4154, National Bureau of Economic Research, Cambridge, Mass.

Krug, W. and Ott, A. (1990), 'Personelle Auswirkungen der Bevölkerungsentwicklung auf die Alterssicherung', in Felderer, B. (ed.), *Bevölkerung und Wirtschaft, Schriften des Vereins für Socialpolitik, Gesellschaft für Wirtschafts-*

und Sozialwissenschaften, 202, Duncker and Humblot, Berlin

Krugman, P.R. and Obstfeld, M. (1991), *International Economics: Theory and Policy*, Second Edition, Harper Collins, Glenview

Krupp, H.-J. (1991), 'Den neuen Ländern müssen schnell geholfen werden', *Wirtschaftsdienst*, *II*, pp. 63–8

KrV (1992a), 'Notizen aus Bonn', *Die Krankenversicherung*, 44 (6), pp. 153–4

—— (1992b), 'Eckpunkte der Bundesregierung zum Gesundheitsstrukturgesetz 1993', *Die Krankenversicherung*, 44 (7), pp. 195–6

Küchle, H. and Müller, G. (1990), 'Währungsunion zwischen BRD und DDR – Chancen und Risiken für beide', *WSI Mitteilungen, 42* (5), pp. 256–81

Kudo, A. (1992), 'The United Germany and the Future of German Firms: a Japanese View', in Sung-Jo, P. (ed.), *Managerial Efficiency in Competition and Cooperation*, Campus, Frankfurt/New York

Kühl, J. (1987), 'Labour Policy in the Federal Republic of Germany: Challenges and Concepts', *Review of Labour Economics and Industrial Relations, 1* (3), pp. 25–56

Kühlewind, G. (1974), 'The Employment of Foreign Workers in the Federal Republic of Germany and their Family and Living Conditions', *The German Economic Review, 12* (4), pp. 356–64

Külp, B. *et al.* (1972), *Der Einfluß von Schlichtungsformen auf Verlauf und Ergebnis von Tarif- und Schlichtungsverhandlungen*, Duncker und Humblot, Berlin

Külp, B., Knappe, E., Roppel, U. and Wolters, R. (1984), *Wohlfahrtsökonomik I. Die Wohlfahrtskriterien*, Werner Verlag, Düsseldorf

Labour and Social Affairs, *Reports* (various), FRG Embassy, London

Lambsdorff, O. von (1980), 'Goals for the 1980s – Competition, Price Stability and Adjustment', *World Economy, 2* (4), pp. 415–25

Lammers, K. (1989), 'Regionalförderung und Schiffsbausubventionen in der Bundesrepublik', *Kieler Studien* No. 224, Kiel

Lampert, H. (1985), *Lehrbuch der Sozialpolitik*, Springer-Verlag, Berlin

Lampert, H. and Bossert, A. (1992), *Sozialstaat Deutschland: Entwicklung-Gestalt-Probleme*, Verlag Franz Vahlen, München

Landeszentrale für Politische Bildung (1984), 'Abbau der Arbeitslosigkeit durch Verkürzung der Arbeitszeit. Gewerkschaftliche Argumente für die Einführung der 35-Studen-Woche', Nachdrucke 1/1984, Hamburg

Lang, F.P. (1990), 'Can the German "Economic Miracle" be Repeated?', *Intereconomics, 25* (5), pp. 248–52

Lange, C. (1992), '. . . und dann werden auf unseren Stühlen Asiaten sitzen! – Situationsanalyse der deutschen PKW-Industrie', *technologie & management, 41* (2), pp. 22–31

Langer, J. (1974), *Ziele und Auswirkungen der Subventionierung der Werftindustrie in der Bundesrepublik Deutschland*, Veröffentlichungen des HWWA – Institut für Wirtschaftsforschung, Hamburg

Laursen, K. and Pedersen, J. (1984), *The German Inflation 1918–1923*, North-Holland Publishing Company, Amsterdam

Lawrence, P. (1980), *Managers and Management in West Germany*, Croom Helm, London

Legler, H. (1992), 'Europa im Technologie-Wettbewerb: Stärken und Schwächen', *technologie & management, 41* (4), pp. 16–24

Leibfritz, W. (1990), 'Economic Consequences of German Unification', *Business Economics, XXV* (4), pp. 5–9

Leibfritz, W. and Nierhaus, W. (1991), 'Gesamtwirtschaftliche Auswirkungen der Steuererhöhungen', *Ifo-Schnelldienst*, July, pp. 24–6

Leibfritz, W. and Thanner, B. (1990), 'Chancen und Risiken einer Wirtschafts- und Währungsunion zwischen der Bundesrepublik und der DDR', *Ifo-Schnelldienst, 7*, pp. 7–12

Leibfritz, W., Nierhaus, W. and Parsche, R. (1990), 'Probleme des Zusammenwirkens von Sozialsystem und Steuersystem', *Ifo-Schnelldienst, 21*, pp. 9–17

Leienbach, V. (1990), 'Die soziale Dimension des Europäischen Binnenmarktes', *Die Ersatzkasse, 70* (8), pp. 301–24

Leipold, H. (1991), 'Die Politik der Privatisierung und Deregulierung: Leben für die Wirtschaftsreformen im Sozialismus', Forschungsstelle zum Vergleich Wirtschaftlicher Lenkungssysteme, *op. cit.*

Lembruch, G. and Lang, W. (1977), 'Die Konzertierte Aktion', *Der Bürger im Staat, 27* (3), pp. 202–8

Lenel, H.O. (1983), 'A Review of the Third Report of the Monopolies Commission of

West Germany', *The Antitrust Bulletin, 28* (2), pp. 757–81

—— (1989), 'Evolution of the Social Market Economy', in Peacock, A. and Willgerodt, H. (eds) (1989a), *op. cit.*

Leptin, G. and Melzer, M. (1978), *Economic Reform in East German Industry*, OUP, Oxford

Limmer, H. (1966), *Die Deutsche Gewerkschaftsbewegung*, Günter Olzog Verlag, München-Wien

Link, F.L. (1992), 'Westdeutscher Maschinenbau unter Anpassungsdruck', *IW-Trends, 4*, pp. 77–89

Lipschitz, L. and McDonald, D. (eds) (1990), German Unification: Economic Issues, *Occasional Paper No. 75*, International Monetary Fund, Washington DC

Löbbe, K. (1991), 'Standort Deutschland', *Der Bürger im Staat, 41* (3), pp. 53–71

Loesch, A. von (1983), 'Privatisierung öffentlicher Unternehmen: Ein Überblick über die Argumente', *Schriftenreihe der Gesellschaft für öffentliche Wirtschaft und Gemeinwirtschaft, 23*

—— (1988), 'Privatisierungen und Privatisierungsdiskussion in der Bundesrepublik Deutschland', *Annals of Public and Co-operative Economy, 59* (1), pp. 67–83

Lösch, D. (1990) , 'The Post-War Transformation of West Germany's Economy: A Model for the GDR?', *Intereconomics, 25* (2), pp. 88–96

Lowe, P. (1990), 'Some British Views of the West German Social Market Economy and its Influence on British Economic Thought and Policy', in Spahn, H.P. (ed.), *op. cit.*

Lumley, R. (1992), 'Business Education and employment relations: the case of Germany', *Industrial Relations Journal, 23* (4), pp. 284–92

Lydall, H. (1968), *The Structure of Earnings*, OUP, Oxford

McKinnon, R.I. (1979), *Money in International Exchange*, Oxford U.P.

McPherson, W.H. (1951), 'Co-determination: Germany's Move Toward a New Economy', *Industrial and Labor Relations Review, 5* (1), pp. 20–32

—— (1971), *Public Employee Relations in West Germany*, Institute of Labor Relations, University of Michigan Press, Ann Arbor

McWilliams, D. (1991), 'Is Short-Termism Holding Back the Anglo-Saxon Economies?', *Siemens Review, 3/91*, pp. 34–7

Mäding, H. (1989), 'Federalism and Education Planning in the Federal Republic of Germany', *The Journal of Federalism, 19*, pp. 115–31

Mahnkopf, B. (1992), 'The 'Skill-Oriented' Strategies of German Trade Unions: Their Impact on Efficiency and Equality Objectives', *British Journal of Industrial Relations, 30* (1), pp. 61–82

Maldonado, Rita M. (1976), 'Why Puerto Ricans Migrated to the United States', *Monthly Labor Review, 99* (9), pp. 7–18

—— (1977), 'Analyzing Puerto Rican Migration – A Reply', *Monthly Labor Review, 100* (8), pp. 34–5

Manchester, W. (1969), *The Arms of Krupp*, Michael Joseph, London

Mann, G. (1974), *The History of Germany Since 1789*, Pelican Books, Harmondsworth

Marburg, T.F. (1964), 'Government and Business in Germany: Public Policy Toward Cartels', *Business History Review, 38* (1), pp. 78–101

Marburger, H. (1990), 'Sozialversicherungsgesetz der DDR', *Wege zur Sozialversicherung, 44* (7/8), pp. 193–208

Marfels, C. (1984), 'Fortschritte bei der Konzentrationserfassung (Progress in Concentration Measurement)', *The Antitrust Bulletin, 29* (2), pp. 607–11

—— (1986), 'Economic Criteria for the Application of Antitrust – Overview and Assessment of the Fifth Report of the Monopolies Commission of the Federal Republic of Germany', *The Antitrust Bulletin, 31* (4), pp. 1067–87

Markert, K. (1981), 'Merger Control in Western Europe: National and International Aspects', in Schachter, O. and Fellawell, R. (eds), *Competition in International Business*, Columbia UP, New York

Markmann, H. (1964), 'Incomes Policy in Germany: A Trade Union View', *British Journal of Industrial Relations, 2* (3), pp. 322–39

Marsden, D. (1981), 'Vive la différence: Pay Differentials in Britain, West Germany, France and Italy', *Employment Gazette*, Department of Employment, HMSO, London, *89* (7), pp. 309–18

Marsh, D. (1992), *The Bundesbank: the Bank that Rules Europe*, Heinemann, London

Marshall, A. (1932), *Industry and Trade*, Third Edition (reprint), Macmillan, London

Martin, P.L. (1981), 'Germany's Guestworkers', *Challenge*, pp. 34–42

Martin, P.L. and Miller, M.J. (1980), 'Guestworkers: Lessons from Western Europe', *Industrial and Labor Relations Review, 33* (3), pp. 315–30

Masur, G. (1971), *Imperial Berlin*, Routledge and Kegan Paul, London

Maurer, R., Sander, S. and Schmidt, K.-D. (1991), 'Privatisierung in Ostdeutschland', *Die Weltwirtschaft, 1*, pp. 45–66

Maydell, B. von (1990), 'Die Rentenversicherung auf dem Wege zur deutschen Einheit', *Deutsche Rentenversicherung, 7*, pp. 387–96

—— (1992), 'Gesundheitsstrukturgesetz 1993 – Auswirkungen auf die Selbstverwaltung im Gesundheitswesen', *Die Sozialversicherung, 47* (9), pp. 242–7

Mayer, G. (1984), 'Arbeitskampf um die 35-Stunden-Woche', *Marxistische Blätter, 5*, pp. 76–86

Mayer, T. (1988), 'Economic Structure, the Exchange Rate and Adjustment in the Federal Republic of Germany: A General Equilibrium Approach', *IMF Working Paper*, WP/88/79, IMF European Department, 1 September

Mayhew, A. (1969), 'Regional Planning and the Development Areas in West Germany', *Regional Studies, 13*, pp. 73–9

MBR (Midland Bank Review) (1975), 'The German Inflation of 1923', November, pp. 20–9

Medley, R. (1981), 'Monetary Stability and Industrial Adaptation in West Germany' in *Monetary Policy, Selective Credit Policy, and Industrial Policy in France, Britain, West Germany and Sweden*, a Staff Study prepared for Joint Economic Committee, Congress of USA, Washington DC

Mellor, R.E.H. (1978), *The Two Germanies* (a modern geography), Harper and Row, London and New York

Mendershausen, H. (1974), *Two Postwar Recoveries of the German Economy*, reprinted by Greenwood Press, Westport, Connecticut

Ménil, de G. and Westphal, U. (eds) (1985), *Stabilization Policy in France and the Federal Republic of Germany*, North-Holland, Amsterdam, New York, Oxford

Mestmäcker, E-J. (1980), 'Competition Policy and Antitrust: Some Comparative Observations', *Journal of Institutional and Theoretical Economics (Zeitschrift für die gesamte Staatswissenschaft), 136* (3), pp. 387–407

Methner, C. (1991), 'Finanzausgleich auf Landesverbandsebene bei überdurchschittlichen Bedarfssätzen', *Wege zur Sozialversicherung, 45* (2), pp. 33–40

Meyer, S.A. (1992), 'Saving and Demographics: Some International Comparisons', *Federal Reserve Bank of Philadelphia*, No. 2, pp.13–23

Michaelis, J. (1991), 'DM – Exchange Rate Policymaking', *Discussion Paper No. 14/91*, Institut für Finanzwissenschaft der Albert-Ludwigs-Universität Freiburg im Breisgau, Freiburg

Michie, J. (1992), *The Economic Legacy*, Academic Press Ltd., London

Mierheim, H. und Wicke, L. (1978), *Die personelle Vermögensverteilung in der BRD*, JCB Mohr, Tübingen

Milbradt, G.H. (1991), 'Finanzierung der ostdeutschen Länder', *Wirtschaftsdienst, 71* (11), pp. 59–68

Miller, D. (1978), 'Trade Union Workplace Representation in the Federal Republic of Germany', *British Journal of Industrial Relations, XVI* (3), pp. 335–54

Miller, M. (1989), 'Die Sozial Marktwirtschaft-Modell für den Gemeinsamen Markt oder Standortnachteil für die deutsche Wirtschaft?', *Arbeit und Sozialpolitik, 43* (8/9), pp. 218–26

Milner, C. and Pentecost, E. (1993), *Locational Advantage and US Foreign Direct Investment in UK Manufacturing*, Conference Paper, Department of Economics, Loughborough University, mimeo.

Milward, A.S. (1965), *The German Economy at War*, Athlone Press, University of London

Ministerium für Medienpolitik/Presse- und Informationsamt der Bundesregierung (1990), *Der Staatsvertrag*, Berlin/Bonn

Ministry of Labour and Social Affairs (1980), *Co-determination in the Federal Republic of Germany*, Bonn

Minshull, G.N. (1990), *The New Europe, into the 1990s*, Fourth Edition, Hodder and Stoughton, London

Mittelstaedt, A. (1991), 'Comparative Advertising in German Law', *European Intellectual Property Review, 13* (3), pp. 75–7

MKI (Monopolkommission) (1977), *Mehr Wettbewerb ist möglich*, Hauptgutachten I, 2. Auflage, Nomos Verlag, Baden-Baden (see also Documentation (1977) *op. cit.*)

MKII (Monopolkommission) (1978), *Fort-*

schreitende Konzentration bei Großunter-
nehmen, Hauptgutachten II, Nomos Verlag,
Baden-Baden

MKIII (Monopolkommission) (1980), Fusionskontrolle bleibt vorrangig, Hauptgutachten
III, Nomos Verlag, Baden-Baden (see also
Cable, J.R. (1981) op. cit. and Lenel, H.O.
(1983) op. cit.)

MKIV (Monopolkommission) (1982), Fort-
schritte bei der Konzentrationserfassung,
Hauptgutachten IV, Nomos Verlag, Baden-
Baden (see also Marfels, C. (1984) op. cit.)

MKV (Monopolkommission) (1984), Ökon-
omische Kriterien für die Rechtsanwendung,
Hauptgutachten V, Nomos Verlag, Baden-
Baden (see also Marfels, C. (1986) op. cit.)

MKVI (Monopolkommission) (1986), Gesamtwirtschaftliche Chancen und Risiken
wachsender Unternehmensgrößen, Hauptgutachten VI, Nomos Verlag, Baden-Baden
(includes an English summary)

MKVII (Monopolkommission) (1988), Die
Wettbewerbsordnung erweitern, Hauptgutachten VII, Nomos Verlag, Baden-Baden
(includes an English summary)

MKVIII (Monopolkommission) (1990), Wettbewerbspolitik vor neuen Herausforderungen, Hauptgutachten VIII, Nomos,
Baden-Baden (includes an English summary)

MKIX (Monopolkommission) (1992), Wettbewerbspolitik oder Industriepolitik, Nomos
Verlagsgesellschaft, Baden-Baden (includes
an English summary)

Molitor, B. (1992), Wirtschaftspolitik, Fourth
Edition, Oldenburg, München

Molle, W. (1990), The Economics of European
Integration, Dartmouth Publishing, Aldershot

Morris, M. (1976), The General Strike,
Penguin Books, Harmondsworth

Möschel, W. (1987), 'Use of Economic
Evidence in Antitrust Litigation in the
Federal Republic of Germany', The
Antitrust Bulletin, XXXII (2), pp. 523–50

—— (1989), 'Competition Policy from an
Ordo Point of View', in Peacock, A. and
Willgerodt, H. (eds) (1989a), op. cit.

MRDB (Monthly Report of the Deutsche
Bundesbank) (various), Frankfurt a.M.
(There are five statistical supplements (Beihefte) to the Report which are occasionally
accompanied by Annexes (Beilage).)

Muellbauer, J. (1992), 'Anglo-German
Differences in Housing Market Dynamics',

European Economic Review, 36 (2/3), pp.
539–48

Mueller, R., Heidenhain, M. and Schneider, H.
(1981), Das Recht gegen Wettbewerbs-
beschränkungen/German Antitrust Law,
Second Edition, Fritz Knapp Verlag, Frankfurt a.M. (The most recent edition has been
written by only two of these authors – see
Heidenhain, M. above.)

Mueller, R., Steifel, E. and Brücher, H. (for the
Dresdner Bank), (1978), Doing Business in
Germany: A legal Manual, Eighth Edition,
Fritz Knapp Verlag, Frankfurt a.M.,

Mühlenkamp, H. (1991), Die Ausgaben in der
Gesetzlichen Krankenversicherung, Duncker
and Humblot, Berlin

Müller, K., 'Geld- und währungspolitische
Aspekte der Wirtschaftsreform', Wirtschaftsdienst, II, pp. 78–84

Müller, L. (1992), 'Demographic Development
and its Impact on Taxation', Deutsche
Bundesbank: Auszüge aus Presseartikeln,
No. 59, pp. 4–5

Müller-Armack, A. (1978), 'The Social Market
Economy as an Economic and Social Order',
Review of Social Economy, 36 (5), pp.
325–31

Müller-Jentsch, W. (1986), Soziologie der
industriellen Beziehungen, Campus, Frankfurt a.M.

Müller-Merbach, H. (1992), 'Die fünf großen
industriellen Wirtschaftszweige im Vergleich', technologie & management, 40 (1),
pp. 26–34

Münch, J. (1991), Vocational Training in the
Federal Republic of Germany, Third
Edition, CEDEFOP – European Centre for
the Development of Vocational Training,
Berlin

Muir, R. (1935), A Brief History of Our Own
Times, Second Edition, George Philip and
Son, London

Mukherjee, S. (1976), Governments and
Labour Markets, Political and Economic
Planning, London

Murswieck, A. (1990), 'Politische Steuerung
des Gesundheitswesens' in Beyme, K. von
and Schmidt, M.G. (eds), Politik in der
Bundesrepublik Deutschland, Westdeutscher
Verlag, Opladen

Mussel, G. (1992), 'Wirtschaftsstandort
Deutschland', Fortbildung, 37 (4), pp. 101–6

Naujoks, P., Sander, B. and Schmidt,
K.-D. (1992), 'Von der Privatisierung
zur Sanierung – Kursänderung bei der

Treuhandanstalt', *Die Weltwirtschaft*, Heft (4), pp. 425–51

Neal, A. (1987), 'Co-determination in the Federal Republic of Germany: An External Perspective from the United Kingdom', *British Journal of Industrial Relations*, 25 (2), pp. 227–45

NEDO (National Economic Development Office) (1980), *Iron and Steel SWP : Progress Report 1980*, London

—— (1981a), *Toolmaking: A Comparison of UK and West German Companies*, London

—— (1981b), *British Industrial Performance*, London

Neifer-Dichmann, E. (1991), 'Working Time Reductions in the Former Federal Republic of Germany: a dead end for employment policy', *International Labour Review*, 130 (4), pp. 511–22

Nell-Breuning, O. (1962), 'Subsidiaritätsprinzip', in *Staatslexikon*, 7, Sixth Edition, Herder Verlag, Freiburg/Basel/Wien

Neu, A.D. (1990), 'Zum Strukturellen Wandel des Energiesektors in der DDR', *Institut für Weltwirtschaft*, 2, pp. 111–37

Neubauer, R. (1988), 'Wettbewerbspolitik: Deutscher Elefant und Europäisches Mäuschen', in Biskup, R. (ed.), *Europa – Einheit in der Vielfalt*, Paul Haupt, Berlin

Neuberger, D. and Neumann, M. (1991), 'Banking and Antitrust: Limiting Industrial Ownership by Banks?', *Journal of Institutional and Theoretical Economics (Zeitschrift für die gesamte Staatswissenschaft)*, 147 (1), pp. 188–99

Neuman, K.-H. (1986), 'Economic Policy towards Telecommunications Information and the Media in West Germany', in Snow, M. (ed.), *Marketplace for Telecommunications: Regulation and Deregulation in Industrialised Democracies*, Longman, New York

Neumann, F. (1990), 'Industrie verstärkt Engagement in Ostdeutschland', *Ifo-Schnelldienst*, 34, pp. 8–10

—— (1991), 'Bestandsaufnahme und Perspektiven der Direktinvestionen in Ostdeutschland', *Ifo-Schnelldienst*, 3, pp. 7–11

Neumann, M.J.M. (1991), 'German Unification: Economic Problems and Consequences', *Discussion Paper* No. 584, Centre for Economic Policy Research, London

Neumann, M.J.M., Schmidt, R. and Schulte, E. (1990), 'Determinants of Contract Wages in Germany', *European Economic Review*, 34 (6), pp. 1233–45

Neumann, M. (1990), 'Deutscher Kapitalexport – eine Bremse für den Abbau der Arbeitslosigkeit?', *Volkswirtschaftliche Korrespondenz der Adolf-Weber-Stiftung*, 29 (4)

Neumann, M., Böbel, I. and Haid, A. (1980), 'Marktmacht, Gewerkschaften und Lohnhöhe in der Industrie der Bundesrepublik Deutschland', *Kyklos*, 33 (2), pp. 230–45

Neuthinger, E. (1989), 'Germany's Enduring Current Account Surplus', *Intereconomics*, 24 (3), pp. 138–48

Newton, K. (1980), *Balancing the Books*, Sage Publications, London

Nicolaides, P. (1992), 'Industrial Policy in an Interdependent World – Promoting National Markets or Global Firms', *Intereconomics*, 27 (6), pp. 269–73

Nicolaides, P. and Thomson, S. (1992), 'The Impact of 1992 on Direct Investment in Europe', *European Business Journal*, 1, pp. 8–16

Niedenhoff, H.-U. (1979), *Praxis der betrieblichen Mitbestimmung*, Deutscher Instituts-Verlag, Köln

Nierhaus, W. (1990), 'DDR: Kaufkrafteffekte durch Währungunion?', *Ifo-Schnelldienst*, 13, pp. 24–6

Nierhaus, W. (1990), 'DDR: Währungunion bringt Kaufkraftplus', *Ifo-Schnelldienst*, 25, pp. 9–11

Nikolinakos, M. (1973), *Politische Ökonomie der Gastarbeiterfrage*, Rowohlt Taschenbuch Verlag, Reinbek bei Hamburg

ndc (Noyes Data Corporation) (1973), *European Stock Exchange Handbook*, New Jersey and London

Nunnenkamp, P. (1992), 'Die wirtschaftlichen Herausforderungen der Umwandlung der ostdeutschen Wirtschaft', *Zeitschrift für Wirtschaftspolitik*, 41 (1), pp. 51–70

Nutzinger, H.G. and Backhaus, J. (eds) (1989), *Codetermination: A Discussion of Different Approaches*, Springer-Verlag, Berlin

Oberhauser, A. (1975), 'Death Duties and Property Taxation as a Means of a More Even Distribution of the Stock of Wealth', *The German Economic Review*, 13 (1), pp. 1–15

—— (1991), 'International Capital Movements and Distribution of Income', in Dams, T. and Matsugi, T. (eds), *Protectionism or Liberalism in International Economic*

Relations?: Current Issues in Japan and Germany, Duncker and Humblot, Berlin

Oberhauser, A. and Joß, S. (1988), 'Employment Policy by Shortening Working Hours', in Dams, T. and Mizuno, M., *Employment Problems under the Conditions of Rapid Technological Change*, Duncker and Humblot, Berlin

Obst/Hintner – Kloten, N. and Stein, J.H. von (eds) (1991), *Geld- Bank- und Börsenwesen*, Thirty-Eighth Edition, Verlag C.E. Poeschel, Stuttgart

Obstfeld, M. (1982), 'Can We Sterilize? Theory and Evidence', *American Economic Review, 72* (Papers and Proceedings), pp. 45–55

—— (1983), 'Exchange Rates, Inflation, and the Sterilization Problem: Germany 1975–1981', *European Economic Review, 21* (1/2), pp. 161–202

OECD (Organisation for Economic Cooperation and Development), *Economic Outlook* (various), bi-annual, Paris

—— *Economic Surveys* (Germany) (various), annually, Paris

—— *National Accounts* (Volume II): detailed tables (various)

—— (1972), *Reviews of National Policies for Education (Germany)*, Paris. (A classification of educational systems, including Germany, was published by OECD in the same year.)

—— (1979), *Unemployment Compensation and Related Employment Policy Measures*, Paris

—— (1981a), *Guide to Legislation on Restrictive Business Practices*, Seventh Supplement to Fourth Edition, Vol.1 (Germany), Paris

—— (1981b), *Income Tax Schedules: distribution of taxpayers and revenues*, Paris

OEEC (Organisation for European Economic Cooperation) (1960), *Industrial Statistics 1900–1959*, Paris

Ogger, G. (1992), *Nieten in Nadelstreifen: Deutschlands Manager in Zwielicht*, Droemer Knaur, München

Ohr, R. (1992), 'Außenwirtschaftliche Konsequenzen der Wiedervereinigung', in Rühl, C. (ed.), *Konsolidierung des Binnenmarktes in den neuen Ländern – Strukturpolitik und westeuropäische Integration (Die ökonomische und institutionelle Integration der neuen Länder 2)*, Metropolis Verlag, Marburg

O'Mahony, M. (1992), 'Productivity Levels in British and German Manufacturing Industry', *National Institute Economic Review*, 1/92, pp. 46–64

Opie, R. (1962), 'West Germany's Economic Miracle', *Three Banks Review*, March

Oppenheimer, J. and Bödecker, D. (1992), 'Long-Term Trends in West German Trade, Direct Investment and Aid, An Inquiry into Third-World Diversification and African Marginalisation', *Journal of World Trade, 26* (2), pp. 43–62

Oppenländer, K.-H. and Gerstenberger, W. (1992), 'Direktinvestitionen als Ausdruck zunehmender Internationalisierung der Märkte', *Ifo-Schnelldienst, 10*, pp. 3–11

Oßenbrügge, J. (1991), 'Impacts of Environmental Protection on Regional Restructuring in Northern Germany', in Wild, T. and Jones, P. (eds), *op. cit.*

Ott, A.E. (1978), 'Arbeitszeitverkürzung als Mittel zur Bekämpfung der Arbeitslosigkeit?', *Der Bürger im Staat, 28* (3), pp. 218–21

Ott, N. *et al.* (1991), 'Demographic Changes and their Implications on some aspects of Social Security in the Unified Germany', IIASA, Laxenburg, Austria, mimeo. (CP-91-002)

Oudenhoven, J.P. van (1989), 'Privatization in Europe', in Finley, L.K. (ed.), *op. cit.*

Oursin, T. (1956), *Das staatliche Schlichtungswesen in Deutschland. Entwicklung und Bedeutung in den Jahren 1923–1933*, unpublished PhD Thesis, Nürnberg

Owen, R. and Dynes, M. (1992), *The Times Guide to the Single European Market*, Times Books, London

Owen Smith, E. (1979), 'The Federal Republic of Germany', in Maunder, P. (ed.), *Government Intervention in the Developed Economy*, Croom Helm, London

—— (ed.) (1981), *Trade Unions in the Developed Economies*, Croom Helm, London

—— (1983), *The West German Economy*, Croom Helm, Beckenham, Kent

—— (1989a), 'A Survey of Economic Policy', in Koch, K. (ed.), *West Germany Today*, Routledge, London

—— (1989b), 'Federal Republic of Germany' in *Western Europe 1989*, Europa Press

—— (1991), 'Banks' Equity Stakes', *Banking World*, June

—— (1993), 'Federal Republic of Germany' in *Western Europe 1993*, Europa Press

Owen Smith, E. *et al.* (1988), 'Public Sector Pay Determination in the Federal Republic of Germany and the UK', *Management Research News, 11* (3), pp. 21–30

Owen Smith, E., Frick, B. and Griffiths, T. (1989), *Third Party Involvement in Industrial Disputes: A Comparative Study of West Germany and Britain*, Avebury Press, Aldershot

Paine, S.H. (1977), 'The Changing Role of Migrant Workers in the Advanced Capitalist Economies of Western Europe', in Griffiths, R.T. (ed.), *Government, Business and Labour in European Capitalism*, Europotentials Press, London

Panic, M. (ed.) (1976), *The UK and West German Manufacturing Industry 1954–72*, NEDO Monograph 5, National Economic Development Office, London

Papagmi, E. (1992), 'High-Technology Exports of EEC Countries: Persistence and Diversity of Specialization Patterns', *Applied Economics, 24* (8), pp. 925–33

Paprotzki, M. (1991), *Die geldpolitschen Konzeptionen der Bank von England und der Deutschen Bundesbank*, Peter Lang, Frankfurt a.M.

Paqué, K.-H. and Soltwedel, R. (1993), 'Challenges Ahead. Long-term Perspectives of the German Economy', *Kiel Discussion Papers*, 202/203, IfW Kiel

Park, Y.S. (1974), *The Euro-bond Market: Function and Structure*, Praeger, New York

Patel, P. and Pavitt, K. (1989), 'A Comparison of Technological Activities in West Germany and the United Kingdom', National Westminster Bank *Quarterly Review*, May, pp. 27–42

Peacock, A. (in collaboration with R. Grant, M. Ricketts, G.K. Shaw and E. Wagner) (1980), *Structural Economic Policies in West Germany and the United Kingdom*, Anglo-German Foundation for the Study of Industrial Society, London

Peacock, A. and Willgerodt, H. (eds) (1989a), *German Neo-Liberals and the Social Market Economy*, Macmillan (London) for the Trade Policy Research Centre

—— (1989b), *Germany's Social Market Economy: Origins and Evolution*, Macmillan (London) for the Trade Policy Research Centre

Peffekoven, R. (1987), 'Zur Neuordnung des Länderfinanzausgleichs', *Finanzarchiv, 45*, pp. 180–228

Peltzer, M. (1972), *The German Labour Management Relations Act*, McDonald and Evans, London

Peltzer, M. and Nebendorf, K. (1973), *Banking in Germany*, Fritz Knapp Verlag, Frankfurt a.M.

Pen, J. (1974), *Income Distribution*, Pelican Books, Harmondsworth

Pera, A. (1989), 'Deregulation and Privatization in an Economy-wide Context', *OECD Economic Studies, 12*, pp. 159–204

Perlitz, M. (1993), *Internationales Management*, Gustav Fischer Verlag, Stuttgart and Jena

Pettman, B.O. and Fyfe, J. (eds) (1977), *Youth Unemployment in Great Britain and the Federal Republic of Germany*, MCB Publications, Bradford

Petzina, D. (1977), *Die Deutsche Wirtschaft in der Zwischenkriegszeit*, Franz Steiner, Wiesbaden

Pfaff, A.B., Busch, S. and Rindsfüßer, C. (1992), 'Die Reform der Gesundheitsreform: Auswirkungen auf die Versicherten', *Sozialer Fortschritt, 41* (9), pp. 216–21

Pfeffer, M.J. (1989a), 'Part-time Farming and the Stability of Family Farms in the Federal Republic of Germany', *European Review of Agricultural Economics, 16* (4), pp. 425–44

—— (1989b), 'Structural Dimensions of Farm Crisis in the Federal Republic of Germany', in Goodman, D. and Redclift, M. (eds), *The International Farm Crisis*, Macmillan, London

Phelps Brown, E. (1977), *The Inequality of Pay*, OUP, Oxford

Picot, A. and Kaulmann, T. (1989), 'Comparative Performance of Government-owned and Privately-owned Industrial Corporations – Empirical Results from Six Countries', *Journal of Institutional and Theoretical Economics (Zeitschrift für die gesamte Staatswissenschaft), 145* (2), pp. 298–316

Pilz, F. and Ortwein, H. (1992), *Das vereinte Deutschland: Wirtschaftliche, soziale und finanzielle Folgeprobleme und die Konsequenzen für die Politik*, Gustav Fischer Verlag, Jena and Stuttgart

Pöhl, K.O. (1990), 'Prospects of the European Monetary Union', in *Britain & EMU*, Centre for Economic Performance

Pohl, M. (1986), 'Entstehung und Entwicklung des Universalbankensystems', *Schriftenreihe des Instituts für bankhistorische Forschung*, Fritz Knapp Verlag, Frankfurt a.M.

Pomfret, R. (1991), 'What is the Secret of the EMS's Longevity?', *Journal of Common Market Studies*, 29 (6), pp. 623–33

Ponto, J. (1971), 'Die Macht der Banken', *Schriftenreihe Rechts- und Staatswissenschaftliche Vereinigung Frankfurter Juristische Gesellschaft, 8*

—— (1976), *Die Chance der Freiheit*, Vorlesung vor dem Tabak-Kollegium im Alten Rathaus zu Bremen aus Anlaß des 200-jährigen Bestehens der Vereinigten Staaten von Amerika

Porstmann, R. (1990), 'Economic Problems of Reunification in Germany', *International Journal of Social Economics, 17* (10), pp. 42–7

Porter, M.E. (1990), *The Competitive Advantage of Nations*, The Macmillan Press Ltd, London and Basingstoke

Pounds, N.J.G. (1966), *The Economic Pattern of Modern Germany*, Second Edition, John Murray, London

Power, J. (with A. Hardman) (1976), *Western Europe's Migrant Workers*, Minority Rights Group, London, Report No. 28

Prais, S.J. (1981), 'Vocational Qualifications of the Labour Force in Britain and Germany', *National Institute Economic Review*, Number 98, pp. 47–59

Prais, S.J. and Wagner, K. (1985), 'Schooling Standards in England and Germany: Some Summary Comparisons Bearing on Economic Performance', *National Institute Economic Review, 112*, pp. 53–76

Pratten, C.F. (1976), 'Labour Productivity Differentials within International Companies', *Occasional Papers*, No. 50, Department of Applied Economics, University of Cambridge, Cambridge UP

Preller, L. (1978), *Sozialpolitik in der Weimarer Republik*, Athenam, Düsseldorf

Press and Information Office of the Federal Government (1986), *The Basic Law in the Federal Republic of Germany*

Priewe, J. (1992), 'Probleme der schnellen Privatisierung einer (ehemaligen) Volkswirtschaft. Kritische Überlegungen zur Treuhandanstalt', in Ipsen, D. and Nickel, E. (eds), *op. cit.*

Prittie, T. (1979), *The Velvet Chancellors: A History of Post-War Germany*, Frederick Muller, London

Propp, P.D. (1990), *Zur Transformation einer Zentralverwaltungswirtschaft sowjetischen Typs in eine Marktwirtschaft*, Edition Deutschland Archiv im Verlag Wissenschaft und Politik, Köln

Pünnel, L. (1981), *Die Einigungsstelle des BetrVG 1972*, Luchterhand, Neuwied

Rajewsky, X. (1970), *Arbeitskampfrecht in der Bundesrepublik*, Suhrkamp Verlag, Frankfurt a.M.

Ramm, T. (1971), 'West Germany', in Aaron, B. (ed.), *Labor Courts and Grievance Settlement in Western Europe*, California UP

Ramser, H.J. and Riese, H. (eds) (1989), *Beiträge zur angewandten Wirtschaftsforschung*, Springer-Verlag, Berlin

Ray, G.F. (1966), 'The Size of Plant: A Comparison', *National Institute Economic Review*, No. 38, pp. 63–6

—— (1972), 'Labour Costs and International Competitiveness', *National Institute Economic Review*, No. 61, August, pp. 53–8

Reichel, H. (1971), 'Recent Trends in Collective Bargaining in the Federal Republic of Germany', *International Labour Review, 104* (6), pp. 469–87

Reichert, H. (1991), 'Geldvermögenspolitik in neuer Bewährungsprobe', *Wirtschaftsdienst, 71* (1), pp. 40–3

Reuss, F.G. (1963), *Fiscal Policy for Growth without Inflation*, John Hopkins Press, Baltimore, Maryland

Richter, A. (1990), 'Europäische Notenbank: Eine Krone für den Binnenmarkt', in Vorkötter, U. (ed.), *Aufbruch nach Europa*, Stuttgarter Zeitung, Stuttgart

Riedmüller, B. and Rodenstein, M. (eds) (1989), *Wie sicher ist die soziale Sicherung?*, Suhrkamp, Frankfurt a.M.

Riemer, J.M. (1983), *Crisis and Intervention in the West German Economy: A Political Analysis of Changes in the Policy Machinery During the 1960s and 1970s*, PhD Thesis, Cornell University, University Microfilms International, Ann Arbor, Michigan

—— (1985), 'West German Crisis Management: Stability and Change in the Post-Keynesian Age', in Vig, N.J. and Schier, S.E., *Political Economy in Western*

Democracies, Holmes and Meier, New York, London

Riese, H. (1987), 'Strategien der Wirtschaftspolitik: Wohlfahrtsimport versus Wachstumsimport', *Vierteljahresheft zur Wirtschaftsforschung*, No. 3, Duncker and Humblot, Berlin

Riha, T. (1985), 'German Political Economy: The History of an Alternative Economics', *International Journal of Social Economics, 12* (3/4/5), pp. 10–231

Ritter, G.A. (1986), *Social Welfare in Germany and Britain*, Berg Publishers, Warwickshire

Roberts, I.L. (1973), 'The Works Constitution Acts and Industrial Relations in West Germany: Implications for the United Kingdom', *British Journal of Industrial Relations, XI* (3), pp. 338–67

Robinson, A. (1991), 'Financing Europe's Regions in the 1990s', *European Trends* Economist Intelligence Unit, No. 1, pp. 66–70

Röhling, E. and Molnfeld, J. (1985), 'Energy Policy and the Energy Economy in FR Germany: An Overview', *Energy Policy, 13* (6), pp. 535–45

Roll, E. (1939), 'Germany', in Marquand, H. (ed.), *Organised Labour in Four Continents*, Longmans Green, London

Rommelspacher, P. (1978), *Schlichtung und Tarifautonomie*, unpublished PhD Thesis, Köln

Roppel, U. (1988), 'Die Auswirkungen auf das System sozialer Sicherung', in Wehling, H-G. (ed.), *Bevölkerungsentwicklung und Bevölkerungspolitik in der Bundesrepublik*, W. Kohlhammer, Stuttgart, Berlin, Köln, Mainz

— (1990), 'Gesamtwirtschaftliche Größenordnung und Entwicklungsperspektiven des Wohlstandsgefälles zwischen Ost- und Westdeutschland', *Arbeit und Sozialpolitik, 44* (11/12), pp. 378–88

Rose, R. (1989), 'Privatization: A Question of Quantities and Qualities', in Fels, G. and von Furstenberg, G.M., *op. cit.*

Rosen, H.S. and Windisch, R. (1992), *Finanzwissenschaft I*, R. Oldenbourg Verlag, Munich, Vienna

Rosenschon, A. (1990), 'Zum System der sozialen Sicherheit in der DDR', *Die Weltwirtschaft*, 1, pp. 91–100

Ross, A.M. (1962), 'Prosperity and Labor Relations in Europe: the case of West Germany', *The Quarterly Journal of Economics, 76* (3), pp. 331–59

Rosset, R. (1952), *Die staatsrechtlichen Grundlagen des Schlichtungswesens*, unpublished PhD Thesis, Freiburg

Roth, W-H. (1991), 'The Application of Community Law in West Germany: 1980–1990', *Common Market Law Review, 28* (1), pp. 137–82

Rowley, A. (1974), *The Barons of European Industry*, Croom Helm, London

Rudolph, H., Appelbaum, E. and Maier, F. (1990), 'After German Unity: A Cloudier Outlook for Women', *Challenge*, November–December, pp. 33–40

Russig, V. (1990), 'Regionale Unterschiede in der Bautätigkeit', *Ifo-Schnelldienst, 31*, pp. 3–10

Rutherford, M. (1974), 'West Germany: People Before Profits', in Rowley, A. (ed.), *op. cit.*

RWI, *Mitteilungen* (various)

Rybczynski, T.M. (1993), 'International Perspective: Structural Changes and the Integration of Europe', *Business Economics, 28* (1), pp. 25–30

Sadowski, D. (1981), 'Finance and Governance of the German Apprenticeship System', *Journal of Institutional and Theoretical Economics (Zeitschrift für die gesamte Staatswissenschaft), 137* (2), pp. 234–51

Sadowski, D., Frick, B. and Stengelhofen, T. (1988), 'Wer beschäftigt Schwerbehinderte?', *Zeitschrift für Betriebswirtschaft, 58* (1), pp. 37–49

Sadowski, D. and Frick, B. (1992), *Die Beschäftigung Schwerbehinderter*, Schultz-Kirchner Verlag, Idstein

Sauer, W. (1978/9), 'The Contribution of Small Units of Enterprise to the German Economic Miracle', *Occasional Papers*, Siena Series No. 13, Acton Society Trust

Sauernheimer, K. (1990), 'Die Standortqualität der Bundesrepublik Deutschland', *Fortbildung, 35* (1), pp. 3–5

Saunders, C. (1978), 'Engineering in Britain, West Germany and France: Some Statistical Comparisons of Structure and Competitiveness', *Sussex European Papers*, No. 3, Sussex European Research Centre, University of Sussex

Saunders, C. and Marsden, D. (1981), *Pay Inequalities in the European Communities*, Butterworths, London

Schackmann-Fallis, K.-P. (1989), 'External

Control and Regional Development within the Federal Republic of Germany', *International Regional Science Review, 12* (3), pp. 245–61

Scherf, W. and Oberhauser, A. (1990), 'Interactions Between the External Economy and the Fiscal and Monetary Policy of the Federal Republic of Germany, in View of Stabilisation Policy', in Dams, T. and Matsugi, T. (eds), *Adjustment Problems in Advanced Open Economies: Japan and Germany*, Duncker and Humblot, Berlin

Schiller, G. (1975), 'Channelling Migration: A Review of Policy with Special Reference to the Federal Republic of Germany', *International Labour Review, 111* (4), pp. 335–55

Schinasi, G.J. (1989), 'European Integration, Exchange Rates and Monetary Reform', *The World Economy, 12* (4), pp. 389–414

Schlesinger, H. (1991), 'The Road to European Economic and Monetary Union', *Intereconomics, 26* (4), pp. 151–8

Schmähl, W. (1990), 'Alterssicherung im sich vereinigenden Deutschland', *Wirtschaftsdienst, 70* (4), pp. 182–7

— (1992), 'Transformation and Integration of Public Pension Schemes – Lessons from the Process of the German Unification', *Public Finance, 47* (Supplement), pp. 34–58

Schmid, G. and Peters, A.B. (1982), 'The German Federal Employment Program for Regions with Special Employment Problems: An Evaluation', *Regional Studies and Urban Economics, 12* (1), pp. 99–119

Schmid-Schönbein, T. and Hansel, F.-C. (1991), 'Die Transformationspolitik der Treuhandanstalt', *Wirtschaftsdienst, 71* (9), pp. 462–9

Schmidt, M.G. (1990a), 'Staatsfinanzen' in Beyme, K. von and Schmidt, M.G. (eds), *Politik in der Bundesrepublik Deutschland*, Westdeutscher Verlag, Oplade

— (1990b), 'Sozialpolitik', in Beyme, K. von and Schmidt, M.G. (eds), *Politik in der Bundesrepublik Deutschland*, Westdeutscher Verlag, Opladen

Schmieding, H. (1990), 'Der Übergang zur Marktwirtschaft: Gemeinsamkeiten und Unterschiede zwischen Westdeutschland 1948 und Mittel- und Osteuropa heute', *Die Weltwirtschaft, 1*, pp. 149–61

— (1992), 'Alternative Approaches to Privatization: Some Notes on the Debate', in Siebert, H. (ed.), *op. cit.*

Schnabel, C. (1989), 'Determinants of Trade Union Growth and Decline in the Federal Republic of Germany', *European Sociological Review, 5* (2), pp. 133–46

— (1991), 'Trade Unions and Productivity: the German Evidence', *British Journal of Industrial Relations, 29* (1), pp. 15–24

— (1992), 'Structural Adjustment and Privatization of the East German Economy', in Welfens, P.J. (ed.), *op. cit.*

Schneider, H. (1990), 'Die Sozialversicherung in der DDR ab 1. Juli 1990', *Betriebs-Berater, 45* (21), pp. 30–2

— (1992), 'Entgeltgrenzen in der Sozialversicherung für das Jahr 1993 für die alten und die neuen Bundesländer', *Die Sozialversicherung, 47* (12), pp. 324–32

Schneider, H., Hellwig, H-J. and Kingsman, D.J. (1978), *Das Bankwesen in Deutschland/ The German Banking System*, Fritz Knapp Verlag, Frankfurt a.M.

Schneider-Lenné, E.R. (1992), 'Corporate Control in Germany', *Oxford Review of Economic Policy, 8* (3), pp. 11–23

— (1993), 'The Germany Case', in G. Bognetti (ed.), 'What Bank Model for Europe?', *Annals of Public and Cooperative Economics, 64* (1), pp. 63–70

Schneider, M. (1989), *Kleine Geschichte der Gewerkschaften: Ihre Entwicklung in Deutschland von den Anfängen bis heute*, Verlag, J.H.W. Dietz Nachf., Bonn

Schnitzer, M. (1972), *East and West Germany: a Comparative Analysis*, Praeger, New York

Schöler, K. (1992), 'Probleme alternativer Privatisierungsstrategien im Transformationsprozeß, *List Forum, 18* (4), pp. 267–75

Scholl, W. (1986), 'Codetermination and the Quality of Working Life' in Stern, R.N. and McCarthy, S. (eds), *The Organisational Practice of Democracy* (Vol.3), John Wiley & Sons, Chichester, New York, etc.

Schöller, P., Puls, W.W. and Bucholz, H.J. (1980), *Federal Republic of Germany: Spatial Development and Problems*, Schöningh, Paderborn

Schoser, F. (1988), 'Die Vollendung des Europäischen Binnenmarktes – Ende- oder Zwischenstufe der europäischen Integration?', in Birskup, R. (ed.), *Europa – Einheit in der Vielfalt*, Paul Haupt, Bern and Stuttgart

Schrettl, W. (1992), 'Transition with Insurance: German Unification Reconsidered', *Oxford Review of Economic Policy, 8* (1), pp. 144–55

Schulin, E. and Müller-Luckner, E. (1989), *Deutsche Geschichtswissenschaft nach dem Zweiten Weltkrieg (1945–1965)*, R. Oldenbourg Verlag, München

Schulte-Mimberg, U. (1989), 'Das Gedankengebäude der Krankenversicherung unter dem Einfluß des Gesundheits-Reformgesetzes', *Sozialer Fortschritt, 38* (7), pp. 148–52

Schulz, E. (1990), 'Veränderte Rahmenbedingung für die Vorausberechnung der Bevölkerungsentwicklung in der Bundesrepublik Deutschland', *DIW Vierteljahrsheft, 2/3*, pp. 169–84

Schupp, J. and Wagner, G. (1990), 'Die DDR – Stichprobe des Sozio-ökonomischen Panels', *DIW Vierteljahresheft, 3/9*, pp. 152–59

Schuppert, G.F. (1992), 'Die Treuhandanstalt – Zum Leben einer Organisation im Überschneidungsbereich zweier Rechtskreise', *Staatswissenschaften und Staatspraxis, 3* (2), pp. 186–210

Schuster, D. (1973), *Die deutschen Gewerkschaften seit 1945*, Verlag W. Kohlhammer, Stuttgart

Schwalbach, J. (1987), 'Entry by Diversified Firms into German Industries', *International Journal of Industrial Organizations, 5*, pp. 43–9

Schwappach, J. (1989), 'Chancen und Risiken des gemeinsamen Binnenmarkts für das deutsche Handwerk unter besonderer Berücksichtigung des Niederlassungsrechtes' in Wirtschafts- u. Sozialwissenschaft Gesellschaft Trier (ed.), *Berufliche Freizügigkeit im EG-Binnenmarkt*

Secretariat of the European Commission for Europe (United Nations) (1990), 'The Unification of Germany', *Economic Bulletin for Europe, 42*, pp. 89–108

Seifert, H. (1991), 'Employment Effects of Working Time Reductions in the Former Federal Republic of Germany, *International Labour Review, 130* (4), pp. 495–510

Seitz, K. (1992a), 'Die japanisch-amerikanische Herausforderung – Europas Hochtechnologieindustrien kämpfen ums Überleben', *Aus Politik und Zeitgeschichte*, B10-11/92, 28 February, pp. 3–15

—— (1992b), 'Do We Need a Strategic High Technology Policy? – The Case for a Federal Government High Technology Policy', *Intereconomics, 27* (4), pp. 103–7

Sengenberger, W. (1984), 'West German Employment Policy: Restoring Worker Competition', *Industrial Relations, 23* (3), pp. 323–43

Shearson Lehman Hutton (1990), 'German Reunification: Wunderbar!', *International Economics*, 4 May

Sherman, H.C. (1990), 'The Economics of German Unification', *Tokyo Club Papers No. 4*, Part 2, pp. 39–72

Shonfield, A. (1965), *Modern Capitalism*, OUP, Oxford

Siebert, H. (1985), 'Perspektiven der internationalen Arbeitsteilung – Thesen zum deutschen Außenhandel', *Marketing, 7* (2), pp. 109–18

—— (1989), 'Anpassungsprobleme in einer offenen Volkswirtschaft', in Gahlen, B. *et al.* (eds), *Wirtschaftswachstum, Strukturwandel und dynamischer Wettbewerb*, Springer Verlag, Berlin/Heidelberg

—— (1990), 'Lang- und kurzfristige Perspektiven der Deutschen Integration', *Die Weltwirtschaft, 1*, pp. 49–59

—— (1991a), *The New Economic Landscape in Europe*, Blackwell, Oxford/Cambridge

—— (1991b), 'German Unification: the Economics of Transition', *Economic Policy, 13* (with discussion and appendix), pp. 287–340

—— (1992a), *Das Wagnis der Einheit*, Deutsche Verlags-Anstalt, Stuttgart

—— (ed.) (1992b), *Privatization. Symposium in Honor of Herbert Giersch*, J.C.B. Mohr (Paul Siebeck), Tübingen

—— (1992c), 'Standortwettbewerb – nicht Industriepolitik', *Die Weltwirtschaft*, No. 4/1992, pp. 409–24

—— (1993), 'Junge Bundesländer: Gibt es wirtschaftliche Alternativen?', Kiel *Discussion Papers*, No. 200

Siebert, H. and Koop, M.J. (1993), 'Institutional Competition versus Centralization: Quo vadis Europe', Kiel *Working Paper* No. 548, The Kiel Institute of World Economics

Siebert, H. and Schmieding, H. (1990), 'Restructuring Industry in the GDR', Kiel *Working Paper* No. 431

Sievert, O. (1992), 'Bundesbankpolitik: Einspruch gegen Übertreibungen', Dresdner Bank *Trends*, September, pp. 6–9

Simon, H. (1992), 'Lessons from Germany's Midsized Giants', *Harvard Business Review, 70* (2), pp. 115–23

Sinn, G. and Sinn, H.-W. (1993), *Kaltstart – Volkswirtschaftliche Aspekte der deutschen Wiedervereinigung*, Second Edition, Beck and DTV, München. (English version:

(1992) *Jumpstart: the Economic Unification of Germany*, MIT, Boston, Mass.)

Sinn, H.-W. (1991), *Macroeconomic Aspects of German Unification*, NBER Working Paper

— (1992a), 'Macroeconomic Aspects of German Unification', in Welfens, P.J. (ed.), *op. cit.*

— (1992b), 'Privatization in East Germany', *Public Finance, 47* (Supplement), pp. 152–71

Smeets, H.-D. (1990), 'Does Germany Dominate the EMS?', *Journal of Common Market Studies, XXIX* (1), pp. 37–52

de Smidt, P. (1992), 'International Investments and the European Challenge', *Environment and Planning A, 24*, pp. 83–94

Smigielski, E. (1989), 'EG-Binnenmarkt und Harmonisierung der europäischen Gesundheitssicherungssysteme', *Arbeit und Sozialpolitik, 43* (8), pp. 224–6

Soltwedel, R. (1987), 'Wettbewerb zwischen den Regionen statt koordinierter Regionalpolitik', *Die Weltwirtschaft, 1*, pp. 129–45

— (1988), 'Employment Problems in West Germany – The Role of Institutions, Labor Law, and Government Intervention', *Carnegie-Rochester Conference Series on Public Policy, 28*, pp. 153–220

Sonderdrucke der Deutschen Bundesbank (1976), *Jahresabschlüsse der Unternehmen in der Bundesrepublik Deutschland 1965 bis 1976*, No. 5 (updated in 1977: No. 6)

Soskice, D. (1990), 'Wage Determination: the Changing Role of Institutions in Advanced Industrialised Countries', *Oxford Review of Economic Policy, 6* (4), pp. 36–61

— (1991), 'The Institutional Infrastructure for International Competitiveness: A Comparative Analysis of the UK and Germany', in Atkinson, A.B. and Brunetta, R. (eds), *Economics for the New Europe*, Macmillan, London

Sozialpolitische-Informationen (1990), *Arbeits- und Sozialrecht im einigen Sozialstaat Deutschland, XXIV*, September

Spahn, H.-P. (1989), 'Competition Between the D-Mark and the Dollar – The Policies of the Bundesbank in the 1970s and 1980s', *Economie Appliquee*, Tome XLII, No. 2, pp. 5–33

— (1990), *Wirtschaftspolitische Strategien*, Transfer, Regensburg

Spahn, P.B. (ed.) (1978), *Principles of Federal Policy Coordination in the Federal Republic of Germany: Basic Issues and Annotated Legislation*, Research Monograph No. 25,

Centre for Research on Federal Financial Relations, The Australian National University, Canberra

Spahn, P.B., Kaiser, H. and Kassella, T. (1992), 'The Tax Dilemma of Married Women in Germany', *Fiscal Studies, 13* (2), pp. 22–47

Spiro, J. (1954), 'Codetermination in Germany', *American Political Science Review, 48* (4), pp. 1114–27

Stadermann, H.-J. (1990), 'Besitzstandssicherung versus marktgerechte Strukturen', *Wirtschaftsdienst, 70* (5), pp. 240–6

Städler, G.N. (1991), 'Infrastrukturengpässe in den neuen Bundesländern', *Ifo-Schnelldienst, 6*, June, pp. 3–4

Stafford, F.P. (1988), 'Employment Problems in West Germany: A Comment', *Carnegie-Rochester Conference Series on Public Policy, 28*, pp. 221–30

Starbatty, J. and Vetterlein, U. (1988), 'Must the Semi-Conductor Industry be Subsidised?', *Intereconomics*, May/June, pp. 109–15

— (1992), 'Europäische Technologie- und Industriepolitik nach Maastricht', *Aus Politik und Zeitgeschichte*, B10-11/92, 28 February, pp. 16–24

Statistisches Jahrbuch für die Bundesrepublik Deutschland (various), Statistisches Bundesamt, Wiesbaden Verlag, W. Kohlhammer, Stuttgart und Mainz

Stehn, J. and Schmieding, H. (1990), *Spezialisierungsmuster und Wettbewerbsfähigkeit: Eine Bestandsaufnahme des DDR – Außenhandels*, Institut für Weltwirtschaft

Stein, J. (1977), *The Banking System of the Federal Republic of Germany*, Tenth Edition, Bundesverband deutscher Banken, Cologne

— (1990), *Das Bankwesen in Deutschland*, Seventeenth Edition, Bundesverband deutscher Banken, Köln

Steinherr, A. (1991), 'The German Banking System on the Eve of 1992', in Imbriani, C., Roberti, P. and Torrisi, A. (eds), *Il Mercato Unico del 1992: Deregolamentazione e Posizionamento Strategico dell'Industria Bancaria in Europa*, Bancaria Editrice S.p.A., Rome

Stephen, D. (1973), 'Immigrant Workers and Low Pay', in Field, F. (ed.), *Low Pay*, Arrow Books, London

Stern, S. (ed.) (1992), *Germany: Doing Business with Europe's New Giant*, Times Books, London

Stevens, B. (1992), 'Prospects for Privatisation in OECD Countries', National Westminster Bank *Quarterly Review*, August, pp. 2–22

Stewart, S. (1980), *The Significance of the German Case*, mimeo.

Stille, F. (1990), 'German Unification and Harmonization of the Labor Market', paper presented at the EALE Conference on Labor Markets and Labor Market Policy in Europe in the 1990s, Lund, Sweden, 20–23 September, Deutsches Institut für Wirtschaftsforschung

Stingl, J. (1977), 'Role and Structure of the German Federal Employment Institution', *International Labour Review, 116* (2), pp. 197–207

Stolper, G., Häuser, K. and Borchardt, K. (1967), *The German Economy 1870 to the Present*, Weidenfield and Nicolson, London, 1967. (Contains bibliographical history of previous German and English editions – page references are to the first joint German edition.)

Stolper, W.F. and Roskamp, K.W. (1979), 'Planning in a Free Economy: Germany 1945–1960', *Journal of Institutional and Theoretical Economics (Zeitschrift für die gesamte Staatswissenschaft), 135* (3), pp. 374–404

Stonham, P. (1982), *Major Stock Markets of Europe*, Gower, Aldershot

Streeck, W. (1984a), 'Co-determination: the Fourth Decade' in Wilpert, B. and Sorge, A. (eds), *International Perspectives on Organisational Democracy* (Vol.2), John Wiley & Sons, Chichester, New York, etc.

—— (1984b), *Industrial Relations in West Germany: A Case Study in the Car Industry*, Heinemann for the Policy Studies Institute, London

Streit, M. (1977), 'Government and Business: the Case of West Germany', in Griffiths, R.T. (ed.), *Government, Business and Labour in European Capitalism*, Europotentials Press, London

—— (1989), 'Ordnungspolitische Überlegungen zur Systemkrise in der DDR', *Wirtschaftsdienst, XIII*, pp. 600–4

Studienkommission für die Reform des öffentlichen Dienstrechts: Bericht der Kommission (1991), Nomos, Baden-Baden

Sturm, R. (1989a), 'The Role of the Bundesbank in German Politics', *West European Politics, 12* (2), pp. 1–11

—— (1989b), 'The Industrial Policy Debate in the Federal Republic of Germany', in Bulmer, S. (ed), *The Changing Agenda of West German Public Policy*, Association for the Study of German Politics, Avebury, Aldershot

—— (1990), 'Die Politik der Deutschen Bundesbank', in Beyme, K. von and Schmidt, M.G. (eds), *Politik in der Bundesrepublik Deutschland*, Westdeutscher Verlag, Opladen

—— (1992), 'Regionalisierung der Industriepolitik', *Aus Politik und Zeitgeschichte*, B10-11/92, 28 February, pp. 25–35

Sturmthal, A. (1964), *Workers' Councils*, Harvard UP

Subsidy Reports (various), Bundesministerium der Finanzen, *Subventionsberichte*, Bonn

Süddeutsche Zeitung (various), Munich

Sullivan, T. (1976), 'Industrial Relations in West Germany', Industrial Relations Unit *Occasional Paper*, No. 2, November

Suntum, U. van (1990), 'Kaufkrafteffekte der Wirtschafts- und Währungsunion', *Wirtschaftsdienst, 70* (8), pp. 398–401

Svejnar, J. (1981), 'Relative Wage Effects of Unions, Dictatorship and Codetermination: Econometric Evidence from Germany', *Review of Economics and Statistics, 63* (3), pp. 188–97

SVR (1990) – Sachverständigenrat zur Begutachtung der gesamtwirtschaftlichen Entwicklung (1990), 'Zur Unterstützung der Wirtschaftsreform in der DDR: Voraussetzungen und Möglichkeiten', *Sondergutachten* vom 20. Januar

Taft, P. (1952), 'Germany', in Galenson, W. (ed.), *Comparative Labor Movements*, Prentice Hall, New Jersey

Tangermann, S. (1979), 'Germany's Role within the CAP: Domestic Problems in International Perspective', *Journal of Agricultural Economics, XXX* (3), pp. 241–59

Taylor, A.J.P. (1978), *The Course of German History*, Methuen (University Paperback edition), London, reprint

Tew, B. (1985), 'Monetising Government Debt', *Research Paper*, No. 19, Loughborough University Banking Centre, November

—— (1988), 'Financial Deregulation and Monetary Policy', in O'Brien, R. and Datta, T., *International Economics and Financial Markets*, Oxford, OUP

Thanner, B. (1990), 'Privatisierung in

Ostdeutschland und Osteuropa: Probleme und erste Erfahrungen', *Ifo-Schnelldienst, 31*, pp. 11–17

— (1991), 'Privatisierung im Widerstreit der Interessen und Meinungen', *Ifo-Schnell dienst, 16–17*, pp. 24–8

Thieme, G. (1991), 'Spatial Aspects of Socioeconomic Disparities in West Germany: A Comparison of Indicators', in Wild, T. and Jones, F., *Local Taxation and Local Economic Development in Britain and Germany*, Anglo-German Foundation Publications, London

Thimm, A.L. (1981), 'How Far Should German Codetermination Go?', *Challenge*, July–August, pp. 13–22

Thirlwall, A. (1992), 'The Balance of Payments and Economic Performance', National Westminster *Quarterly Review*, May, pp. 2–11

Tietmeyer, H. (1992), 'The Economic Situation in the Nineties', Deutsche Bundesbank: *Auszüge aus Presseartikeln*, No. 68, pp. 2–6

Tietz, B. (1991), *Optionen für Deutschland: Szenarien und Handlungsalternativen für Wirtschaft und Gesellschaft*, Second Edition, Verlag moderne Industrie, Landsberg/Lech

Tillotson, J. (1980), 'The GKN-Sachs Affair: A Case Study in Economic Law', *Journal of World Trade Law, 14* (1), pp. 39–67

Tilly, R.H. (1989), 'Banking Institutions in Historical and Comparative Perspective: Germany, Great Britain and the United States in the Nineteenth and Early Twentieth Century', *Journal of International and Theoretical Economics (Zeitschrift für die gesamte Staatswissenschaft), 145* (1), pp. 189–209

Time International (various), London

Time Magazine (various), London

Tipton, F.B. (1976), *Regional Variations in the Economic Development of Germany During the Nineteenth Century*, Wesleyan University Press, Middleton, Connecticut

Tofaute, H. von (1976), 'Gesellschaftliche und ökonomische Aspekte der Privatisierung unter besonderer Berücksichtigung gewerkschaftlicher Gesichtspunkte', *WSI Mitteilungen, 29* (7), pp. 370–92

— (1993), 'Gesamtwirtschaftliche und arbeitnehmerbezogene Bedeutung der Privatisierung von Bundesbeteiligungen', *WSI Mitteilungen, 46* (1), pp. 11–22

Tomann, H. (1990), 'The Housing Market, Housing Finance and Housing Policy in West Germany: Prospects for the 1990s', *Urban Studies, 27* (6), pp. 919–30

— (1992a), 'Towards a Housing Market in Eastern Germany', *Diskussionsbeitrag*, 8/1992, Institut für Wirtschaftspolitik und Wirtschaftsgeschichte, Berlin

— (1992b), 'Der Wohnungsbedarf eilt voraus', *Tagungsvortrag*, mimeo.

Toscano, D. (1981), 'Labor-Management Cooperation and West German Codetermination', *Industrial Relations Journal, 12* (6), pp. 57–67

Trapp, P. (1987), 'West Germany: Why Reflation does not Work', *Economia Internazionale, XL* (2–3), pp. 237–46

Trehan, B. (1988), 'The Practice of Monetary Targeting: A Case Study of the West German Experience', *Economic Review*, Federal Reserve Bank of San Francisco, 2, pp. 30–44

Turner, H.A. and Jackson, D.A.S. (1968), 'On the Stability of Wage Differences and Productivity-Based Wage Policies: An International Analysis', *British Journal of Industrial Relations, 6* (3), pp. 322–9

TVF (Trierischer Volksfreund) (various), Trier

UNESCO (United Nations Educational, Scientific and Cultural Organisation) (1969), 'Science Policy and the Organisation of Research in the FRG', *Science Policy Studies and Documents*, No. 12, Paris

Vanberg, V. (1988), '"Ordnungstheorie" as Constitutional Economics – The German Conception of a "Social Market Economy"', *ORDO Jahrbuch für die Ordnung von Wirtschaft und Gesellschaft, 39*, pp. 17–31

Vaubel, R. (1992), 'Comment on Holger Schmieding, "Alternative Approaches to Privatization: Some Notes on the Debate"', in Siebert, H. (ed.) (1992b), *op. cit.*

Vaubel, R. and Barbier, H.D. (eds) (1986), *Handbuch Markwirtschaft*, Neske, Pfullingen

Vernon, R. (1966), 'International Investment and International Trade in the Product Cycle', *Quarterly Journal of Economics, 80*, pp. 191–207

VÖB (Verband Öffentlicher Banken) (1981), *Wir, die Öffentlichen Banken*, Bonn

Vogl, F. (1973), *German Business After the Economic Miracle*, Macmillan, London

Vogler-Ludwig, K. (1989), *The Changing Nature of Employment*, Study of the German Situation for the Commission of the European Communities, Final Report,

Contract No. 87 534, Ifo-Institute for Economic Research, Munich, June

— (1990) 'Verdeckte Arbeitlosigkeit in der DDR', *Ifo-Schnelldienst, 24*, pp. 3–10

Voigt, F. (1962), 'German Experience with Cartels and their Control during the Pre-War and Post-War Periods', in Miller, J.P. (ed.), *Competition Cartels and their Regulation*, North-Holland Publishing Company, Amsterdam

Völker, G.E. (1973), 'Impact of Turkish Labour Migration on the Economy of the Federal Republic of Germany', *German Economic Review, 11* (1), 1973, pp. 61–77

Vollmer, R. (1981), 'The Structure of West German Foreign Trade', *Journal of Institutional and Theoretical Economics (Zeitschrift für die gesamte Staatswissenschaft), 137* (3), pp. 575–89

Wächter, H. (1992), 'German Codetermination: An Outdated Model?' in J.J.J. van Dijck and A.A.L.G. Wentink (eds), *Transnational Business in Europe – Economic and Social Perspectives*, Researchgroup Transnational Business in Europe, Faculty of Social Sciences, Tilburg University

Wächter, H. and Stengelhofen, T. (1992), 'Human Resource Management in a United Germany', *Employee Relations, 14* (4), pp. 21–37

Wagner, H. (1991), *Einführung in die Weltwirtschaftspolitik*, R. Oldenbourg Verlag, München and Wien

Wagner, W. (1990), 'Die Dynamik der deutschen Wiedervereinigung. Suche nach einer Verträglichkeit für Europa', *Europa Archiv, 3*, pp. 78–97

Walderfells, von G.F. (1991), 'Eine sofortige Einbeziehung in den Länderfinanzausgleich ist nicht verkraftbar', *Wirtschaftsdienst, 71* (2), pp. 67–8

Wallich, H.C. (1955), *Mainsprings of the German Revival*, Yale UP, New Haven. (German version: *Triebkräfte des deutschen Wiederaufstieges*, Fritz Knapp Verlag, Frankfurt a.M. All the pages cited in the text are to the English edition.)

— (1968) 'The American Council of Economic Advisers and the German *Sachverständigenrat*: A Study in the Economics of Advice', *Quarterly Journal of Economics, 82* (3) pp. 349–79

Walter, N. (1992), 'The Heyday of German Trade – Past, Present or Future?', in Stern, S. (ed.), *op. cit.*

Walters, A. (1989), 'Supply-Side Policies: The Lessons from the UK', in Fels, G. and von Furstenberg, G.M. (eds), *op. cit.*

Wanik, B. (1984), 'The Development of Wages of German Industrial Corporations', *The Journal of Industrial Economics, XXXIII* (1), pp. 113–21

Watrin, C. (1979), 'The Principles of the Social Market Economy: its Origins and Early History', *Journal of Institutional and Theoretical Economics (Zeitschrift für die gesamte Staatswissenschaft), 135* (3), pp. 405–25

— (1991), 'Treuhandanstalt: Transformator im Prozeß der Systemänderung', *Wirtschaftsdienst, 71* (4), pp. 167–70

Wehling, H.-G. (ed.) (1991), *Außenwirtschaftspolitik*, Kohlhammer Verlag, Stuttgart

Wehling, H-W. (1991), 'The Crisis of the Ruhr: Causes, Phases and Socioeconomic Effects', in Wild, T. and Jones, P., *op. cit.*

Weinrich, C. and Worzalle, M. (1990), *Betriebsverfassungsgesetz mit Erläuterungen*, Heider-Verlag, Bergisch-Gladbach

Weiss, F. (1989a), 'Die außenwirtschaftlichen Beziehungen der Bundesrepublik Deutschland', in Weidenfeld, W. and Zimmermann, H. (eds), *Deutschland-Handbuch – Eine doppelte Bilanz 1949–1989*, Bundeszentrale für politische Bildung, Bonn

— (1989b), 'Domestic Dimensions of the Uruguay Round: The Case of West Germany in the European Communities', in Neu, H.R. (ed.), *Domestic Trade Politics and the Uruguay Round*, Columbia University Press, New York

Weiss, G. (1978), *Die ÖTV. Politik und gesellschaftspolitische Konzeptionen der Gewerkschaft ÖTV von 1966 bis 1978*, Second Edition, Verlag Arbeiterbewegung und Gesellschaftswissenschaft, Marburg

Weiss, M. (1985), 'Zu den Kosten der Betriebsverfassung, insbesondere der Einigungsstelle', in Dieterich, T. and Kissell, O.R. (eds), *Das Arbeitsrecht der Gegenwart*, vol.22, Erich Schmidt Verlag, Bielefeld

— (1987), 'Federal Republic of Germany', in Blanpan, R. (ed.), *International Encyclopaedia for Labour Law and Industrial Relations* (Vol.5), Kluwer, The Netherlands

— (1991), 'Legislation: Federal Republic of Germany' in Blanpan, R. (ed.), *International Encyclopaedia for Labour Law and Industrial Relations* (Legislation 1), Kluwer Law and Taxation Publishers, Deventer-Boston

Weisser, W. (1984), *Der Kampf um die*

Arbeitszeit in der Metallindustrie 1984, Deutscher Instituts-Verlag, Köln

Weizsäcker, C.C. von (1990), 'Soziale Marktwirtschaft und Demokratie', *Zeitschrift für Wirtschaftspolitik, 39*, pp. 5–40

Weizsäcker, C.C. and Waldenberger, F. (1992), 'Wettbewerb und strategische Handelspolitik', *Wirtschaftsdienst, 72* (8), pp. 403–9

Weizsäcker, C. von and Wieland, B. (1988), 'Current Telecommunications Policy in West Germany', *Oxford Review of Economic Policy, 4* (2), pp. 20–39

Welcker, J. (1990), 'Die Mark der DDR: Konvertibilität jetzt', *Wirtschaftsheft, 5*, pp. 247–51

Welfens, P.J.J. (1991), 'International Effects of German Unification', *Intereconomics, 26* (1), pp. 10–18

—— (ed.) (1992), *Economic Aspects of German Unification*, Springer Verlag, Berlin, Heidelberg

Well, van G. (1990), 'Zur Europapolitik der BRD', *Europa Archiv, 9*, pp. 292–301

Welsch, J. (1992), 'Akute "Standortschwäche" oder Strategiedefizite? – Industrie- und unternehmenspolitische Versäumnisse als Zukunftsrisiken für den Industriestandart Deutschland', *WSI-Mitteilungen, 5*, pp. 283–93

Welter, P. (1958), *Entwicklung, Stand und Problematik der vereinbarten Schlichtung in der Bundesrepublik*, unpublished PhD Thesis, Marburg

—— (1992), 'Die Spaltung von Treuhandunternehmen als Weg zur Entflectung von Staatsunternehmen beim Übergang zur Markwirtschaft', in Ipsen, D. and Nickel, E. (eds), *op. cit.*

Weltz, F. and Schmidt, G. (1976), *Innovation, Beschäftigungspolitik und industrielle Beziehungen*, Vol.1, Anglo-German Foundation for the Study of Industrial Societies

Wenger, E. (1987), 'Managementanreize und Kapitalallokation', *Jahrbuch für Neue Politische Ökonomie, 6*, pp. 217–40

—— (1990), 'Die Rolle der Banken in der Industriefinanzierung und in der Unternehmenskontrolle am Beispiel der Bundesrepublik Deutschland', *Wirtschaftspolitische Blätter, 2–3*, pp. 155–68

—— (1992), 'Universalbankensystem und Depotstimmrecht', in Gröner, H. (ed.), *Der Markt für Unternehmenskontrollen,*

Schriften des Vereins für Socialpolitik, Gesellschaft für Wirtschafts- und Sozialwissenschaften, 214, Duncker and Humblot, Berlin pp. 73–118

Westdeutschlands Weg zur Bundesrepublik 1945–49 (1976), Symposium, Verlag C.H.Beck, München

WestLB Information (various), Düsseldorf

Westphal, A. (1991), 'Economic Consequences of German Unification', *EIU European Trends*, No. 42, The Economist Intelligence Unit, London

Weyman-Jones, T.G. (1987), *Energy in Europe: Issues and Policies*, Methuen, London

Whitesell, R.S. (1989–90), 'Estimates of the Output Loss from Allocative Inefficiency – a Comparison of Hungary and West Germany', *Eastern Europe Economics, 28* (2), pp. 95–125

Wiedemann, H. and Stumpf, H. (1977), *Tarifvertragsgesetz*, Fifth Edition, C.H. Beck, München

Wienert, H. (1990a) 'Was macht Industrieregionen "alt"? – Ausgewählte sektorale und regionale Ansätze zur theoretischen Erklärung regionaler Niedergangsprozesse', RWI-*Mitteilungen*, pp. 363–90

—— (1990b), 'Stahlpolitik: Ein Lehrstück für die Risiken der industriepolitischen Intervention?', *Wirtschaftsdienst, 70* (4), pp. 207–11

Wiesner, G.E. (1990), 'Zur Gesundheitslage der DDR-Bevölkerung – Stand und Entwicklung der Lebenserwartung', *Arbeit und Sozialpolitik, 44* (3), pp. 101–2

Wild, K.-P. (1991), 'Die Treuhandanstalt ein Jahr nach Inkrafttreten des Treuhandgesetzes – eine aktuelle Zwischenbilanz', in Hommelhoff, P. (ed.), *op. cit.*

Wild, K.-P. and Pfeifer, M. (1971), 'Stellung und Aufgaben der Länder, in Eberstein, H.-H., *Handbuch der regionalen Wirtschaftsförderung, Achtzehnter Rahmenplan*, Verlag Dr Otto Schmidt KG, Köln

Wild, T. (1979), *West Germany – A Geography of its People*, Dawson, Folkestone

Wild, T. and Jones, P. (1991) (eds), *Deindustrialisation and New Industrialisation in Britain and Germany*, Anglo-German Foundation Publications, London

Williams, K. (1988), *Industrial Relations and the German Model*, Avebury Press (Gower), Aldershot

Wilmes, B. (1992), 'Arbeitnehmerhaftung', *Arbeit und Arbeitswelt, 47* (3), pp. 75–8

Wilpert, B. (1975), 'Research on Industrial Democracy: the German Case', *Industrial Relations Journal, 6* (1), pp. 53–64

Windolf, P. and Haas, J. (1989), 'Who Joins the Union? Determinants of Trade Union Membership in West Germany 1976–1984', *European Sociological Review, 5* (2), pp. 147–65

Winterhager, W.D. *et al.* (1980), *Comparative Study of the Financial, Legislative and Regulatory Structure of Vocational Training Systems: Federal Republic of Germany, France, Italy, United Kingdom*, European Centre for the Development of Vocational Training, Berlin

Wirtschaft und Statistik (various), Wiesbaden

Wirtschaftswoche (various), Düsseldorf

Witschi, D. (1992), 'The Mechanics of Bundesbank Policy', *Economic and Financial Prospects* (Swiss Bank Corporation), 1/92, pp. 1–4

Witte Commission (1987), 'Neuordnung der Telekommunikation', *Bericht der Regierungskommission Fermeldewesen*, von Drecker Verlag, Heidelberg

Wohlers, E. (1988), 'Internationale Wettbewerbsfähigkeit, Wechselkurse und Außenhandel – einige Anmerkungen zur gegenwärtigen Diskussion in der Bundesrepublik', *Hamburger Jahrbuch für Wirtschafts- und Gesellschaftspolitik, 33*, pp. 27–40

—— (1990), 'Enwicklung und Bestimmungsgründe der deutsche Exportüberschüsse im Handel mit den europäischen Ländern', *Hamburger Jahrbuch für Wirtschafts- und Gesellschaftspolitik, 35*, pp. 271–90

—— (1992), 'Außenhandelsefekte der deutschen Vereinigung', *Hamburger Jahrbuch für Wirtschafts- und Gesellschaftspolitik, 37*, pp. 124–42

Woolcock, S., Hodges, M. amd Schreiber, K. (1991), *Britain, Germany and 1992: the Limits of Deregulation*, Royal Institute of International Affairs/Pinter Publishers, London

WSI (Wirtschafts- und Sozialwissenschaftliches Institut des Deutschen Gewerkschaftsbundes), *Pressedienst* (various), Düsseldorf

—— *Mitteilungen* (various), Düsseldorf

—— (1991), *Tarifpolitisches Taschenbuch*, Bund Verlag, Köln (appears annually)

Wunden, W. (1969), *Die Textilindustrie der Bundesrepublik Deutschland im Strukturwandel*, Kyklos-Verlag, Basel/J.C.B. Mohr (Paul Siebeek), Tübingen

Xideas, E. (1986), 'A Study of the Determinants of Migration: The Case of Greek Migration to West Germany 1960–1982', unpublished PhD Thesis, Loughborough University of Technology

Yeager, L.B. (1976), *International Monetary Relations*, Second Edition, Harper and Row, New York, Evanston, San Francisco, London

Zachert, U. (1979a), *Tarifverträge. Eine problemorientierte Einführung*, Bund, Köln

—— (1979b), 'Der Ablauf einer Tarifverhandlung', *Gewerkschaftliche Monatshefte, 3*, pp. 172–8

Zängl, W. (1989), *Deutschlands Strom*, Campus Verlag, Frankfurt a.M/New York

Zell, S.P. (1977), 'Analysing Puerto Rican Migration: Problems with the Data and the Model', *Monthly Labor Review, 100* (8), pp. 29–34

Zimmermann, H. (1985), 'The Integration of Policies of Fiscal Equalisation and Regional Policies', *Environment and Planning C: Government and Policy, 3* (4), pp. 451–61

Zinn, K.-G. (1991), 'International Aspects of an Alternative Economic Policy', in Graf, W.D. (ed.), *The Internationalization of the German Political Economy*, St. Martin's Press, New York

Zohlnhöfer, W. (1990a), 'Das Schlüsselproblem der deutsch-deutschen Wirtschaftsunion: Schaffung wettbewerbsfähiger Arbeitsplätze in der DDR', *List Forum, 16* (3), pp. 191–219

—— (1990b), 'Sozialpolitik – Achillesferse der Sozialen Markwirtschaft?' in Bundeszentrale für Politische Bildung, *Wirtschaftspolitik*, Bonn, pp. 305–29

INDEX

(The principal synthesised headings appear in bold print)